INDIA'S ECONOMIC PROBLEMS

An Analytical Approach

INDIA'S ECONOMIC PROBLEMS

An Analytical Approach

J S Uppal, **Ph.D. (Minnesota)**
Professor of Economics
State University of New York at Albany
Albany, New York, U.S.A.

Tata McGraw-Hill Publishing Company Ltd
New Delhi

The proceeds of the royalty for this book will go to the Prime Minister's Relief Fund.

This edition can be exported from India only by the publishers, Tata McGraw-Hill Publishing Co. Ltd.

PUBLISHED BY TATA MCGRAW-HILL PUBLISHING COMPANY LIMITED, C-98-A, SOUTH EXTENSION PART II, NEW DELHI–49, AND PRINTED BY K. K. GHOSH AT THE INDIAN PRESS PRIVATE LTD., ALLAHABAD.

Foreword

INDIAN ECONOMICS has long since come of age. In addition to the excellence of research at several long-established centers such as the Indian Statistical Institute and the Gokhale Institute, we also now have the establishment of new constellations of research in Trivandrum (under Dr. K. N. Raj), in Bangalore (under Dr. V. K. R. V. Rao), in Ahmedabad (under the initial leadership of Dr. D. T. Lakdawala) and in other areas of the country. Much of this research has been truly indigenous and this is a source of pride for us.

At the same time, a number of young Indian economists have now left a strong imprint on the international scene: in the theory of international trade, in welfare economics, in planning theory, in econometrics, and so on. Many of our economists now edit international journals (not on the basis of their regional origin but on the tougher basis of individual professional achievement), lead research projects, have been elected to Fellowships in distinguished professional societies, and are at the very top of the professional elite. And this has happened, not merely in the United Kingdom where our achievements must be discounted because we have traditional ties and also because the excellence of economics research has declined with the ebb of the Empire, but also in the United States which has been the center of basic and fundamental research in the subject since the War.

How far have the vast achievements of the Indian economists been reflected in the quality of teaching in our country? This has been a much slower process. Some of the economists of excellence have been drawn away into official work—something that is unavoidable and even socially desirable in a poor country—whereas many have been overwhelmed by the pressures of educational expansion into struggling to maintain, rather than improve, standards. Nonetheless, at some of the universities there have been steady improvements and this is reflected again in the ease with which the students of these universities tend to get into fellowship programmes for Ph.D. at the world's top Economics Departments such as MIT and Harvard, and in fact are sought actively by the next-best Departments such as Stanford, Berkeley, and Rochester.

This steady trend in the improved teaching of the best Indian universities needs to be strengthened by *both* diffusion to other universities—even equality of opportunity to students from different parts of the country requires that this be considered a top priority—*and* the contribution of the better-trained economists to the writing of better and more suitable textbooks and teaching materials.

Hence, I am glad to see that this group of U. S. based Indian economists has seen fit to make its own contribution in this regard by adding this collection of essays on the Indian economy to the growing literature on the Indian economy which is now becoming available to students at the Indian universities. It is to be hoped that the university bodies in charge of recommending reading materials to their students in B.A. and M.A. courses will take cognizance of such materials and utilise them with profit.

JAGDISH N. BHAGWATI

Professor of Economics
Massachusetts Institute of Technology

Introduction

In recent visits to India, I had the privilege of exchanging views with my former colleagues about the teaching of economics in the colleges and universities there and abroad. Many of them complained that most of the books on Indian economics now being used are too descriptive—they fail to analyse critically the economic problems facing Indian society. The result is that students, especially at the undergraduate level, do not learn to examine such problems within a theoretical and logical framework. They are unable to grasp as fully as they might the cause-and-effect relationships between different policy variables. Their knowledge of the Indian economy is often restricted to a set of statements, many of which may be based merely on "conventional wisdom".

These books have another limitation. They are usually cast in a narrow framework. Little effort is made to compare India's problems to those of other developing countries, or, for that matter, to those of more advanced countries in their earlier stages of development. Students thus end up with a rather parochial view of the Indian economy in a day and age when societies have so much to learn from one another and from the rich store of human experience—sometimes known as the "knowledge explosion".

In view of those deficiencies in the currently used books on the Indian economy, we—as economists who were raised in India, educated there as well as in western countries, and who are now teaching abroad—have tried to produce this anthology that would present the economic problems of India in a more analytic manner. The book is intended primarily for undergraduate students, though students working on the master's degree and studying for competitive examinations will also find it beneficial.

Each economist has contributed a paper on an Indian economic problem closely related to his major interest and field of specialization. The papers are comprehensive in that they discuss the problems in their various aspects—including the nature and the causes of the problems, their importance in the process of India's economic development, the Indian government's attempts to solve the problems, and possible solutions based on experiences of other developing countries. It is hoped that a fruitful international perspective has been attained by this reference to the experience of other countries together with the inclusion of western views on Indian economic problems.

The contributors were asked to place emphasis on linking the apparatus of theoretical economic analysis with the facts of Indian economic conditions. The papers are meant to be neither exercises in theoretical analysis nor journalistic presentations of economic facts. They seek to strike a reasonable balance between abstract theory and living reality, difficult though that objective may be.

Events in the Indian economy are moving fast. Since the manuscript went to the press in 1972, several developments have taken place in the economy which the reader should be aware of. These developments, along with the relevant chapter numbers may be noted here: (i) There has been the unprecedented inflationary trend, whose explanation may be sought in factors like the drought in 1972-73, deficit financing and the energy crisis (Chapter 19); (ii) Licensing has been liberalised, by the industrial policy statement of February 2, 1973, which identifies core industries of national importance in which foreign concerns and large houses (with assets of not less than Rs. 20 crores) will be eligible to participate (Chapter 8); (iii) The summary of the Approach to the Fifth Plan, has been given in the document 'Towards an Approach to the Fifth Plan'. (Chapter 10); (iv) The Report of the Banking Commission, 1972 has also been made available (Chapter 17); (v) The recommendations of the Sixth Finance Commission and recent allocations by the Finance Commission to various states throw light on the Centre-State relations and the regional priorities the government has set down (Chapter 21).

As with every compilation of articles by different authors, some differences in treatment remain in spite of the editor's efforts. There are variations in coverage of material, methods of analysis, and writing styles. This is the price that must be paid for the inclusion of analysis by 25 experts in one volume. The editor is grateful to the contributors for their efforts and hopes that readers will find that the merits of this composite volume outweigh the disadvantages of its multiple authorship.

The book is dedicated to the students of India by 'Indian economists based abroad'. All royalties from the sale of this book will be contributed to the Prime Minister's Relief Fund for India.

State University of New York at Albany, New York

J. S. Uppal

***The Editor*:**

Jogindar Singh Uppal, *(b. 1927) did M.A. in Economics from the Punjab University in 1952. After teaching at the Government College, Ludhiana and Mahindra College, Patiala (Punjab, India) for a number of years, he proceeded to the United States for further studies at the University of Minnesota where he took M.A. (1961) and Ph.D. (1965) degrees. He has also taught at the University of Hawaii, Michigan State University and is currently with the State University of New York at Albany as a Professor of Economics. Professor Uppal's other books are: Can Cities Survive? The Fiscal Plight of American Cities, (St. Martin's Press, New York, 1974); Disguised Unemployment in an Underdeveloped Economy, (Asia Publishing House, New York, 1973); Africa—Problems in Economic Development, (The Free Press, The Macmillan Co., 1972); and India and China: Studies in Comparative Development, (The Free Press, The Macmillan Co., 1971). Professor Uppal has also published several papers in professional journals, including the Oxford Economics Papers; Indian Economic Journal; Canadian Journal of Economics, Journal of Developing Areas, Economia Internationale, and Asian Survey. He has been a recipient of the John Cowel Fellowship, Ford Foundation Fellowship & research grants from the State University of New York Research Foundation.*

***The Contributors*:**

Jaleel Ahmad: *M.S. (Pittsburgh), Ph.D. (Massachusetts Institute of Technology), Associate Professor of Economics, Sir George Williams University, Montreal, Canada; and consultant to the United Nations Conference on Trade and Development, Geneva, Switzerland.*

Ramsingh K. Asher: *B.Com. (Bombay University), M.B.A. & M.A. (Syracuse University), Assistant Professor of Economics, Hartwick College, Oneonta, New York, U.S.A.*

V. N. Balasubramanyam: *M.A. (Mysore University), A.M.; Ph.D. (Illinois University), Senior Lecturer in Economics, University of Lancaster, U.K.*

Balwir Singh Cheema: *M.A. (Punjab University), Ph.D. (American University), Associate Professor of Economics, Wittenberg University, Springfield, Ohio, U.S.A.*

Krishan A. Chopra: *M.A. (Punjab University), Ph.D. (Rajasthan University), formerly on the faculty of Economics, Punjab University Colleges and Rajasthan University, presently Professor of Economics, State University of New York College, Oneonta, N.Y., U.S.A.*

Ram L. Chugh: *M.A. (Punjab University), Ph.D. (Wayne State University), Associate Professor of Economics, State University of New York College at Potsdam, New York, U.S.A.*

James Cutt: *Studied Economics at the University of Edinburgh, Ph.D. (University of Toronto), formerly Assistant Professor of Economics, York University, Toronto, Canada, presently on the faculty of Economics, the Australian National University, Canberra, Australia.*

Ramesh Diwan : *B.A. (Punjab University) M.A. (Delhi School of Economics), Ph.D. (University of Birmingham), formerly Lecturer, Punjab University, University of Glasgow, Economist, United Nations, presently Professor of Economics, Rensselaer Polytechnic Institute, Troy, New York, U.S.A.*

G. C. Dorai : *B.A. (Punjab University), M.A. (Delhi University), Ph.D. (Wayne State University), formerly Lecturer Sri Venkateswara College, Delhi, presently Associate Professor of Economics, The William Paterson College of New Jersey Wayne, New Jersey, U.S.A.*

A. Thomas Eapen : *B.Sc. (Honours) Madras University, M.B.A.; PhD. (University of Michigan), Associate Professor of Economics, State University of New York, U.S.A.*

Prem P. Gandhi : *M.A. (Delhi University), M.B.A. (New York University), Ph.D. (New School for Social Research), Associate Professor of Economics, State University College at Plattburgh, New York, U.S.A.*

G. S. Gupta : *M.A. (Baroda), Ph.D. (John Hopkins University), formerly Lecturer in Economics, M.S. University, Baroda, presently on faculty of Economics, Indian Institute of Management, Ahmedabad, India.*

Kumar Kangayappan : *B.A. (Madras University), M.A. (Annamalai University), M.A., Ph.D. (University of Wisconsin), formerly faculty of College of Rural Higher Education, Coimbatore, India. Visiting Professor, the National Institute of Bank Management, Bombay, presently Assistant Professor of Economics, University of Wisconsin, Green Bay, Wisconsin, U.S.A.*

Subbiah Kannappan : *M.A. (Madras University), M.A. (Tufts University), Ph.D. (University of Chicago), formerly Director, Research, Xavier Institute, Jamshedpur, presently Professor of Economics, Michigan State University, East Lansing, Michigan, U.S.A.*

Manjulika Koshal : *B.A., M.A., Ph.D. (University of Patna), formerly Lecturer in Labour Economics, Patna University and Visiting Research Associate, Shri Ram Center for Industrial Relations and Human Resources, New Delhi, India.*

Rajinder K. Koshal : *M.S. (Gauhati University), Ph.D. (University of Rochester), formerly Planning Commission, India, presently Associate Professor of Economics, Ohio University, Athens, Ohio, U.S.A.*

Surendra N. Kulshreshtha : *M.S. (Agra University), Ph.D. (University of Manitoba), formerly taught Agricultural Economics, Agra University, affiliated college; presently Associate Professor of Agricultural Economics, University of Saskatchewan, Saskatoon, Canada.*

Sudhin K. Mukhopadhyay : *B.A.; M.A. (University of Calcutta), Ph.D. (University of Minnesota) member of research and teaching faculty, Indian Statistical Institute and University of Kalyani.*

Inder Pal Nijhawan : *M.A. (Delhi School of Economics), Ph.D. (University of North Carolina), Associate Professor of Economics, Fayetteville State University and Associate Member of Graduate Faculty, North Carolina State University, U.S.A.*

Ulaganathan Sankar : *B.A. (Madras University), M.A. (Annamalai University), Ph.D. (University of Wisconsin), formerly Lecturer in Economics, Annamalai University, presently Associate Professor of Economics, University of Wisconsin-Milwaukee, U.S.A.*

Ismail Shariff : *B.A. (Honours), M.A. (Mysore University), Ph.D. (University of Wisconsin), Associate Professor and Chairman Economics Department, University of Wisconsin, Green Bay, Wisconsin, U.S.A.*

Vidyapati Singh : *M.A. (University of Calcutta), Ph.D. (Case Western Reserve*

University), formerly Post-graduate Lecturer in Commerce, Gauhati University, presently, Professor of Economics, Illinois College, Jacksonville, Illinois, U.S.A.

Rohini Pati Sinha : *B.A. (Bihar University), M.A., Ph.D. (New School for Social Research), Associate Professor of Economics, Muhlenberg College, Allentown, Pennsylvania, U.S.A.*

Mahmood A. Zaidi : *B.A. (Honours), M.A. (University of California, Los Angeles), Ph.D. (University of California, Berkeley). Formerly, instructor in Economics at both the Los Angeles and Berkeley Campuses of University of California; presently Professor of Industrial Relations Center, University of Minnesota, U.S.A.*

Contents

Part One

THE HUMAN FACTOR

1

Population Growth in India

RAM L. CHUGH

1. India's Population Growth: Facts and Figures

India ranks second in terms of world population and seventh in terms of land area. She supports nearly 15 per cent of the world's population on a 2.4 per cent of the world's land area and shares only 1.5 per cent of the world's income. According to recent estimates, India's population in 1971 was 564 million, registering an increase of 125 million in a decade. The present population of India exceeds the combined population of the United States and the Soviet Union. In contrast to India, U.S.A. and U.S.S.R. cover about 22 per cent of the world's land area and share nearly 40 per cent of the world's income and support only 12 per cent of the world's population. To provide another interesting comparison, the population of India nearly equals the population of all 55 countries of Africa and Latin America put together. These comparisons are made to stress the high density of population in India. For a predominantly agricultural economy, this pressure of population is very high. At the present rate of growth, estimated to be 2.5 per cent a year, India's population is increasing at the rate of 13 million a year. It is as though the entire population of a country like Australia is added every year. What does the addition of nearly 13 million people mean to India's economy? It means making available every year, among other things, "tons of food, 2.5 million houses, 4 million jobs, 126,500 schools, 372,500 teachers and 188 million metres of cloth."[1] Thus, such a massive annual increase in population imposes a heavy burden on an already overburdened economy and almost completely wipes out the progress which the country makes.

Let us examine the pattern of India's population growth from a historical perspective. According to the estimates of Kingsley Davis, the population of the Indian subcontinent was 125 million in 300 B.C., and it remained very much the same for about 2000 years.[2] The major reason for the zero growth was the existence of

[1] S. P. Sinha, "India's Uphill Battle," *Far Eastern Economic Review*, vol. 76, no. 18, April 29, 1972, p. 57.

[2] Kingsley Davis, *The Population of India and Pakistan* (Princeton: Princeton University Press, 1951), Chapter 4.

high birth and death rates which, in the long run, balanced each other. "With the establishment of British rule and the restoration of a measure of internal peace in the sense of averted wars, and the setting up of a skeleton health and medical service,"[3] the pattern of population growth was gradually modified. Population increased at a very slow pace until 1921, and thereafter it increased quite rapidly. The population of India for the period 1891 to 1971 is given in Table 1.

Table 1. Growth of India's Population 1891-1971

Census Year	Population in millions (adjusted to the present area)	Increase or decrease in millions
1891	236.7	..
1901	236.3	— 0.4
1911	252.1	15.8
1921	251.4	— 0.7
1931	279.0	27.6
1941	316.7	37.7
1951	361.1	44.4
1961	439.2	78.1
1971	564.2	125.0

SOURCE: S. Chandrasekhar, *India's Population: Facts, Problems and Policy* (Delhi: Meenakshi, 1967), p. 4. The figure for 1971 is from C. Subramaniam, "Indian Planning Comes of Age," *India News*, vol XI, no. 15 (June 30, 1972), p. 3.

The above figures show that the population growth of India prior to 1921 was not only slow but also sporadic. After 1921, the population increased at a steady pace and then at an accelerating rate. The year 1921 is regarded as the year of "great divide" in the demographic history of India. Thus, for example, the population increased by 15 million during the three decades of 1891 to 1921, but during the next three decades of 1921–1951, it increased by 110 million which is seven times the increase of the previous period. During the next two decades of 1951-1961 and 1961–1971, the population increased by 78 million and 125 million respectively. These increases are phenomenal. It took India hundreds of years to attain a population of 250 million in 1921 but it took only 45 years to double it. And, at the current rate of growth, the population will double every 30 years. Such an accelerating growth was not foreseen by the Indian planners. The first two Five Year Plans were formulated on the assumption that the population would grow at an annual rate of 1.25 per cent which, as we know now, was a serious underestimation. The actual rate of growth was closer to 2 per cent as shown by the 1961 census. The findings of the 1961 census were a shocking revelation and were responsible for bringing a new sense of urgency to the family planning programme. If the current trends of the population growth are projected into the future, the resulting figure is even more frightening. It is anticipated that at the present rate of growth India's population will reach the billion mark before the end of this century and there is nothing which India can do to stop this. According to demographers, even if India was to take drastic measures to reduce its birth rate to the replacement level by 1985, its population will still reach the billion mark by A. D. 2000.[4] This is the inevitable consequence of having an age structure which is heavily skewed towards the younger age-group. Nearly 54 per cent of the present population is below 15 years of age and this group has many fertile years ahead. The thought of one billion Indians by A. D. 2000 is quite alarming.

The skyrocketing of India's population is an entirely new phenomenon which has seriously aggravated the problems of economic development. Demographers call it a period of population explosion to dra-

[3] S. Chandrasekhar, *India's Population: Facts, Problems and Policy* (Delhi: Meenakshi Press, 1967), p. 3.

[4] *See* Population Reference Bureau, "India: Ready or Not, Here They Come," *Population Bulletin*, vol. 26, no. 5, Nov. 1970, p. 2.

matize the severity of the situation. Figure 1 portrays the "vertical" nature of this demographic explosion.

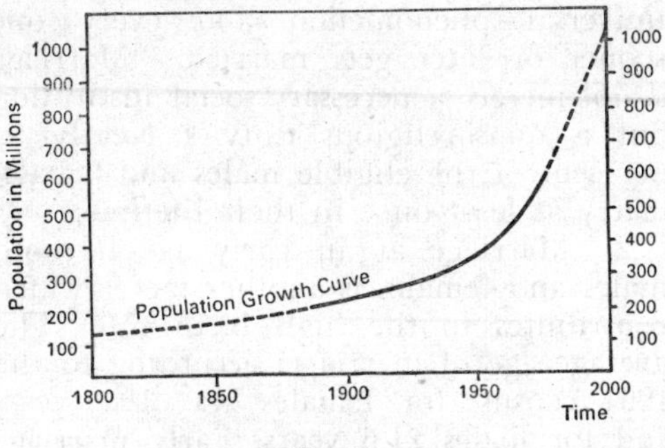

Fig. 1

2. Causes of India's Exploding Population Growth

It is the difference between a nation's birth and death rates which determines its population growth. Consequently, differential movements in these two rates can provide an explanation of the pattern of population growth. For instance, the main reason for the slow and erratic growth of population prior to 1921 was the prevalence of high birth and death rates, leaving little room for population expansion. After 1921, the death rate declined sharply. But the decline in the death rate was not accompanied by a similar reduction in the birth rate. The death rate declined from 47 per thousand in 1911–20 to 14 per thousand in 1968, while the birth rate fell from 48 per thousand to only 39 per thousand during the same period. It is the imbalance between these two rates, brought about mainly by the sudden and rapid decline in the death rate, which is responsible for the explosive growth of India's population. The trends in India's birth and death rates are given in Table 2.

The figures indicate that the decline in the death rate was slow until 1950, and that thereafter it was quite rapid. The birth rate, on the other hand, has remained high and relatively stable. The figures indicate the widening gap between these two rates. Figure 2 depicts this widening gap. The main challenge is to reduce this gap not by increasing the death rate but by reducing the birth rate.

Table 2. India's Birth and Death Rates

Years	Estimated birth rate	Estimated death rate	Increase in population
1901-10	52.4	46.8	5.6
1911-20	48.1	47.2	0.9
1921-30	46.4	36.3	10.1
1931-40	45.2	31.2	14.0
1941-50	43.0	30.0	13.0
1951-60	40.9	22.0	18.9
1968	39.0	14.0	25.0

SOURCE: S. Chandrasekhar, *India's Population*, p. 16, except for 1968 which are from Government of India Planning Commission, *Fourth Five Year Plan : 1969-74* (Delhi : Manager of Publications), p. 31.

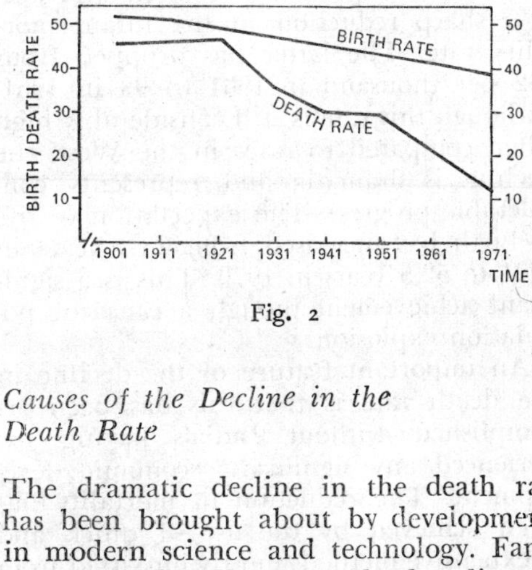

Fig. 2

Causes of the Decline in the Death Rate

The dramatic decline in the death rate has been brought about by developments in modern science and technology. Famines, epidemics, diseases, and other disasters which used to take a heavy toll of human lives have been greatly controlled. With the application of science and technology to agriculture, the supply of food has kept pace with the demand. Moreover, the distribution of food has been considerably facilitated by improvement both in the means of transportation and in the methods of food storage. As a result, the threat of famines has been virtually eliminated. That, however, does not mean there are no periodic food shortages either due to the failure of monsoons or due to some other natural calamity. Such situations can now be met by quick imports. The international community has so far responded splendidly to any threat of famine in any part of the world. International cooperation has been responsible for staving off many deaths due to starvation. Similarly, deaths from epidemics like cholera, plague, smallpox, and other such diseases have been greatly reduced because of the widespread use of immunization, antibiotics, and other products of modern medicine. The eradication of malaria by D.D.T. has had a spectacular effect in reducing the death rate. Better water supplies and improved sanitary conditions brought about mainly by the public health programmes have helped reduce the incidence of death.

The successful attack on the factors causing high mortality is reflected in an increased life expectancy at birth and also in a sharp reduction in the infant mortality rate. The latter has dropped from 232 per thousand in 1901 to 98 in 1961. Although this rate is still considerably high when compared to rates in the West, the decline is dramatic and represents considerable progress. The expectation of life at birth has increased from 23.6 years in 1901 to 52.5 years in 1970. This is a significant achievement though a cause of population explosion.

An important feature of the decline in the death rate is that this has been accomplished without India's having experienced any significant economic development. The reduction in mortality has been achieved by the use of quick and inexpensive methods mostly imported from abroad for fighting diseases. The western countries had to struggle hard to attain a similar decline in their death rates. It took them 70 to 80 years to achieve a decline in mortality which took India hardly 20 years.

Causes of the High Birth Rate

The birth rate in India continues to be very high. Efforts in the direction of reducing the birth rate have not yet been successful. There are various reasons for this.[5]

1. Marriage in India is an almost universal phenomenon and every one sooner or later gets married. "Marriage is not merely a necessary social institution but a quasi-religious duty."[6] Nearly 99 per cent of the eligible males and females marry at least once in their lifetime.

2. Marriage at an early age in both males and females is another factor which contributes to the high birth rate. The average age of marriage, according to the 1961 census, for females was 15.8 years and for males 21.6 years. Early marriage is greatly facilitated by the institution of the joint family system. The married partners need not be economically self-supporting and the husband does not need to have any independent household. Thus, there are no economic restraints to marriage. Marriage at an early age among females contributes to the high birth rate in two ways. First, it prolongs the period of child-bearing, and second, the fertility in the younger age-group is very high. It is estimated that in 1961 nearly 70 per cent of females in the age group of 15–19 years were already married. The corresponding figures for a developed country like Sweden is only 3.7 per cent.

3. The widely prevalent desire to have sons also leads to a high birth rate. This desire is based primarily on economic grounds but also has some religious justification. Sons are expected to provide economic support to their parents when they are sick, unemployed or old. For a country like India with no comprehensive social security programme, this desire is understandable. Because of the high mortality in the past, it was necessary for a couple to have a large number of children in order to ensure the survival of one or two. This attitude persists even though

---

[5] India's birth rate is not any higher than the birth rates of other developing countries. But, considering the already excessive population of India, the present birth rate constitutes a serious threat.

[6] S. Chandrasekhar, *India's Population*, p. 15.

there has been a sharp decline in mortality.

4. The decline in maternal mortality and increase in life expectancy have also led to the higher birth rate. This is a necessary consequence of improvements in health facilities.

5. There is also the absence of widespread use of family planning methods among both urban and rural population, especially among the latter who constitute 80 per cent of the total. Most people regard children as a gift of God and uncontrolled procreation is regarded as one of the laws of normal life.

These factors when taken in conjunction with the entire social and economic structure of the country, tend to maintain the birth rate at a high level. In reality, the birth rate of a country is a highly complex phenomenon and is determined by socio-economic, cultural-religious, and biological factors. All these factors are interrelated with each other in a very complicated manner. Because of their inter-dependence, it is extremely difficult to indicate precisely the manner in which each of these influences the birth rate. Thus, to provide an adequate explanation for the existence of a high birth rate for a poor country like India, which is still caught up in its age-old traditions, religious taboos, and rigid social institutions, becomes a difficult task.

The next section attempts to provide an economic explanation for the existence of the high birth rate in India but it is strongly emphasized that economic factors must be studied in conjunction with non-economic factors.

3. An Economic Theory of Family Formation[7]

An economic explanation for differing levels of birth rates in different countries is based on the theory of cost-benefit analysis. It is argued that in a poor country costs of raising children are low and benefits large, and there is an economic incentive for having large families. Conversely, costs of raising children for an average family in a rich country are very high and benefits small which necessitates a small size family. Let us now analyze this theory in detail.

The underlying economic rationale for different sizes of families is based on the familiar principle of utility maximization. This approach treats a couple as a consumer unit and a child as a special kind of consumer-producer good. A child is like a consumer good because he satisfies certain needs of his parents, and he is like a producer good because investment made in him yields a stream of economic returns. These attributes make a child an economic asset and thus worth having. There are, however, costs of acquiring and maintaining a child which make him not a free good but one with a price tag. A child, therefore, is both a source of benefits and costs. Like any consumer, a couple also operates within a given budget constraint and has to allocate the limited resources among several competing assets (one of which happens to be a child) in such a way as to maximize their utility. Consequently, a rational couple is hypothesized as weighing the satisfaction and other returns anticipated from a child against the costs of raising him before deciding to have one. A couple is expected to have a child if expected benefits exceed costs. They would stop having further children when the additional benefits from the last child equal the additional costs. The last child becomes the marginal unit and satisfies the equilibrium condition of equating marginal benefits with marginal costs. Because couples differ in their budget constraints and in their preference functions, we find differing sizes of families.

Costs and Benefits of Having Children

A child imposes two kinds of costs on his parents. These are financial and opportunity costs. The first covers the complete

[7] The discussion of this section is based on the work of Warren C. Robinson and David E. Horlacher, *Population Growth and Economic Welfare*, Reports on Population/Family Planning, no. 6, Feb. 1971, (New York: The Population Council).

cost of acquiring and maintaining a child until he is grown up. Expenses for prenatal care, delivery, postnatal care, food, clothing, shelter, medical care, and education, which arise due to a child are included in financial costs. Some of these may be borne by the state which would then reduce the cost to the parents. The second covers the earnings foregone by the working mother during the period of her confinement and expenses of extra-parental care. It is argued that the costs of raising children are directly related to the economic status of the parents.

Parents expect to enjoy two types of benefit from their off-spring. These are economic and non-economic. The former includes the economic contribution which a child is expected to make to his family's income when he grows up. The latter includes the joy experienced by the parents of having a child at home, playing with him, and seeing him grow to adulthood. The desire to have a male child for continuing the family line and to perform religious rites at the time of the parents' death are also part of non-economic benefits. While economic benefits are assumed to be inversely related to the economic status of the parents, the non-economic benefits are dependent upon several factors, such as social, cultural, religious, and psychological.

Why Do Countries Have Differing Birth Rates?

Using the cost-benefit approach to family formation, one can now rationalize the existence of high birth rates in developing countries and of low birth rates in developed countries.

Developing Countries. In a typical developing country like India, nearly 80 per cent of the people live in villages and work on land; their living standards are deplorably low. In such a set-up, where the people are poor and illiterate, costs of raising children are low and constitute a very small portion of the family budget. In most cases, prenatal care is rare, delivery takes place within the house, usually with the help of a village midwife whose fee is nominal. Expenses of food, clothing, and shelter do not impose additional financial burden because most of it comes through reallocation within the existing budget. Medical and educational expenses are negligible. Most often, a child does not go to school at all. Similarly, opportunity costs are almost zero because women generally do not work outside the home, and there are thus no extra-parental care expenses. Moreover, the institution of the joint family system makes it easier to raise a child because the direct burden of looking after him does not fall exclusively on the individual parents. Consequently, costs of acquiring and maintaining children are low in a poor society.

On the other hand, benefits are relatively large. A child starts helping his family on the farm at an early age. He learns the skills of farming by observing others and does not require any outside training. At the time of harvest, a farmer normally needs a lot of labour, and the availability of non-wage family labour makes a big family an asset. And, as already stated, because of lack of social security programmes in such countries, children are the best form of social insurance.

Since costs of raising children are low and benefits large, there is an economic incentive for having a large number of children. In other words, it is with a large number of children that a couple satisfies the equilibrium condition of equating marginal costs and marginal benefits.

Developed Countries. In a typical developed country, nearly 80 per cent of the people live in urban areas and derive their income from non-farm occupations, and the average living standard is high. In such a society both literacy and mobility are high. Costs of raising children in such a society are quite high. An average family spends a considerable sum of money in the form of prenatal care, hospital delivery, postpartum care for both mother and infant. The annual cost of upkeep, which includes food, clothing, shelter, medical care, and education, is very high and constitutes a sizable part of the family's budget. Opportunity costs both in terms of earnings foregone by the working mother and expenses for extra-parental care are not insignificant. There is a strong desire on the part of the parents to maintain their living standards even when the family grows big. In fact, it is observed that parents often desire their children to enjoy even higher standards which means more investment in them. In short, costs of raising children in developed countries are high and impose a heavy financial burden on an average family.

Moreover, parents do not ordinarily expect economic support from their children. Most often, when a child becomes an earner he leaves his parents' home. The existence of extensive welfare programmes makes the economic argument for a large family redundant. A child is mainly a source of non-economic benefits. The psychic satisfaction which parents derive from their children declines sharply with the addition of each child.

Thus, in developed countries children are more of a burden and less of an asset which, therefore, necessitates a small size family.

Graphic Presentation

The above analysis can be neatly presented diagrammatically to illustrate the behaviour of two typical couples—one belonging to a developing country and the other to a devloped country—in arriving at the equilibrium sizes of their families. In Figure 3, the vertical axis represents the benefits and costs of having children, and the horizontal axis indicates the number of children. MC_1 and MC_2 refer to the marginal costs of raising children for an average couple in developing and developed countries respectively. The costs of raising the first child equals OB in a developing country and OC in a developed country. It is assumed that the cost of raising further children stays constant at these levels. This is indicated by the horizontal marginal cost curves. MB_1 and MB_2 refer to the marginal benefits which an average couple expects in a developing and developed economy respectively. OD indicates the benefits expected from the first child and, for the sake of simplicity, these are assumed identical for each couple in both countries. But the marginal benefits from additional children drop at a slow rate for the couple in the developing country and at a much faster rate for the couple in the developed economy. These differing rates of marginal benefits are indicated by differing slopes of marginal benefit curves.

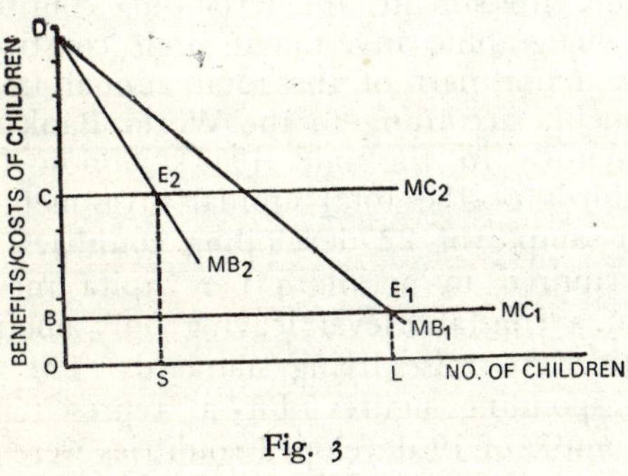

Fig. 3

The couple in the developing country reaches an equilibrium size of family at point E_1 where MB_1 intersects MC_1. The other couple in the advanced economy attains an equilibrium at point E_2 where MB_2 intersects MC_2. These points are represented by letters S and L on the horizontal axis indicating that a couple with low economic status would have a larger number of children than a couple with a higher economic status.

Limitations of this Approach

Even though the cost-benefit approach to family formation has explained the existence of differential family sizes, the presentation of this approach has been rather at an elementary level.[8] The inherent

[8] For example, spacing of children, economies and diseconomies resulting from a large number of children, have not been taken into consideration.

limitations of this approach necessitate caution in accepting the validity of the analysis in its entirety. First, it assumes that an average couple is rational and well-informed. Most couples in a developed country are reasonably well informed but this may not be so in a developing country. Secondly, it assumes that family planning techniques are known and contraceptives are available and accessible so that a couple has children not by chance but by choice. Again, this knowledge may not exist among most couples in a poor country. Thirdly, this is a micro approach which analyzes each family in isolation. The social costs and benefits of differing family sizes are not discussed. Fourthly, the approach does not discriminate between the sex of the child. This may be of no relevance for a developed country but it has great significance for an average couple in a developing country. Lastly, this is mainly an economic approach and treats the child as a consumer-producer good which to some may sound cold and dry.

Despite these limitations, it is generally felt that this approach does provide a reasonably sound explanation for differing sizes of families. The analysis also contains some policy implications for controlling the population growth. For example, a government may succeed in reducing the desirability for a large size family by adopting certain measures such as compulsory education, declaring child labour illegal, and devising a suitable social security programme.

Having discussed the causes for the rapidly growing population of India, we now examine its impact on economic development.

4. Population Growth and Economic Development

The major task facing the developing countries like India is to bring about economic development so as to raise the living standards of their people. A rising living standard means improvement in the economic well-being of the people so that they can afford more and better amenities of life. For most people in India, it means access to more and better food, clothing, shelter, education, and medical facilities. For no other better indicator, economic development is still measured by rising real per capita income, which is the growth of real national income adjusted to the growth in population. And, if the standards of living are to improve, it is essential that the rate of economic development must be higher than the rate of population growth. As we shall see below, a rapidly growing population makes the task of economic development more difficult. In fact, most developing countries are discovering that their efforts to advance into the modern industrial age are being thwarted by a rapidly growing population, and that they need to work hard even to stay at the same place. The reason is that the expanded outlay for food, shelter, clothing, and other social services for meeting the needs of a growing population limits the availability of funds for capital formation.

Demographers draw a distinction between two kinds of investment—demographic and economic. The former refers to the investment required to maintain the per capita income of the growing population at a constant level, and the latter to the investment required for raising the per capita income. While the first is determined by the rate of population growth, the second is determined by the population growth and the rate of increase in per capita income desired. There can be no economic development without economic investment. In developing countries, demographic investment itself constitutes a major part of the total annual investment. According to the World Bank estimates, "In the mid 1960's, almost two-thirds of the total annual investment in a sample of 22 developing countries was required to maintain per capita income at a constant level leaving only about a third to raise living standards. The corresponding figures for a representative sample of 19 developed countries were one quarter and three quarters."[9] This helps explain why India has not made any significant increase in per capita income. Most of the investments are used primarily to provide an increasing population with a constant living standard. While reviewing the economic and social progress the country has made, the Fourth Five Year Plan had this to say: "Per capita real income in 1965–66 was about the same as it was in 1960–61, the results of the meagre growth rate of national income having been completely neutralized by the 2.5 per cent rate of population growth."[10] Clearly, the major objective of economic development of raising the living standards is being jeopardized by the population explosion.

Population Growth and Capital Requirements

Investment is a necessary condition for economic growth. A country with a fast growing population needs to devote a larger proportion of its national income towards capital formation than a country with a slow growing population for obtaining the same increase in the per capita income. How much a country should actually invest depends upon the rate of economic growth desired and its capital-output ratio. The rate of growth in per capita income can be obtained by subtracting the rate of population growth from the rate of economic growth. The capital-output ratio indicates the amount of capital required to produce one unit of output. This ratio is about 3:1 for most developing countries such as India. This means that that a country needs three additional units of capital to get one additional unit of output. The investment required to achieve a certain rate of economic growth can be estimated by multiplying the rate by the capital-output ratio. For instance, if a developing country with its population growing at 3 per cent a year desired its per capita income to increase at 2 per cent a year, it will have to grow at 5 per cent a year, and it will need to invest 15 per cent of its national income annually. On the other hand, if the population of this country was increasing at one per cent a year, it will need to invest 9 per cent a year for getting the same increase in per capita income.

Using the above analysis Table 3 gives the rates of investments which India must make to obtain different rates of growth in per capita income.

Table 3. Investment Required for Different Rates of Growth

Population growth %	Growth in per capita income %	Growth in national income %	Capital-output ratio %	Investment required %
2.5	0	2.5	3 : 1	7.5
2.5	1.0	3.5	3 : 1	10.5
2.5	3.0	5.5	3 : 1	16.5
2.5	7.0	9.5	3 : 1	28.5

To keep the per capita income from falling, India must invest 7.5 per cent of its national income annually. The entire amount becomes demographic investment. An investment of 10.5 per cent will be required to obtain an annual increase of one per cent in per capita income. If India wants per capita income to rise at 3 per cent a year, so as to double it every 23 years, it must invest 16.5 per cent a year. And, if the aim is to double the per capita income in one decade, India must achieve a growth rate of 7 per cent a year in per capita income, and for that it must be prepared to invest as much as 28.5 per cent a year.

Currently, India's per capita income is growing around one per cent a year. At this rate, it will double in 70 or 80 years. This is a long way to go. The Fourth Plan estimates that aggregate domestic savings should rise from 8 per cent of the national income in 1968–69 to 13.2 per cent in 1973-74, and to 16.6 per cent in

---

[9] World Bank, *Population Planning*, Sector Working Paper (Washington, D.C.: March 1972), p. 5.

[10] Government of India, Planning Commission, *Fourth Five Year Plan: 1969–74* (New Delhi: Publication Division), p. 5.

1980-81.[11] If these savings can be actually mobilized, India should be able to achieve an annual growth rate of 3 per cent in per capita income by the end of the Fifth Plan. This projection and the ones in Table 3 are based on the assumption that population continues to grow at the current rate. A decline in this rate will accelerate the process of economic development.

Consequences of the Population Explosion

The foregoing analysis indicates that a country with a fast growing population needs to invest a large amount to raise the per capita income. Unfortunately, a rapidly growing population has features which hamper the process of economic development by reducing the availability of investible funds. These features are: 1. higher dependency ratio, 2. increasing demand for food, 3. unemployment problem, and 4. diversion of investment to social services. The implication of these for economic development will now be examined.

Higher Dependency Ratio. The population of a country can be divided into two groups: economically active and economically inactive. The former refers to the population in the age-group of 15-59 years which is a working population. The latter refers to the population in the age-groups of below 15 years and over 59 years. This is the non-working group which depends for its consumption needs on the economically active group. In most developing countries, the economically productive group constitutes nearly 55 per cent of the population, and the corresponding figure for developed countries is around 65 per cent. This implies a higher dependency ratio in developing countries, i.e., a working adult supports a relatively larger number of people than his counterpart in a developed country. Higher dependency ratio is a necessary consequence of population explosion. A high birth rate results in an age structure heavily skewed towards younger people. And also, reduction in infant mortality increases the number of dependent children. A higher dependency ratio has an adverse effect on the availability of savings. A worker has to meet his own consumption needs and those of his dependents before he can think of saving.

According to the 1961 census, productive and non-productive consumers constituted 55 per cent and 45 per cent of India's population respectively. It is anticipated that with further decline in the death rate and with no change in the birth rate, the dependency ratio will rise. The problem in India is even worse because not everyone in the working age-group is gainfully employed. Consequently, the actual percentage of dependents is much higher.

Population Growth and the Demand for Food. The most widely shared concern about the population growth is the fear that it will outrun the growth in food supply and bring the population closer to starvation. The Malthusian spectre of overpopulation based on the assumption that the food supply will not be able to keep up with demand has long been invalidated in most of the developed countries where agriculture has made tremendous advances. But the Malthusian spectre of mass starvation and hunger still hangs like Damocles' sword over most developing countries. In most of these, the supply of food has not kept pace with the demand. With population growing at an explosive rate, these countries will witness an accelerating demand for food in the coming decades. Food and other farm products constitute major consumption items for an average family. It is estimated that the average income elasticity of demand for food in India is around 0.8 which is very high.

In India, until recently, the demand for food exceeded the supply of food and the deficit was met by imports. During the Third Plan alone, India imported 25 million tons of foodgrains. While im-

[11] Government of India, *The Fourth Plan,* p. 46.

ports of foodgrains constituted 5 to 6 per cent of the total demand, it, however, meant a great loss of valuable foreign exchange which could have been utilized for imports of capital goods. It is now felt that India has reached the stage of near self-sufficiency in food because of the emerging green revolution. The success of the green revolution has brought a new sense of confidence and hope in Indian agriculture. But, will this revolution continue at this rate? India has brought most of its land under cultivation. The Fourth Plan expects to increase the area under cultivation by an additional 2 per cent only. Thus, increase in output has to come through intensive cultivation and higher yields per acre. The Fourth Plan estimates that the output of food and other farm products must increase at the rate of 5 per cent a year so as to be self-sufficient. To meet these goals, India will require a successive series of green revolutions, which means huge investment in the agriculture sector. According to Dr. Lester R. Brown, a leading expert in agriculture, improvements in agriculture brought about through intensive cultivation and use of improved variety of seeds can only give breathing time during which countries must take measures to control their population growth. He says:[12]

> ...the new seeds [do not] offer a solution to the food problem, but they do buy some precious time perhaps an additional 10–15 years in which to stabilize world population growth. If within 15 years we are not well on our way to stabilize world population growth, Dr. Borlaug's monumental contribution will have been in vain. Let it not be so.

It may be possible to increase food production to meet the increasing demand by the application of advances in science and technology. But, as mentioned above, this will call for huge investment in the agriculture sector, which will have to be diverted from other areas. It is the diversion of investment to agriculture from other crucial sectors which causes the planners great concern. If population growth could be controlled and the demand for food did not increase so rapidly, India's investible resources could be used in non-agricultural areas, such as industry, communication, transportation.

Population Growth and the Unemployment Problem. Another serious consequence of a rapidly growing population is the resultant manpower explosion—the swelling stream of fresh entrants to an already over-glutted labour market making the unemployment situation still worse. Despite the best efforts to create more jobs through Five Year Plans, the unemployment problem in India is much more serious today than at any time before. Every plan ends up with a greater backlog of unemployed people. For example, the backlog of unemployment at the end of the Second Plan was 9 million. The additional labour force expected during the Third Plan was estimated at 17 million. The Third Plan anticipated additional employment for 14 million, thus ending up with a backlog of 12 million. This backlog includes open unemployment. But in India nearly one-fourth of the labour force is under-employed. It is anticipated that during the 70's and 80's, the manpower problem is going to be extremely serious. This will be the result of the extraordinary expansion of population which occurred in the 50's and 60's. The babies born during that period will enter the labour market in the 70's and 80's. And, "No program of family planning, public or private, surgical or spiritual, chemical or mechanical, will have the slightest effect whatsoever on the labour force explosion of the 70's."[13] It is expected that nearly 90 million people will enter the labour force during the 70's alone.

To provide jobs for such a rapidly growing labour force is an extremely difficult task and requires huge investment and

[12] Lester R. Brown, "Nobel Peace Prize: Developer of High-Yield Wheat Receives Award," *Science,* vol. 170, no. 3957 (October 1970), p. 519.

[13] Population Reference Bureau, "India: Ready or Not", p. 10.

careful planning. But for a developing country like India, it is difficult to mobilize resources on such a large scale. Governments often end up encouraging labour-intensive projects even though such investments may be less productive from the long-run growth point of view. In short, a rapidly expanding population makes it even more difficult to raise employment and per capita income simultaneously.

Diversion of Investment to Social Services. In addition to the diversion of investments discussed above, a rapidly growing population also leads to increased expenditure on social services, such as health, education, and housing. A rising population means a growing proportion of young people which creates heavy demand for these services. Undoubtedly, expenditure on these services adds to the productive capacity of the nation by improving the quality of the labour but such investments are ordinarily capital-intensive and have long-gestation periods. These investments constitute a sizable part of the total annual investments and the proportion is expected to go up as population keeps growing. During the Third Plan, Rs. 9.36 million were spent on education, health, and housing and urban development. The Fourth Plan has made provision for Rs. 8.23 billion for education, Rs. 4.35 billion for health, and Rs. 2.37 billion for housing and urban development.[14] This outlay does not include non-plan expenditure by the government and expenditure by the private sector. Expenditures on such a large scale impose a great burden on the limited resources of the country. If population growth could be reduced, some of these resources could then be diverted to other projects. Coale and Hoover have shown that, if India could reduce its population growth by half between 1956–81, the country could save as much as Rs. 60 to 65 billion during the thirty years' period of 1956–86 from housing and education alone.[15]

[14] Government of India, *The Fourth Plan,* p. 66.

The above discussion has shown that while a rapidly growing population requires a large investment to raise the living standards, it has the features of reducing the availability of investible funds, thereby making the task of economic development extremely difficult. The Fourth Plan has stressed the serious threat which India's rapid population growth poses to development plans. It says:[16]

> Population growth on this scale can be a crippling handicap since our population in relation to resources is already large, incomes are low and economic development is a desperate need. The speed at which a country develops depends largely upon its ability to direct a larger part of its growing resources to investment rather than current consumption. A growing population with a high proportion of dependent children will find it increasingly difficult to do so. If population keeps growing rapidly, the major part of investment and national energy and efforts may be used up for merely maintaining the existing low living standards. Population growth thus presents a very serious challenge.

Will the population explosion in India continue indefinitely ? The answer is a clear no. The growth of population will have to slow down. The resources of India are not limitless. They, therefore, cannot sustain a rapidly growing population for all time. But what factors will bring about a slow-down ? To answer this question, let us look at the pattern of population growth as experienced by the advanced countries.

5. The Theory of Demographic Transition

The theory of demographic transition postulates a three-stage relationship between economic development and the population

[15] A. J. Coale and E. M. Hoover, *Population Growth and Economic Development in Low Income Countries* (Princeton : Princeton University Press, 1958), p. 254.

[16] Government of India, *The Fourth Plan,* p. 31.

growth. According to this theory, as a country advances economically, its population passes through the stages of low growth to high growth, and then finally to low and stable growth. These stages of population growth are shown in Figure 4, where the horizontal axis indicates diffe-

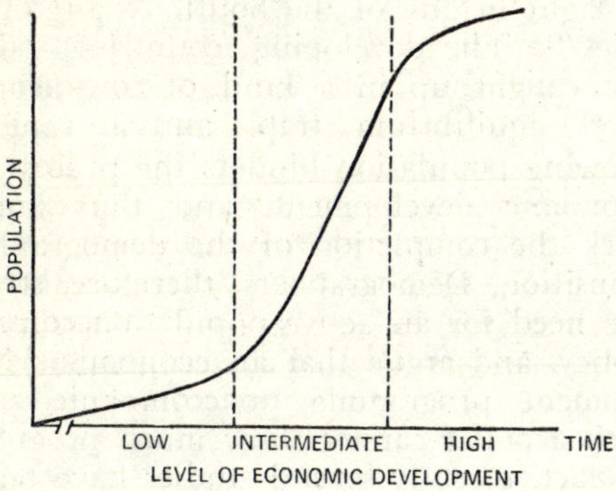

Fig. 4

rent levels of economic development, and the vertical axis population.

During the first stage, a country is at a low level of economic development. Agriculture is the major occupation, and it is conducted in primitive form. The average living standard is extremely low. Most people are illiterate, and are ruled by age-old customs and religious beliefs. Such a society is characterized by a high and relatively stable birth rate and a high but fluctuating death rate, leaving little room for population expansion. The rate of population growth in this stage is below one per cent a year.

As an economy advances, the living standards of the people improve. They now eat better and live longer. Developments in science and technology, and in medicine make means available to control the forces of death. As a result, the death rate starts declining. The birth rate still continues to be at a high level because of the resistance to change the long-established customs and traditions. The imbalance between the high birth rate and the declining death rate leads to a high population growth. The rate of population growth ranges between one to three per cent a year. Demographers call this a period of population explosion. This is a stage of disequilibrium because the population of a country cannot keep growing indefinitely at a high rate.

As economic development continues, the structure of the economy undergoes a change. Industry comes to dominate, which creates a massive shift of population from rural to urban areas. Most people are literate and highly mobile. The status of women also undergoes a change and they start joining the labour force in increasing numbers. These factors tend to make children more of a burden and less of an asset. Thus, small families are preferred. This leads to a decline in the birth rate. In this stage, we ultimately have a low birth rate, a low death rate, and a low but stable population growth, around one per cent a year.

All developed countries have passed through these stages and are now in the final stage. Some demographers observed that when a country becomes highly affluent, there is a tendency for the birth rate to go up, as has happened in the United States during the post-war period. This is regarded as a very temporary phenomenon. It is estimated that most of the European countries entered into the second stage in the latter part of the 18th century and remained in that stage for nearly 100 years.

Most of the developing countries today are in the second stage, and are experiencing population explosions. To answer the question raised at the end of section 4 about the future of population explosion in India we must first ask whether these countries will also experience the same type of demographic transition.

The Relevance of the Demographic Transition Theory to Developing Countries

Will a developing country like India follow a similar population cycle on its own ? Many population experts do not think so. They cite several factors which they feel hinder the application of the transitional theory to the presently over-populated developing countries. They base their arguments on the contrasts they observe between the economic conditions and demographic situaton in the developing countries today with those prevailing in the developed countries at the corresponding stage of their development. They emphasize the following differences.[17]

1. The decline in the death rate in the developed countries was slow and gradual, and was the result of overall economic development. On the other hand, the decline in the death rate in the developing countries has been sudden and rapid and it has not been accompanied by any economic development.

2. The developed countries never experienced birth rates above 40 during their development period. Moreover, after a time lag, these countries registered a decline in their birth rates. On the other hand, the birth rates in the developing countries today range between 40 and 60 and we do not observe any significant decline in their birth rates even though the death rates have declined considerably.

3. Thus, the magnitude of the population explosion being experienced by the developing countries today is much more severe. Such high rates of population growth were never experienced by the developed countries.

4. The developing countries today are relatively more densely populated than was the case for most developed countries during their period of development.

5. The developing countries today are at a much lower level of economic development than was the case for the developed countnies in the past.

6. The opportunities for large scale international migration as existed during the 18th and 19th centuries do not exist any more.

7. Unlike most developed countries, the developing countries today have no colonies to exploit.

Because of the above differences in the circumstances of the developing countries today, there is little hope that they will automatically follow the traditional demographic cycle and attain demographic equilibrium. According to Myrdal, "the population cycle which would restore near balance between births and deaths, is not in sight in any of the South Asian countries."[18] The developing countries today are caught up in a kind of low-income level equilibrium trap, and a rapidly growing population hinders the process of economic development, and thus holds back the completion of the demographic transition. Demographers, therefore, stress the need for an active population control policy, and argue that an economic development programme unaccompanied by such a policy cannot show much progress. In fact, recently several studies have been conducted showing that a developing country will grow faster with a reduced population growth.

One such study, which is of relevance to India, has been conducted by Coale.[19] In this study, the question raised is as to what will be the effect on income per consumer if a country decides to reduce its fertility rate by 50 per cent over a 25 years period? India is used as a case study. The findings indicate that income per consumer would grow faster with reduced fertility. It is shown that after 30 years, income per consumer in a population with reduced fertility would be 40 per cent higher than income per consumer in a population with unchanged fertility. The difference in income would increase to 100 per cent after 60 years, and to 600 per cent after 150 years. The study demonstrates very clearly that a country stands to gain, and will grow at a faster rate, if it is able to reduce its population growth.

---

17 Cf. Ashish Bose, "The Population Puzzle in India," *Economic Development and Cultural Change*, vol. 7, no. 3 (April 1959), pp. 245–46. The article contains a useful summary of these differences.

18 Gunnar Myrdal, *Asian Drama*, vol. 2 (New York: The Twentieth Century Fund, 1968), p. 1402.

19 A. J. Coale, "Population and Economic Development," in Philip M. Hauser (ed.), *The Population Dilemma* (Englewood Cliffs: Prentice-Hall, 1963).

6. Population Policy in India

It is encouraging to note that the Planning Commission in India itself recognized in the beginning that a rapidly growing population can be a menace to economic development and advocated the need for family planning. The Government of India took a courageous stand on this question and displayed great foresight by adopting family planning as an integral part of its overall national development programme. In fact, India is credited to be the first country in the world to adopt family planning as a state policy.

The first indication of the official attitude towards the population problem was contained in the First Plan which, *inter alia,* stated that "there is no doubt that given a stuation in which shortage of capital equipment rather than of labour is the main limiting factor in development, a rapidly growing population is apt to become more a source of embarrassment than of help to a programme for raising standards of living."[20] And, it advocated the need for "reduction of the birth rate to the extent necessary to stablilize the population at a level consistent with the requirements of national economy."[21] Accordingly, a sum of Rs. 6.5 million was made available for family planning. Since the reaction of the people to this new public policy was not known, a cautious approach to the family planning programme was suggested.

The need for population control was stressed even more strongly in the Second Plan, which stated:[22]

> The logic of facts is unmistakable and there is no doubt that under conditions prevailing in countries like India, a high rate of population growth is bound to affect adversely the rate of economic advance and living standards *per capita.* Given the overall shortage of land and capital equipment relatively to population as in India, the conclusion is inescapable that an effective curb on population growth is an important condition for rapid improvement in incomes and in levels of living.

During the Second Plan period, the family planning programme was organized on a nation-wide basis. A Central Family Planning Board was instituted and a Director of Family Planning was appointed in the Ministry of Health at the Centre. Similar boards were also formed at the state level and family planning officers appointed to head these. It was expected that such an organizational set up would help generate a country-wide awareness of the population issue and the need to check the population growth through family planning. The principal method for expanding the programme was still to be the birth control clinics which were to be increased during the Plan. A sum of Rs. 50 million was allocated for family planning.

Even though both plans indicated an official desire to control the population growth, the actual implementation of the programme was half-hearted and lacked a sense of urgency. Both plans failed to fully spend the amount allocated. The First Plan spent hardly 25 per cent of its budgeted amount, and the Second only 45 per cent. The Second Plan, no doubt, created a general awareness of the need for family planning; the programme, however, lacked enthusiastic support, leadership, and a sense of direction. Several reasons have been advanced for the indifference with which the programme was implemented. First, India was the first country in the world to launch a publicly-supported family planning programme, and was thus breaking new ground. The government was not sure of the kind of response such a programme would receive from the political parties, religious groups, and the public at large. It, therefore, adopted a very cautious and exploratory kind of approach. Secondly, the programme relied heavily on the traditional clinical-referral approach, and treated

20 Government of India Planning Commission, *The First Five Year Plan* (New Delhi: Govt. of India Press, 1960), p. 18.

21 Ibid., p. 522.

22 Government of India Planning Commission, *The Second Five Year Plan* (New Delhi: Publications Division), p. 7.

family planning as medical rather than a social and economic problem. Thirdly, which perhaps might be the most important reason, the planners seriously underestimated the population growth. The Second Plan estimated the rates of population growth to be 12.5 per cent for the decade 1951–60, 13.3 per cent for 1961–70, and 14.0 per cent for 1971–80.[23] The family planning programme was based on these projections about the population growth.

But this attitude of neglect did not last long. The results of the 1961 census were a shocking revelation to the planners and brought forth a new seriousness and determination to the family planning programme. This was reflected in the subsequent plans. For instance, the Third Plan emphasized that "the objective of stabilizing the growth of population over a reasonable period must be at the very centre of planned development."[24] And it strongly recommended that "the greatest stress has to be placed in the Third and subsequent Five Year Plans on the programme for family planning."[25] This indicated a clear recognition of the gravity of the country's population problem and the resolve to check it. A sum of Rs. 500 million was provided for family planning, which was more than nine times the combined allocation of funds under the previous two plans. The programme was to be suitably reorganized so as as to reach the people both in urban and rural areas. The Plan emphasized the need for educating the people through various media, and to motivate them to accept the norm of a small family size. The programme was to be expanded through the clinical-cum-extension approach. Though, towards the middle of the Plan, the emphasis shifted more towards the extension approach.

The Fourth Plan described family planning as a programme of "the highest priority." It reiterated that "In order to make economic development yield tangible benefits for the ordinary people, it is necessary that the birth rate be brought down as early as possible.[26] It proposed that the programme should aim at reducing the birth rate from 39 per thousand to 25 per thousand within the next 10–12 years. This was the first time that a Five Year Plan contained a specific recommendation for setting a particular target for reducing the birth rate. It was suggested that to achieve this goal, the programme must expand its activities, and should encourage eligible couples to adopt family planning as a way of life through, "(i) group acceptance of the small sized family; (ii) personal knowledge about family planning methods; and (iii) ready availability of supplies and services."[27] A sum of Rs. 3.15 billion was provided for implementing the programme. It appears certain that family planning will receive a high priority in the future plans as well.

The problem of population growth is also being attacked through changes in socio-economic factors. Some of these changes are: raising the age at marriage for both males and females, improving the economic and social status of women, making education compulsory, declaring child labour illegal, and provision of old age security programmes. It is expected that these changes, in addition to family planning, will help reduce the birth rate. The recent passage of the liberal abortion bill by Parliament was also a step to this end. There is no doubt that India is now strongly determined to control its runaway population growth.

The Family Planning Programme in India

The family planning programme as it exists today has the following essential features.

1. The guiding philosophy of the programme is to educate the people about

[23] Government of India, *The Second Plan*, p. 8.

[24] Government of India Planning Commission, *Third Five Year Plan* (New Delhi: Govt. of India Press), p. 675.

[25] Ibid., p. 675.

[26] Government of India, *The Fourth Plan*, p. 391.

[27] Ibid., p. 391.

the need for family planning and to motivate them to accept it on a voluntary basis rather than through force. "In its implementation, the programme shuns any force, coercion or compulsion and depends on long-term education and motivation of the people on a sustained basis."[28] It is encouraging to note that there does not exist any kind of organized opposition to family planning either from political parties or from religious groups. The knowledge, attitude, and practice surveys have shown that the majority of Indian couples, nearly 70 per cent urban and 50 to 70 per cent rural, favour family planning.

2. The programme has adopted the "cafeteria approach" which means making available a variety of medically tested and proven contraceptives, such as sterilization, IUCD, pills, condoms, foam tablets, jellies, and other conventional contraceptives. The objective is to allow the couple to choose a method among many which suits them the most. Even though there are several contraceptives "on the shelf," the programme has, however, relied heavily on sterilization and on IUCD. Efforts are made to make family planning services available to clients as close to their place of residence as possible. A large network of rural and urban birth control clinics has been established. In 1968, "there were 7057 static and 754 mobile units, 1086 urban centres and 5130 rural centres with over 19000 sub-centers and 9000 other medical institutions where family planning advice and supplies were available."[29]

3. In 1965 when the government accepted the inter-uterine contraceptive device (IUCD) as one of the contraceptives, the family planning programme got a real breakthrough and the movement gained momentum. Since then, the programme has become time and target-oriented. Currently the goal is to reduce the birth rate by 23 per thousand by 1978–79.[30] To accomplish this, annual targets for sterilizations, IUCD insertions, and other contraceptives are specified for each state. These targets are fixed on the basis of the state's population and its past performance.

4. The actual implementation of the programme is in the hands of the state governments. But it is a centrally sponsored programme and is entirely financed by the Central Government. In 1966, a separate Department of Family Planning was created at the Centre to coordinate the family planning programme at the Centre and in the states. For family planning services to reach the people, every state has developed an organizational set-up from the state headquarters to the peripheral level.

5. The family planning programme is highly flexible and dynamic. It allows for periodic evaluation of its working both by internal and external agencies. The Programme Evaluation Organization of the Planning Commission and other officially appointed committees have frequently investigated the working of the programme. The United Nations, at the request of the Government of India, sent two missions—one in 1965 and the other in 1969—to evaluate the performance of the programme and to suggest measures to improve its working. Such periodic evaluations have helped the programme to improve its efficacy. Similarly, the programme also encourages research in medical and biological aspects of family planning. Field studies to investigate the attitude of the people towards family planning are often conducted.

Performance of the Family Planning Programme

Despite so much emphasis on family planning, India's population explosion continues almost at an unabated rate. The programme has not yet succeeded in bringing about any significant decline in

[28] Govind Narain, *India: The Family Planning Program Since 1965*, Studies in Family Planning, no. 35, (New York: The Population Council, November 1968), p. 1. Mr. Narain provides an excellent review of the working and performance of the family planning programme in India.

[29] Ibid., p. 2.

[30] Ibid., p. 7.

the birth rate. There is no doubt that some births have been prevented but the number is very small. It is estimated that during the three year period of 1965–66 to 1967–68, nearly 1.2 million pregnancies were prevented.[31] Even this figure is not very reliable because the recording of vital statistics still continues to be incomplete and defective. It is, however, unambiguously clear that the programme has not yet made any spectacular progress the way similar programmes have done in South Korea and Taiwan. As indicated earlier, it is argued that even though the programme was officially launched in 1952 it suffered from a great deal of uncertainty and lack of initiative for a long time, and it was in 1965 that the programme got a real start. It is, therefore, too early to judge its performance. Its success or failure will not be known until the 1980 census. Nonetheless, the following general comments can be made on its performance up till now.

1. The initial response to the IUCD insertions programme was amazingly high. In 1965 when the programme was introduced, nearly 0.8 million insertions were made and the number shot up to one million in the following year. Such a high performance within the first two years brought great optimism to the programme and much higher targets were fixed for the next several years. It was anticipated that at the rate the programme had gained acceptance, India should be able to reduce the birth rate within a short period of time. Such optimism, however, proved to be short-lived. The programme soon suffered a setback. The rate of IUCD insertions started declining at an increasing rate. In the year 1967–68, only .67 million insertions were made and the number declined to .48 million in the following year. The main reason for this backlash was the lack of follow-up medical facilities for dealing with the complications experienced by the users. In some cases the loop would be expelled involuntarily, while some experienced pain and bleeding. The lack of post-insertion medical facilities created a great deal of anxiety and misgiving in the mind of the present users which in turn spread to potential users. As a result, the IUCD insertion programme, which was supposed to have performed a miracle for India, proved a failure just because it was not carefully planned. The 1969 United Nations Mission has strongly recommended for rehabilitating the IUCD programme and has stressed the need for creating an effective medical machinery for providing post-insertion care to the users.

2. Fortunately the decline in the IUCD insertion programme was somewhat offset by a rise in the popularity of sterilization. During the four year period of 1965–66 to 1968–69, nearly 5 million sterilizations were performed, of which 3.5 million were carried out during the last two years. This is the highest number of sterilizations any country has ever attained both in absolute number and in per capita. Initially, the Central Government was reluctant to include sterilization among other contraceptives mainly because of its irreversibility. But some states like Tamil Nadu, Kerala, Maharashtra, and Gujrat went ahead with the sterilization programme and were able to register considerable success. Subsequently, the Central Government also accepted it as a part of the nation-wide family planning programme. The programme extends monetary incentives to individuals to compensate them for any loss of wages and other out-of-pocket expenses incurred for coming to the clinic. The amount of incentives differs from state to state. So far the programme has been based on a voluntary basis. But many people advocate making it compulsory for couples with more than two or three children. Dr. Chandrasekhar, an eminent demographer and a former Central Minister for Health and Family Planning, is one of the staunchest supporters of compulsory sterilization. He considers sterilization the most suitable method under the Indian conditions. Impressed with the success which the sterilization programmes have made in certain states, he argues that

---

31 Govind Narain, *The Family Planning Program,* see Table 6, p. 10.

"Had India embarked on this policy fifteen years ago with fervour the country by now could have cut its birth rate by half."[32] It is even asserted that sterilization may do the same thing for India that abortion did for Japan. The United Nations Mission of 1969 has cautioned against expecting too much of this programme. The Mission has also stressed the need for intensive research in the after effects of sterilization before deciding to make it compulsory.

3. One of the reasons for the slow progress of family planning is the lack of an effective organization and manpower. "Clearly, the limitations of the family planning programme arise not from finances but essentially from considerations of organization and personnel which affect the scale and intensity at which the programme can be implemented."[33] The Fourth Plan contains specific provisions for expansion of training facilities to meet the manpower needs of the programme. One of the factors contributing to the dearth of personnel (especially medical staff) is that the expansion of family planning depends heavily on the traditional clinical approach. It has been indicated before that despite the cafeteria approach the programme relies greatly on sterilization and on IUCD. Both these methods require individual medical attention, and in the case of the latter there is also a need for follow-up medical service. If the programme can popularize other family planning methods requiring little or no medical services, the manpower problem would then be less serious.

4. The results of surveys indicate that most couples (urban and rural) accept the norm of a small size family and would be willing to practise birth control if such knowledge was made available to them. It has, however, been observed that the willingness to learn about birth control only expresses interest and not the strong motivation to translate this into practice even if such facilities are made available. This kind of behaviour has been observed by the India-Harvard-Ludhiana Population Study: "While 80 per cent of the couples reported willingness to learn a contraceptive method, only 45 per cent used some method at some time during the study period and after about $2\frac{1}{2}$ years of sustained efforts only 17 per cent of the couples were found practising."[34] The results of the field experiences in other areas are even more disappointing. For example, the results of the pilot experiment in the city of Madras indicated that, while 92 per cent of the women were desirous of limiting their families, only 4 per cent did anything about it.[35] Obviously, there is something which prevents these people from translating their desires into action. The major reason seems to be the resistance to alter the long-established norms of life. Family planning is something new, and its acceptance implies breaking away with the age-old tradition of uncontrolled procreation. Thus, while there is no visible opposition to the programme, there also does not exist any enthusiastic support for it among the people. The programme cannot make any significant progress unless it succeeds in breaking the forces of ignorance and superstition which inhibit the people from practising family planning. This appears to be the most difficult task. These obstacles can be overcome only through a well organized massive educational programme designed to free the people from the hold of out-dated beliefs, and to motivate them to actually practice family planning. This is a necessary condition for the success of the programme.

It is evident that the family planning programme has not yet made any significant impact on the population growth. Its achievements have been far below its

32 Chandrasekhar, *India's Population,* p. 47.

33 Government of India, *The Third Plan,* p. 676.

34 As quoted in M. V. Raman, "Attitudes toward Family Size and Fertility Control in India—An Assessment," *Proceedings of the World Population Conference,* 1965, vol. 2 (New York: United Nations, 1967), p. 166.

35 R. A. Gopalaswami, "Family Planning: Outlook for Government Action," in Clyde V. Kiser (ed.), *Research in Family Planning* (Princeton: Princeton University Press, 1962), p. 73.

goals. It is true that the task of reducing the birth rate for a country like India is not only enormous but also highly complex. But it is also true that the economic future of India is inextricably bound up with the population growth. If India desires to break the vicious circle of poverty and to get on to the road of modern economic development, the rate of population growth must be slowed down. India cannot afford to waste any time. The solution to the population problem becomes more difficult every year because of the rapidly growing population. It is, therefore, imperative that the family planning programme direct all its energies to this problem and show some tangible results soon. If the programme fails to do this, the country may be compelled to adopt some drastic policies, such as compulsory sterilization and other similar antinatalist measures. The programme, therefore, faces a serious challenge and it is essential that it meet the challenge successfully.

BIBLIOGRAPHY

Bose, Ashish: "The Population Puzzle in India," *Economic Development and Cultural Change*, vol. 7, no. 3 (April 1959), pp. 230–48.

Chandrasekhar, S.: *India's Population: Facts, Problems and Policy* (Delhi: Meenakshi, 1967).

Coale, Ansley J. and Edgar M. Hoover: *Population Growth and Economic Development in Low-income Countries* (Princeton: Princeton University Press, 1958).

Dow, Thomas E.: "The Population of India," *Current History*, vol. 54, no. 320 (April 1968), pp. 219–24, 241–42.

Davis, Kingsley: "The Amazing Decline of Mortality in Underdeveloped Areas," *American Economic Review*, vol. 46 (May 1956), pp. 305–318.

Hauser, Philip M. (ed.): *The Population Dilemma* (Englewood Cliffs, N.J.: Prentice-Hall, 1963).

Higgins, Benjamin: *Economic Development* (New York: W. W. Norton, 1968).

Jones, Gavin W.: *The Economic Effect of Declining Fertility in Less Developed Countries* (New York: The Population Council, 1969).

Madalgi, S. S.: *Population and Food Supply in India* (New Delhi: Lalvani Publishing House, 1970).

Myrdal, Gunnar: *Asian Drama*, vols. 2 and 3 (New York: The Twentieth Century Fund, 1968).

Narain, Govind: *India: The Family Planning Program Since 1965*, Studies in Family Planning, no. 35 (New York: The Population Council, November 1968).

Ohlin, Govan: *Population Control and Economic Development* (Paris: OECD Development Centre, 1967).

Robinson, Warren C. and David E. Horlacher: *Population Growth and Economic Welfare*, Reports on Population/Family Planning, no. 6 (New York: The Population Council, February 1971).

Population Reference Bureau: "India: Ready or Not, Here They Come," *Population Bulletin*, vol. 26, no. 5 (November 1970).

United Nations: *An Evaluation of the Family Planning Programme of the Government of India* (New York: United Nations, 24 November, 1969).

Zaidan, George: "Population Growth and Economic Development," *Finance and Development*, vol. 6, no. 1 (March 1969), pp. 2–8.

2

Socio-Political Institutions, Cultural Values, and Attitudes: Their Impact on Indian Economic Development

INDER P. NIJHAWAN

1. Non-Economic Aspects of Economic Development

The precise role of non-economic factors in economic problems in general and economic development in particular is subject to considerable controversy. The controversy stems from and centres around the following issues.

A. *Recognition.* Economists have for two centuries debated the issue whether or not boundaries of economics should be delimited to encompass other disciplines. Opinions are sharply divided. A brief review of the controversy may be rewarding as it will provide insights into the need for and justification of the study of the role of social processes in Indian economic development and also warn the reader against the limitations of such a study. The major arguments against the study of "non-economic" phenomena within the purview of economic science are as follows:

1. Specialization presupposes a narrow scope of study. Therefore, the need to restrict the scope of economics exclusively to the study of economic phenomena.[1]

2. "Non-economic" factors are difficult to measure and therefore lack objectivity.[2]

3. Socio-political factors change but slowly. Therefore, in the short period analysis they can justifiably be treated as parameters. From this premise, the moral is derived that less developed countries should not strive to change social and cultural milieu as they cannot afford to wait (owing to pressure of population and rising aspirations). It is, therefore, recommended that the less developed countries should instead focus attention on econo-

[1] Vincent J. Trascio, *Pareto's Methodological Approach to Economics* (Chapel Hill: University of North Carolina, 1966), p. 56.

[2] Sarjent Florence, *Industrial Organization* (London: Macmillan, 1958).

mic factors which are crucial to the immediate increase in per capita income.[3]

4. Some economists deem changes in social and political milieu as the consequence rather than the cause of economic growth.[4] It is, therefore, logical that change in economic variables must precede change in the socio-political framework.

This atomistic conception of the social process provoked strong reactions. It was forcefully asserted that "economic man" is a myth.[5] It was argued that the "unity of social life" and its inseparable connection between its elements precludes any dissection of concrete reality into political, social, cultural, ethical and economic parts. Besides the whole being something greater than the sum of its parts, any attempt to comprehend reality by atomism would be misleading and even dangerous.[6] The relevance of economics, after all, is with social and cultural reality. The tendency to abstract from the social whole will make prediction perilous.

J. R. Hicks believes that since policy is a reconciliation between political, social, cultural, sociological, and economic considerations, any attempt to recommend policy without due consideration of "non-economic" factors will be singularly misleading.[7]

K. Boulding expresses his disenchantment with the efficacy of "applied economics" in dealing with concrete problems. Boulding voices his concern as follows :

> I have been gradually coming under the conviction disturbing for a professional theorist, that there is no such thing as economics—there is only social science applied to economic problems.[8]

Thus, from analytical, operational, and policy standpoints, "non-economic" factors cannot realistically be precluded from economic analysis.

B. *Identification.* "Non-Economic factors" is a loose term used to include a wide variety of factors. However, not all factors branded as "non-economic" and stressed by different economists could be critical in economic development; if it were so, no country of the world could be adequately developed. This leads to the problem of identification: Which of the several "non-economic" factors are relevant to economic growth ? On this issue consensus of opinion is singularly lacking.

Chronologically, the origin of the term "non-economic factors" is to be traced to the reaction against free competition and its concommitant unequal distribution of income. The United Nations' Research Institute for Social Development includes in social factors any phenomenon or variables immediately influencing welfare.

Parson[9] and Levy[10] stress that the relation of the individual to society is critical in transformation process. Economic development presupposes the existence of rationality in cognition, universalism in membership and specificity in relationship. The former implies that the individual's interpretation of the universe must be based on reason rather than on superstition. Universalism in membership presumes absence of nepotism and selection of roles in society by merit, and specificity in relationship requires that production relations be governed by contract, rather than by friendly and family ties. Kuznets[11] is merely endorsing the views of Parson and Levy when he singles out secularism, egalitarianism, and nationalism as preconditions of the Industrial Revolution.

Lerner[12] pinpoints the critical importance of the behavioural deviance in eco-

3 United Nations, *Economic Survey of Asia and Far East* (Bangkok : 1962).

4 Karl Marx, *Capital, A Critique of Political Economy* (New York : The Modern Library, 1956).

5 J. Schumpeter, *History of Economic Analysis* (New York : Oxford University Press, 1954).

6 Schumpeter, op. cit., Chapter III.

7 John R. Hicks, *Essays in World Economics* (Oxford : Clarendon Press, 1956).

8 K. Boulding, *A Reconstruction of Economics* (New York : John Wiley, 1950), p. vii.

9 T. Parson, *Toward a General Theory of Action* (Massachusetts : Cambridge University Press, 1951).

10 M. J. Levy, *The Structure of Society* (Princeton, 1952).

11 S. Kuznets, *Modern Economic Growth* (London : The University Press, 1965), Chapter 1.

12 D. Lerner, *The Passing of Traditional Society* (Glencoe : Free Press, 1958).

nomic change. Hagen[13] stresses the relationship between personality, society, and economic growth. Like Hagen, McClelland[14] also attempts to study variables which produce innovative and creative personalities. The number of people with *n* achievement is one of the most important determinants of economic development.

Ralph Linton,[15] however, believes that most of the factors which affect adoption and integration of new ideas by society can be explained more effectively in terms of cultural rather than psychological factors.

Like Linton, Sole[16] also singles out certain specific types of cognition and culture as most significant "non-economic" factors in economic transformation.

Religion is considerably stressed by Max Weber[17] and R. Tawney.[18]

Erich Fromm,[19] Hoselitz,[20] and Rostow[21] pinpoint the importance of institutional factors in economic development and believe that proper institutional framework is a precondition for "take off."

Mead[22] stresses the relevance of the size of the social unit to economic development.

According to Denison[23] the single most important social factor, which accounts for as much as 23% of growth in the U.S.A. between 1909–1929, is education.

Hoselitz[24] and Wolf[25] stress the importance of values and institutions in economic transformation.

Adelman and Morris[26] adopt a broader definition of "non-economic factors" and define socio-political factors in terms of extent of dualism, extent of urbanization, character of basic social organization, importance of indigenous middle class, extent of social mobility, extent of literacy, extent of mass communication, degree of modernization of outlook, degree of national integration and sense of national unity, extent of centralization of political power, strength of democratic institutions, degree of freedom of political opposition and press, degree of competitiveness of political party system, strength of labour movement, political strength of traditional elite, degree of administrative efficiency, extent of leadership commitment to economic development, and extent of political stability.

Surely not all of these factors are important from the standpoint of Indian economic development. Therefore, the problem of identification.

C. *Causal Relationship.* Another issue which has plagued economists for a long time is whether socio-cultural factors determine or are determined by economic development. According to Marx,[27] the mode of production is the fundamental determinant of the socio-political structure which in turn determines ideas and insti-

13 E. Hagen, *On the Theory of Social Change: How Economic Growth Begins* (Illinois: Dorsey Press, 1962).

14 David McClelland, *The Achieving Society* (Princeton: D. Van Nostrand, 1961).

15 Ralph Linton, "Cultural and Personality Factors Affecting Economic Growth" in David E. Novack and Robert Lekachmon (ed), *Development and Society* (New York: St. Martin's Press, 1964).

16 Robert A. Sole, *Economic Organization and Social Systems* (New York: Free Press, 1955).

17 Max Weber, *Protestant Ethic and Spirit of Capitalism* (New York: Scribner, 1956).

18 R. H. Tawney, *Religion and Rise of Capitalism* (New York: Harcourt and Brace, 1952).

19 Erich Fromm, *Psychoanalysis and Religion* (New York: Yale University, 1950).

20 Bert F. Hozelitz, "Non-Economic Factors in Economic Development," in B. Okun and R. W. Richardson (eds), *Studies in Economic Development* (New York: Holt, Rinehart and Winston, 1961).

21 W. W. Rostow, *Stages of Economic Growth* (London: Cambridge University); *The Process of Economic Growth* (New York: Norton, 1962).

22 M. Mead, *Cultural Patterns and Technical Change* (Paris: UNESCO, 1953).

23 E. Denison, *The Sources of Economic Growth in the U.S. and the Alternative before the U.S.* (New York: Committee for Economic Development, Supplementary Paper Number B, 1962).

24 Bert F. Hoselitz, "A Sociological Approach to Economic Development" in his *Sociological Aspects of Economic Growth* (Glencoe: Free Press), pp. 23–84.

25 Charles Wolf, Jr., "Institutions and Economic Development" in Okun and Richardson, op. cit.

26 Irma Adelman and Cynthia Taft Morris, "An Econometric Model of Development," *American Economic Review*, December 1968.

27 Marx, op. cit.

tutional framework. Hagen,[28] on the other hand, believes that cultural personality is the basic explanatory variable in economic development. Hagen regards economic variables as mere parameters or conditioning circumstances within which specific types of cultural change sparks off the process of economic development.

Katona[29] hypothesizes that economic processes are the result of people's behaviour and are influenced by different patterns of behaviour.

Tinbergen[30] and Rostow[31] take the middle ground and treat the relationship between economic and "non-economic" factors as one of interaction.

Suffice to say that the role assigned to social processes in the economic development of India and the consequent policy recommendations would vary in accordance with whether these are considered as the cause or consequence of economic change.

D. *Methodology*. Even if issues of recognition, identification, and causal relationship are resolved satisfactorily, there remains the fundamental problem of methodolgy. Often attempts to extend growth analysis to include "non-economic" factors are frustrated by the absence of empirical knowledge about the manner in which they operate. There are two distinct approaches: (1) Economists can widen the scope of their positive research to encompass "non-economic" variables, and (2) economic theory can be supplemented with the theories developed in other social sciences which deal with "non-economic" phenomenon. In the latter approach, the study of interaction "between economic" and "non-economic" variables is through a clearly defined division of field of research rather than by an integrated attack on the concrete problems. The emphasis, therefore, is on synthesis of knowledge rather than on integration and assimilation. The former approach is adopted by Hicks,[32] Tinbergen,[33] Viner,[34] Marschak[35], and Boulding.[36] The latter approach is recommended and practised by Rostow.[37]

2. Methodological Considerations and the Framework for Analysis

The four fundamental issues and the controversy which centres around those issues (summarized in the previous section) broadly provide the framework for analyzing the role of socio-political factors in the economic transformation of India. The first issue pertains to relative weight, the second to selection of relevant factors, the third to direction of relationship between economic growth and social processes, and the fourth to methods of analyzing the relationship. The relative weight of socio-political factors in Indian economic development can be determined by Denison's type study[38] where growth in each input is compared with growth in output and by weighing the inputs against each other, their relative contribution to total output can be ascertained. While Denison's type study will provide an analytical framework, data problems will preclude any such study in the Indian context. Besides, as in the Denison's model, unexplained variation (growth in GNP not explained by growth of labour, natural resources, capital and technology) will be attributed to the whole gamut of factors; among them would also be non-economic factors. This

[28] E. Hagen, op. cit.

[29] George Katona, *Psychological Analysis of Economic Behaviour* (New York: McGraw-Hill, 1951).

[30] J. Tinbergen, "Social Factors in Economic Development," *Zeitschrift Ges Staatswists,* 1968.

[31] Rostow, *The Process of Economic Growth,* op. cit.

[32] Hicks, op. cit.

[33] Tinbergen, op. cit.

[34] Jacob Viner, *International Trade and Economic Development* (Oxford: Clarendon Press), p. 2.

[35] Jacob Marschak, "Measurement for Policy and Prediction," in J. Hood and T. C. Koopmans (eds), *Studies of Econometric Method* (New York: John Wiley, 1950), p. 10.

[36] Kenneth Boulding, *A Reconstruction of Economics* (New York: John Wiley, 1950), p. vii.

[37] Rostow, *The Process of Economic Growth,* op. cit.

[38] Denison, op. cit.

will further pose the problem of disentangling the non-economic variables from economic variables and the relative weight of each.

In the absence of empirical data and the lack of appropriate analytical framework to disentangle the contribution of non-economic factors *vis-a-vis* economic factors, it will not be possible to empirically determine the relative weight of socio-political factors in the economic development of India.

Difficulties in measuring "non-economic" factors and their relative contributions to growth of total output makes it hard to identify the socio-political factors which are critical for the success of planned economic development in India. Among the "non-economic" factors, those frequently discussed in the literature of Indian growth are : religion, attitude towards life, political stability, traditions and customs, values, caste system, and socio-political institutions. Other factors such as class structure, literacy, degree of social tension, national integration, and national unity, degree of freedom of political opposition and press, strength of labour movement, degree of administrative efficiency, behavioural deviance, the number of people with *n* achievement, and size of social unit, have received little, if any, attention in Indian literature. It may well be that these factors are not pertinent to and|or are less important in the Indian context. However, any such conclusion should be based on analysis rather than on presumption and, if possible, vindicated by empirical data. Of late, some attempts have been made to quantify some of the variables enumerated above. Literacy, educational attainment, political stability, and *n* achievement have been measured with some degree of success.[39] However, economists still debate the relevance of proxy variables used for measurement. Measurements of more encompassing concepts such as "social development" and "national integration" is particularly shaky.

In what follows, we shall discuss some of the factors iterated above without implying that these alone are of greatest import in the Indian context.

As regards the direction of relationship between socio-political and economic variables, it is now generally conceded, and it is assumed in this paper, that economic and "non-economic" variables interact on each other rather than being tied in a cause-effect fashion.[40]

Analytically, there are two distinct approaches to study the interaction between economic and non-economic variables.[41] According to some psychologists and economists, the individual's internal state (comprising motives, needs and personality) is the most important determinant of human behaviour and actions. Others stress the environment (reflected in and by values, norms, etc.) as the sole explanation of human behaviour.

Kunkel[42] calls the former psychodynamic models and the latter behavioural models. The two approaches have different implications from the standpoint of economic development. Psychodynamic models, by their very nature, are somewhat *fait accompli.* To the extent that man's internal state consisting of innate and acquired characteristics is largely determined in early childhood, change in behaviour of adults would be either difficult or can, at best, occur over a long period of time.[43] Additionally, innate nature being unconscious, its exact determinants can hardly be identified.

---

39 See UNESCO, *Social Aspects of Economic Development in Latin America,* Vol. I (Paris, 1963), pp. 88–89; D. Lerner, *The Passing of Traditional Society,* op. cit.; S. M. Lipset, *Political Man : The Social Bases of Politics* (New York : Doubleday, 1960); David McClelland, op. cit.; and Adelman and Morris, op. cit.

40 See G. Myrdal, *Asian Drama: An Inquiry into the Poverty of Nations* (New York : Twentieth Century Fund, 1968); Viner, Marshack, and Boulding, op. cit.

41 For an excellent discussion on this subject, see John H. Kunkel, *Society and Economic Growth* (New York : Oxford University Press, 1970), pp. 16–25.

42 Kunkel, pp. 19–25.

43 Hagen and McClelland's models provide classic illustrations in point.

Behavioural models, at least, analytically afford considerable scope for change in behaviour, at any stage, without substantial lapse in time. Main determinants of behaviour are rewarding and punishing consequences of certain activities which are determined by social environment. Since the mechanism of reward and punishment is amenable to change, social behaviour can be tailored to the needs and requirements of economic transformation.

have an unfavourable attitude towards thrift. This reduces the probability of saving, and, therefore, when income increases people tend to spend rather than save. Low marginal and average propensity to save result in, *ceteris paribus,* low rate of investment, and other things remaining the same, low rate of growth. In a situation such as this, only a substantial or no amount of rise in interest rate (economic variable) may overcome the stigma

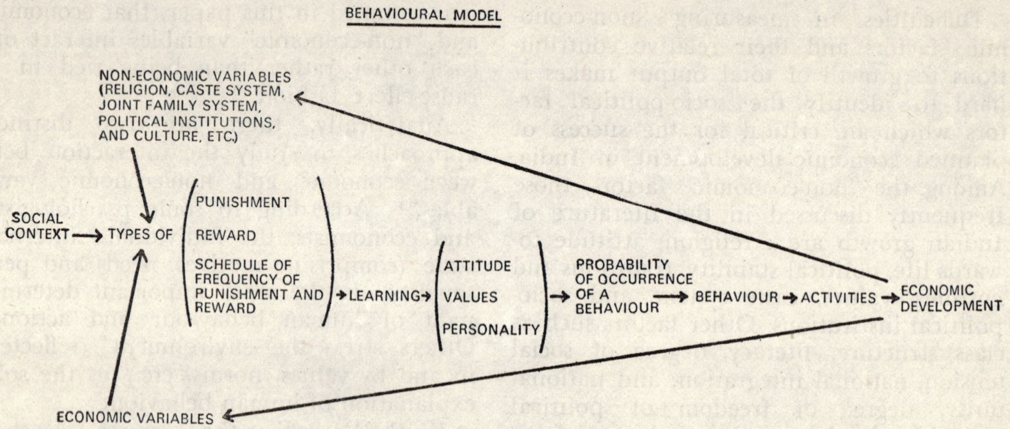

Fig. 1

The discussion on the role of socio-political factors in economic development in general and in India in particular, is often marred by unconscious blending of psychodynamic and behavioural models. Since, in what follows, we shall use the behavioural model in the Indian context, it is essential to briefly summarize it's main features.[44] The model is illustrated by a chart as on this page. The basic features of this model are:

1. It is evident from the chart that the distinction between "economic" and "non-economic" variables is academic. Behaviour (which determines the activities and, hence, rate of growth) is influenced by both "non-economic" and "economic" factors.

2. It is wrong to argue[45] that change in economic variables can, by themselves, spark the process of economic growth. For example, in a society where frugality is treated as greed owing to social customs, or culture, or religion, people learn to

on saving, and hence, facilitate an increase in per capita output.

3. It is evident that if socio-political variables are changed simultaneously with economic factors, considerable increase in output can be achieved without substantial changes in the latter. For example, in the case cited above, if taboos on saving are removed, small changes in interest rate may be enough to generate sufficient resources for economic development (assuming saving is interest-sensitive).

4. It is equally clear from the chart that it is erroneous to believe that social and psychological fetters on economic development can be removed or weakened by changing the values, attitudes, and personality of individuals in less develop-

---

44 For details, see Kunkel, op. cit.

45 See J. Bhagwati, *The Economics of Underdeveloped Countries* (New York: McGraw-Hill, 1970), p. 100.

ed countries.[46] Values and attitudes state the probability of occurrence of behaviour. They are the symptoms or inferences from behaviour, and not the causes of changes in behaviour.

5. Behavioural changes conducive to substantial increase in per capita income, in most cases, result from changes in types and frequency of stimuli and/or presence or absence of punishment.

3. Socio-Political Institutions, Values, and Attitudes in India

In this section, we shall attempt to analyze how "non-economic" factors impinge on the process of transformation in the Indian economy. The behavioural model discussed and illustrated in Section 2 will provide the analytical framework.

Among the "non economic" factors, Indian religion has been subject to maximum controversy and debate.[47] The exact mechanism by which Indian religion impinges on economic change is rarely, if ever, spelled out in detail. However, broadly the relationship postulated is as follows:

Religious Teachings and Interpretation ⟶ Values and Attitudes ⟶ Actions ⟶ Economic Development

The model does not explain how and why religious teachings are internalized in the form of values and then translated into actions. The link between religious teachings and behaviour, therefore, remains clouded. The basic links are clearly laid out in the behavioural model (See page 28). The effect of religious teachings on economic development can be elucidated by an example. The philosophy of renunciation is traced to holy scriptures in Asia. It is often argued that this philosophy militates against economic growth. If people are taught that human desires are the source of misery and unhappiness and that lasting mental peace can only be attained through renunciation, it follows that there is a religious merit in reducing desires or not indulging in material things. People, therefore, learn to value deprivation more than affluence. Limited aspirations warrant limited efforts to attain them. Thus, a worker may not work the whole day if it takes half a day's work to earn two meals. The government may spend crores of rupees on irrigation projects to boost production on farms and yet fail to induce farmers to use the new facilities if the existing facilities are enough to provide subsistence to the farmer and his family. The net result, among other things, would be small marketable surplus, inadequate division of labour, and constrained supply of efforts. Thus, the philosophy of renunciation will run counter to the assumption of non-satiation which is the very premise of economic development.

Having discussed the mechanism by which religion impinges on economic change, in what follows, we shall attempt to answer the fundamental question : whether Indian religion is conducive or inimical to industrialization. This would inevitably call for identification of the basic tenets of Hinduism. Even though the basic tenets of Hinduism are subject to considerable controversy, the philosophers generally agree that there is dualism of thought in Hinduism.[48] There are certain elements in Hindu philosophy which are "other worldly." The varied versions of this view are: Asceticism—the world is essentially an illusion, human desires are the source of misery and unhappiness, and law of Karma—relating present rewards to past actions and present actions to future life. However, there are other elements which sanction the materialistic values of an industrialized society. The Shukranitisara, for example, lauds wealth

[46] McClelland and Hagen are champions of this belief.

[47] See M. Singer, "Religion and Social Changes in India: The Max Weber Thesis, Phase Three," *Economic Development and Cultural Change*, 1966; John Goheen, "A Comment on Professor Singer's Cultural Values in India's Economic Development," *Economic Development and Cultural Change*, October 1958; M. N. Srinivas, "A Note on Mr. Goheen's Note," *Economic Development and Cultural Change*," October 1958.

[48] Ibid.

as the means to all pursuits and favours its accumulation by "...legitimate ways, as by learning, service, valour, agriculture, commerce, the practice of crafts and even by mendicancy."[49] The *Gita,* the well-known Hindu scripture, and the theory of Varnashrama Dharma, like Protestant ethic, exhort every one to do his duty to the best of his ability, whatever his station of life may be. No wonder the *Mahabharata* denounces poverty as a sin and asserts, "He that has no wealth has neither this world nor the next."[50] Similarly, the *Panchatantra* attributes most evils and vices to lack of money.[51] In some quarters it is even argued that Hindu philosophy contains and sanctions all the "character traits" of Protestant ethic such as:

> ...A belief in an orderly universe subject to deterministic laws, the ability to anticipate a course of events and behave accordingly, with the possibility of control based on knowledge; a strong sense of responsibility for one's actions and their consequences; and a capacity to organize one's life under a systematic methodical discipline which will maximize the goals one has set oneself.[52]

The authority of *Bhagvat Gita* and other Hindu scriptures is invoked to substantiate the sanction of the typical "character traits" of Protestant ethic in Hindu philosophy.[53]

It is, therefore, evident that Hinduism blends together disparate and conflicting elements—some elements which are conducive and others that are inimical to economic growth. The controversy stems from and centres around the relative weight of "this worldly" and "other worldly" elements in Hindu philosophy. Here, consensus of opinion is singularly lacking. Dr. T. M. P. Mahadevan, in his address to the Thirtieth Indian Philosophical Congress, disparages the role of material goods and material pursuits in Indian philosophy.[54] Instead he invokes the authority of the Vedas to prove that non-materialism is a dominant theme of the Hindu religion. To quote Mahadevan, "If he [man] should be saved, he must be made to turn back from his meaningless race of material power. Not by adding things to oneself can one be happy. True happiness lies within."[55]

Singer on the other hand, however, argues that Hinduism contains not only all the "character traits" of Protestant ethic (religion which is highly conducive to economic growth), but Hindus in their day to day activities are as materialistic as Western men.[56] Srinivas[57] endorses Singer's viewpoint when he claims that abject poverty of the Indian farmer and the constant threat of starvation forces him to be nothing but practical. He cannot afford to be "other worldly." In Srinivas's words:

> He [peasant] is naturally deeply interested in agriculture and everything related to it—land, rain, water, manure, cattle, labour, pests, etc.—one often comes across pretty strict bookkeeping, even between the members of elementary family. Money from the sale of surplus crops belongs to man, while the money obtained by the sale of milk, butter, butter-milk, eggs and fowl belongs to the wife. The better-off peasant teaches his son the value of money and thrift early in life.[58]

It is no wonder that Max Weber thinks, "The acquisitiveness of Indians of all strata left little to be desired and no-

---

49 M. N. Srinivas, "A Note on Mr. Goheen's Note," *Economic Development and Cultural Change,* October 1958.

50 *Mahabharata* XII, Chapter 8, quoted by Gokhale, p. 52.

51 Transl. A. W. Ryder, p. 211; quoted by Ajit Dasgupta, "India's Cultural Values and Economic Development: A Comment," *Economic Development and Cultural Change,* October 1958, p. 101.

52 Singer, *Religion and Social Change,* p. 501.

53 Ibid.

54 "The Rediscovery of Man," Proceedings of Thirtieth Indian Philosophical Congress, December 1955, quoted by Goheen, op. cit.

55 "The Rediscovery of Man," quoted by Goheen, op. cit., p. 3.

56 Milton Singer, "Cultural Values in Indian Economic Development," *Annals of American Academy and Social Sciences,* pp. 81–91.

57 Srinivas, op. cit., p. 4.

58 Srinivas, op. cit., p. 4.

where to be found so little antichrematism and such evaluation of wealth."[59]

Singer forcefully argues that "this world ly" and "other wordly" elements are not necessarily incompatible.[60] It is possible for an Indian to believe in meditation and Karma and yet possess all the "character traits" (frugality, rationality, hard work, and spirit of adventure, etc.) essential for economic development. Singer quotes several instances (based on personal observations and interviews) where belief in Karma did not prevent a Hindu householder from discharging his wordly duties or in case of merchants, from pursuit and accumulation of wealth. The most befitting example is provided by the "Banya"—a traditional business community in India—which, while it worships the Goddess of Wealth, is most miserly in the personal use of wealth it amasses.[61]

To resolve the issue of relative weight and to ascertain the extent of belief of the younger generation in "other worldly" elements in Hinduism, we took a random sample of 61 students in an all-girls' school and 46 students in an all-boys' school at Kalkaji Colony in New Delhi. The sample is statistically neither large nor representative enough to yield meaningful and trustworthy results. However, we state below the results for what they are worth.

Surprisingly enough, not even one respondent (out of a sample of 107) listed "other worldly" tenets such as asceticism, Karma, and renunciation, among the fundamental tenets of Hinduism. A majority of the respondents deem the following as the salient tenets of Hinduism. Truth always triumphs, union is strength, honesty is the best policy, love one and all, non-violence, respect elders and teachers. God is omnipresent and resides in every being.

The survey results cannot permit generalization owing to statistical inadequacy of the survey. However, this evidence coupled with the evidence presented earlier does suggest that "other worldly" elements are not the dominant theme of Hinduism.

Thus, we may sum up: (1) Hinduism contains "this wordly" as well as "other worldly" elements; (2) "other wordly" elements, even though preached in Indian religion, are practised by very few; (3) these two categories are not mutually exclusive; (4) Indian religion sanctions most of the character traits of Protestant ethic—often considered prerequisites of economic development.[62]

However, religion may impinge on Indian economic development through a different route. It may (1) drain the surplus and (2) affect the investment preference in a manner which is inimical to economic growth.

The ceremonies pertaining to deity and demon in Hinduism are so elaborate and warrant such an enormous investment of food, money, and effort as to absorb a significant proportion of saving of an average household. No breakdown of expenditure on religious ceremonies is available. However, the total ceremonial expenditure in rural India is estimated at 7.2 per cent of per capita income.[63]

It is often hypothesized that the bulk of household savings in India are diverted to unproductive assets like currency and gold hoards. It has been estimated that the stock of gold in India constitutes about 10 per cent of total tangible wealth in India.[64] There are several rather diverse factors which explain the investor's predilection for gold. However, part of the

---

59 Max Weber, *Religion in India* (Glencoe: Free Press, 1958), p. 4.

60 Singer, *Religion and Social Change,* op. cit., p. 501.

61 Ibid.

62 Max Weber over-stressed the role of Protestant ethic in the rise of capitalism. Even if we identify all religions conducive to economic development with Protestant ethic, there is enough evidence in history to prove that the same traits elsewhere did not spark of the process of economic change. As a matter of fact, there are several instances where altogether different "character traits" in religion facilitated industrialization. Japanese religion is a classic illustration in point.

63 Richard D. Lambert and Bert F. Hoselitz, *The Role of Saving and Wealth in Southern Asia and the West* (UNESCO: 1963), p. 307.

64 Hugh Patrick, "Financial Development and Economic Development," *Economic Development and Cultural Change,* January 1966.

explanation can be sought in the sanction it receives in the Hindu religion. Its importance springs from three factors: (1) It is treated as the metal of God. Often idols and temples are either gold-plated or are in fact made of gold. Lord Srivenkateswara's temple in Southern India and the Golden Temple at Amritsar are classic illustrations in point. (2) Gold is often used to worship and propitiate the Goddess of Wealth. The amount of gold collected as charity by some of the temples in India (e.g., Lord Srivenkateswara's Temple of Tirupati defies imagination). (3) Gold ornaments are part of the attire on religious occasions.

The effect of gold hoardings on the growth potential of India can scarcely be understated. Contrary to the generally held view that investment in gold involves only a transfer of purchasing power or assets from the purchaser to the seller, it affects the availability of real resources, comsumption (saving), investment, employment, the price level, allocation and growth of entrepreneurial skill and organization of resources.[65]

Another factor related to, but not necessarily contained in and synonymous with religion, is the "world view" of the masses.[66] The basic component of the world view is the perception and interpretation of the relationship between activities (actions) and consequences (results). An individual may find, perceive, or interpret this relationship as (1) capricious or, (2) systematic and orderly. In the former, the consequences are often distributed randomly and there is no direct, logical, and explicable connection with the activity. Thus, a foreign element like luck (*kismat*), providence, spirits, God, etc. must be invoked to explain the consequences—good or bad. The following paragraph provides a classic illustration of the "capricious universe" view:

> Good luck in the form of fine harvest, freedom from robbery or sickness, finding buried treasure, or acquiring a helpful patron, is the principal hope for improvement in position and, conversely, bad luck explains failure...People rarely speak in the future tense, without qualifying proposed or hoped for action with *si dius me da licencia,* if God gives me permission... Divine providence, above all, is the good fortune that spells out human well-being. But accepting divine providence does not imply belief in a grand design, a pattern and system, which rules the universe. Rather, the universe about one is marked by absence of law and order: It, and God's plan as well, is capricious and unpredictable, quixotic and surprising. Something happens, not because of pre-ordained regularities in the universe and in the world but because God—or whoever the ultimate authority in a particular instance may be—has willed it. A child dies: It was part of God's plan. The highway comes to town: General La'Zaro Cardenas willed it. Chance and accident are the mainspring of the universe, systematic expectations and consistent behaviour are seen as valueless. Western-style foresight is a positive value only within a predictable system.[67]

The generalization is dangerous in the Indian context. However, the masses in rural India show most of the characteristics detailed above.

In the systematic universe view correlation between contingency and activities is strong and predictable. There is, therefore, little or no scope for intervention from non-human elements. What is knowable, predictable, and strongly correlated to human activities is evidently also controllable. There is, no doubt, constant struggle of man against nature but man is not deemed powerless or inferior to nature.

It may be instructive to briefly examine the factors which affect the world view of the masses. The three most important

65 For details refer to my dissertation, Asset Preference and Economic Development—with special reference to India (University of North Carolina at Chapel Hill: January 1971).

66 For a lucid and detailed discussion on this subject, see Kunkel, op. cit.

67 George M. Foster, *Tzintzuntzan: Mexican Peasants in Changing World* (Boston: Little, Brown, and Company, 1967), p. 117; quoted by Kunkel, op. cit., p. 22.

sources of world view are: (1) personal experiences; (2) observation of other's experiences; (3) knowledge of events, experiences described in stories, proverbs, religious teachings, etc. Since the formulation of the world view involves interpretation of relationship between the actions and results, the maintenance and form of the world view may differ among different members of the same community—even though experiences, observations, and source of knowledge of events is the same.

Having examined the forms of the world views and its sources, it will be instructive to analyze the role of the world view in the industrialization of less-developed countries in general, and of India, in particular. The basic links involved are explained in the behavioural model. (See page 28). The world view will impinge on the interpretation of relationship between contingency and actions. If the universe is deemed capricious, the individual will learn to expect little or no correlation between actions and results. This will result in a fatalistic attitude. Owing to uncertainty about the future arising out of the capricious universe view and the overriding importance of non-human elements like luck, providence, and spirits, men learn to be subservient to physical environment.

The attitude of helplessness and resignation pervades the masses. These attitudes impinge on all activities including saving, investment, long-range perspective, supply of efforts, and family planning. If a higher standard of living and amassing of wealth is treated as the result of providence rather than springing from hard work and saving, there is little rationale for saving, hard work, innovations, and enterprise. The Indian farmer, owing to the zamindari system, demonstrated this attitude of resignation and helplessness. No matter how hard he worked or how much he improved his cultivation techniques, a lion's share of the produce was appropriated by the landlord. So much so, the farmer was forced to believe that poverty is a curse. Behavioural response regarding family size is no different. If more children are born, it is believed that God must have ordained it. It is also believed that if God increases the size of family by unwanted children. He will also provide the means to feed them.

Similarly, the attitude of "here and now" pervades all spheres of life. Households avoid assets which yield return over a long period of time or are relatively illiquid or involve considerable risk. No wonder households in India show marked preference for assets like gold, land, and inventories rather than bonds and stocks. As stated earlier, preference for these assets, far from increasing the productive capacity of the economy, adversely affects the saving, investment, entrepreneurial skill, and organization of resources.

Planning and capital formation presupposes a long range perspective. In a society where the future is not only uncertain, but also distrusted owing to the capricious universe view, the desire and incentive to save, invest, and plan are conspicuously lacking. Entrepreneurship and innovations also warrant long range perspective because rewards of these activities do not accrue over a short period.

However, the adverse effects of the capricious universe view should not be overstressed. Fatalistic attitude or faith in nonhuman elements may not be inimical to industrialization if the former is invoked to rationalize one's failure despite efforts. God helps those who help themselves—is a common aphorism in India. Thus, the fatalistic attitude may not necessarily imply inaction or slothfulness or lack of desire and incentives to save, invest, and innovate. Singer rightly argues that the fatalistic attitude "does not create man's condition—it "explains" and "justifies" it. Whatever a man can or cannot do may be explained with reference to a law of Karma but this explanation does not determine what he will or will not do."[68] In fact, it may be a blessing in disguise. Often, individuals undertake extremely risky ventures in the name of God. Since failure is not entirely accounted for by the individual's efforts, the individual may never cease trying again and again. Each failure may strengthen the need to pro-

68 Singer, *Religion and Social Change,* op. cit.

pitiate the Almighty but leave the will to work intact. Not surprising that despite a low per capita income, india's *n* achievement score (index of initiative, enterprise, and entrepreneurial skill) ranks high[69] and household saving rate compares favourably with many advanced contries of the world.[70]

Related to the capricious universe view is the oft repeated allegation : the Indian farmer is irrational and, therefore, his behavioural response run counter to most theories in economics which are founded on the rationality premise. An ardent supporter of the irrationality premise is Kusum Nair.[71] She argues forcefully that the aspirations of the Indian farmer have a low ceiling. Therefore, the "non-satiety" assumption is not valid in the Indian context. Nair quotes several instances (from her extensive All India Village survey) of the perverse behavioural response of the Indian masses. She cites the example of a worker who does not return to work after lunch because he has earned enough money to purchase meals for the day, even though he suffers from abject poverty. Similarly, a farmer, who does not care to use irrigation facilities made available by a million-rupees project, reveals during the course of an interview that, since his requirements for the year consist of two bags of rice which are currently met by existing facilities, there is no incentive for him to utilize the new facilities. The backward sloping supply curve of labour and food grains is a trite proposition in the Indian context.

The opponents of the "irrationality" premise, however, argue that the Indian farmer is as rational as his counterpart in advanced countries. The "practical" and "down-to-earth" approach of the Indian peasant was stressed elsewhere in this paper. The point can be further illustrated with reference to the use of the Indian wooden plough which is often cited as the proof of the Indian farmer's irrational behaviour. The wooden plough is usually considered outdated and outmoded as a method of farming. Recent research has, however, shown that the Indian plough is not necessarily outmoded. It is argued that in certain types of crops where the moisture content of soil is critical, deep ploughing is inappropriate. Since the wooden plough does not dig deep, it is particularly suitable for these crops. The wisdom and knowledge of the Indian peasant regarding changes in weather and the consequent need for crop rotation is vindicated by innumerable research studies.

It must be, however, conceded that a few examples in support of the rationality or irrationality premise are not enough to vindicate either of these hypotheses.

There is, however, an indirect way of empirically testing the hypotheses. If it were possible to gauge the efficiency with which existing resources are allocated and utilized within given institutional framework in rural India or/and show whether or not institutional framework responds to profit considerations—the rationality premise can be refuted or proved.[72] Hopper's study shows that the Indian farmer uses his resources rationally as each resource is employed to the point where its earning is equal to its estimated marginal product.[73] Similarly, Raj Krishna illustrates how farmers in Punjab switched to new varieties of cotton when they were convinced that longer staple cotton would sell in larger quantities and at a higher price than the old varieties.[74]

Desai, however, reaches a conclusion diametrically opposed to that of Hopper's. Invoking the linear programming technique, Desai shows that actual returns to farming are significantly less than the opti-

---

[69]See McClelland, op. cit.

[70] See my dissertation, op. cit.

[71] Kusum Nair, *Blossoms in the Dust* (New York: Frederick A. Praeger Inc., 1962).

[72] For a detailed and lucid discussion, see Jagdish Bhagwati and Sukhamoy Chakravarty, "Contributions to Indian Economic Analysis: A Survey," *American Economic Review,* Vol. LIX, No. 4, Part 2 (September 1969). The following section is based on this survey article.

[73] W. D. Hopper, "Allocation Efficiency in a Traditional Indian Agriculture," *Journal of Farm Economics,* August 1965, quoted by Bhagwati and Chakravarty.

[74] Raj Krishna, *Farm Response in the Punjab (India-Pakistan): A Case Study of Cotton* (Unpublished Ph. D. dissertation, University of Chicago, 1961).

mum-reflecting inefficiency.[75] However, Desai's argument does not refute the "rationality premise." The peasant may attempt to maximize his profits and yet fail to allocate resources in an optimum manner owing to ignorance or inadequate knowledge. Since the analytical models used by Hopper and Desai are subject to considerable limitations and the scope of study is narrow (Hopper's study, for example, is based on selected crops and Desai bases his study on data from forty farms in two districts) their conclusions must be accepted with a grain of salt.

Regarding the institutional framework, Hanumantha Rao argues that choice of institutional arrangements in rural India is, in most cases, based on predominantly economic considerations.[76] The peasant resorts to crop-sharing only if returns are certain; when returns are uncertain he chooses the fixed contractual payment system. Similarly, Raj argues that notwithstanding the sanctity of the cow in Hindu belief, Hindus sometimes slaughter them if "ecological and price considerations make it economically advantageous to do so."[77]

Thus, the available evidence, even though limited and shaky, does not support the hypothesis that the Indian peasant is "irrational." The success of the so-called green revolution, if anything, refutes the irrationality premise.

Another "non-economic" factor which has attracted the attention of Indian and foreign economists alike, is the caste system in India. It is often hypothesized that the caste system in India is inimical to economic growth. The assumptions underlying this hypothesis are :

1. The close and rigid ties between caste and occupations prevents occupational mobility vital to economic transformation. As a rule, Brahmins associated themselves with priestly occupation and government service, Vaishyas with business and trade. Kshatriyas specialized in military and government careers and Shudras in scaveing, sweeping, tanning and shoemaking.

2. Occupational structure is governed by caste and traditions rather than by merit and skill.

3. The caste system tends to limit the loyalty of individuals to a group and hence prevents or obstructs the development of the sense of nationhood, which is considered an important prerequisite of economic development.[78]

4. In certain quarters it is argued that the institution of the caste system blunts the sense of adventure: "Crossing the sea meant becoming outcaste."[79] This will militate against the growth and formation of entrepreneurial skill and scientific and technical progress.

Most of these assumptions are specious. The link between caste and occupation is not as rigid as is generally assumed. More than one caste often practise the same occupation. Agriculture which absorbs nearly 60–65 per cent of the Indian population is not a prerogative of any one caste. Similarly, in the Indian army, people belonging to different castes rub shoulders with one another. Recent studies by anthropologists and sociologists particularly stress that whenever better and more favourable opportunities arose people seized it notwithstanding the nature of occupation and caste.[80] It is no wonder that Brahmins enter the army, Vaishyas hold high ranking jobs in the Government of India, Shudras practise trade and business, and Kshatriyas are teachers. The occupational and vertical mobility is particularly marked among Shudras—sometimes, called the untouchables. Recently in the proximity of Delhi "some of the out-caste groups have deliberately given

[75] D. K. Desai, *Increasing Income and Production in Indian Farming* (Bombay: 1963) quoted by Bhagwati and Chakravarty, op. cit.

[76] C. H. Hanumanha Rao, "Entrepreneurship, Management and Farm Tenure Systems," February 1967, mimeographed, quoted by Bhagwati and Chakravarty, op. cit.

[77] K. N. Raj, "Investment in Livestock in Agrarian Economies: A Theoretical and Empirical Analysis," December 1967, mimeographed, quoted by Bhagwati and Chakravarty, op. cit.

[78] Kuznets, op. cit.

[79] Srinivas, op. cit., p. 5.

[80] See M. N. Srinivas, *Religion and Society among the Coorgs of South India* (London: Oxford University Press); N. A. Toothi, *Vaishnavas of Gujrat* (London: Longmans, 1935).

up their traditional occupations and taken to construction labour as a way of affirming their changed status."[81]

It is equally wrong to argue that the caste system restricts geographical mobility. Historically there has been little or no connection between caste and area. Travelling abroad was restricted to a few due to prohibitive financial costs rather than owing to caste restrictions.

The effect of the caste system on entrepreneurial skill formation is equally dubious. Acquisition of wealth was sanctioned for all castes even though the mode of acquisition may differ. As a matter of fact, the caste system was responsible for the growth of a special class—Vaishya or Banya—whose main objective was to perform, practise and specialize in entrepreneurial activities. As Gore points out:

> The [Vaishya] worshipped and propitiated the Goddess of Wealth. Their pursuit of wealth was single-minded. In search of it they took considerable financial and personal risks. The long trade routes which passed through mountains and overseas could not have been maintained by people who were afraid to take risks of this kind. The Vaishya will leave his country and migrate hundreds of miles in search of suitable place for his work.[82]

No wonder in terms of *n* achievement motive (one of the most important determinants of enterpreneurial skill) India ranks high; the achievement score is estimated to be 2.11.[83]

However, it cannot be denied that sometimes roles in Indian society are chosen on the basis of caste rather than merit and capacity. This results in nepotism, waste of ability and, hence, loss of potential output. Loss of output will be substantial if the selection in the upper rungs of hierarchy in political and economic roles is caste-rooted, rather than if it is confined to the military. Fortunately, selection for key governmental and economic services in India is made on the basis of competitive examinations—which excludes caste.

Nationalism is often regarded as one of the prerequisites of "take off." The caste system, in so far as it limits the loyalty of the individual to a caste or group, militates against nationalism.

The role of the family structure in Indian economic development has been subject to considerable discussion. It is often hypothesized that the extended or joint family system inhibits or obstructs the process of transformation. Under the joint family system, kinship is extended to include not merely immediate family members, but also distant relatives: cousins, nephews, uncle, etc. The rights and obligations are shared by the family members. It is this feature of shared obligations and rights which is deemed inimical to savings, investment, mobility, risk taking, and labour supply. Since the fruits of labour are shared, individuals stint in supplying the labour. Similarly, it is argued, there is little incentive to invest and undertake risky ventures because, whereas risks are borne by the investor, fruits are shared by all the family members. This also dampens the spirit of entrepreneurship and innovation. Similarly the basic motivation for saving is lacking, because family members share the cost of insurance for dependents and security against old age. The filial obligations and ties also limit the geographical and occupational mobility. The institution of the joint family system is also extended to management and operation of business enterprise. Often recruitment in these family type enterprises are based on familial considerations rather than on competence.

It is evident that most of the disadvantages of the joint family system spring from the tacit assumption that there is a fundamental discontinuity or cleavage between the initiator and the beneficiary. While the existence of this discontinuity cannot be denied, its extent seems to be blown out of proportion. It can be argued that in most cases, family members not merely share the fruits but also the risk, labour, and management responsibility of

---

[81] M. S. Gore, "India" in Lambert and Hoselitz, op. cit., p. 181.

[82] Gore, op. cit., p. 187.

[83] David C. McClelland, *Motivational Trends in Society* (New York: General Learning Press, 1971).

the family projects. There are several instances where the joint family system was instrumental in undertaking risky ventures rather than being a deterrent to it. The joint family system, through its "net work of family obligations, particularly among business communities, does provide a way of spreading risks and of collecting capital at a lower cost than would be required on the open market."[84] In certain cases, the money is apportioned according to effort, capital input, and responsibility, even though returns are deposited in the common pool. Similarly the effect of the joint family system on supply of efforts needs to be examined empirically. Logically one may argue that family ties, family honour, and welfare, coupled with monetary stimuli, are better motivating factors than merely monetary rewards and impersonal arrangements. Japan represents a classic illustration in point where great increase in production is achieved "within a paternalistic, particularistic, diffused, and non-rationalized form of social organization, common in large, technologically advanced companies."[85]

The distinct, but characteristic, features of most Japanese industries are : (1) lifetime commitment to labour; (2) familistic management; and (3) seniority system. Most of these features are common to enterprises run by a joint family.

The joint family system also improves the quality of labour force by imparting skill from one generation to another.

Similarly, the effect of the joint family system on saving is dubious. Even though reasons for the origin and existence of this institution are complex, the contribution of economic factors can hardly be denied. Economies arising out of joint consumption and better utilization of certain indivisible items of consumption—such as house, car, furniture, electricity, and other appliances reduce consumption expenditure and hence provide a larger saving margin out of a given income. It is true that the extended family obligations can drain the family savings but if these obligations are not fulfilled by the family, the state may have to bear this burden. Thus, the overall saving rate may not be adversely affected.

The effects of the joint family system on Indian economic development are mixed. The arguments are far from conclusive owing to lack of empirical data. Even if it is granted that it restricts occupational and geographical mobility and also dampens the incentives to save, invest, and work, its relative weight will depend on the prevalence of the institution in India. It can be safely surmized that the joint family system is disintegrating in urban areas and even in rural India it is no longer as appealing as it used to be in the past.

The role of political institutions in Indian economic development has received relatively little attention, and yet it is one of the most important determinants of economic transformation. Its importance stems from its control over the contingencies (taxes, subsidies, differential remuneration) which, according to the behavioural model postulated, are the critical determinants of the behaviour, activities, and, hence, industrialization. Through its control on the contingencies and their schedule of reinforcement political institutions can establish and reinforce types of behaviour which are conducive to industrialization and discourage those which are averse.

Political institutions assume paramount importance in the Indian context because India represents a unique case where the process of planned economic development is conceived within the democratic framework. Detailed planning encompassing the entire economy presupposes coercive powers to an extent that can be ruled out under democracy. Since in democracy the authority is vested with the masses rather than with the chosen few, constant fear of losing votes results in policies and framework which militate against a fast rate of growth. The point can be elucidated by certain examples. Nowhere has Indian planning failed so miserably as in agriculture (the so called green revolution is a recent phenomenon). The sluggishness

---

84 Lambert and Hoselitz, op. cit., p. 400.

85 Robert N. Marsh and Hiroshi Mannari, "A New Look at Lifetime Commitment in Japanese Industry," *Economic Development and Cultural Change,* Vol. 20, Number 4 (July 1972).

in Indian agriculture cannot be solely attributed to the inadequacy of special inputs like irrigation facilities, fertilizers, seeds, and farm equipment. The fact that such facilities as are available have not been fully utilized clearly reveals that the trouble also lies somewhere else. Part of the explanation must be sought in the democratic institutions which put a powerful leaverage—the vote—in the hands of the "common man," which makes the implementation of a plan an uphill task. Speaking frankly Mr. Dhebar once said, "Whenever they tackled the problem of landlordism, the question, 'What will happen to Congress if Zamindari is abolished ?' raised its ugly head." The fear of losing votes thwarted any attempt to introduce sweeping changes in the institutional and organizational framework in the agriculture sector. The introduction of modern inputs within the framework of outdated and outmoded production relations which militate against any improvement in production is bound to prove abortive. Lajdgensky's report in this connection is revealing.

Our disappointing performance on the saving front is no less patent. There is no other road to economic development than to withhold an increasing share of national income from consumption and use it for investment. In any case, the consumption of the masses should be reduced or, if not actually reduced, it should not be allowed to rise as fast as income. History has known only two ways of achieving this. It may be done by allowing the capitalist to increase the share of profits in national income, and then ploughing back the profits in expanding industries and/or let the state amass the savings through taxation and other coercive measures. The first method was the *modus operandi* of capitalist development and the second, that of socialist. But, in India, both methods are subject to severe limitations. The application of the first method will run counter to our avowed objective of reduction in inequality of income and wealth. The method of taxation and other coercive measures are also subject to severe limitations for the same reason. Agriculture produces within itself half of the national income, but the burden of taxation does not in any case exceed 7 per cent of the aggregate income. The scarcity of resources on the one hand and high marginal propensity to live off the peasantry on the other, merely emphasizes the need for, mopping up large resources from agriculture. But the masses, since they are poor and have the ballot paper, cannot be taxed. The rich peasants, since they control the precious "votes" or the political machinery of the state itself, must be exempted. Uttar Pradesh faced a veritable political crises as a result of its government's attempt to increase land tax by a moderate amount.

The fate of the compulsory deposit scheme as originally conceived is another illustration in point. In its original form, the scheme had to be shelved not because resources were not desperately needed but because of vehement opposition from Chief Ministers who saw in this scheme a highly explosive political bomb which might blow off the ruling party.

The much-controverted gold control rules is another instance showing how the implementation of a plan like its formulation, is largely a political process. The goldsmiths offered tooth-and-nail resistance to the government's attempt to prevent gold smuggling which was making a serious drain into our lamentably small, but precious, foreign exchange resources. The goldsmiths were singularly active in Rajkot where Mr. Masani recorded a thundering victory over his rival—the Congress candidate. The latter, while furnishing the reasons for his grand failure, singled out the unpopularity of gold control rules as the most important. It is no wonder that the gold control scheme was soon shelved.

Thus, the problem of resource mobilization becomes difficult in most of the underdeveloped countries :

> both because of their much greater poverty and also because of new ideology which had no real counterpart in early history of developed countries, but is now being spread by their generous support—that purpose of economic development is to raise the level of living of masses of people. It becomes more diffi-

cult in so far as democratic governments are being adopted, giving the vote to the masses.[86]

The day to day strikes by one section of the community or the other, whether justified or otherwise, do corroborate the contention, "The task of organizing a democracy for rapid and coordinated advance along several lines is one of special difficulty."[87]

4. Present Policies and the Call of the Future

It is evident that the whole gamut of non-economic factors impinge on economic development in a wide variety of ways. The precise mechanism by which influence is exerted is rarely, if ever, delineated. However, following Kunkel, a behavioural model is postulated to explain the interaction between economic and non-economic factors. It is assumed that the process of transformation is dependent on certain activities which are determined by behaviour. It is further postulated that most behavioural patterns are induced, learned, and determined by the nature and types of contingencies. It follows, therefore, that by appropriate changes in contingencies certain types of behaviour can be altered and other types can be established and/or reinforced. For example, the capricious universe view can be altered by building a framework in which rewards and efforts are strongly correlated. In the Indian context this would necessitate a change in the production relations on land, better irrigation facilities to save peasants from the vagaries of nature, more objective and competitive type of examinations for selection and evaluation. Though the significance of the latter is self-evident, the former needs explanation. Owing to absentee landlordism or the zamindari system in India, an average peasant learns painfully that there is little or no correlation between efforts and rewards. No matter how hard the peasant works, the landlord (by virtue of his position as an owner of land) will always appropriate a lion's share of the produce. The massive expenditure on irrigation projects in the Indian plans and land reform programme with its stress on "land to the tiller," if implemented, should gradually change the capricious universe view. The Community Development Programme with its stress on self-help and village level planning should also alter the fatalistic attitude of rural people.

As stated earlier, Indian religion is characterized by "this wordly" and "other worldly" elements. Our survey of two schools in Delhi (though hardly an adequate or representative sample) shows virtually little knowledge of there "other wordly" elements among the younger generation. A deliberate policy to underscore materialistic elements *vis-a-vis* non-materialistic elements can reduce some of the inimical effects of religion on industrialization.

The grip of the caste system and the joint family system in India is apparently on the wane. The Gandhian Movement against untouchability and the avowed policy of the government to uplift this minority by granting scholarships and reserving a certain quota of vacancies for Harijans are steps in the right direction. The role of competitive examinations in this context cannot be understressed.

In general, two factors are of critical significance from the standpoint of policy: (1) communication, and (2) education.[88]

Communication. Since most of the behaviour patterns are learnt, the role of mass media in economic development is self-evident. In rural India where much of the information is derived from observations within village and personal experiences, and knowledge imparted by adults, by stories, proverbs, and past incidents, there is considerable uncertainity and lack of knowledge about the outer world. Yet it is in rural India where the hold of reli-

---

[86] Gunnar Myrdal, *Economic Theory in Underdeveloped Regions* (Bombay: Vora and Co., Private Ltd., 1958), pp. 94–95.

[87] Planning Commission, *First Five Year Plan* (New Delhi: Government of India Publication), p. 8.

[88] For details, see Kunkel, op. cit.

gion, the caste system, and the joint family system is the maximum. Evidently, the craving for money will be limited if the image of "good living" is provided by the rich person in the village. Communication with the outer world and the broadening of the horizon beyond the narrow confines of a village is desiderature if some of the existing behavioural patterns are to be changed and new ones are to be established to further economic development.

Education. Assuming behaviour patterns are learnt, education can serve as a powerful tool for reinforcing, shaping, and establishing the types of behaviour patterns which are conducive to industrialization. Education not only enables individuals to know and grasp the range of alternatives available and activities required, but also to interpret, verify, and countercheck the information gathered from hearsay, stories, myths, parents, and friends within the village. By dint of education, the individual can gain access to historical knowledge. The extension of the horizon through knowledge of the rest of the world permits subjects to look beyond the purview of personal experiences and observations. It also enables the individual to relate himself to the environment and successfully manipulate it. Kunkel rightly points out that the capricious universe view can be partly changed by education, even if personal experiences point towards it. In Kunkel's words:

> ...for education may provide a youth with information concerning the principles of national and regional governments, ideals of justice, the operation of economic systems, law, etc. The study of national and regional history as a series of interrelated events, with more or less logical sequence of human activities and governmental, economic, and political forms, would help the individual gain the conception of a systematic universe and lengthened time perspective.[89]

Education is no panacea. But it can, to some extent, reduce the inimical influence of non-economic factors on economic development.

Recent research experiments in South India reveal how psychotherapeutic techniques can be used sucessfully to inculcate and/or stimulate enterpreneurial activities.[90] An achievement training course was organized through the Small Industries Extension Training Institute at Hyderabad. Comparisons between the pre- and post-course candidates showed marked improvement in achievement motivation and consequent entrepreneurial activities. Though the results are tentative, it does suggest that behaviour and personality changes are not only theoretically conceiveable, but also practicable.

5. Conclusions

1. The role of non-economic factors in economic development is subject to considerable controversy. The fundamental issues involved pertain to (a) relative weight of non-economic factors *vis-a-vis* economic factors; (b) identification of non-economic factors most pertinent to economic change; (c) direction of relationship between economic and socio-political phenomenon; and (d) the methods of analyzing the relationship. There is no consensus of opinion on either of these issues owing to lack of relevant and/or sufficient data.

2. There are two distinct approaches to the study of interaction between economic and non-economic factors: (a) psychodynamic model; and (b) behavioural model. The latter approach is deemed more appropriate for the study in question.

3. Philosophers generally agree that there is dualism of thought in Hinduism: There are certain tenets which are "this worldly" and others which are "other worldly." The controversy stems from the relative weight of each in Hinduism in practice. Our survey (even though statistically inadequate) reveals that

[89] Kunkel, op. cit., p. 245.

[90] David McClelland and David G. Winter, *Motivating Economic Achievement* (New York: Free Press, 1969).

the younger generation does not deem "other worldly" tenets important let alone practise it. It was argued that, even if some people believe in these tenets, it does not necessarily prevent them from performing activities which further economic development. It was shown that Hinduism exhibits all the "character traits" of Protestant ethic which, according to Max Weber, are most conducive to industrialization. However, it was established that certain religious activities in India may: (a) absorb a relatively high proportion of lamentably small surplus and (b) result in a pattern of asset preference which is inimical to economic growth.

4. The "capricious universe" view of the Indian masses can obstruct the process of economic expansion through its effect on saving, investment, and supply of labour and family planning. However, the crux of the matter is whether a fatalistic attitude *creates man's condition* or "explains" and "justifies" it. If the latter provides the *raison d'etre* for a fatalistic attitude, its inimical effects should not be overstressed.

5. It is often argued that "economic man" is a myth in the Indian context. The available evidence (even though limited and shaky) does not support the view that the Indian peasant is irrational.

6. It is hypothesized that the caste system in India obstructs the process of economic expansion by (a) limiting the occupational and geographical mobility; (b) breeding nepotism; (c) obstructing the development of a sense of nationhood; and (d) discouraging the entrepreneurial skill formation by blunting the sense of adventure. Available evidence does not support the allegations (a) and (d), which are more critical from the standpoint of economic development.

7. The major disadvantages of the joint family system (such as its adverse effects on saving, investment, mobility, labour supply, and risk-taking) stem from the tacit assumption that there is a fundamental discontinuity between the initiator and the beneficiary. Since the family members are not bound with each other by any contractual arrangement, a wide variation in the criteria and method of apportioning the income are conceivable. It is our contention that in most families not only fruits but also obligations are shared by everyone. The joint family system has certain advantages (such as sharing possible risks familistic management, lifetime commitment to enterprise, and economical utilization of fixed inputs) which should be underscored.

8. Democracy and planning are often regarded as a contradiction in terms. Even though Indian experience refutes this contention, it cannot be denied that the democratic framework and the consequent stress on winning votes do impair the rate of growth.

9. Among other policy instruments, communication and education are of paramount importance in abating or removing the inimical effects of socio-political factors on Indian economic development.

BIBLIOGRAPHY

Adelman, Irma and Cynthia Taft Morris: "An Econometric Model of Development," *American Economic Review*, December 1968.

Boulding, Kenneth: *A Reconstruction of Economics* (New York: John Wiley, 1950).

Goheen, John: A Comment on Professor Singer's "Cultural Values in India's Economic Development," *Economic Development and Cultural Change*, July 1958.

Hagen, Everette: *On the Theory of Social Change: How Economic Growth Begins* (Illinois: Dorsey Press, 1962).

Hoselitz, Bert F: "Non-Economic Factors in Economic Development," in Bernard Okun, and Richard W. Richardson (eds), *Studies in Economic Development* (New York: Holt, Rinehart and Winston, 1961).

Karve, D.G.: "Comments," *Economic Development and Cultural Change*, July 1968.

Karve, Irawati: "What is Caste?" and "Caste and Occupation," *Economic Weekly*, March 22, 1958.

Kindleberger, C.E.: *Economic Development* (New York: McGraw Hill, 1966).

Kunkel, John H.: *Society and Economic Growth* (New York: Oxford University Press, 1970).

Lambert, Richard and Bert F. Hoselitz (eds): *The Role of Savings and Wealth in Southern Asia and the West* (UNESCO, 1963).

Lambert, Richard: "The Social and Psychological Determinants of Savings and Investments in

Developing Societies," in Hoselitz, Bert F., and Wilbert E. Moore (eds), *Industrialization and Society* (The Hague: UNESCO, 1963).

McClelland, David G.: *The Achieving Society* (Princeton: D. Van Nostrand, 1961).

Mishra, V. B.: *Hinduism and Economic Growth* (New York: Oxford University Press, 1962).

Myrdal, Gunnar: *Asian Drama: An Inquiry Into the Poverty of Nations* (New York: Twentieth Century Fund, 1968).

Raulet, Harry and J. S. Uppal, "The Social Dynamics of Economic Development in Rural Punjab," *Asian Survey,* April 1970.

Singer, Milton: "Cultural Values in India's Economic Development," *Annals of American Academy and Social Science,* 1956.

——— "India's Cultural Values and Economic Development: A Discussion: A Postscript," *Economic Development and Cultural Change,* July 1958.

"Religion and Social Change in India, The Max Weber Thesis, Phase Three," *Economic Development and Cultural Change,* July 1966.

Srinivas, M. N.: "A Note on Mr. Goheen's Note," *Economic Development and Cultural Change,* July 1958.

Tawney, R. H.: *Religion and Rise of Capitalism* (New York: Harcourt and Brace, 1952).

Weber, Max: *Religion of India* (Glencoe: The Free Press, 1958).

——— *Protestant Ethic and Spirit of Capitalism* (New York: Scribner, 1956).

Part Two

THE ECONOMIC SECTORS

3

Agriculture in India: Problems and Prospects

ROMESH DIWAN

"That system alone will prevail which the villagers after mutual discussions and understandings approve of. No system or arrangement would be thrust upon them from outside. If each of them prefers separate individual cultivation of land, he can do so; and if two, four or even more persons want to come together or even if the whole village wants to have collective farming they are welcome to follow their inclination. All will, however, work with complete unanimity. If the opinion seems to be divided, both the experiments will be undertaken. *But the ownership of the land will vest in the village as a whole* and consequently there would be real village self-government in each village."

—*Acharya Vinoba Bhaveji on Bhoodan and Gramdan.*

1. Introduction

The word "agriculture" comes from the Latin words : agri, field, culture, cultivation. Accordingly, *Webster's Collegiate Dictionary* defines it as, "the science or art of cultivating the soil, producing crops and raising of livestock; farming." In economic literature, this term has been given much broader meanings. It encompasses everything pertaining to the activity of farming. The basic purpose of farming used to be the production of "wage-goods." "Wage-goods"[1] are those goods that are consumed by people at large to satisfy their basic needs of existence, such as wheat, rice, maize, etc. These are the necessities of life. Without these goods people will literally die. Over time, farming activity has been extended to the production of raw materials[2] used in the manufacture of industrial goods. Examples of raw materials are: cotton, jute, rubber, etc. They are different from wage-goods in so far as the raw materials cannot be consumed directly by the people. These have to be processed before

[1] In the terminology of welfare economics, wage-goods may be defined as those goods the consumption of which leads directly to the production of utilities. In Marxian economics, these are the "basic" goods.

[2] In terms of welfare economics, the utility comes from consumption and raw materials are not directly consumable. To become consumable, these goods have to be processed. Their utility, therefore, is contingent upon the nature and availability of the facility processing them into the consumable form.

these can be consumed. It need be mentioned, however, that some of these raw materials, after dully processed (sometimes in homes), do enter into the consumption of people at large. Some of these, therefore, may be classified as wage-goods since these relate to social necessities. Thus, sugar and cotton would relate to wage-goods. Jute, on the other hand, is strictly a raw material. Even though the distinction between wage-goods and raw materials depends upon the nature and structure of consumption of the society, it is still a useful and analytically meaningful distinction. In this chapter, we will divide the total agricultural production into these two categories.

Sometimes a distinction is made between agriculture and plantations. Plantation economy also produce both wage-goods,[3] like tea, and raw materials; such as cocoa, rubber, cotton, sugar cane, etc. However, the distinction is an important one and follows from the way plantation economy was introduced. While agricultural activity was fundamental to the very existence of the society, plantation activity was superimposed on an existing socio-economic structure by an alien investor. While the purpose of the output of the agricultural production was the consumption by the members of the country in which production took place, the purpose of the output of the plantation economy was pure and simple export to the country of the investor.[4] As a result, the institutional set up was, and still is, very different in the plantation economy. As the countries, which were ruled by foreign governments, have become independent, they have been, and still are, making attempts to integrate the plantation economy with the agricultural economy. This process of integration has problems of its own. In this chapter our analysis will focus only on the agricultural economy.

2. Total Agricultural Output

Since wage-goods satisfy the basic needs of the members of a society, the society, if it has to exist, has to obtain these goods. There are two[5] ways by which it can obtain these goods: (i) produce these goods itself, and (ii) produce other goods, say non-wage goods, and exchange these non-wage goods for wage-goods by trading with another country which produces wage-goods and is willing (or under pressure) to exchange. Generally, countries with large land areas, such as Brazil, Canada, China, France, India, Nigeria, the U.S.A. and the U.S.S.R., produce wage-goods themselves. It is only countries with small land areas and high density of population, like Belgium, Britain, Netherlands, etc., that obtain wage-goods both by producing themselves and through trade.

In the context of India, production of wage-goods is essential. It is particularly so if we examine the nature of the Indian economy. A large part of the total production in the Indian economy is carried on in the agriculture sector. The following table on the shares of agriculture in the National Income of India corroborates this observation.

---

[3] Initially, the plantation economy did not produce wage goods. Over time some of these goods have become a part of general consumption. Thus, tea was produced purely for export. Over 150 years, tea has entered the consumption of every household.

[4] The plantation of tea in India and Ceylon, rubber in Malaysia, cocoa in Ghana, to take a few examples only, was enforced by the British government for export to England.

[5] Actually, there are three additional ways as well, namely, (1) beg, (2) borrow, and (3) steal. (1) In the international arena, begging is rarely possible. There is hardly any nation that gives away these goods in charity. Some propagandists (prestigious professors can also be, and frequently are propagandists) of Western countries have generated a myth, by the use of such terms as "aid," "grants," etc., that the Western countries are giving away in charity these goods to the poor countries. In reality such charity is only a myth and the poor countries pay through their noses via political influence. Thus, in 1966, when India suffered a serious shortage of these goods, as a result of underproduction due to two very bad droughts, the U.S. government was able to force three policy changes: (i) devaluation, (ii) liberalization of trade restrictions, and (iii) the permission to the U.S. Corporations to produce fertilizers in the private sectors, in exchange for the "aid" in food grains. (2) Borrowing is simply trade over time. It is, thus, another form of trade. (3) Stealing is done only by militarily strong countries. Unfortunately, poor countries are also militarily weak.

Table 1. Share of Agriculture in National Income

Year	Percentage of agriculture in national income
1960-61	51.2
1965-66	42.7
1969-70	44.1

Notes : (i) These data are taken from *Economic Survey* : *1970-71*.
(ii) The year refers to the agricultural year; from July to June.
(iii) The estimates of percentages are based on the data for 1960-61 prices (revised series).

Thus half of the total production in the economy is accounted by the agriculture sector. Agriculture, thus, is the most important activity in the country.

The question that arises is: is the production from agriculture enough, or sufficient, to satisfy the basic needs of the members of the Indian society? Before attempting to answer this question, it is necessary to understand what we mean by "the production from agriculture." Also, the percentage share of agriculture in the above table is estimated by dividing the "total agricultural output" by the national income. To appreciate and interpret the numbers in the above table, therefore, it is necessary to define the term, "total agricultural output," which is, basically, the same thing as "production from agriculture." The "total agricultural output" is a fictional concept. However, it is a useful concept for analytical purposes. The "total agricultural output" is made up of various types of agricultural production; such as wage-goods, raw materials. This much is obvious common sense. Yet, there is no easy way to define the total agricultural output as a simple sum of the various types of production. The problem is that different productions are measured in different units. For example, wheat is measured in maunds and tons and cotton in bales. The question is, how does one add, say, wheat to cotton? Thus, how does a particular total agricultural output, say, composed of 10 tons of wheat and 10 bales of cotton, compare with another total agriculture output, say, composed of 15 tons of wheat and 5 bales of cotton? To put this question in a more precise form, let us assume[6] that agricultural production is made up only of two commodities; one representing wage-goods and the other raw materials, and denote A, A_1 and A_2 for the amount of total agricultural output, wage-goods, and raw material respectively. Then, the question is : is $A=A_1+A_2$?[7]

Since A is a purely fictional quantity, in the sense that one cannot find a quantity called A in the real world, and A_1 and A_2 are real life quantities; the sum does not make sense. The reason is that the quantities A_1 and A_2 are measured in different units. Accordingly, these cannot be added together.

In order to express A as a sum of A_1 and A_2, it is necessary to represent all these quantities in the same units. There are various ways of doing so. One of these ways is to write A, A_1 and A_2 in value terms. Thus if we write p, p_1, p_2 for the price per unit of A, A_1, and A_2 respectively, we may write the equation.[8]

$$pA=p_1A_1+p_2A_2 \quad (1)$$

Equation (1) means that the total money spent on total agricultural output is equal to the total money spent on wage-goods and on raw materials. This makes sense, since it is a sum in money terms. In other words, we are adding up quantities in the same units. It may be pointed out however, that p like A is a fictional concept. (pA), on the other hand, is a real life number;

6 This is only a simplifying assumption.

7 More generally, we may ask the question: Is $A=\sum_{i=1}^{n} A_i$? Where A_i refers to the amount of production of the ith commodity. For example, $A_1=$ rice; $A_2=$ wheat; $A_9=$gram; $A_{11}=$sugarcane; $A_{13}=$ cotton; $A_{16}=$tea, etc.

8 More generally, $pA=\sum_{i=1}^{n} P_i A_i$; where p_i refers to the price of the ith commodity. For example, p =price per ton of rice; p_2 =price per ton of wheat; $p_9=$price per ton of gram; p_{11} price per ton of sugarcane; $p_{13}=$price per bale of 180 kilograms of cotton; $p_{16}=$ price per ton of tea, etc.

even though both p and A are fictional.

If we divide equation (1), we get,[9]

$$A=(p_1/p)\,A_1+(p_2/p)\,A_2\,;=c_1\,A_1+c_2\,A_2\,;$$
$$c_i=p_i/p\ (i=1,2) \qquad (2)$$

We can, thus, define the concept, "total agricultural output" as a weighted sum of the production of wage-goods and raw materials. It will be noticed that, even though a simple sum does not make sense, a weighted sum does seem legitimate. The simple sum is possible only in the particular case when $c_1=c_2=1$. This, it will be appreciated, is a very stringent condition indeed.[10]

In the last few paragraphs we suggested that A_1 and A_2 are real life quantities while A is a fictional quantity. The implication of this statement is that we can find data on actual quantities of A_1 and A_2. Table 2 gives such information.

Before we analyze these data, it needs to be mentioned that we cannot write a similar row the "total agriculture output." The total agricultural output can be expressed only in the form of an index number. Thus, we present the data in Table 2 along with the data on "total agricultural output" in Table 3.

Table 2. Production of Agricultural Commodities

Commodity Year		1950-51	1955-56	1960-61	1965-66	1968-69
Rice	(,000 tons)	23.5	27.6	34.6	30.7	39.8
Wheat	(,,)	6.4	8.8	11.0	10.4	18.8
Cereal	(,, ,,)	46.8	55.8	69.3	62.2	83.6
Pulses	(,, ,,)	8.1	11.0	12.7	9.8	10.4
Cotton	(,, bales)	2.9	3.9	5.3	4.7	5.3
Tea	(,, tons)	3.27	.31	.32	.37	.40

Note: The table has been taken from Statement 8, page S14, *Report on Currency and Finance, 1969-70*. The necessary notes regarding these data are given there.

Table 3. Index Number of Agricultural Production
(Agricultural Year ended June 1959=100)

Commodity / Year	1950-51	1955-56	1960-61	1965-66	1968-69
Rice	88	114	138	122	157
Wheat	101	131	163	154	259
Total cereal	90	115	138	124	166
Pulses	92	118	129	98	102
Cotton	111	154	202	184	203
Tea	104	107	121	138	143
Total agricultural output	96	117	142	132	159

Notes: (i) The table has been derived from Statement 9, page S16, *Report on Currency and Finance, 1969-70*.

(ii) The actual figures have been rounded off to whole numbers.

(iii) The original table gives many more details. Necessary notes regarding these data are also given there.

These tables suggest that over the 20 years or so, since 1950, the total agricultural output has increased by 60 per cent; or at the rate of approximately 3 per cent per year. However, this increase has not been evenly spread over individual commodities. It is wheat whose production has

[9] In the general case, $A=\sum_{i=1}^{n} c_i\ A_i\ c_i=(P_i/p)$; $(i=1,\ \ldots\ldots n)$. Since p is only a fictional number, it is legitimate to divide by p.

[10] It is suggested that the reader should analyze the implications of this condition.

increased the fastest: at the rate of 8 per cent per year. Other fast growing crops are maize, cotton, and sugarcane, all of these approximately 5 per cent per year. Coffee and rubber have grown still faster; at the rate of 11 and 17 per cent per *annum* respectively. On the other hand, pulses have remained virtually at the same level as in 1950. Production of jute has actually decreased.

From equation (2) we can see that increase in A can come about in many ways. Thus it is quite possible that there may be an increase in the total agricultural output along with a decrease in one of the commodities. In other words, we can have a situation where the people at large are becoming actually poor (the wage-goods are decreasing) even when the total agricultural output is increasing. It is, therefore, important to look into the production of individual commodities and one must be very careful in interpreting the quantity "total agricultural output."[11]

There are other ways of determining the weights.[12] We suggest another method. Equation (2) can be derived by formulating weights from the amount of manual labour used in producing one unit of the agricultural commodity labour per unit of production—to use the economic jargon. Thus, if we write n, n_1 and n_2 for labour used per unit of A, A_1 and A_2, we get back equation (2) except that now $c_i = n_i/n$ $(i=1, 2)$.[13]

---

[11] National income is also a fictional quantity and it is quite possible that national income may be increasing while people feel more miserable. Some observers think that such a situation is already taking place in the U.S.A.

[12] It is suggested that the reader should find for himself/herself the weighting scheme used in the determination of the index for "total output" in Table 3.

[13] The general case follows from the equation: $L = \sum_{i=1}^{n} L_i$ where L_i and L_i refer to total labour used in all agriculture and total labour used in the production of commodity A_i respectively. Thus $n = L/A$ and $n_i = L_i/A_i$. It is suggested that the reader should develop some other methods to determine $c_?$ so that the meanings of the weighting can be fully appreciated.

3. Sufficiency of Agricultural Production

In Tables 1, 2 and 3 we notice the following facts: (i) Agricultural production forms a large part of total production in the economy. (ii) The production of food grains (cereals and pulses) has gone up from 55 thousand tons in 1950–57 to 95 thousand tons in 1968–69. (iii) The total agricultural production has grown at the rate of 3 per cent per year. By themselves, these facts are quite interesting. However, the fundamental question is: Do these facts suggest that India is producing "enough" wage-goods to satisfy the needs of the members of its society? Obviously, we cannot answer this question from the facts above. We need more information. We need two types of information: (1) What is meant by "enough?" (2) What is the size and nature of the members of the Indian society? Still, this question is of fact.

Before we answer this question, there is a prior question: namely, why should the production be "enough" to satisfy the needs of the members of the society? This question is of value, world views, etc. and not of facts. We can answer as follows. By definition the consumption of wage-goods is essential for the very existence of life of the members. If the members do not live, the society dies. Thus, the production of these goods has to be at least as much as the needed consumption for existence. If the production is less than the needed consumption, those members who cannot get the consumption will die and the size of the society will shrink. On the other hand, if the production is greater than the needed consumption, then the members will not only be able to exist but be even healthier so that they can produce more. Also in the theories of economic development, it is generally believed that excess of this production is necessary for the development of industry. In other words, this surplus production provides the base on which an industrial sector can be built. Without this surplus, there is no way of having an industrial sector.

Now we come back to our question: is the production "enough" to satisfy the needs of the members of the society? The term "enough" can be defined in terms of the floor. Thus, by "enough" we mean the very minimum of food that is needed for simple existence. Experts on nutrition have estimated that in Indian climatic conditions an intake of around 2,000 to 2,400 calories are adequate for living. These calory requirements differ with type of work, age, etc. Our question then is: is the production sufficient to provide at least 2,000–2,400 calories for all the members? There are two ways of looking at this question. One, we can estimate the total amount of calories produced. This can be done if we express all types of food production in terms of calories. Estimates of this nature have been made. Professor K. N. Raj[14] produced evidence to this effect. "His evidence is based on the fact that on nutritional grounds the average food grains requirements of an adult under Indian conditions is 13 ounces per day. Taking into consideration the age composition and provision for seed and wastage, the average requirement would be $15\frac{1}{2}$ ounce per day. From the data he concludes that in no year in the last decade and a half has the per capita availability of food grains fallen below this level and, except in two years (1951–52 and 1952–53), it would have been possible to ensure this from domestic production."[15]

The other approach is to analyze the conditions of actual consumption. Very meagre data are available on the actual consumption of wage-goods by the people at large.[16] Estimates of consumption can be, and are, made from the expenditures on consumption. Recently, Dandekar and

Table 4. Distribution of Consumer Expenditure by Major Items

Monthly per capita expenditure (Rs.)	Percent of population	Annual per capita expenditure (Rs.)	*Percentage distribution of total expenditure*				
			Food grains and substitutes	Other items of food	Fuel and light	Clothing	Others
1	2	3	4	5	6	7	8
Rural							
0-8	6.38	79.3	64.42	18.35	8.74	1.23	7.36
8-11	11.95	116.6	63.57	17.43	8.56	2.51	7.93
11-13	9.88	147.2	60.25	19.09	7.36	5.70	7.60
13-15	9.82	170.8	58.12	20.44	7.48	4.63	9.33
15.18	13.79	200.0	54.50	23.66	6.93	5.23	9.67
18.21	11.44	237.3	50.31	24.10	6.67	6.97	11.95
Urban							
0-8	2.15	77.6	63.79	17.87	8.93	0.63	8.78
8-11	2.49	118.3	52.67	26.65	8.23	1.13	11.32
11-13	7.19	145.0	48.32	27.35	8.64	2.27	13.42
13-15	6.86	169.7	45.73	29.11	8.03	2.87	14.26
15-18	10.71	201.2	41.72	31.37	7.38	3.57	15.96
18.21	11.40	235.7	37.17	33.40	7.49	3.41	18.53
21-24	9.68	271.7	36.45	33.81	7.12	3.94	18.68
24-28	11.04	315.4	32.72	34.56	6.91	5.29	20.52

Notes: (i) This table is made up of Dandekar and Rath, Table no. 1.2 and 1.3; p. 26-27
(ii) For details regarding the Table, see the original article by Dandekar and Rath

14 K. N. Raj, "Food Shortage: Failure of a Policy," *Times of India,* January 20, 1966, p. 8. In this connection also see, M. L. Dantwala, "Food Policy: Misplaced Criticism," *Times of India,* February 10, 1966, p. 8 and Romesh Diwan, "The Debate on Food in India: Some Relevant Variables," *Economic and Political Weekly,* December 31, 1966, pp. 849–56.

15 Romesh Diwan, Ibid, page 851.

16 These data are collected by the National Sample Survey in its various rounds.

Rath[17] have done a somewhat detailed analysis of the actual consumption of a large section of the population. They provide the evidence in Table 4.

Dandekar and Rath argue, and few disagree, that "in 1960–61, an annual per capita consumer expenditure of Rs. 170 was essential to give a diet adequate at least in respect of calories"[18] in the rural areas. In urban areas the equivalent expenditure is Rs. 271. Using, the minimal needed annual expenditure, one can derive the conclusions regarding consumption from Table 4. Dandekar and Rath conclude that, in 1960–61, about one third of the rural population and nearly half of the urban population lived on diets inadequate even in respect of calories.[19] The implication is that a sizable proportion, more than two-fifths, of the Indian society does not get even an adequate diet. On the other hand, the production in the country is sufficient to provide an adequate diet. This contradiction can be explained on the basis of two reasons. One, the contradiction arises due to the problem of maldistribution. This author has argued that the explanation lies in analyzing the urban and rural situations separately.[20] Two, the actual production of food grains is just not sufficient, particularly when one takes into consideration the inequalities generated by regional disparities. In other words, there may be a problem of distribution, but the total output is not sufficient if we wish to remove the poverty of the masses. The policy, therefore, has to be in terms of increasing the production and not merely distributing what is already being produced.

In this chapter we will not discuss the problem relating to the distribution of output. We will concentrate on issues concerning production. The important question here: Why does not Indian agriculture produce sufficiently large quantities of wage-goods and raw materials? It need be mentioned here that the sufficiency of raw materials is determined by the size of the industrial sector. We have not discussed the question whether sufficient quantities of raw materials are produced. The total agricultural output index gives a weightage of 66.9 per cent to total food grains production and only 33.1 per cent to total non-food grains production. We leave the reader with the assertion that the production of raw materials is also not sufficient for India's needs.[21]

4. Productivity in Agriculture

We, thus, come back to our question: Why does not Indian agriculture produce sufficiently large quantities? To answer it we must first understand the factors that determine production. Production of a commodity generally, and an agricultural commodity particularly, is influenced by two major facts concerning: (a) the technological relationships between inputs and outputs, and (b) the institutional set-up in the producing country. *These factors, technology and institutional framework, are not independent of each other.* Instead they are very interdependent. Actually one depends on the other. We shall study these separately in order to shed light on the characteristics of these two factors. The technological relationship analyzes various methods of producing the particular commodity. It refers to the question: How can, and does, actual production take place? The emphasis here is on the alternative forms of combining the different inputs. Institutional set-up, on the other hand, deals with the

[17] V. M. Dandekar and Nilakantha Rath, "Poverty in India," *Economic and Political Weekly*, January 2, 1971, pp. 25–48; January 9, 1971, pp. 100–146.

[18] Dandekar and Rath, Ibid, p. 29.

[19] The reader is advised to analyze Table 4 in order to understand and appreciate the gravity of this conclusion. In this connection, also see Ranjit Sau, "Poverty in India, A Comment," *Economic and Political Weekly*, March 20, 1971; "The New Economics," *Economic and Political Weekly*, Special Number, 1972, pp. 1571–80; and Romesh Diwan, "Planning for the Poor," *Economic and Political Weekly*, August 21, 1971, pp. 1809–14.

[20] Romesh Diwan, "The Debate on Food in India: Some Relevant Variables," *Economic and Political Weekly*, December 31, 1966, pp. 849–856. More precisely, the analysis is couched in terms of a dual economic system.

[21] It is suggested that the reader should question this assertion and prove or disprove it by defining certain criteria and testing it with the actual production data.

relationship between decision makers and actual producers. It is concerned with some of the basic decisions regarding production: (1) What will be produced? (2) Why will it be produced? (3) Who will produce it? (4) and How will the production be distributed between the producers and decision makers? We study these factors in detail as under:

5. Technological Relationships

Production is a process in which a certain number of inputs are so combined as to result in the production of the particular commodity. For example, if wheat is the particular commodity desired to be produced it will require the inputs of (1) land, (2) seeds and manure, (3) water, (4) sunshine, (5) time, (6) energy, and (7) tools. There are large variations in the types of these inputs. Land can be more or less fertile. Water can be obtained through rain or irrigation; irrigation, in its turn, may be from water tanks, tubewells, canals, etc. Seeds can be of different variations. These can be more or less resistant to insects. The timing of the sunshine is very important.[22] No production is possible without time. However, different methods of production take more or less time. Energy comes in various forms: (a) human, (b) animal, (c) electrical, and (d) mechanical. In economic literature, human energy is separated from other forms of energy. Human energy is of two types: (i) mental and (ii) physical. Mental energy refers to the capacity for decision making while physical energy involves the performance of physical tasks. Physical energy can be substituted by other forms of energy.[23] The important thing here is that in a human being one form of energy cannot be separated from another. The tools needed are fully dependent upon the form energy takes. Thus electric energy can be obtained only through an electric generator. Mechanical energy, on the other hand, requires a different motor. The ploughs needed to be pulled by bullocks are of a different nature from ploughs fitted to a tractor. In the last analysis, the purpose of tools is, basically, to facilitate the use of energy. It will be noticed that all the various inputs are heavily interdependent. The relation between them is both of complimentarity and substitution.

A particular combination of these inputs generates a particular technique of production. Since every particular input has a number of forms, the combination of these forms gives a very large number of techniques indeed.[24] We will pick out and concentrate only on two of these techniques. These are well defined and very distinct.[25] These are discussed both in popular and academic literature. Quite a few names have been given to these: *desi* and *farmi*, old and new, traditional and modern, premodern and modern, low and high yielding, high and low quality, Asian and Western, etc. It will be noticed that all of these are emotive words pronouncing judgments that one is better than the other. To avoid value judgments, not that these are not important, and help facilitate understanding and analysis, we shall call them Technique I and Technique II.

Technique I

This is a method of production which has been carried on in India, also in Asia, for quite a few centuries. Over such a long time, it has been improved to the point of being perfected. It has adapted itself to the resources in India. The seeds used are very resistant to any sort of disease, so that even in bleak years there is a minimal production. The water is obtained from whatever sources are available. It is because of this that Indian agriculture is called a gam-

---

22 One of the reasons why some of the agricultural crops cannot be grown in Britain, Sweden, etc. is the lack of sunshine.

23 Some argue that computers may be a substitute for mental energy. However, there is a lot of controversy on this issue.

24 A reader fascinated with some forms of algebra may work out these combinations. The questions is as follows: There are 7 inputs and these have n_1, n_2, n_3, n_4, n_5, n_6, n_7, forms. A combination of the 7 inputs generates a technique. How many techniques are there?

25 It may be pointed out that the effect of a change in technique is not only to change the input combination but also to change the physical qualities of the output.

ble in the rains. The energy used is a low one and in the form of bullocks. The tools are those that can be pulled by bullocks. The production per acre of land by this method is low. On the other hand, the costs of production per acre of land are also low so that even a poor farmer can adopt this method of production. The risk factor is also low. It is a method which is ecologically sound. This is labour intensive and not capital intensive.

Technique II

It is a method of production that has been introduced in India in the very recent past. In this method, the seeds used are least resistant to disease so that insecticides are very important. The manuring involves intensive doses of fertilizers. Fertilizers are effective only if there are rather large quantities of water available. Since a large quantity of water is essential, it cannot depend upon rain alone. Water has to be obtained either from canals or from tubewells; ordinary persian wells are not sufficient since these do not deliver large quantities of water. Thus, if canal water is not available, there is a need for a large capital investment in tubewells, fertilizers and insecticides. The energy needed for this method is in large doses so that simple bullock power is no more sufficient. Such doses of energy can only be channelled through machinery like tractors, etc., which involves further capital investment. Since machinery and tubewells have its own economies of scale, the land holding using this method is comparatively large. The production per acre of land is high[26] so is the cost per acre of land. The risk factor is also high. A poor farmer cannot adopt this method. The method is capital intensive and ecologically unsound. Since this method has been used extensively in Western countries, it conforms to their resource mix.

6. Production Function

In economic theory, the methods of production are analyzed by the means of a production function; an abstracted, simplistic, and somewhat unrealistic device. The production function is generally represented by a mathematical equation :

$$A_1 = f\ (L, K, Ld)$$

Where, A_1, L, K, Ld stand for, respectively, the final output, quantity of labour employed, quantity of capital used, and acreage of land used in production. It will be noticed that seed, manures, water, tools, bullocks, etc. have all been aggregated into the capital K. The function completely ignores the inputs such as time and sunshine. However, these are fairly constant for a particular method of production. Function f is a general form and can express a particular relationship; e.g. linear homogeneous function.[27] f also determines a particular technique of production. Thus f_1 implies one method of production and f_2 another.

The implication of the production function is that if we increase the units of the inputs, L, K and Ld, then the output A_1 will increase. If a one per cent increase in all the inputs leads to more than, equal to, and less than one per cent increase in output, we have, respectively, increasing, constant, and diminishing returns. It is generally believed that the law of diminishing returns to scale operates in agriculture. It will be noticed that a one per cent increase in all the inputs does not change the proportions between inputs; these are written as K/L, L/K, K/Ld, Ld/K, L/Ld, Ld/L. Sometimes the increase may take place only in one input, say, L. In that case, the total output will change but so will the proportions. In the textbooks, production function is expressed in this form. To elucidate some of the concepts and concerns, we make use of these two concepts. Thus taking L as the variable input, holding both Ld and K constant, we may draw the graphs as in Graph I on page 54.[28]

The two curves I and II represent the total output of A_1. The curve I is drawn by holding K and Ld constant at a particular

26 When in literature they talk of the "green revolution" it is this method they have in mind.

27 This is the form associated with the Cobb—Douglas production function.

28 I am indebted to Professor Radha Sinha for elucidating the argument from this graph.

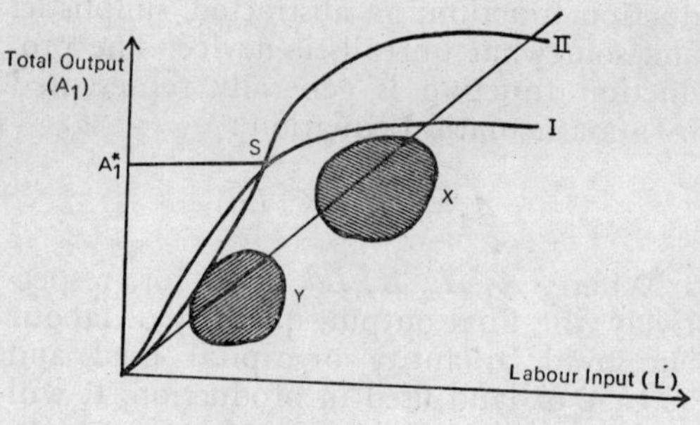

Fig. 1

value, say K^* and $Ld.^*$ Similarly II assumes that K and Ld are constant, however, at a different value K^{**} and Ld^{**}. In this particular example, for every level of output beyond A_1^*, the output on curve II is higher than on curve I. Since the labour employed in both cases is the same, it implies that the output per unit of labour on curve II is higher than the output per unit of labour on curve I. The output per unit of labour (A_1/L) is also known as labour productivity; sometimes simply productivity.

Labour productivity in Indian agriculture is considered quite low. Table 5 compares productivity in India with other countries.

Table 5. Average Labour Productivity per Year in Agriculture

Country	Average productivity in U.S. dollars
India	105
Norway	973
United Kingdom	2057
Canada	2126
Japan	2265
U.S.A.	2408
New Zealand	3481
West Germany	3495

Notes: 1. This table has been taken from Ruddar Datt and K. P. M. Sundharam, *Indian Economy*, Niraj Prakashan, 1971, p. 231.

2. A million problems arise when comparing productivity for the whole of agriculture. More meaningful comparisons could be made between particular commodities.

3. It is not clear what years these estimates relate to.

Even though comparisons have large pit falls, the large difference in the estimates for India and Western countries does suggest that the labour productivity in Indian agriculture is not high.

Before one analyzes the evidence on productivity, it is important to ask the question, namely, what is the relevant concept of productivity? Just as we have labour productivity, we can also define land productivity and capital productivity. In the context of Indian agriculture, it is land and not labour which is, perhaps, the scarce input. A case can, therefore, be made for land productivity, (A_1/Ld), i.e., output per unit of land. Table 6 gives data on land productivity and trends therein.

Table 6. Rates of Growth of Agricultural Production and Land Productivity (1949-50 to 1968-69)

Commodity	(Growth rate per cent per annum) Production	area	land productivity
Rice	3.02	1.22	1.78
Wheat	4.20	2.26	1.90
All food grains	2.79	1.19	1.65
Cotton	3.93	1.91	1.98
Sugarcane	3.97	2.74	1.20
All commodities	2.92	1.37	1.53

Notes: 1. The table has been taken from the *Fourth Five Year Plan.*, p. 117.

2. If we write P_d for productivity, and define it as A_i/Ld, then $\frac{\dot{A}_1}{A_1} = \frac{\dot{Ld}}{Ld} + \frac{\dot{P}_d}{P_d}$ Dots represent rates of change and three values represent the columns rspectively.

Thus the land productivity has been growing in the production of food grains at the rate of 1.65 in the past 20 years.

7. Causes of Law Labour Productivity

Coming back to the evidence of labour productivity, the question arises: why is the labour productivity so low in India? The reasons lie in many causes. Some of the causes deal with the institutional set-up. The institutional set-up affects very strongly the motives for and capacity of labour to work on production. We shall study these in the next section. The other reasons are purely technological. From the graph it is obvious that the labour productivity under Technique II is larger than under Technique I.

Some economists maintain that India is in the area X on the graph. Professor Radha Sinha[29] calls it the "pre-modern high level equilibrium trap." By this he means that in India we have reached the limit posed by the existing technology—Technique I. Any amount of juggling with the factors would not help. Actually, he has made an interesting use of the graph to elucidate his argument. He maintains that the actual production is always less than the potential output defined by the curve. The difference lies in the various imperfections and institutional limitations. The total output cannot be increased beyond the curve. The only way to do so is to shift the whole curve. This is possible if there is a change in the method of production—Technique II. His point is that in the case of India we have already reached the point of virtual maximum. This is also the contention of some other economists, like T. W. Schultz.[30]

The implication of Professor Radha Sinha's argument is that further increases in production can only come from the use and hence availability of the "new" type of inputs, like "new" seeds, fertilizers, insecticides, tubewells, etc., the inputs needed for the "green revolution." These inputs have to be either (i) produced domestically or (ii) obtained by imports from abroad. In one case, the increases in agricultural production depend upon the growth of the industrial sector. In the other, it depends upon the increase in trade with Western countries. In any case, endogeneous increases in agricultural production are not possible. From now on, the agricultural sector is tied up with the industrial sector or the Western economy. Another interesting implication is that contrary to the earlier situation where industry depends upon agriculture (for demand of the industrial output and the supply of industrial inputs), now it is agriculture that depends upon industry for the agricultural inputs.

8. Institutional Framework

So far we have concentrated on the methods of production and the technical relations between the output and its inputs. The production process, however, is also influenced, in a large measure, by the institutional set up. Some social scientists, including economists, argue that the method of production itself depends upon the nature of institutions.[31] In any case, some of the most important and very basic questions regarding production are defined, if not completely determined, by the nature and type of the institutions. Some of the basic questions are: Why produce? What should be produced and who should produce?

We have used the term "institutions" without in any way defining or describing it. There are various ways of defining an institutional set-up. Either one can define the particular institutions prevalent in India or outline the general nature of the institutional framework. We follow the latter. We distinguish three major institutional frameworks, namely, (i) feudalism, (ii) capitalism, and (iii) socialism. These are, unfortunately, amorphous terms hardly well defined. There is, therefore, a large area where there can be, and generally is, a lot of disagreement. Our purpose here is not to engage in defining these systems, but a rather limited one of, hopefully, bringing out the different principles involved in these forms. It is asserted that a particular form can be created from various combinations of these three systems. Actually, various combinations of the principles of these three systems do generate a large number of rather complex institutional framework.[32]

29 Professor Radha Sinha has not yet published his paper in which he has made this argument. He has very kindly allowed me to quote him.

30 Theodore W. Schultz, "Transforming World Agriculture."

31 Interestingly, it is this question that separates the classical from the neo-classical economists. Classical economists believed in the importance of institutions. Neo-classicals believe that the institutions hardly play any role.

32 It is suggested that the reader should analyze the various principles in these systems and apply these to a concrete situation. For example, does share-cropping involve capitalistic or feudalistic

9. Feudalistic Modes of Production

The fundamental basis of the feudalistic agriculture is the relationship between the landlord (or zamindar[33]) and the actual tiller of the land. The land belongs to the landlord. The tiller of the land is attached to the land, hence to the landlord. Various names have been given to the tiller. In England he was called "the serf"; in the U.S.A. he was the "nigger." The nigger or the serf was basically a slave. To my knowledge, there is no such extreme case in India, though some tenancy laws did tend to serfdom and slavery.[34] The legal structure in the feudalistic system is that the landlord had legal rights over his slaves or serfs.

The zamindari system in India, in any form, represents a feudalistic institution. The zamindari system, some remnants of which are visible in today's India, emerged during the British occupation of India.[35] One of the forms of British exploitation of the Indian masses involved the collection of land revenue. Some of the Indian intermediaries, who performed the dirty work of the British masters and collected the land revenue to pass it on the British superior, eventually became zamindars.

In the feudal system, the relations between the tiller and the landlord are well defined. Not only is the tenant attached to the land, but the land is also attached to the tenant. It is the zamindar who owns the land and decides what to produce. Since he also owns the tenants and the tenants are needed to produce whatever he desires, he has to provide for the subsistence of the tenants. Thus, he is forced to produce enough wage-goods so as to maintain the tenants at the "level-of-existence." To that extent, the tenant's livelihood is secure. However, the landlord has to live too. And this at the "level-of-luxury." Thus the tenants have to produce those goods which can maintain the landlord and his class at the "level-of-luxury." Thus, the limits of production in feudalism are defined by the limits of consumption by the zamindars. It needs to be emphasized that the zamindar class itself did not participate in production zamindars, like their feudal lords elsewhere in the world, spent their lives in luxury in towns. The production was made up of two types: (i) necessary production, from the social point of view, to keep producers (tenants) alive and in production, (ii) surplus production, savings from the social point of view, to keep the landlords in luxury. In the case of the Indian zamindari system, this surplus had to be divided between the zamindar, the petty exploiter, and the British government, the super exploiter.

Since the production is carried on by the tenant, there is a limit to the exploitation. Beyond a certain point, the exploitation becomes counterproductive to the zamindar—not to the British exploiter.[36] Also the zamindar spends his/her time in luxury and has thus less time to supervise exploitation.

On the production end, there is no incentive for either the tenant or the zamindar to improve the quantity of production. Investment in land by the landlord involves the reduction in time and expenditures for consumption.[37] Also there is no way to make the tenants work harder. On the other hand, the tenant has no resources to invest in production. Further, since the gains of any additional improvements will be appropriated by the landlord, there is no incentive for him to produce more. Hence, the institution of zamindari is not

modes of production? Again, is the cooperative movement, particularly the cooperative farming, a capitalistic or a socialistic institution?

33 It will be noticed that the term zamindar is made up of zamin (=land) and dar (=possess). Thus zamindar is the person who possesses the land, the lord of the land.

34 The princely states in India, perhaps, had similarities with the serfdom type of tenants.

35 For an understanding of the zamindari system in India, See Romesh Dutt, *Economic History of India*, Vols. I and II, Oxford University Press. These volumes were written around 1900 and Romesh Dutt represented the interests of the landlords. The books analyze, inter-alia, the economic impact of the various forms of the zamindari system: Permanent Settlement versus Temporary Settlement.

36 This distinction is very important and needs to be understood well.

37 Feudalism is not only a mode of production but also a way of life. For lucid expression of this idea see Satyajit Ray's movie, "Jalsaghar," translated in English as "Music Room".

capable of producing high yields of production per acre. Major studies show that labour as well as land productivity is low in such a system. The institution of zamindari encourages the method of production which is land intensive, i.e., it uses more land per unit of output, in other words, land productivity is very low indeed.[38] Production is carried on purely by custom or tradition. Some economists argue that the method of production described under Technique I is also suitable to the zamindari system, the emphasis in this method of production being to use the least amount of inputs.

Some economists argue that the reasons, why the productivity in India is low, can be sought in this institution. If we go back to Graph I, these economists argue that the situation in India is in the region Y. Thus, if the institutional framework can be changed so as to make more production worth the while of the tenants or tillers or farmers, then, even with Technique I, the productivity can be increased. It is on this basis that they argue for land reforms. However, zamindari has been, at least legally, abolished in all states by the laws pertaining to the "land ceilings."

10. Capitalistic System of Production

Development of the capitalistic system of production involves the generalization of commodity production. "Everything that is the object of economic life, everything that is produced is henceforth a commodity, all foodstuffs, all consumer goods, all raw materials, all means of production, including labour power itself."[39] In other words, everything is now produced to be sold in the market for exchange. The production is not decided because it satisfies a basic human need but because it can be exchanged for money. This process extends also to the producer and the worker. "The producers separated from his means of production is no longer master of the products of his labour and can live only by selling, that is, by making a commodity of his own labour power, in exchange for a wage which enables him to acquire these means of life. The transition from petty commodity production to capitalistic production appropriately described, is thus marked by two parallel phenomena. On the one hand, the transformation of labour power into a commodity, on the other, the transformation of means of production into capital"[40]

In terms of agricultural production, it means that land is no more a matter of prestige and aristocracy. There is no one to lord over the land. Instead land is now a means of production, hence capital. The owner now is not a landlord but a capitalist.[41] The motivation of the capitalistic production is to make as large a profit as he can. To do so, he must choose those crops which are most profitable. Most profitable crops are those, the difference in whose price and cost per unit is the largest. There are two ways to make profits:[42] (i) produce crops that are in high demand, whose price is high, assuming the cost of production is the same, and (ii) produce as large a quantity as possible. Since the very purpose of production in the capitalistic system is to make a profit, the system is conducive to production in larger quantities. However, it is quite possible that a part, even a large part, of this production may not be socially useful.[43]

38 Eugene Genovese has convincingly argued that the U.S. Civil War can be explained by the institution of slavery (another way of saying landlordism). The land productivity of the slave-owning white landlords in the South was so low that they could compete with the North only by acquiring more land; hence the Civil War. See, Eugene D. Genovese, *The Political Economy of Slavery*, Random House, New York, 1965.

39 Ernest Mandel, *Marxist Economic Theory*, Monthly Review Press, 1969, Vol. I, p. 126.

40 Ernest Mandel, ibid., pp. 119–20.

41 It is not necessary that the capitalist must be rich or his land holding large. The owner could be a small capitalist as well. The important thing is that the owner behaves like a capitalist.

42 We refer here only to the so-called "legitimate" methods of making a profit. There are other methods, like plundering, looting, stealing, etc., which are used quite commonly. Once one decides to make profits, there is nothing sacrosanct about a particular method. In this case, ends fully justify the means.

43 There is a growing school of thought that argues that many of the poor countries devote a comparatively large part of their resources to satisfy the demand of the rich countries and far less resources to satisfy the needs of the people of the poor countries.

In this system, the actual tiller of the land becomes a wage-earner. The capitalist treats the actual tiller of land like any piece of capital. The wage-earner is now a commodity. The capitalist will employ the tiller so long it is profitable for the capitalist. If the production is not profitable, the tiller of the land is thrown out of a job and becomes unemployed. Thus, in this system, though the actual production is liable to be greater than in feudalism, the actual tiller of the land has no security and, generally speaking, the wage rate is not high. The actual tiller then remains poor and loses the little security he had under feudalism.

Since the capitalist has no personal relations with the actual tiller of the land, he can easily substitute other forms of energy for the human energy. The change in the form of energy may be more productive of output, but it is certainly very destructive of the human being whose energy is being substituted.

In the past history of Indian agriculture, the Ryotwari system[44] or peasant proprietorship provided the capitalistic institutions of production. By and large the land holdings were not large enough to need the employment of wage-labour. The family itself worked hard. One of the reasons why labour productivity in Punjab is higher than in other states is because of the early introduction of this institution in Punjab. Of course, there are other reasons as well; availability of more water, larger size of holdings, etc. The land reform movement is basically a movement to develop capitalistic institutions—and wind up a feudalistic one. This happens because ceilings are being placed on the ownership of land. Thus, a particular family cannot hold land beyond a certain size. Since the zamindari system involves the ownership of large areas of land, ceilings on land will replace feudalism.

11. Green Revolution

The example, par excellence, of the capitalistic modes of production in Indian agriculture are the farms that have been involved in, what has been euphorically called, the green revolution. What has happened is that some of the capitalistic farmers, with comparatively larger holdings, centred in Punjab and Haryana, buttressed by large dozes of "aid" by the government in the form of research, raw materials (fertilizers, insecticides, "better" type of seeds, etc.) and subsidies support (insurance of buying the output at a particular price and low prices for tools and implements, etc.) as well as "aid" by some of the aid giving agencies of the U.S.A. in India, have successfully substituted Technique II for Technique I.

The nature of the capitalistic mode of production is judged by the evidence from Ashok Rudra.[45] According to this evidence only large farmers can make the type of investment needed for Technique II. Table 7 below provides some of this evidence.

Table 7. Capital Expenditure (in rupees) on Some Items on the Big Farms in Punjab (1967-68)

Size & group in acres	Tractors	Tubewells & equipment	Repairs	Building* Land repair set
20-25	1,900	2,000	500	1,100
30-40	4,400	2,200	900	1,850
50-75	7,600	4,700	1,900	3,500
100-150	21,000	..	7,000	6,750

Notes: The table has been derived from Ashok Rudra, ibid.

*Expenditure on buildings, etc. is an average of two years (1966–68)

With such large capital expenditure, the capitalist has to decide whether to invest in industry or agriculture. Investment in agriculture becomes rational only if it is

[44] There are quite a few varieties of this system. Basically, these were determined by the method of payment of the land revenue. Still in these systems, land ownership vested in the person or family who actually carried on the production.

[45] Messrs Ashok Rudra, Majid and Talib of the Agriculture Centre of the University of Delhi conducted research in capitalistic farming in Punjab. Some of the results of this research are contained in Ashok Rudra, "Big Farmers of Punjab," *Economic and Political Weekly*, December 27, 1969.

profitable. There is now some evidence that the investment in Technique II is more profitable than investment in Technique I. This evidence is contained in Table 8 below, which gives information on productivity, expenditures, and incomes on the production of different varieties of wheat crop in a particular area. The different varieties of wheat involve different techniques of production. Thus, *"Desi"* wheat involves Technique I and the Mexican variety "Kalyan" is produced by Technique II.

Table 8. Yield, Income, Expenditure and Profit per Acre in different Varieties of Wheat in Amritsar (Punjab)

Varieties	Yield (in maunds)	Income (Rs)	Expenditure (Rs)	Profits (Rs)
Desi	16.84	521	124	397
Kalyan	38.45	1,223	390	833

Notes: 1. The table has been derived from H. Laxminarayan, "The Small Farmer should be the Strategy Base," *Yojana*, December 8, 1968, p. 5
2. Profit is defined as income-expenditure.
3. Income is defined as output multiplied by price.

The switch to Technique II from Technique I has resulted in both larger profits and output. Since the capitalist farmer is interested in larger profits and the government in the increase in the quantity of food grains production, both these interests have coincided in Technique II. The government is, thus, encouraging the spread of Technique II. The result has been a continuous growth in the use of Technique II. All the indices confirm this growth process. Table 9 below gives the data on the targeted and actual area under the Technique II type of production. Technique II is sometimes referred to as high-yielding varieties (hyv) of seeds.

Table 9. Area under High Yielding Varieties of Seeds (Thousand Hectares)

Food grains	1966-67		1968-69		1969-70
	Target	Actual	Target	Actual	Target
Rice	1,315	887	3,440	2,630	3,240
Wheat	644	540	2,023	4,050	4,050
Total food grains	2,860	1,837	8,499	8,500	10,920

Notes: The table has been derived from Ruddar Datt and K.P.M. Sundharam, *Indian Economy*, 1971, pp. 486.

Also, the consumption of fertilizers has increased rapidly as suggested by the following table 10.

The growth of consumption of fertilizers is obviously large. In the past twenty years it has virtually increased by 20 times.

Table 10. Consumption of Fertilizers

Year	Consumption (100 tons)
1950-51	69
1955-56	130
1960-61	289
1965-66	785
1968-69	1760
1973-74 (anticipated)	5500

Notes: Table taken from Ruddar Datt and K.P.M. Sundharam, ibid, p. 487.

The effect of the introduction of Technique II has been to increase both the output and land productivity. Table 11 below gives some idea of the magnitudes involved.

Table 11. Production and Average Yield of Principal Crops (Production in Million Tons and in Kilograms per Hectare)

	1960-61	1964-65	1969-70
Rice	34.6	39.0	40.4
	(1013)	(1,073)	(1,073)
Wheat	11.0	12.3	20.1
	(851)	(913)	(1,209)
Maize	4.1	4.7	5.7
	(926)	(1,009)	(968)
Bajra	3.2	4.4	5.3
	(286)	(380)	(426)
Jawar	9.8	9.7	9.7
	(533)	(503)	(532)

Notes: 1 Figures in brackets refer to yield in kilograms per hectare (the land productivity).
2. The table is taken from Ruddar Datt and K.P.M. Sundharam, ibid, p. 485.

Since Technique II has demonstrated its capacity to increase the total output and since the government accords high priority to the increase in the production of good grains, Technique II is here to stay. In 1968–69 some 17 million acres were under Technique II. In view of the technicalities of production in Technique II, Technique II can be used only in irrigated areas. The total irrigated area in 1968–69 was 67 million acres. Technique II, thus, can be extended to an additional 50 million acres. Assuming, Technique II produces an additional (to Technique I) 6 tons per acre of food grains, the extension of Technique II will, then, produce an additional 30 million tons of food grains. Considering that in 1968–69 the total output was around 95 million tons, the additional 30 million tons should virtually "solve the problem of food and agriculture in India." Hence, the "new strategy," the "new technology," as our Technique II is generally called, seems very attractive indeed.

12. Prospects

The needs for increased food grains production continues with population growth. Government policy has recognized this fact. Since the Bengal famine in 1943, the government policy, through the mediums of "grow more food campaign" and "five year plans," has been fully involved in the promotion of increased production. The following policy steps have been taken.

(i) More area has been brought under cultivation.
(ii) Irrigation has been extended to larger area.
(iii) Food grains have been imported in large quantities.
(iv) More financial resources have been provided to encourage investment in agricultural production.
(v) Attempts have been made to change the institutional framework by the so-called land-reforms legislation.
(vi) Research has been conducted in varieties of seeds and technical relations of inputs that lead to higher production.
(vii) Supplies of inputs like fertilizers, insecticides, etc. have been imported to encourage the adoption and spread of Technique II.
(viii) Price-support policies have been promulgated to ensure profitability in production.

The current emphasis of policy is to further spread Technique II. So far this technique covers only 25 per cent of the irrigated area. Even if it is extended to the whole irrigated area, it will still not cover all the area in the country. However, even this extension is a very large task. The problems arise from two sources: (i) availability of the supply of the necessary inputs, (ii) contradictions of Technique II itself. Again these are interrelated. Let us take these individually.

1. *Availability of Supplies of Inputs*

Ranjit Sau[46] has estimated the cost of production in Technique II. He provides the following Table (12).

Table 12. Cost per Acre of Wheat Under Technique II

Item	Expenses(Rs)	% of total cost
(A) Current		
(i) Human labour	54.54	10.7
(ii) Bullock labour	56.08	10.9
(iii) Seeds	14.22	2.7
(iv) Insecticides	10.00	1.9
(v) Irrigation	30.00	5.8
(vi) Fertilizer & manure	195.00	38.5
Total current	359.84	70.5
(B) Capitalt (i nteres on capital depreciation and other changes on marketing)	150.00	29.5
(C) Total costs	509.84	100.

Note: For details see the source; Ranjit Sau, ibid.

The largest costs in production are fertilizers, capital equipment, and irrigation. Both fertilizers, manure, and capital equipment are not produced in the country. By and large these have to be imported. The extension of Technique II, thus, implies a large demand for these inputs. Since the domestic industrial production is small, the question arises, can these, be imported in sufficiently large quantities? The balance of payment in India is already negative, the imports being larger than exports. The only way this imports is possible is to change the composition of imports which

[46] Ranjit Sau, "Resource Allocation in Indian Agriculture," *Economic and Political Weekly*, Review of Agriculture, September 25, 1971.

implies that the industry will have to suffer; there are very few consumer goods that are imported.

Again, no studies have been made regarding the availability of water for extended periods of production through this technique. At the moment, water may not be a scarce resource. However, there is the experience of Western countries which suggests that water itself may become a scarce resource.

2. *Contradictions of Technique II*

Any capitalistic system has its inner contradictions. These may be listed under two separate headings: (a) economic contradictions, and (b) ecological contradictions.

(a) *Economic contradictions.* Economic contradictions emerge in three different areas.

(i) *Unemployment.* Technique II requires large doses of energy which cannot be supplied by human and bullock labour. Accordingly, successful adoption requires capital investment in tools and implements, such as tractors. As Table 12 suggests, the capital costs are 150 per cent of the total costs of human and bullock labour. Generally, the tools and implements displace human labour. Martin Billings and Arjan Singh have done a study[47] to this effect. They conclude that by 1983–84, the displacement of labour will be of the order of 17.4 per cent of the total agricultural labour force: one person in every six. In other terms, 146 million man-days will be replaced. Fifty-five per cent of the total labour displaced will be by tractors and pump sets and thirty-seven per cent by thrashers and reapers.

In itself displacement of labour is not undesirable. If the displaced labour is fully employed elsewhere in industry, there is no problem. Actually, the theories of economic development are hopeful of developing a process whereby displaced labour is employed. However, in the context of Indian reality, it may be extremely undesirable. Inspite of the planning efforts and preoccupation of the planning body with employment policy, the economic system in India in the past 20 years has not been able to employ those people who freshly join the labour force. If you add a displacement of another 17 per cent, the unemployment problem will be so large as to literally generate a political revolution.

(ii) *Imports.* The effect of Technique II is to make the production of food grains import intensive. It makes the country dependent upon the Western industrialized countries, particularly when the Western world is not very helpful. The concept of "self reliance," therefore, goes through the window. The effects of such imports is also to export the effective demand thus making the situation still worse. "Take the case of wheat, for instance, under the New Agricultural Strategy. Of the total costs per acre of wheat, fertilizers and manures account for 38.5 per cent, while capital expenses per year claim 29.5 per cent.... As such nearly all of the cultivator's expenses on fertilizer and agricultural capital equipment go out of the country in course of payments for imports. Let us round it off at 60 per cent, and observe that three-fifths of the cost of production of wheat under the New Agricultural Strategy finds its way out of India through import trade, leaving only Rs. 40 within the country for every Rs. 100 spent to produce the wheat. Clearly in that case there would be a deficiency of demand for wheat. All the signs of over production would raise their heads no matter how many millions of people are starving side by side. The market does not recognize you if your wallet is empty."[48]

(iii) *Inequalities.* Technique II is certainly more profitable. It is also more profitable for larger farms. Thus it encourages the capitalist to increase the size of the farm. This is done by continuously buying up the small land holders. Thus the small land holders are joining the rank of wage-earners. Further, the technique leads to

47 Martin H. Billings and Arjan Singh, "Mechanisation and Rural Employment," *Economic and Political Weekly,* June 27, 1970.

48 Ranjit Sau, "The New Economics," Special Annual Number, 1972, *Economic and Political Weekly,* p. 1575.

displacement of labour; it substitutes capital for labour. Accordingly, more people get unemployed while a small number of farmers become richer. The inequalities of income are thus becoming wider. Virtually every commentator or thinker has already pointed to this effect. It is this contradiction in terms of inequalities that is reflected in the statement that the "green revolution leads to the red revolution."

(b) *Ecological contradictions.* Technique I is ecologically sound. It has adapted itself to the larger environment. Technique II, however, is ecologically unsound. It does not fit into the biological cycle.

The ecological problem arises from breaking the biological cycle. The biological cycle is broken at two ends: (i) at the level of production of inputs (a. pesticides and b. inorganic fertilizers), and (ii) at the level of their disposal. Since both the inputs have to be produced industrially, it requires the process of making artificial chemical compounds. To do so, first the natural (organic) chemicals have to be broken into its constituents and then compounded together into artificial chemicals. Both these processes require large doses of energy. The use of energy is one of the sources of pollution. According to the Second Law of Thermodynamics, the uses of large doses of energy implies an increase in entropy.

Having produced these chemicals, they are used in the agricultural production process. The agricultural production cycle may not, and actually does not, have the capacity to completely bio-degrade or utilize these chemical compounds. A part of these chemicals, thus, seep into the environment and lead to environmental degradation.

When pesticides are applied (the high yielding varieties do need an application of pesticides), the most susceptible insects die, leaving the least susceptible insects to reproduce. Because natural selection[49] promotes the evolution of resistance in pesticide targets, it becomes necessary to increase the dose and frequency of spraying the pesticides. It is, thus, a process that feeds on itself. The more pesticides are used, the more they are needed. Being a self-generating process, it is of the nature of an addiction. Actually, in some parts of the world, resistance to three major groups of insecticides—chlorinated hydrocarbons, organic phosphates, and carbonates—is now widespread. There are also indirect effects of pesticides. One group of pesticides, the chlorinated hydrocarbons, like DDT, DDD, DDE, etc., is highly resistant to oxidation and enzymatic attack. This resistance plus insolubility in water result in its concentration at the top of the food chain which leads to the extinction of some species.

Inorganic fertilizers also have similarly harmful effects. Fertilizers (nitrates as well as phosphates) seep into water. The nitrate content of water rises which is conducive to algae growth. Algae consumes large amounts of oxygen so that the living organism in water, like fish, die. This is what water pollution is all about. Inorganic fertilizers "loosen" the nitrogen cycle in the soil by shortcutting certain steps. Just like pesticides, the more fertilizers are used, the more they are needed. They are also addictive. Also, like pesticides, fertilizers do not remain where they are applied but are dispersed and contaminate in unexpected places. Fertilizers spread through rain and underground water.

In view of the ecological contradiction just as the productivity of Technique II is large, so is its probability to lead to a disaster.

---

49 This is based on the Darwinian principle of survival of the fittest.

4

Reorganization of Indian Agriculture and Land Reforms

KUMAR KANGAYAPPAN

1. Introduction

In a country like India where more than 70 per cent of the population is dependent upon agriculture as the predominant means of livelihood, the structure of land relation with its legal, social, and economic implications become very important. Historically, the country's lack of economic development can be partly attributed to the traditionally backward agriculture which has been characterized by lop-sided landownership patterns. In this context, therefore, land reforms have a place of significance in the reorganization and development of agriculture and hence of the Indian economy. Land reforms can provide the socio-economic base and the requisite institutional framework for achieving a systematic agricultural advancement and rapid economic development.

A viable agricultural sector, which the land reforms can evolve, would provide an impetus to the economic development. In a developing economy, the fact that the agricultural sector must grow in harmony with the industrial sector cannot be exaggerated. The contributions of agriculture for economic development can be summarized as follows:[1] (a) providing increased food supplies which would save much-needed foreign exchange, (b) enlarged exports which would provide a surplus for capital importation, (c) transfer of manpower from the agricultural to the non-agricultural sector, (d) agriculture's contribution to capital formation through higher productivity and taxation, and (e) increased spendable net cash income which acts as a stimulus to consumer demand and hence to industrialization.

2. Land Reforms and Economic Development

Land reform is at once a necessary and highly desirable condition of economic development. It is a pre-condition as well as a

[1] B. E. Johnston and J. W. Mellor, "The Role of Agriculture in Economic Development," *American Economic Review*, (September 1961), pp. 566–93.

consequence of the very development process. As Arthur Lewis[2] rightly indicates, from the point of view of economic development, land reform would include policies relating to tenure of agricultural land, the size of farms and the related issues such as economic incentives, capital formation and technical innovation.

Land reform in the traditional and accepted sense of the term means the redistribution of property in land for the benefit of small farmers and agricultural workers. There is also a wider definition now in use, in which land "reform" is understood to mean any improvement in agricultural economic institutions. The object of using this broader definition is to widen the conception of reform policy in order to emphasize that governments undertaking reform measures should not confine their policies only to the redistribution of land, but should also undertake other things—the regulation of rents, conditions of tenancy and farm wages, and the improvement of farm credit systems, co-operative organization, agricultural education and so on. We would delineate the issues such as the regulation of rent, dealing with tenancy system and intermediaries and the ceilings on land holdings for the purpose of our discussion in this paper.

In an agricultural economy, land reforms provide one of the more promising means of improvement. The mass appeal and the general effectiveness of land reforms as a levelling device in redistributing the basic form of wealth—the land—makes it a popular and potentially powerful tool. If land reforms are to have a notable effect on economic development, more emphasis must be given to the integration and joint planning of these programmes. Among other things, the programme should stimulate local desire for economic development and capital accumulation and investment, higher per worker and per acre productivity and an increase in total production.

The developing countries are trying to adopt different types of land reform measures in the context of development. These may broadly be classified as follows:

(a) Reforms involving some degree of regulation and government assistance with limited controls.
(b) Programmes incorporating stronger controls.
(c) Land expropriation from some owners for redistribution purposes.
(d) Collectivization programmes.

It is interesting to note that these objectives may be in conflict with each other. An attempt to implement one may counteract measures undertaken to implement another. So careful consideration must be given to the choice of a combination of policies which do not basically conflict with each other. Any set of policies must fundamentally fulfil the broad objectives: (a) a much more productive agriculture as a base for national economic development and (b) a sense of protection to the peasants giving them the psychological ingredient of security of expectations. The importance of these broad objectives cannot be exaggerated, especially in the context of a developing country such as India.

Land reform in itself does not provide increased production or increased efficiency. Other schemes such as reclamation projects, provision for more adequate credit facilities and the assurance of greater security of tenure are to be undertaken. In those countries where population pressure is high, emphasis must be placed upon means for increasing both individual productivity and productivity of land. The long-run improvement of agriculture and the social welfare in these areas might well involve measures that will either attract or move the surplus farm population to urban areas where it can provide the nucleus for an industrial labour force. In addition, programmes should be developed that will extend opportunities for industrial employment in rural areas through the establishment of cottage and small-scale industries.

The impact of land reform on economic development varies considerably according to the nature of the land reform programme, the manner in which it is carried out,

---

[2] Arthur W. Lewis, *The Theory of Economic Growth* (Homewood: Richard D. Irwin, Inc., 1955), pp. 120–21.

the resources of the country and the extent to which they have already been developed and the social, economic, political and legal institutions of the country. The main contribution that land reform can make in some countries lies in its ability to improve the institutional setting within which economic development is expected to be achieved. And if the main objective of land reform is the attainment of distributive justice, these programmes may have only an incidental impact on economic development.

One approach to assess the effect of land reform on economic development involves separate consideration of the impact that land reform has on some of the more important aspects of economic development. A favourable climate for economic activity and socio-economic progress requires the desire on the part of both the people and government for increased production and levels of living. In addition to the popular willingness, economic development requires institutions that favour the development of individual initiative and business enterprise. Public help and subsidies to private operators may facilitate the creation of new enterprises and improvement of existing industries. Also political and economic institutions should offer reasonable security of expectations to the investor.[3]

In most of the under-developed countries, a major objective of land reform is improvement in the well-being of the peasant. The redistribution of land may satisfy the farmer's hunger for land. But the aim further calls for higher peasant incomes and opportunities for achieving a higher standard of living. Reduction in rent, higher incomes through increased production and assurances of security of tenure may lead to improvement in peasant life. Reforms of this type permit additional productivity and income, and thus enable operators to raise their standards above the subsistence level. The higher standards may also generate higher demand for better markets, improved educational facilities, research and extension, greater use of co-operatives, and other similar measures.

In sum, the process of economic development involves the interplay of a large matrix of factors—economic, political, and social in nature—many of which may occupy a more strategic place in the usual process of development than land reform. A well developed land reform programme can often act as the catalyst that sets in motion the whole stream of economic, social and political changes that go with economic development.

3. Land Systems in India

The land systems and land reforms in India are to be examined in the light of the above considerations. The land tenure systems during the pre-British period were static in character. The systems developed by the British were not greatly conducive to economic development. The changes introduced were in the direction of ensuring the revenue flow to the government.

A brief discussion of the land systems during the pre-Independence period is in order. There were three types of land tenures: (i) the Zamindari, (ii) the Mahalwari and (iii) the Ryotwari.

At the advent of the British influence in India, the East India Company and later the representatives of the Crown had to deal with the landed interests. The Company was confronted with long-established customs and usages. The land revenue system prevailing at that time originated in the days of Hindu kings prior to the Moghul rule. Under the later system, the king was entitled to one-sixth of the gross produce. Towards the end of the Moghul Empire, some reforms, such as the form of cadastral survey, were introduced. The payment of revenue in kind or cash was left to the option of the cultivator. Later on, the collective assessments superceded others. Settlements were made with the provincial chief or other persons in authority for a fixed annual revenue and the imperial share was raised to fifty per cent of the produce. The obvious result was the oppression of cultivators by revenue farmers. The cultivators were forced to pay exor-

3 Raleigh Barlowe, "Land Reform and Economic Development," *Journal of Farm Economics*, (February 1963), p. 172.

bitant rents. The East India Company continued the system by assigning the collection of land revenue to the zamindars and chiefs in the provinces of Bengal, Bihar and Orissa.

During Warren Hastings' period, Temporary Settlements were tried but with disastrous results. Lord Cornwallis introduced the Permanent Settlement in Bengal. Under this system, the zamindars, who were only the agents of the government, were declared full proprietors of the areas where they collected land revenue. The land revenue assessment was fixed at 10/11ths of what the zamindars collected as rent from the cultivators, the balance going to the zamindars as remuneration. The system gave an open hand to the zamindars and landlords to extract quite high rents from the cultivators. They in effect became a parasitic class interested only in extracting the maximum of rent from the peasants.

The system of Permanent Settlement was extended to Banaras, north Madras and certain parts of south Madras. The attempt ran into difficulties and was therefore given up in favour of the ryotwari system.

There were two noticeable phenomena which constituted the outgrowth of the Permanent Settlement. First, the zamindars enriched themselves by collecting exorbitant rents, thereby impoverishing the peasants; second, the cultivators were reduced to mere intermediaries.

The mahalwari or joint village system was first adopted in Agra and Oudh and later extended to Punjab during the early 1800's. Under this system, individual villages were considered as units in themselves. The joint ownership of property was recognized. The villages or *mahals* were settled with directly. The primary liability of paying the land revenue was generally assigned to a co-sharer of standing in the village. The state share varied between 40 to 70 per cent of the rental. In spite of the joint character of the village and the method of payment of land revenue, the system led to the break-up of the old village community and the growth of individualistic attitudes amongst the the cultivators.

The ryotwari system was introduced in Madras by Thomas Monroe in 1792 and was later extended to Bombay. Under this system, the land holder was recognized to be responsible for paying the land revenue to the government. There were no intermediaries between the cultivator and the government. Under the ryotwari system. the lands were heritable, transferable and alienable without the sanction of government. Failure to pay the land revenue would result in the forfeiture of the abovementioned right. The element of discretion on the part of the settlement officer coupled with the possibility of a periodical enhancement of land revenue deprived the system of benefits that would have otherwise accrued to the proprietor. Moreover, the claim of the state led to the destruction of the collective basis of village organization and life.

4. Land Reforms in India

In India after Independence, three major land reform programmes were introduced. They were the abolition of intermediaries, the tenancy reforms and the ceilling on land holdings.

At the time of Independence, the zamindari or the intermediary tenures were predominant in Bihar, former Hyderabad, Uttar Pradesh, West Bengal and parts of Andhra and Madras. The legislative measures gave the powers to the State governments to acquire all rights of the zamindars or intermediaries on the payment of compensation. Included in the process of acquisition were tenant-cultivated land, all waste lands, communal lands, forests, mines, minerals, rivers, channels and fisheries.

Altogether, about 173 million acres of land were acquired for which the total compensation, including rehabilitation grants payable to the intermediaries, amounted to Rs. 513.6 crores.[4]

The largest amount, Rs. 240 crores, was to be paid in Bihar. In Uttar Pradesh it stood at Rs. 178 crores and in West Bengal, Rs. 70 crores.

Acquisition of the intermediary rights

[4] Planning Commission, *Progress of Land Reform* (Delhi: Government of India, 1963), p. 4.

by the state brought the statutory tenant into direct relationship with the state. Some tenants acquired full ownership rights, including the rights of transfer, while others had to make some payment to the state for acquisition of full occupancy rights.

Land under personal cultivation of the intermediaries was exempted from acquisition. This enabled several big zamindars to retain considerable portions of land, defeating the very purpose of the legislation. Some of the zamindars took to mechanized capitalistic farming to evade the legislation. They also took their cases to the court of law and won several rounds.

The effects of zamindari abolition were varied. The abolition of the system by itself could not provide the impetus for agricultural production. The laws of inheritance continue to reinforce the processes of sub-division and fragmentation of land holdings, attendant with their negative effects. Zamindari abolition should have been accompanied by a thorough re-orientation of the entire agrarian organizational pattern. The States should have taken effective steps for consolidation of holdings. The payment of compensation to zamindars and other intermediaries carried the possible effects of inflationary pressures. The staggered payments certainly have helped somewhat in neutralizing these pressures. It would have been advantageous had the compensation arrangements been linked up with schemes of productive investment as were recently done in Taiwan and earlier in Japan.

In India, excessive population has indirectly led to the exploitation of tenants. Farm tenancy reforms are helpful in mitigating the hardships of the tenant-farmers by securing social justice for them.

During the pre-Independence period some legislations were enacted in Bombay, Punjab, Himachal Pradesh, and Madhya Pradesh for guaranteeing security of tenure to tenants. The provision of security of tenure carried with it an incentive effect. It instilled greater interest in the minds of the tenants for introducing improvements on land. In Hyderabad, Rajasthan and Punjab legislations were enacted to fix the maximum limits to the amount of rent payable to the landlord by the tenants. These measures prevented the exploitation of the tenants by the landlords. The tenant, because of the legislation, could initiate improvements on the land. In Bombay, Punjab, Delhi, Uttar Pradesh, Hyderabad, and Rajasthan legislation was passed to provide tenants with rights of purchasing the holdings they cultivated. Such legislations would have had better results, had the States arranged simultaneous credit facilities on easy terms. In a few other States laws were passed incorporating the idea of compensation for the tenants who did make investments for improving the land.

Under the Five Year Plans, comprehensive measures aimed at regulating (reducing) rents, providing greater security of tenure to the tenants and permitting the tenants to purchase the land taken under lease were proposed.

Maximum payable rents in several states have been fixed as follows:[5]

State	Maximum Rent
Andhra Pradesh	1/4 of gross produce (irrigated land)
	1/5 of gross produce (other land)
Bihar	7/20 of gross produce or 50 per cent of rental value
Jammu and Kashmir	1/4 of gross produce (wet land); 1/3 of gross produce (other land)
Madhya Pradesh	2 to 4 times the land revenue
Tamil Nadu	2/5 of gross produce (irrigated land); 1/3 of gross produce (other land)
Mysore	1/3, 1/6 or 2/5 of produce according to local conditons.
Orissa	1/4 of gross produce but not exceeding 4 to 6 (maunds of paddy per acre)
Punjab	1/3 of gross produce

The Planning Commission has felt that it is important to ensure the security of tenure which would prevent sudden evic-

[5] Dhiren Bhattacharya, *Understanding India's Economy* (Calcutta: Progressive Publishers, 1969), p. 116.

tion of the tenants by the owners. The Fourth Five Year Plan recognizes the necessity for specific measures in this direction.

The plan[6] further proposes the following measures:

1. To declare all tenancies non-resumable and permanent (except in cases of land holders who are serving in the Defence Forces or suffering from a specified disability).

2. Where resumption has been permitted and where applications have already been made, arrangements for quick disposal of such applications; where there is a likelihood of a large number of evictions as a result of resumption, for further restricting it with a view to reducing the number of cases of resumption.

3. Regulation of "voluntary surrenders" prohibiting landowners from taking possession of land at present tenanted and empowering the government at local levels to settle other tenants there.

4. Provision for complete security of tenure in respect of homestead lands on which cultivators, artisans and agricultural labourers have constructed their dwelling houses.

5. Implementation of legislation relating to security of tenure to sub-tenants and ensuring that the provisions of law are not circumvented by the landlords.

6. Provision for penalty for unjust evictions.

In addition, creation of tenancy in the future has been prohibited in some states.

In view of the excessive population on the land and the consequent increase in the number of landless agricultural workers and the lop-sided distribution of land holdings, measures relating to ceilings on land holdings have become necessary.

Considering the inequality in the distribution of land, it is felt that no cultivating family should be allowed to retain more land than it can cultivate by its own labour. The general principle which the Planning Commission has recommended is that the size of the holding should not exceed three times the family holding, this being defined as the area which, given the existing techniques of production, can be cultivated by a family of average size. This will, however, vary according to the condition of the soil and methods of cultivation in different parts of the country.

Legislative measures have been undertaken in almost all States providing for a ceiling on land holdings. There are variations from State to State, on the level of ceilings, transfers, and exemptions from ceilings.

The following table provides the data on net area sown and surplus area in some States.

	In thousand acres	
State	Net area sown	Surplus area
Assam	5,758	534.0
Gujarat	23,620	38.8
Jammu & Kashmir	1,724	450.0
Maharashtra	44,490	162.5
Madhya Pradesh	40,392	67.1
Tamil Nadu	15,067	20.2
Punjab	18,732	368.5
West Bengal	13,427	776.5
Uttar Pradesh	42,652	222.7

SOURCE: M.B. Nanavathi and J.J. Anjaria, *The Indian Rural Problem* (Bombay: Indian Society of Agricultural Economics, 1970), p. 265.

The Planning Commission[7] recognizes the defects in the existing laws relating to ceiling on land holdings. The legislation as it exists has not been implemented effectively. A large number of loopholes still exist, making it possible for the landholders to retain their hold on the land. In some States adequate provision has not been made for disregarding the transfers and partitions subsequent to the date of announcement of the decision to impose ceilings. In Andhra, the government have decided to take possession of surplus land only when funds are available for payment

6 Planning Commission, *Fourth Five Year Plan* (Delhi: Government of India, 1970), p. 177.

7 Ibid., p. 179.

of compensation. Though the programme of distribution of surplus land has been initiated in a number of States, there is still a large gap in most of the States between the area taken possession of and of the area distributed.

5. Conclusion

In spite of the progress that has been made in passing the legislation for land reform, it cannot safely be concluded that the problem has been satisfactorily solved either in terms of providing an equitable, efficient land use and management or in terms of evolving an appropriate social structure in the rural areas. The legislative reforms since Independence have only laid the ground work for more positive steps to be undertaken. One can observe the existence of widespread evasive practices which nullify the effects of land reform measures. Practices such as informal tenancy, large scale evictions, voluntary surrenders, and *mala fide* transfers defeat the provisions of the various enactments.

Moreover, there are serious problems in the implementation of the land reform programmes.

An important constraint on the expeditious implementation and also on the availability of credit and other inputs to the cultivating tenant has been the lack of correct and up-to-date records including the record of tenancies.[8] In many states, lack of adequate administrative machinery poses another problem. A noticeable trend is the lack of commitment on the part of State governments to fully implement all the provisions of the land reform legislation. The recommendation in the Fourth Five Year Plan to institute a permanent set-up for constant review and evaluation of land reforms is in the right direction.

India can learn a few lessons from countries of small-farm agriculture such as Japan. Japan, with very high man-land ratio, has developed a viable, productive agricultural sector through land reforms, intensive methods of cultivation, and significantly an appropriate small-scale agricultural technology. A combination of effective land reform policy which would put the land in the hands of the tiller and the development of small-scale technology and the availability of adequate and cheap inputs will go a long way in revolutionizing and reorganizing the Indian agriculture. In particular, emphasis on the equity aspect will contribute towards changing the attitudes of the peasantry. In Myrdal's view, "the promotion of social and economic equality is a pre-condition for attaining substantial long-term increases in production. Success with such an approach to policy is by no means easy to achieve and depends on a host of complementary conditions. But it can at least be said that policies for agricultural reform that ignore the problem of inequality are not likely to achieve major and especially lasting results."[9] Land reform measures, to be successful in India, should also be accompanied by suitable measures such as provision of adequate credit and marketing facilities to increase the productive efficiency of Indian agriculture.

8 Ibid., p. 182.

9 Gunnar Myrdal, *Asian Drama* (New York: Twentieth Century Fund, 1968), Vol. II, p. 1369.

5

Large-Scale Industries in India

BALWIR SINGH CHEEMA

1. Introduction

One of the major reasons which kept India from making significant economic progress before Independence war the slow pace of industrialization. The process of industrialization, defined broadly, means the organization of production based on the principles of specialization and division of labour among enterprises as well as within them, necessitated by, as well as resulting in, the application of new technology and mechanical and electrical energy with a view to maximizing returns and minimizing the per-unit cost of production.[1]

Thus defined, the process of industrialization requires accumulation of capital for the creation of productive capacity and the building of social and economic overhead capital. In this sense, industrialization represents an approach which seeks to develop all sectors of the economy. In fact, in the case of the developed countries like the U.S., Japan, Australia, Canada, New Zealand, the U.K., Germany, France, and other European countries, it is very difficult to draw distinctions between the agricultural and industrial sectors of the economy on the basis of usual indicators such as: the investment and productivity per worker, the degree of specialization and division of labour, sophistication of marketing and management techniques, the use of mechanical and electric power, and the application of science and technology. Viewed in this sense, one may find many more similarities between the agricultural sector of the developed economies and the organized industrial sector of the underdeveloped economies rather than between the agricultural sectors of these two types of economies. Furthermore, one can make a strong case that the process of industrialization, thus defined, must first take place in agriculture to some minimum level in order to generate sufficient surplus, both in terms of manpower and capital needed, to develop industry and guarantee sufficient demand for its products. In this respect one can cite the experience of England and the U.S. in the eighteenth and nineteenth centuries. There are the interesting cases of New Zealand and Australia where the agricultural sector, even after the attainment of a high level of economic development,

[1] Harry G. Johnson, *Economic Policies towards Less Developed Countries* (New York: Frederick A. Praeger,1968), pp. 45–46.

continues to play a dominant role. However, on the basis of these arguments it will be wrong to advocate that developing economies should concentrate exclusively on modernizing their agriculture to the neglect of establishing industries in their quest for economic development. In recommending the establishment of organized large-scale industries in India, we cannot deny either the mutual dependence of agricultural and industrial development or the importance of the agricultural sector for the national economy. The purpose is simply to point out that the industrial sector has to play an important role in the economic development of India, and in the long run it has to assume the role of the dominant sector, especially in view of the present and potential size of the market for industrial products and the availability of raw materials and abundant labour.

The following are some of the basic objectives often cited for development of the industrial sector : First, to provide gainful employment for the backlog of underemployed and unemployed manpower in the agricultural sector, estimated at approximately 30 per cent of the total labour force in India,[2] and for the increasing number of new entrants to the labour force. Second, to increase the per capita productivity for raising the living standards of our poor masses and generate sufficient savings for capital formation. Third, to improve the balance of payments situation of the Indian economy by producing goods for import substitution and increasing exports. These objectives have been affirmed by the Indian Planning Commission in our Five Year Plans. The emphasis placed on the development of the industrial sector and within the industrial sector on "the basic heavy industries for the manufacture of producer goods to strengthen the foundations of economic independence,"[3] as stated by the late Professor Mahalanobis in his Draft Plan-Frame, has remained unchanged. This emphasis on the development of the large scale and organized industrial sector in the case of India is justifiable not only on the basis of the historical experience of developed economies, but also because of the basic economic facts which characterize the Indian economy at present.

The industrial sector in general, and the basic industries in particular, failed to grow in relative importance in the economy in spite of the ample availability of natural resources to support a sizable industrial advance, early development of transportation system, and the fairly early start made in establishing consumer goods industries like cotton textiles, jute, and paper around the middle of the nineteenth century. The major reason for this lack of industrial development up to 1947 was the dominance by an alien power, whose main objective was to utilize India as a supplier of raw materials to feed its growing industries and as a market for its manufactured goods.[4] In England, due to industrialization, a gradual change from mercantilistic ideology, based on protectionism and geared to the goal of having a surplus balance of payments, to free enterprise was made around the middle of the eighteenth century. This change proved disastrous to the Indian industrial development. In the beginning, the Indian exports of handicrafts, which competed successfully with the products of England, were discouraged by the British. In the case of products like fine muslins, brocades, inlaid arms, for which India was known throughout the world, their production declined with the gradual disappearance of native Indian rulers and their retinues who were their major patrons. Wherever the handicraft industries survived, the quality of their products deteriorated sharply for several reasons including the tendency on the part of the Indian elite classes to copy Western designs, to cater to the cheap tastes of the masses. The ban on the carrying of arms eliminated, to a great extent, the need for arms; and this led to the

---

2 Government of India, Planning Commission, *The First Five Year Plan* (New Delhi : 1952), p. 652.

3 The Publications Division, Government of India, *Second Five Year Plan* : *The Framework* (New Delhi : Publications Division, December 1955), p. 13.

4 R. Palme Dutt, *The Problem of India* (New York : International Publishers, 1943). See chapters VI and VII for an interesting study of the role of British imperialism in Indian economic development.

demise of cottage industries producing weapons like swords and shields of excellent quality.[5] Later, when the Indian market was flooded with foreign goods, the products of Indian manufacturers were no match, in price and quality, to the products of British industry. The advantage enjoyed by the Indian manufacturers in the local market was progressively cut because of the decline in transportation costs and of the safety and speed with which British products could be carried to Indian markets as a result of the development of the railroads and steamships. The marketable surplus of agricultural products which could, under favourable circumstances, be used to finance industrial growth, declined due to the increase in population and failure of agricultural productivity to increase. The gifts, exactions, and tributes received by the East India Company and its officials, monies spent on numerous battles to subjugate powerful Indian princely states, and the military expeditions into Afghanistan, Persia, and Tibet in order to protect and strengthen British interests out of general revenues, hindered the formation of capital. Further, the "home charges" (which included interest in the management of debt and annuities on account of railways and irrigation works; payments due in connection with civil departments in India; army and marine charges, including pensions and gratuities; payments for stores purchased in India; and furlough allowances) amounting to about 20 million pounds annually before First World War and almost double the amount thereafter, represented a tremendous drain of capital to England which could hardly be justified on grounds of advantages derived by India.[6]

However, in spite of these difficulties, a beginning in the establishment of the organized industry was made in the latter half of the nineteenth century. The process of industrialization picked up further momentum in the first half of this century because of changes in the British attitude due to independence movement, and also in consequence of the natural protection afforded to the Indian industries during the First and Second World War years, when the supply of foreign manufactured products to India was cut off. However the real growth of the industrial sector—specially the basic industries—started after Independence, with the advent of economic planning.

In this chapter we will make a brief survey of some major and key Indian industries. This is necessary in order to develop a clear understanding of the rapidly changing industrial scene and its significance in the growth of the Indian economy; to determine the impact of the industrial strategy adopted quite early during the planning to develop a broadly based capital goods industry which could in time meet the needs of a widely diversified consumer goods industries. In the concluding section of this chapter an attempt will be made to evaluate the impact of the industrial strategy and the progress made towards the future growth of the Indian economy.

2. Iron and Steel Industry

In spite of the growing importance of aluminium and synthetic materials as substitutes for steel, steel is still considered an indispensable basic input for industrialization. With the development of the iron and steel industry, a tremendous demand may be expected for such primary products as iron ore, coal, manganese, limestone, and refractory materials of which India has considerable deposits. Also from it flows social overhead capital in the form of transportation and trained labour force; and it, of course, satisfies the need for development of engineering, transportation, defence, and construction industries. This process is known as backward and forward linkages in the economic development process.[7] Rightly, therefore, the Planning Commission has given the steel industry

[5] D. R. Gadgil, *Industrial Evolution in India in Recent Times* (London and New York: Oxford University Press, 1954), p. 38.

[6] Vera Anstey, *The Economic Development of India* (London: Longmans, Green and Co., 1931), pp. 509–11. Also see R. Palme Dutt, *The Problem of India* (New York: International Publishers, 1943), pp. 45–70.

[7] Albert O. Hirschman, *The Strategy of Economic Development* (New Haven: Yale University Press, 1958), p. 100.

the place of prime importance in the development of basic industry. This is reflected in the fact that up to the end of 1970–71 nearly a third of the total investment made in public sector undertakings was in steel.[8]

The production of carbon steel in India can be traced to about 2000 B.C., but the foundation of the modern iron and steel industry had to wait till 1907, when the Tata Iron and Steel Co. Ltd., which up to the Second World War was one of the biggest in the world, was started by Jamshedji Nusserwanji Tata at Jamshedpur. In the next fifty years, in spite of this comparatively early successful start, availability of raw materials and their favourable location and expanding demand, the industry failed to make any significant progress. During the inter-war years, subsidized continental steel was dumped in India and the steel prices fell sharply. The small protective duty granted from 1924 proved inadequate. Between 1939 and 1947, steel production in India remained about a million tons, whereas the demand for steel had increased quite rapidly. Further, the steel industry faced the problem of replacing the worn out equipment, some of which had operated for over thirty years without any major modernization. The Iron and Steel Panel, headed by Sir Padamji Ginwalla, recommended in 1946 the establishment by government of two integrated steel plants with an initial ingot capacity of half a million tons each in case the private sector failed to do so. Provision of an investment of Rs. 80 crores, of which Rs. 30 crores were to be incurred during the First Plan for the establishment of a new steel plant,[9] was also made, but no tangible steps were taken for the establishment of any new plant. It was during the Second and Third Plan period, 1956–66, or about fifty years after the establishment of Tata's large-scale integrated steel mill, that the three steel plants at Rourkela, Bhilai, and Durgapur were established in the public sector. The expansion and modernization of the Tata Iron and Steel Company and the Indian Iron and Steel Company was also undertaken during the period. Initially, the three steel plants in the public sector had a capacity of a million tonnes each, but because of the subsequent expansion of the Rourkela steel plant to 1.8 million tonnes, the Durgapur steel plant to 1.6 million tonnes, and the Bhilai steel plant to 2.5 million tonnes, the total steel producing capacity increased from roughly, 1.5 million before 1947 to 9 million ingot tonnes. The total output in 1971–72 amounted to 6.41 million tonnes.[10] The three public sector steel plants at Rourkela, Durgapur, and Bhilai account for roughly two-thirds of the total steel capacity.[11] By the end of the Fifth Plan, the national steel development programme provides for more than doubling the existing capacity of 9 million to about 19 million ingot tonnes. During the Fourth Plan, a new integrated steel plant at Bokaro is being built with an initial capacity of 1.7 million tonnes, with a provision to enlarge the capacity subsequently to 4.7 million tonnes. This will then make it the largest steel complex in Asia. The first blast furnace of the Bokaro steel plant was commissioned on October 3, 1972, and the plant is expected to turn out 2.5 million tonnes of steel by 1973–74. A further expansion of the Bhilai steel plant from 2.5 million to 4 million ingot tonnes capacity is being undertaken. To meet the target of 19 million tonnes of steel by the end of the Fifth Plan, three new steel plants will be built—two integrated steel plants of two million ingot tonnes capacity each at Visakhapatnam and Vijayanagaram, and an alloy and special steels plant of 250,000 tonnes ingot capacity at Salem.[12]

Since the beginning of the Second Plan, India has acquired considerable indigenous know-how, and the industrial potential to build steel plants without foreign help. And so nearly 67 per cent of the supplies of equipment needed to establish the Bokaro steel mill is being obtained from with-

[8] Embassy of India, Washington, D. C., "Public Sector Undertakings," *India News* (April 14, 1972), p. 3.

[9] *First Plan*, p. 428.

[10] Government of India, *Economic Survey: 1972–73* (New Delhi: Publications Division, 1973), p. 110.

[11] Mohan S. Kumaramangalam, "More Steel for the Seventies," *India News* (Washington, D.C., March 17, 1972), Vol. X, No. 50, p. 2.

[12] Ibid., p. 2.

in the country. Not only is this a great achievement in itself, but it has also opened the way for the future industrialization of India and has reduced its dependence on foreign countries. Except for specialized steel, the industry is now able to meet the expanding domestic demand for steel and has emerged as the largest foreign exchange earner in the non-traditional exports sector. The exports value of iron and steel as a proportion of total exports value has increased from Rs. 8.7 crores in 1960–61 to Rs. 77.2 crores in 1969–70. In 1970–71 and 1971–72 they declined sharply to Rs. 67.2 and 25.6 crores respectively mainly due to growth in internal demand and decline in output.[13]

3. Aluminium and Non-Ferrous Metals

Aluminium is the youngest but quite an important non-ferrous metallurgical industry in India. During the past decade, a phenomenal expansion in both the production and consumption of aluminium has been registered. This has been possible because of the availability of sufficient quantities of bauxite deposits in India and the large increase in the production of electricity. The rapid development of the aluminium industry can also be attributed to the relative scarcity of other non-ferrous metals like copper and to the ease with which aluminium could be substituted for them. Because of its versatility, aluminium has found many new uses leading to rapid expansion in its demand. The output increased from 18.3 thousand tonnes in 1960–61 to 181.5 thousand tonnes in 1971–72.[14] The Fourth Plan target for 1973–74 is set at 220,000 tonnes. This expansion in aluminium production will take care of the immediate domestic requirement and also contribute marginally to exports.

The production of copper, zinc, lead, and other non-ferrous metals is severely restricted because of the limited availability of raw materials within the country. During the Fourth Plan, it is planned to increase copper producing capacity from 9,600 to 47,500 tonnes primarily by exploiting newly found Khetri-Kolihan copper deposits in Rajasthan. It is also planned to expand zinc producing capacity from 18,000 to 36,000 tonnes, and the lead producing capacity from 20,000 to 40,000 tonnes per annum.[15]

4. Engineering and Machine Tool Industries

Next to the establishment of the steel industry, priority was given to the engineering industries. The inspiration in this respect came perhaps from Prime Minister Nehru's slogan, "Build Machines, Build India," and this has been amply justified by subsequent events. The investment in the engineering industry in 1970 was estimated at over Rs. 2,000 crores with an annual production capacity of Rs. 2,500 to 3,000 crores. There were about 4500 manufacturing units with an employment of 1.4 million.[16] This represents an annual growth rate of 12 per cent for the years between 1950 and 1970.[17] As a result of this rapid advance, engineering industries are now mostly able to meet the domestic demand for consumer as well as capital goods; they have also succeeded, to some extent, in selling their wares in foreign markets. From a mere Rs. 24 crores in 1964–65, the exports of engineering goods increased in 1971–72 to 118 crores and are expected to reach a level of Rs. 160 crores in 1973–74, the final year of the Fourth Plan.[18]

5. Machine Tool Industry

A good indicator of the level of scientific and economic advance made by an economy and its potential for further growth is the size and sophistication achieved by its machine tool industry. The machine tool industry in India was started during

13 *Economic Survey: 1972–73*, pp. 73 and 163.
14 Ibid., p. 110.

15 Government of India, Planning Commission, *Fourth Five Year Plan*, (New Delhi, 1970) p. 318.
16 K. Easwaran, "Exports and the Engineering Industry," Blue Supplement to *Monthly Commentary on Indian Economic Conditions*, vol. 12, no. 1 (August 1970), p. IX.
17 Ibid., p. IX.
18 Ibid., p. IX.

the Second World War and it grew rapidly, during 1939–45, by government assistance, which became essential due to lack of foreign supplies to meet the increased domestic demand. After the war the production of machine tools fell and no real headway was made in developing the industry till March 1, 1953, when the management and control of the machine tool factory near Bangalore, established during the war as a result of an agreement between the Government of India and a Swiss firm, was taken over by the Hindustan Machine Tools Ltd. Since then, in order to increase and diversify the production of machine tools, the Hindustan Machine Tools Ltd. has built almost half a dozen new plants. Further, several other large concerns, such as the Machine Tool Corporation of India Ltd., Praga Tools Ltd., National Tools Ltd., and National Instrument Factory have been started. In July 1965, the Central Machine Tool Institute for the designing training, standardization, prototype manufacture, research documentation, etc. started functioning at Bangalore. Simultaneously, several large- and small-scale firms have been established in the private sector for the production of machine tools. The public and the private sector enterprises at present are producing all kinds of lathes, milling machines, radial drills, grinders, milling, shaping, and planing machines, pneumatic hammers and tools, and various kinds of special machines. The production of machine tools increased from Rs. 70 million in 1960–61 to 294 million in 1965–66. However, between 1965–66 and 1968–69, though the capacity to produce machine tools was more than doubled from Rs. 300 million to Rs. 610 million, the actual output declined from Rs. 294 million to Rs. 247 million[19] due to the general slowdown in industrial activity. During 1969–72, a partial recovery was made and machine tools worth Rs. 550 million[20] were produced in 1971–72. In the Fourth Plan, emphasis is placed on the fuller utilization of the installed capacity rather than on its further expansion.

[19] *Fourth Plan*, p. 299.
[20] *Economic Survey : 1972–73*, p. 110.

6. Electrical Engineering Industries

At the time of India's Independence, the electrical engineering industry was small in size and produced mainly light bulbs and small household appliances like electric fans, heaters, irons, radios, etc. for domestic use and small electric transformers and motors for industrial use. Even these were made primarily by assembling imported components. In line with the dual strategy of rapidly increasing the electric generating capacity of the country for industrial, agricultural, and domestic use, and of making India self-reliant it was essential that domestic production of generators, turbines, transformers, circuit breakers, etc. for the production and distribution of electricity be undertaken with utmost speed.

As a result of Plan provisions and their implementation, generating capacity has increased from 2.3 million kw at the beginning of the First Plan to 17 million kw in 1971–72. Over 50 per cent of India's population now derives the benefits of having electricity, against only 2.5 per cent in 1947.[21] Overall shortage of power in the country still persists. Against the Fourth Plan target of 23 million kw a capacity of only about 20.2 million is expected to be created by the end of March 1974.[22] Along with this increase in the generating capacity of electricity, the heavy electrical industry in India has been able to develop a measure of self-reliance in design, technology, and manufacturing of the wide range of equipment for the generation and distribution of electricity.

The development of the heavy electrical industry has been mainly in the public sector. During the Second and Third Plan periods, Heavy Electricals (India) Ltd. (HEIL) and Bharat Heavy Electricals Ltd. (BHEL) were established. In addition to main power generating equipment, these public enterprises produce capacitors, rectifiers, industrial boilers and turbines, compressors used in fertilizer and chemical industries, high pressure valves, and a wide range of heavy electric machines.

[21] Information Service, Embassy of India, Washington, D. C., *India News*, September 22, 1972, p. 2.
[22] *Economic Survey : 1972–73*, p. 26.

India has also started producing equipment for atomic powered generating plants, and has successfully exported power generating and distribution equipment. The existing plans envisage, in the next decade, an increase in the generating capacity from 17 million kw to 52 million kw.[23]

On the basis of the progress made thus far, "India need no longer import thermal or hydro-electric power equipment for the projects that are to come up in the Fifth Five Year Plan period" (1974–75 to 1978–79).[24] However, in spite of this rapid expansion and optimism expressed, according to Dr. K. L. Rao, Minister of Irrigation and Power, "The current [1972] shortage of power was 1 million kw without taking into consideration the suppressed demand for power in rural and urban areas which makes the current shortage of power in reality much greater."[25] On the basis of the current trends, the Indian Institute of Public Opinion estimates that by 1973–74 the shortage of power will amount to about 4 million kw, representing approximately 25 per cent of the total power requirements in the country. If these estimates are correct then, even if the most optimistic projections regarding indigenous capacity to produce power generating and distribution equipment come true, India will have to depend on imported equipment, to some extent at least, in the near future. The power shortage crisis from which India has been suffering in recent years can be eased by more efficient use of electricity. Indian thermal stations, for instance, generate about 3,740 kwh of energy per kw of installed generating capacity against 4,700 kwh and 5,625 kwh respectively in the U.S.A. and Japan. The losses in transmission and distribution are about 20 per cent against about only 6 to 13 per cent in most European countries.[26]

In case of the light electrical engineering industry significant progress has been made in the private sector. In addition to meeting the rapidly increasing internal demand for most electrical goods, such as fans, radios, electric heaters, irons, etc., Indian manufacturers have been successful in selling electrical goods, in increasing quantities, to the Middle Eastern, African, and East Asian countries.

Table I. Production in Selected Electrical Engineering Industries

Industry (unit)	1950-51	1955-56	1960-61	1965-66	1971-72†	*Target* 1973-74
Power transformers (lakh kvs.)* . .	1.8	6.2	14.1	44.6	88.71	119.0
Electric motors (,000 h.p.).	99	2,72	7,28	1,753	2,348	3,400
Electric fans (lakh nos).	2.0	2.9	10.6	13.6	20.67	30.0
Electric lamps (lakh nos)	1.40	2.50	4.35	7.21	12.06	NA
Radio receivers (,000 nos)	54	1,02	2,82	6,06	2,004	3,800
Electric cables and wires						
(i) Aluminium conductors (,000 tonnes)	1.7	9.4	23.6	40.6	79.7	NA
**(ii) Bare copper conductors (,000 tonnes)	5.0	8.7	10.1	3.1	0.7	1.25

*lakh = 1,00,000

**Decline in the production of bare copper conductors since 1960-61 is due to rapid increase in the use of aluminium conductors.

†Provisional.

NA = not available

SOURCE: *Fourth Plan*, p. 334. *India*: *1971-72*, p. 352. *Economic Survey*: *1972-73*, p. 112

Production figures in respect of selected electrical engineering industries are given in Table I below. This will give some idea regarding their rapid growth.

23 *India News*, September 22, 1972, p. 2.

24 Ibid., p. 3.

25 Indian Institute of Public Opinion, "Planning for Power: The Crisis Ahead," Blue Supplement to the *Monthly Commentary on Indian Economic Conditions*, vol. 13, no. 10 (May 1972), p. 1.

26 Ibid., p. III.

7. Mechanical Engineering Industries

Over the past twenty years, India has developed a heavy and light mechanical engineering industry of a diversified character. Even a simple but comprehensive listing of engineering goods, presently made in India, is not an easy task. The purpose of the following discussion, therefore, is to highlight some of the salient features of their development and to point out the significance of their growth in the changing industrial scene in India. Accordingly, actual production figures for 1950–51, the last year of the First Plan (1955–56), the Second Plan (1960–61), and the Third Plan (1965–66), 1968–69, and 1971–72 for selected industrial machinery and engineering industries are given in Table 2 below. This Table also includes actual installed capacity figures for 1968–69 and the target output figures for 1973–74, the final year of the Fourth Plan.

In the field of rail and road transport and communications, virtual self-sufficiency for the supply of equipment and rolling stock (including diesel and electric locomotives) has been realized since 1951. Machinery manufacturing capacity for a variety of traditional industries like textiles, sugar, cement, and paper has been developed. Shipyards for building ships for the merchant marine as well as the Indian navy have been built. The capacity to produce automobiles, especially commercial vehicles, has increased to such an extent that in this regard India has become self-

Table 2. Production in Selected Engineering Industries

Industry (unit)	1950-51	1955-56	1960-61	1965-66	1968-69 *Capacity*	1968-69 *production*	1971-72*	1973-74
Industrial machinery								
Cotton textile machinery (Rs Mill)	NA	40	104	216	400	138	335	450
Sugar mill mach. (Rs Mill)	NA	1.9	44	77	210	118.0	177	210
Cement machinery (Rs Mill)	NA	3.4	6	49	230	81.8	22	190
Paper & pulp mach. (Rs Mill)	Neg.	Neg.	Neg.	17	64	27	NA	140
Mechanical engineering industries								
Machine tools (Rs Million)	3.4	7.9	70.0	294.3	610	247.8	550	650
Railway wagons (,000 nos)	2.9	15.3(c)	8.2	23.5	NA	15.8	8.5	21.5
Locomotives	7	179	272	233	NA	185	NA	NA
Automobiles (total) (,000 nos)	16.5	25.3	55.0	70.7	NA	78	91.3	NA
Commercial vehicles (,000 nos)	8.6	9.9	28.4	35.3	57.6	34.4	39.5	85.0
Passenger cars etc. (,000 nos)	7.9	15.4	26.6	35.4	NA	43.6	51.8	NA
Motor cycles & scooters (,000 nos)	—	0.9(c)	19.4	40.7	149.0	70.8	112.7	2,10.0
Power driven pumps (,000 nos)	35	37	1.09	244	350	322	208	4,50
Diesel engines (stationary) (,000 nos)	5.5	10.4	44.7	93.1	125	119.5	69.9	200.0
Bicycles (,000 nos)	99	513	1,071	1,574	2,175	1,957	1,766	3,200
Sewing machines (,000 nos)	33	111	303	430	450	429	312	600

NA = not available
Neg. = negligible
(c) = for calendar year = provisional

SOURCES: *Fourth Plan*, p. 299
India: 1971-72, p. 252

Government of India, Planning Commission, Statistics and Surveys Division, *Basic Statistics Relating to the Indian Economy 1950-51 to 1968-69* (New Delhi, December 1969).

Economic Survey: 1972-73, p. 111.

sufficient. Manufacturing of construction, mining, and agricultural machinery has been taken up in significant quantities. Considerable progress has been made in establishing defence industries, including the manufacture of military vehicles, tanks, aeroplanes, heavy guns, and small arms and ammunition. The production of sewing machines, bicycles, motor cycles, and scooters has increased many-fold. It will be seen from the foregoing review that the development of the engineering industries has made India nearly self-sufficient in many respects and this has also made it possible for India to export her engineering goods in increasing quantities.

8. Textile Industry

Long before the advent of the British rule, India was known for its cotton textiles. The industry was ruined by the British in order to afford Lancashire a vast market in India for its rapidly growing production of cotton textile goods. The destruction of the Indian textiles was so ruthless that Lord Bentinck, the then Governor General of India, while commenting on the plight of cotton textile workers, reported in 1834, "the misery hardly finds a parallel in the history of commerce. The bones of the cotton-weavers are bleaching the plains of India."[27] However, only in a matter of two decades, by 1854, the cotton textile industry regained a firm footing around Bombay. This was possible because of the availability of indigenous cotton, large domestic market, cheap supply of labour, and the humid climate. From the beginning, the entrepreneurship and capital invested in the cotton textile industry have been Indian. The second half of the nineteenth century also witnessed the growth of the jute and woollen industries. The rayon, nylon, and other synthetic textile industries were started only after the Second World War, and they are still of minor importance compared to the cotton and jute industries, but they have become almost as important as the woollen industry. From the outset, the textile industries assumed the place of prime importance in the industrial sector of the economy in terms of employment generated, contribution made to the gross national product, and export trade.

9. Cotton Textile Industry

The growth of the cotton textile industry between 1879–80 and 1968–69 is shown in Table 3 below.

Table 3. Growth of Cotton Textile Industry (1879-80 to 1968-69)

Year	Number of spindles (thousand)	Number of looms (thousand)	Mill production: Yarn (m.kg.)	Mill production: Piece goods (m. metres)
1879-80	14.80	13.3	..	..
1889-90	29.35	22.1	..	..a
1990	48.41	40.5	260	54
1911	60.95	85.8	283	121
1921	72.78	1,33.5	312	1,315
1931	90.78	1,75.2	421	2,456
1941	100.26	2,00.0	603	3,445
1947	103.54	2,03.0	597	3,509
1950-51	..	..	534	3,401
1960-61	157.00	2,04.0	873	4,649
1968-69	177.50b	2,09.0	959	4,297

a. Million kg. b. Figures for July, 1970

SOURCES: Government of India, Ministry of Information and Broadcasting, *India: A Reference Annual, 1966* (New Delhi, 1966), p. 294. *India, 1971-72*, p. 355. *Fourth Plan*, p. 336.

In 1947, as a consequence of partition, out of a total of 423 cotton mills India got 409 and Pakistan only 14.[28] By December 1971, the number of textile mills had increased to 670 of which 379, were spinning and 291 composite mills. All these together had an installed capacity of 1807 million spindles and 209 thou-

[27] Jawaharlal Nehru, *The Discovery of India* (New York: Anchor Books, Doubleday & Company, Inc., 1960), p. 211.

[28] M. R. Chaudhuri, *Indian Industries Development and Location* (New Delhi: Oxford & IBH Publishing Co., 1970), p. 356.

sand looms.[29] In March, 1968, the cotton textile industry afforded employment to roughly eight hundred thousand workers, which was about one-fifth of the entire labour force in India.[30] The production of cotton yarn increased from 534 million kg. in 1950–51 to 902 million kg. in 1971–72, and that of cotton cloth from 3,401 million metres to 4,039 million metres. In 1971–72, the export of cotton fabrics increased to Rs. 76.6 crores from Rs. 69.7 crores in 1970.[31] However, this increased production of cotton textiles has failed to keep in with increase in demand from increase in population and improvements in living standards. This had an upward pressure on prices. In spite of considerable expansion of the cotton textile industry and the efforts made to resolve the major problems confronting it at the time of Independence, it cannot be said that the industry, as a whole, is in a healthy state.

The industry is still heavily concentrated around Bombay, where 60 per cent of the existing spindles and looms are installed. The industry grew there at first because of the following advantages: the required humid climate; early development of major ports of entry and railroad centres, which provided an easy access to the cotton-growing areas and also to markets for finished textiles; and the nearness of South African coal, initially used as a source of power, and also of Lancashire and other industrial centres of the world, from where textile machinery, chemicals, and engineers were imported. The textile industry can now be located with equal advantage either close to the cotton growing areas or to the markets for textile products. Minimization of transportation costs, as a result of double savings on freight, is achieved by locating the industry in the middle of the cotton growing areas as well as of the markets for textile goods. As cotton is grown over large areas in India, better location of the cotton textile industry can be achieved by dispersing it away from the centres of concentration, such as Bombay, where wages are also comparatively high.

Since Independence, the cotton textile industry has suffered from the shortage of cotton, specially of the long staple variety. Periodically, this chronic shortage becomes critical, either because of adverse weather conditions leading to a drop in domestic output or because of decline in imports due to balance of payments difficulties or because of an increase in the international price of cotton. The production of cotton increased from 3 million bales in 1950–51 to 6.5 million bales in 1971–72,[32] but it has failed to keep pace with the increase in demand. In India cotton is at present grown mostly in unirrigated areas, where the average yield per acre is only 32.85 kg. and this also is subject to extreme variations due to variations in rainfall. Compared to this, 112.5 kg. per acre is grown in irrigated areas.[33] To stabilize and increase the domestic output of cotton, it is, therefore, necessary not only to increase the area under cultivation, but also to increase irrigation facilities. The necessity for extending irrigation is futher indicated by the gradual shift in demand from short and medium staple to long staple cotton, required for making finer grades of cotton textiles. Long staple cotton requires greater use of fertilizers, insecticides, and irrigation. The Fourth Plan provides for raising the production of cotton from 6 to 8 million bales annually, and bringing 0.3 million hectares under irrigation for growing cotton.[34] However, for overcoming shortage of cotton in years of bad crop and high international prices, it is essential to create a buffer stock in order to stabilize the availability of cotton to the mills from year to year.

Shortage of cotton in bad years forces the mills to operate below capacity. This leads, on the one hand, to higher costs per unit, as fixed costs have to be spread over smaller output, and, on the other hand, to a lower demand for textiles because of the decline in agricultural incomes. In

29 Government of India, Ministry of Information and Broadcasting, *India 1973* (New Delhi, 1973), p. 275.

30 Chaudhuri, p. 151.

31 *Economic Survey*: *1972–73*, pp. 114–162.

32 *Economic Survey*: *1972–73*, p. 98.

33 Dubey, p. 235.

34 *Fourth Plan*, pp. 163 and 184.

recent years, power shortage has also frequently forced the textile mills to work considerably below their installed capacity. Further, the advantage of lower labour costs is lost to a very large extent because many of the mills are too small to enjoy fully the economies of scale. Many mills have obsolete or worn out machinery. The percentage of automatic looms to total looms is only 8.3 in India against 100 in the U.S.A., 77.5 in Japan, 55.6 in Germany and 22.8 in Britain.[35] According to the Bombay Mill Owners Association, nearly 90 per cent of the machinery in the Bombay mills is over 25 years old.[36] The Fifth Plan, like the Fourth Plan, lays stress on the fuller utilization of the existing capacity and modernization of the mills. At present, the replacement demand for textile machinery cannot be satisfied by over 200 indigenous producers. The country has, therefore, to depend on imported machinery to the extent of almost Rs. 20 crores annually.[37] The domestic production of cotton textile machinery should be increased and until this has been done, its import from abroad should be permitted.

10. Jute Industry

From the beginning, the jute industry has been localized in West Bengal in a narrow belt, approximately 60 miles long and two miles wide, on both sides of the Hooghly river in the Greater Calcutta area. It employs roughly 7 per cent of the industrial labour force and is a major earner of foreign exchange.[38] In 1947, because of partition, India got all the jute mills and East Pakistan (now Bangladesh) most of the jute growing areas. In 1965, there were 97 jute mills with a total employment of 2.71 lakhs and fixed capital of Rs. 56.06 crores. The output of jute goods increased from 10.52 lakh tonnes in 1947 to 13.35 lakh tonnes in 1965, and then declined to 9.89 lakh tonnes in 1969,[39] because of the general slow-down of the economy between 1966–68. In 1971–72 on the basis of provisional estimates 11.29 lakh tonnes of jute textiles were produced. The attempts made till now to make India self-sufficient in terms of jute have met with only modest success. In spite of the increase in production from 3.3 million bales in 1950–51 to 5.7 million bales in 1971–72[40] India still has to depend on large quantities of jute import. The jute industry suffers from the same kind of problems as the cotton textile industry, such as obsolete and worn out machinery, dependence on imported jute, especially of finer qualities, and scarcity of power. As jute can be imported only from Bangladesh, the imports of jute have in the past been greatly influenced by political consideration. This has affected the jute industry adversely. On top of such acute problems, during the last twenty years, the industry has had perhaps more labour difficulties than any other industry in India. This is partly due to its being located in Greater Calcutta which is very prone to such difficulties. The competition facing the Indian jute goods in the international market from other producers of jute goods and from substitutes such as synthetic products has also been increasing with the passage of time. For the healthy growth of the industry in the future the pace of rationalization by organizing production into economically viable units of production equipped with modern machinery should be increased and a vigorous research programme to find new uses for jute and to develop new jute products be undertaken.

11. Chemical and Petrochemical Industries

Development of a basic chemical industry forms an indispensable link in the industrial and agricultural development process of an economy. The increasing use of chemical fertilizers and insecticides in agriculture, of dyes, acids, alkalies, and other chemicals by various industries and the increase in demand for paints, varnishes, building materials, soap and detergents, drugs and pharmaceuticals, etc., on the

35 Chaudhuri, p. 169.
36 Dubey, p. 472.
37 Chaudhuri, p. 169.
38 Chaudhuri, p. 171.
39 *India: 1971–72*, p. 356.

40 *Economic Survey: 1972–73*, pp. 99 and 113.

part of consumers have led to a rapid increase in the demand of basic chemicals. India is not well endowed with basic raw materials needed for the development of a heavy chemical industry. Sulphur, the basic raw material used in the production of sulphuric acid, which in turn is used in the production of other acids and a wide variety of chemical compounds, is not found in India. Sulphur is imported from the U.S.A., Japan, and Italy. In spite of the scarcity of indigenous raw materials, chemical and petrochemical industries have grown quite satisfactorily during the last two decades.

12. Heavy Chemicals

The term heavy chemicals is generally applied to chemicals like sulphuric acid, soda ash (sodium hydroxide) and caustic soda (sodium hydroxide) which can be produced on a large scale at a relatively low cost and are extensively used as raw materials by various industries. The production figures, indicating a phenomenal growth, in case of important heavy chemicals for selected years from 1950–51 to 1971–72 with installed capacity in 1968–69 and target production figures for 1973–74 are given in Table 4.

Table 4. Production in Selected Heavy Chemical Industries

Industry (unit)	1950-51	1955-56	1960-61	1965-66	*Capacity* 1968-69	*Output* 1968-69	1971-72	*Target* 1973-74
Caustic soda (,000 tonnes)	12	36	101.0	218.0	400	304	385	500
Soda ash (,000 tonnes)	45	82	152.0	331.0	430	405	489	555
Sulphuric acid (,000 tonnes)	101	167	368.0	662.0	1900	1038	975	2500

SOURCE: *Fourth Plan*, pp. 334-335. *Economic Survey*: *1972-73*, p. 113.

The increase in production of caustic soda by the electrolytic process has resulted in a considerable increase in the production of chlorine, a byproduct. The demand for heavy chemicals as a result of the general expansion of the economy has outstripped the increase in supply in the past. This was also true when from 1960 to 1970, the production of heavy inorganic chemicals registered an annual increase of 12.9 per cent,[41] and consequently the import of chemicals went on increasing. Between 1966–67 and 1968–69, the imports of various chemical elements and compounds amounted, on the average, to Rs. 71.37 crores per year against Rs. 37.64 crores per year during 1960–61 to 1962–63.[42] Increase in the production of sulphuric acid has necessitated import of sulphur in increasing quantities. Between 1966–67 and 1968–69, the import amounted to Rs. 22.38 crores on the average. In order to reduce this increasing pressure on the country's scarce foreign exchange resources, greater use of pyrites and byproduct smelter gases should be made in the production of sulphuric acid and the pace of development of the chemical industry should be increased further.

13. Fertilizer Industry

The fertilizer industry had its start in India with the establishment of the Sindri Fertilizer Factory on October 31, 1951. Since then, as a result of the establishment of a large number of fertilizer factories, both in the public and private sectors, production of fertilizers has increased rapidly. Table 5 gives figures on the rapid growth in the domestic production, installed capacity, and imports of fertilizers.

41 *Reserve Bank of India Bulletin* (April 1972), p. 727. Figure computed on the basis of actual data.

42 *Basic Statistics, Relating to the Indian Economy, 1950–51 to 1968–69*, pp. 76–77.

Table 5. Production of Fertilizers and Pesticides

	1950-51	1955-56	1960-61	1965-66	1968-69 Capacity	1968-69 Production	Target 1973-74
Domestic Production							
Nitrogenous (,000 tons) (in terms of N)	9	80	101	232	1,024	541	2500
Phosphatic (,000 tons) (in terms of P_2O_5)	9	12	53	123	421	210	900
Pesticides (,000 tons)	—	—	8	13	34	19	65
Imports							
Fertilizers crude (Rs. Lakhs) and manufactured	1,235	224	1,213	4,482	—	15,019	—

SOURCE: *Fourth Plan*, p. 300. Government of India, Planning Commission, *Basic Statistics Relating to the Indian Economy, 1950-51 to 1968-69*, pp. 76-77. *India: 1971-72*, p. 353.

In 1971–72, the production of nitrogenous fertilizers increased to 952 thousand million tonnes and of phosphatic fertilizers to 278 thousand tonnes.[43] This was achieved partly through the erection of new plants, partly through the expansion of the existing plants, and partly through efforts made to ensure uninterrupted supply to fertilizer plants of power and adequate wagons for the movement of raw materials and finished products. In spite of this increase in production between 1950–51 and 1971–72, the need for fertilizer imports continued to increase because of greater and greater use of fertilizer by Indian farmers. In view of this increased demand and greater determination on the part of India to become self-sufficient in food, the Fourth Plan lays great emphasis on the production of fertilizers. However, the total installed capacity is expected to amount to only 2.3 million tonnes in 1973–74 against the planned target of 3 million tonnes.[44]

14. Pharmaceuticals, Petrochemicals and Plastics

Drugs and pharmaceutical industries have made good progress since 1950. The value of pharmaceuticals produced by large and medium scale firms during 1970 amounted to roughly Rs. 250 crores against Rs. 225 crores in 1969.[45] India produces different kinds of surgical instruments, antibiotics, and other drugs including a variety of synthetic hormones. In spite of this growth, India had to import medicinal and pharmaceutical products worth Rs. 17.50 crores in 1968–69,[46] against Rs. 9.97 crores in 1950–51 because of enormous expansion in medical and hospital facilities in the country.

The production of petrochemicals was undertaken on a large scale in December, 1966, when the first menthol plant in India was commissioned by the Fertilizer Corporation of India. The figures on growth in the production of selected petrochemicals from 1960–61 along with targets for 1973–74 output are given in Table 6.

[43] *Economic Survey: 1972–73*, p. 112.
[44] *India News*, July 7, 1972, p. 2.

[45] *India: 1972–73*, p. 368.
[46] *Basic Statistics Relating to the Indian Economy*, p. 79.

Table 6. Production of Selected Petrochemicals

			Capacity	Output	Target
	1960-61	1965-66	1968-69		1973-74
Polyvinyl Chloride (,000 tonnes)	—	12.5	44.0	23.4	90.0
Polyethlene (,000 tonnes)	9.5	13.5	39.1	25.2	90.0
Polystyrene (,000 tonnes)	—	5.6	17.5	9.5	30.0
Polypropylene (,000 tonnes)	—	—	—	—	15.0

SOURCE : *Fourth Plan*, p. 335.

As a result of this, rapid increase in the production of petrochemicals and large availability of phenol formaldehyde and urea formaldehyde, a sizable plastic and synthetic rubber industry has developed in India. The production of synthetic rubber amounted to 26 thousand tonnes in 1968–69 and the target output figure for 1973–74, laid down in the Fourth Plan, is 70 thousand tonnes.[47]

15. Sugar, Cement, Paper and Paperboard

Sugar and paper industries were started in India in the second half of the last century and the manufacture of cement was started in the first part of this century. The First World War gave these industries a great impetus and they not only struggled through the depression in the thirties and the Second World War, but showed a significant growth. The relative growth of these industries since 1950–51 is shown in the Table 7.

The growth of these industries since 1947 can be attributed primarily to the expansion of the economy in general rather than to any special factors. It can hardly be said that the progress made by them acted as a catalyst, as the progress made by the steel and machine tools industry. These industries, however, suffer from the general problems in our industrial structure, such as worn out or obsolete equipment, uneconomic location, etc.

16. Overall Evaluation of Industrial Growth Since 1955-56

1955–56, the year just before the beginning of the Second Plan, is selected as the starting point for evaluating the growth of the Indian industry because, only in the Second Plan, was development of the industrial sector given top priority. Again it was only after 1955–56 that key industries, such as iron and steel, aluminium, machine tools, heavy electrical, mechanical engineering, and heavy inorganic chemicals

Table 7. Growth of Sugar, Paper, Paperboard and Cement

Industry (unit)	1950-51	1955-56	1960-61	1965-66	1969-70	1971-72	Target 1973-74
Sugar (Nov.-Oct.) (lakh tonnes)	11.3	18.9	30.2	35.4	35.6*	31.10	47.0
Paper and paperboard (,000 tonnes)	116	190	350	558	646	803(c)	1,000
Cement (lakh tonnes)	27	47	80	108	122	150	180

*Sugar year relates to October-September since 1967-68. (c) Figure for calendar year.

SOURCES : Government of India, Planning Commission, *Basic Statistics Relating to the Indian Economy, 1950-51 to 1968-69*, p. 69. *India : 1971-72*, pp. 357-359. *Fourth Plan*, pp. 324 and 336. *Economic Survey : 1972-73*, pp. 113-14

[47] *Fourth Plan*, p. 32.

were established, and they started changing the industrial scene in our economy. The general index of industrial production which stood at 72.7[48] in 1955–56 (base 1960=100), climbed to 180.8 in 1970 and increased further to 198 in August 1972.[49] During the ten years from 1961 to 1970, basic industries, incorporating mining and quarrying, heavy inorganic chemicals, cement, basic metals, and electricity, registered an annual growth of 8.3 per cent; capital goods industries, incorporating industrial machinery, railroad equipment, and motor vehicles, an annual growth of 8.4 per cent; intermediate goods industries, an annual growth of 4.5 per cent; and consumer goods, the lowest annual growth rate of only 3.2 per cent.[50] The over all annual growth of the industrial sector amounted to 6.1 per cent during this period.

The industrial sector for the first five years from 1961 to 1965 registered an annual growth rate of about 9 per cent against only 3.4 per cent during the five years from 1966 to 1970. This was because of the general slow-down of the economy in 1966 when the industrial production actually declined by 1.5 per cent. However, this downward trend was reversed in 1968.[51] The installed capacity registered a slightly higher increase of 6.4 per cent[52] from 1961 to 1970 as compared to 6.1 per cent[52] in industrial production. Consequently, the level of utilization of the potential installed capacity fell from 87.7 per cent in 1960 to 80.4 per cent in 1970.[53] The level of potential-utilization ratio declined in the case of basic industries from 84.6 to 83.9, in the case of capital goods from 76.8 to 59.2, in the case of intermediate goods from 89.9 to 79.5, and in the case of consumer goods from 90.3 in 1960 to 86.2 in 1970[54]

[48] *Basic Statistics Relating to the Indian Economy: 1950–51 to 1968–69,* p. 1.

[49] *Economic Survey 1972–73,* p. 23.

[50] *Reserve Bank of India Bulletin,* April 1972, p. 729. Percentage rates of growth have been calculated in the basis of the absolute figures given

[51] Ibid., p. 729.

[52] *Reserve Bank of India Bulletin,* March 1972, p. 403.

[53] Ibid., p. 406.

[54] Ibid., pp. 406–7.

p. 730.

The growth rate of industrial production declined sharply from 7.5 per cent in 1969 to 3.1 per cent in 1970 and to 2.9 per cent in 1971. This prolonged and sharp decline in the growth rate of industrial production was reversed only in 1972 when it amounted to approximately 7 per cent.[55]

The major factors responsible for this slowdown were the same as in most other previous periods of industrial slowdowns since Independence. The shortage of raw materials, especially in the case of cotton and jute, adversely affected the industrial performance. Shortage of steel, due to decline in steel production and lack of demand for railway wagons, and of capital goods in general adversely affected the utilization of existing installed capacity, particularly in engineering industries. Capacity constraints, imposed by government in important industries like paper, caustic soda, soda ash, and other heavy chemicals, limited the growth rates of these industries which, in turn, adversely affected the performance of other industries. Industrial labour and management disputes also had their toll.

17. Conclusion and Future Outlook

The overall performance of the industrial sector since 1950–51, though not spectacular, has been impressive. Steel and power plants, modern factories for making machine tools, locomotives, ships, pharmaceuticals, and petrochemicals have been built and made operational. All this successfully and unequivocally demonstrates India's ability to use modern technology. The technical and managerial know-how has developed to such an extent that India is now in a position to plan and build large hydro-electric projects, modern steel plants, ships, locomotives, jet planes, industrial machines and the sophisticated tools required to make all these. The economy has developed a considerable degree of self-reliance, and this can be utilized successsfully to foster a much more rapid growth of the industrial sector during the seventies, which is still relatively small. The momentum which the green revolution has

[55] *Economic Survey: 1972–73,* p. 22.

made since the middle sixties, first in the wheat-growing areas, such as Punjab and Haryana, and now in the rice-growing areas, specially in Andhra Pradesh and Tamil Nadu, has led to an enormous increase in the demand for fertilizers and agricultural implements. Very soon the increased demand for industrial consumer goods, which have already been felt in Punjab and Haryana, is likely to create a powerful and new chain of demand for industrial products all over India. In view of these developments in the past, the industrial sector of the economy, which has already emerged out of its infancy, is poised to take-off in the seventies. For the full exploitation of this newly created potential, it is essential that measures should be taken to eliminate the factors which not only hindered, in the past, a more rapid growth of the industrial sector, but even imposed periodically formidable obstacles to maintaining the steady rate of industrial growth achieved in the first half of the sixties.

The criticism that in the past investment in heavy industry, power generation, and transportation has been excessive and could not be justified on the basis of the high capital output ratio and the long gestation period seems unwarranted, considering the frequent shortages of steel, cement, electricity, and transportation facilities, which often forced sizable segments of the industrial sector to work below capacity and have now become chronic. In providing for the future development of such heavy industries, the Planning Commission should act more boldly and with greater imagination rather than being slavishly guided by the future projections of their demand based on current trends. It is not being suggested here that in the planning of their future growth, demand considerations should be ignored. Rather what is intended is to point out that, if errors in the estimation of the demand for them cannot be avoided because of the long gestation periods involved, then the errors of overestimation should be preferable to those of underestimation; as, on the basis of the past experience, not only are the chances of overestimation small but, even if made, they are likely to prove less expensive than the cost of underestimation.

The reorganization and rationalization of the traditional industries, such as cotton, jute, cement, and sugar, to name only a few, should be emphasized further. Uneconomic units should be closed and obsolete and worn out equipment should be replaced to lower the cost of production and to give their products a competitive edge in the domestic as well as international markets. The labour unions, which have developed a comparatively greater amount of strength in India at considerably lower levels of economic development than was historically achieved by labour unions in economically advanced nations of today, have successfully resisted rationalization with the help of politicians both in and outside power. There is a strong need for education on the part of all concerned, for steady development cannot be maintained without making the most efficient use of capital and without increasing the productivity of labour. In order to make more intensive use of capital equipment, multiple shifts, wherever possible, should be instituted. This has generally been resisted by labour thus far.

Greater consistency in industrial development should be planned by the simultaneous development of mutually consistent industrial projects. This can be done by proper coordination of decisions on the demand and supply sides. A flexible but effective organization should be built at the Central government level to resolve bottlenecks which may be difficult to foresee and hard to avoid. For achieving the optimum rates of industrial growth it will be essential to revamp the managerial cadres both in the public as well as in the private sector and to streamline the decision-making processes. In the public sector, most of the time the ultimate decision-making power is vested in the top echelons of bureaucratic hierarchy in central ministries rather than in the plant managers at the spot. By nature the people occupying these positions are trained to be conservative in their approach and cannot afford to be daring and independent because their decisions are always subject to review by the minister in charge, the cabinet, and ultimately, parliament. In this kind of environment, survival rather than the exercising of initiative, becomes the objective as the most well-paid positions go to those who manage to survive the longest. When the decision affects more than one ministry, as is quite often the case, simple survival can be assured merely by leaving the ultimate decisions to others. This sort of administrative set-up in the past has resulted in very costly delays in starting important key industrial projects. The private sector enterprises are not immune from the inadequacies of government machinery in these respects, for most decisions made by them cannot be implemented without the sanction of the needed license, foreign exchange permit, or even a loan. Specially since the nationalization of the large commercial banks, the dependence of the private sector on public sector financial institutions for financing medium- and large-scale projects has increased. Because of the dual role of the capitalist-cum-entrepreneur played by the managing agents, under the managing agency system, there is a greater concentration of decision-making authority at the top even in the private sector than in most western economies. The prevalent system has, therefore, to be changed, as ultimately nothing affects the rate of industrial growth more than the quality of the human element, which occupies the top entrepreneurial and managerial positions. There is no doubt that India has a large number of people with the capabilities and qualities demanded of top managers and entrepreneurs, but it has still to demonstrate the ability to create the environment and the institutional set-up which will enable them to flourish. This has been realized for some time now and some steps have already been taken, specially in the private sector, to delegate a grater amount of authority to middle management. The degree of success achieved in these respects will determine the destiny of the Indian industries in the future.

6

Small-Scale and Cottage Industries in India

RAMSINH K. ASHER

1. Introduction

During the quarter of a century preceding India's Independence, Mahatma Gandhi had called upon the nation to solve the problem of tragic poverty among India's teeming millions, by creating work opportunities through cottage industries in hundreds and thousands of isolated villages for utilizing the valuable unutilized asset—the billions of manhours of the labour of her people. In the post-Independence period, the Planning Commission recognized the need for utilization of rural manpower as an important weapon of war against poverty.

On the other hand, the Indian Planning Commission also emphasized the development of large-scale and heavy industries as a means towards achieving balanced and rapid growth of the economy. Indeed, large-scale industries also create employment opportunities, but their development do not have the advantages peculiar to the cottage industries in the village: an egalitarian distribution of work (specially in rural areas), income, economic power, and human dignity. With a rapidly growing population, the labour force has grown, and so has unemployment, as seen from the following figures:

Year	Labour force in crores	Unemployment in crores	As % of Labour force
1951	14.5	.25	1.7
1956	15.4	.50	3.2
1961	16.6	.80	4.8
1966	18.3	1.15	6.3
1971	20.6	1.55	7.5

This post-Independence record of the economy, from the point of view of employment opportunities, calls for a closer look at the policies, the problems and the potential of small-scale and village industries in India. After a brief introduction to the sub-sector of small-scale and cottage industry in India, some theoretial issues will be discussed to formulate the rationale for these industries, and to provide some criteria for evaluating the policies towards this sub-sector. Next, the measures taken during the four Five Year Plans will be reviewed, and the problems of the small-scale industries will be examined in some detail.

2. The Cottage Industry in India

The pre-Independence Indian economy can be characterized by two features: (*i*) The predominance of agriculture and the relative smallness of the manufacturing sector. In 1911, as well as in 1951, agriculture provided livelihood to around 70 per cent of the population, while only about 10 per cent derived their livelihood from manufacturing.[1] The agricultural sector contributed about 50 per cent of the net national income and 70 per cent of the total employment in 1911 as well as in 1951. In contrast the manufacturing sector contributed about 14 per cent of the net national income in 1911 and 17 per cent in 1951. (*ii*) Not only was the Indian manufacturing sector small, it was composed mainly of the cottage and small-scale industries. The 1911 census estimated that only 15 lakh workers were employed in factories, while some 160 lakhs worked in the cottage and small-scale industry sub-sector. The figures for 1951 were 29 lakhs in factories and 115 lakhs in the non-factory work.[2] For comparison, we may look at the situation in other countries.

The manufacturing sector in the U.S.A. was already well developed in the early 1950s's. But 91 per cent of all manufacturing establishments in 1954 employed less than 10 workers each and accounted for 25 per cent of the manufacturing employment and 22 per cent of the output of all manufacturing establishments.[3] In a capital-abundant economy characterized by mass production on a large scale, there was still some role for small enterprises. The proportion of output originating in the small industry sub-sector is less than the proportion of employment in that sub-sector which is sometimes taken to indicate a lower labour productivity (output per worker) in the small scale sector.

The relatively smaller role played by the small enterprises in the U.S.A. is in contrast with the role played by small industries in Japan. In 1953, 99.5 per cent of all establishments were defined as small, i.e., employing less than 300 workers each. These establishments employed 71 per cent of all persons employed in manufacturing industries and contributed 54 per cent of the total value of manufacturing output.[4] The role of small industries in Japan was quite significant. From the point of view of comparative efficiency, the small Japanese producers successfully competed in export markets in those lines of production which in the industrial countries are generally characterized by large-scale production.

In comparing the industrial structures of these three economies (U.S.A., Japan and India) it should be remembered that the definition of the small-scale industry differs for each country. The American small enterprises use capital intensive and labour saving technologies. The technology employed by Japanese small enterprises may not be as capital intensive as that in the U.S.A., but the definition of small enterprises covers a fairly large ground when factories employing up to 300 workers are included. This, more than anything else, explains the apparent importance of small-scale enterprises in Japan. In contrast, the cottage industry which predominates the Indian manufacturing sector uses traditional techniques which are mainly labour intensive, and produces traditional consumption goods for local markets using locally available resources. The Japanese and the American small enterprises have to be efficient to survive among the industrial giants, either as competitors or as auxiliaries, whereas our cottage industries and our modern industry fall in two separate, practically independent, sectors, except perhaps in the case of the textile industry where both the modern and the traditional sectors compete for the raw material cotton, and the market. In the light

1 Kedarnath Prasad, *Technological Choice under Development Planning* (Bombay: Popular Prakashan, 1963), p. 3.

2 These figures are not comparable in the absolute as the geographical coverage of the census in these two years is different.

3 M. C. Shetty, *Small-Scale and Household Industries in a Developing Economy* (Bombay: Asia Publishing House, 1963), p. 13.

4 Ibid., pp. 14–15.

of this dualism of modern and traditional sectors, neither the policies, nor the efficiency criteria of the advanced economies apply readily to our industrial structure. On the other hand, most of our factories, small or large, are not part of the traditional sector, and hence the criteria of efficiency applicable to the modern sector should apply to our small factories. This was the main conclusion of Dhar and Lydall's analysis of the Indian small-scale industry.[5] They emphasized efficiency in the use of the scarce resource capital as more important than the ability to absorb a surplus resource labour on the basis of their finding that the large factories use capital more efficiently than the small ones. Our somewhat cursory analysis, however, rejects their finding.

3. Theoretical Setting and Rationale for Cottage and Small-Scale Industries

Theoretically, two interconnected issues must be raised in determining the appropriate industrial policy. The first issue concerns the choice of technique, and the second, the size of enterprise.

Some goods can be produced by using either a large input of capital with a small input of labour, or a large input of labour with a small input of capital. The former technique may be called capital intensive and the latter technique labour intensive. If such alternative techniques are available, then there is a basic problem of deciding as to which technique should be preferred.

Several factors are taken into account in choosing the technique to be used. We look at the resource endowment of the economy. The Indian economy possesses capital scarcity but abundant supply of labour. It would thus appear that a technique of production which utilizes a large amount of labour (a large labour/capital ratio) would be preferable in the Indian context. This choice assures a high rate of utilization of labour. But does it do so efficiently? Professor Reddaway has pointed out that for productive efficiency some measure of output must also be taken into account.[6] This can be done when we look at the capital/output ratio and labour/output ratio. The capital/output ratio tells us, in general, the amount of capital used in producing a unit of output. Similarly, labour/output ratio—a reciprocal of labour productivity—tells us the amount of labour required per unit of output. Thus, from the point of view of efficiency in the use of labour and capital, we must select those techniques which have lower labour/output and capital/output ratios. In other words, we should look for techniques which give higher output per unit of capital and a higher output per worker.

Suppose technique A has a lower capital/output ratio and a higher labour/output ratio, when compared with technique B. In such a case, indeed, the choice can be determined with reference to the factor endowment. For a labour surplus economy, the efficiency criterion coincides with the full utilization of the labour criterion and gives us a unique choice of technique A. It must be noted that from a selective, partial point of view of the labour productivity alone, technique A is less efficient than technique B. Yet, given the factor endowment, technique A will give a larger total output than technique B, ensure efficient use of capital, and permit a greater, if somewhat inefficient use of labour.

Can the efficiency or productivity criterion come in conflict with the full utilization criterion? Unfortunately, it can. The conflict must then be resolved with reference to the overall economic policy of the country. We can decide to emphasize full employment of labour and select a technique with high labour/capital ratio, although the associated labour/output ratios and the capital/output ratios may be higher (less productive) than those for some other technique with low labour/capital ratio. In such a case a mere comparison of techniques from the efficiency point of view may be insufficient.

Our theoretical discussion so far has been partial because it did not take into

[5] Dhar and Lydall, *The Role of Small Enterprises in Indian Economic Development* (Bombay: Asia Publishing House), pp. 11–19.

[6] W. B. Reddaway, *The Development of the Indian Economy* (London: George Allen and Unwin Ltd., 1962), pp. 71–78.

account other factors of production, and considerations on the demand side. Production needs raw materials, short-term financing capital, entrepreneurship, some economic overheads and infrastructure besides labour and capital. When selecting among techniques on efficiency grounds, we must consider all these factors and not just capital and labour. It can be readily seen that production with traditional techniques can be easily organized with locally available resources and a fairly low level of development of other factors, such as the government, law and order, market mechanism with availability and mobility of resources, financial institutions, and transport and communications, without which modern production cannot be achieved. In comparing the efficiency of traditional production techniques with the modern ones we must take into account the costs of all of these, a task fairly difficult and rarely attempted.

The demand considerations enter into the selection of production technique because the output is measured in value terms. If the demand for capital-intensive production of machine-made goods is greater than the demand for labour-intensive hand-made goods, their relative prices would reflect this difference. Now, if one measures labour or capital efficiency in producing output in terms of money, it clearly contains an element of relative demand. This further limits the applicability of the efficiency criterion in selecting a proper technique.[7] Similarly, the labour intensity or capital intensity of a technique of production may be evaluated in terms of its relative costs, because a unit of labour cannot be compared directly to a unit of capital and also because neither factor is homogeneous.

Economic theory tells us that in a purely competitive free market economy the factor prices (wages and the cost of capital) will reflect factor endowment at least in the long-run. Such factor prices readily resolve the question of selecting the technique as seen from Figure 1.

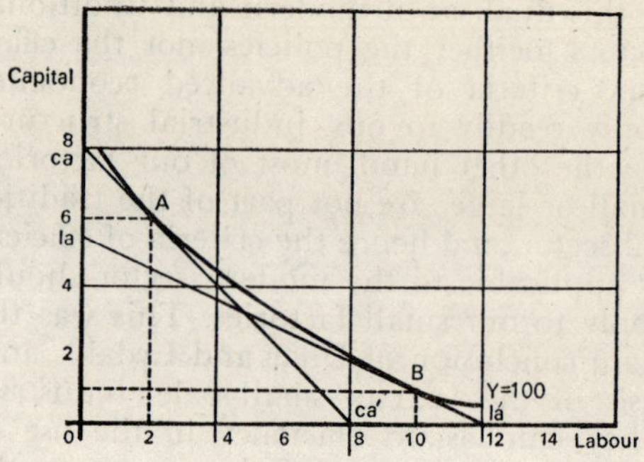

Fig. 1

Suppose that the same output Y=100 can be produced by using various combinations of labour and capital in conjunction with a given constant quantity of all other factors of production. Then, each combination represents a different technique of production. Technique A is capital intensive (capital/labour ratio is 6/2), while technique B is labour intensive (capital/labour ratio is 1/10). If the prices of one unit of capital and labour are the same (as identified by the line *ca-ca'*), then the figure shows that technique A would be selected, regardless of the factor endowment situation. On the other hand, if the factor prices are indicated by the line *la-la'*), then technique 3 will be selected. Now, if factor prices reflect factor endowment, then, for a labour surplus economy, the relative prices of labour would be less (such as *la-la'*) than the relatively higher labour price (such as *ca-ca'*) for a capital abundant economy and the appropriate labour intensive technique B would be selected. However, if for some reason, the factor prices are distorted, then a conflict of interest between the producers and the rest of the economy would result. For instance, if the government subsidizes capital by encouraging imports, and if the wages are artificially raised to levels unwarranted by abundant supply of labour, the producers will find it profitable to use capital intensive techniques of production even in a labour surplus economy.[8] If the

[7] For an excellent theoretical discussion of the subject see A. K. Sen, *Choice of Techniques* (Oxford: Basil Blackwell, 1968).

[8] Foreign enterprises in India are reputed to pay much higher salaries and wages than the market rates, while bringing in obsolete capital equipment at lower rates and enjoying special invest-

relative prices of captial (interest rate) and labour (wage rate) were not distorted, and if all the costs of production associated with each technique were taken into account, for a labour surplus and capital poor economy, the labour intensive technique would emerge as the efficient one. Employment would increase and the interests of the entrepreneurs and the society would coincide.

The second theoretical issue about the industrial policy relates to the size of enterprise. In some cases, the choice of technique determines the size of the enterprise; for example, capital-intensive steel production can be conceivable only as a large-scale industry. Where various plant sizes are possible under a given technique, a different set of considerations must be taken into account. These considerations deal with the economies and diseconomies of scale. Briefly, we look at what happens to output/capital and output/labour ratios as output increases. If the ratios increase in value over a range of output, a larger scale is preferable, and vice versa. Of course, these criteria are applicable only where the same output can be produced by a variety of plant sizes.

4. Efficiency Analysis of the Indian Industrial Sector

The Indian industrial sector can be divided into two categories. The first includes the medium and large-scale manufacturing enterprises which have a capital investment of Rs. 5 lakhs or more (Rs. 7.5 lakhs since 1966) in plant and machinery excluding building and land. The second includes small-scale manufacturing industries with fixed assets of less than the above limit.[9] According to one estimate, the large enterprises contributed Rs. 824 crores to the 1959–60 national income as compared to Rs. 898 crores estimated contribution of the small enterprises.[10] This somewhat larger contribution of the small enterprise sector can be further broken up into two categories. The small enterprises registered as factories (i.e., those employing more than 10 persons and using power, or employing 20 or more persons without using power) contributed Rs. 112 crores, while the share of the nonfactory producers was estimated at Rs. 786 crores.[11]

The non-factory producers include traditional craftsmen such as potters, blacksmiths, carpenters, leather tanners, handloom workers, sericulturists, and other handicraftsmen. This sub-sector provides full- or part-time self-employment to a large proportion of the rural population. It is believed that this sub-sector requires a small amount of capital inputs, and offers a large employment potential. The subsector draws upon local agro-based resources for raw materials and produces generally for the local markets, some places on barter terms.

Figures for enterprises registered as factories are more readily available than those for the non-factory sub-sector. The factory enterprises grouped by value of their fixed assets can be compared in terms of their output and the characteristics of their inputs from Table 1 (see the Appendix for all the tables).

Several questions can be asked and tentatively answered on the basis of these data. It can be readily seen from Table 1 that more than 90 per cent of the factories are small-scale, but in aggregate, these factories own a little less than 7 per cent of the fixed capital of the factory sub-sector, employ about 33 per cent of the factory workers, produce 28 per cent of the gross factory output and contribute about 19 per cent to value added by manufacture. In contrast, the large-scale factories possess over 86 per cent of the fixed capital of the manufacturing sector employing about 50 per cent of the factory workers and producing 54 per cent of the total

ment rebates and depreciation allowances which make capital costs low. Predictably, they find capital intensive techniques more profitable in a labour surplus economy.

9 R. K. Vepa, "Modernizing Small Industries," *Small Industries Bulletin for Asia and the Far East*, no. 8, 1970, p. 130.

10 S. L. Sharma, "Small-Scale Industries in India–Case for Modernization," *Small Industries Bulletin for Asia and the Far East,* no. 1, January 1963, p. 126.

11 Ibid.

factory output and contributing even a larger per cent—almost 65 per cent—in terms of value added by manufacture. The relative importance of the size of the factories can be seen from Table 2.

Table 2 shows a fairly close association between the asset size on the one hand and employment and output on the other. The larger the factory in terms of fixed capital, the more workers it employs, the more output (in money terms) it produces, and contributes more in terms of value added. But, this cannot be interpreted to indicate that a larger size factory essentially is more efficient. For instance, the average large-scale factory takes about 350 times as much capital as a small-scale factory (228.6÷.65), but employs only 40 times more people (1486÷36), produces 54 times as much gross output (244.5÷4.6) and only 90 times as much value added (72.2÷.8) as compared to a small-scale factory. Now if it were desirable to produce as much as possible in the fewest number of factories regardless of cost or efficiency (some of the factors which may favour and encourage the concentration of fixed assets in few industrial enterprises are technology, desire for monopoly control of the market, and a misconception that large size is always more efficient) one would conclude that large-scale factories should be preferred. But if other criteria, such as (i) most economical use of the scarce factor capital, (ii) maximum productivity of labour, or (iii) maximum employment, etc., were to be considered quite a different picture would emerge.

Before leaving Table 2, however, it should be noted that between 1963 and 1964 the average size of the fixed assets of all types of factories have increased, with a Rs. 22 lakh or almost 11 per cent increase for a typical large scale factory and a Rs. 4000 or about 6 per cent increase in the assets of a typical small-scale factory. The 11 per cent increase in capital employed in an average large factory is accompanied by a decrease in employment, a less than 2 per cent increase in average output, and a negligible increase in value added, while the 6 per cent increase in the capital in an average small factory is accompanied by almost 3 per cent increase in employment along with 15 per cent increase in output and value added. Caution must be exercised in jumping to any conclusion from this analysis. The observations are too close really to warrant any conclusions on the incremental changes of the type considered. For instance, new investments in large-scale factories may drive up the average capital assets per factory considerably without increasing employment and output significantly during the initial gestation period. However, if a series of observations over a period of 5 to 10 years indicate similar results, then one may conclude statistically that small-scale factories are more efficient. Even then, nothing is said about the inter-industry relationship. Small factories could very well be more productive because of the fact that the large factories directly supply some inputs or buy the products of the small factories, or they indirectly provide what are known as the external economies.

To examine efficiency in the use of capital and labour one can recast the data in Table 1 in terms of output per worker and output per rupee worth of capital for the three types of factories. Table 3 shows capital, gross output and value added per employee and Table 4 gives figures on employment, output and value added per rupee's worth of fixed capital. Table 3 shows that in 1964 an average worker in a large-scale factory worked with fixed assets worth Rs. 15,400 or more than eight times those available to a worker in a small factory, and contributed Rs. 4,870 to value added (a rough measure of labour productivity), or more than twice that of a small factory worker. Clearly the average worker in the large factory needed eight times as much fixed capital to be only twice as productive as his counterpart in the small factory.

The marginal productivity of capital per worker may be estimated roughly by comparing the figures for 1964 with those for 1963. An increase in fixed capital per worker of Rs. 63 or about 3.6 per cent (63 ÷1757) is accompanied by an increase in value added per worker of Rs. 78 or about 3.7 per cent (78÷2072) for the small scale factory. A much larger increase in fixed capital per worker of Rs. 2014 or over 15 per cent (2014÷13386) in large factories is accompanied by an increase in value added per worker of only Rs. 215 or 4.5 per cent (215÷4655). This indicates that the additional fixed investment per worker in the small-scale factories leads to a larger increase in labour productivity than in the large-scale factories. This conclusion is justifiable even when the comparison is made between the marginal labour productivities over the period 1960–65. This simple statistical analysis suggests that additional capital investment in smaller factories is likely to yield a larger increase in the labour productivity.

Table 4 shows the average labour/capital ratio, the gross output and value added per rupee's worth of fixed capital by size of the factory. It clearly indicates that the small-scale factory combines the largest number of workers with a rupee's worth of fixed capital; that a rupee worth of fixed assets produce almost seven times an output in small as compared to large factories, and that the value added by a rupee worth of fixed investment in small factories is at least three times as large as that for a large factory. On the basis of the figures of 1964 it may be concluded that additional investment should be made only in the small-scale factories rather than in the large ones. But such a conclusion disregards important factors which can explain the records in a way more meaningful for policy than that suggested by a mere comparison of the ratios. For instance, we must take into account the rate of utilization of the fixed assets, the degree of special subsidization enjoyed by small factories, the effects of the difference in fiscal and other regulations applicable to the factory types, and so on. One may very well ask what good then is the statistical analysis of this sort? If the record extended over a period of years confirms the conclusions of our tentative analysis, at least we could then spot the area which clearly must be investigated, and if little can be done about the problem areas (e.g., increasing utilization of capacity), one may invest in small-scale factories, although the large-scale factories, when working at full capacity, may theoretically, be more efficient. The usefulness of such aggregate analysis is admittedly limited, and more industry by industry analysis needs to be done to formulate appropriate policy.[12] However, if these indices of efficiency retain their pattern over a period of time, criteria for policy formulation can be developed from them.

5. Cottage Industry in India's Industrial Policy

The importance of the cottage industry in India was acknowledged in the thoughts of Dadabhoy Naoroji as early as at the turn of this century. Mahatma Gandhi's movement clearly laid its policy priorities on village uplift in Sarvodaya. Eminent economists like G.D.H. Cole recognized the propriety of Gandhiji's spinning wheel as the effective means to attain universal economic independence and prosperity.[13]

So immense was the impact of his ideology that the plan for economic development put forward by a group of Indian industrialists, which was to be dubbed by some a bourgeois plan later on,[14] had left the production of consumer goods explicitly to the traditional rural based decentralized cottage industry, while confining the large-scale capital and intermediate goods production to the modern industrial sector. This was specifically suggested in view of the widespread unemployment problem and with a view to sharing both the effort and the fruits of economic development among as large a number of people as possible. In the light of the modern-traditional type dualism that characterized the Indian economic structure, the Bombay Plan, although opposed to state ownership and socialism in essence, seems to have recognized the responsibility for the uplift of the rural masses through cottage industries.

---

12 One such excellent study is by B. Subba Rao and V. G. Kalkundrikar entitled "A Comparative Study of the Economics of High-Capital-Cost and Low-Capital-Cost Technologies: The Manufactures of Cycle Gear Cases," *Small Industries Bulletin for Asia and the Far East,* no. 6, 1968, pp. 107–109.

13 P. A. Wadia and K. T. Merchant, *Our Economic Problem* (Bombay: Vora and Co., 1957), p. 695.

14 R. Das Gupta, *Problems of Economic Transition* (Calcutta: Nation Publishers, 1970), p. 51.

The Industrial Policy Resolution of 1948 reiterated the importance of cottage industries and the small enterprises. While the major thrust of this policy resolution was to lay directions for the future growth of modern industry in the public sector, the fear of nationalization, which the private sector claimed it created, was spared so far as the cottage and small-scale industries were concerned. If anything, this subsector was to receive a preferential treatment.

The next significant policy statement came in response to the report of the Village and Small-Scale Industries Committee (Karve Committee) in 1955. The Karve Committee's proposals were three-pronged: (i) to avoid, as far as possible, further technological unemployment in traditional village industries; (ii) to provide for greater employment opportunities through different village and small industries; and (iii) to provide the basis for a decentralized society with progressive economic development at a fairly rapid rate.[15]

The Committee's conception of the industrial structure as described in their own words was that "Positive pattern of industrial activity that should gradually emerge is that of a group of villages having its natural industrial and urban centre. These small urban centres will be related to big ones. Thus a pyramid of industry broad-based on a progressive rural economy will be built up."[16]

The community development programmes which began in 1952 had already emphasized the employment aspect. By the end of the Second Five Year Plan, the rural action programme using local labour in more intensive agriculture, rural industry or construction had spread almost nationwide. The negative influence of the modern industry upon employment in competing cottage and small-scale industry were to be contained by restrictions imposed on the modernization and "rationalization" of the large-scale industry. Even production quotas were imposed at one time on textile mills, while subsidies were given to small-scale producers.

Towards the end of the Second Plan, the International Perspective Planning Team made a plea for the use of the micro-efficiency criteria in policies purporting the small industries. This emphasis on efficiency orientation is reflected in other influential writings, such as Dhar and Lydall's book. At this stage the planners seem to have combined the Karve Committee emphasis on employment creation and the other opinion emphasizing efficient use of capital. Increasingly, policy began emphasizing only those labour intensive activities that were more complementary and less competitive with modern and capital intensive ventures. Following the recommendations of the Second International Perspective Planning Team sponsored by the Ford Foundation in 1963, the Third Plan accorded preferential treatment to the urban-based small industries, such as the sewing machine, bicycle, metal processing, etc. But, contrary to the warnings against geographical decentralization of that Team's report, the Third Plan also promoted in a big way the industrial estates and rural electrification. The Plan stressed decentralized development. Some 25 lakh new jobs were expected to be created in the rural areas. The significant policy change since 1966 can be inferred from the reclassification of factories and a redefinition of small-scale factories as those with less than Rs. 5 lakhs in fixed capital. This definition in effect broadens the scope of activities which would be assisted by various governmental programmes. The impact of the Second International Team's efficiency orientation was echoed in the report of the Khadi and Village Industries Committee (Asoka Mehta Committee) which extended this emphasis on productive efficiency to khadi and handloom industries where the major policy aim had always been employment for the rural masses.

These changes in policy direction are reflected in the Fourth Plan's objectives as will be seen presently.

6. Cottage and Small-Scale Industries in the Five Year Plans

The industrial policy gets a more precise form in the planned outlays on invest-

---

[15] Government of India, *Report of the Village and Small-Scale Industries Committee,* 1955, p. 22.
[16] Ibid.

ment in industry and other sectors. Investment in the industrial sector has been considered a key to rapid economic development. Accordingly, new investment has been made mostly in the large-scale modern industry as seen from Table 5.

The share of the cottage and small industries has been small, 5 per cent in the First Plan and has declined to 3.4 per cent in the Fourth Plan. Another significant feature of the Plan provisions for the small industries is that a large part of the investment in this subsector has been left to the private sector.

The small outlays of the First Plan were devoted to laying the organizational foundation for affecting the future development of the small-scale sector. During the First Plan, a network of various all-India boards, such as the Khadi and Village Industries Board, the Handloom Board and the Sericulture Board were established. Also, four regional Small Industries Service Institutes (SISI) were set up to provide technical assistance to small enterprises. At the same time, the National Small Industries Corporation to market the small-scale industries' products was set up. During the Second Plan, 60 Industrial Estates were set up, and the SISIs were spread to all the States with 42 Extension Centres.

The Third Plan proposed to achieve the following policy objectives with regard to the small industries: (i) to increase labour productivity; (ii) to make available institutional finance, subsidies, sales rebates, sheltered markets; (iii) to encourage the spread of small industry to rural areas and small towns, and progressively make it an ancillary type industry to the large-scale industry; and (iv) to organize artisans and craftsmen on cooperative basis. The total public sector outlays on small and village industries during the Third Plan was to be Rs. 264 crores (Rs. 150 in net investments and Rs. 114 on current outlay). The actual public sector outlays for the Third Plan were Rs. 236 crores. However, an additional Rs. 144 crores were also spent during the inter-plan period of 1666–69.

The Fourth Plan reviews the development of the village and small industries over the period 1961–69.[17] The highlights of the review can be seen from Table 60.

While most of the value figures are in current prices and inflate the actual progress, at least some of the plan objectives seem to have been met. The village crafts have been organized in co-ops, and a much larger number of small units have come under the purview of the SIDs.

In a few cases the progress of small industries has been remarkable. The handloom and powerloom cloth production rose from around 200 crore metres or about 30 per cent of the total production of cloth in 1960 to over 300 crore metres or 40 per cent of total cloth production in 1965, and to over 350 crore metres, almost 45 per cent of cloth production, in 1968. Khadi production increased from 5.4 crore sq. metres in 1960–61 to 8.5 crore sq. metres in 1965–66, but declined to 6.6 crore sq. metres in 1968–69.[18]

Between 1960 and 1965 the employment in small factories alone has increased by 8.6 lakhs from 6.7 laks to 15.3 lakhs, while that in medium and large-scale factories together has increased only by 9.4 lakhs, from 21.3 lakhs to 30.7 lakhs (see Table 1). It is conceivable that some of the workers now employed in the small-scale factories were previously in the unorganized village or household industries sector, and this increase may reflect a mere organizational change rather than the creation of new employment. However, the figures seem to indicate some progress in achieving the labour-intensivity employment orientation recommended by the Karve Committee. So far as the productivity objective is concerned, Table 3 indicates that value added per worker increased from Rs. 1657 in 1960 to Rs. 2352 in 1965, or a 42 per cent increase for the small factory, while it increased from Rs. 3816 in 1960 to Rs. 5221 in 1965 (a 36 per cent increase) for the large-scale factory. In absolute terms labour productivity in large industry is greater, but as seen earlier it is at a cost of a more than proportionate

[17] Government of India, *Fourth Five Year Plan, 1969–74*, pp. 284–95.
[18] Ibid.

rise in capital intensity. Our analysis of the marginal ratios has already shown that in the context of a capital-short economy the small-scale industry has shown a preferable record. A reduction in the allotment of Plan outlays to village and small industries clearly can be questioned on the basis of the actual performance of these sectors.

7. The Problems of the Cottage and Small-Scale Industry

While the bulk of the modern small-scale industry in India is a post-Independence phenomenon, the problems they face are also peculiar to a rapidly changing economic scenario of the planning years. Scarce resources, such as imported raw materials, and finances for the initial investment and working capital, do not readily flow to small and relatively unknown entrepreneurs. The rapid technological development has led to a universal increase in the rate of obsolescence of machinery. The shifts in the policy emphasis between capital intensive and labour intensive technologies in the modern industrial sector only add an element of uncertainty to the problem of obsolescence.

New production on a decentralized basis calls for creating new markets. If these are decentralized local markets, the problem may be somewhat milder. If not, a new distributive organization would be required which will mobilize final products from decentralized producer to central markets. Decentralized production not intended for local consumption certainly presupposes a well developed market organization. Furthermore, the production itself calls for dissemination of technical information, development of entrepreneurial abilities, and provision of certain basic facilities such as transport, power, and water. These problems and the measures taken to solve them should be examined to evaluate the future prospects of this sector.

Financing and Credit Facilities

Smaller units constitute the largest proportion of new business and business failures in most economies. The shortage of internal financing makes them particularly vulnerable to market fluctuations. This instability in its turn makes them a poor credit risk.

It was recognized during the early years of planning that in the absence of a proper money market for short-term financing of the working capital needs of the small firms and in the face of the inadequacy of the capital markets for financing the long-term investment needs of the small firm, the government would have to take proper measures geared to meet the financial needs of these industries.

In 1960 a Credit Guarantee Scheme was introduced by the Reserve Bank of India. Under this scheme the Bank would guarantee the repayment with charges of advances made to small enterprises up to Rs. 2 lakhs per enterprise. The number of applicants for the Guarantee Scheme went up from 2,285 in 1961–62 to 32,923 in 1968–69. The amount of loans sanctioned went up from Rs. 76 crores in 1961–62 to Rs. 163 crores in 1968–69.

The State Bank of India, in conjunction with the Reserve Bank, has endeavoured to coordinate various measures to finance small industry. The State Bank itself has advanced Rs. 69 crores to over 12,000 applicants to finance expansion and modernization, and to provide for working capital.

Various state departments of industries have advanced to small-scale industries Rs. 13 crores in the Second Plan and Rs. 17 crores in the Third Plan under the State Aid to Industries Act.

The commercial banks had also participated in lending to small industrial enterprises the amount of Rs. 28 crores in 1960 and Rs. 90 crores in 1966. After nationalization in July 1969 the 14 major banks formulated special schemes for financing small-scale projects. By March 1970 these 14 banks had sanctioned credit limits in excess of Rs. 390 crores to over 37,000 small units.

Besides these measures, financial assistance was provided by the National and State Small Industries Corporation, and the Industrial Cooperatives to some extent.

Raw Material Availability

One of the reasons given by the 1963 International Team for the relative inefficiency of the small enterprises was that the scarce raw material, particularly the imported ones, were allocated more favourably to the large industries by the government. The small units' interests were to be represented by the State and National Small Industries Corporations. However, the Fourth Plan expects regular and adequate supplies of imported and scarce indigenous raw materials to units producing priority items.[19]

The Problems of Marketing

Quality variations in the product and inability to compete with large-scale producers who enjoy marketing economies of scale clearly calls for some organized effort to ensure quality and assist in bringing the product of the small industry to the attention and proximity of the consumer. The National Small Industries Corporation has been active in this field since 1955. The Corporation acts on behalf of small enterprises in bringing government orders and stimulating exports of the output of small enterprises.

There are 17 State Small Industries Corporations for the purpose of distribution of scarce raw materials, supply of machinery on hire-purchase basis, and rendering marketing assistance. The National Small Industries Corporation has supplied machines, both imported and indigenous. This consisted of imported machinery worth Rs. 206 crores and 15 crores of indigenous origin as of 1969. Also, in 1969, 18,223 small scale enterprises were registered with the NSIC for participation in Government Stores Purchase Programme. As of the same year, 24,284 government supply contracts valued at Rs. 161.2 crores have been secured by the NSIC for small enterprises.

Technical Assistance

The shortage of trained and experienced technical and supervisory personnel, and the employment orientation in selecting the technique of production in the earlier years have left the small-scale industries technologically backward. The agency which implements the policy to alleviate this problem is the Central Small Industries Development Organization (CSIDO). The CSIDO, through its Service Institutes and Extension Centres, provides a staff of technically qualified people who advise small industries on technical matters.

In more recent years the thinking of the planners in response to the International Team's recommendations seems to have moved in favour of modern technology, quality control and general efficiency orientation.

As of 1968 the various CSIDO agencies have made available management training to 22,000 persons, completed 252 In-Plant Studies, 150 Industry Analysis Reports, and 272 Industry Prospect Sheets.[20]

8. The Fourth Plan and the Future

The Fourth Plan envisages the modernization of techniques of production for the village and small industries, to improve the quality of their products, to make the enterprises viable and self-sufficient. This emphasis on efficiency emerges from the recommendations of the Khadi and Village Industries Committee (Ashok Mehta Committee). In this connection two factors may be noted: (i) The traditional village industries have the inherent advantage of providing employment on a widespread basis. They require protection from labour displacing modern industries. But to modernize and reorganize the village industry may seem to be a misguided policy, if employment were a major objective. Unlike its predecessors, the Fourth Plan explicitly omit any mention of employment as an objective in connection with the small-scale and village industries. The Plan's employment potential is expected in the large-scale manufacturing, agriculture, construction, etc.;[21] (ii) In analyzing the

---

19 Ibid., p. 290.

20 Government of India, Small-Scale Industries Development Organization, *Development Commissioner's Report for 1968–69,* pp. 2–3.

21 *Fourth Five Year Plan,* pp. 20–21.

factory sector, we saw that the additional rupee invested in the small factory leads to a larger increase in output and in value added, and provides more employment than it does when invested in the large-scale factory (Table 4). If the cottage industry resembles the small factory in this respect, then from the point of view of efficiency also the village and small-scale industry seems to deserve greater attention than it gets in the Fourth Five Year Plan.

In as much as the smaller provisions in the Fourth Plan for village and small industries will be directed towards modernizing (in keeping with the recommendations of Dhar and Lydall, the Second International Team and the Ashok Mehta Committee), its impact on both efficiency and output is likely to be positive. But the reduced share alloted to small industries in comparison with a large increase in the Fourth Plan investment going to the large-scale industry seems to need justifications to counter the findings of our statistical comparisons above. The present policy completes the break away from the Karve Committee's emphasis on providing work to the door-steps of village workers with a view to improving the incomes and living conditions of the great majority of people, and forges its way towards an efficiency-oriented policy.

BIBLIOGRAPHY

All India Khadi and Village Industries Board, *Planning for Full Employment* (Bombay: 1954).

Dey, Sushil K., *Industrial Development: A New Approach* (Calcutta: Thacker, 1955).

International Perspective Planning Team, *Development of Small-Scale Industries in India: Prospects, Problems and Policies* (Delhi: Govt. of India Press, 1963).

Mehta, Vaikunth L., *Decentralized Economic Development* (Bombay: Gramodaya, 1964).

Mitra, Lalit K., *Employment and Output in Small Enterprises in India*, 1967.

Prasad, Kedarnath, *Technological Choice under Developmental Planning* (Bombay: Popular Prakashan, 1963).

Sen, Amartya K., *Choice of Techniques: An Aspect of the Theory of Planned Economic Development*, Third Edition (Oxford: Basil Blackwell, 1968).

Shetty, M. C., *Small-Scale and Household Industries in a Developing Economy* (Bombay: Asia Publishing House, 1963).

Rao, Ch. Umamaheshwara, *Small-Scale Industries: Some Economic Aspects* (Bombay: Popular Prakashan, 1965).

APPENDIX

Table 1. Capital, Employment and Output Estimates for Indian Factory Sector by Value of Fixed Capital 1960, 1963, 1964 and 1965[2]

		Small-scale factories with fixed assets of Rs 5 lakhs or less	%	Medium-scale factories with fixed assets of Rs 5-25 lakhs	%	Large-scale factories with fixed assets of over Rs 25 lakhs	%	Total, all factories including those taking fixed assets on lease or rent basis
Number of Factories	1960	5,421	64.0	1,560[1]	19.0	858[1]	10.0	8,391
	1963	41,851	91.5	2,063[1]	4.5	1,293[1]	2.8	45,757
	1964	41,877	90.5	2,286[1]	4.9	1,499[1]	3.3	46,268
	1965	43,657	90.1	2,477[1]	5.1	1,679[1]	3.5	48,456
Fixed capital (in crores of Rs)	1960	73	5.0	176	14.0	1,040	81.0	1,289
	1963	257	8.1	232	7.3	2,672	84.6	3,161
	1964	274	6.9	260	6.6	3,427	86.5	3,961
	1965	308	6.4	276	5.7	4,248	87.9	4,832
Persons employed (in lakh)	1960	6.7	23.0	6.7	23.0	14.7	51.0	29
	1963	15.0	34.8	7.1	15.7	20.0	47.5	42
	1964	15.0	33.2	7.0	15.7	22.0	49.1	45
	1965	15.3	32.5	6.8	14.5	23.9	51.0	47
Gross output (in crores of Rs)	1960	518	16.0	745	24.0	1,837	58.0	3,151
	1963	1,681	28.9	950	16.3	3,125	53.8	5,811
	1964	1,917	28.5	1,075	16.0	3,665	54.4	6,730
	1965	2,014	26.5	1,172	15.4	4,341	57.2	7,596
Value added by manufacture (in crores of Rs)	1960	111	13.0	182	21.0	561	65.0	864
	1963	302	20.4	217	14.9	929	63.6	1,460
	1964	323	19.4	246	14.7	1,083	64.9	1,669
	1965	360	19.1	260	13.8	1,248	66.3	1,883

SOURCE: *Annual Survey of Industries*, Government of India, Calcutta: Central Statistical Organization, 1963, '66, '68 and '69 issues, Table I.

Notes: 1. Does not include factories taking fixed assets on lease or rent basis.

2. Ratios in subsequent tables are based on rounded figures while figures in Table 1 are rounded.

Table 2. Average Capital, Employment and Output Estimates for Indian Factories by Value of Fixed Capital, 1963-1964

	Year	Small-scale factories	Medium-scale factories	Large-scale factories
Average fixed capital per factory, Rs in lakhs	1963	.61	11.2	206.7
	1964	.65	11.4	228.6
Persons employed average per factory	1963	35	319	1544
	1964	36	311	1484
Gross output per factory, Rs in lakhs	1963	4.0	46.0	241.7
	1964	4.6	47.0	244.5
Average value added per factory, Rs in lakhs	1963	.7	10.5	71.5
	1964	.8	10.8	72.2

Source: Table 1

Table 3. Average Fixed Capital, and Value Added per Employee 1960, 1963, 1964 and 1965

	Year	Small factories	Medium factories	Large factories
		Rs	Rs	Rs
Fixed capital per employee	1960	1,089	2,666	7,075
	1963	1,757	3,521	13,386
	1964	1,820	3,660	15,400
	1965	2,013	4,059	17,757
Gross output per employee	1960	7,731	11,288	12,496
	1963	11,206	13,571	15,625
	1964	12,780	15,357	16,659
	1965	13,163	17,235	18,163
Value added per employee	1960	1,657	2,757	3,814
	1963	2,072	3,299	4,655
	1964	2,150	3,460	4,870
	1965	2,353	3,823	5,221

Source: Table 1

Table 4. Average Employment, Output and Value Added per Rupee Worth of Fixed Capital by Factory Size, 1960, 1963, 1964, 1965

	Year	Small-scale factories	Medium-scale factories	Large-scale factories
Persons employed per rupee worth of fixed capital	1960	.00092	.00038	.00014
	1963	.00058	.00030	.00008
	1964	.00054	.00027	.00006
	1965	.00049	.00025	.00005
Gross ouput per rupee worth of fixed capital	1960	7.09	4.23	1.76
	1963	6.54	4.09	1.16
	1964	6.99	4.13	1.07
	1965	6.54	4.25	1.02
Value added per rupee worth of fixed capital	1960	Rs 1.534	Rs 1.03	Rs 0.53
	1963	1.179	.94	.34
	1964	1.178	.95	.32
	1965	1.169	.94	.29

SOURCE: Table 1

Table 5. Net Investment in the Industries and Total Investment in the Five Year Plans

	First Plan 1951-55 Crore Rs	%	Second Plan 1956-60 Crore Rs	%	Third Plan 1961-65 Crore Rs	%	Fourth Plan 1969-74 Crore Rs	%
Small-scale and cottage industries	175	5	270	5	425	4	746	3
Public sector	25	(15)	120	(45)	150	(35)	185	(25)
Private sector	150	(85)	150	(55)	270	(65)	560	(75)
Large-scale industry including power	865	23	1,810	29	3,632	35	7,821	35
Public sector	380	(44)	1,190	(66)	2,532	(73)	5,747	(73)
Private sector	485	(56)	620	(34)	11,000	(27)	2,064	(27)
Total net investment	3,500	100	6,200	100	10,400	100	22,635	100
Public sector	1,850	(53)	3,800	(61)	6,300	(62)	13,655	(60)
Private sector	1,650	(47)	2,400	(39)	4,100	(38)	8,980	(40)

SOURCE: Various Five Year Plan Documents.

Table 6. Development of the Village and Small Industries, 1961-69

	1960-61	1968-69
Number of small units registered with the State Industries Directorates (SID)	36,000*	140,000
Value of machines supplied on hire-purchase terms	Rs 1.8 crores	Rs 4.5 crores
Value of purchases by Central Government Departments from small industries	Rs 6.5 crores	Rs 28.6 crores
Number of industrial cooperatives including handloom, handicrafts, and processing societies	37,000	51,000
Membership in these Cooperatives	29.2 lakhs	38.8 lakhs
Value of sales by Cooperatives	Rs 111.9 crores	331.9 crores

*1962 figures

7

Transport System and India's Economic Development

VIDYAPATI SINGH

1. Introduction

The transport system of a country consists of different methods of moving commodities or people over space. Among these traffic modes, the major ones are rail, road or highway, water, air, and pipeline, each having a comparative cost and service advantage over other modes in respect to certain types of traffic. Extensions and improvements of these transport modes to provide an economical access to markets as well as to sources of supplies constitute a *sine qua non* for the economic development of a country. The reduced production and marketing costs and increased mobility stemming from the improved transport systems, promote economic development by facilitating the optimal use of resources. Conversely, deficiencies in the transport system inhibit economic development by obstructing the full realization of the production potential. In the light of this role of transport in economic development, this chapter will discuss the crucial importance of improved transport in the Indian economy and will then highlight the deficiencies that exist in her present transport system.

2. Role of Transport in Economic Development—A General Analysis

Improvements in transport capacity contribute to economic development by producing two sets of effects which facilitate and stimulate production leading to an increase in the net national product. They are: 1. incentives for the optimal use of resources and 2. socio-cultural changes conducive to economic progress.

3. Optimal Use of Resources

The extension and improvement of transport facilities generally result in the reduction of transport cost per unit of freight haulage and an improvement in the quality of transport services in the form of faster, safer, smoother, and more dependable transport. All these cost and service dimensions of improved transport promote the optimal use of resources by facilitating productive activities and increasing the productivity of resources employed therein.

Expansion of Productive Activities

As the above features of improved transport reflect in the reduced costs of production and distribution and in the enlargement of product choice, an increase in production becomes profitable except in the extremely limited cases of perfectly inelastic demand in a purely competitive market, and in falling demand. This generally leads to an expansion of productive activities.

Transport and production process. In the production process cost reductions resulting from improved transport take the form of lower costs of assembling the inputs and of maintaining inventories. Assembling costs are affected by the reductions in the costs of hauling the inputs as well as by the reductions in the spoilage or damage to inputs while in transit. When an improvement in transport permits the movement of a given quantity of goods between two points with fewer inputs and the savings in costs in the transport sector are wholly or partly passed on to the users in the form of lower transport charges, the input procurement cost to the producer is correspondingly reduced. Similarly, the safer, smoother, and faster transport service reduces the damage and spoilage of inputs in the course of their movement to the production centre, and thus reduces the input cost by the amount of damage, loss, or insurance cost otherwise incurred. Producers also experience a reduction in the cost of inventory holding as the speed and dependability of transport service allow them to carry on their production with smaller inventories. The decrease in inventory holding reduces the interest and storage costs to the producers. At the same time, the dependability of the transport service allows them to schedule their operations more efficiently.

Transport and distribution process. Costs pertaining to the distribution process are likewise reduced as a result of improved transport. Due to lower transport charges, the producers incur lower costs per unit of freight haulage in moving their products to the market. Also, as in the case of procurement of inputs, marketing costs decline on account of reduced spoilage of the products in transit.

Transport and product choice. In addition to increase in profit potential created by the reduced costs of production and distribution, improved transport widens the range of product choice available to the producers. In particular, the products, which deteriorate so rapidly in course of slow and rough haulage that they cease to be marketable by the time they reach the market, tend to be produced for the market when the relevant service dimensions of transport are improved.

As a result of the above effects of improved transport, productive activities are facilitated and the output of products, particularly of those having elastic or growing demand, is increased. In this process idle resources are put into production and, as explained below, the productivity of the resources so employed rises.

Increase in Input Productivity

Improvements in transport contribute to gains in input productivity by promoting (1) large scale production, (2) geographical specialization, (3) change in product mix, and (4) other production economies.

Large scale production. By providing economical access to both the sources of inputs as well as to the markets, improved transport encourages the establishment of large production units in the industries characterized by large scale economies. In this way, it permits the realization of the resultant scale economies arising from greater division of labour, use of specialized machines, proportionally less idle reserve capacity, etc. As a result of these economies, the productivity of the employed inputs increases, since a larger output is produced with a given amount of inputs.

Geographical specialization. Reduced transport costs also permit the territorial specialization of production whereby each community specializes in the production of goods for which it has the greatest advantage, sells the marketable surplus to other communities, and obtains other commodities from them. Thus, the resources of each community are more effectively employed, bringing about an increase in their productivity.

Change in product mix. Similarly, improved transport facilitates the allocation of resources away from the production of less valuable products to that of more valuable products relative to their production and distribution costs. This, too, results in an increase in the productivity of inputs so shifted.

Other production economies. Gains in input productivity also occur as improved transport permits the given level of production with smaller inventories and reduces the spoilage and damage to inputs and products in transit. There is an increase in productivity in the transport sector as well, as improvements and innovations in this sector make it possible to move a given quantity of goods or people with fewer inputs.

4. Socio-Cultural Changes

In addition to creating economic incentives for the optimal use of resources, improvements in transport promote socio-cultural changes conducive to economic development by facilitating the movement of people and ideas. Contacts with modern and progressive communities influence the attitudes and values of the formerly isolated communities in favour of more productive economic pursuits and overcome their prejudices which are barriers to these pursuits. This may lead them to undertake new enterprises and to increase the duration and intensity of work, thereby causing an increase in their labour productivity. Also, by promoting national cohesion and political and social unity, the improved transport network creates a favourable environment for national economic progress.

5. Historical Experience

The contributions of improved transport to economic development discussed above have been, in fact, experienced by the present developed countries. In all these countries, economic development proceeded as the transport barriers were overcome. The experiences of the United States and Britain are illustrative of this. Until the early thirties of the nineteenth century the United States economy, except coastal plantations, remained, a subsistent agricultural economy, due to high costs of overland transport. But when the construction of canals and turnpikes reduced transport costs considerably, a territorial division of labour followed, New England and the East specializing in manufacturing, the South in sugar, and the West in wheat. Later, the construction of railways further reduced the cost of internal transport and brought new areas and products into the stream of commerce. The railway boom also increased the demand for railway supplies and equipment which, in turn, further stimulated the industrialization process by supporting development in other sectors such as coal, iron, steel, etc.[1] Similarly, transport played a key role in British economic development. The development of her shipping industry gave a great impetus to her economy by carrying the products of her industries to mass markets, by providing access to new resources and technical progress in primary producing countries, and by creating world demand for her new products,[2] while improvements in her internal transport unified the economy, removed barriers to urbanization, and directly stimulated the development of her heavy industries.[3]

On the other hand, the shortage of improved transport and absence of appropriate transport policy of colonial governments in less developed countries inhibited their economic development. In India, agriculture remained largely subsistent in character and her internal industrial development

[1] Wilfred Owen, *Strategy for Mobility* (Washington, D. C. : The Brookings Institution, 1964), pp. 22–31.

[2] W. W. Rostow (ed.), *The Economics of Take-Off into Sustained Growth* (London : Macmillan, 1965), pp. 77–80.

[3] Phyllis Deane and W. A. Cole, *British Economic Growth, 1688–1959 : Trends and Structure* (London : Cambridge University Press, 1962), pp. 238–240.

Table 1. Basic Transport Data, Selected Countries, 1969

Country	Railway density[a]	Paved road density[b]	Vehicles per 1000 population
France	0.072	1.142	262.0
Germany	0.136	1.168	209.3
Japan	0.065	0.344	119.6
United States	0.038	0.270	491.9
India	0.018	0.099	2.5

SOURCE: World Bank, *Transportation: Sector Working Paper* (Washington, D.C., 1972), pp. 42-45.

[a]Railway route length in kilometres divided by area of the country in square kilometres.

[b]Paved road length in kilometres divided by area of the country in square kilometres.

and social transformation suffered in the absence of adequate and efficient transport. Table 1, gives basic data pertaining to India's transport capacity compared to those of selected developed countries. This information also illustrates the relative inadequacy of her transport system and highlights the needs for improvements therein to meet her development requirements.

6. Crucial Importance of Transport to Indian Economy

In view of the developmental role of transport analyzed above, the state of India's transport system has acquired a crucial importance in the context of her successive Five Year Plans for economic development and social transformation. As these Plans seek to achieve the above objectives by developing India's agriculture and industries and by changing the structure of socio-economic relations, appropriate improvements in her transport capacity are a prerequisite to the success of these efforts.

7. Role of Transport in Agricultural Development

One of the major obstacles to progressive agriculture in India has been the lack of all-weather village-to-market roads. A large number of villages still lack road links with market towns and with one another.[4] In 1968 it was estimated that 85 per cent of the roads linking villages to the nearest surfaced roads were mere tracks unsuitable for vehicle movement.[5] The effects of such inadequacy of rural transport are reflected in the prevalence of subsistent farming and low agricultural productivity in most regions of the country. The subsistent character of Indian agriculture is evident from the findings of the All-India Rural Debt and Investment Survey, according to which in 1961–62 as much as 69 per cent of the total value of the agricultural output of the country was retained for self-consumption by the cultivator households themselves.[6] The resultant low agricultural productivity in India is similarly evident from the comparative world data. Just to mention two crops, rice and wheat, as illustrative of low productivity, the yield of rice per hectare in 1966–67 was 1,290 kilograms in India compared to 5,090 kilograms in Japan and 4,850 kilograms in U.S.A., and that of wheat was 890 kilograms in India compared to 3,840 kilograms in the United Kingdom and 2,830 kilograms in France.[7]

It is by facilitating the transformation of largely subsistent and less productive agriculture into highly productive commercial agriculture that rural road improvements

4 Planning Commission, *Fourth Five Year Plan, 1969–74* (Delhi: Government of India, 1970), p. 344.

5 Wilfred Owen, *Distance and Development: Transport and Communications in India* (Washington, D. C.: The Brookings Institution, 1968), p. 52.

6 "All India Rural Debt and Investment Survey 1961–62," *Reserve Bank of India Bulletin* (December 1965), pp. 1860 and 1866–67.

7 Ruddar Datt and K. P. M. Sundharam, *Indian Economy* (New Delhi: Niraj Prakashan, 1969), p. 305.

would make a prime contribution to the development of Indian agriculture. The incentives for such transformation would arise from the improvements in village-to-market roads in the form of reduced costs of production and marketing. As a result of these incentives, agricultural productivity would rise because of an increase in agricultural production per hectare of farm land and a change in agricultural production mix.

Increase in Agricultural Production

Road improvements would contribute to a decline in both average and marginal costs of production by encouraging the use of more productive inputs and farming techniques as well as by reducing the costs of holding inventory of inputs and of procuring inputs from the market. Improved communication and mobility provided by all-weather roads would expose farmers to modern agricultural practices that have proved profitable elsewhere. Visits to model farms and contact with progressive farmers would, thus, motivate them to adopt similar farming methods leading to a significant decrease in the average and marginal costs of their production. At the same time, the year-round access to the market would obviate the need for acquiring commercial inputs much in advance of their timely application. The resultant saving in interest and storage costs otherwise incurred in maintaining the inventory would similarly reduce the average and marginal costs of production. In addition to these sources of reduction in production costs, the access to all-weather motorable roads would also reduce the input costs to the farmers by permitting them to substitute low-cost motor truck transport for high-cost bullock cart transport in the procurement of farm inputs from the market.

In the marketing of farm products as well, rural road improvements would contribute to cost reductions by lowering the costs of transporting them to market and by reducing their spoilage while in transit. As in the haulage of farm inputs, improved roads would permit a shift to truck transport in the marketing of farm products and would thus reduce the marketing costs. That cost savings do arise from such a shift has been corroborated by the findings of the case studies conducted in the Kanpur area during 1963–64. The studies showed that in the marketing of ground nuts, the average transport charge paid by farmers was only 2.1 paises per maund per mile when 150 maunds were hauled by truck over a distance of 50 miles compared to the average transport charge of 5.5 paises per maund per mile for a 20-mile trip by bullock cart.[8] As to the reduction in spoilage of farm products, it is estimated that one-fourth to one-third of all the fruit and vegetable production in India is lost through poor handling, much of the loss occurring in transit.[9] Improved and expeditious haulage of these products would reduce such losses considerably, and would thereby cause a further reduction in marketing costs.

While the cost reductions permitted by improved rural transport would create incentives for expanding production for the market, there is no likelihood of a sharp decline in the prices of farm products to completely offset these incentives. The market demand for agricultural commodities in India is potentially very high due to population growth, increasing urbanization, progress in industrialization, and rising income. As such, in spite of a large expansion in agricultural output, the agricultural price level would tend to remain relatively stable. Thus, the (average and marginal) revenue from the sale of farm products remaining largely unchanged, the reduction in the (average and marginal) costs of production and marketing would induce farmers to adopt improved farming techniques to expand output for sale so as to maximize their returns from farm operation.

Change in Agricultural Production Mix

Athough access to all-weather roads would promote the production of all agricultural commodities, its impact is likely to be relatively greater in the production of soft and

8 Wilfred Owen, Ibid., pp. 53–55.

9 Ibid, p. 71.

highly perishable farm products. These are products, such as milk, eggs, poultry, fresh fruits, fresh vegetables, etc., which lend themselves to year-round production and, therefore, require almost daily use of the road for their marketing. These products are also easily susceptible to spoilage on account of rough and slow haulage. Because of these characteristics, the lack of all-weather village-to-market roads act as a great deterrent to the expansion of their production for the market.

But these are products which have prospects of high returns relative to the costs of their production. The income elasticity of demand for these products being much greater than for the so-called hardware farm products (such as cereals and pulses), the demand for them would continue to increase at a faster rate than for the latter group of products. The extent of demand advantage which these products have can be inferred from the coefficients of income elasticity calculated by the Food and Agriculture Organization of the United Nations for 1957–59 for India. They are: 2.2 for eggs, 1.7 for milk and milk products, 1.4 for meat, and 1.0 for fruits and vegetables compared to 0.5 for cereals, 0.3 for pulses and nuts, and 0.2 for starchy roots.[10] As a result, with an improved access to market, it would be profitable to allocate a progressively increasing portion of farm resources to the production of these products, leading to a further increase in agricultural productivity. Wherever improved roads have been provided, such changes in the agricultural production pattern have already occurred. As an instance, when a 12-foot tarred road was built to connect the village of Wazirpur (Gurgaon district, Haryana) with a neighbouring town, the commercial production of vegetables and milk in the village increased significantly.[11] Similar effects of rural road improvements have also been observed in other developing countries.

10 John W. Mellor, Thomas F. Weaver, Uma J. Lele *et al., Developing Rural India: Plan and Practice* (New York: Cornell University Press, Ithaca, 1968), p. 25.

11 Wilfred Owen, ibid., p. 59.

8. Role of Transport in Industrial Development

While improvements in village-to-market roads are a prerequisite to the development of Indian agriculture, it is the improvements in inter city transport which would play a crucial role in facilitating the industrialization of the country. The progress in industrialization involves a large increase in the movement of freight and people to supply industrial plants and urban population with inputs and food and to deliver industrial products to the market. An indication of the transport needs arising in this process is provided by the relationship between the growth of freight and passenger traffic and the growth of net national product. As experienced in India, during the period, 1948–57, which covered her First and the initial phase of her Second Five Year Plan, the net national product of the country grew at an annual rate of only 2.5 per cent, but her rail and road freight traffic increased at the annual rate of 8 per cent, and her rail and road passenger traffic rose at the annual rate of 5 per cent.[12] In view of such a disproportionate increase in transport needs, a concurrent improvement in transport capacity is crucially important for the achievement of industrialization goals. This is specifically relevant to the conditions in India as her basic transport plant and equipment were inadequate and mostly in a state of disrepair when she launched her First Five Year Plan, and in spite of progress since then, the relative lag in appropriate improvements, integration, and coordination has inhibited the full realization of the industrial development potential.

To permit the realization of such potential, it is of vital importance that each component of her industrial complex has access to the most economical mode in terms of its specific transport needs. As the transport needs of heavy industries differ in character from those of light and agricultural processing industries, the improvement of the relevant modes to meet their respective transport needs is essential for their optimal development.

12 Wilfred Owen, *Strategy for Mobility*, p. 49.

Transport and Development of Heavy Industries

Heavy industries involve a relatively long haulage of bulk inputs and heavy products in order to exploit their inherent scale economies. At the same time, their inputs (such as coal, mineral ore, etc.) command low value relative to their bulk, and therefore, cannot stand high transport charges. The same is largely true in respect to their products as well. Similarly, the food grains that have to be hauled from progressively long distances to feed the industrial population are, too, low-value high-bulk commodities. As such, for their development, heavy and mining industries need access to transport modes that provide the cheapest possible long haul transport for their inputs and products. As railways, along with water transport and pipelines as supplementary modes, have a technological comparative advantage in this regard, cost-reducing improvements and innovations in them would facilitate and promote the development of these industries.

The inherent superiority of railways and water transport in the long distance movement of bulk commodities lies in their very low line-haul costs and high terminal costs. Because of the mass transport units used by these modes, their line-haul costs are very low per unit of freight (or passenger) haulage. However, their high terminal costs (e.g., loading and unloading, forming and breaking of trains, switching of wagons, turning round of ships, etc.) make them high cost transport modes for the short haul but as the terminal cost per unit of freight (or passenger) haulage decreases with the increase in the length of haul, these transport modes are technologically capable of offering low cost transport services for long hauls. The technological superiority of these modes increases as improvements and innovations are effected by the use of diesel locomotives, electrification of railway line, use of unit trains, introduction of microwave and computers in railway communications, mechanization of port operations, etc., which reduce the line haul and terminal costs significantly. A further reduction in terminal costs as well as in transit time and packaging costs arises from operational integration between rail, water, and truck transport by the introduction of interchangeable containers and piggy-back operations (carrying truck-trailers on railway flat cars).

The reduction in transport charges and increase in speed and dependability of the transport service, resulting from the above mentioned improvements and innovations, reduce the production and distribution costs of heavy mining, and large industries, and thus promote their development. As regards the reduction in these costs, it may be specifically pointed out that, apart from reduced procurement and marketing costs and greater scale economies, these improvements would substantially reduce the inventory costs inasmuch as Indian firms at present hold excessive quantities of raw materials and intermediates in their inventories, one of the chief reasons being slow and undependable transport.[13] The improvements in internal transport and port operations would also promote exports and Indian shipping, thereby augmenting the scarce foreign exchange earnings of the country. In addition to railway, shipping, and port improvements, pipelines have a specialized role in the development of gas, oil, and petroleum industries as they are the most economical mode for moving a large volume of these products.

Transport and Development of Light Consumer Goods and Agricultural Processing Industries

As India is a densely populated country with a rising per capita disposable income, most plants producing consumer goods and processing agricultural products can fully realize their scale economies even if each serves a relatively small market area. Furthermore, by being located close to the market, they can also reduce their distribution costs significantly. In promoting these industries, therefore, improvements in inter city road transport would play a key role in view of the comparative advantage of this mode in providing short haul and protective transport. Because of its insignificant terminal costs, its short haul costs

---

[13] Jagdish N. Bhagwati and Padma Desai, *India: Planning for Industrialization* (London: Oxford University Press, 1970), pp. 324–25.

are lower than those of railways and other modes in spite of its relatively high operating variable costs. In addition to the lower short haul costs of truck transport, it can also offer a personalized, flexible, and fast service, thereby reducing the packaging and inventory costs of the producers. It can be economical for intermediate hauls too.

As such, the improvements of inter city roads and growth of truck transport would stimulate the establishment of these plants near the market, and would thus promote the geographical dispersal of these industries. In the case of agricultural processing industries, there would be an additional incentive for their dispersal since their location close to the sources of inputs as well, would permit them to reduce the costs of hauling the weight that is lost in the course of processing.

9. Social Transformation

There are certain social institutions in India which discourage effort, savings, factor mobility, and adoption of highly productive techniques that are vital for economic development. At the same time, these institutions often facilitate the economic exploitation of one social class by another. They are the caste system and joint family system. The caste system hinders the occupational mobility of labour, discourages productive manual work on the part of high castes, disfavours productive techniques that are considered impure, encourages waste of scarce resources on unproductive caste rituals, and has created a non-homogeneous society. It has also permitted the economic exploitation and social humiliation of low castes and untouchables by the high castes. Similarly, the joint family system discourages initiative, enterprise, thrift and hard work by providing economic security to all the members of the joint family and by removing the direct relation between one's effort and its rewards. It also contributes to factor immobility and family tension by encouraging stay-at-home habits.

These institutions are predominant in rural India due primarily to the ignorance of modern values and lack of access to better socio-economic alternatives. Improvements in rural-urban transport would reduce their adverse effects by facilitating interactions between rural and urban populations and by providing access to employment opportunities and largely impersonal social environments in urban centres. The constant inflow of modern and dynamic views made possible by improved mobility and communications would embolden the members of the rural castes and families to effectively protest against oppressive and unproductive actions and to adopt modern productive techniques and behaviour. Thus, the socio-economic restrictions and exploitation would decline to the benefit of economic progress, social cohesion, and better understanding.

While the growth of the rural-urban bus service in combination with the rail passenger service would play a key role in this regard, the growth of all general modes of traffic would further help in promoting national political unity by facilitating the nationwide mobility of people and other inputs as well as by permitting the fast movement of police and army in the event of internal disturbance or external aggression.

10. Transport System in India Today

The present transport system of India consists of railways, roads, coastal and overseas shipping, inland waterways, air transport, and pipelines. The capacity of these modes as it existed in 1968–69 is depicted in Table 2.

Although the transport capacity presented in Table 2 represents a great improvement over the condition prevailing at the beginning of the First Five Year Plan period, a number of deficiencies and problems still characterize the Indian transport system. A brief discussion of the progress and problems of India's major transport modes, viz. railways, road transport, shipping, and civil air transport, follows.

11. Railways

At the beginning of the First Plan period, the Indian railways had less than 54,000

Table 2. Indian Transport System, 1968-1969

Plant and Equipment	Capacity
Railways route length (kms.)	59,553
Surfaced roads (thousand (kms.)	325
Commercial road vehicles (thousand nos.)	386
Shipping (thousand grt.)	2,140
Major ports traffic handled (lakh tons)	550
Inland waterways (kms.)	13,500
Airlines capacity (lakh ton-kilometres)	6,700
Pipelines (kms)	3,166

SOURCE: Government of India, Planning Commisssion, *Fourth Five Year Plan, 1969-74* (Delhi: Publications Branch, 1970), p. 337; Data for inland waterways and pipelines are for 1966 from Planning Commission, *Committee on Transport Policy and Coordination, Final Report, 1966*, pp. 142 and 152-53.

kilometres of lines and their rolling stock was in urgent need of replacement. To meet the growing rail transport needs arising out of the planned economic development of the country, a significant improvement has since been made in the railway capacity by way of construction of new lines and modernization of their equipment and operation. The modernization process has included dieselization, route electrification, conversion of metre gauge lines into broad gauge, and doubling of track. The resultant increase in railway capacity since 1950–51 is shown in Table 3.

Table 3. Railway Route Length and Traffic, 1950-51 to 1968-69

Year	Route length (kilometres)	Freight traffic (crore ton-kilometres)	Passenger traffic crore passenger (kilometres)
1950-51	53,596	4400	6700
1955-56	55,011	6000	6200
1960-61	56,247	8800	7800
1965-66	58,399	11700	9600
1968-69	59,553	12500	10700

SOURCE: Government of India, Planning Commission, *Fourth Five Year Plan 1969-74*, (Delhi: Publications Branch, 1970), p. 337; earlier data from Government of India, *India, A Reference Annual, 1971-72*, p. 428 and Wilfred Owen, *Distance and Development*: *Transport and Communications in India* (Washington, D. C; The Brookings Institution, 1968), pp. 17 and 42.

However, there are three areas in which improvements have been found lacking or inadequate. First, there has been only a limited introduction of direct trains and computerized communications in railway operation and communications. Direct trains can move large quantities of bulk commodities between points of major traffic origin and destinations such as mines, ports, and industrial plants, bypassing intermediate freight yards, and can thus reduce the hauling costs and time considerably. Similarly, the introduction of modern computerized (or micro-wave) communications on traffic demands and rolling stock availability can greatly increase railway capacity and performance. Second, the railway transport is not integrated and adequately coordinated with other modes. The increasing adoption of interchangeable containers, piggyback operations, pick-up and delivery services, and coordination measures (to be discussed subsequently) can reduce the costs to shippers and to the economy significantly. Third, the present railway rate structure, in spite of recent revisions, still fails to reflect the regional transport cost variation in the rates and provides concessional rates to certain commodities which do not cover the costs of moving them. As a result, the users of high density lines are denied the advantage of the lower costs of these lines, and the industrial location is distorted. Similarly, railway rates in excess of costs of transport service charged for the long distance haulage of general cargo tend to divert such freight to a mode (such as truck transport) which is inherently inefficient as a long-haul carrier. Such a diversion likewise results in a misallocation of resources by misdirecting transport development and industrial location.

12. Roads and Road Transport

The road system of India was very inadequate in terms of both its kilometreage and condition when the First Five Year Plan went into effect. During the First and Second Plan periods, road development programmes broadly followed the recommendations of the Nagpur Plan. At the end of the Second Plan, a new twenty-year road development plan for 1961–81 was formulated which provided for the increase in road mileage, improvement in road surface, and the road development in a way so that no village should remain more than four miles from a metalled road or more than $1\frac{1}{2}$ miles from any type of road. The progress in road development and road transport since 1950–51 is shown in Table 4.

Table 4. Progress in Road Development and Road Transport, 1950-51 to 1968-69

Year	Surfaced roads (kilometres in thousand)	Unsurfaced roads (kilometres in thousand)	Trucks & buses (number in thousand)	*Road Traffic* Freight (ton-kilometres in crore)	Passenger (passenger kilometres in crore)
1950-51	156	242	116	6	2300
1955-56	182	314	166	9	3200
1960-61	236	448	225	17	5700
1965-66	287	551	333	34	8200
1968-69	325	639	386	40	9800

SOURCE: Government of India, Planning Commission, *Fourth Five Year Plan 1969-74*, (Delhi: Publications Branch, 1970), p. 337; data for 1950-51 and 1955-56 from Planning Commission, *Committee on Transport Policy and Coordination, Final Report*, p. 62 and Wilfred Owen, *Distance and Development: Transport and Communications in India*, (Washington, D.C., The Brookings Institution, 1967), pp. 17, 26, and 42; unsurfaced road kilometrage are for 1961, 1966, and 1969 from Government of India, *India, A Reference, Annual 1971-72*, p. 436.

In spite of the above-mentioned progress in road development, there are still large deficiencies in the road system. The observations of the Planning Commission in this regard run as follows: "The national highway system has about 400 kilometres of missing road links and 17 missing major bridges. Of the total length of 24,000 kilometres of national highways, about two-thirds have single-lane width. The state road system also suffers from....inadequate road length, ...substandard surfaces, narrow width and weak bridges. .... Many economically backward regions have poor communications. A large number of villages still lack road links with market towns and with one another."[14]

The road transport industry, too, faces several serious problems. Apart from high costs of vehicular operation caused by the poor condition of roads, it is subjected to a very restrictive regulation of the state governments, and is burdened by heavy taxes. Further, there is a scarcity of motor vehicles due to their limited domestic production. The costs of financing the purchase of motor vehicles and the operation of transport service, too, are high because of inadequate and costly financing facilities available to the operators. This has also led to the preponderance of small unviable operators in the industry, and consequently to the loss of the economies of firm size.[15]

13. Road-Rail Coordination

Since rail transport has a comparative cost advantage with respect to long hauls and heavy traffic routes, whereas road transport has a comparative cost advantage in respect to short hauls and light traffic routes, and since the characteristics of their services also differ, the development of both these modes in the light of their respective technological superiorities is essential to ensure the least social cost of meeting the transport needs catered by them. This requires a coordination between them so that, instead of engaging in wasteful competition, they may function as supplementary modes in the transport system.

However, the governmental policies for ensuring coordination between these two modes have in the past been so restrictive of road transport that its development in terms of its comparative cost and service advantage has been handicapped. The Motor Vehicles Act of 1939 specifically provided that goods vehicles were not to be allowed to operate outside the region of the state in which they were registered. In 1950 the Government of India issued a "Code of Principles and Practice" to the state governments which suggested that regional transport authorities should not normally grant, renew, or countersign a carrier's permit for carriage of goods for a distance exceeding 75 miles between places connected by rail, and that in similar circumstances the state transport authorities should not normally issue, countersign, or renew a permit for carriage of goods for a distance exceeding 150 miles. In practice, state governments continued to impose a variety of even greater restrictions on truck transport, particularly in respect of distance. To ease some of these restrictions and to set up the Inter-state Transport Commission for developing inter-state road transport, the Motor Vehicles Act of 1939 was amended in 1956, and recommendations for the liberalization of regulatory practices were forwarded to the state governments in 1959.[16] Such growing recognition of the role of road transport needs to be extended to that of recognizing the declining role of railways in respect to traffic for which road transport provides a more economical and efficient service.

14. Shipping

In view of the importance of India's coastal shipping as a supplement to overland transport in the movement of coal, salt, cement, oil products, and general dry cargo and of her overseas shipping as a means of promoting her international trade and conserving scarce foreign exchange by carrying the growing volume of imports and exports, the Government of India has taken several measures to develop the shipping industry. In 1950 it accepted the policy of reservation of coastal shipping for Indian tonnage. Several private shipping companies have been granted loans by the Government or the Shipping Development Fund Committee to replace their ships. Two shipping corporations (Eastern Shipping Corporation and Western Shipping Corporation) were set up in the public sector in the 1950's to engage in overseas shipping, and they were merged into the Shipping Corporation of India in 1961. In addition, the successive Five Year Plans have provid-

---

[14] Planning Commission, *Fourth Five Year Plan, 1969–74*, op. cit. p. 344.

[15] Planning Commission, *Committee on Transport Policy and Coordination, Final Report, 1966*, (New Delhi: Government of India) pp. 76–94.

[16] Ibid., pp. 78–80.

ed for the construction of shipyards, rehabilitation and modernization of major ports and the development of selected intermediate, minor, and ancillary ports, including the development of Paradeep, Mangalore, and Tuticorin into all-weather major ports and of Haldia and Nheva Sheva as ancillary ports.

As a result of the above policies and efforts, the gross registered tonnage of Indian-owned ships in coastal trade increased from 217 thousand in 1951 to 330 thousand in 1968–69, and that in overseas trade increased from 173 thousand in 1951 to 1,810 thousand in 1968–69. By 1952 the entire coastal trade began moving in Indian ships, and by the end of the Third Plan period Indian tonnage catered about 15 per cent of the overseas trade.[17]

The chief deficiencies that tend to impair the efficiency of shipping industry are: (1) inadequacy of modern ships (e.g., specialized modern bulk carriers, containerized general cargo ships, etc.), and (2) inadequacy of mechanized bulk handling facilities in the ports. They have contributed to high costs of ship operation on account of low productivity and high maintenance and repair costs of old and overaged vessels engaged particularly in coastal shipping. Also, the total tonnage is itself small relative to India's international trade.

15. Civil Air Transport

The growth of civil air transport in India has been primarily a post-war phenomenon. A policy for the development of domestic and international air services with government help was adopted by the Government of India in 1946 under which the Air Transport Licensing Board was constituted to issue licences to a limited number of private firms. Subsequently, in 1950 civil aviation was nationalized and in 1953 the Air Transport Corporation Act was passed. According to this Act, domestic air services are operated by the Indian Airlines Corporation and international air services are operated by Air India. A limited number of private firms operate unscheduled domestic air services. The progress of Indian air transport since 1955–56 is shown in Table 5.

Table 5. Indian Air Transport Capacity and Operation, 1955-56 to 1968-1969

Year	Capacity (ton-kilometres in lakh)		Revenue (ton-kilometres in lakh)	
	Air India	IAC	Air India	IAC
1955-56	560	840	n. a.	n. a.
1960-61	1620	1130	760	830
1965-66	3240	1550	1490	1080
1968-69	4620	2080	2250	1530

SOURCE: Government of India, Planning Commission, *Fourth Five Year Plan, 1969-74*, (Delhi, Publications Branch, 1970), p. 337 and *Committee on Transport Policy and Coordination, Final Report, 1966*, p. 156.

However, there is a need for the further extension of air services to decentralize industrial activity and promote international tourism. As air transport is essential for business travel and for procuring emergency supplies, industrial dispersal and regional development would be promoted by providing air linkage to new and potential industrial-cum-commercial centres. Similarly, the extended air service, along with other tourist facilities, would attract a larger volume of tourist travel and would keep the international tourists in the country for a longer period, thereby increasing the country's foreign exchange earnings.

[17] Planning Commission, *Fourth Five Year Plan, 1969–74*, op. cit. p. 347 and *First Five Year Plan*, p. 467.

16. Overall View

The transport capacity of India has increased significantly since the First Five Year Plan for economic development and social transformation went into effect. Continuous improvements in all modes of India's transport system have contributed to this. However, serious transport inadequacies still prevail which inhibit the pace of economic development and social change.

The state of rural transport is still extremely inadequate. Similarly, the potential contribution of inter city road transport to economic development has not been fully exploited due to the poor condition of roads, restrictive regulation, and other handicaps to which it is subjected.

Also, integration and coordination between transport modes are still inadequate. The lack of integration reflects itself in higher costs and greater delays to the users, and impairs the efficiency of the transport system as a whole. The coordination between transport modes, particularly between railways and road transport, has not progressed enough to realize their respective comparative cost and service advantages. Because of the technological superiority of railways in the long distance movement of bulk commodities and passengers on heavy traffic routes, their operation should be largely concentrated in this area, whereas road transport should be developed to serve other categories of overland traffic.

BIBLIOGRAPHY

Fromm, Gary (ed.), *Transport Investment and Economic Development* (Washington, D. C.: Brookings Institution, 1965), Chapter 3.

Government of India, Planning Commission, *Committee on Transport Policy and Coordination, Final Report* (New Delhi: 1966).

Government of India, Planning Commission, *Fourth Five Year Plan, 1969–74,* Publications Branch, 1970 and also *First, Second, Third Five Year Plans,* chapter on Transport and Communications.

Locklin, D. Phillip, *Economics of Transportation,* seventh edition, Richard D. Irwin (Illinois: Homewood, 1972), Chapters 1 and 4.

Owen, Wilfred, *Distance and Development: Transport and Communications in India* (Washington, D. C.: Brookings Institution, 1968).

———, *Strategy for Mobility* (Washington, D. C.: Brookings Institution, 1964), Chapters 1 and 3.

Wilson, George W., Bergmann, Barbara R., Hirsch Leon V., *et al., The Impact of Highway Investment on Development* (Washington, D. C.: Brookings Institution, 1966), Chapters 1, 7 and 8.

Part Three

ECONOMIC POLICY AND PLANNING

8

Industrial Policy of India: The Nature and Growth of Public Sector in India

U. SANKAR

1. Introduction

EVEN before the attainment of Independence, the need for economic planning was recognized by the National Planning Committee and the authors of Bombay Plan, People's Plan, and Gandhian Plan. While the different planning groups agreed on the role of the state in the development of basic and heavy industries, public utilities, and other infrastructural services, they disagreed on questions such as the respective roles of the state in industrial development, nationalization of industries and on the methods of regulating the economic system.

One of the important tasks of the national government was, therefore, to announce its industrial policy. The First Industrial Policy Resolution, announced in 1948, envisaged a mixed economy for India. It defined the respective roles of the public and private sector in industrial development and outlined the methods of regulating the private sector. Six years later, the government's ideas about the nature and objectives of economic policy were more precisely defined when the Parliament adopted the socialist pattern of society. This phrase means that "the basic criterion for determining lines of advance must not be private profit, but social gain, and that the pattern of development and the structure of socio-economic relations should be so planned that they result not only in appreciable increases in national income and employment but also in greater equality in income and wealth." The adoption of the socialist pattern of society necessitated the announcement of the Second Industrial Policy Resolution in 1956. This Resolution stressed that a large and growing public sector was essential in order to achieve the "socialist ideal" and rapid development. It also emphasized that private enterprises would have to fit into the framework of the economic and social policy of the state and remain subject to various regulations.

The plan of this chapter is as follows: Section 1 deals with the allocation of industries between the public and private sectors. Section 2 reviews the methods used for regulating the private sector and examines their effectiveness. Section 3 reviews the nature and growth of the public sector and examines problems related to planning, initiation, and working of public enterprises. Section 4 contains some concluding remarks.

2. Roles of the Public and Private Sectors in Industrial Development

The first formal enunciation of the relative roles of the public and private sectors in industrial development was outlined in the Industrial Policy Resolution, April 6, 1948. This Resolution stated that any improvement in the economic condition of the country required an increase in national wealth and not just a mere redistribution of existing wealth. It assigned a progressively active role for the state in the development of industries, but admitted that, under existing conditions, "the mechanism and resources of the state may not permit it to function forthwith in industry as widely as may be desirable." The state could contribute to the increase in national wealth "by expanding its present activities wherever it is already operating and by concentrating on new units of production in other fields, rather than on acquiring and running existing units. Meanwhile, private enterprise, properly directed and regulated, has a valuable role to play."

This Resolution classified industries into four categories.

The first category covered arms and ammunitions, atomic energy and rail transport. The central government was to have monopoly in these industries.

The second category covered coal, mineral oils, iron and steel, and the manufacture of aircraft and of telecommunications equipment. "Except where, in the national interest, the state itself finds it necessary to secure the cooperation of private enterprise," the state was to have exclusive access to the setting up of new undertakings in this category. All existing private enterprises in this category would be free to develop for a period of ten years during which they would be allowed all facilities for efficient working and reasonable expansion. At the end of this period, the government would review the situation and if the state decided to acquire any existing undertaking, it would provide compensation on a "fair and equitable basis."

The third category covered 18 industries: automobiles, tractors, prime movers, electric engineering, heavy machinery, machine tools, heavy chemicals, fertilizers, electro-chemical industries, rubber manufactures, power and industrial alcohol, cotton and woollen textiles, cement, paper, salt, sugar, air and sea transport, minerals, and defence industries. The government felt that for industries in this category planning and regulation were essential in the national interest.

The fourth category covering the remainder of the field was left open to private enterprise, but the state would progressively participate and "would not hesitate to intervene whenever the progress of private enterprise was unsatisfactory."

The Resolution also contained promises of assistance to the private sector. The removal of transport bottlenecks, the facilitation of the import of essential raw materials, the imposition of tariffs to prevent unfair foreign competition, and the adjustment of taxation to encourage productive investment were specified as governmental responsibilities.

The declaration of the government's industrial policy within less than eight months after Independence had helped to remove some of the uncertainties facing industrialists on to the role of the public sector and the attitude of the government towards the private sector. The announcement that existing undertakings in the second category would not be nationalized for a period of ten years, and the promise that if the government chooses to acquire any existing undertaking at the end of the period it would pay "fair and equitable compensation" provided a healthy atmosphere for new investments in the private sector.

It appears that the four-fold classification of industries was based more on pragmatic rather than on ideological considerations. Despite the well-known socialist leanings of the government, public utilities (with the exception of railways) and heavy industries, such as heavy engineering, heavy chemicals, and machine tools, were listed only in the third or the fourth category.

The influence of this Resolution on the First Five Year Plan was minimal. In fact, the authors of the First Plan wrote: "The scope and need for development are so great it is best for the public sector to develop those industries in which private sector is unable or unwilling to put up the resources required and run the risks involved, leaving the rest of the field for private enterprise" (p. 422).

Hanson[1] rightly points out that at that time the government was more interested in the control of private enterprises than in the public-private balance (p. 452). The Resolution clearly expressed the government's belief that administrative guidance, promotion and control were essential in the national interest. Three years later, the Industries (Development and Regulation) Act was passed to provide the government with the means of implementing the Resolution.

In December 1954, the Parliament adopted the "socialist pattern of society" as the objective of social and economic policy. In the words of the Second Five Year Plan this phrase means that "the basic criterion for determining lines of advance must not be private profit, but social gain, and that the pattern of development and the structure of socio-economic relations should be so planned that they result not only in appreciable increases in national income and employment but also in greater equality in income and wealth. Major decisions regarding production, distribution, consumption, and investment—and all significant socio-economic relationships—must be made by agencies informed by social purpose."

The adoption of the socialist pattern of society as the national objective of social and economic policy as well as the successful implementation of the First Plan led the government to announce the Second Industrial Policy Resolution in April 1956. This Resolution stated that realization of the objectives of the socialist pattern of society and planned and rapid development "require that all industries of basic and strategic importance, or in the nature of public utility services, should be in the public sector. Other industries which are essential and require investment on a scale which only the state, in present circumstances, could provide, have also to be in the public sector. The state has therefore to assume direct responsibility for the future development of industries over a wide area."

The government classified industries into three categories, regarding the part which the state would play in each of them.

The first category consisted of seventeen industries whose future development would be the exclusive responsibility of the state. These industries were scheduled as: (1) arms and ammunition, (2) atomic energy, (3) railways, (4) air transport, (5) iron and steel, (6) heavy castings and forgings of iron and steel, (7) heavy plant and machinery, (8) heavy electrical plant, (9) air craft, (10) ship building, (11) coal and lignite, (12) mineral oils, (13) mining of iron ore, manganese ore, chrome ore, gypsum, sulphur, gold, and diamonds, (14) mining and processing of copper, lead, zinc, tin, molybdenum, and wolfram, (15) minerals specified in the schedule to the Atomic Energy Order, 1956, (16) telephones and telephone cables, telegraphs, and wireless apparatus (excluding radio receiving sets), and (17) generation and distribution of electricity.

Of these, the first four were to be governmental monopolies. All new units in the remaining 13 industries would be established by the state. However, this did not preclude "the expansion of the existing privately owned units, or the possibility of the state securing the cooperation of private enterprise in the establishment of new units when the national interest so require."

The second category consisted of 12 industries in which the state would increasingly establish new enterprises, without denying the private sector its opportunities.

[1] A. H. Hanson, *The Process of Planning* (*Oxford University Press,* 1966).

These industries were scheduled as: (1) all other minerals except minor minerals, (2) aluminium and other non-ferrous metals not included in the first category, (3) machine tools, (4) ferro-alloys and tool steels, (5) basic intermediate products required by the chemical industries, (6) antibiotics and other essential drugs, (7) fertilizers, (8) synthetic rubber, (9) carbonization of coal, (10) chemical pulp, (11) road transport, and (12) sea transport.

The third category covered all the remaining industries, whose future development would, in general, be left to the initiative and enterprise of the private sector. While reaffirming the right of the state to start any industry, the Resolution stressed that the state's main role would be to facilitate and encourage the development of these industries, by the adoption of appropriate fiscal measures, and the provision of services and financial assistance. Private enterprise in these industries would have to fit into the "framework of the economic and social policy of the state" and remain subject to various government legislations.

This Resolution envisaged an important active role for the state in the development of all industries, except consumer goods industries. All new developments in defense industries, public utilities (except road and sea transport), basic industries and minerals (except minor minerals) would be the state's exclusive responsibility. As for the existing units, it did not repeat the first Resolution's ten-year guarantee against nationalization. The Resolution also envisaged that private enterprises would have to fit into the framework of the social and economic policy of the state and remain subject to governmental regulation and guidance.

The influence of this Resolution on the Second Five Year Plan and later plans was great. The authors of the Second Plan emphasized that the pursuit of socialism meant that the basic criterion for determining the lines of advance must not be private profit but social gain. They felt that a large public sector was necessary to create the type of social order visualized in the socialist pattern of society. They wrote: "The public sector has to expand rapidly. It has not only to initiate development which the private sector is either unwilling or unable to undertake, it has to play the dominant role in shaping the entire pattern of investments in the economy.... In a growing economy which gets increasingly diversified, there is scope for the public and private sectors to expand simultaneously, but it is inevitable that, if development is to proceed at the pace envisaged and to contribute effectively to the attainment of the larger social ends in view, the public sector must grow not only absolutely but also relatively to the private sector."

This was indeed the case. The share of aggregate public sector investment in total investment was raised from 46.4 per cent in the First Plan to 61.3 per cent in the Second Plan. Even though the actual share of the public sector in the Second Plan was only 56 per cent, the Third Plan still allotted 61 per cent of the investment to the public sector. The share of public sector in the group comprising power, organized industry and mining, and transport and communications, was 75 per cent in the Second Plan.

Implicit in the Second Resolution and in the minds of the authors of the Second and Third Plans was the assumption that public enterprises contributed not only to the attainment of the socialist ideal but also to rapid development. Both the Resolution and the Planning Commission contemplated that public enterprises would help to "augment the revenues of the state and provide resources for further development in fresh fields."

Hanson illustrates the tension between ideology and empiricism in the allocation decisions of coal, oil, and steel industries. It may be of interest here to provide one example. The Second Plan postulated an increase in coal production from 38 million tons in 1955 to 60 million tons in 1961. The question was how to allocate the additional 22 million tons between the two sectors. At that time coal production in the public sector was only 4.5 million tons. The Commission did not consider the relative cost of producing coal nor the ability of the two sectors in achieving their targets, but simply referred to the Industrial Policy Resolution of 1948 and said that additional production should be raised to the maximum possible extent in the public sector. Accordingly, it allocated an additional production of 12 million tons for the public sector and 10 million tons for the private sector. By 1959 the public sector showed an increase of only 2.2 million tons while the private sector showed an increase of 6.8 million tons. The Commission attributed the short fall in the public sector to the difficulties in setting up new coal mines. The Third Plan provided for an increase of 37 million tons—20 million tons in the public sector and 17 million tons in the private sector. By the time of Mid-Term Appraisal (November 1963), the public sector had increased its production by little more than 1 million tons, while the private sector had increased its production by more than 7 million tons.

The above example shows that the intrusion of ideological considerations in allocation decisions had affected economic efficiency and slowed down the pace of development.

3. Regulation of the Private Sector

The Industrial Policy Resolution of 1948, as we have seen, had forecast legislation for the control of enterprises in the private sector. The Industries (Development and Regulation) Act was passed in 1951 with the following objectives:

(1) the regulation of industrial investment and production according to Plan priorities and targets;
(2) the avoidance of monopoly and prevention of concentration of ownership of industries;
(3) the protection of small industries against undue competition from large-scale industries; and
(4) the balanced economic development of the different regions in the country so as to reduce disparities in levels of development.

This Act was to be applied to 37 (later extended to 70) scheduled industries. In order to pursue the objectives, the Act provided that:

(1) every existing undertaking covered by the schedule had to register itself with the central government, and no new undertaking could be established, nor any existing undertaking substantially extended, without the prior procurement of a license from the central government;
(2) the government had the power to order a full and complete investigation if it had cause to believe that (a) there had been a substantial reduction in the volume of production or a marked deterioration in the quality of the articles produced, or a rise in the price, where there appeared to be no justification for such a fall, deterioration or rise, or (b) the management of the undertaking was being detrimental to the public interest; and at the conclusion of the investigation, the government might, if necessary, take over its management, directly or through an appointed management;
(3) the government had the power to publish orders for securing equitable distribution and availability at fair prices of any article or class of articles relatable to any scheduled industry;
(4) by order the government could establish Development Councils, one for each industry or group of industries to perform functions such as production targeting, the setting of efficiency norms, the improvements in the utilization of marketing arrangements, and the promotion of standardization, trading, research, and productivity.

Hazari[2] rightly points out that "the major assumption implicit in the Act is that growth and allocation of resources should be looked after wholly or mainly by administrative guidance, promotion and control, and hardly at all by the market mechanism."

In addition to the inspectorial clauses of this Act, the Companies Act of 1956 pro-

[2] R. K. Hazari, *Industrial Planning and Licensing Policy, Final Report,* Vol. 1 (Government of India), p. 17.

vided enough powers to the government to regulate the internal organization of private enterprises. The two main objectives of the Companies Act were (1) to prevent the dishonest practices in the formation and operation of companies, and (2) to limit opportunities for effecting undue concentration of economic power. The Act, together with its amending Acts, Hanson remarks, "constitutes one of the most detailed and stringent codes of business legislation to be found anywhere in the world" (p. 486).

The Essential Commodities Act of 1955 authorized the government to regulate or prohibit the production and control the supply, distribution, and price of certain enumerated commodities and of any other commodities which, by order, may be declared "essential."

It is extremely difficult to evaluate the total effect on the private sector of all these controls. While some of the stringent regulations over the internal organization of enterprises might have dampened entrepreneurial initiatives, there is some evidence to show that these regulations have reduced corrupt practices in the formation of companies and provided some degree of protection to the ordinary shareholder and thereby encouraged investment in equities. From an economic point of view, far more controversial are the powers over the licensing and regulation of industrial investments and control over prices and distribution of commodities. In view of the importance of licensing and price and distribution controls, we review the working of these controls and evaluate their effectiveness.

Industrial Licensing

The purpose of the licensing system was to provide for central government control over the location, expansion, and setting up of private industrial undertakings with a view, *inter alia,* to channelling investments in accordance with Plan priorities and targets. An (Inter-ministerial) Licensing Committee was set up in September 1952 to operate within the framework of the Industries Act. To assist this Committee in making techno-economic evaluation of the applications, the Directorate General of Technical Development (D.G. T.D.) was also set up. Up to 1964 all actual and proposed industrial undertakings employing more than Rs. 10 lakhs in value had been subject to industrial licensing.

In addition to the approval of the Licensing Committee a prospective investor might require licenses from other committees as well. If he wished to raise capital from the public he had to procure a license from the Comptroller of Capital Issues; if he needed foreign exchange, he must get the approval of the Capital Goods Committee; if he needed foreign collaboration, he must obtain the consent of the Foreign Agreements Committee.

The working of the licensing system during the Second and Third Plans revealed a number of deficiencies in the system. The Licensing Committee was supposed to regulate investments in the scheduled industries in accordance with Plan priorities and targets. While the Planning Commission provided specific expansion programmes for the scheduled industries, indicating actual rated capacity and production at the beginning of the Plan periods, and projected rated capacity and production at the end of the Plan periods, it did not provide phasing of the targets to give guidance to the Committee. Hazari points out that "no attempt has been made to synchronize or adjust the pace of licensing and revocation to the actual trends in capacity and output in relation to emerging demand" (p. 18). In the absence of adequate guidance from the Planning Commission, the Committee frequently relied upon various *ad hoc* criteria.

Bhagwati and Desai and the Mathur Team on the working of the D.G.T.D. have drawn attention to the poor quality of the techno-economic work done by the Directorate. Bhagwati and Desai[3] point out that "there is no evidence of any studies having been carried out by the D.G.T.D. on the optimal size, time-phasing, and location of industrial units," (p. 255) in order to guide the Committee in its deliberations.

[3] J. N. Bhagwati and P. Desai, *India, Planning for Industrialization* (Oxford University Press), 1970.

The licensing system was also deficient in a procedural matter. The procedure in general was to proceed on a first-come-first-served basis. This enabled the bigger industrial houses to put in for licenses more readily because they were better informed.[4] These houses also pre-empted licensable capacity in many industries as a means of barring the entry of newcomers into these industries. Analyzing data relating to applications and approvals to certain industrial houses, Hazari comments that the data justify "the presumption that multiple applications for the same product and for a wide, very wide indeed, variety of products are meant to foreclose licensable capacity. This appears to be particularly true of Birlas applications" (pp. 7–8).

The Swaminathan Committee on Industries Development Procedures drew attention to undue delays in the processing of applications. The licensing rules required that an application must be decided upon in three months, but in practice the average time taken for the case disposal was about six months. The Swaminathan Committee attributed the delays to the enormous work load of the Licensing Committee and recommended de-licensing a number of industries.

In May 1966 the government, acting on the recommendations of the Swaminathan Committee, de-licensed 11 industries. By November 1966, 42 industries were de-licensed. The government also raised the exemption limit for licensing to Rs 25 lakhs. In addition, the government announced that enterprises could expand up to 25 per cent more than the registered capacity.

The Administrative Reforms Commission and the Industrial Licensing Policy Committee recommended that the use of licensing as a positive instrument should be confined to industries which come within the basic, strategic and critical sectors. These recommendations resulted in some modifications in the government's policy. According to the Fourth Five Year Plan (pp. 307–9), the broad features of the modified licensing policy are :

(1) There would be a list of 9 "core" industries consisting of basic, critical, and strategic industries for which detailed plans will be prepared and essential inputs made available on a priority basis.
(2) All new investment propositions of over Rs 5 crores shall be deemed to be in the "heavy investment" sector.
(3) In the middle sector, involving investments ranging from Rs 1 crore to Rs 5 crores, license applications of parties other than undertakings belonging to larger industrial houses shall be given special consideration and licenses shall be issued liberally, except where foreign exchange implications necessitate careful scrutiny.
(4) New undertakings or substantial expansion of units (with some exceptions relating to large industrial houses and foreign companies) requiring investment of Rs 1 crore or less will not be required to take a license under the Industries Act.

It is hoped that these modifications would not only simplify the tasks of the Licensing Committee by reducing its workload but also enable them to make a careful appraisal of the applications. We feel that, instead of providing a general exemption limit of Rs 1 crore for all industries, the government should set different limits for different industries based on considerations such as economies of scale.

Price and Distribution Controls

As we have stated before, the Industries Act of 1951 and the Essential Commodities Act of 1956 provided the central government with powers to regulate the production, distribution, and price of certain enumerated commodities. Such powers were exercised

[4] In this connection, the following quote from the Ninth Report of the Monopolies Inquiry Commission (p. 176) is of interest : "Many of the leading industrialists, we understand, have found it necessary to maintain expensive establishments in the capital for facilitating the obtaining of licenses. Those who cannot afford the expenses of running such establishments which include sometimes, it seems, large amounts required to employ high paid 'contactmen' and to give lavish parties—are at a disadvantage."

by the government over a wide range of commodities: iron and steel (production, distribution, and prices), non-ferrous metals (distribution and prices), cement (distribution and prices), coal (distribution, prices, and movement), fertilizers (distribution and prices), cotton textiles (production and distribution), paper (distribution), sugar (production and supply), and motor cars (distribution). In addition, some sort of controls, formal or informal, were exercised over a number of manufactured items.

Two important factors motivated this direct regulation of distribution and prices. The most important factor was the desire to prevent inflation. Until 1963, the country experienced shortages in many commodities and it was felt that these controls would ease inflationary pressures in the economy. Another motivating factor for direct regulation was the desire to ensure allocation of adequate amounts to priority sectors at some reasonable price. This was true of controls over steel and cement.

The working of various price and distribution controls indicate that in many cases the controls were ineffective and in certain circumstances produced "undesirable effects." The Raj Committee Report on the working of steel distribution shows that priorities were not clearly defined and allocations were chaotic. The Committee also points out that the price control enabled the private sector users to buy steel at controlled prices, but it did not require them to price their outputs in such a way as to pass on the benefits to final users.

In 1963 the government freed 16 commodities from price and distribution controls. Subsequently, controls on iron and steel, coal, fertilizers, and cement were relaxed.

The recent shifts in policies towards delicensing of industries and relaxation of controls over distribution and prices mark an important change in the attitude of the government towards the private sector. In the fifties, the government and the Planning Commission emphasized the defects of the market mechanism and suggested that governmental control and guidance over industry were essential for rapid development. Our experience with various controls over the last 15 years have taught us that direct regulation of the economic system by administrative control, promotion, and guidance is also deficient in many respects. In this connection, the following quote from the Fourth Five Year Plan is of interest: "The existing industrial structure has led generally to a high level of costs and the present system does not appear to have prevented concentration. In some cases industry has been inappropriately sited and some desirable adjustments in regional locations have not taken place. Fixation of targets, licensing and some price and allocation controls seem to have affected the care with which entrepreneurs should weigh the long-term prospects of their investment decision...... Sheltered conditions created in part by the operation of existing controls appear to have reduced cost consciousness among entrepreneurs" (p. 27).

4. Economic Performance of the Public Sector

The government had provided the following arguments for the establishment of enterprises in the public sector:

First, a number of basic industries which require large investments and extensive collaboration with foreign firms or governments and which could be undertaken only on the assurance of future prospects, with no immediate gain in sight, would not normally be started if reliance was to be placed entirely on the private sector. Here the implicit assumption is that even with appropriate fiscal and other incentives, private enterprises would not volunteer to undertake such projects.

Second, in the case of industries where, for technological reasons, the plants have to be large, requiring big investments, by organizing them in the public sector, undue concentration of economic and industrial power in private hands can be prevented. It is well known that, in the presence of significant economies of scale, the free market does not produce the best results. Economic efficiency considerations, therefore, require some form of governmental regulation or public ownership. In the United States, firms in electric power, natural gas, telephone and some other industries are being regulated by federal and state regulatory commissions. France, United Kingdom, and some other countries have preferred public ownership.

Third, public enterprises would work towards the attainment of "social gain" and thereby help to create the type of social order envisaged in the "socialist pattern of society." This argument presumes that decision-making units in public enterprises have the knowledge and ability to devise socially optimal rules for allocation and pricing and that these rules could be enforced.

Fourth, rapid expansion of public enterprises would materially contribute to increasing public savings for investment, making it possible thereby to increase the rate of growth.

The first two arguments are valid in the Indian context. At the time of Independence, all planning groups, including the authors of the Bombay Plan, agreed that the state had to play an active role in setting up heavy industries and public utilities. The third and fourth arguments depend crucially on the assumption that the government could play the role of investor and entrepreneur more efficiently than firms in the private sector. Our experience in planning and running public enterprises over the last two decades casts doubts on the validity of this assumption.

Since 1955 there has been a large expansion of the public sector in a wide range of activities, covering fields as varied as mining and manufacturing, generation and distribution of electric power, construction, transport and communications, irrigation, banking and insurance, trade, social services, etc. Undertakings in electricity and road transport are primarily owned by states. Railways, posts and telegraph, and a few undertakings like Chittaranjan Locomotives and Perambur Coach Factory are run as departmental concerns by the central government. The industrial and commercial undertakings of the central government are run by government companies or public corporations.

In view of the importance of the industrial and commercial undertakings of the central government in total investment, our analysis is confined to this group alone. The growth of investment in this group from plan to plan is given in Table 1. From Rs. 81 crores at the beginning of the Second Plan, total investment increased to Rs. 2415 crores at the end of the Third Plan, and at the end of March 1970, the amount was Rs. 4301 crores. Of the 91 undertakings at the end of March 1970, 8 with an investment of Rs. 440 crores were still under construction (see Table 2).

Table 1. Growth of Investment in Public Enterprises (Central Government Undertakings other than Departmental Projects)

Period	Total investment (Rs. crores)	No. of units
At the commencement of the First Plan	29	5
At the commencement of the Second Plan	81	21
At the commencement of the Third Plan	953	48
At the end of the Third Plan	2415	74
As of 3-31-1967	2841	77
As of 3-31-1968	3333	83
At the commencement of the Fourth Plan	3902	85
As of 3-31-1970	4301	91

SOURCE: Annual Report on the Working of Industrial and Commercial Undertakings of the Central Government, 1969-70.

Table 2. Investment in the Public Undertakings (as of 3-31-1970)

		Rs. crores	No. of concerns
1. Undertakings under construction		440.32	8
2. Running concerns		3794.28	69
(i) Hindustan Steel Ltd.	1062.81		
(ii) Others	2731.47		
3. Promotional and developmental undertakings		59.71	11
4. Financial institutions		6.93	3
		4301.24	91

SOURCE: Same as in Table 1.

Table 3 gives a sectorwise distribution of completed investments. About one third of the total investment was in iron and steel and nearly one-fourth in engineering and shipbuilding industries.

Table 3. Sectorwise Distribution of Total Investment in the Public Sector Projects

	As of 3-31-1970 (Rs. in crores)	per cent
Steel	1,419	33.0
Engineering and shipbuilding	1,020	23.7
Chemicals	489	11.4
Petroleum and oils	399	9.3
Mining and minerals	368	86.6
Aviation and shipping	185	4.2
Trading	314	7.3
Financial institutions	7	0.2
Miscellaneous	100	2.3
	4,301	100.0

SOURCE: Annual Report on the Working of Industrial and Commercial Undertakings of the Central Government, 1961-70.

Economic problems of the public enterprises may be grouped under two broad heads: (A) problems related to planning and construction of projects, and (B) problems related to the working of undertakings.

A. Problems Related to Planning and Construction of Projects

The Report of the Study Team on Public Sector Undertakings cited the following deficiencies in the planning of projects.

(1) lack of detailed analysis on scope and pattern of product mix,
(2) selection of site based on inadequate soil investigation,
(3) omission and understatement of several elements of the project,
(4) lack of proper assessment of demand for the products, and
(5) incomplete analysis of commercial profitability and economic forecasts.

Despite the emphasis on "social objectives," the Planning Commission or the Bureau of Public Enterprises has not developed guidelines that clearly define the social criteria and the methodology for project evaluation from the standpoint of social profitability. Bhagwati and Desai note that a careful scrutiny of methods adopted to plan for the projects "underlines the extremely poor quality in general of the work, both from a technical viewpoint and even more so from the point of view of economic, cost and benefit analysis" (p. 158). As an example, they provide the case of Heavy Electricals Limited at Bhopal. According to them, Ian Little, a British economist, found that the actual figures of costs included in the blueprints showed that, even if all expectations about capacity utilization and efficiency of operations were to be fulfilled, the project would yield only 2.7 per cent. A later estimate by Little of the returns on the project by evaluating inputs and outputs at international prices (presumably to take into account correct opportunity costs) showed that the real return in the blueprint project was still dismal.

The draft Fourth Five Year Plan admits that many projects have taken a longer time to complete than was initially anticipated. The fertilizer industry provides an example. Table 4 provides a comparison of the

Table 4. Comparison of Estimated and Actual Time-Schedules in the Construction of Fertilizer Plants

Stage	Normal time-schedule estimated by U.N. Fertilizer mission	Approximate time actually taken in India
	(Time in months)	
(i) Preliminary analysis, project report, initial decision to proceed with the project.	4-5	5-7
(ii) Preparation of tenders, preliminary process and specifications.	3-4	3-4
(iii) Contractor's project bid, review of bids and official decision to construct plant.	4-8	12-20
(iv) Ordering, construction, erection to completion and start-up.	24-30	32-40
Total	35-47	52-71

SOURCE: Report of the Study Team on Public Sector Undertakings (Administrative Reforms Commission), June 1967, p. 84.

normal time schedule needed for completion of fertilizer plants under Indian conditions and the time actually taken for completion of projects. On an average, the actual time taken exceeded the estimated time by 18 months. The important contributing factors for the delays appear to be inadequate project preparation, difficulties in getting foreign aid and bureaucratic red tape.

In many undertakings, the differences between original cost estimates and final construction expenditures were very large. Table 5 compares the original estimate

Table 5. Comparison of Original Estimates and Actual Expenditures in the Construction of Selected Public Enterprises

Name of project-undertaking	Original estimate (Rs. crores)	Actual expenditure (Rs. crores)	Percentage increase
Durgapur Steel Plant	115.00	205.25	78
Rourkela Steel Plant	128.00	230.40	80
Bhilai Steel Plant	110.00	202.34	83
Heavy Engineering Corporation, Ltd.	125.95	206.50	64
Heavy Electricals, Ltd. Bhopal	35.25	49.30	40
Fertilizer Corporation of India, Ltd.			
(i) Trombay Unit	24.34	33.40	37
(ii) Nangal Unit	20.90	31.20	49
Hindustan Antibiotics, Ltd.			
(i) Pimpri Unit	1.15	1.59	38
(ii) Penicillin Expansion	0.45	0.61	36
(iii) Streptomycin Unit	1.73	2.08	20
Gauhati Refinery	13.06	14.51	11

SOURCE: Report of the Study Team on Public Sector Undertakings (Administrative Reforms Commission), June 1967, p. 84.

and the final cost for some selected enterprises. In the case of steel, the final cost was about 80 per cent higher than the original estimate.

B. Problems Related to the Working of the Public Enterprises

One measure frequently used to appraise the performance of an enterprise is the ratio of gross profits (the excess of income over expenditure providing for depreciation, write off of deferred revenue expenditure, but before providing for interest, the taxes, and appropriation to reserves) to capital employed (gross block less depreciation plus working capital). There are some problems in using this measure in appraising the performance of public enterprises.

First, they are expected to maximize social gain and not money profit. Second, their operation is subject to a number of constraints imposed by administrators. Third, a high value of this ratio might indicate monopoly power rather than economic efficiency. For these reasons, it is not possible to attach any welfare significance to this ratio.

Despite these limitations, we use this ratio as a rough indicator of the financial performance of a public enterprise. It may be appropriate to note here that the government and the Planning Commission pointed out on several occasions that public sector undertakings ought to secure adequate return on capital employed and contribute their full share to the increase in the portion of national resources devoted to investment. In a seminar on the working of the public sector, Mr. C. Subramaniam, then minister for iron and steel, expressed the view.[5]

> I think I should take this occasion to emphasize that so far as we in India are concerned, our public enterprises are expected to operate with profit motive as one of their primary objectives. There is nothing vicious or immoral about profit in an industrial unit. Indeed, to cover the costs of running an enterprise and to generate resources needed for paying legitimate charges on capital and meeting depreciation requirements is a legitimate social aim. In a sense, this is the sure test of efficiency of an enterprise.

The Annual Report on the Working of Industrial and Commercial Undertakings of the Central Government provides this ratio. For the year 1969–70, the ratio for Hindustan Steel was only 1.8 per cent. Of 23 enterprises in the group Engineering and Shipbuilding, 9 incurred losses, 5 earned less than 5 per cent, 2 earned between 5 and 10 per cent and 7 earned more than 10 per cent. In Chemicals, out of 10, 5 incurred losses, 3 earned less than 5 per cent, 1 between 5 and 10 per cent and only one more than 10 per cent. In Mining and Mineral group, 2 incurred losses, 4 earned less than 5 per cent and one earned more than 10 per cent. In Petroleum and Oil group, one incurred loss, one earned between 5 and 7 per cent and 3 more than 10 per cent. All concerns in Trading and Aviation Shipping earned more than 7 per cent.

The performances of large concerns, particularly in steel and engineering industries, were poor. In order to study the performances of large concerns through time, we provide in Table 6 the ratios for the years 1960–61 to 1969–70 for all undertakings with investments above Rs. 25 crores. With an investment of over Rs. 1000 crores and several years spent in construction, the performance of Hindustan Steel was poor. Among heavy engineering industries, except Hindustan Machine Tools and Hindustan Aeronautics all others incurred losses. Among other undertakings, Indian Drugs and Pharmaceuticals and Neyveli Lignite Corporation incurred losses in several years.

It appears that three factors—the government's price policy, low utilization of capacity and organizational inefficiency—have contributed to low rates of return in many undertakings.

One of the contributing factors for the negative or low positive rates of return on capital in steel was that until May 1967, the price of steel was fixed by the government. It is now evident that the under-pricing of steel had not served any social purpose. The Raj Committee pointed out that, in many cases, under-pricing of steel merely resulted in increasing the profits of some concerns in the private sector and did not benefit the users of the end products of steel.

In industries such as heavy engineering, heavy electricals, heavy machine tools the problem is low utilization of capacity. In 1968–69, the Heavy Machine Building Project in Heavy Engineering Corporation had a utilization rate of only 16 per cent. Many plants in Bharat Heavy Electricals operated at rates varying between 6 and 29 per cent. Lack of demand due to recession is cited as the contributing factor.

The Study Team on Public Sector Undertakings of the Administrative Reforms

[5] "Public Enterprise," in V. V. Ramanadham (ed.), *The Working of the Public Sector, 1965*.

Table 6. Gross Profits As Percentage of Capital Employed in Large Public Undertakings

Name of undertaking	Investments (Rs. crores)	60-61	61-62	62-63	63-64	64-65	65-66	66-67	67-68	68-69	69-70
Hindustan Steel	1062.81	C	C	L	2.0	3.3	2.4	0.1	L	L	1.8
Hindustan Machine Tools	29.34	12.4	14.0	20.8	21.4	16.5	7.9	6.2	0.6	1.8	1.5
Heavy Electricals	123.36	C	C	C	C	C	L	L	L	L	L
Heavy Engineering	246.97	C	C	C	C	C	C	L	L	L	L
Bharat Heavy Electricals	173.79	Set up in 1964				C	C	L	L	L	L
Hindustan Aeronautics	212.42	3.7	3.7	5.2	5.8	5.8	5.3	2.3	4.4	4.2	4.2
Mining & Allied Machinery	56.00	Set up in 1965					C	C	L	L	L
Fertilizer & Chemicals	70.40			L	3.7	L	L	4.8	5.0	1.6	L
Fertilizer Corp. of India	205.29	2.6	1.2	3.7	4.5	5.2	1.9	1.7	5.0	4.3	3.9
Indian Drugs & Pharmaceuticals	75.43		C	C	C	C	C	L	L	L	L
National Coal Development Corp.	184.82	3.1	1.0	3.3	1.3	L	3.5	0.9	1.7	2.6	2.6
National Mineral Development Corp.	50.06	C	C	C	C	C	L	3.5	L	L	2.3
Neyveli Lignite Corp.	170.47	C	C	C	C	C	1.0	L	L	1.7	0.6
Indian Oil	131.64	L	L	11.8	8.1	7.9	4.5	8.0	9.8	14.2	15.8
Oil & Natural Gas Comm.	203.14	N.A.	N.A.	N.A.	N.A.	N.A.	N.A.	9.0	9.3	8.6	7.3
Food Corp. of India	291.76	Incorporated in 1965						10.9	4.3	4.1	7.3
Air India	49.16	4.8	3.0	8.3	10.7	8.3	3.1	9.7	12.0	10.0	8.6
Indian Airlines	47.30	0.6	0.6	3.6	5.2	9.0	1.3	L	3.7	8.0	7.1
Shipping Corporation of India	81.67	4.0	5.3	6.3	5.3	6.0	6.3	11.1	11.6	9.0	8.3

SOURCE: Annual Reports on the working of Industrial and Commercial Undertakings of the Central Government from 1960-61 to 1969-70.
C=Under construction
L=Loss

Committee pointed out defects in the form of organization and personnel management. It argued that the company form was not suitable for industrial and commercial concerns and recommended public corporation form. It also pointed out the need for improvement in managerial and operational efficiency.

On the basis of the recommendations of the Administration Reforms Committee, the government circulated a memorandum[6] in March 1969 outlining the measures to be taken for improving the working and profitability of public undertakings. To improve the utilization of capacity in steel and engineering industries, it suggested diversification of products, promotion of exports, and better coordination among public enterprises. To improve managerial and operation efficiency, the government announced that (1) more financial and administrative powers would be delegated to enable management to function with greater autonomy; (2) it would assist the enterprises to secure suitable managerial talent; (3) new measures have to be taken and guidelines laid down for improving management techniques in project preparation, economy in construction, financial management, inventory controls, and price policies; and (4) an

[6] This memorandum is reproduced in *Eastern Economist,* March 14, 1969, pp. 586–90.

effective machinery for periodical review and appraisal of their performances would be developed.

There is also a growing awareness on the need for earning some minimum rate of return.[7] The Draft Fourth Five Year Plan suggested that public enterprises must yield not less than 11 to 12 per cent.

5. Concluding Remarks

Our experience in industrial planning, regulation, and public ownership over the last two decades reveals that the present system has contributed to both allocative inefficiency and what Leibenstein calls X-inefficiency.[8] Sheltered conditions, created in part by the operation of various regulations, have reduced competitive pressures and weakened motivation on the part of both private and public managers and resulted in higher production costs.

We recognize that industrial planning and regulation are necessary for some strategic industries in the private sector. It may also be desirable, at the present stage of development, to prohibit or restrict investment in certain "undesirable" economic activities. It is likely that in some industries, the market may not function properly because of market imperfections or because of economies of scale or external economies and diseconomies. Here again, the right approach for the government is not to intervene in the operations of the market by detailed regulations or to take over management. Our experience has taught that the disadvantages of detailed planning are, sometimes, far more serious than the deficiencies of the market system. The government should rather try to strengthen the operation of the market by disseminating information and educating the people, and in the case of divergence between social costs (benefits) and private costs (benefits) devise appropriate taxes and subsidies.

We have established public enterprises (at high costs, of course) in a number of important industries such as iron and steel, heavy engineering, chemicals, power, transport and communications, but we have not yet learned the right methods of managing public enterprises. The French experience[9] in devising optimal policies for investment decisions and pricing may be of some relevance to India. We agree with the Administrative Reforms Committee that the public corporation form of organization is more suitable to industrial and commercial undertakings than the company form which is popular now. We endorse the view of the committee that, unless there are clear and over-riding reasons of public interest (e.g. supplying birth control pills at low prices), public enterprises should aim at earning surpluses, or, at least, earn a reasonable rate of return (8 per cent) on invested capital. Industries such as iron and steel and heavy engineering should always try to operate near full capacity even if it requires temporary adjustments in prices. With huge investment outlays and many years spent in construction, it is a national waste to operate these concerns at low levels of capacity.

---

7 In a white paper on the economic and financial objectives of the nationalized industries, published in November 1967, the British government suggested a target rate of return of 8 per cent.

8 H. Leibenstein, "Allocative Efficiency vs. 'X-Efficiency'," *American Economic Review*, June 1966.

9 For a survey, see J. H. Dreze, "Some Postwar Contributions of French Economists to Theory and Public Policy, with Special Emphasis on Problems of Resource Allocation," *American Economic Review*, June 1964.

BIBLIOGRAPHY

Bhagwati, J. and Desai, P., *India, Planning for Industrialization* (Oxford University Press, 1970).

Government of India (Administrative Reforms Commission), *Report of the Study Team on Public Sector Undertakings*, June 1967.

Government of India (Planning Commission), *Second Five Year Plan*.

———, *Third Five Year Plan*.

———, *Fourth Five Year Plan*.

Hanson, A. H., *The Process of Planning* (Oxford University Press, 1966).

Hazari, R. K., *Industrial Planning and Licensing Policy* (Government of India, 1967).

Ramanadham, V. V. (ed.), *The Working of the Public Sector* (Bombay: Allied Publishers, 1965).

9

Socialist Society— An Analysis of India's Economic Policy

RAJINDAR K. KOSHAL

THIS chapter attempts to examine the pattern of the socialistic society of India and the policies adopted so far to achieve this objective. A "socialistic pattern of society," as defined by the Planning Commission, "means that the basic criteria for determining lines of advance is not private profit but social gains, and that the pattern of development and the structure of socio-economic relations should be so planned that they result not only in appreciable increases in national income and employment but also in greater quality in income and wealth."[1]

1. Historical Background

Pre-Independence. The idea of a socialistic society is not new to Indians. There was a general preference for this pattern of economic development even before Independence. In 1938, the National Planning Committee, set up by the All India National Congress, suggested planning for economic development of India following the path of a socialistic society within a democratic framework.[1] The concept of a socialistic society was provided by Mahatma Gandhi, whose ideas influenced the Five Year Plans.[2] Gandhi's follower, Pandit Nehru, put the aim of Indian planning as follows:

> Our economy and social structure have outlived their day and it has become a matter of urgent necessity for us to refashion them so that they may promote the happiness of all our people in things

[1] Shriman Nayrayan, *Principles of Gandhian Planning,* Kitab Mahal, Allahabad, 1960.

[2] R. K. and M. Koshal, "Gandhi's Economic Philosophy," *American Journal of Economics and Sociology* (April 1973), and M. and R. K. Koshal, "Gandhi's Influence on Indian Economic Planning—A Critical Analysis, "*American Journal of Economics and Sociology* (July 1973).

material and spiritual... We must *aim at a classless society,* based on co-operative effort, *with opportunities for all.*[3]

Furthermore, Tarlok Singh, who served as an economist and a key administrator of the Planning Commission during the first three plans, writes:

> Through many faltering steps, since we gained freedom, we have now the knowledge, the resources, and the social institutions by which it is within the bounds of practical action to achieve a rapid advancing economy and a society integrated from within. In the *Hind Swaraj,* written as far back as 1908, Gandhiji declared that by patriotism he meant the welfare of the whole people. Later he called it *Sarvodaya,* the welfare of all. A few days before the end came, he referred to *Sarvodaya* as true democracy in which we would regard the humblest and lowest Indian as being equally the ruler of India with the tallest in the land. This comes close to defining the mission and the faith which we of this generation and students and youth, who are the harbingers and the leaders of the next phase in our national life, are together called upon to work for, to live for.[4]

Post-Independence. After Independence, in 1950, the Constitution of India was drafted under the guidance of the Indian leaders. The Constitution also includes definite directives with respect to the basic economic policy. Articles 38, 39 and 41 are particularly relevant. These are:[5]

> The State shall strive to promote the welfare of the people by securing and protecting, as effectively as it may, a social order in which justice—social, economic and political, shall inform all the institutions of national life. (Article 38)
>
> The State shall, in particular, direct its policy towards securing
>
> (a) that the citizens, men and women, equally, have the right to an adequate means of livelihood;
> (b) that the ownership and control of the material resources of the community are so distributed as best to subserve the common good;
> (c) that the operation of the economic system does not result in the concentration of wealth and means of production to the common detriment. (Article 39)
>
> The State shall, within the limits of its economic capacity and development, make effective provision for securing the right to work, to education and to public assistance in cases of unemployment, old age, sickness and disablement, and in other cases of undeserved wants. (Article 41)

In 1950, the Government of India set up the Planning Commission to promote a rapid increase in the standard of living of the people by exploiting effectively the resources of the country, increasing production, and offering opportunities for employment to as large a number of people as possible in the service of the community.

Although the planning process started in 1950, it was not until 1954 that the Indian Parliament clearly stated its economic policy. In December 1954, it adopted a resolution containing the following clauses:[6]

(i) The objective of economic policy should be the Socialistic Pattern of Society; and
(ii) Towards this end the tempo of economic activity in general and industrial development in particular should be stepped up to the maximum possible extent.

Five Year Plans and Economic Policy. Basically, the above economic policy has been manifested in all the Five Year Plans.

The Second Five Year Plan explains the term "socialistic pattern of society." It means that the basic criterion for deter-

[3] Tarlok Singh, *Towards an Integrated Society* (Westport, Connecticut: Greenwood Publishing Corporation, 1969), p. 351 (Italics are mine).
[4] Ibid., p. 547.
[5] Planning Commission, *Fourth Five Year Plan*: 1969–74 (Delhi: Government of India Press, 1970), p. 1.
[6] Ibid., p. 2.

mining the lines of advance *must not be private profits but social gains,* and that the pattern of development and the structure of socio-economic relations should be so planned that they result not only in appreciable increases in national income and employment but also *in greater equality in income and wealth.*[7] The planners also realized that in creating the appropriate conditions, the state has to take heavy responsibilities as the principal agency speaking for and acting on behalf of the community as a whole.[8] Consequently, the public sector would have to expand rapidly. Both the Second and Third Plans emphasize the importance of reducing inequalities in income and wealth and a more even distribution of economic power.[9] On the other hand, the Fourth Five Year Plan not only puts a great emphasis on the above objectives, but also suggests further nationalization of enterprises. According to Mrs. Indira Gandhi, the chairman of the Planning Commission :

> The over-riding inspiration must be a burning sense of social justice. While increased production is of the utmost importance, it is equally important to remove, or reduce, and prevent the concentration of wealth and economic power... A reorientation of our socio-economic institutions in this spirit is, accordingly, a first necessity.[10]

As a result, the basic goal of the economic policy lies in a rapid increase in the standard of living of the people, through measures which also would promote equality and social justice.

2. Performance of the Economic Policy

The objectives of the economic policy which India has followed since its independence might be summarized as follows: (a) rapid economic growth through planning, and (b) a more equitable distribution of income and wealth. The means to accomplish these objectives are interrelated in such a way that some of these means might help in achieving both of these objectives while others might aid one objective at the expense of the other. The main policy instruments used to achieve these objectives are (a) economic planning, (b) nationalization, (c) land reform, (d) wealth distribution, (e) income distribution, and (f) taxation. As noted earlier, the planning process has resulted in some progress of economic growth (in terms of increase in national income), but can one make a similar statement with respect to the effectiveness of other policy instruments ? In the following paragraphs, we will examine the effectiveness of other policy instruments used to achieve the above objectives.

Nationalization. One of the methods which might be used to achieve economic growth and to alter the distribution of incomes in a mixed economy is to nationalize the productive enterprises. The idea behind this method is that such a measure would enable the government to increase the public profit by decreasing the share of private profit in the national income. Since Independence, the Government of India has been taking more and more enterprises under state control and the Fourth Five Year Plan has particularly re-emphasized this approach.

Nationalization can help in the process of economic growth and the redistribution of income, provided the public sector is run efficiently and is generating some surplus which could be used for development purposes. If on the other hand, public enterprises are inefficient, and incur losses, they are likely to retard economic growth. Under these circumstances additional taxes might be necessary to compensate for such losses which might then entail transferring scarce resources from other more productive sources.

It may, however, be pointed out that India is not following the policy of nationalization by choice but rather by necessity. This view is accepted even by big

7 Planning Commission, *Second Five Year Plan* (Delhi : Government of India Press, 1956), p. 22.

8 Ibid., p. 22.

9 Ibid., p. 24, and Planning Commission, *Third Five Year Plan* (Delhi : Government of India Press, 1961), p. 48.

10 *Fourth Five Year Plan,* p. iv.

industrialists in the country. J. R. D. Tata, speaking about the Bokaro Steel Plant, said, "India's economy and the standard of living of our people cannot grow without additional steel and it is clear that the private sector, even if permitted to do so, would not be able to undertake on its own a programme of expansion at an average rate exceeding a million tons of new capacity a year.[11] The growth of the public sector in the Indian economy indicated in Table 1.

Table 1. Growth of Government Companies

Year	Number of Companies	Paid-up Capital (in crores of Rs)
1955-56	61	66.0
1960-61	142	547.0
1961-62	154	629.7
1962-63	160	786.0
1963-64	176	960.8
1964-65	183	1114.9
1965-66	212	1214.3
1966-67	232	1391.5

SOURCE: Dagli Vadilal, *The Public Sector in India—A Summary* (Bombay: Vora & Co., 1969), p. 272.

It will be observed that the growth of the public sector in terms of the numbers and the capital, has been quite impressive. The number of companies has increased from 61 in 1955–66 to 232 in 1966–67, and the paid-up capital has increased from Rs. 66 crores to Rs. 1392 crores. Unfortunately, the performance record of the public sector has been rather less than satisfactory. Table 2 gives a statement on return on paid-up capital for central government undertakings[12] according to the type of concern. Although on aggregate basis, the government undertakings have been able to reduce their overall losses in 1969–70 compared to 1968–69. But, from a micro analysis point of view in 1969–70, 33 out of 78 companies incurred losses amounting to Rs. 72 crores. Some of the undertakings which showed losses are: Hindustan Steel, Heavy Engineering Corporation, India Drugs and Pharmaceutical, Heavy Electricals, Mining and Allied Machinery Corporation, Hindustan Photo Films Manufacturing Company, Central Inland Water Transport Corporation, Tannery and Footwear Corporation, and National Building Construction Corporation. The performance of the last six of these companies has been so low that their total losses have exceeded their paid-up capital. Up to March, 1970, the cumulative losses for these six companies was Rs. 93 crores as against their aggregate paid-up capital of Rs. 79 crores.[13] However, there are some undertakings which have shown performance comparable to the private sector. During 1969–70, 24 undertakings declared dividends amounting to Rs. 12.7 crores as against Rs. 11.7 crores in 1968–69, giving the rate of dividend between three and twenty per cent for various undertakings.[14]

On July 19, 1969, fourteen leading banks were nationalized. Besides other benefits this step was expected to ensure an adequate availability of credit for various types of small producers and other business units on reasonable terms.[15] It is remarkable that, since the nationalization of the fourteen major banks, the expansion in the number of branches has recorded notable progress. The number of additional bank offices opened during the period July 19, 1969 to April 30, 1971 was 3,419, of which 2,934 (2,011 in centres without banks in the past) offices were started by the nationalized banks.[16] In

[11] Statement to A.G.M. of TISCO, 29, August 1963 (*Eastern Economist*, 9, August 1963) quoted in A. H. Hanson, *The Process of Planning: A Study of India's Five Year Plans, 1950–69* (London: Oxford University Press, 1966), p. 970.

[12] The data in State Government undertakings is very scanty and therefore no meaningful analysis can be attempted. *See* Raj, K. Nigam, "State Government Undertakings, in *The Public Sector in India—A Survey*, (Ed.) V. Dagli (Bombay: Vora & Co., 1969).

[13] V. Balasubramanian, "A View of the Public Sector," *Eastern Economist*, September 24, 1971, p. 556.

[14] "Performance of Central Government Undertakings for 1969–70," *Eastern Economist*, July 23, 1971, p. 189.

[15] *Third Five Year Plan*, pp. 24–25.

[16] "Bank Offices in Unbanked Centres," *Eastern Economist*, January 1971, p. 94.

Table 2. Return on Paid-up Capital of Central Government Companies (Rupees in lakhs)

	1968-69			1969-70		
	Number	Paid-up Capital	Profit/Loss	Number	Paid-up Capital	Profit/Loss
I. Running Concerns	56	1,35,893.38	(−) 2,685.54	60	1,44,111.61	(−) 283.40
Companies which earned profit	31	38,289.74	(+) 6,438.93	32	42,155.79	(+) 6,818.86
Companies which incurred loss	25	97,603.64	(−) 9,124.47	28	1,01,955.82	(−) 7,102.26
A. Industrial	49	1,34,944.44	(−) 3,898.27	52	1,42,843.42	(−) 1,852.71
Companies which earned profit	26	37,664.74	(+) 5,160.12	25	40,897.60	(+) 5,249.08
Companies which incurred loss	23	97,279.70	(−) 9,058.39	27	1,01,945.82	(−) 7,101.79
B. Trading and services	4	773.94	(+) 1,155.18	4	1,083.19	(+) 1,464.89
Companies which earned profit	2	450.00	(+) 1,221.26	4	1,083.19	(+) 1,464.89
Companies which incurred loss	2	323.94	(−) 66.08	..	..	..
C. Consultancy	1	25.00	(+) 17.26	2	35.00	(+) 43.13
Companies which earned profit	1	25.00	(+) 17.26	1	25.00	(+) 43.60
Companies which incurred loss	..	..	..	1	10.00	(−) 0.47
D. Financial	2	150.00	(+) 40.29	2	150.00	(+) 61.29
Companies which earned profit	2	150.00	(+) 40.29	2	150.00	(+) 61.29
Companies which incurred loss	..	..	..	..	..	..
II. Promotional and Developmental Undertakings	8	756.54	(−) 152.17	9	1,617.44	(−) 22.33
Companies which earned profit	3	203.84	(+) 15.78	5	800.24	(+) 56.83
Companies which incurred loss	5	552.70	(−) 167.95	4	817.20	(−) 79.16
III. Companies under construction (partial operation)	9	26,017.57	..	9	41,830.16	(−) 27.21
Companies which earned profit	..	..	..	1	744.19	(+) 0.26
Companies which incurred loss	..	..	..	1	700.00	(−) 27.47
Companies which have not prepared Profit and loss account	..	..	..	7	40,385.97	..
Total:	73	1,62,667.49	(−) 2,837.71	78	1,87,559.21	(−) 332.94

SOURCES: V. Balasubramanian, "View of the Public Sector," *Eastern Economist*, September 24, 1971, p. 555.

contrast, the annual average growth has been 362 bank offices during the nine years prior to nationalization. This reduced the population per bank from 65,000 in June, 1969, to 47,000 in March, 1971. Table 3 gives the figures on advances allowed by banks in the public sector to various sectors hitherto neglected as a percentage of their aggregate advances.

An examination of Table 3 would show that the proportion of the advance to agriculture and other neglected sectors as a percentage of the total bank advances by the public sector banks has been increasing.

According to some sources, however, the service to clients by the nationalized banks has deteriorated markedly and their net profits have declined.[17] The main reasons for decline of profits might be increase in the wage bill due to union pressures, and

17 "Whither Nationalized Banks," *Eastern Economist*, August 20, 1971.

Table 3. Public Sector Banks' Advances to Various Hitherto Neglected Sectors as Percentage of their Aggregate Advances

Sector	June 1969	June 1970	March 1971*
Agriculture			
(a) Direct finance			
(excluding plantations)	1.26	4.27	5.05
(b) Indirect finance	4.05	3.87	3.28
Small-scale industry	8.34	10.30	11.20
Road transport operators	0.22	0.69	1.00
Retail trade and small business	0.64	1.81	1.95
Professional and self-employed persons	0.01	0.19	0.23
Education	0.02	0.06	0.10
Total	14.54	21.19	22.81

*Provisional

SOURCES: "Banks: Two Years after Nationalization," *Eastern Economist*, August 6, 1971, p. 276.

indiscriminate lending to small borrowers without taking into account their credit worth.

It may be too early to pass any judgment about the future performance of government undertakings. This is especially true when many of the undertakings are not free to determine their price and output policies. For example, railways are subsidizing heavily in the airconditioned and first class passenger traffic, and slow-running passenger trains without much traffic.[18] In addition, these undertakings are required to absorb certain social costs such as the cost of developing new townships. The government of India should allow all the undertakings to follow on cost, output and pricing to maximize profit and the government might subsidize directly only those commodities which on social grounds should be supplied at lower prices. Such a policy would allow the undertakings to compete with the private enterprises for profits in the market, and it would ensure greater efficiency for public enterprises.

Land Reforms. For a long time, small and particularly uneconomic agricultural holdings have been considered as bottlenecks in the development of the rural economy. Being fully aware of this phenomenon, the planners in the beginning emphasized that the measures of land reform have special significance, because (i) they provide the social, economic, and institutional framework for agricultural development, and (ii) they exert great influence on the life of the vast majority of the people. Under such considerations, the objectives of land reforms were mainly: (i) to remove various impediments in agricultural production which arise from the agrarian structure, and (ii) to create conditions for evolving (as speedily as possible) an agrarian economy with high levels of efficiency and productivity.[19] During the last 23 years, some progress has been made in this direction but a great deal more remains to be done.

Although most of the states have enacted legislation for ceilings on land holdings, the provisions regarding level of ceilings, and transfer and exemption from ceilings differ considerably from state to state. On account of this diversity of legislation in different states and loopholes in imple-

18 R. K. Koshal, "Marginal Cost Pricing and Resource Allocation in Transport in India," *Sankhya*, (December 1972).

19 Planning Commission, *Second Five Year Plan* (New Delhi: Government of India Press 1956), p. 178.

mentation, only about 964,800 hectares have so far been declared surplus for redistribution to landless labour and small land owners. However, out of this declared surplus only 640,000 hectares have been actually collected by states, but its distribution has been substantially below 640,000 hectares.

ceiling to about 40 per cent of the irrigated area which is only 22 per cent of total net crop area.[21]

Wealth Distribution. For the year 1961–62, Table 4 gives the distribution of rural households according to value of assets, and Table 5 according to area owned. Table 6

Table 4. Distribution of Rural Households According to Values of Assets, 1961-62

	Cultivators		Non-Cultivators		All Rural Households	
	Percentage of		Percentage of		Percentage of	
Asset Group	Households	Aggregate Value of Assets	Households	Aggregate Value of Assets	Households	Aggregate Value of Assets
Less than Rs. 10,000	82.9	39.7	97.3	62.6	86.7	41.6
Rs. 10,000-20,000	10.7	22.2	1.6	13.2	8.3	21.4
Rs. 20,000 and above	6.4	38.1	1.1	24.2	5.0	37.0
	100.0	100.0	100.0	100.0	100.0	100.0

SOURCE: T.N. Krishnan, "Taxation of Property and Net Wealth in India—A Note," *Economic and Political Weekly*, January 1, 1972, p. 27.

In order to make the ceiling laws unifrom and more meaningful, the Union Agriculture Ministry has proposed that "the ceiling for a family of five members may be fixed within the range of ten to eighteen acres of perennially irrigated land or land under assured irrigation from government sources capable of growing two crops."[20] However, the proposed legislation fails to fill up many of the existing loopholes applying especially to the implementation of reform measures and the interpretation of ceilings on different types and grades of land. In the first place, the phrase "irrigation from government sources" is limited in its scope. This indicates that land which is irrigated by private tube-wells, canals, or tanks, consisting of about 60 per cent of the total irrigated land in 1969–70, is supposed to be excluded from the above phrase and thus from the proposed ceiling. Secondly, this legislation may fail to leave any appreciable impact since government is proposing a

gives distribution of urban wealth in the form of urban residential property. In 1961–62, the aggregate value of assets of cultivators and non-cultivators amounted to Rs. 33,778 crores and Rs. 3,079 crores

Table 5: Distribution of Rural Households According to Area Owned by Size Class of Ownership, 1961–62

Size Class of Ownership Holding	Percentage of	
	Households Owning Land	Area Owned
Below 9.99 acres	86.5	40.5
10-19.99 acres	8.5	23.6
20 acres and above	5.0	35.9

Source: T. N. Krishnan, "Taxation of Property and Net Wealth in India—A Note," *Economic and Political Weekly*, January 1972, p. 27. The figures in this table are based on the data collected by the Seventeenth Round National Sample Survey.

20 "Land Ceiling and the Farm Entrepreneur," *Economic and Political Weekly,* May 6, 197?, p. 915.

21 Ibid., p. 915.

respectively. This implies that about 92 per cent of the total assets of all rural households belonged to cultivator households. Furthermore, 86.7 per cent of rural households claimed 41.6 per cent of aggregate assets, while 5 per cent of rural households accounted for 37.0 per cent of aggregate assets. Land ownership also tells a similar story (see Table 5). As regards urban residential property in 1961–62, the lowest 20 per cent of households owned only 0.4 per cent of the aggregate market value of the residential property, while the share of the highest 20 per cent was 87.3 per cent, with the top 10 per cent accounting for as much as 79.7 per cent. These figures clearly show that even after ten years of planning for an egalitarian Indian society, a considerable degree of inequality in the distribution of incomes still exists. Moreover, there is concentration of economic power in the hands of a numerically small portion of the population.

Income Distribution. As stated earlier although the process of planning has shown some progress in terms of economic growth, the same cannot be said about inequalities in income distribution. A study of literature on the subject would show that nothing concrete has been done by the government more than quantifying the existing inequalities and stating its objectives. The one step worth mentioning in this connection is the step taken by the Planning Commission in 1960 by setting up a committee (the Committee on Distribution of Income and Levels of Living) with the following terms of reference:[22]

(i) to review the changes in the levels of living during the First and Second Five Year Plans;

(ii) To study recent trends in the distribution of income and wealth; and

(iii) in particular, to ascertain the extent to which the operation of the economic system has resulted in concentration of wealth and means of production.

This committee submitted its final report in 1969. In terms of the basic objective of an egalitarian society, the information furnished by this committee and its conclusions are rather revealing. Table 7 summarizes the share of households in different income and in total consumption

Table 6. Distribution of Urban Wealth in the Form of Urban Residential Property in 1961-62

Decile Group	Owner Occupied: Aggregate Value (Rs. Crores)	Owner Occupied: Percentage Share in Aggregate Value	Residential Property: Aggregate Value (Rs. Crores)	Residential Property: Percentage Share in Aggregate Value
0-10	10.01	0.2	10.01	0.1
10-20	29.68	0.7	29.68	0.3
20-30	53.96	1.2	53.96	0.6
30-40	83.65	1.8	83.65	0.9
40-50	121.84	2.7	121.84	1.3
50-60	190.86	4.2	190.86	2.0
60-70	285.15	6.3	285.15	3.0
70-80	446.06	9.8	446.06	4.6
80-90	732.54	16.1	732.54	7.6
90-100	2,588.04	57.0	7,667.09	79.7
ALL CLASSES	4,541.81	100.0	9,620.80	100.0

SOURCE: T. N. Krishnan, "Taxation of Property and Net Wealth in India—A Note," *Economic and Political Weekly*, January 1, 1972, pp. 28-29.

22 Planning Commission, *Report of the Committee on Distribution of Income and Levels of Living, Part I* (Government of India Press, 1964), p. 1.

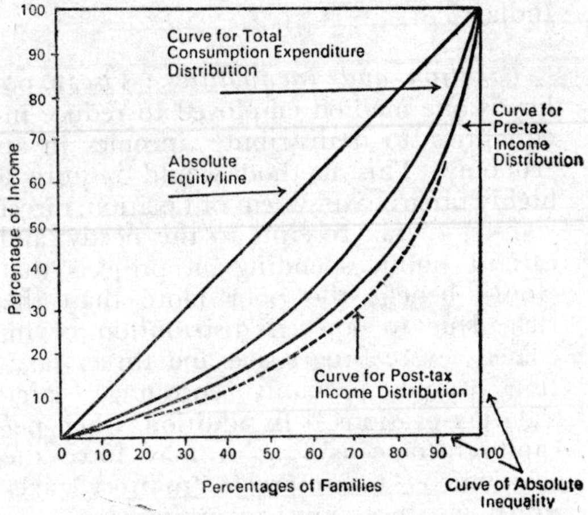

Fig. 1

expenditure brackets. Figure I is a Lorenz curve based on data from urban areas. Lorenz curves show the extent of departure between an equal distribution of income and the actual distribution of income. Along the diagonal line representing equal distribution, the lowest 10 per cent of the families received 10 per cent of total income, the lowest 30 per cent of families received 30 per cent of total income, and so on. The actual line of income distribution reveals considerable inequalities in the urban sector. Table 7 reveals that in 1959–60 the top 10 per cent of the rural households accounted for 26.8 per cent of total expenditures, while the bottom 10 per cent accounted for merely 3.4 per cent. Regarding the distribution of pre-tax income, the top 10 per cent of the rural

Table 7. Share of Consumption and Income in the Aggregate Consumption and Income Among Various Fractile Groups in 1959-60

Fractile Group	Share of total consumption expenditure (July 1959 to June 1960)		Share in aggregate income of different pre-tax income tenths, 1960		Share of household incomes in aggregate incomes by different post-tax income tenths, 1960
	Urban	Rural	Urban	Rural	Urban
1	2	3	4	5	6
0–10	3.33 (3.33)	3.40	1.3 (1.3)	0.7 (0.7)	1.3 (1.3)
10–20	4.66 (7.99)	4.94	2.7 (4.0)	3.3 (4.0)	2.8 (4.1)
20–30	5.67 (13.66)	5.82	3.6 (7.6)	4.5 (8.5)	3.7 (7.8)
30–40	6.34 (20.00)	6.69	4.5 (14.1)	5.6 (14.1)	4.7 (12.5)
40–50	7.44 (27.44)	7.68	5.4 (19.5)	6.6 (20.7)	5.6 (18.1)
50–60	8.30 (35.74)	8.61	6.5 (26.0)	7.7 (28.4)	6.7 (24.8)
60–70	10.21 (45.95)	9.93	8.1 (34.1)	9.5 (37.9)	8.3 (33.1)
70–80	12.17 (58.12)	11.74	10.3 (44.4)	12.1 (50.0)	10.7 (43.8)
80–90	15.88 (74.00)	14.42	15.2 (59.6)	16.4 (66.4)	15.8 (59.6)
90–100	26.00 (100.00)	26.77 (100.00)	42.4 (100.0)	33.6 (100.0)	40.4 (100.0)

SOURCE AND NOTE: Planning Commission, *Report of the Committee on Distribution and Levels of Living, Part I* (Government of India Press, 1964). (i) Figures in parentheses are the cumulative percentages.

households claimed 33.6 per cent of total income, while the bottom 10 per cent accounted for only 0.7 per cent. The corresponding figures for urban population are 42.4 per cent and 1.3 per cent respectively. Meanwhile, for the post-tax income of the urban population, the top 10 per cent accounted for 40.4 per cent of the total income, while the bottom 10 per cent got only 1.3 per cent. These figures clearly reveal the existence of concentration of economic power in a small group in the country. These figures also suggest that the imposition of taxation has not made much difference to the range of variations between the top and the bottom tenth of the population. As is evident, these figures pertain to the last year of the Second Five Year Plan and, therefore, it might be argued that, even after ten years of planning and various policies for taxing the upper incomes, there is a considerable measure of concentration in urban as well as in rural income.

It is quite common for politicians and even for expert committees to conceal the actual facts by making vague statements without giving any factual information. For example, the Committee on Distribution of Income and Levels of Living stated that a considerable measure of inequality in the distribution of income and wealth also existed in several other developed and developing countries.[23] The Committee did not give any comparative data for other countries. A recent expert committee report, namely, the Report of the Banking Commission,[24] has also made a similar remark.

Table 8 gives percentage distribution of the western european countries, and the U.S.A. A comparison of information in this table with that in Table 7 (Columns 4 or 6) shows that in the developed countries (listed in Table 8) except West Germany,[25] the top 10 per cent claimed less share of income than a similar group in India.

Taxation and Inequalities. Fiscal policy is one method employed to reduce inequalities to redistribute incomes in an economy. This method would require a highly progressive system of taxation, direct transfer of tax receipts to the needy, and careful public spending on projects that would benefit the poor more than the rich. Due to uneven distribution of incomes, severe progressive and direct taxation would probably encourage large scale tax evasions.[26] In addition, when per capita income is low, it may force the government to resort to indirect taxes which are not only regressive but may also be inflationary.[27] From this viewpoint, the fiscal policy followed by the government of India—a combination of severely progressive direct taxation and large-scale indirect taxation may actually have widened the distance between the current living standards of the rich and the poor by encouraging the former to consume more and save less.[28] This issue needs further research by Indian economists.

In order to get further insight into the tax policies, it will be useful to study the structure and the growth of taxation since planning in India. Table 9 summarizes the growth of various taxes both at the Centre and the states. At the Centre, between the period 1951–52 and 1968–69, income and expenditure tax revenue increased by 359 percent, taxes on capital and capital transactions increased by 437 per cent, taxes on commodities and services increased by 474 per cent, and total tax revenue increased by 440 per cent. The corresponding figures for the States are 268, 273, 851 and 602 per cent respectively. It is clear that both the Centre and the states have derived relatively more revenue from indirect taxation

[23] Ibid., pp. 29–30.

[24] A. C. Shah, "Source Book, Note Policy Guide," *Economic and Political Weekly*, April 1, 1972, p. 703.

[25] Data for West Germany are difficult to interpret since undistributed profits of private companies are included.

[26] "No Taxes, No Evasion!" *Economic and Political Weekly*, March 25, 1972, pp. 657–58.

[27] John Lindauer, *Macroeconomics* (New York: John Wiley & Sons, Inc., 1971), pp. 344-45.

[28] D. Ghosh, "Garibi Hatao—Making the Capitalist Hen Lay Socialist Egg," *Economic and Political Weekly*.

Table 8. Percentage Distribution of Personal Income Before Tax[a] by Decile[b] and Percentile Groups

	United States		United Kingdom		West Germany			Netherlands		Denmark		Norway		Sweden		France		Finland	
	1955	1965	1954	1964	1955	1960	1964	1952	1962	1953	1963	1957	1963	1954	1963	1956	1962	1952	1962
Decile groups																			
1	1	1	5.5	2.0	1.7	2.0	2.0	1.3	1.3	1.4	1.7	1.1	1.0	2.0	1.6	0.7	0.5	1.0	0.5
2	3	8		3.1	2.9	3.0	3.2	2.9	2.7	3.2	3.3	3.4	3.5	3.6	2.8	2.2	1.4	3.1	1.9
3	4	5	4.5	4.2	3.9	4.4	4.7	4.1	4.2	4.4	4.7	4.6	5.3	5.0	4.1	3.3	2.9	4.8	3.5
4	6	6	5.8	6.0	5.0	5.6	5.4	5.7	5.8	5.8	6.1	6.3	6.8	6.2	5.5	5.4	4.7	5.9	5.2
5	8	8	7.3	7.5	5.9	5.9	6.5	7.0	7.4	7.8	7.7	7.9	8.5	7.8	7.7	6.8	6.4	7.2	6.8
6	9	9	8.6	9.1	7.1	7.1	7.2	8.4	8.6	9.1	9.1	9.7	10.0	9.3	9.7	7.8	7.6	9.0	8.6
7	11	11	10.4	11.0	8.3	8.0	8.4	10.6	10.0	10.8	10.9	11.0	11.3	10.6	11.4	10.3	10.3	10.7	11.1
8	13	12	12.7	12.9	9.2	9.0	9.6	11.7	11.6	13.3	13.3	13.0	13.1	12.7	13.2	12.4	12.5	13.0	13.1
9	16	16	14.8	14.9	12.0	11.5	11.5	14.3	14.6	16.2	16.1	15.4	15.6	15.5	16.1	17.0	16.9	16.4	16.8
10	30	29	30.4	29.3	44.0	43.5	41.4	35.0	33.8	28.8	27.1	27.6	24.9	27.3	27.9	34.1	36.8	28.9	32.5
	100	100	100	100	100	100	100	100	100	100	100	100	100	100	100	100	100	100	100

Sources and Notes: (i) Except the United States, data are from Economic Commission for Europe, *Incomes in Post-War Europe: A Study of Policies, Growth and Distribution* (Geneva: United Nations, 1967), Table 9.19.

(ii) The data for the United States are from Department of Commerce, *The Statistical Abstract of the United States, for 1963 and 1972* (Washington, D.C.: Government Printing Office).

[a]Total personal imcome for the United Kingdom, West Germany, Netherlands and France, assessed income for the Scandinavian countries, data for West Germany provided, before publication, by Professor G. Goseke, Deutsches Institute fur Wirtschaftsforschung, Berlin. The figures include undistributed profits of corporation. Data for Denmark refer to "after-tax" income.

[b]Calculated by reference to the number of taxpayers, except for France where the unit is the household.

than from direct taxation. This fact is further brought out by examining the share of the Centre and states in the various taxes. At the Centre, the share of indirect tax revenue in the total tax revenue has increased from 69.6 per cent in 1951–52 to 75.0 per cent in 1968–69, while at the States the share has increasd from 52.9 per cent in 1951–52 to 74.4 per cent in 1968–69. Thus, it is clear that in India almost 75 per cent of tax receipts are composed of indirect taxes for both the Centre and the States. It is interesting to note that in the United Kingdom in 1968–69, the collection from indirect taxes was about 39 per cent[29] of the total proceeds and in the United States the corresponding figures in 1970 for the federal government were about 10 per cent[30] and for the states were about 54 per cent.[31]

[29] Central Statistical Office, *Annual Abstract of Statistics,* 1969, London: (Her Majesty's Stationary Officer, 1969), p. 289.

[30] United States Government, *Economic Report of the President* (Washington D. C.: U. S. Government Printing Office, 1972), p. 273.

[31] Ibid., p. 278.

Table 9. Growth of Tax Revenue of the Centre and the States in India during 1951-52-1968-69

	Income and Expenditures Tax		Taxes on Capital and Capital Transactions		Taxes on Commodities and Services		Total Taxes
	Rs. Crores	As % of Total Taxes	Rs. Crores	As % of Total Taxes	Rs. Crores	As % of Total Taxes	
				CENTRE			
1951-52	134.74	29.3	4.81	1.1	319.74	69.6	459.29
	100.0)		(100.0)		(100.0)		(100.0)
1955-56	113.23	27.5	2.55	0.6	295.69	71.9	411.47
	(84.0)		(53.0)		(92.5)		(89.6)
1960-61	191.97	26.3	13.49	1.8	524.68	71.9	730.14
	(142.5)		(280.5)		(164.2)		(159.1)
1965-66	453.72	25.4	19.83	1.1	1311.07	73.5	1783.62
	(336.7)		(412.3)		(410.1)		(388.8)
1968-69	484.00	24.0	21.00	1.0	1514.00	75.0	2019.00
	(359.2)		(436.6)		(473.6)		(439.8)
				STATES			
1951-52	57.10	20.3	75.40	26.8	148.60	52.0	281.10
	(100.0)		(100.0)		(100.0)		(100.0)
1955-56	63.10	17.7	111.00	31.2	182.00	51.1	356.10
	(110.5)		(147.2)		(122.5)		(126.7)
1960-61	100.50	16.1	144.40	23.1	379.90	60.8	624.80
	(176.0)		(191.5)		(255.7)		(222.3)
1965-66	133.90	12.0	196.70	17.6	787.20	70.4	1117.80
	(234.5)		(260.9)		(529.7)		(397.7)
1968-69	207.10	12.2	221.00	13.1	1264.00	74.7	1692.10
	(368.0)		(273.10)		(850.6)		(602.0)

NOTE AND SOURCE : (1) Figures in parentheses are index numbers with 1951-52 = 100.0

(2) J. R. Gupta, "The Structure of Indian Taxation, 1951-52-1970-71," *Eastern Economist*, August 13, 1971, pp. xxiv, xxv & xxxi.

The above analysis suggests that in India the tax policy at both the Centre and State level has been relying increasingly upon indirect taxes. This is inconsistent with the social objective of income equality. Furthermore, taxes such as capital and capital transactions taxes which are potential sources for mitigating the inherited inequality are not fully tapped, especially by the States.

3. Conclusions

From the above analysis it appears that the objectives of India's socialistic society have not been met.[32] Even after twenty-five years of Independence and twenty-three years of planning, we have not even made significant progress towards

[32] Op. cit., S. J. Patel.

this objective of a socialistic society. A great deal of constructive effort is needed to (i) run the nationalized undertakings efficiently, (ii) enact a proper land ceiling legislation, (iii) reduce the income and wealth inequalities, and (iv) close the loopholes in the present tax system. It is not sufficient to enact new legislation, rather it is more important to introduce administrative reforms to enforce the existing legislation and tax laws properly. An example may make this point clear. The State excise duty on country liquor in Delhi is higher than in Haryana. This encourages considerable amount of smuggling from Haryana to Delhi. The State of Delhi is not only losing excise revenue but is also spending a considerable amount to reduce smuggling. The simple and costless solution to this problem probably is that the state of Delhi should have an excise duty which would make transporting liquor from neighbouring states unprofitable. This will not only bring more revenue to Delhi, but will also reduce the expenditure on enforcement staff. It is unfortunate that so far no one has given due importance to the administrative reforms; without which it may be difficult to achieve the social objectives of our socialist society.

BIBLIOGRAPHY

Bardhan, Pranab K., "On the Minimum Level of Living and the Rural Poor," *Indian Economic Review,* April 1970, pp. 129–36.

Dandekar, V. M., Nilakantha, R., "Poverty in India—Dimension and Trends," *Economic and Political Weekly,* January 2, 1971.

Gilbey, E. W., *A Primer on Economics of Consumption,* Random House, New York, 1968.

Malenbaum, Wilfred, "Some Political Aspects of Economic Development," *World Politics,* 1958.

Minhas, B. S., "Rural Poverty, Land Redistribution and Development Strategy: Facts and Policy," *Indian Economic Review,* Vol. V, No. 1, 1970, pp. 97–128.

Mukherjee, M., *National Income of India : Trends and Structure,* Statistical Publishing Society, 1969.

Pai, M. R., (Ed.) *A Decade of Planning in India—A Commentary,* Popular Prakashan, Bombay, 1969.

Prakash Om, *The Theory and Working of State Corporations,* Frederick A. Praeger, New York, 1963.

Reid, G. L. and K. Allen, *Nationalized Industries,* Penguin Books, Baltimore, Maryland, 1970.

Swamy, Subramanian, "Structural Changes and the Distribution of Income by Size—The Case of India," *Review of Income and Wealth,* June 1967, pp. 156–174.

Turvey, Ralph, Economic Analysis and Public Enterprises, *Rowman and Littlefield,* Totowa, New Jersey, 1971.

10

Two Decades of Planning in Retrospect

ISMAIL SHARIFF

"A planned policy for economic development is both complicated and comprehensive. It must influence and direct the whole activity of a modern society in all its ramification."

—JAN TINBERGEN

1. Developmental Planning

Planning for an economic policy and more particularly for a development policy is today becoming more and more a part of state activity. More countries are tending to adopt this technique, and the technique itself is constantly improving. The communist countries went over quite suddenly after the Bolshevik Revolution from an unplanned to a planned economy; the transition in other countries was, however, gradual. Whereas, in the past, the state often acted in accordance with the principle of *laissez-faire,* only after natural catastrophe—a war or some other grave crisis or difficulty led to the conscious introduction of "thinking ahead." This thinking ahead is now known as forecasting and it has continued to improve in recent years. We have progressed from the rather naive method of forecasting by extrapolating the line of a graph to the much more sophisticated method of forecasting based on the knowledge of the operation of social and economic forces.

There has also been a change in the basic methodology from a micro to a macro approach as more attention has been given to the mutual relationships between various economic, social, and political forces, with the result that every effort is now made to integrate isolated parts of economic policy. For example, when the west reached the stage of planning and defining its economic aims, there was a marked preference for the use of what are known as macro-economic figures, showing a summary of the national income, national consumption, employment, and so on.[1]

Among the simplifications that have so far been scientifically applied with some

[1] H. Theil, *Economic Forecasts and Policy* (Amsterdam : Zoderdipan, 1968), pp. 71–72.

success can be counted a series of assumptions which may be termed the assumptions of a long-existing development. They include, for example, a constant growth of population, a constant investment quotient (in other words, a constant relationship between investment and a national product), a constant discount for the deferment of consumption, a constant technical development, and the existence of a certain kind of simple law of production, the so-called Cobb-Douglas production function.[2] In general terms the three chief elements of modern planned economic policy are: a looking ahead, co-ordination, and the attainment of a deliberate aim.[3] A given aim no doubt can be achieved by various means or a combination of means, and one of the special functions of the plan is that of choosing the best possible available means. The choice of means is to a great extent conditioned by their effectiveness, although the question of social preference, or valuation will also play a part.

Above all, in spite of the progress made to date in the methodology and technique of planning for development it is to be noted that developmental planning is a comparatively new branch of applied science, barely twenty years old in the west, and over fifty years old in the Soviet Union. In principle it is concerned with the whole economy. It is hardly necessary to say that it is still underdeveloped and unable to provide an answer, or at least a full answer, to many of the questions that arise in the course of formulating a development plan.[4]

2. The Problem in India

The Indian economy at the end of the British rule (in 1947) had practically reached a stage of stagnation. This can be attributed to the passive role of the colonial government about economic development. As a result, per capita income in India had not risen in fifty years, and was in 1951 about one-fortieth of that of the United States, one thirteenth of that of the United Kingdom, and about one-third of that of Japan. The per capita income in India is, in fact, lower than that of the other fifty-four underdeveloped countries for which the United Nations has published the data, including Egypt, Brazil, and Peru.[5]

Very likely also, the standard of living of the large masses of people in India was even lower than indicated by the per capita income, because of the unequal distribution of income, unemployment, and under-employment. In 1950, out of a total working force of about 170 million, about 8 million were unemployed and about 15 million, on a conservative estimate, were under-employed.[6]

If steel output and the educational base, particularly technical education, were to be considered as rough indices of the extent of development, Indian development with regard to the steel output, even in 1955–56, was some 60 to 80 years behind that of the United States, United Kingdom, Germany, France, and Russia. On the other hand, from the point of view of education Indian development was behind all these countries by about 80 to 100 years.[7] Such shortcomings were aggravated by the large absolute size of her population, about 564 million in 1971, to be exact.

In view of this there existed a compelling urgency to generate a process of sustained growth in India. This urgency has become even more pressing due to the widespread poverty and the growing awareness that something must be done, and done at once. Moreover, unlike countries where economic evolution preceded political evolution, India attained political freedom, far ahead of economic freedom. Because of this phenomenon, the

---

[2] E. Phelps, "The Golden Rule of Accumulation," *American Economic Review,* LI (1961), pp. 638.

[3] J. Tinberger, *Development Planning* (New York: McLord University Library, McGraw-Hill Book Co., 1967), pp. 44 and 76.

[4] Ibid., p. 43.

[5] United Nations Statistical Papers, Service 4, Per Capita National Product of Some Selected Countries, 1952–54 (New York: 1957).

[6] Government of India, Planning Commission, *Third Five Year Plan,* Draft Outline, 1960, p. 84.

[7] P. C. Mahalanabis, "Net Step in Planning," *Sankhya,* January 1960, p. 9.

need for economic development became both more imperative, and more difficult. It soon became apparent that if social, political, and economic catastrophes were to be avoided, India needed to accomplish in a very short period the degree and extent of economic development for which the countries that are developed today took more than a century to accomplish under more favourable conditions. As a matter of fact this threat still hangs over India.

In consideration of such pressures, a quarter century scheme of economic development was adopted in 1951, under a strategy 'Five Year Plans'.

3. The First Five Year Plan 1951 to 1956

With the attainment of independence in 1947, the need for a planned development of the Indian economy became urgent, for reasons outlined earlier. Due to the burdens of partition and other political exigencies, the formal inauguration of planning was delayed until the establishment of the Planning Commission in March 1950 (by a resolution of the Government of India) under the chairmanship of Mr. Nehru, the then Prime Minister of India.

Assignment of the Planning Commission

The Planning Commission has been charged with the dual responsibility of first making a thorough assessment of both the tangible and intangible resources of the country, and of formulating a plan for the most effective and balanced utilization of the country's resources. It is supposed to determine the relative priorities and allocate the resources for their completion, to indicate the retarding factors in the economic development and the necessary conditions under the existing socio-political framework for the successful execution of plans. It has also to help in evolving a proper machinery for the implementation, appraisal, and evaluation of the progress achieved. In addition to this, the Planning Commission has also been assigned the task of giving advice on problems referred to it by central or state governments. Thus, in a nutshell, the Planning Commission is assigned the important task of formulation, phasing, implementation, and evaluation of planned programmes.[8]

In keeping with its assigned task, the Planning Commission in July, 1951, presented a draft outline of the plan covering a period of five years (from April 1951 to March 1956). The principal objectives of planning as a whole were set out over a spread of about 25 years, of which the First Five Year Plan marked a beginning. The prime objective of planning was to create a congenial atmosphere in which the living standards are reasonably high, and all citizens, immaterial of sex, may have full and equal opportunity for growth and service. Secondly, it was decided that simultaneously a steady advance should be made towards the realization of wider objectives, such as full employment and the removal of economic inequalities. Thus maximum production, full employment, the attainment of economic equality, and social justice constituted the overall accepted objective of planning.[9]

The First Five Year Plan had dual objectives: first, of correcting the disequilibrium in the economy caused by the war and the partition of the country; secondly, it attempted to provide simultaneously for an all round balanced development, which would ensure a rising national income and a steady improvement in living standards over a period of five years.[10]

However, the First Five Year Plan was based on three assumptions:

1. That population would grow at the rate of 1.25 per cent per annum which was the rate recorded in the last decenial Census) prior to 1951.
2. That postulating the capital output ratio of 3 : 1.[11]
3. That the rate of saving as a proportion of total national income would

---

8 India, Planning Commission, *First Five Year Plan*, pp. 1 to 6.

9 *First Five Year Plan*, p. 28.

10 Review of the First Five Year Plan, May 1957, p. 1.

11 Planning Commission, *First Five Year Plan*, p. 22.

go up from 5 per cent in the base year 1950–51 to 6¾ per cent in 1955–56 to about 11 per cent by 1960–61, and 20 per cent by 1967–68.[12]

On these assumptions, it was asserted that the national income could be expected to double in 22 years by 1972, with per capita income doubled in 27 years, that is, by 1977, or in five years more than the period required for doubling the national income. It was estimated that over these 27 years consumption standards were to rise by a little over 70 per cent as compared to the 1950–51 level.[13]

However, the Planning Commission failed to make any positive prediction regarding employment; nevertheless, under the guise of reservations they observed that "eliminating unemployment in an underdeveloped economy is by its nature a somewhat long term problem which calls for steady and persistent effort." During the period of the First Plan, according to the Planning Commission, "Considerable progress will have been made in expanding irrigation, power, basic industries, transport, and other services and these will provide directly as well as indirectly, new avenues of employment."[14]

These estimates, as was pointed out by the Planning Commission, were considered illustrative and intended only to indicate broadly the implication in terms of the assumed behaviour of the various parameters over a period of time. On the basis of these assumed parameters, along with the detail assessment of both the tangible and intangible resources of the country, the Planning Commission decided on the relative priorities in the First Plan.

Relative Priorities in the First Plan

A detailed study of the magnitude of the relative priorities over the major heads (between agricultural and non-agricultural sector) shows clearly that the first priority was given to the development of agriculture, including irrigation and power, which formed a little over 44 per cent of the aggregate outlay in the plan, as shown in Table 1.

Table 1. The Allocation of Resources in the Order of Priority*

	Rs. in crores	per cent of total
Agriculture & community development	361	17.5
Irrigation	168	8.1
Multipurpose irrigation projects	266	12.9
Power	127	6.1
Transport and communication	497	24.0
Industry	173	8.4
Social Services	340	16.4
Rehabilitation	85	4.1
Others	52	2.5
Total	2,069	100.0

*SOURCE: *First Five Year Plan*, p. 3. P33

In determining the distribution of outlay between agricultural sectors and non-agricultural sectors, the main considerations taken into account by the Planning Commission were:

1. The need for initiating a process of development that would form the basis for the much larger efforts needed in the future.

2. The necessity of completing the projects initiated by the central and state governments prior to the commencement of the plan.

3. The realization that without a substantial increase in the levels of food and raw materials production, it would be impossible to make a breakthrough in the industrial sector, and finally,

4. The need to correct maladjustments in the economy caused by the war and partition.

In view of these considerations the Planning Commission laid heavy emphasis on agricultural development by allocating 44.6 per cent of the total expenditure.

The emphasis on agricultural development was justified by the Planning Commission on the following grounds:

1. Firstly, the Planning Commission asserted that there is an immediate need to

12 *First Five Year Plan*, p. 21.
13 *First Five Year Plan*, pp. 21–22.
14 *First Five Year Plan*, p. 23.

initiate a process of development that will form a basis for future development. For without a substantial increase in the production of food and raw materials a higher tempo of industrial development cannot be long sustained. Furthermore, the realization that an increase in agricultural output would not only serve as a stimulus for expansion in other sectors, but would also help to save, if not also earn, the foreign exchange needed for the purchase of capital equipment from other countries.

2. Secondly, in spite of the fact that a large proportion of the total population remains engaged in agriculture (about 70 per cent) there was still a shortage of food and agricultural raw materials. This state of affairs demanded immediate attention.

3. Finally, the most important factor which influenced the Planning Commission's decision was an attempt to reduce imports of food and industrial raw materials.

Between 1946 and 1959 the total imports of agricultural products amounted to 18 million tons valued at more than 122 million dollars. Table 2 shows the quantity of food imports made by India in the years 1946 to 1950–51.

Table 2. Imports of Food Grains during 1946 and 1950-1951*

Year	Quantity in million tons
1946	2.25
1947	2.35
1948	2.85
1949	3.74
1950	2.13
1951	4.72
Total	18.04

*SOURCE: Raj Narain Gupta, *Indian Economics Year Book*, pp. 62-62

Therefore, in the view of the Planning Commission, the reduction in such imports and the saving of such imports depended upon the development of the agricultural sector.

The Planning Commission concluded that "for the immediate five year period, agriculture, irrigation, and power must in our view have the top-most priority."[15] For one thing, this emphasis is indicated by the need to complete projects in hand. But, further, "we are convinced that without a substantial increase in the production of food and raw materials needed for industry, it would be impossible to sustain a higher tempo of industrial development. In an under-developed economy with low yields in agriculture, there is of course no real conflict between agricultural and industrial development. One cannot go far without the other; the two are complementary. It is necessary, however, on economic as well as on other grounds, first of all to strengthen the economy at the base and to create conditions of sufficiency and even plentitude in respect to food and raw materials. These are the wherewithals for further development."[16]

Thus, as a part of an overall development strategy, the Planning Commission not only contemplated physical outlays to increase agricultural productivity but also recognized that there was need for reorganizing the entire agricultural sector. Thus the planners proposed various measures to remove any impediments which may obstruct the goal of increasing agricultural productivity.

The first plan formulated a land policy intended to secure an increase in agricultural production. This land policy meant in essence the complete abolition of intermediate interests (such as Zamindari and other forms of intermediate interests in land) restricting the scope of ownership of land, security for cultivators against outside hazards, and, finally, making the tenant the ultimate owner of the land he tills.

In addition to land reforms, the Planning Commission also proposed the construction of more irrigation works, and reclamation, with intensive farming based on the methods of cooperative village management, community development pro-

[15] Government of India, Planning Commission, *First Five Year Plan,* p. 44.
[16] *First Five Year Plan,* p. 44.

jects, and rural extension schemes. Furthermore, the Planning Commission made detailed references to the reform of the organization for providing agricultural credit, better marketing facilities for agricultural products, to a better system of animal husbandary, dairying, and horticulture, increase in the forest areas and soil conservation practices, and, lastly, to the necessity of developing and exploiting fishing operations.

Industrial Development

With regard to the industrial development programme, the private sector was assigned a dominant place. In India there were at that time consumer goods industries, such as cotton and jute textiles, paper, soap, sugar, etc., but there were scarcely any basic industries—steel, chemicals, etc. Without well-developed basic industries, no large country like India can hope to progress economically. But the Indian Government could not embark on such industries, during the first plan period, because of other pressing preoccupations. According to the Industrial Policy Statement of 1948, while certain industries like arms and ammunition were to be the states' exclusive monopoly, coal, iron and steel, aircraft manufactures, ship building, and manufactures of telephones, telegraph and wireless apparatus were to be developed by the central and state governments and other public authorities, if necessary with the cooperation of private enterprise. For the rest, private enterprise was free to operate as it pleased, except that the state could intervene in an emergency. Place of pride was given to the private sector in the iron and steel industry. The private sector was expected also to develop consumer goods industries, such as textiles, sugar, paper, salt, paper board, sheet glass, vegetable oils, etc.

Thus some large scale industries were left in the hands of private investors.

Criticism

The First Five Year Plan was naturally subjected to various specific criticisms. They were :

(a) The Plan gave a much greater importance to agricultural development to the neglect of industrial development on the ground of completing the several already established projects in order to create a strong basis for subsequent industrial development. Some critics held that the Planning Commission had made wrong assumptions in placing emphasis on agricultural development. This was asserted to imply that Indian industry had already developed to the extent that the existing agricultural development would justify. This, however, was not the case. Anyone familiar with Indian conditions (at the time of the formulation of the First Five Year Plan) with regard to the then existing output of agricultural raw materials and foodstuffs, etc. could easily understand the real significance of attaching more importance to the development of agriculture, under the First Plan, than to the development of industry. Subsequently, for the same reason the point was made that India could have attained a much bigger industrial development of the country, even with the existing deficit gaps in agricultural production. This can be regarded as an unsound and unhealthy criticism of the overall planning strategy.

(b) Secondly, the plan left industrial development mostly in the hands of the private enterprises. There was no harm in this as business enterprises in the past were entirely in the hands of private corporations. But the criticism against the plan was that, while leaving industrial development mostly to the private sectors and specifying targets of output, it did not provide sufficient resources for the use of private enterprise.[17] Moreover, industry needed not only finance but also many other facilities. Their supporters argued for such privileges as exemption from taxation, greater depreciation allowances, etc. The critics held that it was not possible for private enterprise to do full justice to industrial development.

(c) Thirdly, one of the serious defects of the First Plan was its excessive emphasis on long-period projects; yet there is no doubt that in a planned economy cer-

[17] N. P. Lalwani, *Planning in India, 1955*, p. 39.

tain long term projects cannot be ignored. In some foreign countries, of which the U.S.S.R. is the best example, long term projects formed the main basis of planning. But conditions in India at the time of the formulation of the plan were very difficult. Although the plan needed to have a number of long term projects, the chief emphasis should have been on short period schemes. This would have made it possible to increase the yield of crops per acre of land more quickly and to secure a greater measure of self-sufficiency in food grains in a much shorter time.

Another likely disadvantage of placing greater emphasis on long term period projects has been that the supply of goods, as a result of stepped-up investment (under the plan) increased only slowly but the purchasing power in the hands of the people increased immediately. This had the result of intensifying inflationary conditions. A certain degree of inflation and consequently rising prices were inevitable in a planned economy. But if stepped up investment had increased the supply of goods in the market, the inflationary forces would have been somewhat counteracted. This would have been possible if proper emphasis were placed in the plan on short term projects. In the absence of this, the plan resulted in intensifying inflation much to the detriment of the consumer.

(d) Fourthly, the success of any plan depends in part upon the efficiency of the organization which is set up to make it operational. It was a great weakness of India's First Five Year Plan that it did not set up any special organization for implementing the plan. Some industrial and river valley projects were placed in charge of autonomous corporations over which the government had very little control, with the consequence that much public money was wasted, the schemes had to be revised frequently, and production did not increase as was expected.

But on the whole, in spite of these shortcomings in the plan, there is no doubt that India's First Five Year Plan was a brave attempt at solving the country's economic problems. Though progress under the plan was slow, this marked the beginning of a more concentrated effort to increase agricultural and non-agricultural production and the per capita income of the people.

4. Second Five Year Plan 1956-1961

The progress recorded during the First Five Year Plan period cannot be regarded as more than a modest beginning of the process of generating dynamism in the economy. Also in view of the broad objective of planned economic development, consisting of maximum production, full employment and higher living standards, the achievements of the First Plan can be considered no more than piecemeal effort. Therefore, at the time of the formulation of the Second Five Year Plan, it was felt necessary to achieve a more balanced economic development. This interpretation seems to have been influenced by the tremendous increase (of about 20 per cent) in agricultural production during the First Five Year Plan period. Furthermore, towards the end of the First Five Year Plan (in March 1956), the Government of India declared the new industrial policy,[18] in which an expanding role was assigned to the public sector. Simultaneously, the parliament had accepted the "socialistic pattern of society"[19] as the objective of social and economic policy. These significant developments influenced the overall directions and objectives envisaged in the Second Five Year Plan.

Growth Model

At the time of the formulation of the Second Plan, the planners had to reformulate their long-term growth model, in the light of the performance of the First Five Year Plan. The First Five Year Plan gave a projection of economic growth over a period of 30 years from 1951–1981. In this growth model it was envisaged that national income (1950–51) could be doubled by 1970–71, and the per capita income by 1977–78.[20] In view of the impressive performance in the First Plan it was concluded that the national income would be

[18] *Second Five Year Plan*, p. 28.
[19] *Second Five Year Plan*, p. 21.
[20] *First Plan*, p. 20.

doubled by 1967–68 and per capita income by 1973–74.[21] But this projection was once again based on unrealistic assumptions, with regard to population growth, capital output ratios, and savings and investment. The planners projected that, during the period of Second Five Year Plan, population would continue to increase at the rate of 1.25 per cent (which was far from the actual figure). Though consideration has been taken of the increase in population and its trends, but even with a continual rate of growth in national income of more than 5 per cent per annum, it would seem impossible to attain the target of doubling the 1950–51 level even by the end of the Fifth Plan period.

With regard to the capital output ratio, in view of highly favourable capital output ratio of 1.8 : 1 realized during the First Plan, the planners for the Second Five Year Plan contemplated that an investment of 6,200 crores was expected to result in an increase in national income of 2,680 crores. This gives a capital output ratio of 2 to 3 : 1. For the Third, Fourth and Fifth Plan periods, we have in the present model assumed capital output ratios of 2 : 6, 3 : 4 and 3 : 7 respectively.[22]

As regards the additional employment opportunity, the planners indicated the possibility of creating about 10 million more jobs outside agriculture during the Second Five Year Plan period. Actually the additional employment to be created during the Second Plan was estimated at about 6.5 million outside agriculture.[23] At the end of the Second Plan, the backlog of unemployment was estimated to be prospectively 9 million.

Objectives

The Second Five Year Plan had been formulated with reference to the following four objectives.[24]

(a) A sizeable increase in national income so as to raise the level of living in the country;

(b) Rapid industrialization with particular emphasis on the development of basic and heavy industries;

(c) A large expansion of employment opportunities; and

(d) Reduction of inequalities in income and wealth, and a more even distribution of economic power.

These objectives in the words of the Planning Commission were interrelated and interdependent. A rise in the levels of living and sizeable increase in national income of the order of 25 per cent over the five years could not be secured without increase in production and investment. The substantial increase will not be achieved without building up economic and social overheads and establishment of heavy and basic industries. In a country with surplus manpower, expansion of employment opportunities at a rate sufficient to absorb the increase in labour force assumes crucial importance. For this purpose a programme of proper utilization and technical training becomes imperative. Further, the process and design of development should result in bringing about certain basic changes in social values and purposes. The reduction of economic and social inequalities should be achieved through democratic means. These objectives in the words of the Planning Commission should be pursued in an even manner because too much emphasis on one at the cost of another may damage the economy and jeopardize the realization of the objectives. However, the said objectives, though they appeared sound in view of the inventory of the Indian economy, were too ambitious. They led the entire economy during the latter half of the second plan period into a perplexing situation.

The Order of Priority

In the light of the broad objectives of the Second Plan, the planners assigned top priority to rapid industrialization and diversification of the economy. According to the Planning Commission, if industrialization is to be rapid enough, the country must aim at development industries, and industries which make the ma-

21 *Second Plan*, p. 11.
22 *Second Five Year Plan*, p. 9.
23 *Third Five Year Plan*, p. 4.
24 *Second Five Year Plan*, p. 24.

chines needed for further development. This calls for substantial expansion in iron and steel, non-ferrous metals, coal, cement, heavy chemicals, and other industries of basic importance. The limitation in contemplating this type of development of basic industries before the Planning Commission was the scarcity of resources and the many claims on them. But in view of the fact that the criterion is not merely meeting immediate needs but the continuing and expanding needs in the coming years, the Planning Commission decided that it was desirable to aim at proceeding farthest in the direction of developing heavy and capital goods industries, which conform to this criterion.[25] The primary considerations were :

(a) That agriculture and irrigation have already made considerable progress in the first plan period, and that we can afford to devote more attention to industries which had been comparatively neglected.

(b) With an expanding population it would not be possible to solve the problem of unemployment and under-employment in the country, if we confined our attention mainly to agricultural development; and

(c) The realization of the fact that the economic prosperity of the country in the long run is linked up with industrialization.

The Planning Commission thus justified the shift in emphasis from the development of agriculture in the first plan to the development of basic and heavy industries, without giving adequate reasons for this shift of emphasis, in the whole planning volume. It is said by Mr. Jaya Prakash Narain, the opposition party leader, that Professor Mahalanobis being the chief architect and engineer of the Second Plan, the experts, with whose assistance he was said to have prepared the plan frame, were foreigners mostly, sympathetic to Soviet Russia or her satellite countries. It was perhaps for this reason that Mr. Narain was reported to have remarked in the Indian parliament : "The seven authors of Pandit Nehru's Second Plan are all men from behind the iron curtain."[26]

Wrong Assumptions

Generally speaking, the rate of per capita economic growth of a country, apart from psychological and sociological factors, depends mainly upon (1) the rate of growth of population; (2) the rate of growth of capital formation; and (3) the capital output ratio. In the calculation of these parameters the Planning Commission made grave errors at the time of the formulation of the Second Five Year Plan. As we have pointed out, earlier the Planning Commission had assumed the rate of growth of population at 1.25 per cent per annum, the rate of investment of 5 per cent of the national income and the capital output ratio as 3 : 1 with a time lag of two years. While reviewing the progress of the First Plan the Commission noted that these assumptions were not realized, and, therefore, they should be altered for purposes of future planning. It is here that the Commission committed an error of judgment, both initially and finally.

To start with, the Planning Commission once again underestimated the rate of growth of population during the Second Plan Period, as they had done under the First. As they retained the assumption that the rate of growth of population would continue to rise at 1.25 per cent per annum, when it was actually rising at the rate close to 2 per cent.

Regarding the capital coefficients the Planning Commission calculated that there had been a rise of about 18 per cent in the national income during the plan period. The rate of investment as percentage of the national output was calculated to have risen from 4.9 per cent in 1950–51 to 7.3 per cent in 1955–56. National income at 1952–53 prices rose from Rs. 9,110 crores in 1950–51 to Rs. 10,800 crores in 1955–56, that is, a rise of Rs. 1,700 crores over the five year period. During this period, investment was estimated to be at Rs. 3,100 crores. This gives an incremental capital

25 *Second Five Year Plan,* pp. 24–25.

26 Democratic Research Service, Bombay, "Danger of Physical Planning," p. 7.

output ratio as 1.8 : 1 as against 3 : 1 assumed by the Planning Commission for the First Plan. The Commission had been emboldened by the favourable results and for the next five years has made calculations assuming a capital coefficient of 2.3 : 1.

The Commission was not justified in this assumption. It had not taken all factors into consideration in working out the capital coefficient for the Second Five Year Plan. Increases in national output during the First Plan period were not wholly attributable to investment. Favourable monsoons gave us good crops for two successive years. There was also an increase in production due to utilization of formerly unutilized capacity.

Finally, the planners (under miscalculations) seem to have neglected inter-industry relations in assigning top priority to industrialization. It is from this point of view that the whole planning structure (of the Second Five Year Plan) seems to be more highly idealistic than factual. For it is the same planners who later on, especially during the last two years of the Second Five Year Plan, realized their grave mistake in placing heavy emphasis on the development of basic industries. In fact the bitter experience of the Second Five Year Plan has shown the rate of growth in agriculture to be one of the limiting factors in the progress of the Indian economy. Especially the main factor responsible for the failure of the Second Five Year Plan was the slow growth of the agricultural sector. It is this realization that made the planners rather cautious at the time of formulating the Third Five Year Plan. This led them to shift the emphasis from a rapid industrialization of the country under the Second Five Year Plan to the development of agriculture under the Third.

5. Third Five Year Plan 1961-1966

The beginning of the Third Five Year Plan on April 1, 1961 marked the completion of a decade of planned development strategy. The basic approach of the Third Five Year Plan directly follows from the pattern adopted in the Second Plan. However, in taking a long range view of the economy in general, the Third Plan was directed towards strengthening the agricultural economy, along with a balanced development of industries, power and transport. Thus, in formulating the Third Plan, the planners contemplated the following principal objectives in defining the core of the plan:

1. To secure an increase in national income of over 5 per cent per annum, the pattern of development being designed also to sustain this rate of growth during subsequent plan periods.
2. To achieve self sufficiency in food grains and increase agricultural production to meet the requirements of industry and exports; and
3. To expand basic industries like steel, chemical fuel and power, and to establish a machine building capacity so that the requirements of further industrialization could be met within a period of 10 years or so mainly from the country's own resources. It is with reference to these objectives, along with the revised version of long term growth model, that the specific targets were fixed in the plan for the principal items under agriculture, industry, transport, and communication.

Long Term Growth Model (Revised)

It may be recalled that in the Second Five Year Plan, the Planning Commission had presented a long term projection of economic growth—the revised version of an earlier projection presented in the First Plan. According to this revised projection, the 1950–51 level of national income should be doubled by 1967–68 (a period of 17 years) and that of the per capita income should be doubled by 1973–74 (a period of 23 years). It was in accordance with this projection that against the 18 per cent increase in national income brought about by the First Plan, targets of 25 per cent, 29 per cent and 26 per cent were set for the Second, Third and Fourth Plans respectively. As the Second Plan achievement fell short of the target, the long term projection had to be reconsidered at the time of formulating the Third Plan.

It is estimated under the new projection that over the next 15 years population will increase by a little over 2 per cent per annum. The growth of population of this order will entail expanding demands for food grains, raw materials, transport, employment, education, etc.[27]

With regard to employment, the Planning Commission asserted that the progress included in the Third Plan are expected to provide employment opportunities for about 14 million people. But in view of the sharp increase in population, the number of new entrants to the labour force during the Third Plan period will be as many as 17 million[28] (along with a backlog of unemployment inherited from the Second Plan to the tune of about 9 million), the problem of unemployment will not decrease by the end of the Third Plan. Rather it was bound to increase.

Pattern of Priority under The Third Plan

The pattern of investment indicated in the Third Five Year Plan reflects the priorities and the relative emphasis on different sectors during the plan period. In turn, these derive as much from an assessment of the current economic situation and the likely trends as from the analysis of the basic economic and social problems of the country and the long term goals of national endeavour.

However, contrary to the emphasis on industrialization in the Second Plan, the Third Plan gives priority to the development of agriculture, as under the First Plan. This shift of emphasis from the development of industries under the Second Plan to the development of agriculture under the Third is of considerable significance to the development strategy of the Indian economy as a whole. The experience of the first two (especially the Second Plan) has shown that the slow rate of growth in agriculture is a crucial limiting factor in the overall development of the Indian economy. Agricultural production has, therefore, to be increased to the largest extent feasible. Table 3 shows the importance attached by the Planning Commission to the development of agriculture during the Third Plan, in terms of allocating a greater percentage of plan outlay.

Agriculture under the Third Plan

In the scheme of development (according to the Planning Commission) the first priority necessarily belongs to agriculture. The importance of achieving self-sufficiency in food, and meeting the requirements

Table 3. Comparative Distribution of Plan Outlay in Different Sectors in the Second and Third Five Year Plans*

	Second plan	Third plan	Second plan	Third plan
	(Total in crores)		(% of total)	
1. Agriculture, community development and co-operation	530	1,068	11	14
2. Major and medium irrigation	420	650	9	9
3. Power	445	1,012	10	13
4. Village & small industries	175	264	4	4
5. Industry and minerals	900	1,520	28	20
6. Transport and communication	1,300	1,486	20	20
7. Social services and miscellaneous	830	1,300	18	17
8. Inventories	..	200	..	3
Total	4,600	7,500	100	100

*Ibid., p. 3.

27 *Third Five Year Plan*, p. 27.
28 *Third Five Year Plan*, p. 74.

of agricultural industries and exports were among the major aims of Third Plan.[29] Furthermore, the Planning Commission made quite clear its assessment of the role of agriculture in the total economy of the country, by asserting that the level of agricultural production is an important determinant of the rate of growth of the economy as a whole. It was further envisaged by the Commission that as the plan proceeds (apart from financial outlay already provided in the plan), if large resources are needed for assuring more rapid advance within the rural economy, these will be made available.

In addition to making a rapid headway in the development of the agricultural sector through an extensive net work of community development projects, the Planning Commission recommended, from the technical point of view, five further major programmes around which intensive work was to be organized in an effort to develop agricultural production. They were: (1) irrigation; (2) social conservation; (3) dry farming; and land reclamation; (4) supply of fertilizers and manures; and (5) better ploughs and improved implements.

Proposed Agricultural Targets under the Third Plan[30]

Agricultural production under the Third Plan period was to be stepped up by 30 to 33 per cent. The specific targets of production proposed for various commodities were as follows:

Table 4. Proposed Targets for the Production of Various Commodities between 1960-61 to 1965-1966

Commodities	Annual Production 1960-1961	1965-1966
(million tons)		
Food grains	75	100-105
Oil seeds	7.2	9.2-9.5
Sugarcane	7.2	9.0-9.2
Cotton	5.4	7.2
Jute	5.5	6.5

29 *Third Five Year Plan*, p. 49.
30 *Third Five Year Plan*, p. 62.

In addition to the above targets, it was also proposed to increase the production of food articles, including fruits and vegetables, milk, fish, meat, eggs, etc.

The target proposed for the production of food grains would allow for consumption of about 15 ounces of cereals and 3 ounces of pulses per capita per day, besides providing some margin against emergencies.[31]

Achievement of the Third Plan

According to an early estimate of the central statistical organization, in 1964 the real national income of the country was increasing at the rate of 2.5 per cent against the annual target of 5.6 per cent set by the plan. As the former is about equal to the rate of increase in population, no impovement was occurring in the per capita income, over the plan period. On the face of it, this was economic stagnation. However, the movement of national income in any one, two or three years cannot, by itself, indicate the strength underlying the forces governing the economy. Let us, therefore, look at the picture more closely.

Agriculture. The Third Plan had set a target of 30 per cent increase in overall agricultural production. But production had been almost static, when compared to the 1960 high of 81 million tons. In 1964 it was even less: 79.5 million.[32] Also there were 40 million more mouths to feed than four years ago. Taking all food grains together the area under cultivation showed little change; with output remaining the same, the yield per acre had remained stagnant. Agricultural raw materials were displaying divergent trends. The output of cotton fell by 17 per cent while that of jute rose by 57 per cent. But the increase in jute production was achieved mainly by enlarging the cultivated area rather than by increased yield per acre. This

31 *Third Five Year Plan*, p. 63.
32 John H. Mellow and Lele, "Alternative Trends in Food Grain Production in India," *Economic Development of Cultural Change*, Vol. XIII, No. 2, January 1965, p. 222.

meant diversion of land from other crops, particularly rice.[33]

On the whole food production did not increase because of successive bad crops in the plan period. Some major part of this might be attributed to the erratic monsoons that brought either too much rain or not enough.

Non-agriculture. Though the agricultural sector had under the Third Plan period remained static, the industrial picture was a little brighter. The general index of industrial production advanced by 16.6 per cent, as against the growth rate of 11.2 per cent stipulated under the plan. We often hear that the index of industrial production, as at present compiled, understates the real industrial progress of the country by giving an undue weightage to certain traditional industries and also not taking into account many new industries started since 1951. This is no doubt a valid point, but a closer look at some important industries which could claim to constitute the "core" of the industrial plan do not create any more favourable impressions.

Finished Steel. Output rose from 2.4 million tons in 1960–61 to 3.5 million tons in 1963–64. This 48 per cent increase was, on the face of it, encouraging, but this was still below the Second Plan target of 4½ million tons and a far cry from the target of 7 million tons set for the last year of the Third Plan.

Cement. Production recorded a niggardly advance of a little over 7 per cent from 8 million tons to 8.6 million tons. The plan had envisaged a near doubling of output from 8 to 15 million tons by 1965–66.[34]

The plan laid a great stress on fertilizers, which had a direct bearing on agricultural production. But the production of ammonium sulphate, which could be considered as a representative of the fertilizer group, made a marginal gain during the plan period. The plan had envisaged a trebling of output.[35]

Furthermore, if we consider the employment index in the non-agricultural sector, as a sign of industrial development. The plan had badly failed in creating new employment opportunities in non-agricultural sectors. As such the gain from planning in the field of employment was negligible.[36] The additional employment resulting from the First Plan, outside of agriculture, was 4.7 million and from the Second Plan 6.5 million—an improvement of about 35 per cent despite the steep rise of 110 per cent in the investment outlay from Rs. 3,760 crores in the First Plan to Rs. 7,900 crores in the second. The increase in employment was less than the natural additions to the labour force. The Second Plan, thus, bequeaths to the Third Plan vastly more unemployment—9 million, that is inherited from the First Plan. All calculations in this respect were based on a population increase of five million per year, of which the labour force was assumed to be 40 per cent. But this was upset by the discovery by the 1961 census that the population increase during the past decade was actually at an annual rate of 1.9 per cent. And as of today, even accepting the Planning Commission's view that it was possible to create 14 million new jobs during the plan period, in view of the sharp rise in population, at the close of the Third Plan period the unemployment backlog might rise to 12 million.[37] But here again if we consider the employment trend under the first three years of the plan period, we realized a much higher backlog of unemployment at the end of the Third Plan than the 12 million figure indicated by the Planning Commission.

The one important question that emerges from these dim employment prospects is whether in the future these unemployed millions are ever going to find jobs—are they to be put on relief, or find some gainful employment in non-agricultural pursuits or will they be made to depend upon

33 Government of India, Central Statistical Bureau, Calcutta Crop Index, p. 39.

34 *Third Five Year Plan*, p. 486.

35 *Third Five Year Plan*, p. 478.

36 B. R. Shenoy, *Indian Planning and Economic Development*, p. 23.

37 *Third Five Year Plan*, p. 156.

agriculture. As of today, indications are that in spite of a steep rise in plan investment the prospect of finding any feasible opportunity to employ all the entrants to labour force is pretty dark, thereby forcefully pushing them to depend upon already overburdened agriculture as a residual solution. Fortunately, the backbone of the Indian society and the Indian culture does provide for such an existence (for instance, the most powerful age old institution of joint family existence, is a good example of such an array of institutions).

6. Fourth Five Year Plan 1969-1974

According to a quarter century scheme of economic development as originally envisaged by the Planning Commission in 1951, the Fourth Plan was scheduled to begin on April 1, 1966. Though the first draft of the plan was prepared as early as 1965, the plan never got off the ground. Later on it was declared that the Fourth Plan would start only in 1969–70. There was to be a three year period of "Plan Holiday,"[38] an idea conceived by Lal Bahadur Shastri, the then Prime Minister and Chairman of the Planning Commission. On close examination it is clear that such an action was a product of unexpected circumstances brought about by the conflict with China in 1962 and with Pakistan in 1965 followed by a temporary suspension of foreign aid,[39] the devaluation in 1966, the failure of the monsoons, and the general election in 1967.

However, during this three year period of Plan Holiday, in the interest of continuity, the Planning Commission adopted annual plans on a modest scale both in terms of total outlay and goals. As a result national income rose only by 1.1 per cent and the index of industrial production registered an increase of only 1.7 per cent in 1966–67 and 0.31 in 1967–68 and finally rose by 6 per cent in 1968–69. Whereas national income also registered an increase of 9 per cent in 1968–69 as compared to 1.1 per cent in 1966–67.[40]

Against these achievements under the annual plans, the Fourth Five Year Plan was finally started in 1969 on a solid foundation. It envisaged an outlay more or less equal to that of the past eight years. Compared to earlier Plans, therefore the anticipated tempo of expansion is not as high when the outlays are deflated by the increase in price level since 1960, which was nearly 70 per cent when the Fourth Plan was finalized. The allocations in real terms in some important sectors are lower than in the Third Plan, for instance, the allocation of Rs. 236 crores and Rs. 293 crores for village and small-scale industries, and of Rs. 100 crores and Rs. 142 crores for the welfare of the backward classes. Thus with a 70 per cent price deflator, in real terms the Fourth Plan is no larger than the previous plan.

Objectives

In the interest of growth-with-stability, the byword of the Fourth Plan, the Planning Commission has adopted the following five broad objectives: (1) introduction of safeguards against fluctuations of agricultural production as well as uncertainties of foreign aid; (2) a sustained increase in export by about seven per cent annually to secure balanced foreign trade; (3) considering the poor performance of the public sector in the past, limiting industrial activity in this sector and achieving efficiency and profitability of public enterprises; (4) stepping up the tempo of economic activity to such an extent that it may bring about more productive employment maintaining stable and self-reliant economy; and (5) accentuate the process of industrial dispersal and stimulate the economy of weaker and less developed areas through regional and local planning processes.[41]

The Planning Commission hopes to achieve these objectives by assigning heavy

38 Narayana Pillai, "Unplanning the Plan," *Far Eastern Economic Review*, 58:448–50 (December 7, 1967), p. 448.

39 Davis Derek, "A Cart Without a Horse," *Far Eastern Economic Review*, 56: 305–8 (May 11, 1967), pp. 306–307.

40 *Publications Division, India 1969*, Government of India, 211–212.

41 "Fourth Five-Year Plan, 1969–76—Draft, a Summary," *Reserve Bank of India Bulletin*, 23: 1017–40 (July 23, 1969), pp. 1018–19.

emphasis on agriculture, fertilizers, and steel output. The core of the Plan is undoubtedly agriculture. The agricultural plan has been carefully formulated. Its analytical parts are superior to the formulations in the earlier Plans. An annual growth rate of five per cent in agricultural production is anticipated. In the previous Plans almost half the increase in agricultural production came from an extension in area; now the increase is almost wholly expected from improved productivity. The qualitative change in the effort needed can be easily recognized.

The main input will be the new technology, the key areas of activity being those where high-yielding varieties can provide the needed response. In rice, jowar and bajra such extension has to be three-fold to four-fold: from 9.2 million hectares in 1968–69, of which wheat accounted for 4.8 million hectares or more than half the area, the HYV (high-yielding varieties) programme will be raised to 25 million hectares, of which wheat will only cover 7.7 hectares. "For obtaining optimum results from the high-yielding varieties programme, the main thrust of effort will be in the sphere of extension. The new varieties require more refined and precise cultural practices concerning preparation of seedbed and methods of sowing. Perhaps the most significant aspect relates to controlled irrigations so that water is supplied at critical periods of plant growth. How many state governments, facing the recurring political instabilities, are in a position to provide these extension services and to attend to the technological changeover? Again, in the face of the spreading Naxalite unrest in the rural areas, and the uncertainties maintained there by the constant talk of land reforms without any final transformation, how many agriculturists will be willing to make the investments and undergo the discipline that a technological changeover demands? A five per cent annual rate of growth in agricultural production is, of course, desperately needed and indications are that this target will be met. The following table shows the specific agricultural target contemplated by crops in the fourth plan:

Table 5. Fourth Plan Targets of Agricultural Production*

Commodity	Unit	Base Level Production (1968-69)	Estimated Production (1973-74)
Foodgrains	Million tonnes	98	129
Oilseeds	Do	8.5	10.5
Sugarcane (Gur)	Do	12	15
Cotton	Million bales	6	8
Jute	Do	6.2	7.4
Tobacco	Million kgs.	380	480
Coconut	Million nuts	5600	6600
Cashewnut	Do	160	236
Arecanut	Thousand tonnes	126	150
Pepper	Do	23	42
Lac	Do	35	52
Tea	Do	418	450

*SOURCE: *Reserve Bank of India Bulletin*, 23: 1017—70 (July 1971).

In keeping with the campaign (1971) promise of the ruling party to reduce unemployment drastically, programmes have been initiated to provide as many jobs as possible through the emphasis on labour-intensive employment–generating industries. But a word of caution is in order, in achieving any significant progress in re-

ducing unemployment, particularly in the light of past experience in the three five year plans.

Though the Fourth Plan is in its third year, its achievements are rather obscure, at best mixed, and by far short of the Fourth Plan targets. For example, national income rose five per cent in 1969–70 compared to the base of the previous year but per capita income rose only 2.5 per cent. Industrial production increased by 5 per cent in 1969–70 and 4.5 per cent in 1970–71 due to shortages of certain raw materials, especially steel and raw cotton.[42] However, agriculture on the other hand is making, if not remarkable, steady progress. As a matter of fact for the first time India is contemplating export of wheat and wheat products to the Middle East during the next year.[43] However, in assessing the overall progress of the Fourth Plan one has to take note of the proceedings of the newly constituted Planning Commission on October 6, 1971 :

> The appraisal of the progress made so far is still not complete, but tentative findings are that the Centre has done badly. Shortfalls in expenditure in each of the first two years have been of the order of Rs. 200 crores (though the States have overshot their expenditure, making the overall shortfall in the Plan outlay in the first two years just slightly over Rs. 200 crores).
>
> The Planning Commission has come to the conclusion that poor performance has led to serious distortions and imbalances in the economy. Shortfalls have been mainly on the industrial front and investments have fallen well below targets in such crucial fields as heavy industry, mining, etc.
>
> But it was acknowledged today that, taking into account the rise in prices in the last two years, achievement in real terms has been around 15% less than the targets aimed at. This has been mainly in industry, but certain sectors of agriculture have also not done well.
>
> The position regarding cereals was reported to be sound—the target of a 5.5% annual rise in production is being maintained—but production of pulses, cotton, oilseeds and sugar has lagged behind and caused further distortions in the economy.
>
> Since the satisfactory position on the cereals front is attributed to a technological breakthrough, it was decided today that expenditure on research into production problems of other crops should be stepped up.
>
> A far bleaker picture has emerged on the industrial front... Various factors, such as shortages of raw materials, non-utilization of capacity and bad labour relations have been identified, for the shortfall.[44]

In addition to this assessment, we should also take into consideration the effect of the 17 day war with Pakistan, with an influx of 10 million refugees (though most of them have returned to Bangladésh) in the overall performance of the Fourth Plan.

Some Observations

The foregoing general observations are made not with a view to criticizing the basic strategy of the plan, which is perhaps the one the country should have adopted under the circumstances, but with a view to seeing whether the implications flowing from the strategy have received full and conscious acceptance and attention.

Consider, for instance, the incremental capital output ratio. The performance of the Second Plan shows a capital output ratio of 2.8 : 1. Advance calculations of investment output relation in a growing economy is a difficult exercise but world experience would suggest that the ratio becomes higher as the economy progresses on the path of industrialization.[45] One would,

---

42 Information Service, Embassy of India, *India News*, Vol. IX, No. 47 (Washington : D. C. : 1971), p. 2.

43 *New York Times*, May 7, 1972.

44 *The Statesman Weekly* (Calcutta : Saturday, October 9, 1971), p. 7.

45 Ismail, Shariff, *The Development of Indian and American Agriculture—A Comparative Study* (Chicago : Interstate publishers and printers, 1968), pp. 14–15.

in the normal course, have expected the Planning Commission to assume a slightly higher ratio for the Third Plan, that is, unless the pattern of investment adopted in the plan were to suggest a reversal of the trend of heavy industrialization. As a matter of fact, however, the Third Plan appears to have been formulated on the assumption of a capital output ratio of 2.4 : 1. In view of the bold advance towards industrialization conceived by the Third Plan, and the accent it lays on basic industries, the adoption of a capital output ratio lower than the one that prevailed in the Second Plan would seem to have been unrealistic. The adoption of a higher capital output ratio would have been in conformity with the basic strategy of the plan, and might have also led to more intensive efforts at resource mobilization.

Secondly, the assumption in the Third Plan of a rise in the rate of saving to 11 per cent at the close of the plan is unattainable, unless we adopt totalitarian techniques of direct physical restraints on the masses of the people. Under full individual freedom over the disposal of one's earnings as between spending and saving, we may not reasonably expect the rate of saving to rise above 6 per cent.

Thirdly, in the formulation of a policy for accelerating the national product, we must take note of the following factors more thoroughly than it has been given under the four successive plans. First, 50 per cent of the Indian national income comes from agriculture, and 70 per cent of the population draws its living from it. Manufacturing industries account for less than 20 per cent of economic activity. Peasant farming dominated agriculture on a crude traditionalistic basis. This in itself is manifest and suggests the need for a rapid development of agricultural industry. For the basic necessity of life is food. Then comes clothing and housing. But food has the priority. That India until recently was not able to produce enough food for its own people is a very sad commentary on the Indian economy. The first thing, therefore, that India should plan for is to produce more food for the growing millions. Accordingly, India has to devote a greater percentage of her total plan investment, to the development of agriculture. This will not only provide food (or at least more than what the people have today), but also, at the same time, with the development of agriculture, we will be placing the Indian economy on a more solid and dependable basis. It will also pave the way for a sound development of other nonagricultural sectors at a more rapid rate. Nobody would deny the importance of industries in a modern world. However, besides manufacturing industries we should have plants for producing machinery. But all manufacturing industries require labour. In many industries half the cost of production consists of wages of labour. If industries are to prosper labour must be cheap and also efficient. But cheap and efficient labour can be had only if food is cheap and abundant. Make food available in plenty, and make it cheap, and automatically this will lead to laying a sound foundation for our economy. Manufacturing industries have been complaining of a lack of balance between price and costs. Cost-price ratio has been adversely affected in recent years and the industries are not making the progress they could have.[46] The only way to bring about this proper balance is to make food cheaper. The Indian Government has in some cases fixed the wages of the labourers too high, in other cases have fixed the prices of raw materials like sugar cane and cotton too high. This was done, it seems, in an attempt to provide the labourers and growers of cane and cotton with more income. But one cannot increase the supply of food by putting more money in the pockets of consumers. Rather one has to put more money in enterprises that produce more food.

The Fourth Plan is based upon various assumptions, such as price stability and 7 per cent annual increase in exports. In the first year of the Plan, the price level has risen by 6 per cent, manufacturing industries have registered a growth in output of only 6.3 per cent instead of the expected 9 per cent and exports have in-

---

[46] "Trends in Industrial Production, 1962," *Indian Statistical Series,* No. 9.

creased by only 3.8 per cent. If the Plan targets are to be reached, the effort needed in the remaining two years will have to be greater than envisaged in the Plan: for instance, exports will have to rise by 8 per cent per year. Though the Plan covers the years 1969–1974, the document was finalized only in the middle of 1970. Unfortunately, it has neither been revised in the light of the first year's experience nor have indications of corrective action been provided. No indications are available from the government either. At the first meeting of the AICC of the Ruling Congress after the finalization of the Plan, there was no discussion on the Plan and therefore, no light has been thrown on how the Government proposes to buttress the crumbling assumptions of the Plan.[47]

The Plan envisages a marked increase in domestic savings. The total domestic savings are to go up from 8.8 per cent to 13.2 per cent of the national income at the end of the Plan period. Household savings will register a small increase from 6.4 per cent of the national income to 7.6 per cent; corporate savings are expected to remain relatively constant—from 1 per cent to 1.1 per cent. Public savings will jump from 1.4 per cent to 4.5 per cent of the national income. The success of the Plan thus depends upon the Government's capacity to mobilize adequate savings and channel them to desired areas of investment. The trend is expected to continue up to 1980–81, when public saving will have to rise to 8.2 per cent while the two other streams of savings will have only minor increases—of 0.8 per cent and 0.3 per cent respectively. The order of effort, in absolute terms, is indicated thus; given the objective of dispensing with net aid after 1980–81 the volume of domestic savings will have to rise from Rs. 2,530 crores in 1968–69 to approximately Rs. 10,450 crores by 1980–81 or a four-fold increase in twelve years.[48]

The Plan assumes the generation of an additional income of about Rs. 1,800 crores a year, of which about Rs. 700 crores will be invested.

The draft Fourth Plan had expected the balance from current revenue to be Rs. 2,400 crores. The final document has brought it down to Rs. 1,625 crores. In the Third Plan the expectation was Rs. 460 crores but the actuals turned out to be minus Rs. 642 crores. For the succeeding three annual plans, the total expectations were Rs. 621 crores; the actuals proved to be Rs. 184 crores. During the first two years of the Fourth Plan, the balance from current revenue at the Centre (the combined picture of the State remains dismal) has been Rs. 117 crores and Rs. 180 crores respectively. If the remaining Rs. 1,327 crores are to be realized, the annual accomplishment in the subsequent two years must be about Rs. 450 crores a year. Nobody knows what positive steps are being taken, or are under active consideration, for this advance.[49] In the past, the centre managed to raise its share of additional taxes and it is well poised to achieve the Fourth Plan target. The states, however, have recently become less energetic. In the first year, they were expected to raise Rs. 122 crores through additional taxes: they raised only Rs. 37.4 crores inclusive of Rs. 8.8 crores from lotteries. It is possible that a full year's impact may be somewhat larger, but it cannot possibly be Rs. 84 crores needed to meet the expected target.

Above all, the planning mechanism in India has suffered from lack of implementation, from its very inception mainly because of the fact that the Planning Commission's role is subjected to political dependency as it lacks any autonomy in its thinking. In any democratic government, planning, in the last analysis, must be a political process, and we Indians have never fallen into any delusion to the contrary. Yet this basic feature condemns the Planning Commission as a central staff agency charged with performing a quasi-expert, and also quasi-political function to an inherently precarious ambivalent set of relationships with the central government's ministries and other major

---

47 *The Statesman Weekly* (Calcutta: Saturday, July 6, 1970), p. 2.

48 Ibid., p. 4.

49 Ibid., p. 4.

lines of organizaton, as well as India's eighteen state governments. The precariousness of the Commission's position is intensified by the fact that lacking political independence, the Commission's political bargaining power depends almost wholly on the liveliness of the support it draws from the Prime Minister.[50]

As a consequence of this, the very texture of the Planning Commission's operations lacks flexibility in its basic thinking and hence in implementation of its objectives. A plan is of little value, no matter how good it looks on paper, if its execution is faulty. This would create even more problems for a developing economy. Rightly a success or failure of a planning effort depends not in the flawless blue print but in its execution. Countries like India took to planning as a way to achieve a more rapid growth rate than is expected from a relatively free economy. But such planning to be effective, requires an independent judgment based on facts without any outside influence, political or otherwise.

Despite such shortcomings and difficulties it is encouraging to note that India is desperately trying to change the economic spectrum of the country through a planned endeavour.

[50] John P. Lewis, *Quiet Crisis in India*, The Bookings Institution, 1962, pp. 114–136.

BIBLIOGRAPHY

Alexander, R. J. *A Primer of Economic Development* (New York: The Macmillan Co., 1962).

Bruibanti, R. and Spengler, J. J., *Administration and Economic Development in India* (London: Duke University Press, 1963).

Galbraith, John K., *Economic Development in Perspective* (Harvard University Press, 1962).

Government of India, Planning Commission. *First Five Year Plan*, December 1952.

Government of India, Planning Commission, *Second Five Year Plan*, 1956.

Government of India, Planning Commission, *Third Five Year Plan*, 1961.

Government of India, Planning Commission, *Fourth Five Year Plan*, 1970.

Hirschman, Albert O., *The Strategy of Economic Development* (Yale University Press, 1958).

Kaldor, S., "Can Under-developed Countries Learn to Tax" in *Foreign Affairs*, January 1963.

Kuznets, S., Moore, W. E. and Spengler, J. J., *Economic Growth: Brazil, India and Japan* (Duke University Press, 1955).

Kuznets, S. *Six Lectures on Economic Growth* (John Hopkins, 1962).

Lalwani, N. P., *Planning in India* (Asia Publishing House, 1959).

Lewis, John P. *Quit Crisis in India* (The Brookings Institute, 1962).

Lewis, W. A., *The Theory of Economic Growth* (Richard D. Irwin, Inc., 1955).

Mahalanobis, P. C., "Next Step in Planning" *Sankya*, January 1960.

Myrdal G. *Economic Theory and Under-developed Regions* (London: G. D. & Co. Ltd., 1957).

Nelson, E., *Economic Growth Rational, Problems, Cases* (Austin: University of Texas Press, 1960).

Nurkse, R., *Problems of Capital Formation in Under-developed Countries* (New York: Macmillan, 1953).

N.C.A.E.R., *Looking Ahead Prospects of India's Economy and Trade*, Trend in 1981.

Pillai, P. P., *Economic Conditions in India* (Asia Publishing House, 1963).

Reddaway, W. B., *The Development of Indian Economy* (Richard D. Irwin, Inc.. 1962).

Shenoy, B. R., *Indian Planning and Economic Development* (Asia Publishing House, 1963).

Singh Tarlok, *Poverty and Social Change* (Longmans, Green & Co. Ltd., 1945).

Shariff, Ismail, *The Development of Indian and American Agriculture—A Comparative Study* (Danville, Ill: Interstate Publishers and Printers, 1968).

Tinbergen, J. *Development Planning*, World University—Library (McGraw-Hill Book Co., 1967).

Vakil and Brahmanand, *Planning for an Expanding Economy* (Vora & Co. Publishers, Private Ltd., 1956).

Venkatasubbiah, H., *Indian Economy Since Independence* (Asia Publishing House, 1958).

Wilfred, Malenbaum, *Prospects for Indian Development* (London: Allen, Ltd., 1972).

11

Structural Change in the Indian Economy

MAHMOOD A. ZAIDI and

SUDHIN K. MUKHOPADHYA

1. Introduction

The national income of India at 1948–49 prices increased from Rs. 89,000 million in 1950–51 to Rs. 1,69,000 million in 1968–69. During the same period of time the composition of the national product also changed. The share of agriculture, animal husbandry, and ancillary activities declined from 50 per cent to about 40 per cent, while the share of industries and services rose correspondingly.[1] These are some of the indications that the economy of India has been developing.

Discussions of economic development generally deal with such changes in the aggregates of national product or its industrial composition. Such aggregative studies are important to understand the broad movements of the economy. But it has to be remembered that there is much more to economic development than surfaces via these highly aggregated magnitudes. What, after all, is an economy? It is a web of numerous activities carried out by the different constituent units—firms, industries, sectors, regions, etc., that generate the macro-economic magnitudes like national income or consumption. As economic development takes place, i.e., as there is a sustained change in the economic aggregates, there usually takes place a change in the network of activities lying behind the simple aggregates. As W. W. Leontief has put it, "it is necessary to penetrate below the surface of global statistics and such round terms as "development." Each economic system—even that of an underdeveloped country has a complicated internal structure. Its performance is determined by the mutual relations of its differentiated component parts, just as the motion of the hands of a clock is go-

The authors of this paper would like to thank Edward Coen, Professor of Economics and the Director of Undergraduate Studies and the Editor for helpful comments and encouragement during the preparation of this paper.

[1] *Economic Survey* (New Delhi: Central Statistical Organization, Government of India, 1965).

verned by the gears inside."[2] At different levels of economic development the volume and nature of the activities of the internal structure are generally different. So, in order to ascertain the nature of the development and to predict the requirements of various inputs for development and to facilitate the formulation of national plans for economic development, it is important to examine the internal mechanism of the economy within its broad macro-framework.

The purpose of this chapter is to present a simplified picture of the "internal structure" that lies behind the changing global aggregates of the Indian economy. After some introductory comments in this section, the methodology of studying economic structure is discussed in simple non-technical terms in section II, and section III deals with some actual measures of the changing economic structure of India.

Economists have long been aware of the need to examine the mechanism of interrelated changes in the economy as a whole and theories were developed as early as in the eighteenth century by the French economist Francois Quesnay in the famous *Tableau Economique,* and in the nineteenth century by Leon Walras in his general equilibrium theory. But in spite of their elegance and depth, these ideas remained far removed from the possibility of actual application to particular economies. The task of constructing the network of interrelated economic changes through equations and measuring them empirically had been considered extremely difficult. In reality, this network consists of flows of goods and services between the micro elements of an economy and the flows involve too many variables and too complicated interrelations. So, rather than attempting to study the economy in its total framework, economic analysis had been long content with a partial equilibrium approach, making the restrictive assumption that there is no significant change outside the given portion of the economy under investigation.

But since the nineteen thirties, due mostly to the research contributions of W. W. Leontief, the theoretical conceptualization of general equilibrium has been rendered empirically verifiable.

The method, known as "input-output" analysis, makes possible an analysis of the detailed statistical picture of the entire economy. The disaggregated structure of the economy and changes in it are now amenable to quantitative measurement.

2. Input-Output Analysis—a simple Exposition

It has been suggested that, in order to understand the mechanism of economic development at the macro level and to formulate plans for aiding and influencing development, it is necessary to know the internal structure of the economy. Input-output analysis is a modern technique designed to study this internal structure and its changes.

The input-output analysis is developed by treating the economy like a fabric which is woven together by the flows of trade or transactions of goods and services that ultimately link the different branches or industries of the economy. The economy is first divided into a number of sectors or branches. Then a simple double-entry method of book keeping is adopted to record the flows between different sectors or branches. The transactions are set up in the form of a two-way table of horizontal rows and vertical columns. The horizontal rows of figures show the way the output of each sector is distributed among all the different sectors of the economy. These sectors will include both production and consumption, so that part of the output of a sector will go as intermediate goods or inputs into production sectors, and part will go to final consumption, be it private or governmental consumption. On the other hand, the vertical columns show how each sector receives its *inputs* in the form of goods and services from the various sectors of the economy. The two-way input-

---

[2] W. W. Leontief, "The Structure of Development", *Input-Output Economics,* (New York: Oxford University Press, 1966), pp. 41–42. Readers are referred to this article for a simple and authoritative treatment of input-output analysis.

output table shows each figure belonging both to a row and a column; it stands as the output of one sector being used as input for another sector. Of course, the output of a sector is used also as its own input in most cases. For example, paddy seeds are the output of the agriculture sector used as an input in the same sector. So the total gross output of a sector may be looked upon in an input-output framework as the sum of the flow of goods to the productive sectors and to final consumption, and the sum of the total gross outputs of all the sectors is the gross national product of the economy.

The input-output relations can be understood clearly with the help of a simple tabular presentation. In Table 1 the economy is divided into two production sectors, 1 and 2.[3] Let X represent output and C represent final consumption. The subscripts refer to the sectors.

Table 1.

From \ To		*Production Sector* 1	2	Final Consumption	Total Gross Out Put
Sector	1	x_{11}	x_{12}	C_1	X_1
	2	x_{21}	x_{22}	C_2	X_2

x_{11} represents the output of sector 1 that is used as input in sector 1 itself. Similarly x_{12}, for instance, stands for the output of sector 1 used as input in sector 2. The column of Total Gross Output gives the sum of the output of each sector that is used as inputs as well as final consumption. This relationship can be written in the form of two balance equations corresponding to the two sectors, namely:

$$x_{11} + x_{12} + C_1 = X_1 \quad (1)$$

$$x_{21} + x_{22} + C_2 = X_2 \quad (2)$$

[3] Theoretically, it is possible to disaggregate the economy into any number of sectors. The level of disaggregation depends on the purpose of analysis and the availability of data.

The grand total of the sectoral outputs will give us the gross total output of the economy. Thus input-output analysis gives us a glimpse into the flows of goods and services that take place behind the global aggregates of gross output.

Input-output analysis enables us to go beyond a simple exposition of the volumes of inter-sectoral transaction as indicated in Table 1. The central concept of input-output analysis is that there is a fundamental relationship between the volume of output of a sector and the inputs used by it. For example, if sector 2 represents cotton textiles industry, then there is a relationship between how much textiles are produced (i.e. output of the Sector 2, X_2) and the amount of cotton that is used by it as input. And if sector 1 includes cotton farming, the entry x_{12} in Table 1 will represent the flow from sector 1 to sector 2, so X_2 and x_{12} are interdependent. Input-output analysis shows how in this way every entry in the table is dependent on each other.

These relationships indicate the structure of the technology of the economy and are measured by calculating the ratio or coefficient of each input to the total output in the production of which the input is used. For an industry or sector we get these input coefficients by dividing the column-wise entries for this industry by its gross output figure. For example, from Table 1, x_{12}/X_2 is the input coefficient of product 1 in industry 2. This coefficient is usually denoted as a_{12}. Similarly, we can compute $a_{22}=x_{22},/X_2$, $a_{11}=x_{11}/X_1$ $a_{21}=x_{21}/X_1$. The input coefficients corresponding to Table 1 are shown in Table 2.

Table 2.

$$\begin{bmatrix} a_{11} & a_{12} \\ a_{21} & a_{22} \end{bmatrix}$$

Each element in this table shows how much of the input of an input-supplying sector is needed to produce one unit of output of the receiving sector. That is, to produce one unit of output, sector 1 needs, for example, a_{11} units of its own output, and a_{21} units of input from sector 2. Table 2 provides a picture of the economy's technological structure at the time to which the table refers.

The input-coefficients of a sector are the measures of its *direct* requirements of inputs per unit of output produced. But to produce the inputs, the supplying sectors would in their turn require inputs also. For example, to produce textile, an input of cotton is required, but the production of cotton in its turn would need the use of possibly some farm machinery or fertilizer which again would need inputs of iron and steel, chemicals, and so on. Thus, to produce a given amount of output in an industry, there is not only a direct input requirement, but indirect or secondary requirements for outputs from industries which supply the first industry, and so on through successive outputs and inputs until the effect of the final demand for the first industry's output has been traced to its last reverberation in the remotest part of the economy. Input-output analysis provides us with this useful information relating to the supplies of different goods and services which are needed to produce a given set of final goods.[4]

3. The Internal Structure of the Indian Economy

The technical structure of an economy reflected in its input-coefficients is determined by engineering considerations, custom or institutional arrangements, and by relative prices of inputs. The data of input-output analysis, on the basis of which the input coefficients are calculated, are the flows of goods and services within the economy that lie behind the summary measures line, gross national product. Since the level of the gross national product varies with different levels of development, it is usually observed that the pattern of transactions between different sectors are similar for economies which are at a relatively high level of development. The input-output tables of countries at low levels of development, with a relatively small gross national product, usually display a pattern that is different from the pattern displayed by the developed countries. At primitive or very low levels of development, the mode of production is largely self-contained, i.e., there is very little or no interaction between the sectors of the economy. As economic development takes place, there emerges increasing interaction between sectors, there is more trade, i.e., more flow of goods and services. This is because the economy moves to higher levels of technology where, due to both engineering and institutional reasons, there is increased specialization within sectors and more interdependence between sectors. For example, consider two sectors, agriculture and chemical industries. At a low development level of agriculture, there is hardly any flow of chemicals, e.g., fertilizer and pesticides, into agriculture, but the flow is substantial in a modernized agriculture. Also, before the development of the modern steel plants in India, there was no scope for the flow of iron ore (mining sector) to the steel industry (manufacturing sector).

Several input-output tables have been prepared for India that make it possible to examine how the structure of the Indian economy has changed. Table 3 provides us with a view of the structure of the Indian economy in 1952–53, 1959 and 1964–65.[5] This table has been prepared on the basis of larger input-output tables. For simplicity the larger tables have been ag-

[4] The coefficient matrix of the total (direct plus indirect) input requirements are known as Leontief Inverse and computed by inverting the (IA) matrix, where I is the identity matrix and A is the matrix of coefficients (e.g., Table 2).

[5] The data for 1952-53 are taken from the 19 sector input-output table prepared by the Indian Institute of Public Opinion; the 1959 data are from the 29 sector table in *Economic Analysis in Input-Output Framework,* edited by P. N. Mathur and R. Bharadwaj, Input-Output Research Association, Poona, 1965; and the 1964-65 table is based on the 77 sector Input-Output Table prepared by the Planning Commission, Government of India. The 1952–53 figures are at 1952–53 prices, 1959 data are at 1959 prices and the 1964-65 data are at 1960–61 prices. It should be mentioned that relative price differences do have some effect on the structures but it has been assumed to be negligible in the present study.

gregated here to only two sectors, the interrelationships between which are displayed in the flows. Sector 1 is called the primary complex because it consists mostly of primary activities and such industries as are primarily engaged in the processing of primary products. Sector 2 consists of all other industries and is called the secondary complex. Such a classification of the economy might throw light on the two crucial sectors and their inter-relationships along with the development of the Indian economy. The rows of Table 3 show the intermediate outputs, i.e., outputs used as inputs. These, added to the output for final consumption (not shown here) would give gross output.

Table 3. Input-Output Transaction, India[5]
(Rs. Millions)

From \ To	1952-53 Primary Complex	1952-53 Secondary Complex	1959 Primary Complex	1959 Secondary Complex	1964-65 Primary Complex	1964-65 Secondary Complex
Primary Complex	2,892	456	35,193	1,004	36,765	3,331
Secondary Complex	397	826	2,604	5,245	3,705	18,670

Table 3 shows how the flow of goods between the primary and secondary complexes have increased during the period. This indicates that in 1952–53, which was the beginning of planning for economic development in India, not only was the gross national product of India relatively low, but the volume of input-output transactions inside the economy was also at a rather low level compared to the volume of transactions in 1959 or 1964–65.

But it is not only in the volume of intermediate goods that the Indian economy has changed, the structure of its technology also has changed considerably as indicated by the coefficients in Tables 4 and 5. As was noted earlier, such structures reflect engineering and institutional factors. These factors are relatively stable rendering the input-coefficient structures quite stable over time[6] in most countries. However, it may be argued that in a country like India, which is at a very low level of development, changes in the input-coefficients are likely to be more than in an advanced country like the U.S.A., which is already on a high technological level. This is mainly because a more mature and stable economy is generally less prone to change than an economy in the very early stages of development. Also at the initial stages of development of an economy, the bases on which the *rates* of change are calculated, for example the level of income, are low so that the rates of change appear to be rather large as compared with more developed economies where the same absolute *amount of change* will mean a smaller *rate of change* because of a larger denominator.

Table 4 shows the input coefficients for both sectors in India for the three selected years. The first point of difference with the volume of transactions in Table 3 is that, proportionately speaking, the coefficients in Table 4 have changed much less than the volumes in Table 3, indicating that the coefficients are more stable than the volumes. Secondly, all the transactions in Table 3 showed increase over time, but all the coefficients in Table 4 did not change in the same direction. For example, the input required from the secondary complex per unit of primary complex output decreased slightly while input from the secondary complex per unit of secondary complex output increased. Again, between 1952–53 and 1964–65, input required

6 W. W. Leontief, "The Structure of Development," in *Input-Output Economics*, (New York; Oxford University Press, 1966).

Table 4. Input Coefficients, India

	1952-53		1959		1964-65	
	Primary Complex	Secondary Complex	Primary Complex	Secondary Complex	Primary Complex	Secondary Complex
Primary Complex	0.222	0.103	0.303	0.061	0.268	0.062
Secondary Complex	0.029	0.124	0.023	0.281	0.027	0.374

from the primary complex per unit of primary complex output increased while the same input per unit of secondary complex output decreased. This shows that the structure of the Indian economy changed such that different sectors moved in different directions in regard to their input use. Moreover, it is noticeable that both in the transactions and in the coefficients the entries on the main diagonals of each table, i.e., the upper left-hand and the lower right hand entries, are larger relative to the other two entries. This signifies a considerable dependence of each sector on inputs from within the sector itself rather than from outside. In general this is a characteristic of a developing economy like India.

The input-coefficients reflect only the *direct* input required per unit of output. But the secondary effects of the production of one unit of any sector's output for final consumption are not reflected in Table 4. For this purpose Table 5 has been computed to show the *total* (*direct plus indirect*) inputs required to produce one extra unit of each sector's output for the market. Table 5 shows that the total input requirements in India did not change in the same way as the direct input requirements in Table 4. To produce one rupee's worth of primary goods, it was necessary to have a total input from the primary sector worth Rs. 1.293 in 1952–53 which rose to Rs. 1.371 in 1964–65. Similarly, to produce secondary output worth one rupee the total input requirement from primary sector was worth Rs. 0.169, 0.122 and 0.130 in 1952–63, 1959 and 1964–65 respectively. The structure of production of the Indian economy changed so that the total input requirements per unit of final goods from the primary sector increased with respect to both sectors. This indicates an increase in the use of industrial inputs in Indian agriculture during the period. On the other hand, the total input requirements for the secondary complex increased with respect to inputs from itself but decreased with respect to inputs from the primary sector.

Changes in the structure of an economy have important implications for the generation of not only output from different

Table 5. Total Input Coefficients[7], India

	1952-53		1959		1964-65	
	Primary Complex	Seconday Complex	Primary Complex	Seconday Complex	Primary Complex	Seconday Complex
Primary Complex	1.293	0.169	1.447	0.122	1.371	0.130
Secondary Complex	0.047	1.279	0.055	1.40	0.057	1.536

7 These are measured by taking (I-A) 1, where I is the identity matrix and A is the input coefficient matrix in Table 4.

sectors of the economy, but also in the creation of employment. An economic activity has implications for employment, first, through the direct employment of labour to work in the given sector, and second, indirectly through creating demand for intermediate output from other sectors. As we have seen in Tables 4 and 5, structural changes in any one sector may result in either an increase or a decrease in the input coefficient associated with each supplying sector. Thus the net effect on employment potential caused by a structural change depends on both the degree and direction of change in each input coefficient and the corresponding employment potential of each sector. On the basis of the employment potentials of the primary and secondary complexes of India and the nature of changes in the input coefficients it seems that the employment potential of the Indian economy has increased substantially.[8]

4. Conclusion

Studies of economic development commonly deal with changes in the aggregative magnitudes of the end results of economic activity like national income or consumption. But behind these expressions there lies an interconnected network of numerous transactions of outputs between the different branches of the economy. In order to understand the mechanism of economic development and to formulate plans for economic growth it is necessary to study this internal structure. Input-output analysis provides a useful tool for such study. Based on two-way tables of the flows of outputs between sectors that use those outputs as their inputs for producing the final goods for consumption, input-output analysis has made possible a general equilibrium analysis of the detailed structure of the economy. The extent to which the different branches of the economy are connected by the flows of intermediate goods is rather small in the earlier stages of development which are characterized by very little inter-sectoral trade. As the economy moves along the path of development there is more specialization within sectors and increased interdependence between sectors and so the inter-sectoral flows of outputs become larger. This is illustrated by the Indian economy which has displayed an increase in the volumes of transactions between sectors during 1952–53 and 1964–65. The internal structure of the Indian economy has changed in such a way that to produce the same amount of output it required in total a much higher amount of input from the industrial sector in 1964–65 than in 1952–53. This shows the increased use of industrial inputs in the Indian economy, or in other words, this is an indication of the industrialization of India.

---

[8] See authors' "Economic Development, Structural Change and Employment Potential," *Journal of Development Studies, forthcoming* (1974).

Part Four

THE LABOUR SECTOR

12

Labour in India —Market and Institution

ROHINI PATI SINHA

1. Introduction

The productive activities of an economy are divided into three main sectors : households, firms, and governmental units. We generally tend to think of business firms as organizers of economic operations in the country. We also recognize the economic contribution of the government—central and state—in areas such as national defense, construction of dams, transportation, postal and telegraph services, public health and education, etc. We are less accustomed, however, to associate households with sources of economic activities. But it is the family which offers labour services for production and is the ultimate destination of all that is produced.

A household decides the allocation of its time between work and non-work activities. The latter will include leisure, household chores, and the education of its children. Our concern here is largely with the former, i.e. the decision of the household in relation to the supply of labour to the economy. The terms and conditions under which labour services are transacted are of vital importance to the family, since jobs constitute the major, and in most cases, the only source of purchasing power for it. If workers find themselves unable to cope singly with the "market," they seek out labour unions to help them deal with it more effectively.

In the market drama, the interests of the two protagonists—labour and capital—essentially coincide. Both have stakes in the smooth functioning of business. However, their unrestrained excesses in pursuit of their individual gains cause them to collide. The government then is compelled to intervene in this foray for the following reasons:

(1) In market relationships, labour, in terms of economic power, is less than equal to capital. This inequality can be exploited to the advantage of the stronger party. The government creates conditions under which fair deals could nonetheless result. This is done mainly by bestowing legitimacy on the workers' organization—the union—and by promoting the institution of collective bargaining. These efforts are in a sense directed to *equalize* the power

differences between the workers and the management.

(2) While the employed and the employers resolve certain problems between them by the courses of action they adopt, they also create some difficulties for the society at large. Strikes and lockouts often inflict heavy damages on the community. A developing country like India can ill afford these troubles. In order to assure the flow of production and income, industrial strife has to be averted.

(3) Labour, in the macro context, is a fixed cost item to the economy. While a worker is idle, his contribution is zero but he is, nevertheless, maintained at least at a subsistence level. India being a labour-surplus economy has to mobilize this surplus resource, which otherwise would be a drag on it in terms of economic development. This is still another reason why government must act to insure industrial peace and harmony so that surplus labour is absorbed into industrialization programmes.

In the present paper, we will address ourselves to this triad: the labour market, the union, and governmental intervention.

2. Labour Market

(A) *Theoretical Framework*

The main function of a labour market is to bring the buyers (firms) and sellers (workers) of labour services together. With the development of such a contact, the terms and conditions of labour employment are negotiated. Spatially, most labour markets are defined as local in character: the supply of machinists in Ranchi, Bihar, for example, does not influence the price of machinists in Bangalore,. Mysore.

Under *purely competitive* conditions, a labour market turns out to be an orthodox market: it has a downward-sloping demand curve and an upward-sloping supply curve for labour, just as we would expect for any other resource or commodity.

Diagram I represents the determination of wages and employment in a labour market. The equilibrium wage—the wage that clears the market—is OW. Any other wage rate can not be sustained. While a wage higher than OW would create a condition where more workers would be available to work than are jobs for them, a lower wage will lead to a shortage of that kind of labour, i.e., there will be more jobs than workers willing to offer their services at such a low price. Competitive pressures by the unemployed, in case of the former, and by the eager employers, in the case of the latter, will restore the wage to OW—the equilibrium wage.

For a firm that operates in a competitive labour market, the market wage becomes a datum for it. Consequently, the WS—line in Diagram 2 reflects the supply condition of labour. Given the wage rate, the decision as to employment will then hinge on the value productivity of labour. The profit-maximizing firm will weigh the economic benefit the worker is likely to

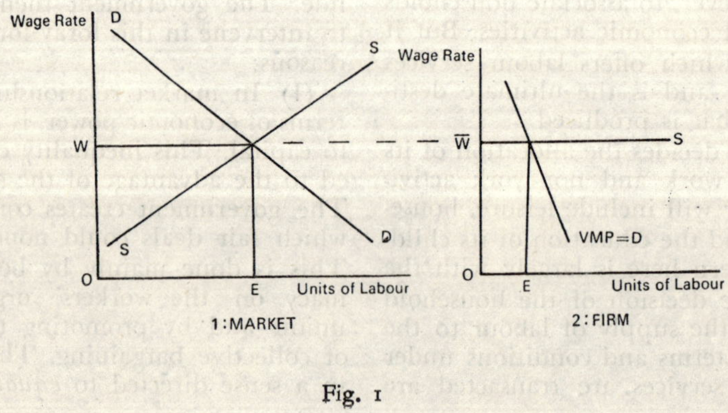

Fig. 1

bring to it against the cost of employing him. The decision rule for such an employer would be to employ labour so long as the revenue from the sale of the product due to that labour exceeds the cost of hiring that labour. It will be to his advantage to continue to hire workers up to the point where the (marginal) product of the last worker employed just pays for the (marginal) expenditure incurred in hiring that worker. In Diagram 2, the equilibrium employment of labour would, thus, be OE. This is essentially what the Marginal Productivity Theory of wage is all about.

The value productivity of labour constitutes the demand for labour. This, in turn, depends upon two conditions: (1) the physical output produced by labour, and (2) the price or prices at which the varying output could be sold. Given the fixed factors, the *marginal physical product* associated with different levels of labour input would be a declining function due to the Law of Diminishing Returns. If the output so produced is sold at the same price per unit—a case of pure competition—the value productivity curve (Price X Marginal Product-curve) will assume the same shape as the marginal physical productivity curve. In the Diagram 2 above, the *Value of Marginal Product* which stands for the demand for labour is, therefore, shown as a downward-sloping curve. Under such a condition, a wage change will provoke the employment adjustment in just the opposite direction; a wage increase would necessitate a decrease in employment and a decrease in wage, symmetrically, would lead to an increase in employment. This inverse relationship between wage and employment would obtain also in the event that the producer operates in a *non-competitive* labour and/or product market.

In the long run, when the employer is allowed to make changes in all the inputs, he will select the resource-mix which would be the least expensive way to produce an output. The supply condition of other factors thus also influence the price and quantity of labour. For instance, a change in the rate of interest (or in the volume of capital) will require appropriate adjustments in the employment of labour. These adjustments will continue until factor market equilibrium consistent with the least-cost combination is reached.

(B) *Empirical Evidence*

From society's point of view, a labour market has two important and inter-related tasks to accomplish: (1) it should provide jobs for persons who are willing and able to work, and (2) it must assure the workers and their families enough means to acquire a decent standard of living. The widespread unemployment in India leads us to question the efficiency of the market on the first count. Its performance vis-a-vis earnings could be evaluated only with reference to actual wages earned by those who were fortunate to hold jobs. In Table 1, the indices of money and real wages for the factory workers earning Rs. 200.00 or less per month for the period 1951–64 are given.

Table 1. Money and Real Earnings of Factory Workers Earning less than Rs. 200.00 per Month, 1951-64.

Year	Index of Money Earnings per Worker (Annual Average) 1951=100	Index of Real Earnings per Worker (Annual Average) 1951=100
1951	100.00	100.00
1952	107.10	109.20
1953	107.70	106.60
1954	107.70	112.00
1955	113.10	123.70
1956	115.40	115.40
1957	120.80	114.30
1958	122.30	110.60
1959	126.40	109.70
1960	134.40	113.80
1961	138.60	115.50
1962	144.00	116.30
1963	145.20	113.80
1964	151.40	104.60

SOURCE: Indian Labour Statistics, 1968, Tables 12.7 and 4.2.

These indices are based on the figures obtained under the Payment of Wages Act of 1936 as amended in 1957. Despite the limited scope in terms of workers included under the Act, Table 1 does yield the following conclusions: (1) The money wages show a definite trend upward. (2) The real wages did not move *pari passu* with money wages. They did have periods of expansion as, for instance, 1951–55 and 1959–62, but they suffered periodic setbacks. The Minimum Wages Act of 1948 was partly responsible for the rise in real earnings index for 1951–55. (3) Over this span of time, the gain in real earnings was not substantial.

The movement of earnings of Class IV employees of railways—the single largest employer of labour in India—shows very much the same pattern of behaviour.

Table 2. Movement of Money and Real Earnings of Class IV Employees of Government Railways, 1949-50 to 1967-68

Year	Index of Money Earnings per Class IV Employee 1949-50=100	Index of Real Earnings per Class IV Employee 1949-50=100
1949-50	100	100
1950-51	103	102
1955-56	122	127
1960-61	142	115
1961-62	143	113
1962-63	152	116
1963-64	157	115
1964-65	168	107
1965-66	182	108
1966-67	196	103
1967-68	215	101

SOURCE: Report of the National Commission on Labour, Ministry of Labour, Employment and Rehabilitation (1969), Table 14.11, p. 197.

The industry which fared relatively better during this period was the coal mines. The possible reasons for this observed improvement in the real earnings series include the fact that the wages in the base year, to start with, were very low in mines.

The failure (or success) of real earnings to move upward could be traced to one or more of the following factors:

1. *Technical Innovation and Capital Formation.* Under competitive conditions, the money wage rate equals the Value of Marginal Physical Product, which is obtained by multiplying the price (P) by the Marginal Physical Product (MPP), That is,

$$W = VMP$$
$$= P.\ MPP$$

Or, Real Wage,

$$W/P = MPP$$

Table 3. Average Annual Money and Real Earnings per Worker: Mines, 1951-1964 (Base 1951= 100)

Year	Index for Real Earnings per Worker		
	Coal Mines	Noncoal Mines	All Minerals
1951	100.00	100.00	100.00
1952	109.50	104.00	107.80
1953	106.40	100.60	104.50
1954	114.00	107.20	112.10
1955	122.80	114.80	120.20
1956	158.70	110.70	143.60
1957	169.20	112.10	151.30
1958	175.70	109.40	154.4
1959	182.60	107.70	158.90
1960	182.00	113.90	160.50
1961	178.90	134.70	165.00
1962	178.70	136.90	165.50
1963	188.20	134.70	171.40
1964	166.90	121.10	152.50

SOURCE: Report of the National Commission on Labour, Ministry of Labour, Employment and Rehabilitation, Government of India (1969), Table 14.9, p. 195.

Thus, the key to real wages lies either in declining prices or increasing productivity. A general fall in prices has to be averted at all costs for the sake of stimulating employment. Therefore, we have to rely only on physical productivity to improve the real wage and to increase the standard of living for the working population. Unfortunately, the productivity in Indian industries has been generally very sluggish.[1] A gain in physical productivity is possible through either increased technical innovation and/or capital formation. Commonly, the two—innovation and capi-

[1] K. K. Dewett, *Indian Economics* (New Delhi: S. Chand & Co., 1972), p. 514.

tal formation—come together. It should, however, be noted that only "capital deepening" and not the "capital widening" type of investment is likely to augment productivity. It seems that in India, the growth in the capital stock has hardly kept pace with increase in labour force. Capital accumulation has been mostly of "capital widening" nature.

2. *Union and Collective Bargaining.* A strong collective bargaining position of the unions vis-a-vis the management can enhance the (real) earnings of the workers. In large measure, this is achieved by affecting the functional share of labour and capital. The state of labour disorganization and weak institution of collective bargaining in India do not lend support to change the share to labour's advantage. As a matter of fact, there is strong evidence that labour's share in national income has been stagnating, even declining somewhat.[2]

3. *Public Policy.* The policy of the government in relation to wages also influences directly the earnings of the workers. The policy takes various forms. For example, legislation pertaining to minimum wages, bonuses, etc. affect the workers covered by these Acts. A critical assessment of the government's involvement in this regard will be made later in section.

(C) *Governmental Involvement*

The state is committed under the Directive Principles of the Constitution to work towards achieving a "living wage" for workers in India. This broadly forms a legal basis for it to intervene in the process of wage formation. But economic reasons for the state involvement are largely the following : (1) The market on its own fails to generate an equitable distribution of income. It is felt that part of the observed bulge in the Lorenz[3] income distribution curve could be eliminated by boosting worker's earnings institutionally. (2) The labour market realities also warrant corrective measures by the government. For instance, India suffers from pervasive unemployment, both open and disguised. In this situation, an increase in demand for labour would not translate itself in a higher wage. Even in the face of increasing productivity, wages would be slow to move upward. They would tend to stagnate at low levels due to an almost perfectly elastic supply of labour. (3) The state of disorganization in labour ranks and the absence of strong economic leverage make bargaining position of workers extremely weak. They cannot negotiate from a position of equality. Under such a condition, exploitation is likely to occur, i.e. workers do not get what they rightfully deserve on the basis of their productivity. To some extent, this is responsible for the worsening of labour's share in production. It has been found that wages as a per cent of total costs in manufacturing industries have suffered a decline in recent years.

Despite its expressed concern and commitment, the government's intervention in matters relating to wages is so far limited in scope. First, its wage policy applies effectively to industrial employment only, even though the agricultural sector is covered under the Minimum Wages Act of 1948. For all practical purposes, the Act is inoperative as far as farm employment is concerned. Second, the wage policy, as stated in the act, has only one part which is mandatory. The other part is primarily recommendatory.

Minimum Wages Act of 1948. The Act empowers central and state governments to fix minimum rates of wages for workers in twelve industries and agriculture. The criteria used in selecting an industry was that it either employs a sizeable number of sweated labour, or that it has the opportunity to exploit its workers. It should be noted, however, that industries covered by

[2] Ministry of Labour, Employment and Rehabilitation, *Report of the National Commission on Labour,* (Delhi :Government of India, 1969), Table 15.1. pp. 224–25.

[3] Lorenz curve indicates distribution of income in a society.

[4] Ruddar Dutt, *Indian Economics* (New Delhi : S. Chand & Co. 1972), p. 623.

the Act are mostly made up of small firms. Large firms manage to escape this statutory regulation.

The Act requires the government to review the fixed rates periodically, at least once every five years. The machinery for enforcing the Act is largely left for the appropriate government to devise. It can set up committees or sub-committees to hold enquiries and to advise the government with respect to the establishment or revision or minimum rates of wages. The Minimum Wages Act also empowers the government—both the state and central—to set up advisory boards to coordinate the work of these committees.

One serious limitation of this Act is that, while it empowers the government to fix minimum rates of wages, it does not set up norms or guidelines which would govern the setting of wage rates. The Committee on Fair Wages in 1948 recommended only some general principles for deciding the rates. The Planning Commission later did recommend an elaborate, a "need-based" formula for fixing the minimum rates of wages. With some modification, this was adopted and recommended by the fifteenth session of the Indian Labour Conference in 1957. But the recommendation has not yet been accepted as an operating standard for official minimum rates of wages.

Wage Boards : Non-statutory Wage Fixation. The Planning Commission, in its programme for Second Five Year Plan, recommended for creation of industry-wise wage boards. This was done at a time when wages were the largest single source of industrial conflicts. The rates set were not always agreeable to the parties involved. It was felt that a machinery which would seek the participation of both the employers and employees in the decision-making process would be much more acceptable than the ones presently available, viz. industrial tribunals. Such boards were not aimed at supplanting the tribunals which are already in existence, but to supplement them. Accordingly, in March 1957, a tripartite wage board for cotton textile industry was constituted. The same year, it was also approved by the Indian Labour Conference. Between 1957 and 1971, wage boards were established in twenty-four major industries.

A wage board is a tripartite body consisting of an equal number of representatives of employers and workers with an independent person to chair it. In addition to them, an economist and a representative of consumer interests are also appointed to the board as independent members.

The approach of the boards has generally been to determine the minimum wage for unskilled workers and then to build upon it a structure of differentials. In determining the lowest wage, the workers' needs carry the heaviest weight. Beyond that level, it is structured so as to provide incentives for workers with different skills and efficiency. The board in its deliberation also takes into account the ability of the industry concerned to meet the rates but not that of a particular employer in the same industry.

The government has ordinarily accepted the recommendations of the board. Since a wage board is a non-statutory body, its recommendations are not binding. In view of this fact, the implementation of such recommendations is achieved through the good offices of the industrial relations machinery in existence.

3. Possible Adverse Effects on the Economy

A wage policy committed to increasing the earnings of the workers can bring about the following adverse consequences: (1) On the micro-level, given the demand for labour, a wage increase necessitates a drop in employment. A worker who continues to hold a job certainly benefits from the wage increase but the one who loses the opportunity for employment because of the rise in wages will be worse off. (2) A general rise in wages, in macro context, will threaten price stability. The Phillips' curve presents the economy with unpleasant choices between unemployment and inflation, if money wages are allowed to exceed productivity gains. (3) The race between wages and prices can trigger industrial strife as workers resort to protests against the erosion of the purchasing power of their money wages. (4) The investment funds which come largely from corporate profits might possibly be reduced. To that extent, the flow of capital formation, and therefore the growth of the country, might be retarded.

In view of our discussion of the wage policy, it is clear to us that the government is facing a dilemma in this area. On the one hand, it is compelled to intercede in the wage determination process on behalf of the workers. On the other hand, it is confronted with serious economic constraints. If undue wage increases are granted, their side effects on the economy could be devastating. The government has resolved this dilemma by making a trade-off, i.e. it is willing to forsake, up to a point, some other economic objectives, such as price stability and economic growth, in favour of obtaining a seemingly better standard of living for the workers. The adverse consequences of its policy are the calculated costs the government is apparently willing to pay for its programmes. In many instances, though, it is the political pressure or the ideological predilection which override the sound economic decisions in terms of costs and benefits.

4. The Union

(A) *Groping for Models*

The history of the labour movement in India is characterized by series of experimentation with union models. In the beginning, the concerted efforts of the workers were directed mainly at attacking specific problems. In 1862, about 1200 railway workers went on a strike at Howrah station for an eight-hour workday.[5] In 1877, the workers of the Empress Mills in Nagpur resolved to strike for higher wages. Seven years later, under the leadership of N. M. Lokhanday, textile workers in Bombay held protest meetings against the working conditions prevailing in their factories. From 1882 to 1890, about twenty-five similar strikes occurred in different parts of the country.[6] The cohesion which emerged on such occasions, however did not last for long. Organizations which were set up to lead the action groups dissolved afterwards. In this respect, they were more like strike committees than trade unions committed to protect the interests of the workers on a long range basis. To all intents and purposes, they were of *ad hoc* nature.

Almost simultaneously, workers experimented with enlisting outside support for their cause. It was felt that in the absence of public help and protective legislation, a battle against poverty and exploitive practices by employers would be difficult for workers alone to win. Socially conscious persons and institutions were drawn into the labour scene. Shapurji Bengali gave considerable aid to N. M. Lokhanday—a factory employee in Bombay, who established the first labour organization, the Bombay Millhands Association, in India. This Association was by no means—a labour union in the traditional sense. Functionally, it worked as a public relations firm for the workers. Its main thrust was to persuade the British Government to enact factory laws similar to those obtaining in England. In this venture, the Association also received moral and political support from textile workers and millowners in Lancashire, whose jobs and profits were threatened by the inexpensive production of textiles in India. Brahmo Samaj also played an important role in this area. Its leaders, especially Shashipada Banerjee and P. N. Majumdar, were active in putting pressure for favourable labour laws as well as in the welfare programmes for the workers. The enactment of Factory Acts of 1881 and 1891 were partly the result of such agitations. Other organizations dedicated to the uplift of the workers also came into being in later years. The most notable among them were the Kamgar Hitvardhak Sabha and the Social Service League, founded in 1909 and 1911 respectively.

Just as childhood experiences influence

[5] Gopal Ghosh, *Indian Trade Union Movement*, (Calcutta : T. U. Publication, 1961), p. 44.

[6] V. B. Karnik, *Indian Trade Union : A Survey* (Bombay : Allied Publishing Private Ltd., 1960), pp. 3–4.

a person's behaviour in his adult life, an institution's behaviour pattern is very much shaped by the experiences of its early encounters. This possibly explains, to an extent, the differences in the nature of labour movements in the United States of America and India. At the early stage of development, the organized labour in America was not well received. The public opinion was hostile to its aspirations. Both the Congress and the courts were less than sympathetic to their cause. This experience forced the American labour to become self-reliant and even somewhat more militant. Instead of seeking governmental help, it sought to develop its bargaining position on its own. The early reception of labour in India, on the other hand, was different from it. The Indian labour was well received by the public at large. It mobilized public support to change the terms and conditions of work through favourable labour legislation. This, among other factors, accounts for the workers' propensity in India to rely on the government to bring about an improvement in their economic status.

In the first quarter of this century, some labour leaders also tried to form a separate *labour party* as a political organization in India. B. P. Wadia toyed with this idea as early as 1918 and a resolution to that effect was introduced before the All India Trade Union Congress in 1923. In Calcutta, a "Labour League of India" was established the same year under the leadership of K. C. Roy Chowdhary. In 1925, Lala Lajpat Rai and his associates went so far as to convene a special meeting for that purpose and decided to frame the constitution for such a party.[7] Even though they did not succeed, the efforts reveal labour's proclivity towards political action. Reasons for such a disposition are not very difficult to discern: (1) The limited success in influencing legislation perhaps worked as a positive conditioning factor. (2) The overlapping leadership in labour and national liberation movements inescapably politicized the ranks of labour. (3) Strong, cohesive labour unions could not be formed along the business lines for several sociological reasons. For example, castes, religions, and languages stood as barriers against worker solidarity. (4) Most workers' involvement in unions was only half-hearted, if at all, because of their tenuous attachment to urban lives. (5) Also, the feeling that the poor and the illiterate workers could not by themselves sustain viable unions compelled their leaders to seek solutions to labour problems by political means.

Some of the events in the aftermath of the First World War catalyzed the unionization process. The increased cost of living, the successful revolution in Soviet Union, and the establishment of International Labour Organization contributed to the strengthening of labour movement in India. The first industrial union, the Madras Labour Union, was formed by textile workers under the stewardship of B. P. Wadia in Madras. In 1920, the Textile Labour Association of Ahmedabad was established. It received guidance and assistance from Mahatma Gandhi, which gave it the ideological direction and stability it needed. The same year, All India Trade Union Congress (AITUC) was formed. In all these organizations, outsiders played key roles. This legacy continues to this day.

Since AITUC at its formation attracted leaders of diverse political persuasions, it was hoped that Indian labour at last would have a unified front of its own. This expectation, however, did not materialize. Within a decade of the birth of AITUC, there was a severe rupture in the movement due to ideological differences existing between union leaders. An All India Trade Union Federation was carved out of the All India Trade Union Congress with moderate leadership. The parent union—the AITUC—came to be dominated now by the communists. There were some attempts in the thirties to restore unity to the movement but they did not succeed. As a matter of fact, any time there was a serious split in a political party, it was almost always followed by a mitosis in the trade union movement.

In 1947, the Indian National Trade Union Congress (INTUC) was born. It

[7] Ibid., p. 30.

maintains close ties with the Indian National Congress, and is the largest of all the central labour organizations. The following year (1948), when the socialists broke away from the Congress Party and established the Praja Socialist Party, they also formed a trade union called the Hind Mazdoor Sabha (HMS). The other central labour organization, the United Trade Union Congress (UTUC), came into being in 1949. Its leaders at one time belonged to the AITUC like most other labour leaders, but later, dissatisfied with its policies, left that union. Its membership strength lies largely in West Bengal and Kerala. In 1970, the Marxist Communists left AITUC and established a new trade union called the Centre of Indian Trade Union (CITU). This is the result of division in the Communist Party of India. Presently, the AITUC is dominated by the Right, while the CITU by the Left, Communists.

(B) *Membership*

The total union membership in India stood at about 4.5 million in the year 1964–65. This was about 24 per cent of the non-agricultural employment in the country. Its strength varied from one industry to another. Industries with a high degree of unionization included the following: tobacco (15 per cent), iron and steel (63 per cent), coal (61 per cent), cotton textiles (56 per cent), banking (51 per cent), mining (51 per cent), railway (33 per cent), insurance (33 per cent) and plantation (28 per cent).[8]

Even though the membership in the unions has continued to grow, organized labour has failed to gain influence commensurately in the industrial realm. This is because of the fact that an offsetting development has occurred within the labour movement. Union proliferation has been going on at a faster rate than the increase in membership. The outcome of this development is that the average membership per union has declined from 3,954 in 1927–28 to less than 600 in 1964–65. We would normally expect that as industrial units become larger due to economic development, unions will also tend to grow larger just to countervail the growing power of the management. So far in India, this has not been the case.

Table 4. Number and Membership of Trade Unions

Year	No. of registered unions	No. of unions submitting returns	Total membership (in millions)	Average membership
1927-28	29	28	.101	3,594
1935-36	236	205	.268	1,309
1947-48	2,766	1,629	1.663	1,026
1951-52	4,623	2,556	1.996	781
1955-56	8,095	4,006	2.275	568
1960-61	11,312	6,813	4.013	589
1963-64	11,984	7,250	3.977	549
1964-65	13,023	7,543	4.466	592

SOURCE: Report of the National Commission on Labour, op. cit., Table 20.2, p. 278.

It should be noted that despite a century of experimentation, the Indian labour movement has not yet evolved a union committed entirely to workers' interests. The movement continues to be torn by internal dissension, deflected by secondary pursuits, dominated by politics from outside, and it exists more as an instrument of the politicians than an agent of the workers they represent.

Of the four central labour organizations for which data are available, the Indian National Trade Union Congress (INTUC) is the largest and fastest growing. The United Trade Union Congress (UTUC) has been losing membership since 1955–56.

[8] op. cit., pp. 278–79.

The record of the All India Trade Union Congress (AITUC) is marked by ups and downs but the membership since 1959–60 seems to be declining somewhat. Besides the INTUC, the Hind Mazdoor Sabha (HMS) shows signs of growing strength. Table 5 below lists both the absolute size and relative share for each of the four unions for selected years.

Table 5. Membership of the Four Central Trade Unions Organizations for Selected Years

Year	INTUC	AITUC	HMS	UTUC	Total verified membership
1952-53	919,258 (56 .3)	210,914 (12 .9)	373,459 (22 .9)	129,242 (7 .9)	1,632,873 (100 .00)
1955-56	971,740 (55 .3)	422,851 (24 .1)	203,798 (11 .5)	159,109 (9 .1)	1,757,498 (100 .00)
1959-60	1,053,386 (53 .8)	508,962 (26 .0)	286,202 (14 .6)	110,034 (5 .6)	1,958,584 (100 .00)
1962-63	1,268,339 (57 .4)	500,968 (23 .8)	329,931 (14 .9)	108,982 (4 .9)	2,208,219 (100 .00)
1966	1,417,553 (59 .5)	433,564 (18 .2)	436,977 (18 .3)	93,454 (4 .0)	2,381,548 (100 .00)

SOURCE: Report of the National Commission on Labour, op. cit., Table 20.4, p. 208.

5. Government and Labour Relations

The control of labour and industrial relations in India, as in most other countries, has been mainly through laws governing hours of work, minimum wages, the employment of women and children, workmen's compensation, social security, trade unions, and the resolution of industrial disputes. In this chapter we will address ourselves briefly to legislation pertaining to only the last two areas, viz. the trade unions and the industrial disputes.

(A) *Trade Union Legislation*

The first Act which gave legal protection to the activities of the union was the Indian Trade Union Act of 1926. Under this Act, the registered unions are granted immunity from certain criminal and civil liabilities. For the first time, a trade union became a legitimate institution. The Act was amended in 1928, 1937, 1947, 1960, and 1964. Except for 1947, all other amendments were largely aimed at removing administrative "bugs" or problems. The 1947 Amendment did contain some important provisions, such as the compulsory recognition of unions and penalties for unfair labour practices by both employers and employees. But for various reasons, the Act has not been enforced.

The main features of the Act are the following: (1) Every state government is to appoint a Registrar of Trade Unions. (2) Any seven or more members of a business unit can apply for registration. It is, however, optional and not mandatory. (3) At least 50 per cent of the executive committee must be union members. This provision is to reduce the influence of outsiders. (4) Union funds may not be used for other than business of the union. They cannot be spent for political campaigns. Separate funds raised voluntarily from within the union may, however, be earmarked and employed for non-union purposes. (5) Minimum membership dues of twenty-five paise per month are to be charged each member.

Two facts of trade unionism which need corrective measures in India are the multiplicity of unions and the jurisdictional or representational feuds between the unions. The present membership requirement of only seven members permits small, unviable unions to exist. Larger specified minimum membership should be required. The jurisdictional disputes which arise so often from simultaneous claims by competing unions to represent the same set of workers would be reduced if there was an election machinery which would determine the union with the largest membership. The present practice of deciding such an issue by membership rolls is filled with pitfalls. An agency similar to the National Labour Relations Board in the U.S.A., with, of course, some modifications to suit Indian conditions, would be worth considering. Under such a system, representational rights would be granted to the union with majority votes at the polls.

The policy of the Indian government with respect to industrial disputes constitutes two sets of measures: (1) preventive measures to reduce friction by attacking the problems at the source of conflict, and (2) the creation of positive machinery to handle disputes. The Payment of Bonus Act of 1965, the formation of Wage Boards, and the promotion of Joint Management Councils have as their targets the prevention of strikes by getting at the roots of labour-management problems. They are aimed at reducing the factors contributing to labour-management misunderstanding. State intervention directly into a dispute first started with the Trade Disputes Act of 1929. It empowered the government to appoint *ad hoc* conciliation boards and/or courts of enquiry. In 1947, this Act was replaced by the Industrial Disputes Act of 1947. This sets up machinery for the resolution of industrial disputes.

The Industrial Disputes Act of 1947 as amended lays out procedure to settle industrial conflicts through conciliation, arbitration and adjudication processes.

Conciliation. The state government is empowered under the Act to appoint conciliation officers to mediate disputes and to reconcile the differences between the industrial combatants—labour and management. If their attempts fail, the government may appoint a Board of Conciliation. In the case of public utilities industries, conciliation is compulsory. In practice, however, it is becoming more and more mandatory. In order to expedite the resolution of disputes, the conciliation officers are required to submit their reports within fourteen days, and the Board to submit its reports within two months. A settlement arrived at in the course of conciliation is binding on both parties for a period mutually agreed upon, or for a period of six months. Beyond six months, term of settlement would be binding unless revoked by either party. While a case is pending before the Conciliation Board, strikes and lockouts are prohibited under the Act.

Arbitration. Voluntary arbitration as a means of solving industrial disputes was attractive to the policy makers in India because of the success of the Gandhian experiment with textile industry in Ahmedabad. The Code of Discipline (1958) voluntarily adopted by labour and management reinforced the role of arbitration in the settlement of disputes. Recently, the government has set up a National Arbitration Promotion Board (NAPB) with a tripartite composition. The Board is to develop norms and principles for arbitration. It would also set guidelines for types of disputes to be brought under its orbit. It may also look into the causes of any delay in the arbitration process. This is in a way an overseer of the arbitration mechanism. Despite governmental support, arbitration has not gained wide currency as a means of settling disputes.

Adjudication. The adjudicative process involves a three-tier system of tribunals; labour courts, industrial tribunals, and national tribunals. A labour court would take up issues arising from an employer's decision, such as a worker's discharge or dismissal. It would examine the propriety and legality of such an action by the employer. An industrial tribunal established by appropriate state government would adjudicate matters pertaining to wages, allowances, hours of work, leaves, and conditions of work, etc. The National Tribunal is appointed by the Central Government to intervene in disputes which involve industries which are either of national importance or have inter-state operation. The verdicts of the tribunals are binding on parties involved.

The main criticism of the machinery for the resolution of industrial strife is that it is over-protective. This possibly chokes the development of collective bargaining. The issues which should ordinarily be the subjects of negotiation at the bargaining table are being handled presently by conciliation and adjudication procedures. A short-sighted over-concern by the State for industrial harmony might possibly smother initiative by labour and management to resolve conflicts by negotiation. It may be beneficial for industrial relations if the State were to adopt an attitude of "benign neglect" for short-term labour problems and were to devote its energies towards building institutional support for strong labour unions.

BIBLIOGRAPHY

Grouch, Harold, *Trade Unions and Politics in India* (Bombay: Manaktalas, 1966), chaps. IV, V, XI.

Dutt, Ruddar, *Indian Economy* (New Delhi: S. Chand & Co., 1972), chap. 39.

Dewett, K. K., *et. al., Indian Economics* (New Delhi: S. Chand & Co.), chapters 35, 36.

Ghosh, Alak, *Indian Economy* (Calcutta: The World Press), chapters 23, 24.

Ghosh, Gopal, *Indian Tarde Union Movement* (Calcutta: T. U. Publication, 1961).

Karnik, V. B., *Indian Trade Unions: A Survey* (Bombay: Allied Publishers Private Ltd., 1960).

Kennedy, V. D., *Unions, Employers and Government* (Bombay: Manaktalas, 1966), chaps. 2, 3.

Mathur, K. & Sheth, N. R., *Tripartitism in Labour Policy* (New Delhi: Shri Ram Centre for Industrial Relations, 1969), chaps. 5, 6.

Ministry of Labour, Employment & Rehabilitation, *Report of the National Commission on Labour* (New Delhi: Government of India, 1969), chaps. 14, 15, 16, 19, 20, 23.

Rothschild, K. W., *The Theory of Wages* (New York: 1967), Augustus M. Kelley, chaps. II, V, XIII.

Varkey, N. K., *A Handbook of Labour Legislation in India* (Bombay: Lalvani Publishing House, 1968), chaps. 1, 2, 6, 8.

13

Economics of Agricultural Labour in India

SURENDRA N. KULSHRESHTHA

1. Introduction

Human resources in an economy constitute a significant input in the production process of goods and services. The study of human resources—their quality, and problems is of immense use in manpower planning in both developing as well as developed economies. Knowledge of this sector is even more crucial for a country such as India where techniques of production are more labour intensive. The industry of agriculture constitutes the major and most staple industry of India, employing about 70 per cent of the total workers (available for work) and contributing about 49 per cent towards total national income of the country.[1] A study of agricultural labour—its problems and possible solutions—in India must, therefore, be considered a topic with a great potential for improvement through Indian economic planning.

The primary objective of this chapter is to theoretically review the agricultural labour situation, analyze some of the major problems facing this sector, and suggest solutions for improvements in its present situation in India.

2. Agricultural Labour in India—A Historical Perspective

Agriculture industry in India has been traditionally managed in the form of a very large number of tiny owner-operated farm units; each tiny unit further fragmented into a number of small pieces. The structure of the industry does approach atomistic competition in the conventional sense. In spite of the large number of farm units, there is a tendency of concentration of production. Comparing the land resource base[2] in India during 1961, a very uneven size distribution is

[1] The figures for employment refer to the year 1961, and that for national income for the year 1960–61. Data to calculate these figures were obtained from Government of India, *India 1970* and its other issues.

[2] It is recognized that size of the holding is a measure of production potential under the rigid assumption of homogeneous quality, identical

noticed. About three-fourths of all farms command only 30 per cent of the total cultivated area, whereas the top 4.6 per cent of farms occupy 29.7 of the total acreage. The pattern is also shown as a Lorenz curve in Figure 1, which clearly

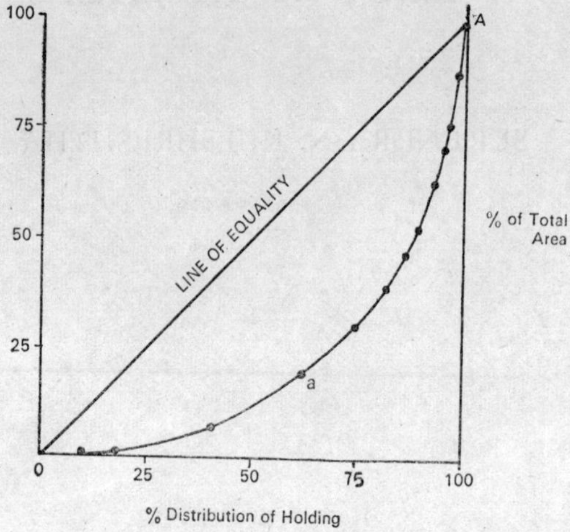

Fig. 1

Lorenze Curve Showing Size Distribution of Agricultural Holdings in India, 1961.

SOURCE : Data obtained from *India 1970.*

indicates the large unequal distribution. Further away the line OaA is from the 45° line of equality, higher is the concentration coefficient.

According to the First Agricultural Labourer's Enquiry Committee,[3] an agricultural labourer is defined as a person who for more than half of the total number of days on which he actually works during the year is engaged in agricultural operations as a hired worker. The definition of agricultural labour force includes these workers plus all the operators of agricultural holdings.

The agricultural labour force during 1961 comprised of 131 million workers, which constituted 69.5 per cent of total labour force in the country. The proportion of agricultural labourers to total varies from state to state. For example, in Kerala this proportion is only 38 per cent, whereas in Madhya Pradesh it is as high as 79 per cent.[4] Historically, the predominance of agriculture in providing gainful[5] employment has not declined as shown in Table 1. Labour force in agriculture

Table 1. Labour Force in Agriculture, India, 1900-1961

Year	Per cent of Workers Engaged in Agriculture to Total
1900	62.5
1911	67.8
1921	68.5
1931	66.4
1951	69.0
1961	69.5

SOURCE : Government of India, *Census of India*, Paper no. 1, 1962.

has increased in proportion to the growth in all workers. During the 1951–61 period, the number of farm operators increased while the hired labour declined. (Table 2). A part of the explanation in the relative reduction of hired labour force may lie in increased alternatives for them in the non-farm sector, and by the fact that small farm units can barely support the hired workers except during peak season. As farms grow in size the dependence on hired labour resources grows. (Figure 2).

Labour force in rural India consists of persons belonging to varying ages ranging from below 14 years to over 60 years. The participation rates vary substantially

technology, comparable product mix and homogeneous set of other factors of production. Given that such a situation very seldom exists in any realistic system the conclusions based on land holding distribution alone would be of limited value.

[3] Ministry of Labour, *Report of the First Agricultural Labour Enquiry in India,* (Delhi : Government of India, 1952).

[4] Figures are based on estimates of the *Report of the Second Agricultural Labour Enquiry Committee, 1956–57,* and *Census of India,* 1962.

[5] The term "gainful" should be interpreted with a great deal of caution. Concept of gainful employment in occupations with a great deal of self-employed labour resources cannot preclude the possibility of a few being underemployed.

Table 2. Change in Agricultural Labour Force, India, 1951-1961

Type of Worker	Total Number 1951	Total Number 1961	Per cent of Total 1951	Per cent of Total 1961	Δ in the per cent during 1951-61
	(No. in Mill.)		%		%
Operators	69.8	99.5	50.0	52.8	+2.8
Hired Labourers	27.5	31.5	19.0	16.7	—2.3
All Agricultural Workers	97.3	131.0	69.0	69.5	+0.5

SOURCE : Government of India, *Census of India*, Paper No. 1, 1962.

Table 3. Labour Force in Rural India—Age Composition and Participation Rates, 1961

Age Groups (Years)	*Distribution of Rural Workers*			*Participation Rates*		
	Male	Female	Total	Male	Female	Total
0-14	7.6	10.0	8.4	10.6	7.6	9.2
15-34	47.7	51.0	48.8	91.1	49.8	70.3
35-59	36.8	34.4	36.0	97.5	52.3	76.0
60+	7.8	4.6	6.7	79.9	24.3	52.0
All Ages	100.0	100.0	100.0	58.2	31.4	45.1

SOURCE : Government of India, *Census of India*, Paper no. 1, 1962.

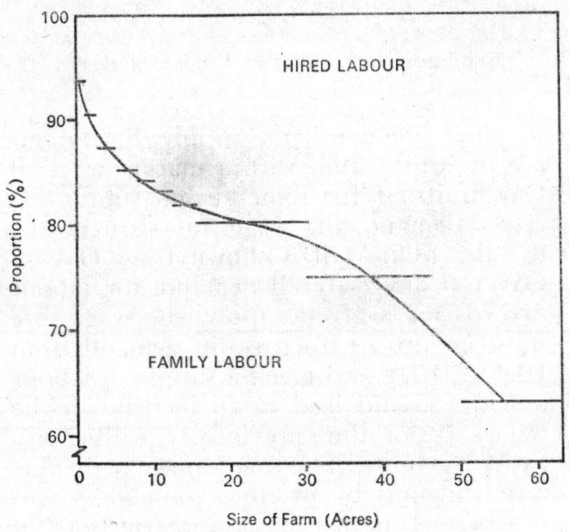

Fig. 2

Proportion of hired : family labour on farms by size.

SOURCE: Data obtained from Kalra, 8, p. 62.

among age groups and for male and female. (Table 3). Participation by workers below the age of 14 years in the labour force is quite unique in economies such as India. Compared to some of the western developed countries, at least two marked differences can be noted: one, that the labour force in India has a relatively high proportion of people under 34 years of age.[6] Two, the participation rates in India for male labour are significantly below those in Canada or U.S.A. In U.S.A. participation rates for male workers in all ages for 1961 were estimated at 79.7 per cent, as against only 57.7 per cent in India.[7]

6 A relatively lower proportion of workers in age brackets over 35 years may be as a result of a relatively shorter production life of an individual, and also as a result of a deliberate policy of some institutions for early retirements in order to create more jobs.

7 For details of these figures see Appendix Table 1.

Part of the explanation for low participation may lie on the opportunity for jobs, prevalence of particular work ethics, and low opportunity cost of being unemployed. One of the serious problems facing hired agricultural workers is the low level of wages. In part, low wages for hired workers are a direct result of low productivity in agriculture, although many other factors may also be held responsible for them. The broad conclusions that can be derived on the basis of the first and the second Agricultural Labourers Enquiry Committee reports are: greater dependence of agricultural labour families on wage employment, a tendency of widening wage differentials between male and female, and a general decline in wage levels.

This section has briefly reviewed various factors underlying in the determination of the economics of labour in Indian agriculture. An understanding of these forces, therefore, would facilitate the basic problems facing this resource sector.

3. Agricultural Labour Market—A Theoretical Expose

In theoretical economics the term "market" refers to the existence of a set of buyers and sellers for a homogeneous factor of production, goods or service. It is not generally given any specific geographic boundaries. In reality, however, the entire industry in a nation can very seldom constitute a single labour market area. Rather one can make distinctions on the basis of geographic regions, and occupational characteristics. Such distinctions become necessary since the characteristics of a perfect labour market can very seldom be satisfied by a country as large and diverse as India. According to Peitchinis,[8] a perfect labour market must possess the following characteristics: (i) the labour force must be homogeneous; (ii) employment conditions are perfectly identical in all forms; (iii) the number of workers on the market must be so large that each worker constitutes an infinitesimal proportion to total; (iv) workers are fully mobile within the labour market; (v) every worker seeks to improve his economic position; and (vi) every employer seeks out that worker who will accept the lowest possible wages, and is always ready to replace anyone of his workers who refuses to accept that rate for which another worker offers his services. If there were a perfect market, there will be only one wage and an employer can hire any number of workers at that market rate. The two basic forces which bring about a change in the market wage rate are the supply for labour, and demand for labour, as shown in figure 3. Given that at a point

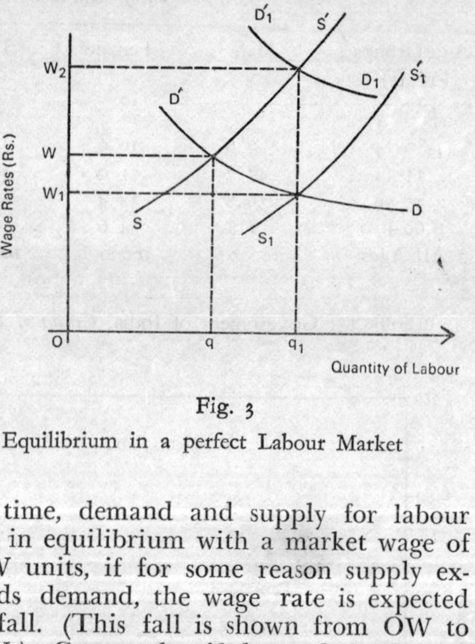

Fig. 3

Equilibrium in a perfect Labour Market

in time, demand and supply for labour are in equilibrium with a market wage of OW units, if for some reason supply exceeds demand, the wage rate is expected to fall. (This fall is shown from OW to OW_1). Conversely, if demand for labour exceeds for a given supply, the wage rate must go up. An increase in demand from DD′ to D_1D_1' and given a supply of labour at Oq_1, should lead to an increase in the wages (from the previous equilibrium) by WW_2 units. This mechanism will operate indefinitely in any economic system if a perfect market exists. Imperfections in labour market are universal and agriculture in India is by no means an exception to these. Some of the major imperfections in labour markets are: absence of a homogeneous service, lack of mobility due to

---

[8] S. G. Peitchinis, *The Economics of Labour* (New York: McGraw-Hill, 1965), p. 43.

cultural, food, and language barriers, lack of communication or knowledge, emigration of workers, and so on. In order to understand the market mechanism concepts of market and demand should be developed further.

(a) Supply of Labour

In common terminology the term supply of labour denotes the number of people able and willing to work. A more satisfactory measure should be the amount of productive work people are able and willing to work at various levels of wage rates. The term "productive" has been used to denote productive of the means of production, and of durable sources of enjoyment.[9] Any form of physical and mental exertion with the objective of production of goods and services (whether immediate or ultimate) is included in labour. This definition includes all types of workers: hired workers, self-employed workers, employees, and unpaid workers.

The size of the labour force in any economic system is determined by factors affecting the participation of population in offering their services. A distinction must, therefore, be made between the potential labour force and actual labour force. Potential labour force includes all those individuals in the civilian population who are over a certain legal age.[10] Actual labour force is composed of that portion of the potential labour force who are able and willing. The participation of the population in labour force is determined by a number of factors: age group and sex; compulsory retirement; unemployment rate in appropriate age, sex, and occupational category; family income; and intensity of progressive income tax. A certain degree of controversy on whether progressive income tax acts as a deterrent to labour supply exists. There is no agreement amongst economists on this question, although it appears that income tax may not affect the number of people in the labour force, it may significantly determine the quantity of labour offered at a given wage.

A labour supply function for an economy (or individual) can be derived from the utility function for the individuals. An equilibrium in employment is reached when the marginal utility of wages is identically equal to the marginal disutility of labour or work. The utility function, therefore, denotes a person's choice between leisure and work at a given wage rate.

Let utility be denoted by U, hours of leisure by L, and hours of work by H, and wage rate by ω. Total wage income of the individual (I) is:

$$I=\omega \qquad (1)$$

and his utility from leisure and wage income can be expressed as:

$$U=\phi\ (I, L) \qquad (2)$$

Assuming that an individual distributes his time between leisure and work, total number of hours (T) can be written as:

$$T=L+H \qquad (3)$$

From equation (1)

$$H=\frac{I}{\omega} \qquad (4)$$

Therefore, equation (3) can be written as a time-budget constraint as:

$$T=L+\frac{I}{\omega} \qquad (5)$$

This budget equation specifies how a person should spend his total time. He has a choice between not earning any income (or purchasing leisure at T units) or earning income. Maximizing his utility in (2) subject to time budget constraint (5), a solution for hours of work can be obtained.

Assume that the utility function is of a Cobb-Douglas type:

$$U=K\ I^{\alpha}L^{\beta} \qquad (6)$$

where K, α, β are constants, such that

$$K > 0,\ 0 < \alpha < 1,\ 0 < \beta < 1.$$

---

9 For more discussion, see A. Marshall, *Principles of Economics* (London: Macmillan, 1926), p. 56.

10 Legal age is determined by the legislative and institutional regulations regarding eligibility for employment.

Using (3) and (5) to express wage income I and leisure L as functions of hours of work H, we convert utility in terms of H. By setting

$\frac{dU}{dH}=0$, and testing $\frac{d^2U}{d^2H} < 0$, we maximize utility and solve for H as a function of wage rate.

As wage rate rises, on an average up to a certain level of income the supply of labour (H) should increase. At a certain income level supply will not respond to an increasing wage and if further increases in wages are experienced it may conceivably reduce the supply of labour. This phenomenon is theoretically denoted by a backward sloping supply curve as shown in Figure 4.

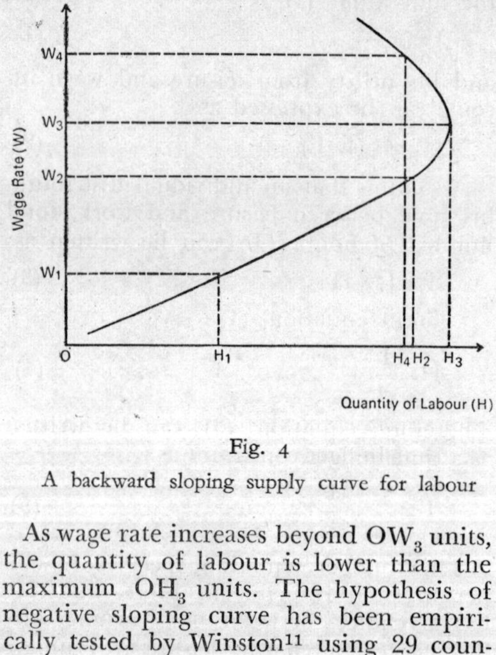

Fig. 4
A backward sloping supply curve for labour

As wage rate increases beyond OW_3 units, the quantity of labour is lower than the maximum OH_3 units. The hypothesis of negative sloping curve has been empirically tested by Winston[11] using 29 countries cross-section data.

Supply of labour is significantly determined by immigration (or emigration) of workers. However, given a limited opportunity for agricultural workers outside India, and pursuance of a very tight immigration policy by Indian government, agriculture labour is not affected by this factor.

(b) Demand for Labour

(i) *Concept of Derived Demand*

Demand for a factor of production in an industry is a derived demand. It is derived on the basis of:

(1) demand for the final good,
(2) nature of the production function (as dictated by technology), and
(3) relative factor prices.

One may be given a production denoting multiproducts and multi-inputs of a firm in the following form:

$$Q(Y_1, \ldots, Y_p; L, X_1, \ldots, X_{k-1}) = 0 \quad (7)$$

where $Y_i \geq 0$ are products $(1, \ldots, p)$

$X_j \geq 0$ are inputs of non-labour factors $(1, \ldots, k\text{-}1)$

$L \geq 0$ is labour input

Simplifying the analysis to assume a single product function, such that

$$Y = f[L, X_1, \ldots X_{k-1}] \quad (7.1)$$

and assuming that P_y is the unit price of output, P_L is price per unit of labour, and P_j is price per unit of jth input, we can develop the profit function of the firm as follows. Denote profit as Π, where

$$\Pi = TR - TC \quad (8)$$

TR=total revenue, and TC=total cost

$$\Pi = [f(L, X_1, \ldots, X_{k-1})]P_y - \sum_{j=1}^{k-1} P_j X_j - P_L L \quad (8.1)$$

Profit is maximized where the marginal net return from the application of an input is zero. This is obtained by taking the first derivative of equation (8.1) and setting it to zero, and then testing if second-order condition is satisfied.[12] The first order derivatives are:

11 G. C. Winston, "An International Comparison of Income and Hours of Work," *Review of Economics and Statistics*, Vol. 48, February 1966.

12 The second order condition is satisfied when $\frac{\partial \Pi}{\partial L} < 0$, $\frac{\partial \Pi}{\partial X_1} < 0$, . . . and so on.

$$\frac{\partial \pi}{\partial L} = \frac{\partial Y}{\partial L} \cdot P_y - P_L = 0$$

$$\frac{\partial \pi}{\partial X_1} = \frac{\partial Y}{\partial X_1} \cdot P_y - P_{x_1} = 0 \qquad (9)$$

$$\vdots$$

$$\frac{\partial \pi}{\partial X_{k-1}} = \frac{\partial Y}{\partial X_{k-1}} \cdot P_y - P_{x_{k-1}} = 0$$

From equation (9) equilibrium condition is obtained as follows:

$$\frac{\left(\frac{\partial Y}{\partial L} \cdot P_y\right)}{P_L} = \frac{\left(\frac{\partial Y}{\partial X_1} \cdot P_y\right)}{P_{x_1}} = \ldots = \frac{\left(\frac{\partial Y}{\partial X_{k-1}} \cdot P_y\right)}{P_{x_{k-1}}} \qquad (10)$$

For the multi-product firm, equation (10) would be extended to equation (11)

$$\frac{\left(\frac{\partial Y_1}{\partial L} \cdot P_{y_1}\right)}{P_L} = \ldots = \frac{\left(\frac{\partial Y_2}{\partial L} \cdot P_{y_2}\right)}{P_L} = \ldots = \frac{\left(\frac{\partial Y_p}{\partial L} \cdot P_{y_p}\right)}{P_L} \qquad (11)$$

The equilibrium condition can also be shown diagramatically in Figure 5.

In order to simplify presentation a case of a firm producing single product and employing only one input-labour is assumed. Total value product (TVP), marginal value product (MVP), and average value product (AVP) for labour are shown. Equilibrium demand for labour is obtained at the point

$$MVP_{\text{labour}} = MFC_{\text{labour}} \qquad (12)$$

where MFC is marginal factor cost

or

$$P_y . \frac{\partial Y}{\partial L} = P_L \qquad (12.1)$$

as shown in equation (10).

(ii) *Concept of Unemployment and Disguised Underemployment*

According to Pigou,[13] in a perfect labour market involuntary unemployment is not possible if the wage structure is responsive to changes in the demand for labour. It is assumed here that if supply of labour exceeds demand, wage rates will drop sufficiently to create extra employment, until the economy reaches full employment. However, in realistic models of an economy it is very seldom that one reaches a zero level of unemployment, and hence

13. A. C. Pigou, *A Theory of Employment* (London : Macmillan, 1933), p. 252.

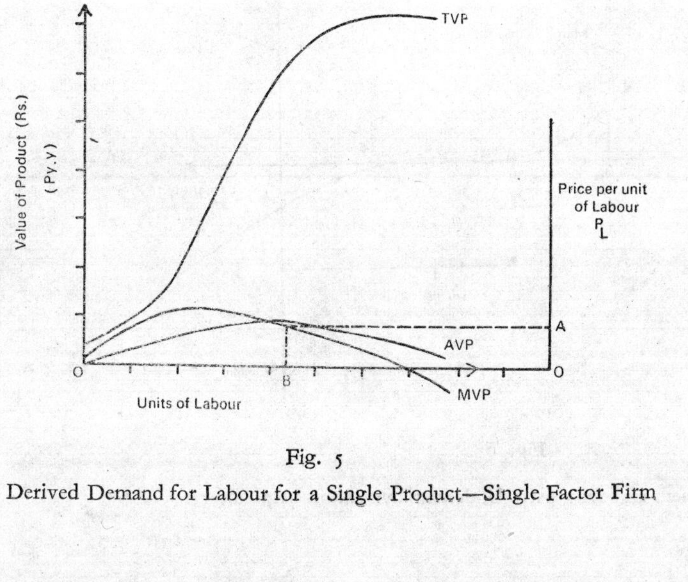

Fig. 5

Derived Demand for Labour for a Single Product—Single Factor Firm

full employment is defined in terms of some minimum level of unemployment. There are at least five types of unemployment which are present. These are:

(i) Cyclical unemployment, caused by contractions in the economic activity.
(ii) Frictional unemployment which is attributed to movement of workers between jobs, industries, and regions.
(iii) Structural unemployment, caused by an imbalance in the structure of the economy and occupational structure of labour force.
(iv) Technological unemployment brought about by changes in the production process.
(v) Seasonal unemployment which can be attributed to both fluctuations in demand and production process within a calendar year.

In addition to various types of unemployment, a developing country suffers from a very serious problem of underemployment and disguised underemployment. Underemployment exists if workers are prepared to offer their services even at wage rates below bare subsistence level. Disguised underemployment prevails in a situation when withdrawal of a certain quantity of labour does not diminish total output of the sector. Diagramatically the situation is depicted in Figure 6. Given a subsistence wage level of OWs the level of labour employment should be OA units. However, if supply of labour is OD and all are being employed then there is AB units of underemployment and BD units of disguised underemployment.

This section has developed a theoretical analysis of labour market, which will be useful in analyzing the agricultural labour problems in India, as presented in the next section.

4. Problems of Agricultural Labour

A comprehensive discussion of all problems facing agricultural labour in India is beyond the scope of this chapter. Instead only a few selected major problems will be described in brevity. These are:

(a) Low labour productivity in agriculture,
(b) Underemployment and surplus manpower,
(c) Landless labour and agricultural mechanization.
(d) Low standard of living.

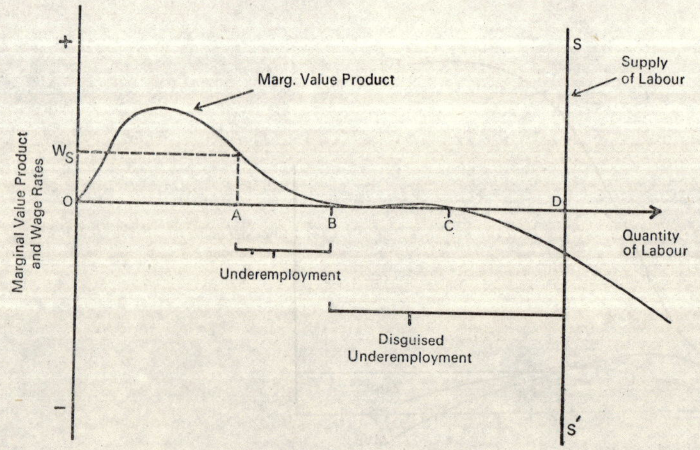

Fig. 6

Underemployment and Disguised Underemployment in Agriculture.

(a) Low Productivity of Agricultural Labour

Productivity of a factor input can be viewed in terms of inter-temporal, inter-region, inter-firm, inter-industry, and international differences. When one analyzes the agricultural labour productivity in India, one faces the insurmountable problem of lack of data and lack of comparability in data. This is not to say that appropriate data does not exist or is not collected. The series of farm management studies sponsored by the Government of India contained a treasure of data useful to research. However, most of this information is published in the form of averages, thereby rendering much of its use in analysis difficult.

(i) *Earnings of Agricultural Workers—An Inter-industrial Comparison*

Data on average wages, number of workers, and duration of employment in various industries are very scanty. Consequently earnings per worker were approximated using gross domestic production, as shown in Table 4. An average worker in agriculture had a gross earning of Rs. 501 per annum, as compared to an amount of Rs. 2952 in construction industry, or Rs. 2320 in manufacturing. Earnings in the non-farm sector are as much as six times the level earned by an average agricultural worker. A great deal of caution must, however, be observed in interpreting these productivity differences. Since the gross earnings is as a result of all factors of production—land, labour, capital, and management—a clearcut comparison of labour earnings cannot be made unless these figures are adjusted for the share of other factors of production.

(ii) *International Comparison of Agricultural Labour Productivity*

Information gathered in the studies carried out by Hayami[14] and by Hayami and Ruttan[15] has been used to illustrate the comparative farm labour productivity in U.S.A. and India. Table 5 summarizes this data. Average farm output per worker (in comparable units of measurement) in India was estimated at 2.2 units, as against 96.2 for U.S.A. In addition, other inputs such as fertilizer, machinery, and land (on a comparable per worker basis) were much lower in India than the levels in U.S.A. These factors, along with education, and

Table 4. Relative Earnings of Workers by Industries, India, 1960-61

Industry	Gross Domestic Production (Crores of Rs.)	Labour Force (in million)	Earnings Per Worker (Rs.)	Index Ag = 100
Agriculture	6570	131.0	501.5	100
Forestry, mining etc.	395	5.2	759.6	152
Manufacturing	1856	8.0	2320.0	463
Construction	620	2.1	2952.3	590
Trade and Communications	1301	7.6	1711.8	342
Trasportation	569	3.0	1896.7	379
Others	2055	21.0	662.9	132
All Industries	133.66	177.9	750.9	143

SOURCE : Estimation by Author

14 Y. Hayami, "Sources of Agricultural Gap among Selected Countries," *American Journal of Agricultural Economics*, Vol. 51, No. 3, 1969.

15 Y. Hayami and V. W. Ruttan, "Agricultural Productivity Differences among Countries," *American Economic Review*, Vol. LX, No. 5, December 1970.

Table 5. Comparative Farm Output and Inputs per Male Worker, India and U. S. A., Average 1957-62

Particulars	Unit	U. S. A.	India
Farm Output	Wheat Units/Worker	96.20	2.22
Fertilizer	Mill. Tons/Worker	2.13	.0038
Machinery	Horse Power/Worker	45.90	.0077
Agricultural Land	Hecter/Worker	129.70	1.99
Literacy Ratio	Per cent	97.0	18.0
No. of Graduates	Per 10,000 Workers	22.8	.4

SOURCE : Compiled from the results reported by Hayami, *op. cit.*

research and development were used to explain the productivity differential (Table 6). A lack of fertilizer and land resources together explained the next 41 per cent differential.

Table 6. Contributions of Various Factors to the Difference between Farm Output per Worker in U. S. A. and India.

Factor	Contribution (Per cent)
Fertilizer	21.0
Machinery	15.0
Land	20.0
Education	38.0
Research, Development and Extension	10.0
Residual	—4.0
Total	100.0

SOURCE : Hayami, op. cit., p. 573.

The evidence presented in these paragraphs tends to support the hypothesis of low productivity of agricultural labour in India. Theoretically, this may be interpreted as an indication of a misallocation of labour resources in the Indian economy.

(iii) *A Regional Analysis of Agricultural Labour Productivity*

Using data collected in the Government of India's Farm Management studies,[16] a regression analysis of the following nature was applied.[17]

$$\frac{O}{A} = f\left[\frac{L}{A}, \frac{NL}{A}, D^L_1, D^L_2, D^L_3, D^L_4, S^D_1, S^D_2, S^D_3\right] \qquad (13)$$

where

O/A gross output per acre
L/A labour cost per acre
NL/A non-labour cost per acre
$D^L_1 - D^L_4$ location binary variable.[18]

(One each for M.P., Madras, Punjab, and U.P. respectively).

$S^D_1 - S^D_3$ size of farm binary variable

(one for each size of farm; < 5 acres, 5–10 acres, and 10–20 acres).

Two variations of equation (13) were estimated. One in linear form using all the variables specified, and the other bringing L/A in non-linear form[19] and deleting NL/A variable. The results obtained are shown in Appendix II.

Mean elasticity of agricultural labour use was estimated at .4906 using a log function implying that a one per cent change in labour cost per acre will increase the gross output by .49 per cent. Labour productivity functions can be de-

[16] Ministry of Food and Agriculture, *Studies in the Economics of Farm Management,* Delhi, 1955–56, for Madhya Pradesh, Madras, Punjab, Uttar Pradesh, and W. Bengal.

[17] A cross-section data for the provinces of Madhya Pradesh, Madras, Punjab, Uttar Pradesh, and West Bengal was used.

veloped for each of the five regions, by appropriate adjustments[20] in equation (A.1), as shown in Table 7. Average gross output per acre was higher in U.P. and Punjab, and was lowest in West Bengal. (Table 7).

Table 7. Regional Labour Productivity Relations

Province	Intercept	Regression L/A	Coefficient for NL/A
M. P.	71.71	.318	.770
Madras	83.78	.318	.770
Punjab	99.86	.318	.770
U. P.	152.61	.318	.770
W. Bengal	62.64	.318	.770

SOURCE : Estimation by Author

From equation (A.2) one can also derive conclusions as to the relative (per acre) labour productivity on farms of various sizes. The regression coefficients with respect to the three size binary variables indicate that average labour productivity per acre is highest on smaller farms (0–5 acres) and consistently decline except a moderate rise for farms over 50 acres. This rise may be interpreted as a result of superior technology applied by these farms relative to smaller size units.

A discussion of regional agricultural labour productivity will be incomplete without introducing the implications of "Green Revolution" (GR) in Indian agriculture. GR is a term which is collectively used for a number of programmes such as:

(i) increase in the area under high-yielding cereal varieties,
(ii) increased use of more nitrogeneous and other fertilizers,
(iii) increase in improved irrigation and drainage facilities,
(iv) better extension efforts to improve the cultural practices.

Success of GR varies from crop to crop, and from state to state. For example, in the case of wheat, in Punjab, change in yield per hectare (in kgs.) in 1968–69 (over 1967–68) was 16.6 per cent, in Bihar 32.6 per cent, in Maharashtra 21.3 per cent, as against an all-India gain of only 5.9 per cent.[21] Recognizing that not all this gain in yields can be attributed to a differential rate of adoption of programme implied in GR, implications of such changes for agricultural labour productivity are significant. An accelerated rate of adoption of GR programme would inevitably mean an improved level of economic performance by the human resources in agriculture of that region. However, a differential rate of adoption in some states would have far-reaching implications. These include: (i) a larger surplus of cereals and increasing inequality in cereal production, thereby causing decline in prices unless a free movement of grain across India is secured; (ii) increased burden on marketing and transportation system and need for improved facilities; (iii) wide interregional disparity in agricultural incomes, thereby resulting in social and political problems.

(b) Underemployment and Surplus Manpower in Indian Agriculture

In this section a review of various estimates of underemployment in Indian agriculture is presented; no attempt is made to make new estimates because of inadequate data. Data limitation is a major problem in India. Similar conclusions were derived by a Committee of experts which inquired

18 A binary variable is one which only takes value 0 and 1, depending upon whether a certain event takes place or not.

19 The non-linear forms were

$(L/A)^2$ and $(L/A)^3$

20 Regional functions are derived as follows: setting $D^L_1 = 1$ and other binary variables to zero, function for M.P. is derived, similarly when D^L_2, D^L_3, D^L_4, are set to one, functions for Madras, Punjab, and U.P. are estimated. When all the binary variables are zero, the function for West Bengal is obtained.

21 Data obtained from Directorate of Economics and Statistics, *Indian Agriculture in Brief,* 10th Edition (New Delhi : Government of India, 1970).

into the estimates of unemployment. To quote:

> ...the data available for estimating unemployment and underemployment in the past have not been adequate and that the conclusions based on them were, therefore, unavoidably subject to an unknown margin of error. Some of the limitations are inherent in the socio-economic conditions of our country and cannot be wholly overcome by the conceptual refinements or improvements in the technique of estimation.[22]

Although this author does not agree with the latter part of the quote, the message that data is scanty and of poor quantity in arriving at better estimates of underemployment is clear.

Three studies dealing with disguised underemployment in agriculture are reviewed. These are by Majumdar,[23] Uppal,[24] and Mathur.[25] Majumdar's study focussed on two facets of underemployment—seasonal and disguised. Disguised underemployment was estimated for Bombay Karnatak region using a standard cultivated holding, which was an arbitrary unit. No adjustments were made for differences in capital, fertility, and irrigation on various farms. Major conclusion of the study was that "roughly about 71 per cent of the farmers are affected by disguised unemployment."[26]

Uppal[27] estimated the disguised underemployment in Punjab agriculture at 8.41 per cent of total labour force, using a standard quantity of labour. This quantity was defined as the minimum number of labour inputs required to produce the existing output with other factors remaining the same.

Mathur[28] estimated disguised underemployment using the following relationship :

$$D(U) = \sum_{i=1}^{n} \frac{(E-d)_i \ (P \times T)_i}{100}$$

where $D(U)$ = disguised underemployment,

$(E-d)_i$ = surplus manpower per acre on size group i,

$\frac{(P \times T)_i}{100}$ = actual cultivated area in size group i.

The estimates of (E-d) were made by using a standard man-land ratio, which was not defined in any meaningful way. Mathur[29] estimated disguised underemployment at 33.1 per cent of rural working force in West Bengal, 4.8 per cent in Punjab and 8.8 per cent in U.P. Although all these estimates vary in magnitude, they do, in general, support the hypothesis of surplus manpower in Indian agriculture—a resource which can effectively be used for non-farm alternatives.

(c) Landless Labour and Agricultural Mechanization

According to the 1961 census, landless labourers were estimated at 315 lakhs an increase of 12.5 per cent over the comparable figure in 1951. This labour constituted 24 per cent of total agricultural labour supply in 1961—a significant part of the industry. One of major problems faced by this sector is that of high seasonal variations, particularly by those whose contractual agreements are not for the entire season. Opportunity in non-farm sector of the economy are meagre for two basic reasons: one, there is in general a lack of employment potential;[30] two, the skills required for the jobs available are beyond

22 Planning Commission, *Fourth Five Year Plan* (New Delhi: Government of India, 1969–74).

23 N. A. Majumdar, *Some Problems of Underemployment* (Bombay: Popular Book Depot, 1961).

24 J. S. Uppal, "Measurement of Disguised Unemployment in Punjab Agriculture," *Canadian Journal of Economics and Political Science*, Vol. XXXIII, November 1967.

25 A. Mathur, "The Anatomy of Disguised Unemployment," *Oxford Economic Papers* (New Series), Vol. 16, No. 2, July 1924.

26 Majumdar, op. cit., p. 208.

27 Uppal, op. cit.

28 Mathur, op. cit.

29 Ibid., p. 186.

30 The backlog of unemployed labour during the 1966–71 period was estimated at 135 lakhs of workers. See, *Fourth Five Year Plan*.

the capability of unskilled farm workers.

Related to the question of hired help is the issue of mechanization of Indian agriculture. It is but obvious that mechanization at a level in some western developed countries, is neither fessible nor desirable. The labour that it would further displace will further accentuate the grave problem of underemployment and unemployment not only in agriculture but in the entire economy. In addition, an average farm unit consisting of tiny fragmented holdings cannot effectively and efficiently utilize machine power, except under the assumption of joint (co-operative) ownership. However, if the concept of mechanization is relaxed only to infer improved implements and machinery as appropriate for Indian agricultural conditions, some merits of such a programme are conceivable. It may even out some of the seasonal fluctuations by reducing labour demand at peak time for agricultural operations; it may reduce the losses in crop production by more timely operations; it may tend to move agriculture from the non-commercial diversified industry to a commercial specialized industry.

(d) Low Standard of Living

As a direct consequence of the low productivity, underemplyoment in agriculture, and lack of opportunities in the non-farm sector, standard of living of many agricultural families is lower relative to that enjoyed elsewhere. In addition, there is a wide degree of regional differences in farm income per person—a variable which determines the level of living a family may maintain. This is a direct result of the productivity per worker, as shown in Figure 7. Inter-regional productivity differentials exist because of differences in resource quality, use, and management, and also because of a lack of mobility of workers due to social, cultural, and diet differences. Differences in the technology for farm production is also a very important determinant of labour productivity differentials.

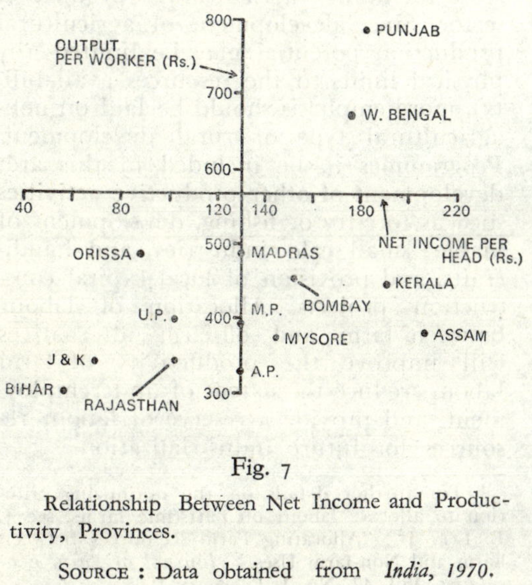

Fig. 7

Relationship Between Net Income and Productivity, Provinces.

SOURCE : Data obtained from *India, 1970*.

All these problems of agricultural labour arise from the same basic problem—problem of farm resource use, and, therefore, a common set of solutions to them may be found.

5. Programme to Improve Agricultural Labour Situation in India

The immediate cause of mounting unemployment in India and many other developing— countries is the inability of the land to provide employment for the growing population. One very important development in India—so called "green revolution" (GR) —raises a series of questions about rural employment which have not been answered, and more research is necessary.

Since the problems of agricultural labour are so diverse among regions, and within a region among farms of various size groups, no one single policy is going to be a panacea. In order that employment policies may be more effective, they should be integrated with general economic development policies. The unsatisfactory rate of employment growth in the development process, together with inadequacies in the present state of planning, point to the need to accord a higher priority to employment creation in development planning and to work out appropriate policies to achieve it.[31]

Planning Commission in the Second Five Year Plan envisaged improving labour conditions through development of agriculture. The same philosophy was extended through the Third Five Year Plan. The Third Plan proposed to improve the conditions of agricultural labour force through improvements in irrigation, soil conservation programmes, and through development of cottage industries. In the draft Fourth Five Year Plan, the Commission acknowledged that the benefits of development had not reached the bulk of hired agricultural workers to any appreciable extent. The plan therefore intended to concentrate on small but potentially viable farms through developing minor irrigation, agricultural credit, and animal husbandry.[32]

The conditions of hired agricultural workers can be improved through an increase in level of employment and conditions of work, and through an improvement in the level of wages. To secure the latter, the Minimum Wages Act of 1948 was passed. The level of wages vary from state to state, and are in general very low. For example, in Punjab, minimum wage level is between Rs. 1.00 to 2.50; in Madras between Rs. 0.75 to 1.25; in West Bengal between Rs. 1.50 to 2.25; and in U.P. between Rs. 1.00 to 1.50.[33] Compared to industrial wages, these wages are extremely low.

Employment level of rural agricultural labour can be improved by a combination of three types of policies:

(a) Polices which tend to increase employment potential of agriculture industry, and that of rural society.
(b) Policies to improve the labour employment in the non-farm sector by choosing a capital extensive industrialization strategy.
(c) Policies to facilitate migration of rural labour.

A discussion of the second type of policy is beyond the scope of this chapter, since it lends more towards the general economic policies.

Policies to increase rural employment potential may be divided further into two broad types: policies for improving labour use in agriculture, and those aimed at rural development. Programmes to improve agricultural labour use may take a variety of strategies, and a comprehensive treatment to all is beyond the scope of this chapter. Suffice it to say that these programmes will include those aimed at technical efficiency of labour resource use, dissemination of better cultural practices, and knowledge for optimum decision making. Training of workers for particular types of operations, and research-cum-development of agricultural problems should constitute a major strategy in such policies.

Rural development can make a very effective strategy for rural employment policies, if proper emphasis is laid on making productive use of underemployed labour and on raising the incomes of poorer segments of the farming community. Rural development is being used in this context to include all sectors of rural life including agricultural production sector. Since development of agricultural production potential may be limited (by physical limits to the resources availability), more emphasis should be laid on non-agricultural type of rural development. Programmes to be included in this are: development of other productive activities such as forestry or fishing, development of viable small-scale industries and handicrafts, and provision of local capital construction projects. Allocation of labour between farm and off-farm alternatives will improve the productivity of farm labour, reduce the extent of underemployment, and provide a reserve of labour resources for future industrialization.[34]

---

31 For further details, see I.L.O., *The World Employment Programme* (Geneva: International Labour Office, 1969).

32 Planning Commission, *Fourth Plan Draft Outline* (New Delhi: Government of India, 1964).

33 C. B. Mamoria, *Agricultural Problems in India*, 6th Edition (Allahabad: Kitab Mahal, 1969), p. 348.

34 For further details on the optimizing criterion to allocate labour on part-time farms, see J. E. Lee, Jr., "Allocating Farm Resources between Farm and Non-farm Uses." *Journal of Farm Economics*, Vol. 47, No. 1, February 1965.

The other type of policy which would improve productivity in agriculture includes those programmes which tend to increase the rate of outmigration of agricultural workers. These programmes include knowledge of work opportunities in various regions, proper job counselling, assistance in moving from one area to another, and so on. Attempts should also be made to reduce the institutional barriers for interregional migration of workers.

BIBLIOGRAPHY

Bachmura, F. T., "Under-employment in Relationship to Macro-Economic Policy," *Indian Journal of Agricultural Economics,* Vol. XIX, No. 3 & 4, July–December 1964.

Galenson, W., (Ed.), *Essays on Employment* (Geneva: International Labour Office, 1971).

I.L.O., *The World Employment Programme* (Geneva: International Labour Office, 1969).

Kao, C. H. C., K. R. Anschel and C. K. Eicher, "Disguised Unemployment in Agriculture: A Survey," edited by C. K. Eicher and L. W. Witt, *Agriculture in Economic Development* (Bombay: Vora & Co., 1970).

Kulshreshtha, S. N., "Measuring the Relative Income of Farm Labour 1941–61," *Canadian Journal of Agricultural Economics,* Vol. 17, No. 1, 1967.

Majumdar, N. A., *Some Problems of Underemployment* (Bombay: Popular Book Depot, 1961).

Mehmet, O., "Disguised Unemployment and Agricultural Development," *Canadian Journal of Agricultural Economics,* Vol. 19, No. 1, July 1971.

Mellor, J. W. and R. D. Stevens, "The Average and Marginal Product of Farm Labour in Undeveloped Economies," *Journal of Farm Economics,* Vol. XXXVIII, No. 3, August 1956.

Ornati, O. A., *Jobs and Workers in India* (The Institute of International Industrial and Labour Relations, Cornell University, 1955).

Peitchinis, S. G., *The Economics of Labour* (Toronto: McGraw-Hill Co. of Canada, 1965).

Rao, R. M. M., "Unemployment and the Demand for Leisure," *Indian Journal of Agricultural Economics,* Vol. XXI, No. 1, January-March 1966.

Uppal, J. S., *Disguised Unemployment in an Underdeveloped Economy* (New York: Asia Publishing House, 1973).

APPENDIX I

Table 1. Age Distribution of Labour in India and Selected Countries

Country	Year	Per cent Distribution in Age Groups 0-14	15-34	35-64	65 +	All
India	1961	7.67	49.32	36.51*	6.50**	100.00
Canada	1961	.27	44.05	52.05	3.70	100.00
U.S.A.	1960	.30	38.73	56.31	4.66	100.00
Japan	1955	.21	52.37	43.18	4.24	100.00

*Belongs to 35-59 age group **Belongs to 60+ age group

SOURCE : Census of India, 1961 Census of Canada U.S. Statistical Abstract 1967.

Table 2. Labour Force Participation Rates in India and Selected Countries

Age Group (Years)	Sex	India (1961)	Canada (1961)	U.S.A. (1960)
		Percentages		
0-14	M	9.45	..	..
	F	6.62	..	..
15-34	M	89.52	82.00	83.50
	F	43.78	35.70	37.30
35-59	M	97.07	90.70*	93.00*
	F	47.62	30.40*	43.80*
60+	M	76.83	28.70**	32.20**
	F	22.38	6.70**	10.50**
All Ages	M	57.70	77.70	79.70
	F	28.02	29.50	36.10

*Belongs to 35-64 age group **Belongs to 65+ age group

SOURCE : See Appendix Table 1

APPENDIX II

The estimated equation for the gross output per acre are[1] :

$$\frac{O}{A} = 62.64 + .318^* \frac{L}{A} + .770^{**} \frac{NL}{A} + 9.07\, D^L_1 + 21.14^* D^L_2 + 37.22\, D^L_3 + 87.97\, D^L_4 + 23.51^* S^D_1 + 17.61^* S^D_2 - 9.67\, S^D_3$$

$R^2 = .930^{**}$ Se = 15.83 dW = 2.17 (A.1)

$$\frac{O}{A} = -48.06 + 8.63^{**} \frac{L}{A} - .120^{**} \left(\frac{L}{A}\right)^2 + .0005^* \left(\frac{L}{A}\right)^3 + 5.93\, D^L_1 + 37.04^* D^L_2 + 16.06\, D^L_3 + 70.08^{**} D^L_4 + 23.82^{**} S^D_1 + 10.38\, S^D_2 - 12.16\, S^D_3$$

$R^2 = .949$ Se = 13.72 dW = 1.84 (A.2)

Both the functions explained over 93 per cent of variations in gross output per acre, and no tendency of auto-correlation was apparent.

* Significant at 5 per cent level.
** Significant at 1 per cent level.

[1] Due to limitation of space, standard error of estimates are not provided.

14

Labour Welfare in India

MANJULIKA KOSHAL

1. Introductory Survey

The word "welfare" is derived from a French phrase "Welfaren," which means to fare well.[1] Labour welfare is an extension of the term 'welfare' to a particular class—labour. This implies that labour welfare originated with the origin of labour as a class as distinct from any other classes. Viewed from this point, it can also be called "a part of social welfare that responds to human needs in society."[2]

In fact, the attitudes towards labour welfare have been changing according to the different stages of economic development. As a result, the issues of labour welfare policy is the result of not only the status labour acquires in the society or the type of work it performs but also of the value system, social institutions, degree of industrialization, nature of the economy and the general level of social development[3] in a country at a particular time. Of all these factors, the "value system" and the "nature of the economy" can be said to be the two most influential factors for bringing about a change in the labour welfare policies of any country. From the transitional stages of economic development (the simple and the feudal economies) to the period of the money economy, one can observe a definite and strong influence of the currently held values on social justice, charity, and humanity in the labour welfare policies. In India today this paternalistic approach seems more intense and paramount than in most European countries. During the mercantilist system, the paternalistic approach was substituted by a strong commercialistic approach, whereby labour welfare was no longer a "charity" but an economic "burden." Even in the form of Poor Relief, welfare was considered by mercantilists as "allowances in aid of wages which could act as a subsidy to the

[1] K. N. Vaid, *Labour Welfare in India* (New Delhi: Shri Ram Centre for Industrial Relations, 1970), Chapter 1, p. 1.

[2] H. N. Crampton and K. K. Keiser, *Social Welfare—Institutions and Process* (New York: Random House, 1970), pp. 5–6.

[3] Ministry of Labour, Employment and Rehabilitation, *Report of the National Commission on Labour* (Delhi: Government of India, The Manager of Publications, 1969), Chapter 10, p. 111.

export market."[4] During the industrial revolution, the commercialistic approach towards labour welfare policies was further intensified. Wages—the only kind of remuneration available—were called by the buyers the "price of labour" and anything beyond it was considered not allowances but added costs to the firms. In India, this trend was obvious in the last forty years of the British regime.

Pre-Independence India

The primary task of the British in India was to maintain law and order. During this period, not much was done to improve the lot of the common man.[5] The labour welfare policy of the administration was concerned mainly with creating statutory right, including those of labour welfare for workers, by creating obligations for employers.[6] In 1931, the Royal Commission on Labour reviewed the labour scene in India and identified a large number of imbalances in the industrial life of the country. Although the Commission made a number of recommendations to provide some of the basic facilities like housing, it was not until the outbreak of the Second World War that the Government of India and the states realized the need for adoption of welfare measures as a means to increase the workers' efficiency and boost their morale.[7] The Coal Mines Labour Welfare Fund Organization under the sponsorship of the Central Government had just begun its work. The states of Bombay, United Provinces, and Bengal had organized welfare centre which provided facilities for workers like indoor recreation and educational activities, ordinary and circulating libraries and dispensaries.[8] The other states as a part of their contribution to the war effort had taken steps to encourage the starting of cost-price (or fair-price) grain shops and co-operative societies in industral establishments.

It was only during the First Five Year Plan in India that a co-ordinated labour policy was adopted in which expenditures on labour welfare were deemed essential and useful, since they met socially desirable ends.[9] Thus, for the first time the concept of added cost was replaced by the notions of inevitable or essential costs.

This concept of labour welfare policy has taken a further turn recently under the name "investment in human capital." According to this theory, since labour welfare activities increase the productive capacity of the country, they are "investments"[10] and not "costs." Some economists, however, object to this treatment of "investment" approach as the *main* justification for expenditures on social or labour welfare. They argue for a "consumption" approach in which welfare expenditure is recommended even on those items that are desirable in *themselves* irrespective of their part in increasing future productivity. This idea does not, however, mean that such expenditure cannot contribute to future productivity.[11] On the other hand, the "investment" approach may overlook this aspect of social desirability.

The difficulty perhaps arises due to regarding consumption as a useless expenditure and investment as a useful one, which, according to the traditional economic notions, is not correct. On the other hand, an over-emphasis on "investment" approach may lead to absurd future policies. So it seems desirable that the labour welfare policy should take the "investment" approach in its proper perspective so that it can be a perfect compromise between the "traditional" approach (of

[4] Richard A. Lester, *Economics of Labour* (New York: The Macmillan Company, 1924), Chapter 3, p. 160.

[5] Planning Commission, *Plans and Prospects of Social Welfare in India, 1951–61,* (New Delhi: Government of India Press, 1963), p. 2.

[6] K. N. Valid, *Labour Welfare in India,* op. cit., p. 27.

[7] Ministry of Labour, Employment and Rehabilitation, *Report of the National Commission on Labour,* op. cit., p. 132.

[8] Ibid., p. 132.

[9] Planning Commission, *The First Five Year Plan—A Summary* (New Delhi: Government of India Press, 1952), p. 116.

[10] A. K. Sen and K. A. Naqvi, "Social Welfare in Relation to Economic Development", working paper, *Report of Seminar on Special Welfare in a Developing Economy,* Planning Commission (Government of India, 22–26 Sept. 1963), p. 32.

[11] Ibid.

the value system) and the "consumption" approach.

In addition, the cost-benefit analysis of welfare expenditures can also help in evaluating an effective labour policy. In a country like India with heavy demands on limited resources, any large number of possible benefits involve a corresponding real cost and so, for an optimal allocation of resources careful analysis of needs and resources or costs and benefits is necessary.

Scope and Growth of Labour Welfare in India

The scope of labour welfare in India was well defined only after Independence. As stated earlier, labour welfare was ignored in British India. Some writers contend that the British policy of "divide and rule" also extended to the field of social welfare.[12] For example, according to Sir Edward Blunt, "Since India presents so great a diversity of physical, economic and sociological features, is it possible to discuss Indian Social Welfare as if India was not manifold but one? Social Welfare is at best a relative term. Its content will differ with the nature of the society and of its environment; but whereas in most countries there will generally be only one society and one environment, in India there are many of both. In other words, is it possible to generalize about 353 millions of people, especially when they are broken up into many heterogeneous units?[13] This suggests that during the British rule government tried to ignore social welfare activities. The Rege Committee (1946) reported that it was only during the Second World War that the British rulers realized the need for labour welfare programmes as a means to increase the worker's efficiency and boost their morale.[14]

The other reasons for neglect of labour welfare during the British regime were (i) the slow growth of factory employment, (ii) scarcity of equipment, and (iii) illiteracy and lack of awareness about welfare measures among the workers.

However, Mahatma Gandhi and many labour leaders, long before the Second World War, had been stressing the importance and need for welfare measures.[15]

The International Labour Organization's (ILO) Recommendation No. 102 and the Directive Principles of State Policy enunciated in the Indian Constitution have precisely defined the scope of welfare. The relevant Directive Principles of State Policy are quoted below:

(i) "The State shall strive to promote the welfare of the people by serving and protecting, as effectively as it may, a social order in which justice, social, economic and political, shall inform all the institutions of national life." (Article 38)

(ii) "The State shall, in particular, direct its policy towards serving—(d) that there is equal pay for equal work for both men and women; (e) that the health and strength of workers, men and women, and the tender age of children are not abused and that citizens are not forced by economic necessity to enter a vocation unsuited to their age or strength." (Article 39)

(iii) "The state shall, within the limits of its economic capacity and development, make effective provision for serving the right to work, to education and to public assistance in cases of unemployment, old age, sickness and disablement, and in other cases of underserved want." (Article 41)

(iv) "The State shall make provision for securing just and humane conditions of work and for maternity relief." (Article 42)

(v) "The State shall endeavour to secure, by suitable legislation or economic organization or in any other way, to all workers, agricultural, industrial or otherwise, work, a living wage, conditions of work ensuring a decent standard of life and social and cultural oportunities and, in particular, the State shall endeavour to promote cottage industries on an indivi-

12 Planning Commission, *Plans and Prospects of Social Welfare in India,* 1951–61, op. cit., p. 2.

13 Quoted in ibid., p. 2.

14 Ministry of Labour, Employment and Rehabilitation, *Report of the National Commission on Labour,* op. cit., p. 132.

15 Rajindar, Koshal and Manjulika Koshal. "Gandhian Economic Philosophy," *American Journal of Economics and Sociology,* April 1973.

dual or co-operative basis in rural areas." (Article 43)

Thus the Directive Principles charge the state to secure for its people more and better food, clothing, shelter, employment, living wages, social security, and public assistance. However, not much emphasis was laid on labour welfare under the First Plan, since it assumed that welfare needs of urban workers were adequately met by the then prevailing state government schemes and of mine workers' statutory arrangements.[16] The plan provided for some welfare measures for plantation labour. It combined health, housing, and education in one group and recommended that when one or the other of these was adequate on any estate, attention should be concentrated on other items which were below standard.[17] The Second Plan made a significant statement, namely: "Though admittedly much remains to be done, especially in matters like covering the distance between the existing wage and 'fair wage' and in industrial housing, progress can only be gradual."[18] It also suggested the constitution of a welfare fund for manganese mining similar to the Coal and Mica Mines Labour Welfare Funds.[19] The Third Plan made no specific reference to welfare, but stressed that for improving work efficiency, welfare within the establishment should be ensured through the implementation of the programmes started under the Second Plan.[20] The Fourth Plan stressed on possible extension of the Employees State Insurance Act (ESI), 1948, so that in future it may turn out to be a national health insurance scheme.[21] However, the present scope of labour welfare in India is quite narrow. As a result, housing, hours of work, wages, employment, education, and social security are considered outside the scope of labour welfare.

The present labour welfare measures in India can be classified as (1) The health, safety, and welfare provisions under the basic Acts: the Factories Act, 1948, the Mines Act, 1952, Plantation Labour Act, 1951 and Dock Workers Scheme, 1961, (2) the labour welfare funds for specific industries, (3) welfare activities of employers, and (4) activities of trade unions. Some acts specifically provide for "welfare" measures while others place them under "health" and "safety" provisions. Appendices I and II give a detailed description of the welfare provisions.

Employers Programmes of Labour Welfare

The credit for pioneering the labour welfare programmes in India goes to the employers; among which are the Ahmedabad Textile Labour Association (TLA), 1917, the Tatas, Sri Ram, Delhi Cloth Mills (1920) and Calico Mills, Ahmedabad (1950).

At present in cotton textiles, the iron and steel industry, sugar, jute, cement, railways, posts, telegraphs, telephones, ports and docks, and the Kolar gold mines, employer-oriented labour welfare programmes are being operated on an extensive scale. The programmes in the railways and in iron and steel are especially effective. In the railways, the labour welfare expenditure both in total amount and on per capita basis rose in one year (1965–66 to 1966–67) from Rs. 137.7 to Rs. 147.8, and in ten years (1955–56 to 1965–66) from Rs. 49.1 to Rs. 137.7.[22] In the iron and steel industry, even in the absence of the ESI Act of 1948 comprehensive medical facilities are available. In the cement industry many factories provide special paid holidays and grants to these workers who underwent vasectomy under the family planning units provided by the govern-

16 Ministry of Labour, Employment and Rehabilitation, *Report of the National Commission on Labour,* op. cit., p. 133.

17 Planning Commission, *First Five Year Plan—A Summary,* op. cit., pp. 121–24.

18 Planning Commission, *Second Five Year Plan—1956,* (Delhi: Government of India, 1956), p. 571.

19 Op. cit., p. 582.

20 Planning Commission, *Third Five Year Plan* (Delhi: Government of India, 1961), pp. 250–63.

21 Planning Commission, *Fourth Five Year Plan, 1969–74* (Delhi: Government of India, 1970), pp. 422–23.

22 Ministry of Railways, Railway Board, *Indian Railways, 1966* (Delhi: Government of India, 1967), p. 72.

ment.[23] In fact, welfare costs are accepted by employers to a point where they become overhead costs. It is estimated that welfare costs, including social security measures, amount to about 24.67 per cent of the wages in most Indian industries.[24] This raises the question of policies involving the concepts of "useful expenditures" vs. "added costs" and the "investment" vs. "consumption" approach as pointed out earlier.

Trade Unions and Labour Welfare

Trade unions in India are not yet mature, self-dependent agencies as they are in the West. Nevertheless, they participate in welfare programmes through co-operating in administration of government-sponsored welfare programmes; participation in welfare planning; demanding various welfare measures through agitations; providing educational programmes through a variety of medias such as study circles, seminars, short term courses, adult education, publications and research.

It may be noted that "in 1969, trade union representatives held more than 180 seats on 150 national or industry level committees."[25] They also participate on committees of industry-wide welfare funds. At present the Indian National Trade Union Congress (INTUC) is sponsoring four colleges and the All India Trade Union Congress (AITUC) supports one college. The Textile Labour Association (TLA) is spending one million rupees a year on its educational programme. The Institute of Labour Studies and the proposed Labour Research Institute are the result of the efforts of the Hind Mazdoor Panchayat and the INTUC, respectively. In addition, managing the co-operative societies either independently or in collaboration with management is an important achievement of trade unions, but, unfortunately, 31 per cent of the establishments allowed to open fair price shops[25] did not open such shops until 1968. However, it is encouraging to know that the coverage was about 95 per cent in the case of the central public sector undertakings.[26] Current information is usually provided by posters or lectures. Important topics are usually family planning, and national savings scheme and housing. Lastly, trade unions also provide recreational facilities in the form of holiday homes and summer camps. The TLA, Baroda City Labour Council, All India Coffee Board Labour Union, and Sakhar Kamgar are some of the examples of Indian trade unions' outstanding welfare activities.[27]

Assessment

According to the reports of the various investigating agencies,[28] the implementation of basic welfare provisions has been rather unsatisfactory in small factories, coal mines, and plantations. The reasons for this may be (1) the ignorance of workers about the significance of safety and hygienic working conditions' contribution to health and efficiency, and (2) a lack of concern among the employers in general. If one compares this state of affairs with that prevailing in some of the advanced countries, one is amazed at the poor standards of labour welfare in India. Many of the basic welfare amenities such as rest shelters, cleanliness, conservancy, sitting facilities, and provisions for drinking water, which are statutorily listed under the laws in India, are taken for granted as a part of daily life in Europe, the U.S.A., the U.S.S.R., Yugoslavia, and Australia.[29] Creches there are usually run by private agencies in eastern Europe and Yugoslavia and canteens by workers. In India the case is just the opposite. Despite statutory provisions and enforcing agencies, the facilities are absent. Cement industry is the only indus-

23 Vaid, op. cit., p. 107.

24 *Report of the study group of the Hind Mazdoor Sabha,* 13th Annual Convention, Madras, March 1965.

25 Vaid, op. cit., p. 131.

25 As recommended by the 20th session of the Indian Labour Conference in August 1962.

26 Planning Commission, *Fourth Five Year Plan (1969–74)* (New Delhi: Government of India

27 Vaid, op. cit., p. 131.

28 The Committee on Labour Welfare (CLW), the National Commission on Labour (NCL), Rege Committee and Labour Investigation Committees of earlier periods.

29 Ministry of Labour, Employment and Rehabilitation, *Report of the National Commission on Labour,* op. cit., p. 118.

try where provisions are adequately enforced.

About 85 per cent of factories provide latrines and urinals in the cement industry as compared to 94 per cent in glass, the same percentage in tanning and leather, and 92.1 per cent in coal mines; but only in the cement industry 100 per cent factories providing conservancy arrangements have sewer or septic tanks and running water near latrines.[30] The figures for other industries providing these two arrangements are very low. Arrangements for conservancy do not mean anything if, along with that, septic tanks and water taps and latrines are not provided. Similarly, all the cement establishments provide washing facilities, such as wash basins with taps on standpipes. No other industry except printing and tanning (where the percentage of establishments providing such facilities is 89 and 86 respectively), comes close to even 70 per cent. Bathrooms, in addition to washing facilities, are provided in 48 per cent of the cement establishments, but in the case of coal mines, only 49 per cent provide bathing facilities.[31] In fact, bathing facilities ought to be the best in coal mines in view of the nature of work and also because of the specific legislation: "The Pit Head Bath Rules, 1959."

As for creches, all the establishments in the cement industry are providing them, although the proportion of women in that industry is the lowest in Indian industries. All the tea plantations employ women, as do 82 per cent of the coal mines, 53.6 per cent of the cotton textile factories, 50 per cent of the glass factories and only 39 per cent of the cement establishments.[32] The position of coal mines regarding creches is the worst because, while 82 per cent are under statutory obligation to provide them, only 56 per cent are complying with this rule.

With regard to canteens, cement industry again comes out with a one hundred per cent implementation rate, while no other industry exceeds 80 per cent; the tea plantations' rate is the lowest at 15.8 per cent.

Suggestions

A survey of the existing situation indicates the immediate necessity for overhauling and tightening the machinery of inspection. The first step requires the appointment of welfare inspectors for different industries. Secondly, a distinction is needed between the duties of mine or factory inspectors and those of welfare inspectors. Also, a distinction is needed between the jobs of the present welfare *officers* (as required for factories and coal mines) and those of the welfare *inspectors*. The welfare officers are management's employees with limited powers, whereas the welfare inspectors will be government employees with powers of enforcement. Also, welfare officers do not inspect the implementation of provisions, but instead facilitate such provisions, control labour strikes and fulfill the letter of the law. Thirdly, welfare inspectors should be required to submit annual and quarterly reports and be empowered to fine in case of default; they should be well informed of current researches and assist the government in collecting useful and appropriate information for future empirical researches. The fear of prosecution, it is hoped, will make the employers vigilant, which in turn will make welfare officers alert.

In case of canteens, three suggestions seem essential. First, there should be a legal requirement for providing one compulsory meal for every worker to be arranged by the government, keeping in view the nutritional aspect and the regional food habits. Secondly, the management of canteens should be either solely in the hands of management or workers' co-operatives, but in no case with contractors. This decision should be arrived at in consultation with the workers. In cement industry, where canteens are successful, 83 per cent of canteens are run by management, and in 80 per cent of these canteens articles are sold at subsidized rates.[33] Thirdly, for port and dock workers

30 Ministry of Labour, Employment and Rehabilitation, *Report of the National Commission on Labour,* op. cit., Table 10.1, p. 121.

31 Ibid., pp. 122–23.

32 Ibid., Table 10.3, p. 125.

33 Ministry of Labour, Employment and Rehabilitation, *Report of the National Commission on Labour,* op. cit., Table 10.4, p. 128.

provisions should be made for mobile canteens, for night shifts and for those performing duties in mid-streams. The Port Trusts Employees Welfare Fund should apply to all casual and contract workers, since a substantial percentage of the labour force constitutes casual workers in ports and docks. For maintaining a creche, the present criteria of employing 50 women or more should be replaced with "any number of working mothers who have a sum total of ten children or more." Various employers in the *Bidi* industry who employ more than 100 women but have no creche should make the necessary arrangements. Also, the welfare inspectors should be given a detailed list of activities to be inspected by them. For example, only providing a creche is not enough in itself, but all accessories such as staff, general cleanliness, cribs, boiled milk, soap, towels, etc. are essential. In India, adequate maintenance of these accessories is lacking in general.[34]

Regarding Labour Welfare Funds, the suggestion for unification of a General Mines Labour Welfare Fund, as recommended by the Committee on Labour Welfare,[35] seems essential. Similar funds for seasonal industries and for coffee, rubber, quarries, tea, and cement should be set up. This would ensure continuous facilities and remove the impression of "excessive cost" phenomena in larger industries by matching a part of the cost by corresponding increases in labour productivity.

Finally, "workers in India can enhance welfare facilities by proper participation provided the bargaining relationships of the trade unions in general are not tense and unstructured and their status recognized."[36] Several developed countries have succeeded by leaving "welfare" entirely to the bargaining capacity of the workers, but for this, one requires a strong, well-informed, and united organization. In India, in the long run, a conscious and organized labour force might help in the proper implementation of welfare measures, but presently there is need for strict measures of implementation by the government.

It is heartening to note that under the Fourth Five Year Plan the government has started taking interest in the improvement of administration of the health, safety, and welfare legislations relating to industrial workers.[37] A provision of Rs. 39.90 crores[38] has been made in the Fourth Five Year Plan for labour welfare programmes.[39] Also the craftsmen training scheme, which until 1968–69 was a centrally sponsored scheme, has been transferred to states, although overall co-ordination and application of uniform standards will still be the task of the Directorate General.[40]

2. Social Security

Social security is the "security that society furnishes through appropriate organizations against certain risks to which its members are exposed."[41] Up to 1880, social security existed in its crude forms under such names as small savings, employer's liability[42] and private insurance[43] but all these methods had their limitations. According to the International Labour Organization, it was only towards the end of the 19th century that the true meanings of social security were recognized through four approaches: (1) social insurance which evolved from a private insurance system, (2) the social assistance which was the result of the Poor Law, (3)

---

34 Ibid., p. 114.

35 Ibid., p. 139.

36 Vaid, op. cit., p. 158.

37 Planning Commission, *Fourth Five Year Plan*, op. cit., p. 425.

38 Ibid. (out of this Rs. 10.0 crores is in the Central Plan, Rs. 27.02 crores in State Plans and Rs. 2.88 crores in Union Territory Plans).

39 Planning Commission, *Fourth Five Year Plan*, op. cit., p. 57.

40 Ibid., p. 424.

41 International Labour Organization, *Approach to Social Security: An International Survey* (Geneva, 1942), p. 83.

42 For details, cf. Koshal Manjulika, "Workmen's Compensation Act 1923 as applied to the Indian Coalmining Industry" (Nov. 1962), Ph.D. dissertation (typewritten manuscript), Patna University, Chapter 1, pp. 19–21.

43 International Labour Office, *Introduction to Social Security* (Geneva: Kundig; 1970), p. 9.

public services which evolved from private insurance and the Poor Law,[44] and (4) the provident fund, which evolved from an individual savings system but is essentially a method of compulsory savings based on regular bipartite contributions. The basic similarities between social insurance and social assistance are that both (1) aim at meeting a minimum standard of need, (2) include persons of meagre resources against risks, (3) grant pensions and benefits as a matter of right, and (4) provide a quasijudicial process.[45] The differences are summarized in Table 1. The term "social security" was first introduced in 1935 in the United States,[46] followed by New Zealand in 1938[47] and later publicized by the ILO in 1941.

Scope

Social security usually covers seven contingencies, but provides nine types of benefits. According to the Social Security (minimum standards). Convention of 1952, these benefits are grouped for organizational purposes in the following categories: (1) Family Allowances, (2) Medical, Sickness, and Maternity Benefits, (3) Invalidity, Old Age, and Survivors' Pensions, (4) Employment Injury Benefits, and (5) Unemployment Benefits.

Table 1. Distinctions in Social Insurance, Social Assistance, and Commerical Insurance,

Part A

Social Insurance	Social Assistance
1. A co-operative device.	1. Purely governmental affair.
2. Payment of contribution as a condition for benefit which becomes returns.	2. Devoid of any conditions and so benefits are favours.
3. Benefits granted as rights.	3. Proof of eligibility needed for granting benefits.
4. Do not depend solely on budget appropriations, thus scientific and stable.	4. Does depend solely on budget appropriations.
5. Tripartite contributions.	5. No contributions.
6. Benefits are compulsory.	6. Not compulsory.

Part B

Social Insurance	Commercial Insurance
1. Relationship between the ratio of contributions and benefits is not exact and actual.	1. The relationship is exact.
2. Minimum standard of living is an objective.	2. No such objective.
3. Compulsory.	3. Voluntary.
4. Designed to meet a chain of contingencies of varied nature and intensity.	4. Insurance against an individual risk.

SOURCE: (1) Hallen, op. cit., chapter 1.
(2) International Labour Organization, *Introduction to Social Security*, op. cit., pp. 10-13.

The Pattern of Social Security in Foreign Countries

From the international experience, there is a variety of combinations concerning the application of various methods in covering social risks. Social insurance is the most common form of social security, as it covers primarily the industrial workers. Germany was the first to introduce this and later Austria, the U.K., the U.S.S.R., Japan, Latin America, the U.S.A., and Canada adopted

44 Ibid.

45 G. S. Hallen, *Understanding Social Security in India, England, U.S.A. and U.S.S.R.* (Meerut: Rastogi & Co., 1959), p. 24.

46 With the enactment of the U.S. Social Security Act, 1935.

47 Their National Health Plan is extensive, involving free and complete medical and dental care for every citizen.

it. In Asia, Africa and the Caribbean region, this system became popular after the end of the Second World War, and synchronized with the achievement of Independence. Social assistance is basically meant for needy citizens and public services exist for the entire population. Denmark was the first to adopt social assistance and the method of public services was adopted by many countries after the Second World War.

New Zealand and England have a national plan covering all *risks,* while Bulgaria, Czechoslovakia, Hungary, and the U.S.S.R. have a national risk and ill-health plan. The United States has a combination of social insurance programmes in case of old age, unemployment, and social assistance in the shape of federal subsidies to non-contributory pension schemes in different states. Provident fund systems exist in Sri Lanka, Ghana, Kenya, Malaysia, Nigeria, Singapore, Tanzania, Uganda and Zambia. Iraq converted its provident fund to a social insurance system in 1964.[48]

The Pattern in India

India has a combination of social insurance and provident fund systems covering primarily the industrial workers, and some central government employees. The social insurance system provides medical, sickness, maternity, disablement and dependants' benefits and the provident fund system covers old age or death.[49] Unemployment and family pension schemes are being considered for adoption. It covers only workers of organized sectors and 94 per cent of the work force in the tertiary service; unorganized and rural sectors are not covered. Judging from international perspective, the Indian social security system seems rather backward, as is evident from the figures on expenditure on social security as a percentage of the GNP in various countries given in Table 2.

Although the Fourth Plan has emphasized the need for broader coverage, India cannot easily adopt a national plan or have broader coverage of social assistance like the advanced countries. India can at best gradually enlarge her social security system, depending upon her pace of economic development.

Table 2. Expenditure on Social Security, 1966

Country	Expenditure on Social Security as percentage of GNP	Income of Schemes as percentage of GNP
Sri Lanka	3.4	4.5
Chile	9.6	11.1
Ghana	1.3	2.7
India	1.8	2.6
Japan	5.8	7.6
Mexico	2.3	2.7
UAR	1.6	2.8
USSR	10.2	10.2

SOURCE: S. Venu, "Economics of Social Security", *Eastern Economist,* Sept. 10, 1971, p. 478

The Economics of Social Security

Social security is often recommended as an efficient and compulsory means of generating savings. In India this can be seen on the basis of the provident fund contributions as a percentage of national income; it increased from 1.0 per cent to 1.6 per cent during the period 1961–67. Other studies of similar nature have furnished the same conclusion.[50] Also it is argued that the programmes of compulsory contributions induce lower income groups to save.

Social security is also favoured as an incentive for greater work effort due to (1)

48 International Labour Organization, *Introduction to Social Security,* op. cit., p. 15.
49 The provident fund schemes.

50 *Reserve Bank of India Bulletin 1965,* pp. 341–43; *Economic Bulletin for Asia and the Far East,* Vol. XIII, Dec. 1962.

the positive correlation between social security and the per capita income, and (2) the income effect of compulsory deductions encouraging more work. But Professor Venu agrees with the first argument under two conditions: (1) if the gain in marginal income is substantial, and (2) the contribution is a flat rate.[51] He refutes the second argument by indicating the role of many variables in the growth process in addition to social security.

Social security savings have also proved helpful in providing funds to finance India's five year plans. In the First Plan, the social security savings amounted to Rs. 92 crores, in the Second Rs. 265 crores, in the Third Rs. 253 crores, during 1966–69 to Rs. 300 crores and in the Fourth Plan to Rs. 660 crores.[52]

Also Titmuss's hypothesis that social security *redistributes* income seems to have some validity for India. Since in India the real wage differentials between the lower ranks of supervisory staff and the industrial worker has been narrowed down, a vertical equity can be said to have been achieved.

Social security systems are also supported by economists on the grounds of elasticity, flexibility, and stability. The argument for elasticity is based on the plea that with wider coverage at the same rates, the yield is flexible in terms of buoyancy and of built-in nature. So, with increasing income, greater amounts of social security deductions are achieved. In India the percentage of increase in social security yield collections from a percentage increase in income, for some major industries has risen from $6\frac{1}{4}$ to 8 per cent.[53] Also with a greater number of large enterprises, the collection becomes easier.

The stability argument rests on the theory that "on the revenue side, the savings constitute an anti-cyclical factor, thus lending stability to the programmes and creating vested rights for contributors."[54]

Social Security in India

The Social Security measures in India may be listed as follows: (1) The Workmen's Compensation Act (referred to as W. C. Act) 1923, (2) The Employees' State Insurance Act (E. S. I. Act) 1948, (3) The Mines Maternity Benefit Act, 1942, and The Central Mines Maternity Benefit Act, 1961. (4) (a) The Employee's Provident Funds Act 1952, (b) The Coal Mines Provident Fund & Bonus Schemes Act, 1946, (c) The Seamen's Provident Fund Act, 1966, (d) various Old Age Assistance Schemes at state levels, (e) The Gratuity provisions, (5) Provisions of "Lay Off" and "Retrenchment" under the Industrial Disputes Act, 1947, (6) Family Pension Scheme, 1971, and (7) Consideration of the Unemployment Insurance Scheme.

The Problem of Unemployment Injury

In India, social insurance made its beginings through the coverage of work-injuries through the Workmen's Compensation Act (1932).[55] At present, there is another legislation[56] which covers work-injuries but its enactment was made primarily on health grounds. The Workmen's Compensation Act of 1923 was enacted to make compensation an automatic, non-obligatory, unconditional, and absolute right of the worker through insurance.[57] On comparing both of these Acts now, it seems that the W.C. Act of 1923 has many loopholes. The Act was amended many times for minor adjustments.

The E.S.I. Act, 1948, covers about 38 lakh employees (1970–71) and the number of beneficiaries per insured person increased from 3.3 in 1963–64 to 3.9 in 1970–71.[58] The W.C. Act of 1923 also covers about 38 lakh workers (1969–70).[59]

An Assessment

Due to the various loopholes in the W.C. Act of 1923, it has been sug-

51 S. Venu, op. cit., p. 475.
52 Ibid., p. 478.
53 Ibid., p. 478.
54 Ibid., p. 478.

55 There were two Acts (the Fatal Accident Act, 1855, and Employers' Liability Act) prior to this but both suffered from many loopholes.
56 The Employees' State Insurance Act, 1948.
57 For details, cf. Koshal. op. cit., pp. 58–61.
58 Department of Labour and Employment, *Indian Labour Statistics* (Delhi: Government of India, 1972).
59 Ibid., p. 158.

gested to replace it either with the E.S.I. Act of 1948 or comprehensive social security legislation; but on a deeper analysis it becomes clear that both the Acts suffer from some common defects such as limited coverage[60] and the inadequacy of the wage-loss compensation in all kinds of disablements. In fact, it is only in the lowest wage groups that maximum compensation is declared under the W.C. Act of 1923, yet it is equal to only 8 years and 4 months' earnings in case of death and 11 years and 8 months' earnings in permanent total disablements.[61] Only in the two lowest groups is there full wage-loss compensation, but the wages seem grossly inadequate.[62] The wage-loss problem under the E.S.I. Act of 1948 will be discussed later; but it seems important to point out that criteria of worker's age, family size, working life expectancy of the Indian worker at each age, and the age of all children are important for full wage-loss compensation in both the fatal and permanent disablements, but are presently lacking in both Acts. The magnitude of the problem can be seen from the figures of the high burden of dependency in India, which is 57 per cent of the total population.[63] For permanent partial cases, foreign experience from other countries such as Germany, France, Mexico, and Japan can be helpful. In India, the Permanent Partial Disablement Schedule needs to be more detailed and should include the factors of age and occupation.

Under the E.S.I. Act of 1948, as the rate of benefits for disablement, dependants, and sickness is half of the "average assumed daily wages," it cannot compensate for the full wage losses. If the standard of full wage losses is difficult to attain, at least the international standard as fixed by the I.L.O. of two-thirds of the wages should be attained. Also, the principle behind the fixation of such "average assumed wages" is not justifiable. A worker earning 3 rupees daily will benefit from such fixation, as his average assumed daily wages will be Rs. 3 As. 3, but those earning above Rs. 3 As. 3 and up to Rs. 3 As. 15 will be at a loss because in their case also, the average assumed daily wages will be Rs. 3 As. 3 and the rate of benefit will be 50 per cent. of Rs. 3 As. 3. In addition, the E.S.I. Act of 1948 also suffers from the inadequacy of the Schedule relating to permanent partial injuries as stated earlier.

The problem of wage-loss compensation appears serious when the existing wage groups under both the Acts are compared to the current Indian economic trends. It is true that the rates were revised under both the Acts in 1962 and 1966, but since 1966 conditions have also changed. With the higher cost of living and rising prices, the real value of the rupee has decreased to a great extent. The working class consumer price index rose from 184 in 1966 to 215 in 1968.[64] Furthermore, the per capita annual money earnings of manufacturing workers earning less than Rs. 200 per month even in 1964 in India were Rs. 1,522, which amounts to about Rs. 126.5 per month.[65] These statistics suggest that all categories covering earnings below Rs. 3 need to be neglected and the exemption limit be raised to Rs. 4. Usually wages are fixed on the factors of standard diet, the family needs, its average size, and the budget of an average family, but in India, since all of these criteria are not taken into account, the need for a full wage-loss compensation seems all the more necessary.

In addition to these common defects the W. C. Act of 1923 suffers from some further disadvantages—(1) in the same wage group, the amount of compensation varies greatly with different wages,[66] (2) with a slight increase in wages in marginal cases, the percentage of compensation

60 The W. C. Act restricts undertakings and excludes casual workers; the E. S. I. Act excludes firms with less than 20 persons and without power.

61 See Schedule IV of W. C. Act, 1923.

62 These are from Rupees 0—10 and more than Rupees 10—13 in schedule IV of the Act.

63 V. G. Kulkarni, *Statistical Outline of Indian Economy* (Vora & Co., 1968), Table 11.9, p. 21.

64 Report of the National Commission on Labour, op. cit., p. 22.

65 Ministry of Labour and Employment, *Indian Labour Statistics, 1968,* Labour Bureau Department of Labour and Employment (Delhi: The Manager of Publications, 1968), Table 4.1, p. 60.

66 A worker earning Rs. 41 will be compensated at the rate of 63.17 per cent of his wages and one earning Rs. 45, at the rate of 57.7 per cent.

varies greatly,[67] (3) the lumpsum gets frittered away and does not last even for the expected years of earnings,[68] and (4) the administrative machinery needs overhauling. Under the E.S.I., on the other hand, with some additional merits such as provisions for medical services, lenient benefit provisions for dependant school children, different rates of dependants' benefits,[69] no time limit for benefits, and payments in instalments, the wage-loss compensation at the rate of even 50 per cent does not seem inadequate.

On the basis of a review of the two Acts, there seem to be four possibilities: (1) modify the W.C. Act of 1923, (2) merge the W.C. Act with the E.S.I. Act of 1948, (3) substitute E.S.I. for W.C., and (4) evolve a comprehensive scheme of social security. The last measure is generally favoured.[70] While there is no support for retaining the W.C. Act even with certain modifications, it seems that this is one of the ways of achieving the least cost for the firms by imposing the full value of society's losses on the firms. It is also an efficient method of accident prevention. Conceptually, it appears to be a tax, but even so, it is a tax for conservation of human lives which can be favoured on the grounds similar "to a tax on effluents being discharged into a river or pollutants being thrown into the air."[71] No doubt, from the viewpoint of administrative costs and distributional aspects, the alternative to workmen's compensation is social security through the E.S.I. or some comprehensive legislation, but considered from the economics of accident prevention and its cost aspects, W.C. seems more suitable.[72] The specialists in the field also generally favour workmen's compensation especially for work-connected accidents.[73]

Maternity Benefit. Before the enactment of the E.S.I. Act, 1948, maternity benefit provisions in India were state-enacted and state-administered. After the enactment of the E.S.I., a separate Act for mines was passed in 1941 as the former did not cover mines. In 1961, a centrally-administered maternity benefit system was instituted covering all factories, mines, and plantations, but this was not a substitution for the other Acts. As a result, maternity benefits are provided today by three sources, but no two Acts can regulate the same industry.

The E.S.I. Act of 1948, the Maternity Benefit Act of 1961, and a few states provide free medical services during pre- and post-natal periods. In addition, the Act of 1961 has provisions for a medical bonus in the absence of medical services, nursing breaks, prohibition of hazardous and strenuous work before delivery, and no work during six weeks after delivery, some definite improvements over other Acts. The qualifying periods vary from 5 to 9 months of attendance under the state Acts, to 5 months 10 days of attendance under the 1961 Act, and of 2/3 of the number of weeks available for employment with a minimum of 12 contributions under the E.S.I. Act, 1948. The benefit period is usually from 8–12 weeks under all the Acts. It seems that the E.S.I. is most liberal with regard to the qualifying period, and the amount of benefit is better under the Maternity Benefit Act of 1961.[74]

For better results, it may be suggested that the Central Act of 1961 should bring under its administration and coverage all industries, including the establishments regulated by the E.S.I. Act of 1948. This will reduce administrative costs and confusion. Bringing mines and plantations

[67] A worker earning Rs. 80 per month is compensated at the rate of 50 per cent of his wages and one earning Rs. 81, at 64.16 per cent.

[68] As explained on p. 342.

[69] This takes into account the size of the family and its needs.

[70] These are the Study Group on Social Security in 1958, India, the E. S. I. (Employees' State Insurance) Review Committee, February, 1966 and the National Commission on Labour 1970.

[71] Monroe Berkowitz, "Allocation Effects of Workmen's Compensation," *Industrial Relations Research Association Series,* Proceedings of 24th Annual Winter Meeting, 1971, pp. 348–49.

[72] Substituting the W. C. Laws by social security or merging them with Occupational Safety and Health Legislation, Berkowitz, op. cit., p. 346.

[73] Cf. Berkowitz, op. cit., p. 343; R. H. Coase, J. M. Buchanan and W. C. Stubblebine.

[74] Under the Act of 1961, the rate is either the average daily wages or Re. 1, whichever is higher.

within the fold of the Central Act was hailed as an important step. Also a provision to discontinue benefits after the third child was consistent with the central government's effort to curtail production. This proposal was considered in February 1966, by the Tripartite Standing Labour Committee.

Old Age

Old age protection is generally provided through provident funds, pension payments, gratuity, assistance schemes, or a comprehensive social security scheme. Provident funds are generally based on tripartite contribution. In West Germany, Italy, the U.K., and Japan it is based on tripartite contributions. In France exceptional grants are made by the government, in eastern Europe only employers contribute, while in the U.S.A. the government is generally not the contributor.

In India a provident fund is the most common form of old age protection; it has usually been a bipartite contribution of employers and workers, and has been instituted for civil servants, industrial workers, and workers of commercial houses. The central government has started contributing, since February 1971, only to the recently developed Family Pension Scheme.[75] The Provident Fund schemes cover coal,[76] plantations[77] and seamen[78] separately, and a central scheme[79] covering workers up to Rs. 1,000 monthly earnings. The rate of contribution for employer and worker each varies from $6\frac{1}{4}$ to 8 per cent and is administered by a Tripartite Board of Trustees. The investments are made generally in interest-bearing government securities. Pension schemes cover departments of defense, railways, post and telegraphs, and a number of commercial houses. Gratuity schemes are voluntary in character and are either due to a contract between the management and the union or a decision of industrial tribunal. Assistance schemes are at state levels, and only in December of 1963 was a central scheme with a Relief and Assistance Fund started. Appendix 3 gives details of the old age assistance and gratuity schemes in India.

There is a controversy about converting provident fund schemes into pension schemes. There are advantages and disadvantages in both the systems and a proper solution in this case can be found only after careful analysis.

The disadvantages of provident fund schemes can be summarized as follows: (1) benefits not matching with contributions, (2) undue advantages for the provision on "non-refundable advances,"[80] (3) delays in investment of provident fund money leading to a drop in the quantum of interest, (4) difficulty in recovery of provident fund arrears, (5) the maldistribution of powers between the state and the central government, and (6) non-coverage of firms with less than 20 persons. The pension schemes are objected to on the grounds of (1) the small intermittent nature of payments which may not be helpful when lump sums are needed; this being more true for a country devoid of any public assistance scheme of subsidized housing, family assistance, facilities for raising loans or for buying property on hire-purchase basis, and (2) a provident fund is a compulsory saving, which with the high cost of living and low wages seems impossible. On the basis of the above analysis, it seems that, for India, a scheme of old age, invalidity, and survivorship pension combined with a provident fund can prove to be an ideal system. For the agricultural workers of India, the joint family system has been serving as a measure of social security, but with industrialization and urbanization and the resultant disintegration of the joint family, the vacuum created by this family system can be filled only by a comprehensive social security system. The provident fund can be modified with respect to an integrated scheme by reshuffling administrative machinery,

---

[75] Dependants of workers dying before retirement are eligible for pensions.

[76] The Coal Mines Provident Fund Act, 1948.

[77] The Assam Tea Plantation Provident Fund Act, 1955.

[78] The Seaman's Provident Fund Act, 1966.

[79] The Employees' Provident Fund Act, 1952.

[80] Such advances are for share in consumer cooperative societies, house constructions and life insurance financing.

imposing strict penalties for provident fund arrears and making default in payment a cognizable offence.[81] As it is, the provident funds have shown a considerable progress. It covers 18 lakhs workers with an investment of Rs. 76 crores in 1969. Receipts rose from Rs. 54.80 crores in 1965–66 to Rs. 74.71 crores in 1970–71[82] and the share of reserves in government securities[83] tripled from 1957 to 1967.

Unemployment—the present provisions and attempts

There are no specific schemes for protecting the unemployed in India except the provisions for "Lay Off" and Retrenchment"[84] under the Industrial Disputes Act, 1947. Lay off compensation is at the rate of fifty per cent of wages and dearness allowances for a maximum of 45 days with a qualifying period of 190 days of attendance in a year for underground miners only and 240 days for other industrial workers. Retrenchment is at the rate of 15 days average pay for a year's service or any part exceeding six months. Furthermore, one month's notice for terminating a worker's employment is required by employers to workers with one year's service. Other provisions such as the National Employment Service or the Dock Workers (Employment of Regulation) Act, 1948 are limited in scope. Even "lay off" provisions do not apply to seasonal workers and firms employing less than 50 persons. In January 1965, an Unemployment Insurance Act[85] was passed by the Parliament, but it has not been enforced because the main criticism was about its contributory nature, which might not have been popular in the presence of retrenchment compensation and without any contributions. On August 19, 1968, the Planning Commission set up a committee of experts on unemployment under Professor M. N. Dantwala to evaluate the methodology used in the previous plans and to advise on alternative methods of analysis that may be adopted in the Fourth Plan. The Committee submitted its reports in 1970, and in January, 1972, the Planning Commission circulated a questionnaire based on the important issues of the Dantwala report to various research organizations for suggestions. A majority of the comments were submitted by April, 1972, and it seems that the government is seriously considering the whole question of unemployment compensation in the light of changed conditions in economy.

3. Housing

Housing is generally regarded as a part of social welfare; like health and education, it is an indirect transfer expenditure and results in subsidized facilities. In India, before Independence, the conditions of housing in general and of housing for industrial labour in particular were appalling, as reported by several reports.[86] It is shocking to know that important factors like ventilation, sanitation, lighting, drainage, and latrines were not even considered, and on the average 8.8. sq. ft. of space was available per worker.[87] After Independence, for the first time in 1947, a "Housing Policy" was framed which had three basic issues: (1) improvement of workers' and low income groups' housing, (2) a subsidy at the rate of 50 per cent to state governments and 25 per cent to employers and workers' co-operative housing societies, and (3) 10 per cent of family earnings to be charged as rent from workers. Under the First and Second Five Year Plans an emphasis was placed on housing by modifying the old schemes and introducing new ones. Under

81 Under the Indian Penal Code.

82 Cf. Venu, op. cit., p. 476.

83 Up to 1967, all reserves had to be held in government securities but after 1967 some flexibility is allowed.

84 Cf. Government of India, *The Industrial Disputes Act, 1947*.

85 For full details, cf. M. Koshal and B. N. Shukla, "Practicability of an Unemployment Insurance Scheme in India, *Searchlight* (May 5, 1966, Vol. LXVI, No. 104), p. 4, Cols. 2–4, Patna.

86 Industrial Commission 1919, the Royal Commission 1929, Labour Investigation Committee 1946 and Rege Committee, 1944–46.

87 "Chawls" in Bombay, "Bustees" in Calcutta, "Ahatas" in Kanpur and "Dhowrahs" in mines are the terminologies for workers' residence for particular regions in India and all relate the same story.

the Third Plan, nine schemes on housing were introduced. Of these, *two* related to industrial workers–(1) The Subsidized Industrial Housing Scheme[88], and (2) The Subsidized Housing Scheme for Plantation Workers.[89] In addition, there are specific housing schemes for coal mines, non-coal mines, and port and dock workers. There are six kinds of schemes for coal mines. The rates of subsidies under all these schemes are listed in Table 3.

cent in the Second and 71 per cent in the Third Plan. For plantations, in 1967, against the target of 1923 houses, only 1350 were constructed. In total, under the three Five Year Plans, 40 per cent of the targets were not fulfilled. Latest estimates show that there is a need for 129 lakh houses in India. The shortage of housing units was 28 lakhs in 1951, 93 lakhs in 1961 and 119 lakhs in the beginning of the Fourth Plan (1969–70).

Table 3

Name of Scheme	Rate (Based on approved cost of construction) *Loan*	*Subsidy*
I. Subsidized Industrial Housing Scheme	Loans recoverable in 30 instalments from (a) and (b) below and in 15-25 instalments from (c)	
(a) State Govts., Housing Boards, Municipal Bodies	50 per cent	50 per cent
(b) Registered Cooperative Societies of Industrial Workers	65 per cent	25 per cent
(c) Industrial Employers	50 per cent	25 per cent
	Loan	*Subsidy*
II. *Subsidized Housing Scheme* For Plantation Workers' Cooperative Societies	65 per cent	25 per cent
III. *Subsidy-cum Loan Scheme*		
1. For Coal Mines	37½ per cent	25 per cent
2. New Housing Scheme	Entire costs are borne by the "Housing Fund" of Coal Mines Labour Welfare Fund Act, 1947	
3. Low Cost Housing Scheme for Coal Mines	Half of the collections of the Fund is spent on housing	
IV. *Subsidy Scheme for ports and Docks* Housing Board	35 per cent	25 per cent

SOURCE : National Commission on Labour, pp. 147-52.

For non-coal mines, housing is regulated by the Subsidized Industrial Housing Scheme, 1952, but employers do not use the facilities. This scheme achieved a target of 57 per cent in the First Plan, 97 per

Some of the important reasons for workers' housing shortages are low priority on housing by state governments, diversion of funds, non-utilization of allocations made for housing, a scarcity of developed urban land, the high cost of building materials and insurance, the inability of workers to pay subsidized rent and a lack of interest on the part of employers. Employers complain in terms of excessive municipal taxes, low ceiling costs, and

88 Was introduced in 1952 but revised in April 1966, and is now known as the "Subsidized Industrial Housing Scheme for Industrial Workers and Weaker Sections of the Community."

89 This scheme was revised in April 1967.

soaring land prices. Reasons for employers' lack of interest have been discussed by the International Labour Organization in its publication "Recommendation No. 115 and Poor Returns on Housing Investment." These observations will be useful to India. In foreign countries, employers either contribute to national low cost housing, offer loans at low interest rates or participate in the state subsidized housing programmes, but do not take *leading* roles in its development. Recommendation 115 deals with workers' housing and merely *expects recognition* by employers of the importance of the problem but does not make them liable to provide housing.

We can offer the following recommendations in this connection: to provide fiscal and monetary incentives to employers aiming at a fair return on housing investment; extension of state co-operative housing societies for low and middle income groups by providing land with minimum formalities and loans at concessional rates to these societies; mass production;[90] standardization and introduction of new techniques in building and materials through research;[91] emphasis on the use of already available land rather on new acquisition; priority to underutilized lands in built-up sections; and pursuance of state-planned land development schemes. Finally, it is strongly felt that under the Fourth Plan housing should be given a priority, because due to the existence of surplus labour, specially in the agricultural sector, and excess capacity in building material, "the multiplier effect of large housing programmes would strengthen economic recovery and improve workers' efficiency."[92]

We may conclude with an encouraging note that the Planning Commission has recently set up a Steering Committee under Dr. B. S. Minhas to formulate a national policy on housing and development. In the future, funds for housing will be earmarked in the National Plan and there will be state budgets for housing schemes. Also, the Housing Ministry has recently initiated a proposal for "social control" of urban land by (1) converting it into lease land, no part remaining as freehold, and (2) providing free house-sites for rural landless labour with a 100 per cent central grant to states amounting to Rs. 300 crores, to be completed by August 15, 1973.[93] These are all encouraging trends in the field of housing for workers.

4. Role of Labour Welfare in Economic Development

Labour welfare contributes to economic development by moulding workers into a productive, efficient, and committed labour force which in the literature is referred to as "the effective human growth agent."[94] The history of labour welfare indicates that in the economies passing through the initial phases of industrialization, the lack of growth of a committed labour force was a serious obstacle to economic development. Consequently, labour welfare and social security measures were adopted as a policy in economic development.[95] These measures boosted employment, reduced absenteeism, increased productivity (per worker), enhanced efficiency and skill, and led to a permanent and stable work force particularly in industries involving higher risks, such as the coal mines. In fact, only increased productivity with efficiency can lead to savings, which, if properly utilized, can facilitate capital accumulation and economic growth of the economy.

Social security and labour welfare measures enhance productivity in several ways —timely medical assistance and continued medical services. Timely assistance reduces

[90] Research efforts by National Building Materials at the centre and mass production efforts by Central Housing Finance Corporation are reported by the Fourth Five Year Plan, op. cit., p. 402.

[91] Ibid.

[92] *Report of National Commission of Labour*, op. cit., p. 156.

[93] "Social Control of Urban Land," *Economic and Political Weekly* (Bombay: July 15, 1972, Vol. VII, No. 29), p. 1349.

[94] J. L. Dholakaia, *Industrial Labour and Economic Development in India* (Ahmedabad: Ananda Book Depot, 1965), p. 1.

[95] Germany, New Zealand and countries of western Europe are glaring examples.

the seriousness of an injury, the total sickness period and hence the cost of sickness.[96] Continued medical services prevent future sickness costs and contribute to efficiency by maintaining a high level of body resistance.

In addition, social security expenses constitute maintenance costs on fixed capital. Contributory social insurance also works as an automatic stabilizer which helps in the process of stable economic development. Since the contributions are progressively related to workers' earnings, during boom periods they help to reduce the disposable income of the workers, but during a slump, it helps in maintaining effective demand due to a greater flow of earnings to the workers in the form of unemployment benefits. Thus, labour welfare and social security measures are not only monetary incentives but are also measures for human development, which, according to Professor J. K. Galbraith, "is an external economy whose benefits accrue to all firms."[97]

[96] These costs are of two kinds: (1) the cost of workmen's compensation or disablement benefits from employers, and (2) the cost of losing one's average earnings from the point of the worker.

[97] J. K. Galbraith, *The Affluent Society* (London: Hamish Hamilton, 1958), p. 214.

BIBLIOGRAPHY

Bose, S.N., *Indian Labour Code* (Revised Third Edition) (Calcutta: Eastern Law House, 1957).

Burns, Eveline M., *Social Security and Public Policy* (New York: MaGraw Hill, 1956).

Committee on extension of employees Provident fund scheme (Delhi: Manager of Publications, 1964).

Committee on Labour Welfare Report (New Delhi: 1969).

Planning Commission, *Fourth Five Year Plan, 1969–74* (Government of India, July 1970).

Hallen, G.C., *Dynamics of Social Security* (Merrut: Rastogi Publications, 1967).

Kinsley G., Thomas and Kristof, Frank S., *A housing programme for Metropolitan Calcutta,* Ford Foundation Advisory Planning Group (Calcutta, March 1971).

Lalwani, K.C., *Economics of Industrial Labour,* (Calcutta: The World Press, 1969).

Mamoria, C.B. and Doshi, C.L., *Labour Problems and Social Welfare in India* (Allahabad: Kitab Mahal, 1966).

Malenbaum, Wilfred, *Modern India's Economy* (Columbus, Ohio, U.S.A.: Charles E. Merrill Publishing Co., 1971; Geneva: I.L.O., Introduction to Social Security, 1970).

Mehrotra, S.N., *Labour Problems in India* (Delhi: S. Chand & Co.).

Ministry of Labour, Employment and Rehabilitation, *Report of the National Commission on Labour* (New Delhi, 1969).

Mitra, Asoke. "Housing of the Urban Poor," *Economic and Political Weekly* (Bombay: Special Number, July 1971).

Nevitt, A.A., *The Economic Problems of Housing* (New York: St. Martin's Press, 1967).

Rai Choudhri, S., *Social Insurance in India and Britain* (Calcutta: The World Press, 1966).

Richardson, Albert H., *Economics and Financial Aspects of Social Security: An International Survey* (London: George Allen & Unwin, 1960).

Sri Ram Centre for Industrial Relations, New Delhi, *Financing and Administering of Labour Welfare*: a paper submitted to the Committee on Labour Welfare, Government of India, October 1968, New Delhi.

Srivastava, G.P. (ed), *Glance at Indian Economy* (New Delhi: Peoples' Publishing House, 1967).

United States Department of Health, Education and Welfare, Social Security Administration. Office of Research ond Statistics: *Social Security Programs throughout the World,* 1967, (Washington, D.C.: U. S. Printing Office, 1968).

Idem: *The role of Social Security in Economic Development,* Research Report No. 27 (Washington D.C.: United States Government Printing Office, 1968).

Vaid, K.N., *Labour Welfare in India* (New Delhi: Sri Ram Centre for Industrial Relation, 1970).

15

Unemployment in India

S. KANNAPPAN AND

J. S. UPPAL

1. Introduction

Unemployment constitutes a serious economic, social and political problem facing India. In its economic aspect, the existence of large numbers of unemployed means waste of human resources and the resultant deprivation of the society from the goods and services the unemployed could produce. Socially, the unemployed become alienated to the social order from the frustration and anger against the economic system. If unemployment persists longer, the disillusioned unemployed could constitute a danger to the political stability of the society as they are prone to be attracted to the subversive elements in the society. The recent Naxalite movement in India and political unrest in Sri Lanka are still fresh in our memory as examples of political consequences of serious unemployment.

In any discussion about unemployment in a huge and populous nation like India it must be noted that sheer numbers are not only overwhelming but also misleading. Factory employment, enrollment in educational institutions, and the unemployed as well as the poor constitute large numbers. But for some perspective, absolute numbers must be set against each other. The unemployment rate does precisely that for the phenomenon we are concerned with. It is obtained by comparing the numbers unemployed with the numbers in the labour force and expressing the result in percentages. Even a large number unemployed, if only a small fraction of the entire labour force, may constitute an "acceptable" rate of unemployment, although, if concentrated in specific areas or industries, it may give cause for anxiety on a selective basis. A major aspect of the intelligent study of unemployment, therefore, is an empirical assessment of its magnitude. This should at least give us some benchmark figures for judging the severity of this problem compared with the many others confronting the Indian economy.

We shall discuss later the considerations which are relevant for determining whether or not observed rates of unemploy-

* *The sections on theoretical aspects represent primarily the contribution of S. Kannapan. The empirical part has been written by J. S. Uppal.*

ment are within acceptable or tolerable limits. We cannot even initiate an intelligent discussion of this without a theoretical understanding of labour market concepts and how supply and demand are brought in alignment. Such conceptual and theoretical clarity is also the foundation for any attempt to measure the numbers unemployed or in the labour force for such measures, to be useful, must proceed on theoretically valid or at least conventionally accepted usages.

This paper will consist of three parts: first, a theoretical discussion of the economist's approach to the study of un-employment; second, we will discuss some of the problems in applying these concepts to the less developed countries, and in particular to India; and third, we will discuss some empirical estimates of unemployment in India and steps taken to solve the problem.

One may become impatient about the need for theory, much of which has inevitably been developed in the economically advanced Western economies. Students of economics hardly need a defence of theory, for theory consists of hypotheses which have been successful in explaining observed phenomena. The mere fact that some of these hypotheses have been developed in a non-Indian setting merely heightens the need for a careful examination of the phenomena they explain, with a concomitant emphasis devoted to explaining phenomena uniquely Indian. As we gain maturity in economic analysis, we will recognize that there are few problems entirely novel or unique to a given environment; conversely, that hypotheses resulting from competent professional work have a universal relevance wherever the phenomena are comparable. Some Indian problems like chronic "underemployment" in the rural areas have their counterparts in the depressed areas in the United States; some "Western" problems like industrial layoffs have their counterparts in India's urban economy; and both have their "poverty" threshold, and somewhat perverse behaviour of those below the poverty line." The rich countries are also richer in the knowledge they have gained of their own economies, and we must build on this heritage for a better understanding of the unemployment problem in India.

2. Labour Markets, Labour Force and Unemployment

The labour market is the medium through which buyers and sellers of labour services conclude their transactions. The labour market is not necessarily tied to a physical location, although inevitably service must be performed at a specific place. The labour market's span is as broad as the range over which job-seekers and employers or, as in the case of the early days of factory development in India, recruiters wish to search. These widely dispersed and generally uncoordinated efforts are governed by three circumstances: freedom to make labour market decisions, information concerning available choices, and a promise of economic gains commensurate to the costs involved. In the case of the employer, it is the relationship of the value of the service provided by the employee relative to what it would cost to hire the services (including wage and non-wage costs); for the employee it is the remuneration in relationship to the costs of providing the service (including the other things he could be doing either at home or elsewhere in employment, the costs of training, travel, etc.). None of these three circumstances, labour market freedom, information, and search for economic gains exists in its pure or absolute form without some restrictions or competing considerations, but taken together they are essential for labour markets to function. And we focus on prevailing wage rates and wage differentials as the market signal to which employers and workers respond and as an indicator of the efficiency of the labour market.

It should be emphasized that labour markets differ from other markets in key respects. Unlike most commodity or physical markets, governments regulate the labour markets with a view to protecting the well-being of the human being who sells his services. Also market transactions are limited to the sale or purchase of the services provided by human beings, but not of the human beings themselves. It is as if one may rent the services of a typewriter or an automobile, but is not permitted to own either. Under such circumstances, an individual is unlikely to affect improvements in the typewriter or automobile or transport them unless he were guaranteed or could in fact appropriate the returns from his efforts. Since the human presents a comparable risk, an employer would not normally find it as attractive to incur expenditures on his employees (for instance, for training or migration) as to invest in his plant or equipment. However, a human being can invest in himself with the assurance that the resultant improvement in the market worth of his services will accrue to him alone. Whether it is the employer or employee, some of the fruits of their expenditures will be realized only in later years. Added to this, one must consider the fact that many individuals lack the resources to finance their own training or mobility from one place to another, except as they are helped by parents, relatives, or philanthropic and public agencies. The importance of the time dimension, and the sluggishness of response to differential economic opportunity must be kept in mind as we later consider some of the issues pertinent to the problem of unemployment.

As implied above, labour market transactions are concluded by the interaction of employers, who buy labour services, and workers, who sell labour services, for an agreed-upon wage or remuneration. Economists portray this in terms of a downward sloping demand schedule, relating employer demand for labour at different wage rates, and an upward sloping supply schedule, relating worker supply of labour at different wage rates. Employer and worker decisions are in alignment when demand and supply schedules intersect.

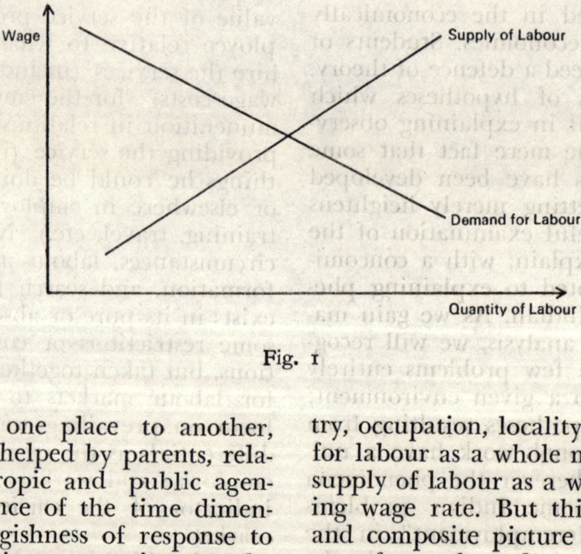

Fig. 1

As long as supply and demand curves are shaped as above, there is no scope for unemployment, for they must intersect at some point, even if only at a negative wage rate. However, unemployment does exist, and it is conceded even by economists who basically subscribe to the behaviour implied by the above demand and supply schedules.

Even where supply and demand are in equilibrium, and there is no unemployment at the prevailing wage rate, a number of adjustments are always taking place in the labour markets. Thus in an industry, occupation, locality or nation, demand for labour as a whole may be equal to the supply of labour as a whole at the prevailing wage rate. But this is an aggregative and composite picture and would not be true for each and every component and constituent unit or subdivision. Thus equilibrium in the larger entity, for instance, full employment equilibrium for the economy as a whole, is perfectly consistent with an individual industry or employer or employee being out of equilibrium, either trying to contract or expand their work force, or moving from one job to another. This type of unemployment is referred to as frictional unemployment. This is a necessary feature of a living, dynamic economy as long as information about alternatives and ability to affect job changes are qualified by their costs or other restrictions so that these adjustments are not instantaneous. Also, the structural characteristics of a nation's educational system and labour markets may dictate some "waiting" between graduation and employment or in effecting job transfers or other changes in one's employment status. It need not necessarily be a sign of ill-health if individuals find it to their advantage to wait, even if it be at the cost of current unemployment. This would be particularly true if some of the costs of unemployment, in the form of foregone earnings, are "absorbed" by the society at large or friends or relatives.

In the same way that disequilibrium may exist for a constituent unit while the economy as a whole is at full employment equilibrium, the economy as a whole may be in imbalance although the fundamental, basic conditions indicate that the economy is providing jobs at about the same rate as people are looking for them. The economy's performance at any one time, indicating conditions of less than full employment may be viewed as a subset of a larger series of observations, again part of a whole. The parts then consist of short-run deviations from the basic or secular feature of the economy. A major reason for the short-run deviations in the advanced western industrial economies (where much of the theorizing for this was initially developed) is the rigidity of the money wage up to the level of full employment (the labour supply curve is horizontal because the organized labour does not allow the wages to fall below OW or the labour supply is zero below OW wages) and a sharply increasing money wage after that point. Graphically, this suggests that whenever aggregate demand for labour falls short of the full employment level, money wage rates do not move downwards (or at least only very sluggishly) and, conversely, efforts to step up labour demand in the entire economy can be accomplished with negligible money wage increases up to the level of full employment. The unemployment total Le–La number of workers, and the rate of unemployment becomes

$$\frac{Le-La}{OLa+(Le-La)} \cdot 100 = \frac{Le-La}{OLe} \cdot 100$$

where OLe is the labour force consisting of OLa employed+ (Le–La) unemployed. The principal reason for the wage rigidity is that in highly unionized and bureaucratic-corporate economies wage and service conditions are not easily altered in the short run.

A third category of unemployment is chronic or secular unemployment, due to deep seated structural characteristics, and

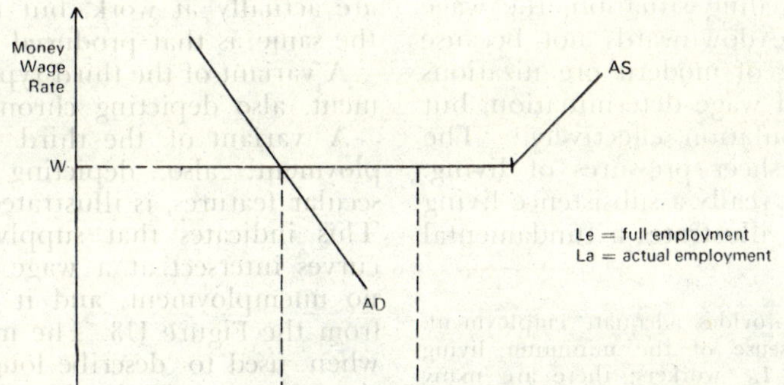

Fig. 2

not self-liquidating, except at the cost of unimaginable and intolerable suffering and misery. This is the situation most often identified with the less developed countries, although in depressed areas or regions of the industrially advanced economies the situation may be similar. Graphically, it may be illustrated as above.

imbalance between the increase in population (and the resultant increase in labour supply) and the economy's ability (technological, managerial, and institutional) to result is unemployed human resources. However, social ingenuity may encourage work and income sharing arrangements such that a larger number, say L_2,

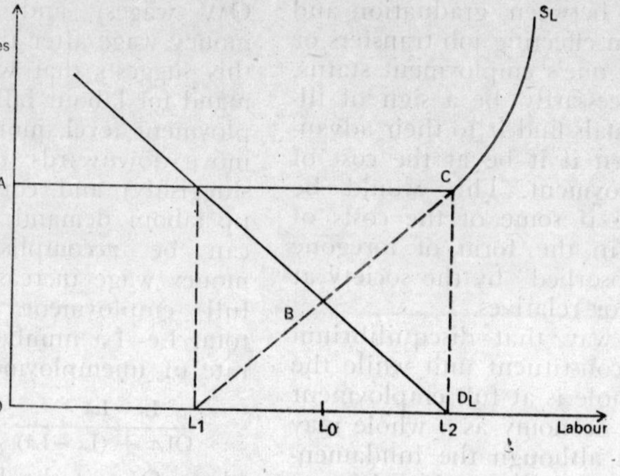

Fig. U.3.

Unlike the preceding situation, the wage rate is inflexible downwards not because of the influence of modern organizations in the process of wage determination, but utilize this population effectively.[1] The because of the sheer pressures of living. The wage rate is really a subsistence living standard, and it illustrates a fundamental

are actually at work, but their output is the same as that produced by L_1 workers.

A variant of the third type of unemployment, also depicting chronic and secular

A variant of the third type of unemployment, also depicting chronic and secular features, is illustrated by Fig. U3B. This indicates that supply and demand curves intersect at a wage where there is no unemployment, and it is no different from the Figure U3. The main difference, when used to describe long term conditions in an underdeveloped economy as a whole, is that equilibrium is established at a real wage too low for human comfort. For convenience, we may refer to this as Unemployment Three B, or U3B. The difference between U3B and U3 should be of greater concern to us as they both purport to represent conditions in less developed countries. In both cases equilibrium is established at a very low real wage, but the main difference is that at the going real wage a large number of additional workers are available and "seeking" work in U3, but not in U3 B. In both cases, output may be increased by shifting demand to

---

[1] The economy provides adequate employment, adequate in the sense of the minimum living standard, only for L_1 workers; there are many more, up to L_2 who would be willing to work at that minimum standard. What actually happens is that the larger number shares the work and income of the smaller number or workers, L_1. However, note that if income or work sharing did not exist, that is, if wage rates were allowed to fall below the subsistence standard, a larger number would be employed at a lower real wage rate, and the total may or may not increase depending upon the elasticity of the demand curve for labour. If we assume an elasticity greater than one, not an implausible one, and flexible wages below the conventional minimum, equilibrium would be established at a wage below OA, L_0 would be employed fully, and total product would be greater than before under full employment of L workers, or a larger number sharing the work to produce the same output.

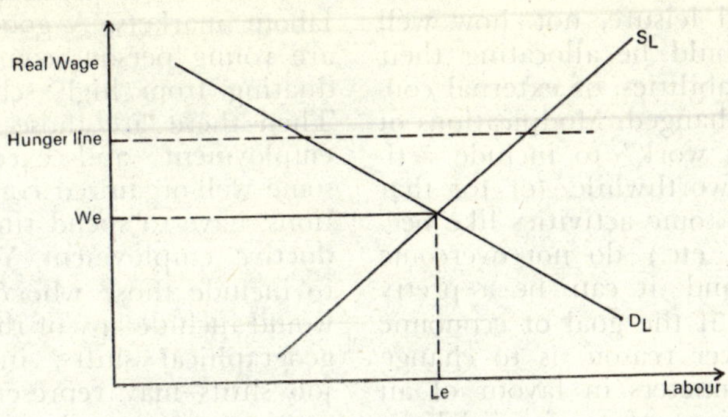

Fig. U3 .B

the right, but in the second case, this would also signify pressures on the real wage. The difference is really an empirical one, the former emphasizing widespread income and work sharing at subsistence levels and the latter emphasizing the low attractiveness of work, and even physical limitations in stepping up the supply of effort, when prevailing earnings are a miserable pittance. At a sufficiently low wage, and when conditions are allowed to prolong, it can be seen that U3 will approach U3B as human tolerance and generosity are strained to their maximum.

3. Problems in Applying these Concepts to less Developed Countries

Many of these concepts and indeed the analytical foundation for the study of unemployment were developed initially in the industrially advanced, Western capitalist economies, and modifications were introduced to include the problems of India and other underdeveloped countries as the focus of attention broadened later. Their greatest limitation is that they do not deal adequately with a situation in which concern arises, not from a short-run condition of unemployment, nor from sectional imbalances in specific industries, regions or occupations, but from a secular condition, affecting the entire nation, of underutilization of human resources associated inextricably with the low productivity of those economically active. This is after all our major problem in India.

First, much of the above analysis centres around supply decisions in labour markets, with the emphasis on goods and services being produced for sale. Economists recognize that prevailing national income accounting methods, which focus on output for the exchange sector, omit a good deal of output produced outside of their sector, even though this leads to human welfare. The effect of this limitation is even more serious when it comes to an assessment of the distribution of time in the nation's households. The time spent outside of the labour market may be misleadingly and conventionally labelled as "leisure" or "involuntary idleness" (that is, unemployment) when it may be nothing of the sort but simply the most effective way in which a household distributes the time of *all* members of a family to produce market and household goods for consumption.[2]

Second, optimality or efficiency in this way of looking at things directs attention to how households individually and in the

[2] Advanced students should read Gary S. Becker, "A Theory of the Allocation of Time." *Economic Journal*, September 1965, Vol. 75, pp. 493–517, where households are treated as producers as well as consumers, their product a function of an optimal combination of goods and the time available at their disposal. For a simpler exposition, see Belton M. Fleisher, *Labor Economics*, Prentice-Hall, 1970, pp. 51–54. Note that "efficiency" refers to optimum allocations at given tastes and "state of the arts" and not what the allocations would be if technology, etc. were to change.

nation as a whole allocate time between market work and leisure, not how well they should or could be allocating their time if attitudes, abilities, or external conditions could be changed. Modifications of the term "market work" to include activities considered worthwhile (or for that matter to exclude some activities like begging, prostitution, etc.) do not overcome this limitation and it can be a pretty serious limitation if the goal of economic policy, for whatever reason, is to change any of these parameters in favour of an increased utilization of a given labour force and greater effectiveness in producing goods and services of market value. A behaviouristic (largely voluntary) measure of labour participation, of what is, may be substituted by a normative measure of what *ought to be*. Much of the discussion about underemployment, particularly applicable to countries like India, is really concerned with a crucial and normative exercise of this sort. In terms of our graphs, this is illustrated by U-3B, except that the theoretical, as well as empirical or measurement, problems become greatly complicated when dealing with long-term changes in a country as a whole.

Additional theoretical problems may be noted at this stage. First, little attention has been given to how well labour markets actually function in urban or rural areas, with the consequence that we have only a poor understanding of the magnitude of frictional unemployment. Frictional unemployment, we know, is consistent with a basic equality between demand and supply in labour markets either in the country as a whole or for industrial, occupational, or geographic sub-categories. And this is dependent upon the changes taking place in the economy on both demand and supply sides, the former due primarily to changes in technology or market demand for products (and in India this could include variations in availability of essential inputs like power or imported material and goods) and the latter due to a number of changes which are always taking place on the supply side. There are always new entrants into the labour force, within rural areas, within urban areas, and some of these represent migrants from primarily rural to urban labour markets. A good number of these are young persons coming of age or graduating from high schools and colleges. Then there are those who seek seasonal employment, and except in the case of some well-organized contract labour situations, have to spend time looking for productive employment. You will also have to include those who change jobs, which would include any of the above-mentioned geographical shifts; in some cases, these job shifts may represent a break in the continuity of employment but not necessarily a change in employers. In all of these cases, the new employment would have to be an improvement over the existing situation, particularly so where individuals migrate or shift from one job to another. Of course, there will also be a number of unrealized expectations, in which case an individual will return to his former status (a rural migrant returning to his village) or scale down his expectations (a high school or college graduate who decides to accept a lower-paying job than the government or business employment he hoped for or his family and friends were protecting as his proper due).

In a country like the United States, this type of frictional unemployment is assumed to require something like 4 per cent of the labour force being idle at any given time and the figure is less for many of the smaller, more integrated European nations. As long as there are changes in supply demand conditions, some frictional unemployment would be inevitable, although one would want this to be as brief as possible. Starting from a position of initial equilibrium, this requirement can be expressed graphically as below: We are talking of four situations, each representing a change from an initial equilibrium: two of these represent demand, and two supply, shifts; and in each case there is an increase as well as a decrease to consider. Each shift causes a disequilibrium so that the demand for, and supply of, labour services at the prevailing wage rate are not equal. However, so long as these are random occurrences, overall equilibrium will be preserved as indicated in

Fig. 1 and the subsequent discussion. (However, our statistics will show a 4 per cent unemployment rate as we measure only two situations, one caused by a leftward shift in demand, D to D_1, and the other by a rightward shift in supply, from S to S_2 and have no accurate measure of job vacancies). The unemployment resulting

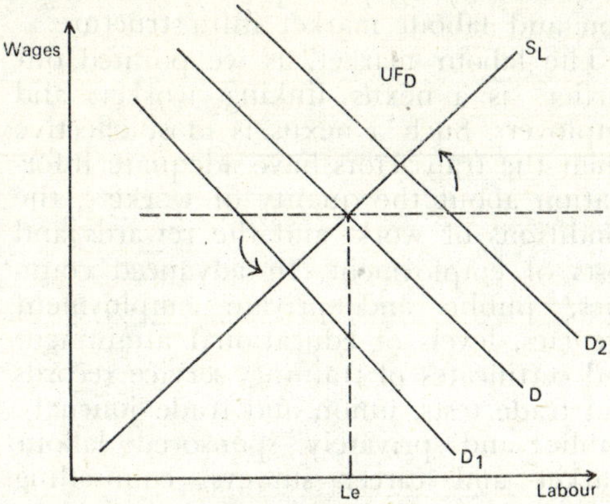

Fig. 4.A

from these shifts will continue until employers and workers adjust to the greater availability of workers, or the reduced availability of work: these adjustments would not in general be instantaneous as the information relating to such change, the resultant revision of expectations and anticipations, and the flexible adaptation of the institutional and contractual arrangements in force will not come about overnight, and may even be delayed indefinitely. This is what the economist has in mind when he talks of positive information and transfer costs. The magnitude of unemployment can be thus seen as a function of two (not necessarily independent) forces: the frequency of shifts leading to an increase in supply or decrease in demand, and the sluggishness in revising prevailing information, expectations, and arrangements. Complete sluggishness would mean rigid money wages and a maximum of unemployment, only slowly resolved by a downward shift D curve on the right. This can be called a function of the "reaction speed" of employers and workers and the supply and demand elasticities involved.

Now what is the situation in India? We have no reliable estimates to parade out, not even informed guesses, for most of the attention given to the unemployment problem has concentrated on the secular mismatch between demand and supply

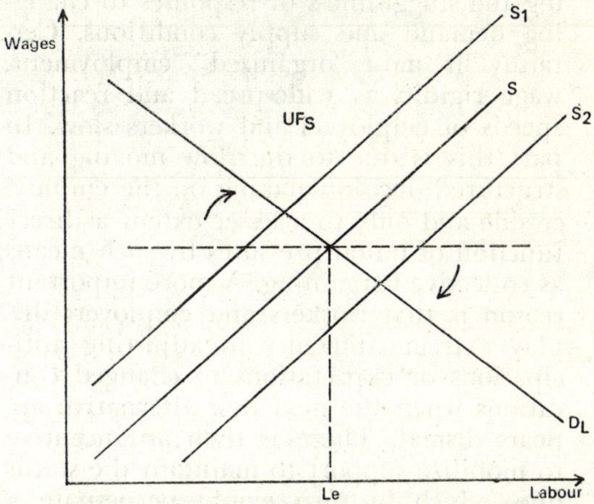

Fig. 4.B

(U3 or U3B), but has ignored the equally important secular condition represented by frictional unemployment. Although our facts are few, we can advance a few pointers.

Contrary to widespread stereotypes, there are continual changes in supply and demand in individual firms or labour markets; there is some evidence that this may be slowed down in the "organized" urban labour markets because of penalties associated with reducing work offered (lay-off benefits) or with leaving a job (a wide range of seniority benefits). On the other hand many markets are "unorganized" and tenure in employment not a particular constraint, as witness the disputes surrounding contract and construction labour or the relatively unsuccessful attempts to organize domestic labour. The Indian transport system also encourages mobility towards the towns and cities, if not with the same frequency as in the United States, certainly with greater frequency than in socialist countries like mainland China. Changes in import policy, of raw materials for finished products and other inputs like power, and climatic variations are also relevant. On the whole, it is difficult to be conclusive about the importance—the frequency as well as magnitude—of these changes in demand and supply conditions in the labour market.

However, the weight of our information is more clearcut when it comes to assessing the sluggishness of responses to changing demand and supply conditions. Certainly in most "organized" employment, wage rigidity is widespread and reaction speeds of employers and workers slow. In part this is due to the slow moving and structured decision-making on the employer side and only to a lesser extent a direct function of union pressures by such means as collective bargaining. A more important reason is that workers and employers display extreme difficulty in adjusting anticipations or expectations to changed conditions when the next best alternative appears dismal. There is then an incentive to mobilize support to maintain the status quo, which in turn would perpetuate a vicious cycle where the alternative to the prevailing position tends to be worse than where such change is taken in stride. Instances of resistance to change, which have this reinforcing effect, are a declining demand for the products of a firm or industry, or changes in demand for labour following reorganization (the so-called "rationalization" issue in textiles, coal mining, etc.), or the termination of construction work on a new project. Workers may react by pressures on the employers to maintain their employment and wages which would in turn dampen the willingness of employers to increase employment or wages when changes in demand favour such a course. This type of apprehension works the other way, too. For various institutional and other considerations, employers, particularly in some public enterprises and ordinance factories, prevent workers from leaving their service or even transferring within public employment. The overall framework is also one of a rigid wage structure. Sluggish employer response to the tightening of labour market conditions naturally dampen workers' ability to accept the lessons of market conditions and encourages them to prefer other means such as political pressure. Most of these comments apply with particular force to "organized" employment, where public regulation is the rule and bureaucratized decision-making prevails. However, this will be true even if these conditions are not present due to the fact that market responses are generally slow in less developed countries. This is best illustrated by the poor quality of information and labour market infra-structure.

The labour market, as we pointed out earlier, is a nexus linking workers and employers. Such a nexus is most effective when the transactors have adequate information about the quality of workers, the conditions of work, and the rewards and costs of employment. In advanced countries, public and private employment agencies, levels of educational attainment and certificates of training, service records and trade tests, union and trade journals, public and privately sponsored labour market and career surveys, counselling centres, etc. perform this role of providing the needed information. Although, at the national level, a good beginning has been made in India to recognize the importance of these services for many parts of the country and for many individual transactors the available information is meagre and even non-existent except for various rules of thumb (place of origin, caste), gossip, hearsay, etc. In Sri Lanka, for instance, there was only one effective employment exchange, in the national capital, and even this had no effective means of trade testing its employees and for many kinds of occupations, there was not much of a mechanism even to certify that an individual had such and such a skill. Although there are more of these offices in India and the public employment services are a little ahead, the available information is seriously inadequate for a country of India's size and needs.

The effect of these considerations, the poor information, discounting of alternatives, employer practices, and public policies regulating labour, are generally to raise the cost of search for jobs in the labour market and to depress the expected benefits. An important component of the cost of search is the period of "waiting" or the time taken in finding a job under prevailing market conditions which represents "frictional" unemployment in our terms.[3] Practices and policies which raise the cost of search while depressing the expected benefits would generally discourage labour mobility, particularly movement from one paid employment to another. In that sense, they lower the incidence of frictional unemployment for any given level of expected benefits. On the other hand, they increase the magnitude of frictional unemployment for any given level or frequency of jobs seeking. Precisely because one has to look much harder and longer to obtain a given benefit, fewer persons would be tempted to look. This takes place for at least three major reasons: there are constant new arrivals in the labour market (persons who come of age, rural to urban migrants, high school and college graduates, seasonal job seekers, etc.), persons who are forced to leave their jobs, and persons who do so "voluntarily" because this is the best means of finding an alternative. The net effect of these opposing tendencies is difficult to determine in *a priori* terms but forces which have tended to increase frictional unemployment in recent years may be briefly noted.

There has been an accelerating urbanization and along with it the growth of many small towns and of wage earning employment. These in turn reflect many new forms of job seeking and productive enterprise where contract rather than custom or status provide the link between employer and employee. There has also been a growth in non-farm rural wage earning employment. There has been a great increase in literacy which may tend to widen the geographic span of job seeking. In some Indian states, e.g. Kerala, with high rates of female literacy there has been an increase in female labour force participation. As yet, research along these lines is too limited for us to go beyond these tentative and broad pointers.

To sum up this discussion on frictional unemployment, defined as unemployment arising due to continual change in demand and supply conditions, we have two things to consider: the frequency of these changes, and the period of search involved. To our knowledge, there is no accepted judgement on the first, and all we know is that enough changes are taking place, particularly where contract rather than custom govern labour market relationships, for us to be concerned about the efficiency of the adjustment process in the labour market. On the second the picture is clearer: the weaknesses of the labour market infra-structure generally raise the costs of job search relative to the benefits to be gained, and would thus discourage either entry into the labour market or voluntary movement between jobs. This may raise the level of idleness but not necessarily of unemployment. But whenever benefit conditions favour labour market entry or job shifts, or these are induced by employers or by such exogenous factors as population growth, etc., prolonged involuntary idleness may precede the finding of employment; in the former case because the benefits to be gained permit the associated costs, and in the latter because a relative decrease in the supply price of labour encourages search at the previously prevailing labour market conditions. A major problem is therefore to distinguish between idleness and involuntary idleness: between a state when an individual is not employed simply because at prevailing conditions the labour market is discouraging and a state when an individual is not employed but is looking for work because his expectations (which could turn out to be wrong) indicate this to be promising behaviour. Thus Dr. S. V. Sethuraman writes in a sad commentary on the lack of integration between theory and empirical work:

> The major drawback of the approaches to measuring underemployment discussed thus far, is that all ignore individual preferences in regard to work and leisure, and workers responses to

[3] The wages to be realized upon employment or the incremental wage (if switching from one job to another) constitute benefits, while the cost of search would include foregone earnings and direct costs, such as out of pocket expenses, commission paid to recruiter, foreman, etc.

changes in incentive. None distinguish between voluntary and involuntary underemployment.[4]

Beyond this, there is a chronic, secular condition of idleness, of the sort that would exist even with no change in supply or demand conditions, due to the structural characteristics of an underdeveloped economy. Perhaps the most important reason for this is the seasonal nature of the greater part of economic activity, especially agricultural production. Such an economy, as contrasted with another where agriculture is a smaller component of national output, would indicate wide swings in the incidence of idleness. Acute shortage of labour (particularly at harvest times and for pre-monsoon operations) at one extreme, and fairly prolonged periods of idleness at the other extreme, market, they do not find it profitable to look for work. But many do, and this is the reason why there is seasonal migration from the countryside to the cities or entry into wage earning employment in the rural areas. This is also the reason for the fluctuation in agricultural wage rates. We also know that some of the relationships between labour contractor and seasonal workers are of the nature as to minimize the search costs and the period of search. What we do not know is the precise measure of idleness among those who seek seasonal work during periods when seasonal demand conditions imply fairly sharp decline in earnings.

A further structural condition deals with secular changes primarily on the supply side, thereby prolonging the degree of unemployment (assuming wages to be rigid) or underemployment (for any

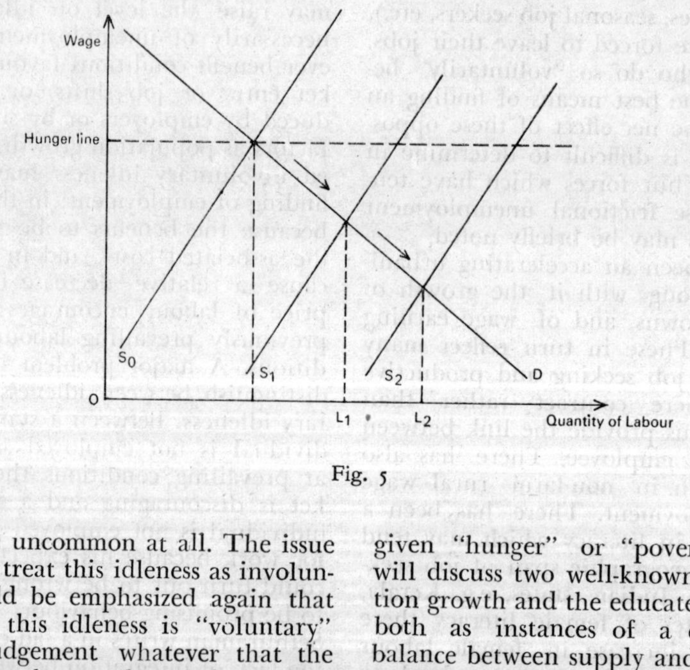

Fig. 5

would not be uncommon at all. The issue is whether to treat this idleness as involuntary. It should be emphasized again that to state that this idleness is "voluntary" makes no judgement whatever that the idle persons are happy about this; all that the term implies is that at the prevailing cost-benefit relationships in the labour given "hunger" or "poverty" line). We will discuss two well-known cases, population growth and the educated unemployed, both as instances of a developing imbalance between supply and demand.

What is the impact of an increase in population, given the absence of an equivalent increase in the demand for human services? Going back to our graphs, U 3 and U 3B, we can visualize the following situation:

As represented here, population increases shift the supply curves to the right which

4 *Underemployment in Rural India: Implications for Rural Works Programme*, U.S. Agency for International Development, May 1972.

initially, at S_0, equalled demand at a subsistence wage measured vertically from 0 to the "hunger" line. An increase of the supply from S_0 to S_1, can have one of two consequences: it can increase unemployment by the distance L_0L_1 or it can produce equilibrium at a new and "hungrier" level of earnings in the labour market, or some combination of both. The longer the time allowed for the market to absorb the impact of the additional labour supply, the more concerted will the pressure be to lower wages.

Now what does happen in the real world? Contrary to the general assumption about these matters, the rigid wage is by no means the dominant phenomenon in the Indian labour market. Much of organized employment, in factories and public offices and the like, obviously follow relatively rigid wage practices reflecting the spirit of unionism or corporate and administrative policy. However, these are not the major employers in the country, nor are they necessarily the major employers even in the biggest cities like Bombay or Calcutta. This means that, to the extent that wages are rigid in organized employment, the pressure for lowering wages will be greater in the traditional or unorganized wage-earning sector in both urban and rural areas. There will also tend to be an increase in the relative advantage of earnings from paid as opposed to self employment. This may also result in an increase in unemployment by L_0L_1, L_1L_2 and so on.

There is definite indication of some visible unemployment of this type in the cities and urban areas, where there are many job seekers who are very persistent in their efforts to obtain employment in the organized sector but are not successful. In some cases, as in the Bombay textile industry, it has even been argued that the Badli system was an attempt to seal off the organized sector and its wages from the depressing effect of the unemployed pool outside. But firm judgments as to whether these job seekers are unemployed and likely to stay there depend in part upon whether they are really as good as those with the better paying jobs and in part upon whether they are actually employed while seeking a better-paying alternative. There is also some evidence that the wage differential between paid and self employment has been increasing in favour of the former, but this is compatible with greater inelasticity of supply to the former as opposed to the latter reflecting developing opportunities in paid as compared to self employment. On the trend in wage differentials between organized and non-organized employment, the evidence is mixed. The impact of industrial adjudication and government wage determination was initially to shift the differentials in favour of organized employment but it is not clear that this upward thrust has been maintainel.

The rigid wages of the organized sector, whatever combination of above consequences result, is thus of use only to explain the frustrations of those waiting for jobs in the corporate and modern sector. For an explanation of the bulk of the phenomena of idleness and frustrations of earning a decent living, we must analyze the consequences of the above supply shifts, assuming wage flexibility. It will be helpful to refer to the graph again, where equilibrium was established initially at the "hunger" or "poverty" line. What is the effect of a shift in labour supply? Will it result in unemployment or a further immiseration of the level of wages?

The answer to this lies in the strength of the supportive social institutions when additional entrants into the labour market are unable to find jobs at prevailing wages. Will they be encouraged to wait by relatives who are themselves at the margin of subsistence? Can this margin of subsistence admit of further economies and deprivation? What combination of stamina, fortitude, and hope is needed to sustain the job seeker's (and his relatives') unwillingness to accept a lower-paying job (and assume the costs of waiting) in an adverse labour market (with a decrease in the expected value of benefits)? It is clear that as time goes by the downward pressure on wages will increase until a new equilibrium is established below the "hunger" line. What we then have is a "poverty" problem, rather than an "unemployment" problem.

The factual position in India is difficult to determine for three major reasons. First, while the growth of population and output is visible and depends mainly on a headcount, supply and demand schedules represent propensities at different market prices and are less easily identified. Our own graphs neglect the fact that population growth, representing supply shifts, may induce, as well as accompany, demand shifts in the same direction. Second, unemployment invites attention because of the misery it represents and misery does not care whether it arises due to a lack of jobs or a lack of adequate income while employed.[5] While it is a technical requirement, with diverse policy implications, that this difference be recognized, most public discussion (including by economists) has blurred the issues and this distinction. Thirdly, the "hunger" line is a normative concept representing social goals and commitment which are variable and as yet needing refinement. Over-riding all of these is the fact that while we have masses of data, there are few breakdowns that are relevant, illustrating the dictum that if you don't ask the right questions you won't get the right answers.

Later we will examine in greater detail the available data pertaining to job seekers and unemployment. For the moment, we need only record that if demand is growing along with population, the incidence of unemployment will be less than otherwise, and if wages are flexible downwards, this will reduce unemployment, although it may increase the incidence of poverty. All of this is of course consistent with increased national output and absolute increases at every level of paid employment or remunerative activity.

When we turn to graduate or educated unemployment, we can use the same theoretical apparatus and can expect some of the same problems in interpreting observed phenomena. However, some noteworthy economic analyses greatly improve our understanding. We will concentrate on the pioneering study by Professor Mark Blaug of the *Causes of Educated Unemployment in India.* According to Blaug, there has been a continual increase in the demand for graduates, but this has been outstripped by the increase in the output of graduates because of a lowered private cost of obtaining the necessary schooling and the expectations of enhanced benefit from schooling. However, the excess supply of new graduate entrants does not get absorbed by the labour market because the benefit-cost relationships encourage the graduate to wait rather than to terminate his unemployment. While he is waiting, and until he gets his job, he is of course unemployed.

What are the ingredients of the benefit-cost relationship which encourage unemployment upon graduation? Many of us are aware that unemployment is costly, particularly if you have a currently useful skill. In that sense waiting is costly. But few of us realize that not waiting, being employed, can be costly, too. A full-time job may mean less time to prepare for a competitive examination qualifying one for a superior service. Procedures for governing entry into the latter may not give sufficient weight to skills acquired while in employment or the skills acquired may be of little general value. Job shifts and even transfers under the same employer might be made costly by cumbersome procedures or onerous requirements. New employers may be selective on where they recruit and even exclude those in employment at jobs below a certain income level when recruiting for the remunerative vacancies. There may also be a certain advantage in waiting in line for the remunerative jobs, in trying repeatedly, and in establishing a preferred position in the "queue" as it were. The *viva voce* (or oral examination) which has such an unsettling effect on many new graduates seeking employment, and is so dominated by the subjective considerations of the examiners, may place a premium on taking time out to "psyche" the examiners and there may be an improvement with each trial.

Our own inquiries throughout the length and breadth of the country, and with graduates at all levels of employment

[5] Current relevant literature in the United States identified this latter phenomenon as "wage poverty."

ranging from humble crane operator jobs to prestigious professorships and scientific positions in national laboratories, clearly convince us that the labour market for graduates encourages waiting—and, therefore, a greater period of unemployment following graduation. This is also the conclusion of Professor Mark Blaug and his team. What is not clear, however, is that this position is worsening. It is also not clear that the secular relationship is one of a more rapid increase in the supply of college graduates than of an increase in the demand for their services. Such a conclusion would be appealing if it can be demonstrated that the return on investment in training college graduates has been falling. In the absence of specific computations such an inference cannot be sustained by *a priori* arguments alone.

Our analysis of unemployment so far has been concerned about workers who are not able to find jobs either because of rigidity of wages or fundamental imbalance between the increase in population (and the resultant increase in labour supply) and the economy's ability to utilize this population effectively. We have not yet considered the question, what would this unemployed labour do? There are various possibilities in this connection. The unemployed may be actively looking for other jobs in those subsectors of the economy which might be expanding and needing their skills. In the interim period, these unemployed might be paid unemployment benefit, if the society has such a provision. This can be classified as "open" or "visible unemployment" in the sense the workers are cognizant of their unemployment status and they are seeking work. This type of unemployment is characteristic of western developed economies and also in the urban, industrial sector in underdeveloped countries. The unemployment among the educated in India would mostly fall in this category. In underdeveloped countries and especially in Asian economies with the institution of joint family (also called as extended family) system, the unemployment or underemployment might not take the "open" or "visible" form. In a joint family, which is a dominant form of family institution in the Asian societies, the members share its work and income as a matter of social obligation. A joint family does not hire any worker; rather the family enterprise work is shared by family members, each receiving a share of the total product. The pattern of employment emerging from such an arrangement is explained in figure above. OL_1 is the initial size of labour force, with the marginal (MP) and average product (AP) curves. W_s is subsistence level of living. In this family enterprise, if all members would share equally in the total product, the share of each would be their average product OW which also happens to be equal to the subsistence level of living or hunger line.

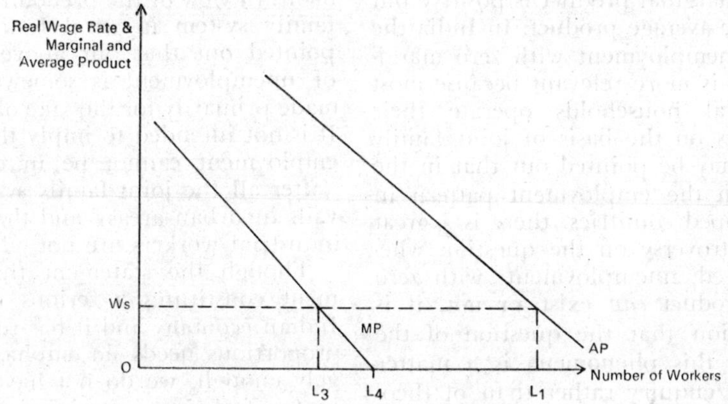

Fig. 6

If this enterprise were a profit maximizing firm, how many workers would have been hired at OW_s wage rate? OL_3, because it is at this level of employment that the wage OW = the MP : a condition of employment of inputs in a profit maximizing firm. L_3L_1 workers are simply there because they are working in a "family type" rather than "profit maximizing firm." In this sense L_3L_1 are disguisedly unemployed, and they can be divided into two categories: (a) Disguised unemployment with zero marginal product L_4L_1. The interesting part of this employment status is that, while they are in fact not contributing anything to the family's total product—akin to unemployment—they consider themselves employed and are not looking for any work. (b) Disguised unemployment of L_3L_4 workers, where the marginal product is positive but less than the average product. In India the disguised unemployment with zero marginal product is more relevant because most of the rural households operate their family farms on the basis of joint family system. It may be pointed out that in the literature on the employment pattern in underdeveloped countries, there is a great deal of controversy on the question whether disguised unemployment with zero marginal product *can* exist or not, it is our contention that the question of the existence of this phenomena is a matter of empirical enquiry rather than of theoretical argument. As we will see in a subsequent section, it is generally believed that disguised unemployment and underemployment is rather a serious problem, specially in the rural sector of Indian economy.

4. Estimates of Unemployment in India

A. *An overall view*

After having analyzed theoretical aspects of unemployment and also the relevance of theoretical models to the underdeveloped countries, we would discuss the extent of the phenomenon in India and major steps being taken to cope with it. For this purpose, we would group unemployment in the following categories:

Urban Unemployment

(*a*) among educated persons: educated unemployment
(*b*) among others: labour and industrial workers.

This category can be assumed to be open unemployment

Rural Unemployment

(a) seasonal unemployment
(b) chronic unemployment

While seasonal unemployment may be open unemployment in the sense that the worker is aware of his being out of work in the slack season, we will, on the whole, consider rural unemployment (both seasonal and chronic) as disguised unemployment, in view of the predominance of joint family system in rural India. It may be pointed out that our above classification of unemployment is somewhat arbitrary, made primarily for the sake of convenience. It is not intended to imply that urban unemployment cannot be in disguise form (after all the joint family system also prevails in urban areas) and that labour and industrial workers are not educated.

Though the statement that unemployment constitutes a serious threat to the Indian economy and it has reached serious proportions needs no emphasis, yet, strangely enough, we do not have precise estimate of the magnitude of the phenomenon. There are so many conceptual as well as statistical difficulties in estimating the magnitude of unemployment that any estimate on unemployment has to be treated with caution. According to the Report of the Committee of Experts on Unemployment Estimates (1970) appointed by the Planning Commission, "In our complex economy, the character of the labour force, employment and unemployment, is too heterogeneous to justify aggregation into single-dimensional magnitude."[6] The estimates made by various organizations on the level of unemployment are given below:

The 1961 census estimated unemployment

[6] Planning Commission Government of India, *Report of the Committee on Experts on Unemployment Estimates* New Delhi; (1970), p. 31.

at 1.41 million (1.29 million males and 0.12 million females) of whom 0.60 million (0.54 million males and 0.06 females) were in rural areas. Unemployed persons consisted of (i) a person who has not been employed before but is seeking employment for the first time, and (ii) a person employed before but now out of employment and seeking employment.

The National Sample Survey estimates:

> The N.S.S. followed a labour force approach under which, persons having some gainful work, however nominal, during the reference period, were classified as employed. Persons without gainful work throughout the reference period and seeking work or not seeking but available for work during the reference period, were reported as unemployed. For the period May–August 1955, the number of employed were estimated at 2.2 million (1.3 million in urban areas and 0.9 million in rural areas).

Here comments on the estimates of unemployment in general and those by the 1961 Census and the National Sample Survey in particular would be in order. As already pointed out, in the context of Indian social institutions—joint family system—open unemployment would assume the form of disguised unemployment or underemployment especially in the rural areas. As the Committee of Experts on Unemployment Estimates pointed out about Indian economy, "In an economy like this, there is very little open or outright unemployment, but there will be considerable unemployment and/or underemployment."[7] The committee cautioned that "The distinction between these two features of overt unemployment and underemployment within household enterprise should be clearly recognized and the estimates pertaining to them should not be aggregated into estimates of full time unemployment."[8] It may be noted that the estimates of unemployment by the National Sample Survey and the 1961 Census are quite low and obviously gross underestimates. The reason for this underestimation is the restricted definition of "unemployment" since, for a person to be considered unemployed, he should not have worked at all during the reference period, this restrictive definition would have the effect of classifying respondents underemployed—

Table 1. Estimates of Employment and Unemployment in the Five Year Plans

	I Plan	II Plan	III Plan	IV Plan
	(in millions)			Three Annual Plans
	1951-56	1956-61	1961-66	1966-69
1. Labour force at the beginning of the Plan	185.2	197.0	215.0	229.0
2. Net addition to the labour force during the Plan	9.0	11.7	17.0	14.0
3. Back-log of unemployed at the beginning of the Plan	3.3	5.3	7.1	9.6
4. Total 2+3	12.3	17.0	24.1	23.6
5. Additional jobs created	7.0	10.0	14.5	0.6
6. Back-log of unemployed at the end of the Plan (6-4-5)	5.3	7.0	9.6	23.0
7. Unemployed as % of total labour force	2.9	3.6	4.5	9.6

SOURCES: Ruddar Datt and K. P. M. Sundharam, *Indian Economy* (New Delhi: S. Chand & Co., 1972), p. 621. Reserve Bank of India Bulletin, December 1969. Planning Commission, Government of India, *Report of the Committee of Experts on Unemployment Estimates* New Delhi: (1970), p. 7

[7] Report of the Committee of Experts. *Ibid.*, p. 30-31.

[8] Ibid., p. 31.

even for few weeks in a year—as fully employed when for all practical purposes they are in fact unemployed. It is, therefore, important to note that these grossly underestimated figures on unemployment are misleading and should be interpreted with caution. It is interesting to note that judged from western style, unemployment statistics of 2–3 million unemployed in a country with 600 million population and more than 200 million persons in labour force, can be considered as full employment. After all in the U.S.A. 2–3% unemploymetnt is considered consistent with full employment of labour force.

B. *Urban Unemployment*

Urban unemployment in India, although a serious economic and social problem wrought with political dangers, also remains largely unmeasured in quantitative terms. Besides the conceptual difficulties regarding "unemployment" and "underemployment" in an underdeveloped economy, as already pointed out, the statistical information in this area is grossly inadequate. This explains why the results of different studies are so varied and complicating. The estimates on urban employment have been provided by the Planning Commission, the ministry of Labour and Employment, the Central Statistical Organization and a few individual studies. These estimates are summarized in Table 2.

Urban employment is due to several factors such as the rigidity of wages in the industrial sector, inadequate economic development to absorb the growing labour force from increase in population and urbanization.

C. *Educated Unemployment*

The growing unemployment among the educated people is a matter of great national concern: For an educated person not to find a job after all the hopes and dreams built during the period of acquiring education, brings great amount of disillusionment and frustration. The educated unemployed, being very vocal, can spread dissatisfaction and cynicism against the political and economic structure. They become easily prone to the revolutionary movements aiming at the destruction of the economic and political order, which cannot provide them with work. The recent uprising of educated unemployed in Sri Lanka (Ceylon) is a case in point.

In view of the serious implications of this category of unemployment, a separate identification of this problem is very important. The attention given so far to measure the trend in the number and composition of educated unemployed has,

Table 2. Estimates of the Volume of Urban Unemployment in India

Source	Period of reference	Urban unemployment (in millions)	Urban unemployment as proportion of total labour force
B. N. Datar	March 1951	2.5-3.0	12.00
National Sample Survey & Employment Exchange Data	Sept. 1953	2.4	11.00
Second Five Year Plan	March 1956	2.5	10.0
Wilfred Malenbaum	March 1956	2.5	10.0
National Sample Survey & Employment Exchange Data	May 1956	3.4	13.6
R. C. Bhardwaj	March 1951	2.5	11.4
	March 1956	3.4	13.5
	March 1961	4.5	15.5

SOURCES: R. C. Bhardwaj, *Employment and Unemployment in India*. (Humanities Press, 1969), pp. 109-126.

however, been very inadequate. Some estimates on educated unemployment (unemployment among persons with educational qualifications of matriculation and above) are given below:

(1) On the basis of figures from the Five Year Plan documents, Bhardwaj[9] estimated that at the end of Second Five Year Plan, out of a total of approximately 6.45 million educated people, around 1 million (or 15.5 per cent) were unemployed.

(2) According to the study Group of National Commission on Labour, the unemployment among educated persons, increased from 244.4 thousands in 1951 to 1087.4 thousands in 1967—more than four-fold increase.

Table 3. Increase in Educated Unemployment in India

Qualifications	1955	1967
Matriculation	187.0	714.1
Undergraduates	30.6	251.8
Graduates & Post-Graduates	26.8	121.5
	244.4	1087.4

SOURCES: Quoted from Ruddar Datt and Sundharam, *Indian Economy*, New Delhi, 1971, P.622

(3) According to a Sample Survey on Unemployment conducted by the Government of Kerala in October 1965, 19 per cent of the matriculates were unemployed in the State, with the corresponding percentages of 7.4 of graduates and 5.7 for post-graduates.

(4) Paradoxically, the unemployment is assuming serious proportions even among educated persons with technical qualifications. In 1968, 17 per cent of total stock of engineering graduates and diploma holders was unemployed. In the decade preceding 1965, the unemployed within this category was estimated at no more than 7 to 8 per cent and according to the Report of the Committee on Experts on Unemployment (1970),[10] even this appears to have been largely due to the waiting period (or no more than one year) that the bulk of the new graduates had to go through before securing employment.

The extent and causes of the deteriorating position about educated unemployment is well described in the Mid-term Appraisal of the Fourth Five Year Plan.

> The technically qualified personnel presented no serious employment problem until about the end of the Third Plan. However, as a result of serious set-back in the mid-sixties, to investment and growth particularly in industry and mining, there was a sharp decline in the demand for technical personnel. This happened just as the large expansion of training facilities during the Second and Third Plan periods was beginning to yield a much larger turn-out of technical personnel. As a result, large scale unemployment appeared even among the technical and scientific personnel including degree holders, diploma holders and science graduates and post-graduates...serious and growing unemployment among the non-technical educated is a chronic problem. In the recent years, the position has been deteriorating even faster than usual.[11]

In other words, the deteriorating unemployment among educated persons is due to big increase in their numbers beyond the ability of the economy to absorb them. The great increase in the number of educated persons during 1950–70 is indicated from statistics in Table 4. To provide employment to this fast increasing numbers of educated persons is a difficult task indeed. The Planning Commission has proposed the following schemes for speedy generation of employment opportunities for the educated unemployed:

(i) Intensification of research and development in identified priority areas.

[9] R. C. Bhardwaj, *Employment and Unemployment in India* (Humanities Press, 1969), p. 83.

[10] Committee of Experts, op. cit., p. 150.

[11] Planning Commission, Government of India, *The Fourth Plan; Mid-Term Appraisal* (February 1972), pp. 44–45.

(ii) Formulation of a shelf of projects from which choices could be made for inclusion in the Fifth Plan.

(iii) Acceleration of construction activities.

(iv) Assistance to technically qualified persons for setting up small-scale industries.

The Planning Commission recognizes the fact that "the lasting solution of the problem must, eventually, be found in greatly intensified tempo of growth. In this context, a sharp step-up in the rate of investment and industrial expansion, particularly in areas that have a high employment potential is essential."[12]

"underemployment" rather than "unemployment" is more relevant in the rural sector of the Indian economy. This explains why the estimates of unemployment made by the National Sample Survey (N.S.S.) in 1960–61 that 1.62 per cent of the rural population was unemployed, is considered a gross underestimate. Underemployment includes (a) underemployment from sharing work on farms owned and operated by joint families, and (b) seasonal unemployment. The N.S.S. provided some estimates on the extent of underemployment. Persons working less than 28 hours per week were considered severely underemployed and those working between 29 to 42 hours as moderately underemployed. The estimates on severe underemployed in Indian agriculture are given in Table 5:

Table 4. Students attending Educational Institutions in India 1950-70

	1950	1970	Per cent increase
1. Number of students in classes VI-VII (in Lakhs)	31.2	122.7	300
Percentage thereof to total population age group 11-14	12.7	12.7	-
2. Number of students in classes IX-XI/XII (in Lakhs)	12.2	65.8	440
Percentage thereof to total population age group 14-17	5.3	19.3	-
3. Number of students at the University Stage (Lakhs)	3.6	16.9	430
Percentage thereof to total population age group 17-23	0.8	2.9	-

SOURCES: Government of India, Ministry of Information and Broadcasting, *India: A Reference Annual 1971-72.*

D. *Rural Unemployment*

It is, this category of unemployment and underemployment, which generally assumes the form of disguised unemployment as already discussed, plagues the Indian rural economy. The Planning Commission in its paper, "Towards an Approach to the Fifth Plan" admits that rural unemployment is the principal cause of our poverty and that goal of the "Garibi Hatao" cannot be achieved without providing work to our unemployed rural workforce.[13]

As already pointed out, in the context of the social and economic structure,

Table 5. Percentage of Employed Males and Females Working for 28 Hours or Less and Available for Additional Work

Year	Males	Females	Total
1958-59	5.78	8.94	14.72
1959-60	5.46	9.08	14.54
1960-61	3.34	6.55	10.39
1961-62	3.96	5.89	9.85

SOURCES: Planning Commission, Government of India, ***Report of the Committee of Experts on Unemployment Estimates***, 1970, p. 10.

[12] Ibid., pp. 45–46.

[13] Planning Commission, *Towards an Approach to the Fifth Plan,* July 1972.

It is interesting to note that there has been a decline in the percentage of "severely underemployed" from 14.72 per cent in 1958–59 to 9.85 per cent in 1961–62. It may be either the result of additional work opportunities created in the rural areas under the Five Year Plans, or due to change in statistical coverage and methods applied. In its Mid-Term Appraisal of the Fourth Plan issued in February 1972, the Planning Commission remarked: "The incidence of seasonal and underemployment remains as heavy as before. It is, perhaps, heavier than before except in some part of the country where the Green Revolution has achieved significant success."[14]

The Indian peasantry continues to depend for work on the vagaries of nature. According to Mamoria: "The period of complete inactivity in each agricultural region varies with the nature and variety of crops and cropping pattern. Broadly speaking, the Indian cultivator is unoccupied anywhere from 4 to 6 months in a year excepting in places where he has undertaken the cultivation of wet crops or where he grows more than one crop from the same soil in a year, while the cultivator's womenfolk are occupied for even longer part of the year."[15] Since the area under double cropping is only 14 per cent of the total cultivated area, this enforced idleness due to seasonal factors inflicts on vast majority of Indian rural workforce.

The extent of underemployment among the agricultural labourers was estimated by the First and Second Agricultural Labour Enquiry Committees in 1950–51 and 1955–56. The seriousness of their underemployment is indicated by the following estimates:[16]

1. Casual adult male workers were employed, on an average for wage for 200 days in 1950–51 and for 197 days during 1956–57. They were self employed for 75 days in 1950–51 ond for 40 days in 1956–57. Thus, they were without work for 91 days and 128 days during 1950–51 and 1956–57 respectively.

2. Casual adult female workers were employed on wages for 134 days during 1950–51 and for 141 days during 1956–57.

In the literature on unemployment in the rural sector, the terms "disguised unemployment," "surplus labour," "underemployment" have been used synonymously to describe the phenomenon. Several estimates on surplus labour have been made by different writers. Tarlok Singh[17] estimated in 1945 that 21 to 22 million persons, out of the working population of 99 to 103 million (i.e. 33–35) per cent of the total population) were surplus in the British India. Shakuntla Mehra,[18] estimated the surplus labour at 17.1 per cent of the agricultural work force on all India basis. Uppal[19] made use of the data compiled by the Indian Planning Commission through its studies in the Economies of Farm Management for the year 1956–57 and estimated disguised unemployed in Punjab agriculture at 8.41 per cent of the total rural work force. On the small size holdings (e.g. on the farms of less than 10 acres in size), more than one-fifth of the labour force was surplus.

The existence of the serious rural unemployment and underemployment is a symptom of general backwardness of the Indian economy and static condition of the rural sector. Historically, the developing countries have followed a definite pattern of development. In a predominantly agricultural economy, as India is, agriculture develops; its productivity increases; lesser people are required on land to produce needed food and raw materials; increasing agricultural productivity creates demand for non-agricultural products; processes of urbanization starts; the sur-

14 The Fourth Plan Mid-Term Appraisal, p. 47.

15 C. B. Mamoria, *Agricultural Problems of India* (Allahabad: Kitab Mahal, 1966), p. 727.

16 Quoted in Ibid., p. 728.

17 Tarlok Singh, *Poverty and Social Change*, 1945, p. 136.

18 Shakuntla Mehra, "Surplus Labour in Indian Agriculture," *Indian Economic Review* (April 1966), p. 112.

19 J. S. Uppal, "Measurement of Disguised Unemployment in Punjab Agriculture," *The Canadian Journal of Economics*, No. 4 (November 1967), pp. 590–96.

plus population in the rural sector is absorbed in the expanding urban industrial centres, and finally, the urban industrial centres and rural areas become complementary to each other in economic expansion. In India, unfortunately we have not been able to tread on this path of development. The productivity in agriculture has not increased sufficiently and urban centres have not grown adequately to absorb the surplus rural population. In fact the cities have not been able even to provide employment to new entrants to their labour force from natural increase in urban population. Serious overcrowding and urban unemployment characterize most of our cities. As a result, the increasing population in Indian villages is being absorbed in the already crowded agriculture. Fortunately for the survival of people, but unfortunately for the economic growth, the joint family system is able to provide sustenance to our increasing but surplus rural work force. Even before independence, Indian agriculture was becoming crowded without any increase in productivity. While the rural population increased from 274.2 million in 1941, the productivity per acre did not register any increase. Surprisingly, the output per acre of major crops actually decreased as indicated in Table 6:

Table 6. Agricultural Yield per Acre of Major Crops in India

(Average yield in pounds per acre)

Crop	1936-39	1945-46	1948-49
Rice	793	703	699
Wheat	618	541	573
Jowar	435	322	303
Maize	659	594	529

SOURCES: Wadia and Merchant, *Our Economic Problem* (Bombay, 1954), p. 202.

The Indian Planning Commission remarked that for the three years ending 1949–50, compared to the period immediately preceding the war, while the area under cereals has not changed appreciably there has been a decline in the yield per acre from 619 lbs. to 565 lbs.[20] Though this decline in productivity was reversed after 1950–51, with huge investments under Five Year Plans, the increase in productivity compared to increase in rural population, has not been very impressive. Between 1949–50 and 1969–70, the agricultural productivity per acre increased annually by the compound rate of growth of 1.57 per cent,[21] against the 1.9 per cent annual increase in rural population. Agriculture is thus, becoming a reservoir of ever increasing underemployed and surplus population. It is the utilization of this surplus manpower which will ultimately determine the effectiveness of economic development of the Indian economy.

5. Policies Aiming at Solving the Unemployment Problem

In view of the importance of providing employment opportunities for not only ameliorating the tragic poverty of teeming millions, but also to promote the nation's economic development, the employment policy has been an integral part of India's Five Year Plans.

The First Plan stressed the need of making maximum use of surplus rural man-power as essential part of programmes for agricultural development. By 1953, with deterioration in the employment situation especially in urban areas, the Planning Commission planned new schemes costing Rs. 309 crores, with high employment potential. Special 11 points programme for expanding job opportunities was undertaken involving labour intensive projects like small scale industries, road transport, slum clearance, one teacher schools in rural areas, and improved training and education facilities. It is estimated that these schemes generated about 7.0 million jobs against the unemployment of 12.3 million workers (9.0 million net addition to labour force during the First Plan and backlog of 3.3 million un-

[20] Planning Commission, *The First Five Year Plan*, pp. 155–156.

[21] Government of India, Ministry of Food and Agriculture, *Indian Agriculture in Brief, 1971*, p. 103.

employed before the Plan) leaving 5.3 million unemployed at the end of the First Plan. Unemployment situation was, by and large, far from satisfactory at the end of the First Plan.

The Second Plan enunciated, as one of its objectives, a large expansion of employment opportunities, by proposing massive investment in the industrial sector, especially labour intensive small scale industries. With a backlog of 5.3 million unemployment from the First Plan, along with 11.8 million new entrants to the labour force, the Second Plan targeted for 10 million jobs within the proposed investment patterns. At the end of the Second Plan, it was discovered that population increase during 1951–61 exceeded the previous forecasts. This enhanced the already grim number of unemployed. The unemployment situation, thus, deteriorated further during the Second Plan. Against the backlog of unemployment of 5.3 million at the beginning, the corresponding figure was 7.1 million at the end of the Second Plan.

The Third Plan, thus, inherited grave unemployment situation. With backlog of 7.1 million, there was 17.0 million net addition force. In other words, while the Second Plan faced 17.1 million unemployed, the Third Plan was confronted with 24.1 million of unemployment. The Third Plan planned for 14 million additional jobs. (10.5 million non-agricultural and 3.5 million agricultural employment) through stepping up investment in labour intensive construction schemes, including irrigation and power, cottage and small scale industries, transport, and communication. By April 1969, however, it was discovered that the new jobs created stood at 7 million (4.5 million outside agriculture and 2.5 million in agriculture). Thus the number of jobless in April 1969, when the Fourth Plan started to operate, was more than 10 million strong.

The unemployment situation at the beginning of the Fourth Plan was even graver than before. It was estimated[22] that the number of employment seekers during the Fourth Plan period might even exceed the staggering figure of 40 million. Some new progrmames were planned to ease the deteriorating unemployment situation. Rural works programmes were initiated involving an outlay of Rs. 100 crores which would provide 3 million jobs in the rural areas. For the marginal farmers and agricultural workers an outlay of Rs. 47.5 crores was planned to start 41 Work-Projects by providing subsidized credit support for agro-small scale industries, like dairy, poultry, fisheries, piggery, and other projects such as planting trees, digging of channels, etc. A sum of Rs 67.50 crores was arranged to provide credit to small but potentially viable farmers to enable them to use new inputs for intentive agricultural development. Agro-Service Centres were sanctioned to provide financial as well as technical assistance to the unemployed graduates and diploma holders in mechanical, agricultural, and electrical engineering. The objectives of the scheme were: to provide self employment opportunities to technical trained personnel; to provide on the farm maintenance and repairing facilities for agricultural machinery and implements; an easily accessible source of supply for spare parts and other engineering services. 5000 such centres were planned during the Fourth Plan and these were to be financed by loans from the State Bank of India and other financial institutions at liberalized credit terms. In April 1971, the government initiated a Rs. 150 crores crash programme for providing rural employment. The programme aimed at providing jobs to 1000 persons for 10 months in a year in every district. In all 336,000 new jobs were to be created under this plan. In addition, each project would generate "durable resources" such as roads, drains, minor irrigation projects in consonance with the local development plans.

Despite all these plans and efforts, the unemployment situation continues to be grave. The resultant loss of human resources has assumed serious proportions. The society is threatened by the loud protests from the unemployed and underemployed poor. The Planning Commission

22 Alak Ghosh, *Indian Economy—Its Nature and Problems* (Calcutta, 1971), p. 78.

once remarked that "the ability to absorb at least the net addition to labour force into productive and gainful employment is a test which a plan of development should endeavour to meet at the very stage of its development."[23] Judging our Five Year Plans from this test, one has to remark with dismay that they have largely been ineffective, since the additional jobs created during the First, Second and Third Plans consistently fell short of the net additions to the labour force during the plan periods. The backlog of unemployed as the end of each plan has been growing larger and this alarming situation calls for a serious reexamination of our planning techniques and methods for effective utilization of our fast increasing manpower. There is need for new thinking and fresh approach since the unemployed have already lost or would soon lose faith in our "work programs," "crash schemes" which have not made even a dent in the problem.

[23] Planning Commission, *Fourth Five Year Plan—A Draft Outline,* p. 106.

Part Five

THE FINANCIAL ASPECTS

16

Capital Formation in the Indian Union–Nature and Composition

BALWIR SINGH CHEEMA

1. Introduction

Since its establishment in March, 1950, the Indian Planning Commission has regarded capital formation as one of the major objectives of the Five Year Plans. This emphasis on capital formation by the planners stems from two basic considerations. First, periods of take-off have always been characterized by an increase in the rate of capital formation, irrespective of the differences in the social and political conditions and institutions.[1] Second, in the growth models, great importance is attached to the rate of capital formation.

In this connection, one cannot ignore the impact of the Harrod-Domar growth model[2] on the thinking of Indian planners. According to Harrod-Domar, the rate of growth is

$$G = s \times \frac{1}{C}$$

Where G=The rate of growth of output, defined as the ratio of the increase in income to total income in a given period ($\triangle Y/Y$);

s=saving expressed as a proportion of income (S/Y);

and C=The incremental output-capital ratio, IOCR.

The rate of growth minus the population rate equals the growth rate in per capita income.

The model is based on the behavioural assumptions that saving depends on the level of income and that investment depends on the rate of growth of income. The level of investment plays a dual role

1 Government of India: Planning Commission, *The First Five Year Plan* (New Delhi: 1952), p. 13.

2 R. F. Harrod, *Economic Essays* (London: Macmillan, 1952, Essay 14), "Second Essay in Dynamic Theory," *Economic Journal*, Vol. LXIXI (June 1960), pp. 277–93. Also see E. D. Domar, *Essays in the Theory of Economic Growth* (Oxford: Oxford University Press, 1957).

in determining the rate of growth. Not only does it generate income, the precise extent of which is determined by the value of the multiplier, but it also enlarges the capacity of an economy to produce, the magnitude of which is determined by the incremental output capital ratio (referred to as IOCR in subsequent discussion). One may ignore lags in the working of the multiplier and the accelerator in a simplified model, but their significance in the formulation of economic plans and their effective implementation can hardly be over-estimated. Thus, given the values of s, the ratio of saving to income, and IOCR, one can easily calculate the rate of growth—or, in case a certain target rate of growth is adopted, given the IOCR, one can easily calculate the saving effort needed to realize the target growth rate on the basis of the Harrod-Domar growth equation.

The postulate that the level of saving is determined by the level of income finds considerable support among development economists who support the theory of vicious circles.[3] However, economic planners, for practical reasons, cannot accept it without qualifications. Furthermore, it cannot be upheld historically as it rules out the possibility that an underdeveloped economy will ever generate sufficient saving to become a developed economy.[4] For instance, in 1965 the proportions of income saved and invested in China and Japan (33.2 and 35.2 per cent respectively) were almost one and a half times those of the U.S.A. and the United Kingdom (20 and 19.3 per cent respectively). By comparison, the per capita income of China was dismally low and that of Japan was roughly half of the U.K. and one fourth of the U.S.A.[5] As against the investment rate of 25.2 per cent in China in 1965–66, the rate of investment in India amounted to only 13.4 per cent, of which 2.3 per cent[6] represented foreign investment, even though per capita income in India was not substantially lower than that of China. Therefore, in addition to the level of income, the proportion saved and made available for investment must be influenced by psychological and institutional factors. Distribution of income, social customs and habits, the rate and direction in which the distribution of income and price levels change, and the degree of effectiveness with which government, banking and other financial institutions mobilize savings are some of the factors which play an important role in determining the rate of saving attained. Thus, without giving serious consideration to these factors, no economic plan can be realistically formulated and successfully implemented.

Along with the saving ratio, the IOCR has been the most important variable in determining the growth rate. In spite of the seeming simplicity of the IOCR, the difficulties involved in its empirical measurement tend to make it appear to be a very crude concept.[7] Nevertheless, empiri-

---

3 R. Nurkse, *Problems of Capital Formation in Underdeveloped Countries* (Oxford: Basil Blackwell, 1953), p. 5.

4 According to Professor Lewis, "No nation is so poor that it could not save 12 per cent of its national income if it wanted to; ...Least of all can those nations plead poverty as an excuse for not saving, in which 40 per cent or so of the national income is squandered by the top 10 per cent of income receivers." Arthur W. Lewis, *The Theory of Economic Growth* (Homewood, Ill.: Richard D. Irwin, Inc., 1955), p. 236. According to national sample survey conducted between July 1967 to June 1968, in India the top 10 per cent of households were responsible for 23.61 per cent of consumption against 28.36 per cent by the bottom 50 per cent. In urban areas the differences in consumption among the rich and the poor were slightly greater than in the rural areas. See Government of India, Planning Commission, *Fourth Five Year Plan* (New Delhi: 1970), p. 36.

5 A. Maddison, *Economic Growth in Japan and the U.S.S.R.* (New York: W. W. Norton & Company Inc., 1969), p. XIX. Also see William W. Hollister, *Trends in Capital Formation in Communist China,* reproduced by Kuan I. Chen, and J. S. Uppal, *Comparative Development of India and China* (New York: The Free Press, 1971), pp. 242–254. The figures are actually investment figures but because of very low component of foreign investment in these countries they are also considered to be equal to domestic saving.

6 Indian Institute of Public Opinion, Blue Supplement to the *Monthly Commentary on Indian Economic Conditions* (New Delhi—Vol. XIII, No. 5, December 1971) p. 11.

7 Everett E. Hagen, *The Economics of Development* (Homewood, Illinois: Richard D. Irwin, Inc., 1968) pp. 185–187.

cally it is a highly useful measure to estimate the need for investment over a period of time to achieve the target rate of growth.

Countries with high growth rates have, without exception, low IOCR's. This shows that a high growth rate is not only the function of saving and investment ratio but also of how effectively additional capital is used. Economic efficiency in the use of capital can only be maintained if other complementary factors of production like land, labour, technical knowhow, and entrepreneurship can be mobilized simultaneously to meet the demands of the optimum production function. In mathematical terms, this means that the IOCR has to be treated as a total derivative. For determining the value of IOCR the supply of all factors of production, except capital, is treated as a variable. The growth of per capita income further depends on the growth rate of population and is indirectly related to it.

2. Long Term Capital Formation Game Plan

Every Five Year Plan has laid down the long-term strategy to achieve the minimum rate of capital formation considered necessary to transform the economy into a self reliant economy in a matter of about two decades. Thus, the First Five Year Plan in 1952 envisaged that the average proportion of income saved and invested could be raised from pre-vail-propensity to save at 20 per cent by 1968–69, by maintainings the marginal propensity to save at 20 per cent up to

Table 1. Planned vs Actual Growth of Domestic and Foreign Saving, Investment and Income and Per Capita and Capital Output Ratio

	Domestic Saving (as a % of national income)		*Foreign Saving* (as a % of national income)		*Investment* (as a % of national income)		*Average Annual* (national income growth rate)		*Incremental* (capital-output ratio)	
	Planned	*Actual*	*Planned*	*Actual*	*Planned*	*Actual*	*Planned*	*Actual*	*Estimated*	*Actual*
First Plan										
1951-52 (Base year)	-	5.0	-	-		5.0	-	-	-	-
1955-56 (Final Year)	7.0	7.3	0.2	0.3	7.0	7.3	2.1	3.4	3.0	2.1*
Second Plan										
1960-61 (Final year)	9.7	8.5	1.0	2.5	10.7	11.0	4.6	3.7	2.3	3.0
Third Plan										
1965-66 (Final year)	11.5	10.5	2.5	3.5	14.0	14.0	5.4	2.5	2.6	5.5*
Annual Plan										
1966-67	-	9.0	3.2		-	12.2	-	1.5*	-	-
1967-68	-	7.9	2.7	-	-	10.6	-	9.3*	-	2.9*
1968-69	-	8.4	2.5	-	-	11.3	-	2.2*	-	-
Fourth Plan										
1973-74 (Final year)	12.2	-	1.3	-	14.5	-	-	-	2.0	-
Fifth Plan										
1978-79	15.7	-	-	-	-	-	-	5.5	-	-

SOURCES: The five Five Year Plans.

*Blue Supplement to the Monthly Commentary on Indian Economic Conditoins, Indian Institute of Public Opinion, Vol. XIII, No. 5 (December 1971), p. VIII B.

Against these figures which are calculated on the basis of actual average annual national income growth rate and the investment rate the Planning Commission figure for the first three Five Year Plans is 2.4. See pp. 44-45 of Fourth Five Year Plan,

1955–56 and 50 per cent thereafter.[8] The existing per capita income was considered to be too low to be tapped for additional saving. If this strategy had worked, the rate of saving as a proportion of income would have risen to 7 per cent by 1955–56, 11 per cent by 1960–61, and 20 per cent by 1967–68. On the basis of a projected IOCR of 3.0, it was considered possible to attain a growth rate of 6.25 per cent in national income by 1967–68. As the population growth rate was assumed to be 1.25 per cent this would have meant an annual increase of roughly 5 per cent in per capita income. In Table 1, figures regarding the planned and actual performance of the Indian economy are given to evaluate the long-term Indian planning strategy.

Because of the fuller utilization of the installed capacity and favourable weather conditions, which resulted in bumper crops, the saving and investment targets were met during the First Plan period of 1951–56. National income registered an increase of 3.4 per cent against the target of 2.1 per cent. The IOCR turned out to be 2.1 against the anticipated 3.0. Because of the initial success, the IOCR estimates were revised downwards to 2.3 for 1956–61 and to 2.6 for 1961–66. These projections proved to be quite low in view of the actually realized ICOR's of 3.0 and 5.5 respectively during the Second and Third Plan periods.[9] At this point, too, the Second Five Year Plan with much larger investment targets, was adopted. Moreover, in the allocation of investment, emphasis was shifted to the development of heavy industry in the IOCR is generally considered to be much higher. The Second Plan at best can be considered a qualified success. In spite of the difficulties of inflationary pressure, mounting deficit in the balance of payments and delay in the execution of key projects experienced during the Second Plan, the Planning Commission did not compromise the long-term objectives laid down in the First and Second Plans in the formulation of the Third Five Year Plan. Instead emphasis was placed on the need for still greater effort to regain the ground lost during 1956–61. Again, during the Third Plan, specially in its last two years, the economy failed to make any headway in raising the savings ratio or in improving the IOCR. National income grew only at 2.5 per cent annually against 5.4 per cent provided in the Third Plan. Coupled with an increase in population of approximately 2.4 per cent this meant an increase in per capita income of only about one-tenth of one per cent. One can blame the poor performance on the two wars with China and Pakistan, in 1962 and 1965 respectively, and on bad weather. However, this does not alter the fact that, measured in terms of crucial economic variables referred to above, the Indian economy failed to make significant progress. This led to a holiday in planning of three years, though the annual plans adopted during 1966–1969 continued to follow the investment strategy laid down in the Fourth Five Year Plan draft. Only the investment target of 14 per cent was fulfilled during the Third Plan. This was made possible

Table 2. Investment, Saving and Foreign Aid in the Indian Economy

(Percentage of Net Domestic Product)

Year	Net investment	Domestic saving	Foreign aid
1960-61	12.0	8.9	3.1
1961-62	10.8	8.6	2.2
1962-63	12.0	9.6	2.4
1963-64	12.7	10.7	2.0
1964-65	12.0	9.8	2.2
1965-66	13.4	11.1	2.3
1966-67	12.2	9.0	3.2
1967-68	10.6	7.9	2.7
1968-69	9.5	8.4	1.1
1969-70	9.2	8.4	0.8
1970-71	9.6	8.3	1.3
1971-72	9.6	8.2	1.4
1973-74 (Planned)	13.1	11.9	1.2

SOURCES: Indian Institute of Public Opinion, *Blue Supplement to the Monthly Commentary of Indian Economic Conditions.* (New Delhi, Vol. XIII, No. 5, December 1971), p. 11.

9 Government of India, Planning Commission, *The First Five Year Plan* (New Delhi, 1952), pp. 20–23.

9 Government of India Planning Commission, *Second Five Year Plan* (New Delhi, 1956), p. 11.

principally because of a large increase in foreign investment listed in Table 2. Domestic savings after touching a high of 11.1 per cent in 1965–66, declined to 7.9 per cent by 1967–68. In 1968–69, during which period the Fourth Five Year Plan was finally adopted, the domestic savings ratio made partial recovery to 8.4 per cent, but it was still below the level attained in 1961–62, the last year of the Second Plan.

According to Professor Rostow, the rate of productive investment must rise from less than 5 per cent to over 10 per cent of net national product for the economy to take off.[10] During the four years between 1968–69 and 1971–72, the net investment fell short of this minimum of 10 per cent. The situation would have been made difficult if foreign aid had not been forthcoming. However, because of India's strained political relations with the U.S., the biggest contributor of foreign aid to India in the past, the flow of foreign aid has declined considerably since 1967–68. It is likely to decline further in the future. Moreover, India in the near future will have to channel considerable amounts of her own resources to aid Bangla Desh. As a result, India will have to rely increasingly on domestic resources for economic development.

After almost two decades of experience in economic planning and the increasing difficulties experienced in their execution since 1962–63, the Fourth Five Year Plan was formulated. Again it was to function in terms of the estimates of IOCR and target saving rates, deemed necessary to make the economy self-reliant, after taking into account the projected population growth rates. The target ratios of net-domestic savings to national income by sectors up to 1980–81 are given in Table 3 above.

Table 3. Target Ratio of Net Domestic Savings to National Income by Sectors : 1968-69 to 1981-82

Sector	1968-69	As a % of Total Saving	1973-74	1980-81	1981-82
1. Household	6.9	75.82	7.6	8.9	8.4
2. Corporation	0.3	3.30	1.1	1.4	1.4
3. Public Saving	1.9	20.88	4.5	6.3	8.2
4. Total domestic Savings	9.1	100.00	13.2	16.6	18.0

SOURCE : *Fourth Five Year Plan*, P. 46.

For achieving the higher savings ratio of 18.8 per cent by 1980–81, a special effort will be required to raise government saving. The success of this measure further depends upon the fulfillment of the following conditions. First, for the realization of government saving of 8.2 per cent, the proportion of taxes to national income must reach approximately 18.5 per cent.[11] Second, the prevalent marginal savings rate of 12 per cent of disposable income must be maintained.[12] Third, the IOCR of 2 during the Fourth Plan and of 2.4 thereafter must be achieved. Fourth, the economy must grow at the postulated rate of 5.5 per cent during the Fourth Plan and at approximately 6.2 per cent after the Fourth Plan.[13]

The long-term projected rate of investment between 18 to 20 per cent, which the Indian planners have upheld so tenaciously, is justifiable, since it exceeds the minimum rate of investment needed to prevent the per capita income from falling in the face of population growth rate of 2.5 per cent at present and 1.7 per cent anticipated for future.[14] If one examines the projected rate on the basis of the feasibility criteria one is likely to come up with widely divergent answers. Theoretically, maximum feasible rate of investment can be considered to involve saving of all income above the subsistence level (though it is difficult to define the level of subsistence in absolute terms). However, in view of the rapid increase in population, the longevity of the life span, and the relatively greater increase in per capita income than the increase in savings

10 W. W. Rostow, *The Stages of Economic Growth* (Combridge : Cambridge University Press, 1963), p. 39.

11 Government of India, Planning Commission, *Fourth Five Year Plan 1969–74* (New Delhi : 1970), p. 47.

12 Ibid., p. 46.

13 Ibid., pp. 30–31.

14 Ibid., p. 31.

during the last two decades, one can safely say that domestic savings thus far generated have fallen considerably short of the maximum feasible. Considering, on the other hand, the political structure of India and the willingness on the part of the different sections of the Indian society to sacrifice voluntarily by abstaining from present consumption in order to assure a higher standard of living in the future, and in view of the past experience, one can say with little hesitation that the savings stipulated in the plan are far in excess of the maximum feasible. Judging from the overall ability of the central and state governments to impose this magnitude of sacrifice by imposing additional taxation and keeping government expenditures from rising, one comes to a similar conclusion. Examining the stipulated rate of investment on the basis of absorptive capacity criterion defined in terms of the availability of natural resources, infrastructure, skilled and unskilled labour one can say that very largely the Indian economy can profitably utilize this level of investment. However, it lacks badly the essential ingredients of devoted and skilled administrators and entrepreneurs.

3. Mobilization of Saving for Capital Formation

For attaining the investment ratio of 18–20 per cent, the Indian planners have laid emphasis on the mobilization of domestic savings. Three essential steps are involved in increasing the rate of capital formation. First, the volume of real savings must increase. This can be accomplished by diverting some of the inputs away from the production of consumption goods or by making greater use of inputs without a corresponding increase in consumption. Second, real savings must be channelled from actual savers to investors with the help of financial intermediaries. Third, investment itself must be encouraged, so that the factors of production are effectively employed to increase the capital stock. In seeking to determine the reasons for India's failure to mobilize savings and to increase the rate of capital formation during the four Five Year Plans, these essential steps in the process of capital formation must be kept in mind. Further, as conditions for generating savings differ in the household, corporate, and government sectors, their study can best be undertaken separately.

Household Sector Savings

The Indian economy places comparatively great reliance on the household sector for saving. In 1968–69 total net domestic saving amounted to 9.1 per cent of the national income. The contribution of household saving to total saving amounted to 75.82 per cent against 3.30 per cent and 20.88 per cent, respectively, by the corporate and public sectors (See Table 3).

Separate saving figures for the rural and urban households are available only up to 1962–63 and are given n Table 4. The rural household savings figure as a percentage of national income between 1951–52 to 1962–63 declined slightly from 1.6 per cent to 1.5 per cent. There is little reason to believe that rural household saving ratio has changed substantially since 1962–63. On the other hand, urban household saving grew from 3.4 per cent in the First Plan to 5.0 per cent during the Second Plan. Between 1967–68 and 1969–70, the household saving stood at 6.8 per cent after reaching the all time high of 8.1 per cent in 1963–64.[15] Because of the general slackening of the economy between 1965–66 and 1966–67 household saving declined to 5.7 per cent in 1966–67. The urban household saving ratio has increased substantially, though in the past it fluctuated considerably. The share of rural household saving, in the total household saving, had declined from 32 per cent during the First Plan to 23.81 per cent between 1961–62 and 1962–63. In general the present household saving and national income ratio in India compares quite favourably with that in developed economies. The United States, for instance had, between 1967–1971 a personal saving to national income ratio of 6.15.[16]

---

[15] Ruddar Datt and Sundaram, *Indian Economy* (New Delhi: S. Chand & Co., 1973), p. 136.

[16] United States Government, *Economic Report of the President: Transmitted to the Congress, January 1973* (Washington, D.C.: 1973), pp. 211, 216.

In the household sector, the number of rural households is proportionately very large, as about 80 per cent of India's population still lives in villages. Between 1951–52 and 1961–62, rural households received slightly less than 50 per cent of the total household income.[17] Relatively more rapid growth of income in large scale manufacturing and mining as compared to the agricultural and allied sectors since 1960–61 has further reduced the share of the rural household sector in the total household income.[18] The income of rural households, therefore, is comparatively low, and the gap between the rural and the urban household incomes is widening.

Table 4. Household Saving as a Percentage of National Income and Total Domestic Saving

	Net domestic saving	House-hold saving	Rural house-hold saving	Urban house-hold saving	Household saving as % of domestic saving	Rural household saving as % of total household saving	Urban household saving as a % of total household saving
First Plan	6.6	5.0	1.6	3.4	75.75	32.00	68.00
Second Plan	8.5	6.6	1.6	5.0	77.65	24.24	75.76
1961-62 to 1962-63	9.5	6.3	1.5	4.8	66.32	23.81	76.19

SOURCES: Kuan-I Chen and J. S. Uppal, *Comparative Development of India and China*, (New York: The Free Press, 1971) pp. 229-241, Reproducing Khathkhate, D. R. and K. L., Deshpande "Estimates of Saving and Investment in the Indian Economy": 1950-51 to 1962-63, *Reserve Bank of India Bulletin* (March 1965) pp. 314-333.

In the rural sector the very rich, who have the greatest capacity to save, get most of their income from rent on land. Traditionally they belong to classes who have had close ties with the governing classes. They are prone to lead a life of luxury and often try to maintain their political influence and social image by spending lavishly on marriages and other social and religious ceremonies. By living frugally, the small landholders and landless labourers may be able to save small amounts in good crop years, but in bad years they are forced to spend more than their income. Over a period of years they are, therefore, unable to generate much of a saving. The very high degree of their indebtedness to the money lenders makes this evident. A very high ratio of defaulted loans to cooperative societies in rural areas further confirms this observation.

Further, most of the income earned by rural households is earned from agriculture or activities closely related to agriculture. Income is generally received in terms of goods and services rather than in cash, and most of the income generated by the household is self consumed. A large portion of the household saving is invested directly by the households in land and buildings, which do not add to productive capacity. Moreover, farmers as well as such rural artisans as cobblers, barbers, weavers, carpenter sand blacksmiths treat their vocation as a way of life rather than as a means of earning a livelihood. As a result, production in the rural sector is rarely organized on business principles. The rural households generally do not understand explicitly the significance of the link between saving and capital formation.

Finally, in the rural sector many transactions are still carried out on the basis of barter. Even when the transactions are carried out in money terms, most of them

[17] Kuan-I Chen and J. S. Uppal, *Comparative Development of India and China* (New York: The Free Press, 1971), p. 239. Figure computed on the basis of the rural and urban household saving figures given as a ratio of national income.

[18] Ibid., *Fourth Five Year Plan*, p. 6.

are carried out on the books of the shopkeeper who also acts as a banker and money lender. It is generally observed that monetization of an economy along with the creation of financial and monetary institutions have a positive influence on the rate of saving. Because of the above features, up to now, the saving generated by the rural households as compared to the urban households has been small. This is especially apparent when such figures are compared to the contribution made by the agricultural sector to total investment during the initial stages of economic development in some of the developed economies of today.

There has been a tendency among the Indian planners and development economists in general to underestimate the actual and potential saving of the rural households, in view of the very low levels of productivity, and in turn to attribute the low levels of saving and investment to it, on the basis of the vicious circles theory of Nurkse. By contrast, the hypothesis relating low investment in agriculture to the constancy of the state of arts or stagnant technology has been given very little attention up to now.[19] This hypothesis seems more plausible in the context of the recent experience in India, especially in the Punjab and other wheat growing areas where the investment and saving picture in the agricultural sector has been radically changed in a matter of a few years, by the green revolution. Even on the basis of the earlier findings of the National Sample Survey and Rural Credit Survey covering the entire country it has been estimated that in case of the agricultural sector the gross saving-income ratio is over 12 per cent, excluding direct investment. Allowing for non-cash saving, and after taking into account repair, maintenance and depreciation, the net cash saving-income ratio works out to be over 8 per cent.[20] This compares quite favorably with the savings in the urban and industrial centres.

Urban households because of their comparatively higher incomes (in contrast with rural households) have a greater potential for saving. Certainly the conditions for the generation of savings and for their mobilization are more favourable in urban areas. The literacy ratio and degree of monetization, for instance, are much greater. The professionals and persons belonging to the capitalist and entrepreneurial classes tend to live in urban areas where there is a greater concentration of business opportunities, and educational and civic amenities. These classes, a great portion of whose income consists of profits and interest, generally tend to save a greater portion at the same levels of income, than the landlords in rural areas.[21] In general, economic development in countries of Western Europe and North America was accompanied by the gradual emergence of a new class of entrepreneurs and a gradual erosion of the political and economic strength of the landed aristocracy. However, higher savings out of profits are unlikely to be generated in India because of the deliberate choice made to create a socialist pattern of society and not to tolerate great concentrations of wealth as well as income. The continued enlargement of the public sector and comparatively higher rates of taxation at a relatively early stage of economic development have also affected adversely the growth of profits and saving out of them in the private sector of the economy.

In urban areas a great preponderance of middle class salaried employees and skilled wage earners are employed by the government and organized industry. They enjoy comparatively high levels of income because the increase in the development rate has generated relatively a greater demand for educated and skilled labour. However, this growing urban middle class is unable to save a large amount of its income because of the pressure felt by them to spend a large proportion of their

---

[19] T. W. Schultz, *Transforming Traditional Agriculture* (New Haven: Yale University Press, 1964), p. 84.

[20] P. G. K. Panikar, *Rural Savings in India* (Bombay: Somaiya Publications Pvt. Ltd., 1970), p. 163.

[21] Lewis, op. cit., p. 226.

income on children's education and on keeping up with the Joneses. The impact of the demonstration effect on their consumption levels is also comparatively great. The income of unskilled labourers is not only close to the subsistence level, but they are unable to save for the same general reasons as farmers in the rural areas.

In view of the democratic nature of Indian society and government, the final choice regarding the extent of saving, through voluntary restraint from consumption, is made by the households. In order to encourage households to save India must, therefore, encourage by propaganda the desire to save. Second, the Indian government must provide incentives to save by providing sufficient returns in real terms on savings. Up to now the returns on savings, especially on small savings, have been very low because of the deliberate policy pursued by the government to keep the interest rates low. A low interest rates policy was considered essential to keep the cost of public debt within reasonable limits and to encourage investment in the private sector. A comparatively high rate of inflation, in the past, however, has rapidly eroded the real value of monetary assets. This has further curtailed returns on savings in real terms. Third, for the mobilization of household saving the government must provide conveniently located facilities for the banking of savings. The service at these facilities should be prompt and courteous.

Even before the start of economic planning the government of India was aware of this problem. This awareness grew further as it was forced to mobilize greater amounts of household savings for financing capital projects within the public sector. The central and state government draft on private savings was originally estimated at Rs. 5,695 crores, representing almost 43.64 per cent of the total estimated savings of the private sector during the Fourth Plan. In the Fourth Plan mid-term appraisal it was raised to Rs. 6,732 crores.[22] In order to meet this need a vast network of organizations consisting of primary co-operative societies, district and central co-operative banks, land mortgage banks, post office savings banks commercial joint stock banks, industrial and agricultural finance and development corporations, the State Bank of India (till June 30, 1955, the Imperial Bank of India), Agricultural Refinance Corporation (A.R.C.), Industrial Finance Corporation, State Finance Corporations, National Industrial Development Corporation, Industrial Development Bank of India, and Investment trusts and Unit-trusts have been created. The role of the Reserve Bank of India, which sits at the apex of these banking and financial institutions to meet their need for financing, supervision, and training of personnel, has grown with the passage of each year. In harnessing small savings the government further depends on the National Life Insurance Corporation of India and provident and pension funds both in the private as well as in the public sector. After the nationalization of the fourteen big commercial banks in July 1969, new branches (especially in rural areas) have been opened at an unprecedented pace.[23] As a result in 1970–71 (July–June) bank deposits increased by 17 per cent.[24] The quality of service at the financial and banking institutions, however, has deteriorated after nationalization, however, because of an increase in red tape.

The institutional arrangements to harness the potential growth in agricultural income into saving and investment have been created, but these are still highly inadequate and inefficient. The basic weakness of the cooperative credit system is the non-viability of a large number of primary agricultural societies because of inefficiency and poor book-keeping. These deficiencies can be ascribed partly to lack of education on the part of members and partly to lack of honest, well-trained, and devoted administrators. Inspite of the programmes of rationalization and consolidation which resulted in the decline in

22 *The Fourth Plan, Mid Term Appraisal,* op. cit., p. 29.

23 Ibid., p. 35.
24 Ibid.

the number of primary agricultural credit societies from 212,000 to 171,800 between 1960–61 and 1967–68, the situation has not improved much. The Fourth Five Year Plan estimates were that further reorganization, leading to consolidation and amalgamation would leave only 120,000 potentially viable societies in operation.[25] However, it seems that, like the many previous attempts to reform the cooperative societies, the present attempts to rationalize them are not succeeding. According to the information recently made available by the Reserve Bank of India, the overdues in case of primary agricultural credit societies have risen substantially between 1969–70 (July–June). An enormous amount of mismanagement and inefficiency also exists in the district and central cooperative banks.

Comparatively speaking, the situation in urban areas (where household savings are mainly channelled for industrial development through the joint stock commercial banks, post-office savings banks, investment and unit trusts, etc.) is much better because of greater literacy, better maintenance of records, less participation in management of local interests, and comparative absence of political pressure. However, here too the situation has been slowly deteriorating and on the basis of very sketchy and partial evidence available so far the nationalization of the large commercial banks has not helped the situation as much as initially expected.

In spite of the above shortcomings, the household savings have continued to grow and have provided the needed financing of investment in the public as well as the corporate sectors of the economy. The increasingly greater emphasis on the more equitable distribution of wealth and income is likely to adversely effect household savings, because in general the propensity to consume among lower income brackets is comparatively higher.

Corporate Saving

Economic development is made possible by the rapid expansion of the capitalist sector at the expense of the subsistence sector. The capitalist sector which can be private, public, or partly private and partly public, employs reproducible capital and wage labour for profit making. Capitalists have been distinguished from other classes by their passion for saving and productive investment. Along with the growth of the capitalist sector the corporate form of business organization emerged, without which it would have been difficult to raise and accumulate capital needed for large-scale production. Well before the Second World War, the privately owned corporations started generating a larger and larger proportion of saving internally by retaining a greater and greater percentage of their growing profits to finance investment in the free market economies. For instance, in the United States during the nineteen sixties corporate saving accounted for roughly 8.83 per cent of the national income.[26] In the Soviet Union and other communist countries, on the contrary, the ownership of the means of production as well as the responsibility to generate saving has been vested in the hands of the state.

In India the government, in line with its objective of establishing a socialist pattern of society, based on equitable distribution of income and wealth, has assumed the major responsibility for the development of the capitalist sector. Under the Industrial Policy Resolution of 1956,[27] the private sector has been given a minor but an important role in enlarging the capitalist sector. With the passage of time, as a result of the nationalization of insurance companies and large commercial banks, the passage of the Monopolies and Restrictive Trade Policies Act of 1969, the Industrial Licensing Policy of 1970, and the new Industrial Policy announced on February 2, 1973, the role of the private sector has been limited further. In view of this, the private corpo-

[25] *Fourth Five Year Plan*, op. cit., p. 217.

[26] *Economic Report of the President: 1973*, op. cit., p. 211. The saving figure has been computed on the basis of corporate profits and inventory valuation adjustment minus dividend figures for 1960–69.

[27] *Second Five Year Plan*, op. cit., pp. 43–50.

rate sector is unlikely to play the same role in the expansion of the capitalist sector and the generation of saving, as has been played traditionally by the corporate sector in the free enterprise developing economies. The raising of equity capital for expansion, because of the nationalization of large commercial banks and insurance companies and the increase in the public sector draft on private savings, has become more difficult. In spite of the above limitations the corporate sector has registered a considerable growth since 1955–56, as indicated by the increase in the paid up capital of the joint stock companies from Rs. 1,024.02 crores in 1955–56 to Rs. 3,565.67 crores in 1968–69. The actual number of joint stock companies, however, declined from 29,874 in 1955–56 to 27,828 in 1968–69.

Because of the relative smallness of the corporate sector of the Indian economy its share in the national saving has been small. During the First Plan period it amounted to 0.5 per cent of national income and constituted 8 per cent of the total domestic saving. It declined slightly during the Second Plan but in 1963–64 reached a peak of 0.8 per cent of national income, representing 6.9 per cent of total saving. Thereafter, it declined sharply and in 1967–68 amounted to only 0.2 per cent of national income, representing 3.1 per cent of total saving. By 1969–70 it had increased again to 0.4 per cent of national income constituting 5.0 per cent of the total saving. This lack in growth of the share of corporate saving to total saving and as a percentage of national income can mainly be attributed to the relatively faster growth of the public and non-corporate sectors (mainly representing agriculture and small scale industry) of the Indian economy. Some of the other important reasons which have adversely affected the growth of corporate savings are discussed below.

The ability of the corporate sector to generate profits, in a developing economy, is directly related to its ability to pay wages close to the subsistence wage. This is made possible because of the presence of a large pool of unemployed labour in the subsistence sector. In India the capitalist sector has been unable to take full advantage of the situation because of the development of strong and well organized labour unions, comparatively early on the road to economic development. Under strong labour union pressure the wage-price ratio instead of remaining close to the subsistence level has risen sharply. Corporate profits have, therefore, faild to increase proportionally to the increase in output caused by the increase in employment in the corporate sector.

The corporate income tax rates in India possess a certain degree of progressivity as corporations are taxed at different rates according to their class (distinction is made on the basis of ownership private or public and foreign or domestic), the priority being given to various industries on the basis of their significance in economic development and size. The surtax imposed on corporate profits as a super profits tax since 1964 along with the penal tax (levied on closely held companies, with the intention of checking tax evasion by the rich through company formations) add further to the progressive nature of the corporate income tax. Justification of a progressive tax is generally based on the principle of ability to pay but the principle is considered to be relevant only in case of individuals. In case of corporate income tax the progressiveness of the tax simply penalizes efficiency, especially where the extent of corporate profits is determined by relative efficiency rather than on the monopoly power exercised. It is very difficult to measure the direction and the extent to which the incidence of the corporate income tax is shifted, since the results of the studies made in this connection differ widely.[28] However, to the extent corporate income tax has affected retentions, corporate saving has been adversely effected.

In view of the above difficulties and on the basis of the past experience it can be safely concluded that the target of 1.1 per cent of national income for corporate saving, laid down in the Fourth Plan for

28 Ved P. Gandhi, *Some Aspects of India's Tax Structure: An Economic Analysis* (Bombay: Vora & Co., 1970), p. 141.

1973–74, is not likely to be reached. For the achievement of the target corporate saving, some substantial changes in the over all role assigned to the private sector in the Indian economy will have to be made. Even major tax concessions by way of tax holiday in case of certain types of new investment-projects, larger depreciation allowances, and more favourable treatment given to export industries, as made in the past, are not likely to affect the corporate saving in a significant manner.

Government Saving

In view of the general inadequacy of the household and corporate savings to meet the needs of rapid growth in capital formation the economic planners in India have acknowledged, from the beginning, the urgent necessity of enlarging public saving. The basic weakness in this connection has been that the government sector has very few resources of its own, by way of surpluses, to finance investment. Public saving, like individual saving, depends upon the relative levels of revenues and expenditures. Public saving can be increased therefore, only by widening the gap between government revenues and government expenditures. Government income can be increased by either raising the ratio of tax revenue to national income or by increasing the income of the factors of production owned by the government. Government expenditures can be lowered by reducing government consumption expenditures or by curtailing government subsidies, paid to the private sector.

In 1950–51, the ratio of tax revenue to national income was 6.6 per cent. Between 1951–52 and 1965–66, it rose rapidly and reached a peak of 14.2 per cent in 1965–66, the last year of the Third Plan. In spite of their rapid increase, the tax ratio in India amounted to about half to one third of the developed economies and remained considerably below the tax ratios of some developing economies.[29] By 1967–68, because of the general slowing down of the Indian economy after 1965–66, it had declined to 12.2 per cent. With resumption of economic growth after 1967–68 it had again increased to 12.8 per cent by 1970–71. However, because of the simultaneous increase in government consumption since 1951–52, government saving during the four years between 1966–67 and 1969–70 remained at 1.5 per cent, the level attained between 1951–52 and 1955–56. This means that the government saving to finance development expenditures can be effectively increased by almost 100 per cent if the tax ratio of 14.2 per cent, attained in 1965–66 is reached again, without a corresponding increase in government consumption expenditures. Because of the growth in national and per-capita income (even though quite small) this should not be difficult.

The income elasticity of taxes as a whole, between 1953–55 and 1966–68, in case of India was 2.4.[30] This meant that every increase of 1 per cent in national income resulted in a 2.4 per cent increase, on the average, in tax revenues. High income elasticity of taxes, as a whole, causes the tax ratio to increase as income goes up. It can, therefore, be considered as a reasonably good indicator of the effort being made to raise the tax ratio. The high income elasticity of taxes in case of India and the success achieved in raising the tax ratio can be attributed to the following factors. First, both the individual and corporate income taxes have been made increasingly progressive. This has meant that as individual and corporate incomes have risen, a relatively greater proportion has been paid in taxes. The progressive nature of direct taxes and high

---

29 Raja C. Chelliah, "Trends in Taxation in Developing Countries," *I.M.F. Staff Papers*, Vol. XVII, No. 2, (July 1971), pp. 302–303. Also see Jorgen R. Lotz and Morss Elliott, "Measuring 'Tax Effort' in Developing Countries," *I.M.F. Staff Papers*, Vol. XIV, No. 3 (November 1967), p. 479.

30 Ibid., p. 265. Income elasticity of taxes $= \frac{\Delta T}{T} \div \frac{\Delta Y}{Y}$, where T and Y stand for taxes and gross national product. Income elasticity of taxes at 2.4 in case of India was the highest among the 27 developing countries considered by Prof. Chelliah.

income elasticity of taxes in general in India also has been mainly responsible for the drop in the tax ratio after 1965–66. Second, during the last two decades new taxes have been levied and the existing taxes have been increased or made more progressive. Third, the tax structure has been changed to incorporate more taxes on production and internal transactions with high income elasticity.[31] In spite of this considerable increase in the tax ratio since 1950–51, among the underdeveloped countries, the Indian tax effort to raise revenues during the last two decades is ranked about average.[32]

There are a number of reasons for the present low tax ratio in case of India and for the problems encountered in trying to raise it. Perhaps the most important of these is the low per capita income in India, even as compared to the most developing economies. Among the democratic countries, where the choice to abstain from consumption is made voluntarily, much greater emphasis has been placed by India on the equitable distribution of income and wealth. This commitment to establish a socialistic pattern of society has resulted in a great reluctance to tax directly a very large proportion of the population at the lower end of the income distribution.[33] The lower income classes also escape largely the payment of indirect taxes, since necessities, on which most of their income is spent, are generally exempt from such taxes. However, in the case of India where a vast majority of the people live in abject poverty it is futile to expect a very small sprinkling of the rich and middle income people to generate enough saving (forced or voluntary) for capital formation. In case of the poor, because of their low income, rising aspirations and the operation of the demonstration effect, the propensity to consume is almost equal to 1. It is, therefore, imperative for the success of the saving effort to force, by the imposition of taxes, a large number of people in low income brackets to save. Usually it is easier to tax exports and imports. However, because of the sheer size of the Indian economy, its dependence on foreign trade is comparatively small. India's annual imports and exports constitute only about 10 per cent of the gross domestic product. In spite of this relatively less openness of the Indian economy taxes on international trade between 1953 to 1955 and 1966 to 1968 generated 25 per cent and 17.8 per cent, respectively, of the total tax revenues.[34] The comparatively low literacy and monetization ratios along with the lack of efficient tax administration no doubt make the task of raising tax revenues more difficult.[35]

The agricultural sector relatively to the mining and manufacturing sector in India is large in comparison to the developed economies.[36] Low levels of literacy, monetization and incomes among the agriculturists make the taxing of agricultural sector very difficult. Agricultural incomes, therefore, remain lightly taxed. Relatively more rapid growth of the agricultural sector and other lightly taxed sectors of the Indian economy has been

31 Ibid. Between 1953–55 and 1966–68 income elasticity of major categories of taxes according to Professor Chelliah were: Income taxes 1.7, taxes on production and internal transactions 4.1, import taxes 1.8 and taxes on international trade 1.5.

32 Lotz, op. cit., pp. 494–495. Also see, Roy W. Bahl, "A Regression Approach to Tax Ezort and Tax Rotio Analysis," *I.M.F. Staff Papers,* Vol. XVII, No. 3, (November 1971), p. 596. Among 52 countries considered by Lotz and Morss, India was ranked 21 and was grouped among averaye tax effort countries after taking into account the difference in the per capita vross national product and exports and imports. In terms of taxable capacity India was ranked 41 among the 49 countries considered by Bahl.

33 In 1963–64 less than a million persons paid income tax. Because of the consistently declining effective tax ratio for the low and middle income classes and a simultaneous shift in the (pre tax) income distribution in their favour, the averabe burden of income tax has declined since 1950–51. See Gandhi, op. cit., p. 29.

34 Chelliah, op. cit., p. 270.

35 Because of the laxity of tax administration, the tax arrears if those tax payers owing Rs. one million or more alone totalled to Rs. 890 million on December 1, 1968, Ibid., p. 31.

36 Empirical studies point out that the share of agricultural income has a significant negative correlation to the tax ratio whereas the mining and manufacturing incomes bear a significant positive correlation to tax ratio. Bahl, op. cit., p. 605.

partly responsible for the comparative drop in the over all tax ratio since 1965–66.[37]

The taxing of agricultural incomes is made more difficult because the power to tax agricultural incomes is given to the states under the constitution of India. Most of the states, including those where the argricultural productivity and incomes have risen sharply because of the adoption of the green revolution technology, are reluctant to tax agricultural incomes for political reasons. A majority of the states, therefore, have no or very low agricultural income tax. The incidence of agricultural income tax has, in fact, always been less than a rupee per hectare.[38] The agriculturists also largely escape the burden of indirect taxes as a large proportion of the consumption of agricultural households consist of their own produce. The tax contribution of the agricultural sector, up to now, has not only been small, but since 1950–51 the intersectoral inequity in tax burdens has further increased in favour of the agricultural sector.[39]

The government of India, over the last two decades, has been consistently pursuing the policy of expanding the public sector in order to raise the income of government owned factors of production. As a result of this emphasis on investment in the public sector, its share in reproducible tangible wealth has increased steadily.[40] Roughly, over half of the actual outlay in the public sector in the past has been made in large scale capital intensive industrial projects, as they have been considered to generate large surpluses for future investment. Nevertheless, the public sector's contribution to total saving has remained disappointingly small.[41]

Public consumption expenditures and the subsidies paid to the private sector, on the other hand, have risen more rapidly than anticipated. This has been mainly due to the rapid rise in prices since 1950–51. The long term increase in prices has been caused in part by the large annual budgetary deficits under-taken to meet the investment targets and in part by the failure to achieve the planned increase in gross national product based on the estimates of capital-output ratio. Concern over employment, especially among the university-educated white collar workers in urban areas, has resulted in unreasonable expansion of employment in the public sector. There has been also a rapid increase in the health, education, sanitary, and welfare and relief services rendered by the government. Defense expenditures have increased rapidly, especially since 1962, due to the difficulties with China and Pakistan. Besides, the need for relief to Bangla Desh, since its creation, has further strained the budgetry resources.

The increase in public consumption expenditures in the past may have been

[37] *The Fourth Plan: Mid-Term Appraisal,* op. cit., pp. 11, 25. During the first two years of the Fourth Plan, 52 per cent of the additions to real national income accrued to the agricultural sector. The share of national income accruing to agriculture, measured in current prices, has been still greater, because of the above average increase in agricultural prices since 1960–61.

[38] Gandhi, op. cit., p. 141.

[39] Ibid., pp. 131–137. In 1952–53, in the income bracket of Rs. 1,200 to Rs. 1,800 urban households paid 5 per cent of their income in taxes against 3.2 per cent paid by the rural households and in the income bracket of Rs. 1,800 to Rs. 3,600 the taxes paid by them amounted to 5 per cent and 3.6 respectively. Due to the increased importance in the Indian tax structure of the indirect taxes, which fall primarily on the monetized urban consumption, it is felt that relatively the burden of taxes on rural incomes has further declined.

[40] In 1965–66, 35 per cent of the entire reproducible wealth was owned by the public sector and was estimated to rise to 43 per cent as a result of the implementation of the Fourth Plan. Please see Planning Commission, Government of India, *Fourth Five Year Plan: A Draft Outline* (New Delhi: August 1966), p. 42.

[41] In the Second and Third Five Year Plans the contribution of public enterprises to public saving consistently fell short of the original estimates by wide margins. In the Fourth Five Year Plan the contribution of public enterprises to public saving, according to the revised estimates, is likely to amount only to Rs. 829 crores against the original estimates of Rs. 1271 crores. This represents a drop of 34.78 per cent. Please see Planning Commission, Government of India, *Fourth Five Year Plan 1969–74, Draft,* p. 78 and the *Fourth Plan: Mid-Term Appraisal,* p. 17.

justified and even unavoidable; nevertheless, this does not negate the fact that, in spite of the considerable increase in the share of the public sector in national income and reproducible tangible wealth, its relative contribution to national saving has not increased significantly. Unless this trend is reversed, any additions in government revenues will only replace private consumption by public consumption and will adversely affect private saving. The greater emphasis placed on the utilization of economic policy to attain more equitable personal and regional distribution of income and wealth in general in order to eliminate poverty (Gharibi Hatao) in the Draft Fifth Five Year Plan (1974–79) is likely to make it more difficult to check the rise in public consumption expenditures.

4. Conclusion

Increase in saving ratio is a necessary condition for more rapid capital formation. In free enterprise economies the necessary incentive for saving and the mobilization and investment of savings have been primarily provided by the opportunity to make profits and to get rich. In communist countries, on the other hand, people have been forced to forego present consumption in order to meet the investment needs of the economy to grow. Acknowledging the need for investment, as well as realizing the improbability of its being realized purely through market mechanism, India has been trying to raise the rate of investment by following a middle of the road policy. In order to preserve the democratic nature of the society and the right to property (within broadly accepted limits) the decision to save has been left primarily with individual households. However, the responsibility to invest has been increasingly shifted to the public sector. An important justification given for enlarging the size of public sector investment has been that increase in the relative size of the public sector will in time lead to an increase in its share of total saving. Besides, public saving adds to the collective wealth and income of the community (which will grow further with every successive round of saving and investment) considered essential for building a society based on a socialistic pattern.

In spite of the failure to achieve planned targets, considerable progress has been made in raising the level of saving. Between 1951–52 and 1963–64 net domestic saving to national income ratio increased from 6.5 per cent to 12 per cent. By 1967–68, it had nosedived to 8 per cent. This reversal in trend was caused primarily by a sharp decline in government saving from a high of slightly over 3 per cent in 1963–64 to a low of 1 per cent in 1967–68. Since 1967–68 the net domestic saving ratio has resumed its upward trend, though it is still considerably below the level achieved in 1963–64.

Household saving has grown considerably, in the face of almost insurmountable difficulties posed by low levels of income, education, and monetization. This has been made possible through education and infusion of national fervour by the adoption of plans and plan targets, as a result of which perhaps an average household has become more conscious of the fact that the saving habit is not only a personal virtue, but also helps in strengthening the national economy by making investment possible. A network of financial and monetary institutions for the mobilization of household saving has created. The effectiveness and efficiency of these institutions, however, still leaves much to be desired. In the past the returns on household saving in real terms have been very modest because of the government policy to keep interest rates low and the rapid decline in the real value of the monetary assets due to inflation. Returns in real terms on household saving, therefore, need improvement.

Corporate saving in India, unlike the corporate saving in free enterprise economies, is likely to remain relatively small because of the limited role assigned to the private sector under the industrial policy adopted by India. Progressivity of corporate income tax has discouraged efficiency and the presence of strong labour unions have adversely affected the corporate sectors ability to make profits. Inspite of the serious limitations placed on the sphere of activity of private sector and the mushrooming of government red tape, which private sector has to confront on a day to day basis in conforming to government regulations, the performance of the private corporate sector up to now has been remarkable. This fact along with the importance of profit motive and individual initiative, considered essential for economic development under democratic set up, needs greater recognition.

The main cause for India's inability to attain the target saving ratio, in the past, has been the incapacity of the public sector to generate adequate saving. As far as raising of the public sector's income is concerned India has been fairly successful. The ratio of tax revenues to gross national product has almost been doubled. In tapping private sector saving for public sector investment, the government has been increasingly successful as evidenced by the rapid growth in the public sector draft on private saving. The share of the public sector in the reproducible tangible wealth of the country has increased rapidly. Besides, the contribution of the public sector enterprises to gross national product has increased. Nonetheless, because of the increase in public sector consumption, delays and high cost of building public sector projects and their inefficient operation, the government sector has so far failed to generate necessary savings. The flow of foreign aid, which had largely enabled India to bridge the gap between investment targets and domestic saving in the past, has declined sharply and the outlook regarding the future flow of foreign aid remains bleak. The need to make the economy self-reliant has therefore become more urgent. The responsibility of meeting the challenge to generate sufficient savings to match investment targets has increasingly come to rest with the public sector, because of the rapid increase in its relative importance in the economy. The provision for rapidly increasing the public saving from 1.9 per cent in 1968–69 to 4.5 per cent of the national income in 1973–74, in the Fourth Plan, was a clear recognition of this responsibility of the public sector by the Planning Commission. In spite of this correct reading of the situation at the beginning of the Fourth Plan, very little progress has been made up to now in raising the government saving. As a result the crisis of saving, which has existed for so long, remains unabated in the Indian economy.

17

Indian Banking System

KRISHAN A. CHOPRA

1. The Economic Role of Banks

Keynes said that the history of money was the history of civilization. One could add that the role of money would have been insignificant without the institution of banks. With the passage of time money became more and more a debt instrument (as currency became token money and the role of demand deposits increased), and thus became intimately connected with the banks—the dealers in debt. There are many species of dealers in debt but the commercial banks have a special role. "The commercial banks are the only private dealers in debt whose own debts are generally accepted as a means of payment."[1]

No economy can be viable without a well developed banking system. The banks receive deposits from those who save and lend money to those who need it. Both these functions, when properly performed, lead to more productive use of national resources. In the former case, the banks mobilize monetary resources, while in the latter, they distribute these between different uses that can help adding to the real capital of the nation. Further, when banks make advances, they add to effective purchasing power. This is because when a bank makes an advance, by allowing its customers to overdraw his account, the bank in effect exchanges its own promise to pay immediately against the customer's promise to pay off the advance later on.[2] Through this exchange of promises between the bank and the borrower the aggregate liquidity increases in the economy.

Banks also affect the aggregate demand in the economy throhgh inflnencing sectoral demand functions like investment by manipulating interest rates. Such a role gives banks strategic importance in affecting such vital variables as national income and employment. There is no doubt, therefore, that the more advanced and developed a country is, the more advanced and sophisticated is its banking system.

The present paper is divided in three parts. The first part encompasses a theoretical discussion of the role of banks in underdeveloped economies. On this as premise, the second part, dealing with the

[1] Hart, Kenen and Entine, *Money, Debt and Economic Activity*, p. 21.

[2] Sayers, *Modern Banking*, p. 3.

Indian banking system and its constituents, is structured. The third part is devoted to the evaluation of the role of Indian banking in the light of the theoretical issues discussed earlier.

Banks and Underdeveloped Economies

The role of banks in the development of underdeveloped economies has come into prominence specially in the post 1945 period since when most of these countries have become free from foreign rule, and have embarked on national economic policies for planned economic growth. The banking system, however, as it exists in these countries, is organizationally different from the integrated structure of banking institutions characteristic of the West. Comparable banks do exist but they are "expatriate banks,"[3] operating in selected industrial and/or trading centres. Mostly, the banking activities are carried on by small and isolated indigenous banks.

In these countries a large part of the economy is non-monetized where some sort of barter system prevails. With the minimal use of money exchange, the role of banks is negligible. Further, even in the monetized sector the use of cash is predominant and "there is a concentration of much of the total deposits in a few groups of large customers,"[4] thus inhibiting the role of banks. Again, these countries do not have a well-developed capital market active in long term loans, nor do they have a money market providing short-term loans. The absence of capital markets in these countries has led to distorted investment patterns seen in the wealth of the richer people being confined to real estate, precious metals and jewellry. Investment in shares of commercial and industrial firms is limited which indirectly constrains the role of banks. Further, the size of business in these countries is small. Most of the firms operate on small and cottage scale. Such firms are not a sound credit risk. The role of banks in their financing is thus limited.

Occupational structure of underdeveloped economies shows that almost all of these are predominantly agricultural and in most of them cultivation is done on small, fragmented pieces of land. The farms are generally family farms and are cultivated on subsistence level. In most of these countries agriculture depends on capricious rainfall and thus a good harvest is a gamble. Majority of the farmers use old and antiquated farm equipment which makes land productivity quite low. The role of institutional finance, in the absence of sound credit-worthiness of the farmer, is thus only a limited one. Rural finance is mostly non-institutional and the farmer turns to the money-lender or the indigenous banker whose usurious interest rates keep him in perpetual indebtedness. It is a common saying that the farmer in these countries is born in debt, lives in debt, dies in debt and bequeathes debt.

The central banks in underdeveloped countries were mostly established either during the interwar period (in Latin America), after World War II (in South and East Asia), or in the 1960's (in newly independent countries in Africa). "The establishment of these central banks was generally aimed at promoting price and exchange stability, full employment, economic development and growth, and the development of the banking structure."[5] They differ from central banks of developed economies in their control operations. Due to narrow scope of the financial mechanism, these banks, unlike advanced central banks, cannot rely on the general control instruments but have to adopt traditional central banking instruments and practices in the light of the circumstances in which they are placed. They have also to develop different techniques to deal with the particular problems of the underdeveloped economies.[6]

The special institutional and structural circumstances obtaining in these economies constrain the scope of central banking. As pointed out earlier, in most of these economies the use of money is large-

[3] Ibid., p. 29.
[4] Ibid., p. 29.

[5] Chung, *Money, Banking, and Income—Theory and Policy*, p. 291.
[6] Ibid.

ly confined to non-rural sectors. Even in urban and semi-urban sectors the use of credit is limited. This is principally the result of low development of banking habits and inadequate banking facilities. Further, the organized money market is undeveloped with limited availability of credit instruments like commercial bills of exchange, short term government securities, banker's acceptances, etc. Due to loose discount markets the central banks have poor contact with the commercial banks. The unorganized money market represented by money lenders, indigenous bankers, etc., is completely outside the sphere of central banking influence. Yet a preponderatingly large part of the money market is controlled by these non-institutional financiers. The money lenders operate with their own funds and seldom come in touch with the commercial banks. This leads to the non-existence of any contact between the organized money market (represented by commercial banks) and the unorganized money market (represented by money lenders and indigenous bankers).

Often, the central banks are handicapped in their control on commercial banks when the latter are self-sufficient and have no need for advance or rediscounting facilities. This is particularly the case in countries with many foreign banks which, in time of tight credit, call on their head offices in foreign money centres to obtain additional reserves for credit expansion instead of depending on local central banks for accommodation.[7]

These countries have a low propensity to save (because of low national income and high propensity to consume) and a general apathy to investments in bonds and shares. This coupled with inadequate institutional facilities, has limited the growth of capital markets and consequently limited central banking influence on long-term investments, income and employment.[8]

Banking and Economic Development

In spite of the fact that the role of commercial banks as well as central banks is restrained in the underdeveloped countries, it is, nonetheless, true that banks are and have been a necessary adjunct to the growth effort in these countries. Banks played a noticeable role in the development phases of developed nations and are presently a crucial factor in the growth of developing economies.

A look at the history of economic development of the presently developed countries shows that during their process of growth these countries successfully changed both economic and non-economic parameters (like tastes, technology, and institutions) into variables. Further, in this process, which involved interaction among various factors, the role of institutions has been very important. For instance, social institutions hindered or facilitated technological invocation, resource mobilization and capital formation. One such institution which played a strategic role in accelerating economic growth was modern banking system.

Schumpeter in *The Theory of Economic Development* (*1933*) regarded banking system and entrepreneurship as the two key factors in the process of development. Some modern economists have disputed the "all pervasive" role of banks, but, nonetheless, no one has denied the role of the banking system as one of important institutions influencing economic development.

Rondo Cameron[10] has pointed out that as an economic institution the banking system might be expected to be more directly and more positively related to the performance of the economy than most non-economic institutions. Such non-economic institutions as government, religious institutions, the education system, ethics and aesthetics influence the operation of the banking system. Thus the banking system is the prime mover in accelerating economic development, while the non-

[7] Ibid., p. 293.

[8] Ibid.

[9] J. G. Gurley is one of them. He points out that the role of banking systems as intermediaries in the economic development of many socialist countries as well as Taiwan, Israel, and Venezuela has been minimal.

[10] Rondo, Cameron, *Banking and Economic Development*, p. 7.

economic institutions act as catalysts or dampers depending on their contribution to the growth process.

Alexander Gerschenkron's[11] writings on the role of banking in the historical process of industrialization are among recent authoritative works in the field; they establish that the greater the backwardness in the economy the greater is the role of special institutional factors designed to increase capital supply to incipient industries and provide entrepreneurial guidance. Gerschenkron made a special study of three countries with respect to capital and entrepreneurship. These countries were England, Germany and Russia in descending order of industrial backwardness. While England started to industrialize from a small-scale level her needs for capital and entrepreneurial guidance were minimal in the initial stages. Growth took place here basically by means of reinvestment. The role of banks in England was not crucial. In the case of Germany things were different. At the time she started to industrialize and develop economically the optimum size of plant was larger requiring comparatively much larger investments. "As a result the banking system became the prime source of both capital and entrepreneurship."[12] In Russia, where the level of industrial backwardness was the highest, the banking system in conjunction with the imperial government played a major role in initiating industrial growth in the last quarter of the nineteenth century.[13] Rondo Cameron, in his studies, however, pointed out that the role of banks in England was not that poor. He said that the law of the land at that time constrained banks from making long-term investments. "Even so, there were numerous instances in which banks made long-term commitments to industrial enterprises; indeed, banks were often founded by industrialists for precisely that purpose."[14] Rondo Cameron further pointed out that the country banks in England played a vital role in the process of reinvestment by enabling the manufacturers to economize on working capital and thus allowing them to plow back earnings into fixed capital.[15]

Case Studies of the Role of Banks in Economic Development of Countries

Case studies of certain countries in Europe and in the United States further underscore the important role of banking system in the process of industrial growth. Richard Rudolph in his study of Austria (1800–1914) researched the role of banks within the overall process of economic development in the country.[1] The joint stocks investment or promotional banking played a less important role in Austria compared to Germany where the banking system developed simultaneously with Austria. Comparatively limited role of the banking system in Austria has been explained by the protectionist policies consistently followed in the cuontry and also by the *limited domestic market*.[17] Banks, however, did play a role in stepping up the economy. Particularly from the 1890's the banks established strong ties with industry. There was a broad extension of a branch network of banks which played an important role in mobilization and provision of short-term credit for a number of industrial firms. The banks played a notable role in financing coal-mining, metallurgy and sugar industries. The banks also many a time undertook commission sales of a number of industries.

The author feels that the Austrian banks would have fared better in their role in industrialization if they were not structurally constrained (the government made certain loans more reliable by fiat).[18]

John S. Cohen in his study of the role of banking in the industrial growth of Italy[19] found that the new industrial credit banks were established in 1894. From 1898 the Italian industry recorded a big spurt which continued till 1913 (the last

[11] *Economic Backwardness in Historical Perspective: A Book of Essays.*

[12] Rondo Cameron, op. cit., p. 11.

[13] Ibid.

[14] Ibid., p. 12.

[15] Ibid.. p. 12.

[16] Ibid., Chapter II, "Austria 1800–1914."

[17] Ibid., p. 17.

[18] Ibid.

[19] Ibid., Chapter III, "Italy 1861–1914."

year of his study). The banks were able to have as high as 40 per cent of their assets used for industrial and commercial needs. Credit was provided through loans, security purchases or advances on uninsured equity. Banks helped firms convert themselves into joint stock companies, provided technical advice on new technology and often played an entrepreneurial role in organizing a group to form a new company under their auspices.[20] The main impetus for the banking system to assist industries came from the Bank of Italy in its chief role as the lender of the last resort in 1894. This reduced the danger of holding portfolios containing a large percentage of non-liquid industrial assets.[21]

Gabriel Tortella's research on the developmental role of banks in Spain[22] shows the important role of banks in the industrial growth of the country. Professor Tortella, however, asserts that much greater and speedier industrialization could have been possible if there were a larger number of small local banks catering to local commerce and industry than the few large banks operating from Madrid. Moreover, had the funds not been diverted from manufacturing and industry to railroad construction (a project backed by the government) the industrial growth of the state would have been far quicker. The banks were thus the victims of structural constraints placed by the government.

In his study of Serbia John R. Lampe[23] found an apparent correlation between the growth of banking system and industrial growth. However, the banking system could not operate at optimal efficiency due to such structural problems as shortage of human capital at the managerial or the entrepreneurial level and throughout the labour force.[24] Similarly, the privileged position of the government in the capital market, and its penchant for unproductive expenditures retarded active contribution of banks to industrial development.[25]

Kozo Yamamura's research[26] on Japanese industrial growth between 1868 and 1930 shows that the modern banking system, strongly encouraged by the government, was extremely important in providing the necessary capital and, wherever necessary, entrepreneurial guidance. To begin with, between 1885 and 1905—when the "spurt" occurred, the banks gave short-term loans to a small select group of firms mainly confined to mining, ship building and other industries. Later. since the end of the First World War and particularly during the 1920's, the banks reached a more diversified clientele and offered long-term loans to such unrelated industries as metallurgy, chemicals and utilities. It is pointed out that in the early period the banks followed the English practice of short-term commercial lending to established enterprises and since the early 1920's they engaged in the German type of universal banking.

Professor Green's study[27] of banking and economic development of the U.S.A. (particularly in Louisiana) shows the positive contribution of banks to the economic welfare of the state's citizens. Bank Finance was not merely a passive or permissive factor in the growth of New Orleans and its hinterland; instead "financial growth was an independent cause, an active contributor to more rapid real economic growth."[28]

In the case of the United States as a whole Professor Sylla[29] demonstrates that from Civil War to World War I, the National Banking System was biased in favour of the industrial sector of the economy.[30] The banking system promoted industrialization and specially encouraged the growth of the North-Eastern States.

An appraisal of the role of banks in the industrial and economic growth of countries in their developing stage as seen above shows that banks do wield influence on economic development. "Where they exist, they do so because there is a demand

---

20 Ibid.
21 Ibid.
22 Ibid., Chapter IV, "Spain, 1829–1874."
23 Ibid., Chapter V, "Serbia, 1878–1912."
24 Ibid., p. 20.
25 Ibid., p. 21.

26 Ibid., Chapter VI.
27 Ibid., Chapter VII.
28 Ibid., p. 22.
29 Ibid., Chapter VIII.
30 Ibid., p. 23. The bias in favour of the industrial sector is obvious because growth in this sector took place, in part, at the expense of agriculture.

for their services, and such a demand is usually evidence of a growing developing economy."[31] The discussion above, however, points out that the banking system does not always make a positive and growth-inducing contribution. So many times the way the banking system is structured can accelerate or retard development. "It is thus a matter of some importance for policy-makers to know what structural characteristics are especially favourable or unfavourable."[32] Similarly, the functional aspects of the banking system are important. The way the banks conduct themselves through their functionaries, their attitudes and behaviour patterns towards their customers and the earnestness in the implementation of policies—all have tremendous influence on the developmental role of banks. Some economists[33] are so influenced by the structural-functional role that they have formulated a structural-function theory of the role of banking in economic development. Of the two the structural aspect is considered more important than the functional. "Whether or not the banking system makes a positive and substantial contribution to economic development does not depend primarily upon the personal qualities of the bankers, although those qualities are not negligible considerations. The structural characteristics of the customs that govern its behaviour, will normally be far more important determinants of its effectiveness."[34]

Like the commercial banks the central banks, despite numerous constraining forces, have a role to play in the underdeveloped economies. In the first place, despite the fact that absence or loose organization of capital and money markets makes the central banking control substantially weak, they "contribute significantly to maintaining stability through the development and use of new central banking techniques and the adaptation of traditional control instruments to their specific problems,"[35] Again they help finance government spending by making loans to government and act as a bridge between the government, the banks and other financial institutions. They also help development of the banking and financial structure by directing and assisting private commercial banks in branch banking. Here they occasionally establish state commercial banks which become pace-setters for other private commercial banks. Lastly, the central banks are a symbol of prestige and an assertion of monetary independence. For underdeveloped countries which gained independence recently from years of colonial rule this fact is of no mean politico-economic significance.

2. The Constituents of Indian Banking System

The Indian banking system comprises the Reserve Bank of India, the commercial banks including the State Bank of India, the indigenous banks and the joint-stock banks. While the Reserve Bank of India performs the central banking functions, the indigenous bankers combine banking with trading, the joint-stock banks—the Indian Commercial banks—specialize in internal financing of primary, secondary and tertiary sectors, and the exchange banks—the foreign commercial banks—finance foreign trade. Besides, the cooperative banks and the land mortgage banks primarily meet the short-term and long-term financial needs of agriculture.

The Reserve Bank of India

The Reserve Bank of India was set up on April 1, 1935. It had a share capital of Rs. 50 millions. The shares were primarily held by private institutions. The Bank was nationalized in 1949.

Efforts to have a banking institution in India to perform central banking functions were made sporadically at the close of the eighteenth century and during the nineteenth century. During the present century, a scheme for a central bank was submitted in 1913 to the Chamberlain Commission which did not fructify. It was in 1926 that the Hilton Young Commission made a powerful plea for the estab-

---
31 Ibid., p. 24.
32 Ibid., pp. 24–25.
33 Rondo Cameron among them.
34 Rondo Cameron, op. cit., p. 8.
35 Chung, *Money, Banking, and Incime,* p. 294.

lishment of a Reserve Bank which was accepted and led to the passing of the Reserve Bank of India Act on March 6, 1934.

Functions

The Reserve Bank of India is the central bank of the country and performs all the central banking functions.

1. *Monopoly of Note-Issue.* The Reserve Bank has the sole monopoly of the issue of currency notes in India. It issues notes of all denominations except one-rupee note which is issued by the Government of India. The Issue Department of the Reserve Bank is separate from the Banking Department and exclusively controls note issue. Originally, in the matter of monetary reserves, the Bank followed the proportional reserve system. It maintained 40 per cent of the total assets of the Issue Department in gold coins, bullion, and foreign securities, of which gold component was not to be less than Rs. 400 million. Due to exigencies of development and need for gold and foreign exchange for development imports the proportional reserve system was changed in 1956 to minimum reserve system. The changed reserve requirements needed Rs. 2,000 millions to be maintained in gold and foreign exchange of which at least Rs. 1,150 millions was to be in gold.

2. *Government's Bank.* The Reserve Bank acts as the banker to the government. It is obligated to keep government's cash balances as deposits free of charge, advances cash to the government in emergencies, transacts foreign exchange business for the government and receives and makes payments on behalf of the government. Further, it manages the public debt and helps the government float loans. It also acts as adviser to the government in banking and monetary matters.

3. *Bankers' Bank.* The Reserve Bank is to the commercial banks as commercial banks are to the general public. The commercial banks keep their surplus money with the Reserve Bank and in times of need borrow from it. It is mandatory for every scheduled bank with capital and reserves of not less than Rs. 500,000 to maintain with the Reserve Bank a cash balance equal to 5 per cent of its demand liabilities and 2 per cent of its time liabilities. The Reserve Bank is thus the custodian of the cash reserves of the commercial banks. This centralization of cash reserves, besides protecting the interests of the depositors, is a source of strength to the entire banking system making possible rediscount facilities. The mandatory reserves also give the Reserve Bank a control on supply of credit in the country.

4. *Lender of the Last Resort.* Since the commercial banks can fall back on the Reserve Bank when they fail to get financial accommodation from all other sources, the Reserve Bank acts as the lender of the last resort. The scheduled banks normally borrow from the Reserve Bank on the basis of eligible securities or by rediscounting bills of exchange.

5. *Controller of Credit.* The Reserve Bank is the controller of credit in the country. Through a number of operations it influences the powers of the commercial banks to create credit. Besides quantitative credit control it can influence availability of credit in selective areas. This is called qualitative credit control. The importance of these controls has been on the increase since 1950.

6. *Maintenance of Exchange Stability.* The Reserve Bank maintains the external value of the rupee. Since the inception of the Reserve Bank till 1946 the rate of exchange for the rupee had been maintained at 1s. 6d. From 1946, when India became a member of the IMF, to June 1946, the Reserve Bank maintained exchange rates with the currencies of the other countries of the world. After June, 1966, when the rupee was devalued and later when the pound was devalued (November 1967), the rate of cxchange of the rupee became 1 pound=Rs. 18 and 1 dollar=Rs. 7.50. With the devaluation of the dollar in 1972 the rate of exchange between the rupee and the dollar has been changed to 1 dollar=Rs. 7.25.

7. *Other Functions.* The Reserve Bank provides the clearing house facility to the commercial banks. This helps in the settlement of mutual obligations of banks through this department of the Reserve Bank of India.

The Reserve Bank has a special agricultural department to help agricultural credit and coordinate the activities of various banking institutions dealing with agricultural finance.

Besides, it has a department of Research and Statistics which provides information about the economic conditions in the country through its publications. It also acts as a link between Indian government and world financial institutions.

The Reserve Bank of India and Monetary Policy

Monetary Policy is a conscious and deliberate policy of the government or its accredited institutions to affect the supply of money with a view to achieving certain economic objectives. By consent these economic objectives can be summed up in the phrase "economic stabilization," comprising price, exchange, income and employment stability, and economic growth. Obviously a disequilibrium in these economic variables has severe economic and social consequences. In India the Reserve Bank monitors economic stability and directs monetary policy to rectify disequilibria. It employs the usual monetary policy weapons comprising bank rate changes, market operations, variable reserve requirements, etc. Over time it is seen that the Reserve Bank has exercised both quantitative controls to direct the supply of money and qualitative controls to select the direction of money supply.

The monetary policy of the Reserve Bank of India before the commencement of planning in 1951 was the cheap money policy with a fixed bank rate of 3 per cent. This was in line with the post-depression trends of the 30's which called for cheap money to lift the economy from the sloth of unemployment and falling prices. Since the advent of planning the monetary policy has been activized to score the twin goals of economic growth and stable prices. The monetary policy pursued during this period can rightly be called as one aiming at growth with stability of purchasing power.

The Reserve Bank of India and the Indian Money Maker

The money market is a meeting ground for the borrowers and lenders of short-term funds. The lenders, comprising financial and other institutions, offer surplus investible funds and borrowers, consisting of individuals, institutions, and others, bid for these funds. The role of the central bank in the country is to regulate the flow of currency and credit into the market.

The Indian money market is composed of an organized sector, viz. the Reserve Bank of India and the Indian and foreign joint stock banks and the unorganized sector representing indigenous bankers and the money lenders.

Before the establishment of the Reserve Bank of India the Indian money market was poorly organized. After 1935, when the Reserve Bank came into existence, some of the deficiencies of the money market were removed. However, many of these still persist. For example, despite the efforts of the Reserve Bank to tighten control on the money market, the unorganized sector is still outside the pale of its influence. This has led to, among other things, the existence of diversity in interest rates, book-keeping and accounting procedures, systems of remittance of funds, etc.

The Reserve Bank has been successful in removing the differences which existed between the different sections of the money market, the discrimination between foreign and Indian joint stock banks, and the seasonal monetary stringency. It has also been successful in knitting the money market and in reducing the differences in rates of interest which existed in different places and at different times.

A marked improvement in the sphere of influence of the Reserve Bank of India was registered with the establishment of the Bill Market in 1952. Under this, the Reserve Bank grants loans to banks against their promissory notes supported by approved bills of their customers. This has facilitated commercial bank financing. Before 1952, if a bank needed extra financial resources, it could do so by selling government securities to the Reserve Bank of India. But after the initiation of the Bill Market scheme, a bank can lend to its customers on their security and further use this security to borrow from the Reserve Bank of India. Since 1957, the scheme has been extended to include export bills. This has gone a long way in helping finance exports. The commercial banks advance loans to exporters against their export bills and can later, on the basis of these export bills, borrow from the Reserve Bank of India. From 1963, the Reserve Bank has introduced the Export Bills Credit Scheme under which eligible commercial banks can borrow from the Reserve Bank on their promissory notes. This has widened the range of collateral borrowing.

3. Commercial Banking in India

Indian Commercial Banking encompasses a large field—from the age-old indigenous bankers to the modern banking system. The latter include commercial banks usually called joint stock banks, foreign commercial banks or foreign exchange banks, cooperative banks, and land mortgage banks—the last two primarily doing short-term and long-term agricultural financing.

Indigenous Banking

The indigenous bankers were the earliest banking institution in India. They combined with banking such other functions as trading, money changing, brokerage, etc. Indigenous banking has differed from modern western banking in primarily being a family business. To a great extent this has been confined to certain social groups who have a natural apptitude to save, conserve, and adhere to traditional methods of banking. Most of the indigenous bankers have been carrying on on a hereditary basis. The size of their business varies from petty money lending to substantial banking activities. They have been called variously as Shroffs, Marwaris. Multanis, Chettis, Sahukars, Mahajans, Kirars, etc. Their field of operation is confined to internal trade only.

The indigenous bankers work with their own capital. Unlike the joint stock banks they generally do not attract deposits from public. They grant loans on the security of gold, jewellery, land, promissory notes, hundis, etc. They also lend against the personal credit of the borrower. The rate of interest charged by them is high, ranging anything between 12 and 18 per cent. They finance trade through direct lending and through discounting internal bills of exchange (hundis). They finance the farmer at the sowing time and also finance the movement of crops from the rural areas to the trade centres.

They carry out their banking business following the traditional methods. They follow the Indian accounting method and use the vernacular system.

Appraisal of Indigenous Banking. The indigenous bankers have been occasionally criticized for carrying on business in the old, out-of-date way, for being unorganized, for charging very high rates of interest, for keeping out of the main commercial banking stream, for combining banking with commerce, and for maintaining accounts in a dubious fashion using vernacular methods.

It has been pointed out that most of this criticism is uncalled for. Indigenous bankers carry on their business with ignorant and illiterate farmers and petty industrialists who feel more at home with the traditional modes of their operations. By sticking to their traditions they can be regarded as organized. They charge high rates of interest because of higher credit risks, higher personal inconveniences, and higher sacrifices. A hind view at their services shows their valuable role in financing agriculture, small industries and internal trade. But for them the co-operative banks and the organized joint stock banks would have met only a fraction of the financial needs of the economy. The Shroff Committee estimated that the indigenous bankers provided 75 to 90 per cent of the financial requirements of the country.

Since 1935, efforts have been made to bring indigenous bankers within the fold of the Reserve Bank of India. The Reserve Bank suggested that the indigenous bankers give up extra-banking functions (i.e., trading and commission business), vernacular system of accounting and get their accounts properly audited and follow the procedures of Reserve Banks' regulations and supervision. This done, the indigenous bankers would be placed in the category of joint stock banks for receiving rediscount facilities. The indigenous bankers, however, did not want to give up their traditional ways of operation and, therefore, declined the offer of the Reserve Bank. Later, in 1954, the Shroff Committee recommended the Reserve Bank to take the initiative by rediscounting the hundis (bills of exchange) of the indigenous bankers through the joint stock banks. But this suggestion was declined by the Reserve Bank.

People have cast doubts about the future of indigenous banking in India. The joint stock banks have expanded rapidly, State Bank of India has opened branches in the remote villages besides new towns and cities and cooperative banks have greater coverage—all leading to expanded sources of financial supply. The nationalization of banks has made the joint stock banks more open to the agriculturist and the small industrialist. All this, it is contended, would diminish the role of the indigenous banker. The future for him is thus dark. But all the same one need not forget the crucial role of the indigenous banker in providing loans on simple and easy conditions least insistence on high margins or credit-worthy collateral or on following any long-drawn formal procedures. The indigenous banker becomes the lender in the last resort for the poor farmer or the entrepreneur who cannot come up to the rigorous standards of credit-worthiness set by the organized banking system. He is deep-rooted in the rural areas and deep-stemmed in the cities. It may be a long time before the institution of the indigenous banking is gone.

4. Joint Stock Banking

Commercial banking on western style started in India in the beginning of the 19th century. These banks were called Agency Houses and were started to serve the commercial and financial needs of the East India Company. These Houses were located in Bombay and Calcutta. The first joint stock bank was started at Calcutta in 1770 and was called the Bank of Hindoostan. This bank was under European management. It failed after a short time.

To facilitate the trading and banking operations of the East India Company three banks, called Presidency Banks, were started. They were the Bank of Bengal started in 1806, the Bank of Bombay started in 1840 and the Bank of Madras started in 1843. The bulk of the share capital of these banks was subscribed by the government and the Europeans. These banks were also given the right to note issue. The first purely Indian joint stock bank called Oudh Commercial Bank was started in 1881. After this a number of other banks with the Indian content were started (notably the Punjab National Bank in 1894 and the Peoples Bank in 1901).

The Swadeshi Movement of 1905 gave a great fillip to the development of joint stock banking in India and the number of these banks grew. However, in 1913 and again in 1921, there were banking crises and a number of banks failed. Bank failures continued in the subsequent years till during the Second World War, due to war-created prosperity, bank liquidations were halted. It is estimated that 21 banks failed between 1911 and 1921, 373 failed between 1922 and 1936, and 620 failed between 1937 and 1948. In 1960–61, seized of the continual bank failures in the country, the Reserve Bank of India forced the banks to stabilize through reconstruction and mergers. As a result, many tottering banks merged with other banks to achieve viability, others went into voluntary liquidation and still some others were ordered by the courts to be wound up.

Looking back at the succession of bank failures one finds various causes, both endogenous and exogenous, responsible for this. Among the most important causes were:

a. *Shortage of Capital.* Most of the joint stock banks that met their doom had been operating on very low capital. They maintained low cash reserves ranging between 4 to 10 per cent with the result that they could not withstand pressure of withdrawals. Maintenance of cash calls for a prudent balance between liquidity and profitability—while liquidity (high cash) means security, it is always at the cost of profits, and while profitability means high dividends for the share holders, it is always at the cost of security. These banks had by and large chosen to be less liquid and thus more insecure.

b. *Severe Competition.* The joint stock banks have been in severe competition with one another to get more and more business. They offered high rates of interest to depositors and to balance this they invested funds in assets which were unsafe but promised high returns. Moreover, in the heat of competition there was rash and unprudent lending. Loans were given to insecure and dubious companies and many a time short deposits were locked up in long-term advances.

c. *Branch Expansion.* Indiscriminate branch banking without taking into consideration the financial outlay involved was also responsible for bank failures. Branches were opened with the rash idea of exhibiting rapid growth.

d. *Mushroom Growth of Small Banks.* A large number of small banks had sprung up without giving consideration to their viability and strength in the highly delicate banking system. Most of them were short of capital and lacked properly trained management personnel. They often advanced loans to their own directors and friends and maintained fraudulent accounts with the help of unscrupulous auditors. It was possible for these banks to go unnoticed because of lack of any strict banking regulation. This state of affairs continued unabated till the Reserve Bank of India was established in 1935.

e. *Inadequate Banking Regulation.* The only regulations under which the banks operated till 1935 were the provisions of the Indian Companies Act of 1913 which were too mild and patchy. It was all the time felt that a separate act was needed for regulating and controlling the banking system. The Imperial Bank of India, which, in the absence of a central bank in the country, should have supervised the banking system, was itself competing with the commercial banks. Banking control was strengthened with the establishment of the Reserve Bank of India and later by the Banking Companies Act of 1949.

f. *Other Causes.* The commercial banks passed through a period of relative stability during the Second World War due to transitory prosperity brought about by the war. However, in the wake of Independence and partition of the country a large number of banks faced crisis conditions in Bengal and the Punjab—the two states partitioned as a result of carving out of Pakistan. There were heavy withdrawals of funds by the depositors. Moreover, large amounts of cash belonging to the banks were frozen in their vaults in branches left in areas forming Pakistan.

Recent Trends in Joint Stock Banking

Indian joint stock banking has undergone many changes since the country became independent in 1947 and particularly since planned development in 1951. Efforts have been afoot to make the banking system a vehicle of growth for the Indian economy. Indirectly, the banks have been influenced by the forward thrust of the economy leading to a variety of changes in the banking system.

Development-Orientation. Banking in India had started in the conservative Scottish tradition. Banks restricted their financial activities to commercial and traditional industries. They had been very chary of financing new enterprises or encouraging new ventures. Recently, the banks are coming out of their traditional mould by entering into non-traditional areas of agricultural and industrial finance. While as late as the end of the First Five Year Plan the amount of advances to industry was less than one-fifth of the total loans advanced by the banks, it is presently over four-fifths. The period of loans is also changing from short-term to medium and long-term. The concept of credit-worthiness is undergoing change and the banks are liberalizing their loaning operations by not sticking to the physical side of collateral as the potential of the borrower. The commercial banks have taken to underwriting of new issues (a major step towards industrial finance). They are also working as a liaison between the Indian industrial houses and foreign companies.

There is a new emphasis on farm finance. An Agricultural Finance Corporation with an authorized capital of Rs. 1,000 million has been established. Agriculturists can now be easily financed in the purchase of agricultural machinery and equipment. Indirectly, the banks are helping agriculture through subscribing to the debentures of land mortgage banks.

Mobilization of Savings, Deposits and Credit. Recent years have seen a marked increase in bank savings and expansion of deposits and credit of scheduled banks. By opening branches in unbanked areas and by adding additional branches in areas directly served by banks but needing additional units, commercial banks have successfully tapped savings in the country. From 1951 to 1973, deposits of the joint stock bank went up by more than 1000 per cent from about Rs. 8,200 million to over Rs. 85,000 million. Per capita deposits and deposits as percentage of national income also went up during the period. Simultaneously, there had been continued expansion in bank credit. The quantum of expansion here has been the same as in the case of deposits for the period 1951–1973—about 600 per cent rise, from Rs. 5,800 million to approximately Rs. 60,080 million. While the expansion in deposits can be attributed to planned economic development and increased money supply, increase in bank credit is accounted for by increased trade and increased production in agriculture and industry.

Deposit Insurance. To protect the interests of depositors and to give the banking system an added look of security the Deposit Insurance Corporation was established in January, 1962. Under this insurance, cover is provided in respect of all deposits up to Rs. 5,000. "The scheme has been helpful in safeguarding the interests of small depositors and has contributed to the strengthening of public confidence in the banking system and the mobilization of deposits by banks." The net amount of claims met by the Deposit Insurance Corporation during 1962–69 amounted to Rs. 2.13 million which indicates a favourable risk experience.

Socialization of Banks. Of all the measures undertaken to give a turn to the banking system to subserve the community interests, the most outstanding is the nationalization of banks. For long there has been a demand from the left-wing of the ruling party to nationalize the commercial banks. They had argued that people's savings should be in the public sector. Further, they maintained that big business was using its hold on the banks to finance their speculative activities as well as for strengthening their monopolistic hold. There were other arguments like the failure of commercial banks to mobilize the savings of the public effectively, discrimination against small business units, failure to be guided by the positive direction given by the Five Year Plans.

Initially, the Government of India reacted negatively to the demand for complete nationalization but acceded to what was termed as the social control of banks. Under the social control the banks were asked to be responsive to the needs of the farmers and the small business enterprises. Also the Reserve Bank of India was made responsible for the appointment of the chairman and the directors of the banks.

While social control of banks was underway, the Prime Minister of India decided in favour of nationalization and on July 19, 1969, 14 major banks with deposits of Rs. 500 million or more were nationalized. Exception was made in the case of foreign banks which were left out of State ownership.

The nationalization of banks is expected to help progress in the direction of socio-economic democracy. This is through ensuring availability of credit for various types of small producers and other business units.

The State Bank of India

The State Bank of India was established on July 1, 1955 as a result of the nationalization of the Imperial Bank of India which in its turn was established in 1921 as a result of the amalgamation of the three Presidency Banks of Bengal, Bombay and Madras. The need for the establishment of the State Bank of India was felt because the Imperial Bank of India had been very slow in opening new branches in rural and semi-urban areas needed for the agricultural development. It has been seen that for more than 90 per cent of their credit needs, the cultivators had to depend upon money lenders, traders, and the marketing intermediaries who charged usurous interest rates. The All India Rural Credit Survey Committee appointed by the Reserve Bank of India in 1951 was highly critical of the tardy progress of the Imperial Bank in meeting the needs of the rural areas. In the opinion of the Committee the establishment of a state-owned and operated commercial bank with branches throughout the country providing vastly extended facilities for rural credit and operating on sound banking principles was the urgent need of the times. To achieve these ends the Committee recommended the establishment of the State Bank of India which was accepted by the Government of India.

Organization and Management. The State Bank of India had an authorized capital of Rs. 200 million and an issued capital of Rs. 56 million. The authorized capital was divided into 20 lakh fully paid up shares of Rs. 100 each. The shares of the State Bank are held by the Reserve Bank of India, insurance companies and the general public—former share holders of the Imperial Bank of India. The State Bank is managed by a Board of Directors of 20 members comprising a Chairman, a Vice-Chairman, two Managing Directors and 16 Directors. The Board of Directors supervises and guides the work of the State Bank. The central office of the State Bank is located at Bombay with local head offices at Bombay, Calcutta and Madras.

Functions. The State Bank of India is the largest commercial bank in the country and performs all the commercial banking functions. It receives deposits, advances loans, makes investments, accepts bills of exchange and promissory notes, buys and sells gold and silver, buys and sells bills of exchange, acts as agent of cooperative banks, etc. It also acts as the agent of the Reserve Bank of India at all places in the country where it has a branch and where the Reserve Bank of India does not have any. More recently a special role has been assigned to it in meeting the credit needs of the agriculturists.

The Bank is prohibited from owning or acquiring any interest in any movable property or discounting bills for any individual or firm at any time in excess of the amount prescribed.

Recent Developments. Ever since the State Bank came into existence there has been a steady increase in its assets and liabilities. In 1971 the deposits of the bank stood at approximately Rs. 1,100 crores as against Rs. 225 crores in 1955. The Bank made rapid progress in opening new branches, particularly in rural areas. Between 1955 and 1960, 400 new branches were opened. During the Second and the Third Plans, more branches were opened so that by 1971 more than 1,600 State Bank offices were in operation.

The bank has taken particular interest in the financing of agriculture and small-scale industries. State bank and its subsidiaries provide special facilities to the agricultural cooperatives by giving concessional loans and by subscribing to the debentures floated by apex cooperative banks. They give advances to marketing and processing societies on easy conditions. Agricultural marketing has been further facilitated through advances against warehouse receipts. In the matter of small-scale industries the Bank has relented many of its stringent conditions of security and credit-worthiness of the borrowers. The rate of interest charged from them is also lower. Besides, agriculture and small industries which received prime attention, the Bank has provided credit facilities for exports, food grains procurement and allied operations.

In evaluating the working of the State Bank of India it can be said that it has successfully executed promotional activities in line with the avowed objectives of the planned economic development in the country. The State Bank and its subsidiaries[36] have acted as pace setters and given direction to the entire commercial banking sector. As the biggest commercial bank of the country the State Bank has a great potential as a mobilizer of financial resources throughout the length and breadth of the country, particularly in the rural and semi-urban areas. In actual operation it has contributed its mite in this direction and cut the right path for the other commercial banks to follow.

5. Evaluation of the Indian Banking System on the Basis of the Theoretical Model

The earliest efforts to establish banks devoted to industrial growth in India can be traced back to the years 1906–13. This was the period of the Swadeshi Movement and there was a strong feeling for developing indigenous industries. The impetus also came from the spectacular achievements of Japan and Germany which had shown great industrial activity during this period and later during and after World War I. However, between 1913–15 most of these newly established banks were gripped by a financial crisis and failed. A second wave of industrial banks started in 1917 but in a few years all of these also closed down. The main causes of their failure were transplantation of the German model on Indian soil without requisite knowledge and experience, reckless lending, non-diversified investments, inefficient administration, etc.[37]

The Industrial Commission in 1918 recommended the establishment of industrial banks on the Japanese model with state assistance. During the inter-war period, the emphasis shifted from industrial banks to industrial mortgage banks.[38] These banks were to grant long-term loans on the mortgage of fixed assets. Such banks had been successful in Finland, Hungary and Poland and were strongly recommended[39] for India. Efforts to have industrial banks in India consummated in the establishment of Industrial Finance Corporation and of various State Financial Corporations for the provision of long-term finance to industries. Besides, the Industrial Credit and Investment Corporation of India, the Industrial Development Bank of India, the Unit Trust of India, and the Small Industries Development Corporation of India—all devoted to industrial finance in one way or the other—were established over the years.

Simultaneously, with the establishment of these specialized institutions, it was felt that commercial banks should provide short-term, medium-term and long-term capital to industries. "The commercial banks through their large number of branches and through their contact with capital and money markets and all lines of business are in an advantageous position to study the prospect of each enterprise against a comprehensive perspective of economic setting as a whole."[40] The Indian Central Banking Enquiry Committee (1930–31), the International Monetary Fund Mission (1953) and the Shroff Committee (1954) recommended such shifts in commercial banking operations in the country.

Since the beginning of the Second Five Year Plan (1956) a perceptible change has been visible in the attitude of the commercial banks in the provision of medium and long-term capital to industries in India. The main forms of long-

---

36 The State Bank of Bikaner and Jaipur, The State Bank of Hyderabad, The State Bank of Indore, The State Bank of Mysore, The State Bank of Patiala. The State Bank of Sourashtra, and The State Bank of Travancore.

37 Kuchhal, *The Industrial Economy of India*, p. 270.

38 Ibid.

39 Dr. P. S. Lokanathan quoted by Kuchhal.

40 Kuchhal, op. cit., p. 273.

term financing by banks have been like investment in shares and debentures, long-term loans against fixed assets, underwriting of securities, investments through specialized finance corporations (e.g. I.F.C., S.F.C.'s, I.C.I.C., etc.) and advances against corporate securities.[41] Provision of short-term finance has been through advances, loans, overdrafts and cash credits, discounting of bills, hundis, and other commercial papers.

Other changes (as a sequel to Shroff Committee recommendations) were structural transformation in the form of consolidation and strengthening of banking system, opening of branches in rural and suburban areas, structural changes in the employment of bank funds (through advancing term loans to industry and financing of small-scale industries) and development of integrated and balanced credit structure "to meet the diversified needs of development."[42]

Despite the fact that ostensible shifts and changes took place in the organization and functioning of the banking system in India since the Second Plan, a hindsight shows many flaws and weaknesses. The very fact that most of the changes occurred simultaneously with the industry-oriented Second Plan the changes in the banking system neglected the primary sector of the economy. Agriculture has thus been bereft of the social and liberal orientation of the banks. Even in the industrial sector everything has not been smooth and as desired. For one thing, the long-term financing is still a vulnerable area. The various corporations established with the exclusive object of long-term financing have only touched the tip of the iceberg. They have circumscribed their loaning operations to a few pet industries (e.g. sugar, and cotton textiles in the case of I.F.C.), have insisted on tedious collateral conditions (personal guarantee plus property mortgage), are subject to bureaucratic delays and finally are open to the justifiable criticism of charging high rates of interest.

More specifically, it can be said that the Indian commercial banks fell short of their role in the developing economy of India. They centred their activities in urban localities to the neglect of rural and sub-urban areas. It was estimated that between 1956 and 1965 the scheduled banks opened only 196 branches in the areas without banks.[43] The idea behind opening branches in thickly populated areas was to attract more deposits. There had been little realization that to develop banking habits among people there had to be more and more spreadout of the banks. In the United States many of the very big banks have branches in places where the population is less than 100 persons.[44]

Again in the large sector of the Indian economy, constituting agriculture, small industries and cottage industries, the provision of credit by the banks had been disappointingly low. In agriculture, for instance, about 90 per cent of credit came from the unorganized monetary sector. According to the Rural Credit Survey, out of Rs. 2300 crores lent to the farmers, less than Rs. 300 crores came from the banks, the cooperatives, and the government, while over Rs. 2000 crores was provided by various types of money-lenders. The position in regard to small and cottage industries was also about the same. While there had been acute scarcity of credit in these sectors it had been strongly argued that the banks had been financing a small number of industrial and business empires. A study showed that two-thirds of bank loans were given only to 650 individual borrowers. In 1965–66, loans to large-scale industries were of the order of 64.3 per cent (Loans to agriculture in this year touched the ridiculously low figure of 0.2 per cent). Further, 188 directors of 20 leading banks held 1452 directorships of other companies and controlled 1100 companies.[45] The Mahalanobis Committee pointed out that interlocking directorship of banks and non-governmental industrial undertakings had helped concentration of economic power.

41 For detailed study see Kuchhal, op. cit.

42 Kuchhal, op. cit., p. 281–282.

43 Excluding the State Bank of India which opened 360 branches.

44 K. A. Chopra, "Social Control of Banks," *A.I.C.C. Economic Review*, p. 29–31.

45 Quoted by K. A. Chopra, *Ibid.*

It is no secret that the resources of the banks were used by the directors of the banks for their personal ends. Funds of the commercial banks had been used for speculation, hoarding, and other anti-social activities. All this, with the concentration of wealth and economic power in a few hands, was negation of the professed socialistic pattern of society—the avowed aim of the ruling party's economic policies. There was an often-heard criticism, basically because of the failure of banks in the crucial economic areas, that in a planned economy private control of a strategic sector like banking was an anachronism. In India this had stood in the way of the achievement of the objectives of the Five Year Plans by not directing financial resources in the priority sectors.

The neglect by the commercial banks of the crucial areas in the economy and their otherwise dubious operations have been due to structural, traditional, and functional environments in which they worked. The history of commercial banking in India highlights the fact that this country had copied the Scottish banking methods and practices with an urban big industrial structure. Modern commercial banks were launched in India with a view to serving industry and commerce in urban areas. It had all along remained so for the urban areas providing a lender's market. Moreover, lending risks had been low in these areas. The nature of the agricultural system, including the land tenure system, had been such that it prevented the banks from taking up the task of financing agriculture.

The Scottish banking tradition was also visible in the traditionally accepted norms of safety where collateral and security were preferred to such other criteria as the record of performance, the integrity and capability of the borrower and the purposes of the loan. The limited role of the banks was understandable in the light of concentration of wealth and economic power. The operation of banks was influenced by the structural-traditional constraints. There was little sense in the bank functionaries being friendly and open-armed to sectors which otherwise were not to be financed.

The role of banks has been a subject of questioning ever since the country embarked on planning. On the mildest level it has been pointed out that the activities of the commercial banks should be more strictly directed towards the priority sectors of the economy. This implicitly meant more rigorous control of commercial banks by the Reserve Bank of India. However, a large majority of people had wanted a complete socialization of finance. The first step in this direction was to be the nationalization of commercial banks.

In deference to the accumulating pressures on the ruling party for public control of banks a via media between private and public control of banks was found by the Banking Laws (Amendment) Act of 1968, as a result of which banks were put under social control. The important provisions of the Act were: reconstitution of the Boards of Directors, restriction on loans to directors, prohibition of illegal activities and the government take-over of defaulting banks. While the social control of banks was in operation, Prime Minister Mrs. Indira Gandhi thought fit to nationalize 14 major banks (with deposits of Rs. 50 crores and over) in July, 1969.

The main arguments offered in favour of nationalization of banks centre round rectifying structural-functional defects of the banking system as pointed out earlier. Prime Minister Mrs. Indira Gandhi said that nationalization was a means to an end—the end being ushering in of a socialist economy. The case against nationalization rested upon such arguments as: nationalization would disrupt established rapport between banks and the business and industry, causing severe economic dislocation; nationalized banking system would be vulnerable to political pressures and be excessively bureaucratic and rule-oriented in operations; earlier experience of nationalized institutions was not encouraging with respect to the role of trade unions of the employees; with liberalized lending policy of the nationalized banks there would be defaults, particularly in the agricultural sector where existing laws were in favour of the farmer and judicial procedures long and time consuming.

Conclusion

It is now over five years since the banks were nationalized in India. It is too short a period within which to form any conclusive view of the success or failure of bank nationalization in the light of its avowed aims and objectives. The Reserve Bank of India carried out in 1970–71 a comprehensive survey on an all India basis on problems in connection with Provision of Bank Finance to Small Scale Industrialists and Small Artisans. Report on the survey was published in 1972 by the Banking Commission, Government of India. From the findings of the survey it is clear that there existed a justified cause for the nationalization of banks. The small entrepreneurs and particularly the handicraftsmen had been very much neglected by the commercial banks. Most of them depended on non-institutional sources of finance paying high rates of interest. The few borrowers who got financial accommodation from the commercial banks had to face delays, favouritism, undue strictness for collateral, irksome questions, etc., at the time of receiving loans. Many of the industrialists were unaware of the facilities provided by the banks, showing lack of publicity by the banks. There were no guidance bureaus attached to the banks with the result that many of the very deserving candidates were not benefitted because they did not succeed in going through the labyrinthine formalities (e.g., the requirement for a projected balance sheet). In many cases technically feasible projects were sacrificed at the alter of anachronistic credit-worthiness principles.

Although the five-year period is too short to show any definite trends in the modus operandi of the nationalized banks, it can be inferred from some regional studies carried out by researchers that there is no immediate discernible shift in the commercial bank's financial activities. In fact, some studies[46] show perpetration of existing practice by banks of preferring high collateral parties. The entrepreneurs have also shown little enthusiasm to shift from non-institutional sources to the nationalized institutional sources. This is probably because their applications for loan in the past did not meet favourable consideration, and they have not been shown any explicit shifts in the lending postures of the new publicly-owned banks.

As said earlier the period to appraise the working of the nationalized banks is too short and, therefore, any findings are only tentative. The future of nationalized banks is certainly promising, particularly in the light of the avowed aims and objectives. With time both the entrepreneurs and the banks are bound to come closer. The new ties will put huge financial resources at the disposal of up and coming sectors of the economy.

---

46 Carried out at Jaipur, Rajasthan by the author in the capacity of Director of Research, Banking Commission, Government of India.

18

Monetary System in India: A Survey

G. S. GUPTA

1. Introduction

The present chapter discusses the significance of a monetary system; the various monetary systems in theory; the history of the Indian monetary system from 1835, i.e. the year in which the rupee was formally adopted as a national monetary unit, to the present; the various money supply components and their relative roles in total money supply; different producers of money and their production systems; the different monetary policy instruments and their operating processes; the significance and potency of monetary policy in India; and the monetary policy objectives, the problems faced, and policy measures adopted since 1951–52 to help solve specific monetary problems faced by the Indian economy. An evaluation of the Indian monetary policy concludes the chapter.

2. Monetary Systems

For money to serve as a good store of value, its own value must remain fairly stable over time. The value of money is expressed in terms of the quantity of goods or services that a unit of money can buy in the market. Thus, the value of money is inversely and proportionately related to the market prices of goods and services. By the simple laws of supply and demand, the market prices of goods and services depends positively on the total quantity of money available to buy all goods and services supplied, and negatively on the total quantity of goods and services available in the market. There fore, in order that money may serve its useful function of a good store of value, the supply of money must be kept within certain limits. Various monetary systems have been designed and used for limiting the total quantity of money. They are nothing but different methods of limiting the total supply of money. India, like all other countries, has at different times used one or the other monetary system to regulate the circulating media in the economy.

The monetary standard of a nation involves the overall set of laws and practices that control the quantity and quality of money in the system. Although numerous variations may exist within each category, there are only two types of monetary standard: (a) metallic standards, and (b) inconvertible managed paper currency standard, also known as gold parity standard.

Metallic Standards

Under a metallic standard, money is tied up with the supply of some precious metal like gold or silver, or both. Therefore, the value of money remains fixed in terms of the precious metal which is chosen as the standard metal. If only one metal, either gold or silver or any other metal is used as the standard metal in terms of which the value of money is fixed, the metallic standard is called mono-metallic standard. The mono-metallic standard where gold is used as the standard metal is called the Gold Standard. Similarly, the mono-metallic standard where silver is used as the standard metal is called the Silver Standard. The monetary system in which money is linked up with gold as well as silver or with any other two metals is called the bimetallic standard.

A metallic standard may take only one of the three forms. Without the loss of generality, we illustrate this for the Gold Standard. The three forms of the Gold Standard are Gold Currency or Full Gold Standard, Gold Bullion Standard, and Gold Exchange Standard. The distinctive features of these forms of a metallic standard will be made clear in the following paragraphs.

The salient features of a metallic standard of any form are:

1. The national unit of account—the rupee, the dollar, the pound, and so on—is defined in terms of a certain weight of the standard metal (s).

2. There is a free flow of the standard metal (s) into and out of the monetary system. That is, the public is free to take the standard metal (s) to the national mint and to convert it into money at the rate fixed by the definition of the unit of account and also to take metallic coins out of circulation and to convert them to industrial use or into bullion.

3. The public has the right to import or export the standard metal free of any restriction.

Besides these common features of a standard metallic standard, each form of a metallic has a peculiar feature. The peculiar feature of a gold currency standard is that only gold coins circulate as money. Under gold bullion standard, token money, defined as the one whose token value is greater than its intrinsic value, circulate as money, and the same is convertible into gold bullion at a fixed rate. Unlike these, under gold exchange standard, the token money, which alone circulates as money, is convertible only into the currency of those countries which are on either gold currency standard or gold bullion standard, and also exclusively for purposes of foreign exchange payments.

Inconvertible Managed Paper Currency Standard

Under the inconvertible managed paper currency standard, money is not linked to any metal but is regulated directly by the government and the country's monetary authority. Under this system, the token money, which alone circulates, is defined in terms of gold, and the exchange rate between token moneys of different countries is determined by gold parity. Therefore, this system is also called Gold Parity System. Under this system, redemption of money merely involves the interchangeability of the different forms of money. Both paper currency notes and token coins circulate as money.

3. Indian Monetary System

The Indian monetary system has had an eventful career. It has experienced a silver standard, a gold exchange standard, a gold bullion standard, and a sterling exchange standard. At present India is a member of the International Monetary Fund (IMF) and has an inconvertible managed paper currency standard. Before fully elaborating the present monetary system, we present briefly the history of the Indian monetary standard.

Past Monetary Systems

A better understanding of the present monetary system in India calls for a brief survey of the monetary systems that existed in India in the past. We start the survey from 1835, the year in which the rupee was formally adopted as the national monetary unit.

1835–1893 : *Silver Standard.* The Currency Act of 1835 established the silver currency standard in the country. The silver rupee weighing 180 grains and 11/12 fine was adopted as the standard coin and legal tender throughout India. Gold coins were not accepted as legal tender. The discovery of new silver mines in 1873 brought down the silver price in terms of gold, which, in turn, caused a rude shock to India's foreign trade. This created difficulties in the smooth working of the silver standard, which ultimately, on the recommendation of the Herschell Committee, was abandoned in 1893. The free coinage of silver was stopped and the rupee became a token coin.

1893–1898 : *Transition Period.* The period 1893–1898 was the period of adjustment, during which the Fowler Committee worked to draw-up a suitable scheme for the introduction of gold standard in the country.

1899–1917 : *Gold Exchange Standard.* John Maynard Keynes hailed the gold exchange standard as the ideal monetary system for an underdeveloped country like India. Influenced by this idea and by the special circumstances of that time, the gold exchange standard was adopted in January, 1899. Under the new system, the silver rupee was the standard coin used for all internal transactions. For external purposes, the rupee was convertible into gold at the rate of 1s. 4d. The system worked smoothly and the Chamberlin Commission, which was appointed to enquire and suggest improvements in the Indian currency system, endorsed in its favour. However, difficulties in its working cropped up in the beginning of 1916; this was caused by an acute shortage in supply of silver. In the face of short supply of silver, the price of silver was rising. Consequently, people in India were melting the silver rupee and selling it as silver for a higher price. Under these circumstances, it became impossible for the government to purchase silver at the higher price and supply rupees at the lower rate of 1s. 4d. Therefore, in August 1917, the silver rupee, it was declared, ceased to be a standard coin, and the gold exchange standard was abandoned.

1917–1920 : *Unstable Exchange Rate.* After the gold exchange standard was abandoned in August 1917, the rate of exchange was left free to be determined by the market price of silver. The exchange rate fluctuated widely and government efforts, to restore the stable gold exchange standard by raising the exchange rate *pari passu* with a rise in the price of silver, were unsuccessful. In December 1919, the exchange rate stood at Re. 1= 2s. 6d.

1920–1927 : *"Masterly Inactivity".* After 1920, the government in desparation gave up efforts to maintain a particular exchange rate and, between 1921 and 1925, it followed the so-called policy of "masterly inactivity." As in all other difficulties, a Commission, the Hilton-Young Commission, was appointed in 1925 to recommend reform of the Indian monetary system. Incidentally, it may be noted that it was this Commission which recommended the establishment of a central bank in the country.

1927–1931 : *Mixture of Gold Bullion and Sterling Exchange Standards.* On the recommendations of the Hilton-Young Commission, the Currency Act of 1927 established a mixture of gold bullion and sterling exchange standards in India. Under this system, the rupee was linked directly with gold but its value was fixed at 8.47 grains of fine gold which was equivalent to 1s. 6d., in terms of sterling. If gold was required for foreign payment, the Indian currency authority had the option of paying sterling for immediate delivery in London. This "hybrid" type of currency system continued in India up to September, 1931.

1931–1939 : *Sterling Exchange Standard.* A significant change in the Indian monetary standard came during the Great Depression that began in 1929. One of the dramatic aspects of this world-wide depression was the disorganization of the monetary system in almost every nation. In September 1931, the U.K. came off the gold standard and the government of India abandoned the mixed gold bullion and sterling exchange standards. The rupee was directly linked with the British pound sterling at the rate of 1s. 6d. Britain was no more on the gold standard. India, thus, adopted the sterling exchange standard and, therefore, India's monetary system became highly dependent on the monetary policy of Great Britain.

During the depression period, Indian exports dwindled considerably without a compensating decrease in imports. Consequently, India had to export gold heavily in order to pay for her excess imports. Devaluation of the Indian rupee was then feared. The Reserve Bank of India was established in January, 1935 and this considerably strengthened the currency and the banking systems of the country. The RBI became the statutory currency authority in India and it was made legally responsible for maintaining the rupee-sterling exchange rate at the par value of Re. 1=1s. 6d. The sterling exchange standard continued up to March 1, 1947, when India became a member of the International Monetary Fund (IMF).[1] Since March 1, 1947, India has been on a single monetary system, which is prevailing even now. We shall discuss this system under the next section. "Present monetary System."

Present Monetary System
Inconvertible Managed Paper Currency (or Gold Parity) Standard

On March 1, 1947, India became a member of the IMF and the rupee obtained a gold parity value which was jointly decided by the IMF and the RBI. The gold parity rate fixed was such that the old rate of Re. 1=1s. 6d., was maintained. The rupee became theoretically convertible into any foreign currency and the issue department of the RBI was required to hold other foreign currencies in addition to sterling. Under this system, as already discussed, the external value of the rupee is linked to the value of gold and so this system is also known as the gold parity standard.

The gold parity system has been working well in terms of the stability of the exchange value of the Indian rupee. The Indian rupee was devalued by 30.5 per cent in terms of gold on September 20, 1949, not because the RBI found it impossible to maintain its exchange value but because the British government decided to devalue the sterling by that percentage and India followed suit as a faithful member of the Commonwealth. The June 1966 devaluation of the Indian rupee by 36.5 per cent in terms of gold was, however, caused by difficulties in maintaining the external value of the rupee.

4. Money Supply Components and their Relative Role in Total Money Supply

Money is a means of payment that possesses universal acceptability within the home country. It is this charecteristic of money that distinguishes it from "near money" assets, such as banks' time deposits. The RBI's definition of money comprises the following items: (a) currency with the public; (b) net demand deposits of banks, and (c) "other" deposits with the RBI.

Currency with the public, the legal tender money, consists of notes and coins in circulation net of those held in banks' coffers. The RBI Act of 1934 permits the home country. It is this characteristic of RBI to issue notes of rupees two, five, ten, twenty, fifty, one hundred, five hundred, and such other denominations, not exceeding rupees ten thousand, as the central government may specify on the recommendations of the Central Board of the RBI. At present all these denominations, except rupees fifty and five hundred, are being issued. Besides notes of these denominations, there are one rupee notes, which are issued by the government of India. Unlike in the U.S.A., where notes of different denomi-

1 IMF was established on March 1, 1947.

nations bear the same colour and design except the photo, the notes of different denominations in India differ in respect of colour as well as of design. This is primarily because of the rather low literacy rate in India, particularly compared to the literacy in the U.S.A. The different colours, designs, and sizes for different currency notes enable the illiterate people to distinguish between the different denominations easily. The colours and designs of these notes have to be approved by the central government.

Since April 1, 1957, when India changed over to the decimal system of coinage, the Indian rupee has been divided into 100 paise, the half rupee and the quarter rupee being equivalent to 50 and 25 paise, respectively. The two-anna, one-anna, half anna, and pice coins of the old coinage system have no counterparts in the new system. Coins of 50, 25, 10, 5, 2 and 1 paise have been issued, and Re. 1 continues. The old coins continued to circulate side by side for some time, but were, in due course, replaced by the new coins. With effect from January 1, 1964, all cupro-nickel one anna, copper double pice, and copper and bronze single pice coins ceased to be legal tender. These coins, however, were to be accepted at all offices of the Reserve Bank and government treasuries till June 30, 1964. Incidentally, note that currency notes in all denominations and one rupee coins are unlimited legal tender, half-rupee coins are legal tender for any sum not exceeding ten rupees, and smaller coins are legal tender only for any sum not exceeding one rupee.

Net demand deposits[2] of banks consist of demand deposits of the public with the commercial banks and of the demand liabilities of state co-operative banks.[3] The last component of money, that is, "other" deposits with the RBI is made-up of deposits of semi-government institutions, such as of the Industrial Development Bank of India, the Industrial Finance Corporation of India, the State Financial Corporations, the Agricultural Refinance Corporation, the Unit Trust of India, the Deposit Insurance Corporation, with the RBI.

The relative shares of the three components of money in India's total money supply in the selected years is provided in Table 1. The currency component of money constitutes over 60 per cent of the total money stock in the economy. This proportion is very high in India as compared to those in the advanced economies, e.g., roughly 22 per cent in the USA, 21 per cent in the UK, 25 per cent in Canada, 22 per cent in Japan, etc. This is one of the main indicators of the poor development of banking in our economy. Within the currency, the proportion of notes and coins, which reveals a change in favour of notes over time, was in the ratio of approximately 10 : 1 in 1970 – 71. Furthermore, "over 80 per cent of the currency in circulation in March 1969 was accounted for by ten (35 per cent) and one hundred (46 per cent) rupee notes. Five rupee notes accounted for about 7 per cent, one rupee notes and coins for about 6 per cent and small coins for about 3 per cent of the currency in circulation."[4]

Demand deposits of banks' component of money accounts for roughly that part of total money supply which is not accounted for by its currency component. For, the only other component of money, i.e., "other" deposits with RBI, accounts for only about 1 per cent of the total money supply. As the banking sector develops in the economy, the deposit component of money increases. It has increased from 29.01 per cent in 1950 – 51 to 38 per cent in 1970 – 71. The share of state co-operative banks' demand liabilities in total money stock is only around 1 per cent; the remainder of the deposits part of money is accounted for by the commercial banks' demand deposits.

Incidentally, it may be noted that the relative proportions of currency and de-

---

2 "Net" because these are net of inter-bank demand deposits.

3 Demand liabilities instead of just demand deposits of state co-operative banks are considered as a part of money, for its relative role in money supply is meagre and perhaps it is difficult to separate these two items.

4 R.B.I. (1970), p. 10.

Table 1. Money Supply Components and their Role in Total Money Stock

(Rs. crores)

Money Supply Component	As on last Friday of the fiscal year (ending March) 1950-51	1955-56	1960-61	1965-66	1968-69	1970-71
Currency	1406.52 (69.77)	1571.01 (70.86)	2098.05 (73.14)	3034.28 (66.99)	3681.97 (63.71)	4379.84* (61.39)
Notes[a]	1195.08 (59.28)	1381.64 (62.32)	1875.34 (65.37)	2744.99 (60.60)	3341.42 (57.82)	4000.60 (56.07)
Coins[a]	211.44 (10.49)	189.37 (8.54)	212.71 (7.77)	289.29 (6.39)	340.55 (5.89)	379.24* (5.32)
Net Demand Deposits of banks	585.03 (29.01)	636.90 (28.73)	757.10 (26.39)	1478.38 (32.64)	2016.41 (34.89)	2711.14* (38.00)
Net Demand Deposits of Commercial banks	576.40 (28.59)	624.97 (28.19)	731.15 (25.49)	1434.99 (31.68)	1945.55 (33.66)	2633.38 (36.91)
Net Demand Liabilities of State Co-operative banks.	8.63 (0.42)	11.93 (0.54)	25.95 (0.90)	43.39 (0.96)	70.86 (1.23)	77.76 (1.09)
"Other" Deposits with RBI	24.44 (1.22)	9.04 (0.41)	13.46 (0.47)	16.72 (0.37)	80.88 (1.40)	43.83 (0.61)
Money Supply (total)	2015.99 (100.00)	2216.95 (100.00)	2868.61 (100.00)	4529.38 (100.00)	5779.26 (100.00)	7134.81 (100.00)

SOURCE: RBI: Report on Currency and Finance 1970-71.

Note: Figures in parentheses indicate the percentage of the total money supply in different money components.

*Provisional.

[a]As no separate figures are available for notes and coins held by the public, the date on coins are taken as the total circulation of rupee and small coins and the date on notes are obtained as the residual difference between total currency held by the public and total coins in circulation.

posits in the money stock are governed not by the producers of money but by the money-using public. The different producers of money supply their part of money only to meet the public demand for it.

5. Producers of Money and their Production System

The three agencies that supply the circulating media are the Treasury (government), the Reserve Bank of India and commercial and state co-operative banks. The Treasury supplies one rupee notes and coins of all denominations. The RBI is the sole issuer of all other currency notes. It also supplies the "other" deposits part of the money stock. The bank deposits component of money is the liability of commercial and state co-operative banks.

The Ministry of Finance undertakes the issue of one rupee notes and coins, more or less on an autonomous basis, to finance that part of plan expenditure which is not covered by other sources of finance, such as taxation and borrowings. The RBI maintains a separate department, known as the "Issue Department," for the purpose of issuing the currency notes. According to Section 33 of the RBI Act of 1934, the assets of the Issue Department against which currency notes are issued are to consist of gold coin and bullion, foreign securities, rupee coin, government of India rupee securities, and such bills of exchange and promissory notes payable in India as are eligible for purchase by the Bank. In practice, such bills and promissory notes have not figured as assets due to lack of a proper bill market. The original Act prescribed a Proportional Reserve System of note issue. Under that system, of the total assets not less than 40 per cent was to consist of gold coin and bullion, and sterling securities, with the proviso that gold coin and bullion were not, at any time, to be less than Rs. 40 crores in value. On India's becoming a member of the IMF in March, 1947, the note-issue system was slightly revised so that foreign currencies other than sterling could also be kept in the 40 per cent reserve. The system of note-issue remained unchanged until 1956, when, in order to meet the needs of developmental planning, the proportional reserve system was replaced by a Minimum (Fixed) Reserve System. Under the new system, the Reserve Bank was required to hold a minimum of Rs. 400 crores in foreign securities and Rs. 115 crores in gold coin and bullion; the former was reducible, under special circumstances, to Rs. 300 crores. Simultaneously, gold was revalued from Rs. 21.24 per tola to Rs. 62.50 per tola, so that the required quantity of gold under the new system remained nearly the same as under the old system. As the foreign exchange crisis deepened, the President issued an Ordinance in November 1957, which sliced down the statutory minimum reserve requirement of gold and foreign securities to Rs. 200 crores; of this, the value of gold was not to be less than Rs. 115 crores, the same as prior to the promulgation of the Ordinance. Further, the Second Amendment Act of 1957 empowered the RBI to reduce its holding of foreign securities in the Issue Department to any lesser amount, with the previous sanction of the Central Government. Thus, under the new system the Bank can dispense entirely with the holding of foreign securities if circumstances so require; it must, however, have gold equivalent of Rs. 115 crores at all times. To take account of the devaluation of the rupee by 36.5 per cent in June 1966, the price of gold was once again raised from Rs. 62.50 per tola to Rs. 98.44 per tola, with effect from February 1, 1969. The statutory gold and foreign exchange reserve requirements were, however, left unchanged, which in effect, meant a reduction of the reserve requirements in terms of gold and the U.S. dollars.

In short, the present note-issue system, which is known as the minimum reserve system, stipulates for all times a minimum reserve requirement, in gold coin and bullion, of only the amount of Rs. 115 crores, gold being valued at Rs. 98.44 per tola. Thus, at present, India has an elastic system of note issue, which satisfies the requirement of an expanded paper currency system, necessary to fulfil the deficit financing programme of her bold and ambitious developmental plans and meet emergencies which might arise from adverse balance of payments.

The bank-deposit part of money is a liability of commercial and state co-operative banks. Its volume depends on the willingness and ability of these banks to acquire assets, which, in turn, depends on their ability to acquire a particular kind of asset, viz., bank reserves held either at RBI or in their own vaults. Bank demand deposits are a certain multiple, called the deposit multiplier, of bank reserves. In India, the value of this multiplier has been around seven. Since bank reserves are the assets of the banking system and are the liability of the Treasury and the RBI, and since demand deposits are the assets of the public and the liability of the banking system, all these segments of the economy play a role in the determination of the deposit multiplier.

From the foregoing discussion it is clear that in the present monetary system, the Treasury, the RBI, the banking system and the public all take part in the determination of money stock in the economy.[5]

6. Monetary Policy Instruments and their Operating Processes

One of the very important functions of the RBI is to control and regulate the availability of credit, the cost of credit, and the use of credit in the country. For this purpose, the RBI possesses in its armoury all the usual monetary policy instruments or techniques that are possessed by a central bank. They are:[6]

1. Bank rate or discount rate
2. Open market operations (OMO)
3. Reserve requirement ratios (RRR)
4. Selective or qualitative credit control (SCC)
5. Moral suasion.

The first three of these are the so-called traditional weapons of the central bank and together they are known as the general or quantitative instruments of monetary policy. All three of these affect, directly, the cost and availability of credit. The SCC is a relatively new instrument and is also known as the instrument of qualitative credit control. Its application affects the use of credit. Every central bank enjoys a unique position in the home country's organized money market, which it supervises and regulates. By virtue of this, the RBI, either by order or exhortation, can influence any or all the aspects of credit: cost, availability, and use. This instrument is known as the "Moral Suasion" instrument in the hands of the RBI. Some writers regard it as a distinct technique of monetary control while others just ignore it.

Bank Rate

In India, in the absence of a well-knit bill market, the bank rate, or the discount rate as it is called in the USA, is the rate at which the RBI makes advances to its member banks against eligible securities.[7] Thus, the bank rate policy has two dimensions: (i) by changing the effective bank rate, it directly affects the cost of member banks' borrowings from the RBI, which, in turn, encourages or discourages member banks to borrow from the RBI, and (ii) by widening or narrowing the list of eligible securities against which member banks could borrow from the RBI, it directly affects the ability of borrowing banks to obtain funds from the RBI, and thence the availability of bank credit. Thus, theoretically speaking, by lowering (or raising) the bank rate and/or widening (or narrowing) the list of eligible securities, the RBI under bank rate policy can generate expansion (or contraction) in the economy. It is an indirect instrument in the sense that by lowering (or raising) the Bank rate and/or widening (or narrowing) the list of eligible securities for loans, the RBI can only encourage (or discourage) banks to borrow more from it, but by doing so it can not make them borrow more (or less).

Since January 9, 1971, the bank rate in India is 6 per cent. The present bank rates in the USA, the UK, Japan, France, Pakistan and South Africa are 4.5, 7.25, 4.75, 5.75, 6 and 6.5 per cent respectively.

Open Market Operations

In the narrow sense, OMO refer to the purchases or sales of government securities and other financial assets (e.g. gold) by the central bank in the open market with a view to affecting the banking system's reserve position, and thence the latter's ability to create credit, and the market rates of interest. In the wider sense, OMO refer not merely to the RBI's purchases and sales of government bonds, etc., in the open market, but also to the Treasury's dealings in its bonds with the banking system and the public.[8] In India, these operations have been confined to short- and long-term government securi-

[5] For the exact role of each of these sectors or institutions in the determination of the total money supply in the economy, see Gupta (1972).

[6] For a detailed discussion of these techniques, see Aschheim (1961).

[7] RBI (1970) p. 41.

[8] Raj (1948), Ch. VII.

ties, excluding Treasury bills, unlike in the United States, where they are confined to bills only." At present there is no restriction on the quantity or maturity of government securities which the RBI can buy or sell and the RBI enjoys full discretion in this respect. Furthermore, the RBI is free to undertake switch operations, i.e., buy securities of one maturity and sell those of the other maturity, in any amount it deems appropriate to bring about a desired term structure of interest rates.

The instrument of OMO has at least two dimensions: (i) by purchasing (or selling) government securities from (to) the public including the banking system, the RBI directly increases (or decreases) the banks' reserves,[9] which in turn, directly increases (or decreases) the banks' ability to bring about a multiple expansion (or contraction) of credit; and (ii) by purchasing (or selling) government securities in the open market, the RBI, in general, increases (or decreases) the price of bonds, and thus decreases (or increases) the yield on government bonds. RBI's dealings in switch operations also obviously affect the term structure of interest rates. Thus, OMO, unlike the bank rate instrument, directly affect both the availability and the cost of credit. There is a good scope for an effective use of OMO in India, for both the RBI and the public, including banks, hold a significant portion of their total financial assets in the form of government bonds. However, OMO have rarely been used in India as an instrument of credit control. "In general the open market operations have been used in India more to assist the government in its borrowing operations and to maintain orderly conditions in the government securities market than for influencing the availability and cost of credit."[10]

Reserve Requirement Ratios

Under the RBI Act of 1934, scheduled commercial banks were required to maintain with the RBI at the close of business on any day, interest free minimum cash reserves of 5 per cent of their demand liabilities and 2 per cent of time liabilities. Non-scheduled commercial banks were brought under the same requirements by the Banking Companies Act of 1949 except that a non-scheduled commercial bank was free to maintain the required reserves either with itself or with the RBI. However, RRR was not an instrument at that time, for the RBI was not permitted to vary them. It became an instrument effective from October 1956, when the Amendment Act of 1956 empowered the RBI to vary the minimum reserve requirement ratios between 5 and 20 per cent and 8 per cent against demand liabilities and between 2 and 8 per cent of time liabilities. Subject to these limits the RBI was also empowered by this Act to require scheduled commercial banks to maintain up to a 100 per cent reserve on the increase in their demand and time liabilities after a specified date. The Amendment Act also made it optional for the RBI to pay a variable interest on scheduled commercial banks' reserves with the RBI in excess of required reserves at its discretion. All these clauses of the Amendment Act of 1956, gave this instrument the required flexibility.

The instrument of variable reserve requirement ratios like the Bank rate and OMO instruments, has bearings both on the availability and cost of credit. A change in RRR, which leave total reserves unaltered, directly affects the amount of required reserves for a given level of banks' deposit liabilities. Required reserves are yield barren, so an increase in RRR, *ceteris paribus,* renders banking less profitable. In their endeavour to compensate for the decreased profitability, banks attempt to increase their lending rate. Quite the reverse follows when RRR are decreased. Thus a change in RRR directly affects the cost of credit. Furthermore, an increase in RRR adversely affects the availability of credit through decrease in banks' loans, banks' investment and/or banks' holdings of excess reserves to compensate for increased required reserves.

---

9 Whether the RBI deals in OMO with the non-bank public or with banks, its effect on bank reserves would be the same if non-bank public keeps all its cash balances with banks. Otherwise, the effect would be different.

10 RBI (1960) p. 799.

Thus theoretically, the RBI can produce an expansionary monetary policy by reducing the RRR and a contractionary monetary policy by raising the RRR.

In India, since September 1964, the RRR is 3 per cent for all scheduled and non-scheduled commercial banks against both demand and time liabilities and this rate can be varied by the RBI between 3 per cent and 15 per cent. Since August 1966, scheduled State Co-operative banks also are subject to the same reserve requirement; non-scheduled State Co-operative banks are required to hold 2.5 per cent of their demand liabilities and 1 per cent of their time liabilities in the form of reserves. As a contrast to this, the current primary reserve requirements in the USA are 17 per cent against demand deposits of under five million dollars and 17.5 per cent against demand deposits of five million dollars and over for Reserve City banks, 12.5 per cent against demand deposits of under five million dollars and 13 per cent against demand deposits of five million dollars and over for Country banks, and 3 per cent against time deposits of any amount for all banks. These rates can be varied by the US monetary authorities between 10 per cent and 22 per cent against demand deposits of Reserve City banks, between 7 per cent and 14 per cent against demand deposits of Country banks, and between 3 per cent and 10 per cent against time deposits of any group of these banks.

Besides the (primary) RRR, under the Banking Companies Act 1949, every bank was also required to maintain in India in cash (vault cash + balances with the RBI + balances with notified banks), gold and/or unencumbered approved securities a minimum amount of 20 per cent of the aggregate demand and time liabilities in the country. The Amendment Act 1962, raised this requirement to 25 per cent plus the minimum primary RRR of 3 per cent, making a total of 28 per cent effective September 1964. The Amendment Act thus ensured that with every increase in the primary RRR, the overall liquidity obligations were also correspondingly raised. The Amendment Act further empowered the RBI to vary the overall liquidity requirement for Scheduled banks from 28 per cent to 40 per cent effective September 1964. However, this instrument of credit control has not been used by the RBI to date. Furthermore, banks in India have always held bonds in excess of their requirement. In the USA, there is no secondary reserve requirement and yet banks there have maintained 25 per cent to 30 per cent of their deposits in US Central and State government securities.

In principle, the instrument of RRR for monetary controls is very powerful, for by changing it slightly the RBI can release or freeze bank reserves, which forms the basis for banks' multiple credit creation. However, its practical use is obscured by the RBI's promotional objective of leaving the banking institutions profitable and thereby promoting the organised banking system in the country.

Selective Credit Controls

The quantitative instrument of credit controls discussed above enable the RBI to regulate the volume and the cost of bank credit. They are of no significance in directing credit to selective uses. The regulation of the use of bank credit is achieved through the use of the techniques of selective or qualitative credit controls. The distinctive feature of this technique is that it seeks to influence the specific sectors of the economy which are crucial and need to be controlled without affecting the other sectors. Under these techniques a central bank can make it obligatory for the banking system to discriminate between the customers with different loan purposes and thereby help check the various imbalances in the economy, i.e., sectoral imbalances, regional imbalances, and imbalances in the context of planning. The Banking Companies Act, 1949, conferred upon the RBI permanent powers to effect selective controls on bank credit. Its operating process needs no explanation.

In India SCC take the form of fixing margins for lending against the commodities in short supply or ceilings on credit to certain undesirable sectors. As against this, in the USA margins are imposed on advances against shares, consumer durables, real estate, etc., under SCC.

Moral Suasion

Moral suasion describes the use of central banking power upon the lending activities of banking institutions through exhortations. In other words, it consists of the central bank's requests to the particular banking institutions that in the interest of the economy they themselves should adopt certain credit policies voluntarily, instead of by force of law as in the other techniques of monetary controls. Such a request can be either general or selective or both in character and so the instrument of moral suasion is both a quantitative and qualitative instrument of credit controls. The success of the instrument positively depends on the concentration of banking. Indian banking is neither as concentrated as in the UK nor is it as diffused as in the USA. The 15 nationalized commercial banks account for more than 85 per cent of total deposits and credit.

The various instruments of monetary controls discussed above are complementary rather than competitive. The choice of one over the other, if relevant, depends largely on the monetary problems these instruments are used to help overcome.

7. Significance and Potency of Monetary Policy in India

Government Policies and their Complementary Role

A variety of policy instruments are available to any society that wishes to regulate the levels of its ultimate target variables: output, price, employment, and balance of payments. As far as India in its post-Independence period is concerned, the range of available instruments includes (i) monetary policy instruments, (ii) fiscal policy instruments, and (iii) direct instruments or controls. Monetary policy instruments have been discussed in the previous section. They influence the target variables only indirectly through the market-mechanism, i.e., through their impact on financial variables: interest rate, supply of money, supply of bank credit, etc., called intermediate target variables. Fiscal policy instruments: taxation, government consumption and investment expenditures, transfer payments, government debt management, etc., which also work through the market-mechanism, normally produce direct directional effects on the economic activity. As against these, direct controls—industrial policy, industrial licensing policy, monopoly control, capital issues control, import licensing policy, price controls, etc., are normally expected to produce directly certain desirable directional effects on the economic activity.

Although, monetary and fiscal policies and direct controls are the alternative instruments in the hands of the public authority for regulating and controlling the economic activity, they are mutually complementary rather than competitive instruments. Where there is a clearly visible need to expand or restrain the economy, all these instruments can be used in the same direction. They can also be used in more subtle ways in order to acommodate special problems within the total economy. Depending upon the specific problem (s) which these policy instruments are expected to arrest, at times one policy might be preferred to the other. In general, monetary policy is more effective with respect to monetary variables: money supply, bank credit, interest rate, etc. While fiscal policy is more effective with respect to real magnitudes: output, employment, etc. In India, which has adopted a programme of planned economic development, in which the public sector has an important part to play, fiscal policy would be concerned largely with effective structural changes in the economy, while monetary policy would be aimed at regulating investment in the private sector and short-run management of the economy. Direct controls would be used when the targets sought are crucial and urgent. Thus, all the three types of policy measures are an integral part of a progressive economy.

The three policy measures are not always independent. For instance, monetary and fiscal policies are inter-linked through the management of public debt: a budget deficit or surplus has repercussions on the stock of money. In passing it may be noted that while monetary policy is easy to deploy and reverse, fiscal policy is difficult to deploy and reverse.

Potency of Monetary Policy in India

Since monetary policy influences the ultimate target variables only indirectly through its influence on financial variables, the potency of monetary policy with respect to ultimate target variables hinges on two important causal links: (i) a link between the monetary policy instruments and the financial variables, and (ii) a link between the financial variables and the ultimate target variables. In the absence of either link, monetary policy remains impotent. It is now clear that the monetary authority through its policy instruments—bank rate, OMO, RRR, and SCC—can influence the financial variables, interest rate, money supply, supply of bank credit, etc., though it does not control them exactly. However, the non-zero effect of financial variables on the target variables is not yet universally acceptable. It is because of the vagueness in the second link that the significance of monetary policy has remained ambiguous.

The limitations to an effective use of monetary policy arise from the factors that cause the above two links weak. The link between the monetary policy instruments and financial variables is weaker in India than in advanced countries like the USA, UK, Japan, France, etc., because of its relatively large unorganized money and capital markets. The indices of the organized banking sector indicate that, in 1966, population per bank office in India was 86,000 as compared to 7,000 in the USA, 4,000 in the UK, 16,000 in Japan, and 5,800 in France; the percentage of aggregate bank deposits to national income was 15 in India as against 47 in the USA, 35 in the UK, 96 in Japan, and 39 in France; deposit money as percentage of total money supply was 36 in India as contrast to 78 in the USA, 79 in the UK, 78 in Japan and 63 in France. The unorganized money market, which comprises indigenous banks, is synonymous with what Gurley and Shaw call non-bank financial intermediaries. This market lies outside the purview of monetary controls and thus it reduces the significance of monetary policy in the economy. The nationalization of the 14 major commercial banks effective July 1969, which is expected to reduce the size of the unorganized money market through the expansion of organized banking in rural India, is likely to increase the effectiveness of monetary measures in the country.

It is a truism that monetary policy is superfluous in a barter economy, for the above mentioned second link is then absolutely missing. Though one can still find people trading goods against goods in remote Indian villages, barter is not, in present-day India, the usual method of exchange. "The non-monetized sector may be put at between one-quarter and one-third of the whole, but it is shrinking possibly at an annual rate of $\frac{1}{2}$ per cent of the economy."[11] Further, the link between the financial variables and the ultimate target variables is perhaps relatively weak in India as compared to that in the advanced countries, because of India's relatively

1. low level of investment, particularly in the private sector, and of its
2. excessive dependence on agriculture and other primary industries.

The rate of investment in India is about 12 per cent as compared to about 31 per cent in Japan, 26 per cent in Canada, 22 per cent in France, 18 per cent in the UK, only 11 per cent in the USA, and so on. Furthermore, the share of public sector investment in the country's total investment is about 60 per cent in India as against 48 per cent in USA, 20 per cent in UK, 12 per cent in Japan, and so on. The share of agriculture in national income is as large as about 48 per cent in India in contrast to 3 per cent in the USA, 3 per cent in the UK, 7 per cent in Canada, 7 per cent in France, 12 per cent in Japan, and so on.

[11] Madan (1965).

The causal link between the financial variables and the ultimate target variables comes mainly through the effect of interest rate and/or bank loans on the private sector's investment expenditures. For, the public sector's investment and the private and public sector's consumption expenditures are not quite sensitive to interest rate variations. Similarly, because agriculture, particularly in India, largely depends on the finance from the non-organized money and capital markets, its dominant role in the aggregate output renders monetary policy less effective. To the extent the recent nationalization of 14 major commercial banks in the country will reduce these bottlenecks for an effective use of monetary instruments, it will help increase the potency of monetary controls in India.

8. Monetary Problems and Monetary Policy in India

Monetary problems and policy should be discussed in relation to the objectives of monetary policy. We, therefore, first discuss its various objectives and then take up the survey of monetary problems and policy in India since 1951–52.

Objectives

Monetary policy is, as the Radcliffe Committee puts it, "economic policy of government in the monetary field." The objectives are, therefore, the same as those of any other economic policy of the government. They are:

1. A high and stable level of employment,
2. A high and growing level of income,
3. A reasonable stability of the price level,
4. A margin in the balance of payments, and
5. A stable exchange rate.

It is easy to see that these various objectives are inter-related. For instance, usually high levels of employment and income, rising prices (inflation), and deficits in the balance of payments go together; and low levels of employment and income, falling prices (deflation), and surpluses in the balance of payments also go together. In other words, the objectives of a high level of employment and income, and surplus in the balance of payments conflict with the objectives of price stability. Furthermore, the objectives of price stability may also conflict with the objective of exchange rate stability. Faced with these conflicting objectives monetary authorities, who implement the monetary policy, have to resolve these conflicts constantly by assigning different degrees of importance to these objectives in different economic situations. India's being a planned developing economy, she has been following a monetary policy of controlled expansion since 1951. The rationale of this policy is to increase money supply sufficiently to match the growth of real national income without generating inflation.

Problems and Policy in India

Monetary problems faced by the economy and monetary policy followed in India since 1951–52 may conveniently be discussed separately during India's different Five Year Plans periods:

First Plan Period: 1951–52 to 1955–56. The First Plan was launched at a time when the country was experiencing inflation first in consequence of the devaluation of the rupee in September 1949 and later because of the Korean War from June 1950 onwards. Further, this was the time when the Finance Ministry was headed by Mr. C. D. Deshmukh who, in his previous position as a Governor of the RBI, had already made it clear that he disliked cheap money policy and favoured dear money in a limited sense. His views were also popular in developed countries, particularly in Britain.

In order to control inflation and the high level of credit maintained by banks, which was being used by traders for a speculative build-up of inventories, the following three restrictive measures were undertaken by the monetary authorities at the beginning of the plan:

1. Effective November 15, 1951, the Bank rate was raised from 3 to 3.5 per cent.

2. RBI refused to buy government securities from banks except in special circumstances and instead it undertook large sales of government bonds. During the plan period as a whole the net sales of govement bonds (sales-purchases) in the open market amounted to Rs. 55.47 crores.

3. Effective March 1951, banks were required to keep a minimum of 20 per cent of their demand and time liabilities in the form of cash and unencumbered securities.

As a consequence, not only the money supply fell during the first two years of the plan but the bank credit also contracted by 8.9 per cent in the year 1952–53. Perturbed by these trends, the RBI turned to the cheap money policy by announcing the introduction of the Bill Market Scheme effective since January 1952. Under this scheme, eligible banks could borrow from the RBI against the security of promissory notes of their customers at a concessional rate; borrowing against the security of government bonds at the Bank rate was also permitted as before. The trend of monetary policy during the next four years, i.e., 1952–53 to 1955–56, remained nearly the same. Among the various effects of all these monetary measures, during the First Plan period as a whole were: an increase in the money supply by 10 per cent, an increase in commercial banks' credit by 39.5 per cent, an increase in real national income by 18.4 per cent, and a decrease in wholesale price index by 17.3 per cent (Appendix, Table 2). It is important to note that in this period the increase in national income was not matched by the increase in the money supply. During the first three years of the Plan, in which the natio-

Table 2. Change in Money Supply, Bank Credit, National Income and Prices Since 1951-52

(Percentage)

During	Change in			
	Money Supply	Commercial banks' credit	National income at constant prices	Wholesale price index (all commodities)
First Plan:				
1951-52 to 1955-56	10.0	39.5	18.4	—17.3
Second Plan:				
1956-57 to 1960-61	29.4	68.0	21.5	35.0
Third Plan:				
1961-62 to 1965-66	57.9	70.7	15.0	32.2
Three Annual Plans:				
1966-67 to 1968-69	27.6	26.0	13.6	25.7
Fourth Plan:				
1969-70	10.5	16.8	5.3*	3.7
Fourth Plan:				
1970-71	11.7	17.1	5.5*	5.5
Whole Period				
1951-52 to 1970-71	253.9	710.3	112.3*	113.0

SOURCES : (a) RBI: Various issues of *Report on Currency and Finance.*

(b) Central Statistical Organization : Various issues of *Statistical Abstracts of India.*

*Provisional.

nal income increased very fast, the money supply contracted; on the other hand, the money supply expanded fast in the last two years of the Plan, when the national income either did not rise or rose slowly or even declined. The paradox of an increase in national income with a decrease in money supply was due to the fact that the bulk of the increase in national income accrued in that sector of the economy, i.e., agriculture, the production of which was elastic neither with respect to money supply nor with respect to prices; it was elastic perhaps with respect to weather conditions.

Second Plan Period : 1956–57 to 1960–61. Like the First Plan, the Second Plan began with an inflationary potential, which began in the last year of the First Plan. In the last year of the First Plan, the money supply increased by about 14 per cent, bank credit by about 22 per cent, price index by about 8 per cent and the real national income by only about 2 per cent. Further, the Second Plan envisaged a deficit financing of the order of Rs. 1200 crores, one-fourth of the Plan's proposed outlay. This had its impact on the increase in money supply, on which the RBI had no control. In addition to these inflationary tendencies in the economy, the balance of payments position turned adverse from May 1956 and foreign exchange reserves had started falling. New credits of a medium-term nature were granted against imports of capital goods and for other purposes. There was also a heavy demand for bank credit to meet the tempo of investment activity in the private sector. Consequently, banks remained in over-extended positions and there was stringency in loanable funds even in slack seasons. Thus, the economy was ripe for a great wave of inflation.

Faced with these inflationary trends, the monetary authorities undertook, during the Second Plan period the following major monetary measures with a view to achieving stability in the economy:

1. The concessional rate on eligible banks' borrowings from the RBI under the Bill Market Scheme which was 0.5 per cent below the bank rate at the beginning of the scheme and 0.25 per cent below the bank rate effective March 1, 1956, was further raised to be equal to the bank rate effective November 21, 1956. Besides, effective from the same date, the stamp duty, i.e., charge on converting a demand promissory note into an usance bill, was raised from practically zero to 0.5 per cent so that the effective rate under the scheme moved to 0.5 per cent above the bank rate.

2. Effective May 1956, selective credit controls to curb banks' advances against food grains, oilseeds, and shares and debentures were made a regular feature of the monetary policy in India. In the order of timings, these controls were levied on scheduled commercial banks' advances against rice and paddy (May 1956), wheat (September 1956), sugar (June 1957), shares and debentures (August 1958), groundnuts (February 1959), etc.

3. Moral suasion, in the form of requests to banks and conferences with the representatives of selected banks, to achieve a positive reduction in the level of bank credit without diminishing assistance to the essential sectors of the economy, was used by the RBI quite frequently during the Second Plan period.

4. Effective May 16, 1957, the bank rate was raised from 3.5 per cent to 4.0 per cent.

5. Effective March 11, 1960, the reserve requirement ratios on additional (new) demand and time liabilities of scheduled commercial banks were raised from 5 and 2 per cent of demand and time liabilities respectively to 25 per cent of demand and time liabilities. On May 5, 1960, the additional reserve requirement ratio was further raised to 50 per cent. However, these additional requirements were abolished in November 1960.

6. A back door increase in the effective bank rate was announced effective October 1, 1960, when the quota-cum-slab rate system, also known as the tier system of the RBI's lending rates, was introduced for eligible banks' borrowings from the RBI. Under this system, borrowings up to 50 per cent of the borrowing bank's average statutory reserves in the preceding quarter with the RBI were

available at the Bank rate, borrowings up to the next 50 per cent were charged 1 per cent above the bank rate, and borrowings above 100 per cent of average statutory reserves in the preceding quarter were made available at 2 per cent above the Bank rate.

7. During the five years of the Plan, the RBI undertook net open market sales of government bonds in the amount of Rs. 188.81 crores (Table 4).

Table 3. Bank Rate of the RBI Since 1951-52

(Percentage)

Date	Effective Rate
Prior to November 15, 1951	3.0
November 15, 1951 to May 15, 1957	3.5
May 16, 1957 to January 2, 1963	4.0
January 3, 1963 to September 24, 1964	4.5
September 25, 1964 to February 16, 1965	5.0
February 17, 1965 to March 1, 1968	6.0
March 2, 1968 to January 8, 1971	5.0
January 9, 1971 to date	6.0

SOURCE: Various issues of *Reserve Bank of India Bulletin.*

These various measures were not always in the direction of dear money policy. In times of stringency in the credit market, they were relaxed towards cheap money policy. The margins under selective credit controls and requests under moral suasion were changed from time to time to create desirable conditions in the market. It is clear that monetary policy was used more intensively and extensively during the second plan than ever before.

During the period 1956–57 through 1960–61, the money supply increased by 29.4 per cent, commercial bank credit by 68 per cent, real national income by 21.5 per cent, and the wholesale price index by 35 per cent (Appendix Table 2). In these five years, the real national income declined (by 1 per cent) only in the year 1957–58, the year in which the wholesale price index fell by 0.2 per cent.

Third Plan Period: 1961–62 to 1965–66. The Third Plan was launched at the time when the country was on a stronger path of expansion than ever before, though it was also in the grip of inflation. In the last year of the Second Plan, the real national income and the wholesale price index had increased by 7.3 per cent and 7.2 per cent respectively in contrast to only a 1.9 per cent and 8 per cent increase in them, respectively, in the last year of the First Plan. The Third Plan envisaged an acceleration of the industrialization programme that was initiated in the Second Plan and a considerable stepping up of agricultural production. In order not to push inflation further, deficit financing was planned only at Rs. 550 crores, as against the actual amount of deficit financing of Rs. 948 crores in the Second Plan, and every effort was to be made to restrict the increase in money supply both on account of the government and the private sectors to the genuine requirements of production. Inspite of fairly liberal foreign aid, the availability of foreign exchange resources continued to act as a severe restraint. The build-up in defence expenditure following the Chinese aggression in November 1962 added to these strains. The low return to investment in agriculture, which continued to be more or less in unorganized sector, was another disturbing factor. To maintain growth with stability in the economy, monetary measures, along with fiscal and direct measures, had to be used rather carefully.

The monetary policy during the Third Plan continued to be characterized by caution with due regard to the needs of the development plan and the changing economy. The Plan began with relaxation of controls, which were again made stringent with time beginning from 1962–63. The various major monetary measures undertaken during the period under review were the following:

1. The larger limits for RBI's loans to eligible banks under the Bill Market Scheme on bills by sugar and jute mills were sanctioned. This measure was taken to enable banks to obviate credit difficulties of these mills.

2. The quota of RBI's loans to eligible banks at the bank rate was increased

by their amounts of loans to co-operative credit and small-scale institutions. This measure was announced to encourage the growth of the co-operative sector and small industries in the country.

3. Selective credit controls on advances against those commodities whose supplies and prices had improved were either relaxed or withdrawn. For example, controls in the case of advances against paddy, rice, groundnuts, and shares were relaxed; while controls in respect of sugar, wheat, raw-jute goods, and clean advances were withdrawn.

4. Controls on advances to all parties except co-operative and marketing societies in respect of stock of paddy and rice against warehouse receipts which were exempted before were imposed, effective January 1963. This measure aimed at discouraging the use of warehousing for speculative hoarding.

5. Bank advances against stock of sugar, through prescribing a minimum margin of 45 per cent on credit limits on advances granted to parties other than those manufacturing sugar and on those granted to parties manufacturing sugar in respect of stock which have left the factory or mill's premises on which excise duty has been paid, were brought under regulation effective April 1963. This measure was aimed at checking the rising sugar prices.

6. The three-tier system was replaced by the four-tier system of the RBI's lending rates effective July 1962. Under the new system, the first, second, and third slabs of 25 per cent, 25 per cent and 50 per cent of the borrowing bank's average statutory reserves in the previous quarter were charged, respectively, at the bank rate, at 1 per cent above the bank rate, and at 2 per cent above the bank rate. Borrowings in excess of 100 per cent of reserves were charged at 2.5 per cent above the bank rate. This system of graded lending rates was intended to make the cost of credit more flexible to match the seasonal variability of the demand for liquidity.

7. Ceiling at 100 per cent of its average statutory reserves was imposed on a member bank's borrowings from the RBI in normal cases with effect from October 1962. Thus, the four-tier system was changed to the three-tier system of the RBI's lending rates.

8. The bank rate was raised from 4 per cent to 4.5 per cent effective January 3, 1963, to 5 per cent effective September 25, 1964, and to 6 per cent effective February 17, 1965.

9. The three-tier system was substituted by a two-tier system of the RBI's lending rates effective January 3, 1963. This was done by merging the first two slabs of the earlier three-tier system. Under the new system, 50 per cent of the average statutory reserves could be borrowed at the bank rate and the remaining 50 per cent at $1\frac{1}{2}$ per cent above the bank rate.

10. Ceiling on an eligible bank's borrowings from the RBI was increased from 100 per cent to 150 per cent of its reserves effective October, 1963. The last 50 per cent could be borrowed at 2 per cent above the bank rate.

11. The primary reserve requirement ratios for commercial banks were changed from 5 per cent of demand and 2 per cent of time liabilities, to 3 per cent of demand and time liabilities effective September 1964. As the proportion of commercial banks' demand and time liabilities was about 50 : 50 in September 1964, on the whole the new reserve requirements were less than the old ones.

12. The secondary reserve requirement on commercial banks' demand and time liabilities was raised from 20 per cent to 25 per cent effective September 1964.

13. The quota-cum-slab rate system was replaced by a differential system of interest rates with respect to eligible banks' borrowings from the RBI effective September, 1964. Under the new system, the effective lending rate depends on the bank rate and borrowing bank's net liquidity ratio. Banks maintaining a certain minimum liquidity ratio could borrow at the bank rate; other banks could borrow only at the penalty rate, which went up with every 1 per cent point decline in their liquidity ratio. The penalty rates were revised upward until November 1966, when a slight relaxation in the system of differential interest rates was announced. As a consequence, the effective average

cost of commercial banks' borrowings from the RBI was pushed up from 5.15 per cent in 1963–64 to 5.78 per cent in 1964–65, and to 6.99 per cent in 1965–66.

14. Credit Authorization Scheme was introduced in November 1965. Under this scheme, scheduled commercial banks are required to obtain the RBI's authorization before sanctioning any fresh credit limit of Rs. 1 crore or more to any single party or any limit that would take the total limit enjoyed by such party from the entire banking system to Rs. 1 crore or more on secured and/or unsecured basis.

15. The RBI undertook net open market sales in the amount of Rs. 172.29 crores during the Third Plan period (Table 5).

Table 4. Open Market Operations of the RBI Since 1951-52

(Rs. crores)

Year		Net Purchases(+) or Sales (—)
First Plan	1951—52	11.82
	1952—53	—1.20
	1953—54	—22.14
	1954—55	—28.00
	1955—56	—15.95
Total :		—55.47
Second Plan	1956—57	19.17
	1957—58	—65.22
	1958—59	—88.95
	1959—60	—60.33
	1960—61	—6.52
Total :		—188.81
Third Plan	1961—62	0.81
	1962—63	—11.00
	1963—64	—44.70
	1964—65	—98.60
	1965—66	—18.80
Total :		—172.29
Annual Plans	1966—67	—44.40
	1967—68	—38.20
	1968—69	—53.40
Total :		—136.00
Fourth Plan	1969—70	—30.00
	1970—71	—84.10

SUORCE : RBI : Various *Reports on Currency and Finance.*

We thus conclude that the monetary policy played a very active role during the Third Plan period. During this period, the money supply increased by 57.9 per cent, commercial banks' credit by 70.7 per cent real national income by 15 per cent, and wholesale price index by 32.2 per cent (Table 2). In these years, the wholesale price index fell only once in 1961–62 by 3.1 per cent, the real national income also fell only once in 1965–66 by 2.3 per cent; money supply and bank credit increased in all these years.

Three Annual Plans Period : *1966–67 to 1968–69.* The last year of the Third Plan was characterized by a decline in the real national income by 2.3 per cent, and by increases in wholesale price index by 8.1 per cent, in money supply by 10.6 per cent, and in commercial bank credit by 12.1 per cent. The pressure on prices emanated from both supply and demand sides. The supply position in regard to both consumer goods and industrial raw-materials was tight because of a 16.3 per cent decline in agricultural production and only a 4 per cent increase in industrial output in 1965–66. These trends were largely due to the severe drought over large parts of the country in that year. The expansion in aggregate monetary demand is reflected in the 10.6 per cent increase in money supply in that year. Thus, the year 1966–67 began with a greater pressure on prices and a more severe fall in national output than ever before. In this context the RBI undertook the following important monetary measures in the year 1966–67 and in the next two years.

1. Under the instrument of moral suasion, through letters on May 26, 1966 and June 6, 1966, and a meeting with banks on June 15, 1967, the RBI requested all scheduled commercial banks to strive for a return flow of advances against seasonal commodities and to invest the accretion to their resources by way of deposit increase and the return flow of credit in government bonds, including Treasury bills.

2. In order to meet the increased volume of credit demand generated then

by the expected recovery of agricultural production, a larger quantum to imports, and the expected increase in industrial production, the credit policy for the busy season of 1966–67 provided for larger access by commercial banks to the RBI at the bank rate. Every bank, in addition to the funds it could have earlier obtained if its net liquidity ratio was at or above 30 per cent, was now able to secure a tranche of refinance at the bank rate equal to 10 per cent of its net liquidity ratio at the end of the slack season. Besides, all banks were now allowed refinance at the bank rate up to 10 per cent of their actual net liquidity position at the end of the slack season.

3. Under the selective credit controls instrument, during the year 1966–67 the RBI advised banks to exercise controls over clean advances and advances against all domestic commodities in short supply.

4. Effective August 12, 1966, State Cooperative banks were classified into scheduled and non-scheduled State Cooperative banks, and the former were brought under the same reserve requirements as commercial banks, i.e., 3 per cent of demand and time liabilities.

5. In order to check recession in some of the domestic engineering industries, especially those with export potentialities, the RBI announced, in August 1967, ceilings on rates charged by the banks to the ultimate borrowers at 6 per cent in respect of packing credit advances to exporters of engineering and metallurgical products and at 8 per cent in respect of other packing credit and post-shipment export bills. Simultaneously, refinance from the RBI was made available at a preferential rate of 4.5 per cent (i.e., 1.5 per cent below the bank rate) in respect of scheduled commercial banks' packing credit advances to exporters or engineering and metallurgical products and at the bank rate in respect of packing credits to exporters of other products, as also in respect of post-shipment export bills in all currencies.

6. With a view to directing credit to the priority sectors, on January 29, 1968, the RBI announced a concesssional rate of 4.5 per cent on refinance by the RBI of the total increase in commercial banks' advances over the base period to the priority sectors.

7. The bank rate was reduced from 6 to 5 per cent effective March 2, 1968. This measure was expected to provide a further push to credit liberalization policy followed in those days.

8. Effective March 2, 1968, the RBI imposed a ceiling rate of 9.5 per cent on the scheduled commercial banks' loan rate.

9. Effective June 1968, the RBI advised banks to advance credit to deserving borrowers of small means for productive purposes on the basis of their integrity and credit worthiness even on an unsecured basis.

10. Following the improvement in the supply position and a fall in prices of certain agricultural commodities in 1967–68, selective credit controls on advances against various commodities were relaxed or eliminated, during 1968–69. They were relaxed on scheduled commercial banks' advances against oilseeds and vegetable oils first in January 1968 and again in May 1968; against raw cotton first in April 1968 and again in June 1968; against "other food grains," i.e., food grains excluding paddy and rice, and wheat, in May 1968; and against paddy and rice in March 1969. Controls on advances against raw cotton to cotton mills were completely removed in November 1968.

11. The RBI undertook net open market sales of government bonds to the amount of Rs. 136 crores during the period under review (Table 4).

Thus, it is clear that the RBI made use of all its policy instruments during the period of three years, 1966–69. While the instruments of open market operations and reserve requirement ratios were used to create dear money policy, the instruments of bank rate, selective credit controls, and moral suasion, in general, were directed towards cheap money policy. One important development during this period was to encourage credit to the priority sectors and to the weaker sections of the community.

During the period under review, the money supply increased by 27.6 per cent, commercial banks' credit by 26 per cent, real national income by 13.6 per cent, and the wholesale price index by 25.7 per cent. The country thus obtained a reasonable progress, which was of course not all due to monetary measures.

First Two Years of the Fourth Plan: 1969–70 and 1970. The Fourth Plan began at a time when the country was on a slow growth path with a near price stability. The real national income increased only by 2.4 per cent in 1968–69 in contrast to a 7 per cent increase in it in 1967–68. On the demand side, the increase in money was nearly the same in 1968–69 (7.6 per cent) as in 1967–68 (8.1 per cent). The wholesale price index actually declined by 1.2 per cent in 1968–69 as against an increase in it by 4.2 per cent in 1967–68. The task for monetary policy, as for other policy measures, was, therefore to bring about again a rapid expansion in the economy. The 14 major commercial banks were nationalized with effect from July 19, 1969. This made the task of the monetary authorities easier. During the period under review, the following major monetary policy measures were undertaken by the RBI:

1. In August 1969, the RBI relaxed the Bill Market Scheme with respect to the banks' borrowings from it for financing the distribution of fertilizers. The minimum amount of usance promissory notes in respect of advances granted for distribution of fertilizers was reduced from Rs. 50,000 to Rs. 25,000, and the minimum amount that could be borrowed was reduced from Rs. 5 lakhs to Rs. 1 lakh. A similar concession was made for refinancing advances granted by banks to small-scale industries.

2. Owing to the improved supply position and the considerable fall in their prices, control on advances against gur was withdrawn on January 21, 1970, and against sugar on May 4, 1970.

3. The 9.5 per cent ceiling rate of interest on bank advances was removed with effect from January 21, 1970.

4. In view of the tight supply position and the sharp rise in prices of certain agricultural commodities, selective credit controls were tightened on credit against such commodities. The minimum margin on advances against oilseeds and vegetable oils was raised uniformly for advances to all parties to 60 per cent of the value of stocks, against food grains to 50 per cent, against cotton and kapas to the parties other than these mills to 60 per cent and to the mills 40 per cent, etc., effective January 21, 1970.

5. The minimum rate on advances against foodgrains, oilseeds, vegetable oils, and cotton and kapas was prescribed at 10 per cent effective January 21, 1970, and the same was raised to 12 per cent effective April 28, 1970. These measures endeavoured to check the persistent rise in prices of these commodities.

6. In order to check the sharp rise in bank credit as well as in the borrowings of banks from the RBI, through a letter on February 5, 1970, the RBI withdrew the refinance facility at the bank rate for food procurement advances, discontinued the availability of refinance up to the total of short-term lending to agriculture at $1\frac{1}{2}$ below the bank rate, and permitted only direct lending to agriculture for refinance at the bank rate.

7. The minimum liquidity ratio qualifying for bank rate refinance was raised from 30 to 31 per cent effective February 19, 1970, to 32 per cent effective April 24, 1970, to 33 per cent effective 1970, and to 34 per cent effective January 29, 1971.

8. The bank rate was raised from 5 to 6 per cent with effect from January 9, 1971. Simultaneously, the ceiling rates on saving deposits were increased from 3.5 to 4 per cent, on fixed deposits for 15 days to 45 days from 1.25 to 2 per cent, and on those for 46 days to 90 days from 2.5 to 3 per cent. The ceiling rates on fixed deposits of other maturity categories up to one year was raised by 0.25 per cent and of one year up to five years maturity categories by 0.5 per cent. The maximum rate payable was fixed at 7.25 per cent in respect of deposits for periods above five years.

9. The RBI undertook net open market sales of government bonds in the amount of Rs. 30 crores in 1969–70, and of Rs. 84.1 crores in 1970–71.

Thus, during the period under review

all instruments of monetary controls, except the variable reserve requirement ratio, were used. The percentage increases in the money supply, bank credit, real income, and wholesale prices were, respectively, 10.5, 16.8, 5.3 and 3.7 per cent in 1969–70, and 11.7, 17.1, 5.5, and 5.5 in 1970–71. It is instructive to note that inspite of all these monetary measures and many fiscal and direct measures, the inflationary trends persisted in the economy.

9. Evaluation of the Monetary Policy

The survey of the RBI's monetary policy over a period of the last 20 years indicates

Table 5. Reserve Requirement Ratios for Commercial and Co-operative Banks Since 1951-52

(Percentage)

Date	Effective rate on: Demand Liabilities: Commercial banks	Demand Liabilities: State Co-operative banks	Time Liabilities: Commercial banks	Time Liabilities: State Co-operative banks
Prior to March 11, 1960	5	2.5	2	1
March 11, 1960 to May 5, 1960	5 on existing + 25 on additional	2.5	2 on existing + 25 on additional	1
May 6, 1960 to November 10, 1960	5 on the level existed on march 10 + 25 on addition upto May 5 + 50 on further additions	2.5	2 on the level existed on March 10 + 25 on addition upto May 5 + 50 on further addition	1
November 11, 1960 to September 24, 1964	5	2.5	2	1
September 25, 1964 to August 11, 1966	3	2.5	3	1
August 12, 1966 to-date	3	3% for Sch. banks 2.5% for non-sch. banks	3	3% for sch. banks 1% for non-sch. banks

Source: RBI: *Functions and Working* (1970)

that the RBI is making extensive and intensive use of both traditional and modern instruments of credit control to help achieve growth with stability in the economy. The use of modern techniques, selective credit controls in particular started in 1956 and now it has become a dominant technique of monetary controls. This is quite in line with the objective of leading towards a socialist pattern of society.

On the whole, the monetary policy in India has followed the objective of "controlled expansion" by keeping down the rate of expansion of aggregate bank credit and by favouring certain types of borrowings. The RBI has been unable to arrest inflationary trends in the economy, for it does not have much control over the two important factors, which contribute to inflation. They are production and deficit financing. The production, particularly agricultural production in India, depends more on weather conditions, etc., than on the availability, cost, and the use of credit. Similarly, the amount of deficit financing, which causes a direct increase in the money supply, is decided by the government autonomously on the basis of plan expenditures and revenues. The fiscal policy and the non-monetary measures, such as a suitable policy regarding wages, and price-control and rationing, should play an important role and these should be better co-ordinated with monetary policy measures to achieve price stabilization.

The progress achieved by the country during the period of 20 years under review seems quite satisfactory. The money supply has increased by 253.9 per cent, commercial banks' credit by 710.3 per cent, real national income by 112.3 per cent, wholesale price index by 113 per cent, and so on. Needless to say, all this progress is not due to monetary policy alone.

REFERENCES

Aschheim, J., *Techniques of Monetary Control* (Baltimore: John Hopkins Press, 1961).

Fousek, P.G., *Foreign Central Banking: The Instruments of Monetary Policy* (New York: Federal Reserve Bank, 1957).

Ghosh, A., *Indian Economy, Its Nature and Problems* (Calcutta: World Press Private Ltd., 1961).

Gupta, G.S. (1972), "Money Supply Determinants and Their Relative Contribution to Monetary Growth in India," *Indian Economic Review*, Vol. VII (New Series). No. 1 (April), 1972.

Madan, B.K., India, in Crick, W. F. (editor): *Commonwealth Banking Systems* (Oxford: Clarenden Press, 1965).

Raj, K.N. (1948), *The Monetary Policy of the Reserve Bank of India* (Bombay: National Information and Publication Ltd., 1948).

Reserve Bank of India (Yearly Issues): *Report on Currency and Finance* (Various Issues).

Reserve Bank of India, (Open Market Operations of the Reserve Bank of India, *RBI Bulletin* (June, 1960).

Reserve Bank of India, *Functions and Working* (Bombay: Reserve Bank of India Press, 1970).

Sethi, J.D., *Problems of Monetary Policy in an Underdeveloped country, with special Reference to India* (Bombay: Asia Publishing House 1961).

19

Inflation and Economic Growth in India

G. C. DORAI

1. Theoretical considerations: an Overview

Inflation, or a secular and persistent increase in the general price level, is a world phenomenon. Almost all countries throughout history have experienced some degree of inflation. During the greater part of the twentieth century, the developing nations as well as the industrially advanced countries have undergone rapid inflation, with relatively very short periods of price stability. The rate, duration, causes, and consequences of inflation may differ from one country to another and from one period to the next. This is because the mechanisms initiating inflation, the attitude and behavioural response of individuals, institutions and groups in society towards it, and the government's ability and willingness to control the inflationary process differ markedly. Other variables that have considerable bearing on the strength and duration of inflation include: the stage of a country's economic development, its degree of dependence on foreign trade, the power and militancy of trade unions as well as the presence or absence of excess aggregate demand.

In order to understand the trend of prices in India during the last two decades, it is necessary to analyse in broad detail some of the features of the Indian economy which make it inflation-prone. The analysis of inflation generally applicable to a developed industrial country like the UK or the USA needs to be modified to take account of the nature and characteristics of a developing economy such as India. Most of the Keynesian-type analyses of inflation in which the overall pressure of aggregate demand pulls prices up in the face of full utilization of available resources, or the monetarist-type theories which seek to explain inflation by correlating the quantity of money in the economy with the availability of goods and services, are not easily applicable in the context of a developing economy. On the other hand, the explanation for persistent inflationary trends has to be sought in the nature of the development process itself. It is not very meaningful to categorize the inflationary process as being that of a simple "demand pull" or "cost push" variety. Accordingly, we shall show a model of inflationary behaviour taking explicit account of the changing structure of the Indian economy during the Five Year Plans, and in terms of the various aggregate economic variables which influence price behaviour.

Understanding the causes and process of inflation is very essential in order to be able to moderate and control its more undesirable consequences. Although inflation is almost always accompanied by an increase in the quantity of money, the latter may be a consequence, rather than the proximate cause of the rise in prices. The monetary authorities or the banking system may passively respond to the additional demand for money generated by the inflationary spiral. Assume, for example, an autonomous decline in the quantity of agricultural output resulting from unfavourable weather conditions. Given the existing demand for final consumption or exports or by the industrial sector for agricultural inputs, there will be a rise in the relative prices of the primary products, in the absence of sizeable imports or compensatory sales from buffer stocks (if any). As the agricultural sector constitutes a significant proportion of total net national product, the general price level will increase. The price index rises not only because of the direct rise in the price of agricultural wage goods, but indirectly because the cost of farm goods used as inputs in industry has risen, and consequently the prices of manufactured goods increase too. Not only this, to the extent that consumers buy manufactured products, their cost of living goes up further. Certain industrial products used as inputs in other user industries go up in price, and those sectors find their costs and prices rising simultaneously. In short, a mechanism causing an inflationary process is already apparent. If workers now clamour for higher money wages to maintain their real incomes and living standards, wages would have to be increased further, providing additional fuel to the accelerating rise in prices. Assuming all industries maintain their initial profit margins, mark-ups will continue to ensure a rising price index throughout the economy. Under these conditions, the monetary authorities would have to increase the quantity of money to satisfy the additional need for means of payment. Otherwise unemployment or a liquidity crisis will ensue. Thus, we find that the quantity of money may respond passively to the inflationary spiral, rather than causing that process initially. In this situation, controlling the quantity of money will not result in the disappearance of the "real" phenomena which is the underlying cause of inflation.

The Need for Balanced Growth

One of the most important causes of inflation in India as well as other developing countries is to be found in the inability of the agricultural sector to expand its output in relation to the growth of demand. It is well known that the income elasticity of demand for food is high at low levels of per capita income. It has been estimated that the average income elasticity for India is in the neighborhood of 0.63.[1] If population grows at an average rate of 2 to 2.5 per cent per year as in fact happened in India during the 50's and 60's, respectively, and if per capita income grows at 3 per cent or thereabouts (as planned), the demand for food may be expected to be roughly rising at 3.8 to 4.4 per cent annually. The minimum annual rate of expansion of output of foodgrains must, therefore, be in this neighbourhood, unless the country has recourse to, or wants to, import food.

The output of commercial crops such as cotton, jute, tea, oilseeds, and other agricultural raw materials must also increase commensurately with the need for them as industrial inputs (as determined by the country's input-output structure), or as exports. Otherwise, there is bound to develop shortages of these commodities, leading to a gradual and persistent increase in their relative prices, as well as shortfalls in the achievement of Plan targets set for industry and export per-

---

1 Economic Commission for Asia and the Far East, *Economic Survey*, 1964, p. 123.

formance. This results in overall inflationary pressures. Exports may suffer because of inadequate supplies or because the pressure of "home demand" and a ready domestic market leave exporters with little incentives to seek foreign markets. India's competitiveness in these commodities also suffers as a consequence. As a result, the country's capacity to import is reduced, foreign exchange earnings decrease, and overall shortages of essential imports ensue. In addition, imports of these very commodities (food and agricultural raw materials which could be produced at home) are required to meet domestic needs of an expanding population and growing industry. But this means diversion of foreign exchange from other uses which suffer in consequence.

This theoretical model explains, in large part, the achievements as well as failures observed in the Indian Government's concern with maintenance of price stability during the decades of the 50's and 60's. More importantly, it helps to identify the real causes and consequences of inflationary pressures in India, rather than concentrate on the usual quantity theory approach. Many other relevant factors, such as fiscal and monetary developments, large budget deficits, outlays on non-developmental expenditures in excess of planned magnitudes, defence spending, and overall industrialization policy and performance, affect price trends in the economy. These will be examined in the following pages.

In the next section, we shall briefly examine the case for and against inflation as a stimulant to economic growth, since this will help us understand India's recent inflationary experience in proper perspective. It is interesting to note that India provides us with a good real-world example of government-engineered capital formation in a democracy, using many of the techniques advocated by a generation of planners, and development economists, including inflationary methods of financing of economic development. Also, governmental policies and actions during the Plan periods to control the rise in prices can be related to the concern with the consequences of inflation. In Section III, we shall describe the inflationary trends in the Indian economy during the period 1950–51 to 1970–71, and attempt to relate them to the theoretical outline presented in Sections I and II. Some of the conclusions directly emanating from this analysis and the price policy pursued by the Indian Government will be discussed in Section IV. And finally, in Section V, certain concluding comments and observations, which have significance for developing economies generally and India in particular, are set forth.

2. Inflationary Financing of Investment : Pros and Cons

There are two distinct schools of thought among economists about the efficacy of inflation in generating capital formation and rapid economic development. According to the pro-inflationist school, forced savings, brought about through deliberate deficit financing of investment programmes, is a swift method of mobilizing resources for development.[2] It is also argued by some that "a slow and steady rate of inflation provides a most powerful aid to the attainment of a steady rate of economic progress."[3] The theoretical argument for inflation as an engine of growth is based on the assumption that (1) in an under-developed economy, voluntary saving and investment ratios are too low, (2) the tax system is too inelastic to generate the needed investible resources for the public sector, and (3) in the face of supply bottle-necks and institutional rigidities, the private sector's incentives for raising the ratio of investment to national income are limited. Real capital formation is also hampered by lack of mobility of resources. Private capital markets are undeveloped, and financial

[2] See Arthur Lewis, "Economic Development with Unlimited Supplies of Labour," *The Manchester School,* May 1954 (Reprinted in A. N. Agarwala and S. P. Singh (eds.), *The Economics of Underdevelopment* (Oxford University Press, 1963).

[3] A. P. Thirlwall and C. A. Brown, "Inflation and Growth : The International Evidence," *Banca Nazionale del Lavoro quarterly* (September 1971).

institutions as vehicles for transfering savings of rural households and other surplus units (savers) to urban industry or other deficit units (investors) are inadequate or imperfect. It is further argued that the market mechanism does not adequately reflect social priorities and that there exists a large potential for real investment and capital formation by transfering surplus labour from the agricultural sector to modern industry—the urban or capitalist sector. In these circumstances, it is possible to accelerate economic growth by a deliberate policy of credit creation, bidding away resources for real investment and capital formation, thus raising the rate of saving in the economy. Thus inflation is considered as an alternative to increased taxation, which is administratively difficult or politically impossible. Inflationary financing of investment can break the barriers of the "vicious circle of poverty and unemployment," provided it is done judiciously, and suitable projects with low gestation periods are chosen for the investment programme. In this view, inflation is a "growing pain," and is the lesser evil than stagnation or perpetual poverty. In fact, inflation is inevitable for growth; it is beneficial and desirable; its long run benefits far outweigh the shortrun costs. It is a self-liquidating process because, if undertaken in appropriate doses, the fruits of investment projects begin to flow through the pipelines with a minimum time lag.

The opponents of this theory emphasize the undesirable and harmful consequences of inflation.[4] It is pointed out that inflation is a highly discriminatory and inequitable form of tax, imposing intolerable burdens on the poorer sections of the community, leading to social tensions and political instability. Groups with fixed incomes (government servants, retired pensioners, rentiers, wage-earners with limited bargaining power, bond holders, and other saving units) bear the burden of inflation, as the purchasing power of their contractual income shrink in value. Inflation erodes the real value of savings. The incentives to save and invest get distorted, as people try to protect their savings by seeking forms of investment which appreciate in value over time, rather than in terms of calculations of current returns or socially desirable forms. The tendency for speculation abounds with the rising price level. Time and effort are invested in bidding up property values against one another. If the inflationary spiral gathers momentum, expectations are generated which result in eventual loss of confidence in money, and when this happens, the monetary mechanism may break down. The longer inflation lasts, the greater the distortions that it creates. It is difficult to contain the rate of inflation within narrow limits, and it soon gets out of hand. As the internal value of the monetary unit declines, balance of payments difficulties begin to pile up. The currency becomes overvalued under a regime of fixed exchange rates, and exports get priced out of foreign markets. Imports increase as foreign goods become relatively cheaper to buy. Foreign exchange reserves are lost, and capital inflows decline as foreign investors lose confidence in the currency. Government and the monetary authorities are unable to control the deteriorating situation, as they find that they have killed the "goose which lays the golden egg." In sum, forced saving is a self-destructive process, because the inflation soon gets out of hand, and whatever shortrun benefits it provides for stepping up the rate of capital formation are illusory in the long run.

Inflation and Growth : The Historical Evidence

This debate can now be put in historical perspective by assessing the efficacy of inflation in generating or retarding growth in other countries.

There have been several empirical attempts dealing with the relationship between inflation and economic growth.[5] A number of statistical studies have been made to document the evidence from historical country case studies purporting to

[4] See S. Mookerjee, "Financial Stability and Planning," *Finance and Development,* March 1972, p. 5.

[5] See U. Tun Wai, "The Relation between Inflation and Economic Development : A Statistical Inductive Study," *IMF Staff Papers,* October

show whether inflation helps or hampers the process of development. Unfortunately, the results are not clear-cut or conclusive. In the case of some countries, [profit] inflation resulted in redistributing income towards capitalists with a high propensity to save, thus aiding investment, capital formation, and economic growth. Thus, according to Rostow, "In Britain of the 1790's, the United States of the 1850's and Japan of the 1870's capital formation was aided by price inflation, which shifted resources from consumption to profits."[6] However, in an extensive empirical study, Geoffrey Maynard has reported[7] that the rapid growth that took place in the USA during the 1870's and early 1880's was associated with periods of rising as well as falling prices. High rates of growth were observed in the late 90's and early 1900's when prices were rising, but the decade before the First World War witnessed very rapid rates of inflation with slow growth. He has also shown that during the greater part of the 19th century, prices were secularly falling in the United Kingdom, and yet this period was characterised by rapid growth of national income as well as per capita output. After 1895, prices began to rise almost continuously, but during this period, the growth of the economy was slower than in the preceding 40 years.

Japan and USSR both experienced government-sponsored growth through inflationary means. In the case of Japan, inflation did not retard growth, as evidenced by almost continuous inflation coupled with spectacular growth of the economy since the 1870's as well as in the recent post war years.

Russian economic growth and industrialization in the 1930's was accompanied by severe inflationary pressures. In fact the cost of living of urban workers increased by over 650 per cent over a decade. Money wages rose much less, and the worker's real wages fell by one-half! But there is no doubt that a high rate of capital formation and rapid growth of the economy took place during this decade.

Looking at more recent historical evidence from less developed countries, the experience of many Latin American countries during 1946–1966 gives no clear correlation between rates of inflation and economic growth.[8] In some of these countries, high rates of inflation retarded growth: yet in others, rates of growth above average were achieved simultaneously with severe inflationary pressures. Nor did the absence of inflation or relative price stability in some countries necessarily promote growth. In fact, different patterns of overall price trends have been observed with high as well as low rates of economic growth, or even stagnation and retardation. However, there is some evidence for the view that rates of inflation in excess of 10 per cent per year are inimical to growth, whereas rates between 3 to 10 per cent do not seem to influence growth very much one way or the other. The acceptable or tolerable rate of inflation seems to be a matter of getting used to it rather than *a priori* reasoning by economists or statisticians.

3. Price Trends during 1950-51 to 1970-71

The inflationary trends in the Indian economy under the impact of the Five Year Plans can best be studied by looking at the behaviour of prices during each Plan period. Although this procedure is somewhat arbitrary, it will help us to understand how the general and sectoral price levels reacted to the overall imbalance between aggregate demand and supply under the impact of rising development outlays. The ratio of investment (I) to net national income (N.I.) was progressively increased under the first three Plans

1959; R. J. Bhatia, "Inflation, Deflation and Economic Development," *IMF Staff Papers,* November 1960; Graeme Dorrance, "Inflation and Growth: The Statistical Evidence," *IMF Staff Papers,* March 1966.

6 W. W. Rostow, *The Economist,* 15 August 1959, reported in Thirwall & Brown, op. cit.

7 Geoffrey Maynard, *Economic Development and the Price Level,* pp. 117–23.

8 Thirwall and Brown, op. cit. See also Committee for Economic Development, *How Low Income Countries Can Raise Their Own Growth,* (Washington, September 1966), pp. 23–46.

with a view to stepping up the rate of capital formation and economic growth. Domestic savings (s) available (household and corporate and governmental savings) to finance the investment programme were inadequate. The investment and saving ratios were:

	First Plan	Second Plan	Third Plan
I/NI	7.4	10.2	12.8
S/NI	5.7	8.1	9.8

Some of the factors that have a direct influence on the price level would be:

1. The overall size of the investment outlays
2. The strategy of planning and sectoral allocations of Investment.
3. Availability of external aid (or foreign exchange reserves)
4. Methods of financing the gap between Investment and Savings
5. Success of the plan in achieving the targets set.

Given the size of the investment programme and the marginal propensity to consume, national expenditures or aggregate demand would rise. The increase in the supply of goods and services available to satisfy the demand generated would be a function of the productive capacity created by the investment as defined by the marginal capital/output ratio. Such parameters as the capital/employment ratio, the gestation period of the investments chosen and the productivity of the resources employed would determine whether or not aggregate demand and supply are in balance. In order to avoid a rise in the general price level, the supply of wage goods (especially food products and manufactured consumer goods) must keep pace with the spending patterns of income recipients.

As discussed in Sections I and II, the most important criterion for price stability (or alternatively, to prevent an excessive or socially unacceptable rate inflation) is that there must be an overall balance between the output of the agricultural sector and the industrial sector's demand for it. Also since economic development implies urbanisation and monetisation of the economy, the agricultural sector must produce enough food not only to satisfy its own increasing demand consistent with the income elasticity of farmers, but to meet the requirements of the urban workers engaged in the investment projects. The behaviour of marketed surplus of agricultural produce is thus an important determinant of the trend of food prices.

Deflationary Growth during the First Plan

The general price level during the First Plan rose remarkably little because of the tremendous success achieved in the production of agricultural commodities. The Plan outlays were modest in relation to the size of the economy. Investment in agricultural projects was emphasized, and thanks to favourable weather conditions, the index of agricultural production over the Plan period increased by 22.2 per cent, or at an average annual rate of 4.2 per cent. The per capita net availability of food increased from 13.92 ounces per day at the beginning of the Plan to 15.19 ounces towards the end of 1956. Table I below shows the changes in the indices of agricultural production.

The wholesale price index for food articles during the five year period 1950–56 declined 23.0 per cent. The general wholesale price index (WPI) for all commodities declined by 17.3 per cent. In fact, the terms of trade turned against agriculture. The ratio of index of agricultural prices to non-agricultural prices, which stood at 114.3 in 1950–51, declined to 90.1 in 1955–56. The all-India consumer price index (CPI 1949=100) which stood at 101 in 1951, fell 5 points to 96 in 1956.

Several factors account for the stability or decline of the price level during the years 1950–51 to 1955–56. While the planners had anticipated an incremental capital/output ratio of 3.1, the actual ratio turned out to be only 2.4. The growth of net national output (production) at constant prices increased (18 per

Table 1. Change in Indices of Agricultural Production

	First Plan	*Second Plan*	*Third Plan*
All commodities	22.2	21.7	—7.4
	4.2	(4.3)	(—1.1)
Foodgrains	27.4	18.9	—11.5
	(5.3)	(4.0)	(—1.9)
Other Agricultural commodities	13.2	27.3	—0.1
	(2.8)	(5.1)	(—0.3)

SOURCE: Reserve Bank of India Bulletin, June 1967, p. 747.

Note: Figures in brackets represent annual rates of increase in output

cent during the periods), exceeding the growth of net national expenditures at market prices (6 per cent).[9] Many of the crucial targets for production were achieved and in some cases exceeded planned magnitudes. It is interesting to note that the actual monetary outlays of Rs. 1,960 crores turned out to be only 82 per cent of the plan provision of Rs. 2,378 crores for the public sector. In sum, in contrast to the later Plan periods, the First Plan period turned out to be one of relative price stability, and indeed this may be termed as "deflationary" growth.

Growth with Inflation: the Second Plan Years (1956–61)

In contrast to the deflationary price trends observed during the First Plan period, economic growth during the second half of the decade was accompanied by inflationary trends. The general index of wholesale prices (1952–53=100) which stood at 92.5 at the end of last year of the First Plan, rose to 124.9 towards the end of the Second Plan period. The all-India working class CPI (1949: 100) rose from 96 in 1955–56 to 124 in 1960–61. The overall trend in some of the sectoral indices may be observed from Table 2 above.

Table 2. Index Number of Wholesale Prices: Main Groups

Base: 1952-53=100

Groups	weights	1955-56	1960-61	% variation in 1st Plan	% variation in 2nd Plan
All commodities	1000	92.5	124.9	—17.3	35.0
Food articles	504	86.6	120.0	—23.0	38.6
Liquor and Tobacco	21	81.0	109.9	—17.8	35.7
Fuel, power, light and lubricants	30	95.2	120.0	— 2.8	26.1
Industrial raw materials	155	99.0	145.4	—24.3	46.9
Manufactures	290	99.7	123.9	— 3.4	24.3
Intermediate products	41	100.1	130.6	—10.9	30.5
Finished products	249	99.6	122.8	— 2.2	23.3

SOURCE: *Reserve Bank of India Bulletin*, June 1967, p. 767

[9] *Reserve Bank of India Bulletin*, June 1967, p. 746.

It will be seen that most of the rise in the index was accounted for by the increase in agriculture-based commodities: food products and industrial raw materials, which rose 38.6 and 47 per cent respectively. The overall WPI rose 35 per cent during the period, at an average annual rate of 5.9 per cent. Although the annual rate of growth of agricultural production (4.1 per cent) during the period was roughly equal to that attained in the preceding one, there were considerable erratic fluctuations in the output of commercial crops, leading to large year to year variations in the price index. The rapid industrial expansion planned during this period added to the pace of developmental expenditures. Actual outlays in the public sector amounted to Rs. 4,672 crores, about 2.5 times greater than the First Plan. The growth of net national expenditures at market prices rose 44 per cent, or at the rate of 7.6 per cent per year, whereas the growth in output at constant prices was one-half of this rate, 22 per cent (4.7 per cent per year). Thus there was a big gap between aggregate monetary demand and supply. This resulted in a rise of 35 per cent in the WPI during the period, in contrast to the 17 per cent decline registered in the previous plan. The actual increment of total product as a ratio of planned magnitude was 0.86, as the incremental capital/output ratio turned out to be 2.9, instead of the planned figure of 2.3.

Since the Plan emphasized industrialization, the outlays on building up heavy industry in the public sector increased tenfold over the period. In fact, actual expenditures ran ahead of plans, the ratio being 118. However, it was the output of heavy industry or the capital goods sector that grew fastest: an annual growth rate of 11.2 per cent vis-a-vis consumer goods output which grew at 3.5 per cent per annum. The employment and money income generated by the public sector during the Plan period rose 37 per cent and 44 per cent respectively. However, there was a shortage of consumer goods available to satisfy the demand generated by this sharp increase in national expenditure, resulting in an upward pressure on most consumer goods prices. There was a 33 per cent increase in the CPI for food items alone during the period, reflecting the great shortage of cereals, whose price rose 7.5 per cent per annum. The increase would have been still higher without large imports, which were roughly 20 million tons over the Plan period. Cereal imports during the year 1960–61 constituted almost 16 per cent of total imports in value terms.

Although there were shortages of staple commodities, industrial raw materials and consumer goods, the general index of industrial production increased from base year 1956=100 to 133 by 1960–61, or an average annual rate of 5.9 per cent. The net national product (50–51=100) grew at an average rate of 3.9 per cent annually over the Plan period, and, as we shall see, the rate of inflation was considerably less than that during the Third Plan. We now examine the record over the next five years.

Rapid Inflation and Slow Growth : Third Plan period 1961–66

Compared to the two previous Plan periods, the rate of inflation during 1961–66 was very rapid, and the growth rate of the economy was very slow. Inflation became so rampant that several special measures had to be taken by the Government to control prices. (These are discussed later in Section IV). It would not be an exaggeration to say that the accelerating inflation necessitated revision of various index numbers to a new base with 1960–61 as the new starting point to make comparisons with other years meaningful. Money national income grew at an annual rate of 9.1 per cent during the five year period, but real income in 1960–61 prices grew at only 2.5 per cent: taking into account the population growth rate of approximately 2.3 per cent, per capita real income grew at a meagre 0.2 per cent per annum!

In fact, most of the growth that took place during this period was due to industrial expansion. Agricultural production at the end of the Plan period was very much below what it was at the beginning.

Table 3. Index Numbers of Agricultural Production

1949-50 : 100

	Weight	60/1	61/2	62/3	63/4	64/5	65/6
Foodgrains:	66.9	137.1	140.3	133.6	136.5	150.8	121.3
Non-foodgrains:	33.1	152.6	153.9	151.6	156.5	176.7	157.0
All commodities:	100.0	142.2	144.8	139.6	143.1	159.4	133.1

SOURCE: *Economic Survey, 1970-71,* p. 82.

Table 3 brings out some of the important features of this period.

Except for the bumper crop year 1964–65, there was relatively little progress in agricultural production since the beginning of the Plan period. In fact, taking the five-year period as a whole, the rate of growth of production was negative–0.9 per cent. The poor record of agriculture permeated the economy with undesirable consequences. The single most important cause of failure of the Plan in achieving its targets was the failure of agricultural production to expand as had been expected. The planners had targeted for a foodgrains output of 101.6 million tons by 1965–66: the actual output turned out to be 72.0 million tons. This was, in large part, the consequence of the disastrous fall in output during 1965–66.

As a result of this poor performance, the index number of wholesale prices for agricultural commodities rose 42 per cent during the five-year period (1961–62 : 100 to 142 in the final Plan year 1965–66). The terms of trade moved consistently in favour of agriculture year after year. Recall that during the First Plan period, the relative price changes had been in the opposite direction. In fact, agricultural prices throughout the decade of the 60's continued their upward climb: they almost doubled in a decade! The consequences of this shift of relative prices for the growth of the economy, as well as for price stability, were very unfortunate.

Besides the poor performance of agriculture, several other factors contributed to the extraordinary rise in prices of goods and services during this period.

The first year of the Plan started off with the war with China, and the last year of the Plan ended with the war with Pakistan. During this period, defence outlays were increased from Rs. 281 crores in 1960–61 to Rs. 884 crores by 1965–66, a three-fold rise in five years. Defence outlays have continued to increase since then, year after year, and for 1970–71, were estimated to be Rs. 1,152 crores.

Both public and private investment during the Plan period were stepped up substantially as compared to the earlier plans. The public sector's actual outlay of Rs. 8,608 crores was more than Rs. 1,000 crores in excess of the planned figure of Rs. 7,500 crores. This increase was necessitated by the rise in prices that occured during the Plan, in order to carry out the physical targets for investment. It is pertinent to point out that the increased public sector outlays during the five-year period exceeded the total outlay of the First and Second Plans combined, by more than Rs. 2,000 crores. An investment programme of this magnitude was bound to create inflationary pressures in the economy (especially in the market for consumer goods and services) even during normal periods, because the proportion of total investment devoted to the creation of capital goods (heavy industry, power and mining) was to be 35 per cent as against 29 per cent in the Second and 23 per cent in the First Plan.

Although the Plan had visualized deficit financing of the order of only Rs. 550 crores, the actual magnitude turned out to be almost twice that figure: Rs. 1,133 crores. The relevant figures for the three Plans were as follows:

As pointed out in Section II, inflationary financing of economic development results in a rapid increase in the price level unless the economy has an elastic supply of wage goods available to satisfy the added consumer demands. While deficit financing during the First and Second

Table 4. Deficit Financing during the Plans, Annual Averages
(current prices—rupees crores)

	Plan	Actual	Total
First Plan	58	69	345
Second Plan	220	191	955
Third Plan	110	227	1135
Annual Plans 1966-69	104	227	682
		Total	3117

Source: Wilfred Malenbaum, *Modern India's Economy*, p. 103.

Plans could be undertaken with relative ease because of increasing supply of consumer goods (rapid increase in foodgrains production during the first Plan and use of foreign exchange reserves during the Second Plan), the inflationary pressures that it created during the Third Plan period were difficult to contain. The overall aggregate demand created was too large in relation to the economy's capacity to satisfy that demand without a very rapid rise in prices.

The growth of output of consumer goods, which had lagged behind other industrial output growth during the Second Plan, continued during 1961–66. of consumer goods. It is also of interest to note that high-income consumer goods (cars, refrigerators, air-conditioners) grew much more rapidly than middle-class (cycles, fans, sewing machines) or mass consumption goods (soap, kerosene, textiles). The output of the former grew during the 15 year period (1951–65) about 100 per cent, whereas the latter grew less than 50 per cent.

The rise in prices accelerated towards the last two years of the Plan, because the gap between expenditures and output growth widened considerably (in part due to stepped up defence expenditures) as compared with the first three years. The growth in expenditures at market prices was 50 per cent over the five year period, whereas output at constant prices grew only 14 per cent.

It has been estimated that annual payrolls in the public sector alone increased 100 per cent over the Third Plan period, from Rs. 615 crores in 1960–61 to Rs. 1,232 crores in 1965–66. This is an annual growth rate of 15 per cent, compared to 7.7 per cent and 4.8 per cent for the earlier plans.[10] The country did not or could not produce sufficient consumer goods to absorb the demand generated by such expenditures.

Table 5. Percentage Change In Index Numbers of Industrial Production
(Base : 1960=100)

	Weight	1961	1962	1963	1964	1965	1966	1967	1968	1969	Jan-Oct 1970
Mining and Quarrying	9.72	5.4	9.3	6.9	—3.1	10.3	3.3	—0.2	6.2	2.2	1.4
Manufacturing of which	84.91	9.1	9.5	8.0	9.5	8.8	—2.0	—1.7	5.5	—7.0	4.2
Consumer Goods	32.61	7.4	1.6	1.6	6.9	4.3	4.9	—5.1	6.4	10.8	7.4
Intermediate Goods	35.94	8.3	11.0	12.3	6.2	5.6	—0.3	1.0	6.3	5.8	1.8
Capital Goods	10.98	17.3	28.5	10.4	20.7	18.0	—13.6	—6.5	0.5	—1.2	2.7
Electricity Generated	5.37	16.3	12.4	15.5	15.0	10.0	8.9	11.0	15.6	12.9	11.3
All Industries	100.00	9.1	9.7	8.3	8.6	9.1	—0.8	0.8	6.4	7.1	4.7

Source: Economic Survey, 1970-71, pp. 92-93

The percentage change in index numbers of industrial production may be seen from Table 5.

It will be noticed that the lowest rate of expansion in the index was in respect

India's attempt at rapid industrialization by emphasizing the building up of

10 *Reserve Bank of India Bulletin,* June 1967, p. 750.

basic heavy industries, capital goods, and import-replacing types added to the severe inflationary pressures that began at the beginning of the decade of the sixties. The aim during these years was to increase the nation's productive capacity. It became apparent as the Plan progressed, and especially during the latter half of the decade, that capacity creation did not necessarily result in capacity *utilization*. Shortages of foreign exchange, industrial raw materials, lagging demand from user industries and the poor performance of the agricultural sector in two successive years (65–67) added to the strain on the economy.

As a result of inflation, India's competitiveness in foreign markets suffered throughout 1960–67. Although the volume of exports rose during 1960–61 to 1965–66, export performance in general was below expectations. In this respect, the following[11] quotation is of considerable interest:

> An interesting recent analysis of Indian export performance by Professor Benjamin Cohen has shown that while imports from all sources of India's traditional exports by North America, Europe and Japan increased in value during the period 1960 to 1967 by 19 per cent, those from India declined by 3 per cent. On the other hand, Pakistan's share rose by 13 per cent. If India had remained as competitive as in 1960—Professor Cohen argues—she could at least have added some 23 per cent to her traditional exports. Such an increase would have eliminated about 30 per cent of the 1968/69 trade gap.

Thus we find that (1) failure of the agricultural sector to expand production to meet the economy's rising demand, (2) large defence outlays, (3) expenditures in excess of planned magnitudes deficit-financed by large-scale borrowings from the Reserve Bank, and (4) heavy industrialization not matched by a corresponding flow of consumer goods production, were the primary causes of the rise in the price level during the Third Plan period. The rate of inflation was especially severe during the last two years. The price of food articles rose 22 percentage points in 1965–66 alone, and the price of finished goods by 7.4 per rent. Overall rise in the food price index for the five year period was 48.4 per cent and the rise in the general price index was 36 per cent. Unlike the First and Second Plan periods. however, the Third Plan period was characterized by very slow growth during the first couple of years, somewhat higher growth during the next two years, and negative growth in the final year. The annual growth rates were 2.5, 1.7, 4.9, 7.6 and 4.2 per cent. As pointed out earlier, real growth in net national product for the five-year period amounted to only 2.5 per cent per annum.

We shall now discuss the salient features of growth and inflation during the next five years, 1966–71.

Inflation, Stagnation and Resumption of Growth : 1966–71

The Fourth Five Year Plan, which was supposed to have been started in the year 1966–67, was postponed until 1969–70. The interim period, 1966–67 to 1968–69 was marked by the so-called "Annual Plans," drawn up and implemented on an *ad-hoc* basis. During this period, the economy experienced a recession coupled with severe inflation. The shortfall in agricultural output during two consecutive years, 1965–67, adversely affected the economy's performance not only during those two years, but subsequently. The index of agricultural production during 1965–66 and 1966–67 declined from the earlier year (176.7) to 157.0 and 147.4 respectively. Consequently, the rise in food prices in each of these two years was almost 20 per cent a rate which adversely affected not only the living standards of most people, but contributed to increasing wage pressures, and cost inflation throughout the economy. Rice and wheat prices during the year 1967–68 temporarily reached previously unheard of levels: 208 and 186 respectively (with 1952–53 : 100). Only

[11] Austin Robinson, "Economic Progress in India," *The Three Banks Review*, March 1970, p. 27.

large imports under PL 480 helped ease the food situation in the country. Total imports during 1965–68 amounted to 26 million tons. The WPI for agricultural commodities rose 13.8 per cent in 1966–67 and 11.6 per cent in 1967–68, inspite of large imports which amounted to 7 to 10 million tons of foodgrains annually.

The all-India CPI for urban non-manual workers (1960=100) which stood at 132 in 1965–66, rose to 146 in 1966–67 and 159 the next year. The rate of increase was somewhat moderated in the next two years, due mainly to increasing availability of foodgrains, as well as government procurement and distribution through fair price shops throughout urban areas. Some of the important indices reflecting the performance of the economy during the five-year period, 1966 to 1971, are tabulated below Table 6.

national income attained in 1964–65. Net national product (in 1960–61 prices) in 1964–65 was Rs. 15,917 crores, and had fallen to Rs. 15,021 crores in 1965–66 and Rs. 15,243 crores in 1966–67. It reached Rs. 16,660 crores in 1967–68. This was due to the relatively large increase in agricultural production, which had fallen in the two previous years below the level attained in 1964–65. The increased outpht of agricultural goods had a favourable effect on wholesale prices, especially in the following year, and helped to moderate the rise in the price level.

The rate of growth of money supply during these years ranged between 8 to 11 per cent per year. Repeated budget deficits incurred by Central and State Governments resulted in large scale borrowings from the Reserve Bank, and contributed to the rapid increase in money supply

Table 6. Selected Economic Indicators

	Percentage change over previous year				
	1966/67	1967/68	1968/69	1969/70	1970/71
National income at constant prices (provisional)	1.5	9.3	2.4	5.3	5.5
Agricultural production	—1.1	22.4	—1.0	6.5	5.0
Industrial production	0.3	0.5	6.7	6.8	4.1
Wholesale prices	13.9	11.6	—1.1	3.7	5.6
Money supply	8.3	9.1	8.1	10.8	10.6

SOURCE: *Economic Survey, 1970-71*, p. 3.

It is significant that, despite the slow growth of industrial production in the year 1967–68, national income grew rapidly. In part, this rapid growth was no more than a recovery from the absolute level of with the public. Non-developmental outlays (mainly defence expenditures had climbed very rapidly during the years 1967–71, as can be seen from Table 7.

Almost one-third of the non-develop-

Tabe 7. Budgetary Transactions of Central and State Governments, 1967-68 to 1970-71

	Rs. crores			
	1967/68	1968/69	1969/70	1970/71
Developmental outlays	3,676	3,937	4,408	4,697
Non-developmental expenditures	2,772	2,890	3,266	3,249
Total	6,448	6,827	7,674	7,946
Current Receipts	4,516	4,943	5,405	6,023
Gap	1,932	1,884	2,269	1,923
Financed by Capital Receipts	1,675	1,571	1,967	1,512
Overall budgetary deficit	257	313	302	411

SOURCE: *Economic Survey, 1970-71*, pp. 104-05.

mental (or government consumption) outlays were accounted for by defence expenditures. Because real growth in the economy during these years was very limited, inflationary pressures gathered momentum, fueled by increased money supply generated by deficit financing. Between the years 1965, and 1969, population growth was sufficient to absorb the growth in national product, with very little margin left for increase in per capita income. It was only during the years 1969–70 and 1970–71 that national income grew more rapidly than did population. Per capita consumption in 1968–69 was not significantly higher than the level attained in 1960–61!

The rate of growth of industrial production during these years also was slow: in fact, in 1966 and 1967, it was negative, as can be seen from Table 5. Even the production of capital goods, which had continuously increased throughout the previous Plans at a very rapid rate year after year, barely rose, except in 1970. The overall rate of industrial expansion was considerably slower than that achieved until 1965.

Although economic recovery began to take place during the closing years of the decade, shortages of key industrial raw materials like jute, cotton and oilseeds continued to push prices up rapidly. The index for raw material prices, which stood at 170.6 in November 1969, rose to 201.2 in June 1970, and climbed to 206.5 in January 1971, a rise of 20 per cent in one year. Costs and prices throughout the economy continued to increase. The all-India working class CPI rose 5.1 per cent in 1970–71.

In 1969–70, the Fourth Plan was officially inaugarated. The performance of the economy during the first two years of the Plan was a modest improvement over the three years that preceded them. Although overall agricultural production has continued to advance, the output of commercial crops, as mentioned in the preceding paragraph, has fluctuated erractically. The production of foodgrains increased by about 8 per cent in 1970–71, with a favourable influence on food prices and India's balance of payments, which was severely strained during the preceding five years due to large imports needed to feed a rapidly expanding population.

As we have seen, since the middle of the Third Plan, the general price level has continued to increase at a very rapid rate, with food prices raising at an alarming rate. It soon became apparent that such increases in the cost of living were intolerable, and several Government policies were initiated to moderate the price advance. In Section IV, these actions and their results will be reviewed.

4. Price Policy during the Plan Years: How and How much

Indian planners have laid great stress on the need for price stability during the process of economic development. From the very inception of the Five Year Plans, there seemed to be a recognition of the distorting consequences of inflation, as evidenced by the repeated statements in successive Plan documents as well as other government publications and official pronouncements.[12]

The function of the price system in a market economy as a signalling device, (providing incentives for substitution in production and consumption choices) and as a regulating mechanism for directing the allocation of resources, was very well recognised by the government. At the same time, the authorities did not hesitate to intervene in the market process whenever it was considered that such an intervention was called for:

(a) to moderate the inequality of income distribution brought about by natural monopolies or contrived scarcities,

(*b*) to alter the market-determined prices of goods and services to attain equity (which really meant assuring some minimum availability of essential goods to poorer sections of society),

(c) to indicate directions in which resources should be re-channeled, whenever the market determined investment and

[12] See for example, L. K. Jha, "Price policy in a Developing Economy," *Reserve Bank of India Bulletin*, April 1968.

allocation decisions conflicted with the Plan priorities.

We have seen that rapid inflation began to emerge in the Indian economy during the middle of the Third Plan period. The prices of essential consumer goods (especially foodgrains, textiles, sugar, kerosene, and vegetable oils) and industrial raw materials started their steep upward climb during 1963–64. It soon became apparent that some kind of overall control of prices, as well as other administrative measures, were required to ensure implementation of Plan projects, to prevent profiteering and ensure equitable distribution of available supplies of critical items. Until 1963–64, government did not consider it necessary to institute formal price controls, rationing, procurement, and direct distribution policies in respect of foodgrains, although prices of some mass consumption goods such a textiles, sugar, etc. were under constant government review; and production of several goods and services were regulated by licensing, allocation of foreign exchange and capital-issues control. Many commodities included in the WPI were already 'regulated'. By the year 1966, about two-thirds of the items included in the WPI were price-regulated through statutory or informal controls, licensing requirements, and the like, in order to soften the inflationary impact of ever-increasing scarcities. As a consequence, inflation was suppressed, and the actual price indices did not adequately reflect the extent of inflationary pressures in the economy.

However, the main anti-inflationary thrust of governmental policies in recent years was directed at controlling food prices which were rising at an average rate of 20 per cent per year in 1966–67 and 1967–68. Large imports under PL 480 programmes, forced procurement from farmers, opening up of fair-price-shops in urban areas for distribution at controlled prices, prohibition of inter-state movement of foodgrains (to facilitate government procurement from surplus areas at low prices) and increasing government domination of wholesale trading in foodgrains were among the policies adopted by the authorities. A loose rationing system, covering 250 million people through 140,000 fair price shops was in effect to assure minimum supplies of foodgrains at subsidised prices, costing over Rs. 100 crores annually.

These and other policics pursued by the government did not always meet with the desired results. Several critics have pointed out the distorting consequences and disincentives caused by these policies, which, they have convincingly argued, have held back agricultural progress and dampened local production.[13] Price controls, rationing, and subsidized distribution of food are only short run solutions to the problem of insufficient supplies in an expanding economy. Since the demand curve for food cannot be shifted back to the left, and since price controls or subsidies are non-equilibrating devices in the long run, the only sensible solution is to seek ways and means to produce more, or shift the supply curve to the right. Nor are continuous and ever-increasing imports possible, or desirable. They have been a heavy drain on India's foreign exchange earnings throughout the sixties. Food imports as a percentage of total consumption during the last year of the first three Plans were: 2.3, 4.6 and 14.4 per cent. During the years 1965–66 to 1968–69, cereal imports alone have contributed to as much as 18 to 32 per cent of the value of imports (though under PL 480 auspices). Although food imports become inevitable during disaster crop years such as 1965–66, continued dependence on foreign sources of food supply do not augur well for the economy in the long run.

This fact has been recognized by the planners. A number of reforms are now under way to reorient policies designed to encourage agricultural production.

A comprehensive price policy, covering the prices of factors of production and producer as well as consumer goods, cannot long remain operationally efficient. Regulating the prices of innumerable

[13] See A. M. Khusro, "The Pricing of Food in India," *Quarterly Journal of Economics,* May 1967, pp. 271–286; J. N. Bhagwati and S. Chakravarty, "Contributions to Indian Economic Analysis: ,A Survey," *American Economic Review* Supplement, Sept. 1969, pp. 29–66.

inputs and outputs throughout the economy, even in a centrally planned system, become an almost impossible task. It creates its own distorting influences, adversely affecting private incentives, breeds corruption, creates black markets, reduces efficiency by causing administrative delays and proliferates bureaucratic control. There seemed to be a danger that the Indian planning machinery was moving in this direction during the sixties: but there are certain indications that official policy has recently veered towards less control and more freedom for free market decisions to prevail. There are deep conflicts among various social objectives. These will have to be recognized and resolved.

5. Concluding Comments: Implications of the Analysis

The most important cause of inflation in a developing country like India is the inadequate growth of the agricultural sector during a period of rapid industrialization. Unless the primary sector is able to generate adequate supplies of food and raw materials needed for an expanding industrial development programme, severe and prolonged inflation will result. Although the failure of agricultural output to expand can be compensated by imports, this results in a foreign exchange crisis because (1) rapidly growing industry needs imports of capital equipment and industrial raw materials which are locally unavailable, (2) exports of agricultural commodities is the main source of foreign exchange earnings, and (3) there seem to be limits beyond which foreign aid or private capital inflows cannot be depended upon.

During the period of the first decade of Planning in India, the average growth rate of the economy was higher than during the second decade. The annual rate of inflation did not exceed 5 to 6 per cent during the Second Plan period, and growth during the First Plan period was deflationary.

Rapid population growth, coupled with deteriorating and uneven performance of the agricultural sector, resulted in a high degree of inflation during the sixties. Although several other factors, such as (a) Increasing budget deficits (b) Rising defence expenditures (c) Rapid monetary expansion during the sixties (d) too much emphasis on building up (d) too much emphasis on building up of heavy industries and the associated capital-intensity of investment plans, helped fuel the inflationary pressures, control of the money supply alone would not have solved the problem of lagging foodgrains and consumer goods output, in the face of increased aggregate demand.

The Reserve Bank of India played a passive role in the expansion of money supply. Ever-increasing government expenditure plans, which were not adequately matched by domestic savings, foreign aid or tax receipts had to be deficit financed by Reserve Bank credit. Fiscal, rather than monetary policy, was responsible for inflationary pressures.

Inflation did not necessarily promote or retard growth. A rapid and prolonged inflation in excess of what society can tolerate hampers economic growth, but only because adequate growth fails to take place. What is needed is growth-inducing policies and programmes to control inflation. If agricultural and consumer goods output expansion can be accelerated, inflationary pressures will automatically dwindle.

Many developing as well as developed countries have experienced rapid inflation during the sixties. In most of the developed countries, the rate of inflation averaged 3 to 9 per cent in recent years. In developing countries, it has ranged from 2 to 40 per cent. The mechanisms causing inflation and its impact depend on particular circumstances. The instruments needed for control of inflation differ too.

With the resumption of agricultural output growth in India since 1967–68, there is some evidence that inflationary pressures are receding. The renewed emphasis accorded agriculture in the Fourth Five Year Plan and the emergence of the "green revolution" may accelerate economic growth with acceptable rates of inflation in the present decade.

BIBLIOGRAPHY

Bhagwati, J. N. and S. Chakravarty, "Contributions to Indian Economic Analysis: A Survey," *American Economic Review* (Supplement), September 1969, pp. 29–66.

Bhatia, R. J., "Inflation, Deflation and Economic Development," *IMF Staff Papers,* October 1959.

Committee for Economic Development, *How Low Income Countries Can Advance Their Own Growth* (Washington: September 1966), pp. 23–46.

Dorrance, Graeme, "Inflation and Growth: The Statistical Evidence," *IMF Staff Papers,* November 1960.

Jha, L. K., "Price Policy in a Developing Economy," *Reserve Bank of India Bulletin,* April 1968.

Khusro, A. M., "The Pricing of Food in India," *Quarterly Journal of Economics,* May 1967, pp. 271–86.

Lewis, Arthur, "Economic Development with Unlimited Spuplies of Labour," *The Manchester School,* May 1954 (Reprinted in A. N. Agarwala and S. P. Singh (eds), *The Economics of Underdevelopment* (New York: Oxford University Press, 1963), pp. 400–49.

Maynard, Geoffrey, *The Price Level and Economic Development* (London: Macmillan, 1963).

Mookerjee, S. "Financial Stability and Planning," *Finance and Development,* March 1972, pp. 2–9.

Robinson, Austin, "Economic Progress in India," *The Three Banks Review,* March 1970, pp. 5–34.

Thirlwall, A. P. and C. A. Brown, "Inflation and Growth: The International Evidence" *Banca Nazionale del Lavoro Quarterly,* September 1971.

Velayudhan, N. K., "Prince Trends During the Three Plan Periods," *Reserve Bank of India Bulletin,* June 1967, pp. 740–66.

Wai, U Tun, "The Relation Between Inflation and Economic Development: A Statistical Inductive Study," *IMF Staff Papers,* October 1959.

Part Six

PUBLIC FINANCE

20

Taxation and Economic Development in India

JAMES CUTT

1. Introduction: The Objectives of Taxation Policy under Planned Economic Development

The financing of economic development is primarily a "bootstraps" operation. Developing countries must, to a very large extent, finance internally their development programmes. The primary means of internal financing available to such countries is taxation.

It is the object of this paper to examine the role of taxation policy, as one of a set of public policy instruments, in furthering the attainment of the objectives of planned economic development. The explicit context for the examination and evaluation of taxation policy must, therefore, be the specification of the objectives of taxation policy in the context of planned economic development. The objectives of taxation policy reflect the overall goals of planned development articulated in Indian Five Year Plans, namely growth, equity, and stabilization.

The goal of *growth* may be defined as the attainment of *the rate and pattern* of growth of national income considered desirable in terms of planning objectives. In the context of the central planning objective to improve living standards as quickly as possible, taxation policy must be designed to *increase the rate of growth of national income in aggregate terms* but also to *transform the pattern of national income growth* in accordance with planning priorities.

In order to promote an increase in the rate of growth of national income, taxation policy must serve to increase the proportion of national income directed to developmental spending, defined as the aggregate of investment spending in the private sector, and investment spending plus consumption spending of a developmental nature in the public sector. The division of public expenditures into developmental and non-developmental is now made annually in the Economic Survey which precedes the Union budget, and the

[1] For further elaboration see J. Cutt, *Taxation and Economic Development in India* (New York: Praeger, 1969).

broader concept of developmental or growth-oriented spending which this statistical classification facilitates underlines the contribution to economic growth of a considerable proportion of public spending which, though formally classified as of a consumption nature is, in fact, directly growth-promoting in nature.

With respect to the private sector, the growth objective of taxation policy may be couched in both negative and positive terms. On the one hand, taxation policy for increased public revenue must be so designed as to minimize the opportunity cost of increased revenue in terms of private savings (and therefore investment) foregone. On the other hand, and more positively, the tax system must incorporate a set of incentives designed to promote directly an *increased savings ratio* in the private sector.

In sum, the aspect of the growth objective relating to the rate rather than the pattern of economic growth may be defined as the maximization of the incremental ratio of developmental spending to national income, in effect, substituting $\triangle(Y-[C_h+C_{gn}])/\triangle Y$, for the traditional $\triangle S/\triangle Y$, where Y is national income, S is saving, C_h and C_{gn} are, respectively, household consumption and public consumption expenditure of a non-developmental nature, and $\triangle$ indicates an increment in the variable.

The maximization of the ratio of incremental developmental spending to national income will, of course, be constrained by the extent to which the increase in household consumption and public sector non-developmental spending can be limited; the degree of restraint on the increase in household consumption will reflect a compromise between the maximum possible rate of economic growth and the desire to improve living standards in the short run—in effect, an acutely difficult generational trade-off.

The policy of providing incentives to private sector saving and investment, and, possibly, to work of certain kinds, constitutes an active policy of fiscal dirigism. The principle of neutrality, whereby the tax system seeks to avoid interference in the private allocation of resources, is defensible in a developed economy, but, it may be argued, is of little relevance to the problem of economic development, where optimum resource allocation may not unreasonably be defined as that allocation specified as desirable in the national plan.

In addition to a system of incentives to save, invest, and work, it may be argued that the tax system in developing countries should be designed to promote the desired use of resource by taxing in terms of "potential" resource use. This principle is of great importance in agriculture, where the tax base may be defined as "average potential output," and in the case of wealth taxation, where the net wealth tax effectively taxes on an assumed average rate of return on capital, penalizing, respectively, the inefficient farmer on the one hand, and the hoarder and the conservative investor on the other.

The concept of a policy of fiscal dirigism implies not only that growth be maximized—subject to the constraint indicated above—in an aggregate sense, but that the *pattern* of growth be modified so as to conform as closely as possible with the pattern of resource allocation specified in the national plan.

The *equity* objective may be broadly defined to include a basic *principle* of taxation policy and a major *objective* of taxation policy in developing countries. The principle is that of horizontal equity, and requires the equal treatment of taxpaying units in similar circumstances. Although in this broad sense unexceptionable, the principle may be construed in a literal way to require tax neutrality, and may thus be redefined in the planning context to require the avoidance of non-neutral or unequal treatment of taxpaying units in similar circumstances except insofar as such non-neutral treatment reflects deliberate fiscal dirigism, i.e. intended inequalities of treatment intended to induce behaviour of the sort considered desirable under planning objectives.

The second, more controversial, aspect of equity is the objective of redistribution—the moderation of inequalities of income, wealth, and opportunity through the use of taxation policy. The redistribution objective originates in the Indian Constitution and has been re-affirmed in each of the Five Year Plans. Perhaps its most eloquent articulation was by the Taxation Enquiry Commission:

> We can no longer afford to leave the problem of equality to the automatic functioning of economic and social forces... The demand that the instrument of taxation should be used as a means of bringing about a redistribution of income more in consonance with social justice, cannot be kept in abeyance.[2]

The specification of the redistribution objective, i.e. the actual degree of income and wealth equality towards which the tax system—in conjunction with the expenditure side of the budget—should aspire, will reflect the political consensus at any given time as to the desirable state of income and wealth distribution. Although the precise magnitude of the degree of equality is not specified in the planning literature, the evidence on the existing degree of inequality and attitudes to that inequality suggests unequivocally that, at least in directional terms, taxation policy be employed to further diminish inequalities.[3]

Although there is seldom disagreement on the principle of horizontal equity, it is frequently argued that a redistributive tax policy designed to promote the objective of vertical equity will conflict with the objective of promoting private sector growth, and that, accordingly, the vertical equity objective be relegated to the status of a long-term aspiration. There is no question that a redistributive tax policy which retards growth will be self-defeating, and it may be argued that the necessary reconciliation between the private sector growth and the vertical equity objectives can be approached by the introduction of the principle of "functionalism" into the tax structure. Such a principle would provide for concessionary treatment, within an overall progressive tax system, for income or wealth used for specified priority investment purposes. In this manner, "functional" inequalities would be tolerated, while non-functional inequalities—inequalities of consumption in the case of the income tax, and inequalities of unproductive wealth in the case of wealth taxation—would be moderated.

The question of reducing unemployment and underemployment may be subsumed in developing countries under the growth objective. The *stabilization* objective may, therefore, be defined essentially as the prevention of inflationary price increases. The body of evidence suggests that a rate of price increase beyond a rather low maximum—certainly not higher than 5 per cent per annum—retards the rate and distorts the pattern of growth, and worsens the redistributive problem.

It is, of course, important in a growing economy to permit price increases in growing sectors in order to attract resources to these areas. Since equivalent price reductions in declining areas are unlikely, some upward pressure on the general price level may be expected as a result of what may be referred to as "functional" instability. Inflationary price increases, unlike functional price increases, tend to be cumulative and pervasive in nature. It is equally important to ensure that measures to promote stability do not conflict with the growth objective. To this end, the functional exemptions and concessions referred to above under vertical equity objective will serve to ensure that reductions in aggregate spending are primarily at the expense of consumption spending rather than investment spending.

2. An Overview of the Indian Tax System

(a) *Federal Finance*

The Indian Constitution provides for the division of tax powers between the States and the Union. The division closely follows that established by the Government of India Act (1935). Local authorities are

---

[2] Government of India, *Report of the Taxation Enquiry Commission* (New Delhi: Ministry of Finance, 1953–54), Vol. I, p. 145.

[3] Cutt, op. cit., Chapter 2.

considered to fall under the aegis of their respective State governments and thus have no explicit share in the allocation of tax powers. Under the quasi-federal character of the Constitution, fairly wide powers are vested in the States, but residual tax powers belong to the Union.

The Constitution also provides for the distribution of certain revenues between the Union and the States through the agency of a Finance Commission which reports at five-year intervals on the state of federal finance and makes recommendations for changes in the distributional arrangements. The relevant sections of the Constitution are Articles 268, 269, 270 and 275.

In practice, funds allocated to the States by the Finance Commission have amounted to only 25 per cent of the total Union allocation to the States in the planning period. The balance of revenue transfers has fallen under the aegis of the Planning Commission which makes loans and grants to the States for sanctioned Plan expenditure, and the Ministry of Finance, which provides grants-in-aid of non-Plan expenditure where it is considered that such expenditures are of national significance.

(b) *Tax Revenue of the Union and State Governments,* 1950-51—1971-72

(i) *General Survey of Revenue Sources.* The division of Union tax revenue into constituent items over the Planning period is presented in Table 1, Appendix 1; tax revenue accruing to the States over the same period is set out in Table 2, Appendix 1.

The tax revenues of the Union Government are mainly derived from three heads: taxes on income, both personal and corporate, customs duties, and Union excise duties.

In 1950–51, the year before the beginning of the First Plan, net receipts from these three heads accounted for 35.01, 44.0, and 18.92 per cent, respectively, of Union tax revenue. Corresponding proportions in 1970–71 are 20, 20, and 58 per cent. Comparing the First and Third Plans, taxes on income provided 29.7 per cent of Union tax revenue over the First Plan as a whole, and 27.9 per cent over the Third Plan. Corresponding figures for customs revenue were 43.6 and 25.9 per cent, and for Union excise duties, 22.9 and 43.6 per cent.

The remarkable increase in revenue from Union excise duties is accounted for by the extension of coverage to a wide range of commodities, increased consumption, and rate increases. The Report of the Central Excise Reorganization Committee indicated that over the period 1953–54 to 1961–62, the most important factor was rate increases, accounting for 57.8 per cent of the overall increases in excise tax revenue of Rs. 3,310 million. Increased consumption accounted for 19.7 per cent, and additional coverage for 21.3 per cent.[4]

Tax on income formed a relatively stable proportion of Union tax revenue over the planning period to date, in spite of the increasing States' share in personal tax. It is apparent, however, that the maintenance of this proportion is in large measure the result of the rapid increase in revenue from corporation income tax. Revenue from this latter source has moved from 32.2 per cent of net Union revenue from income tax in 1950–51, to 78.34 per cent in 1970–71; viewed as a proportion of gross income tax revenue—before deduction of the States' share—corporation tax revenue has moved from 23.3 to 46.3 per cent over the same period. The greatest relative decline has taken place in customs revenue, from 44 per cent of Union tax revenue in 1950–51 to 19.96 per cent in 1970–71.

The tax revenues of the State governments are derived mainly from their share of Union income tax and excise duties, land revenue, the tax on stamps and transactions, the State excise on alcoholic liquor, and a variety of commercial taxes including the general sales tax, the tax on motor spirit, the entertainment tax, the tax on motor vehicles, and electricity duties.

The States' share of Union income tax has increased from Rs. 526.5 million in 1951–52 to Rs. 3,571 million in 1970–71,

[4] Government of India, *Report of the Central Excise Reorganization Committee,* (Delhi: Manager of Publications, 1963), p. 68.

but the relative significance of this source as a percentage of total States' revenue has dropped from 18.7 to 15.82 per cent. This decline in relative significance has occurred despite the trend towards increasing allocation of income tax revenue to the States—from 50 per cent in 1951 to 66.66 per cent in 1961 and 75 per cent in 1965—and reflects, first, the relatively slow growth of personal income tax revenue to the Union and, second, the more rapid growth of alternative sources of States' revenue, in particular the general sales tax.

The contribution of Union excise revenue to States' revenue began on the recommendation of the First Finance Commission in April 1952 and has grown rapidly; this source provided 17.13 per cent of total States' revenue in 1970–71. This is accounted for by the great expansion of Union excise duties and by the trend towards increasing States' share in their revenues.

Land revenue has declined over the planning period as a proportion of total States' revenue from 17.1 per cent in 1951–52 to 5.11 per cent in 1970–71. The relative decline of land revenue is even more apparent if the 1938–39 percentage (45 per cent of total revenue of the then nine Provinces) is also considered.

(ii) *Direct : Indirect Tax Ratio.* Taxes listed in Tables 1 and 2 under the headings of "taxes on income and wealth" and "taxes on property and capital transactions" will be regarded as direct; "taxes on commodities and services" will be regarded as indirect; this classification adopts the simple "basis of assessment" criterion, whereby taxes levied on the receipt of income are termed direct and taxes levied on expenditure are termed indirect. The Expenditure tax is included under the direct tax head.

Direct taxes as a proportion of total (Union+States) tax revenue have fallen from 41.0 per cent in 1951–52 to 23.7 per cent in 1970–71. Although the present Indian ratio is comparable to that in other developing countries, the diminishing relative significance of direct tax revenue in India runs contrary to a general correlation between the direct: indirect tax ratio and per capita income.

(iii) *Tax Burden or Sacrifice in India.* The simplest measure of tax burden sacrifice in a national sense is that of the *ratio of tax revenue to national income*. Table 3, Appendix 2, presents this information for twenty selected countries between 1950–1964. The tax : income ratio, expressed as a percentage, has almost doubled for India over this period. In this limited sense then, the national tax burden may be assumed to have doubled. The concept of burden or sacrifice is, however, most meaningful in a relative sense, and emerges very poorly from the comparison. India, indeed, ranks eighteenth out of twenty. Does it, therefore, follow, in some sense, that India is making a lesser tax sacrifice than almost all the other countries selected ?

Tax sacrifice may best be considered as a measure of the relative importance to the citizens of the resources given up to government in countries at different levels of income, and must relate taxes to some index of "ability-to-pay." A meaningful index of tax sacrifice must, therefore, incorporate per capita income as well as national income.

Several indices incorporating per capita income have been proposed.[5] The index proposed by Richard Bird takes taxes as a percentage of disposable income, all as a percentage of per capita domestic product.[6]

A further refinement of tax : income ratio analysis provides insight into changing tax burdens over the planning period. In Table 5, Appendix 1, tax revenue and national income figures are set out for the

[5] See, for instance, H. Frank, "Measuring State Tax Burdens," *National Tax Journal,* XII (June 1959), pp. 179–85; R. Bird, "A Note on Tax Sacrifice Comparisons," *National Tax Journal,* XVII (1964), pp. 303–8.

[6] i.e. $\left[\left(\frac{T}{T-Y}100 \div \frac{P}{Y}\right)\right] 100$

where T=tax revenue, Y=Gross National Product and P=Population. Bird uses Gross National Product in the first ratio, and Gross Domestic Product in the second. The same convention has been followed in the present work.

planning period until 1964–65. The tax: income ratio, here interpreted as the average tax rate in the year in question, is calculated for gross Union tax collections, net Union revenue plus State revenue, and State tax collections (i.e. State revenue minus Union transfers). The marginal tax rate on increments in income between years may be obtained from the national income and tax revenue data, and is set out for all three categories in column eleven.

The average tax rate rises steadily from 1959–60 on, the larger part of the increase being accounted for by Union tax collections. A measure of the increasing tax burden imposed by both levels of government in India is the marginal rates of tax imposed in the period after 1959–60. For total tax revenue, the average of the final six marginal rates (column six) is 19.3 per cent; for Union gross collections the average is 27.6 per cent, and for State collections, 8.3 per cent. The inference may again be drawn that the resource mobilization efforts particularly of the Union Government, and the corresponding tax burden on at least the non-agricultural sector, have been not inconsiderable—certainly far greater than the *prima facie* inference suggested by the comparative tax: income ratios.

3. Major Indian Taxes: A Brief Appraisal

(a) *The Personal Income Tax*

Under the Indian personal income tax laws the various sources of income are not taxed separately, as would be the case under a "schedular" income tax, but are aggregated on a "global" basis. Elements of a schedular system persist, however, in the exemption of agricultural income and the concessionary treatment afforded capital gains. Tax is levied at progressive rates on the total income of all individuals, joint Hindu families, unregistered firms, and other associations of persons; total income for tax purposes is reduced by certain exemptions and deductions and tax liability is further diminished by a set of tax assets based on the taxpayer's family status.

The rates of basic income tax on all non-corporate assessees rise progressively from a zero rate on taxable incomes up to Rs. 5,000 to 85 per cent on incomes above Rs. 200,000. A union surcharge is also levied as a percentage of the basic tax; the rate of surcharge is 10 per cent on taxable income up to Rs. 15,000 and 15 per cent on income above Rs. 15,000.

Accretions to capital value—other than in the case of agricultural land outside urban areas and disposal of house property by small house-owners—are subject to tax under the personal income tax. Short-term gains—where the asset is held for less than twelve months—are fully incorporated in income for tax purposes. Long-term gains are subject to tax at concessionary rates.

In developed countries the progressive personal income tax is generally an elastic and productive revenue source; it is an extremely flexible fiscal device, in that a variety of forms of selectivity, discrimination, etc., can be introduced into the tax if so desired; it tends to be the most useful tax instrument in stabilization policy, in terms of both built-in stabilization and as a discretionary stabilization device; and, finally, by dint of its progressive nature it is considered the most appropriate tax instrument for the pursuit of vertical equity.

In developing countries, on the other hand, the personal income tax generally has a very limited coverage, frequently is inapplicable to the agricultural sector—for either constitutional or administrative reasons—and tends to be subject to widespread avoidance and evasion. For these reasons, the personal income tax generally plays a less significant role in the tax structure than in developed countries.

The Indian case provides a classic illustration of the relative inadequacy of the personal income tax as a source of public revenue, and as a tool of stabilization and redistribution.

Although the number of assessees under the personal income tax in India has tripled from the figure of just under 500,000 at the inception of the Second Five Year Plan, the coverage of the tax

is still limited to a very small proportion of the total population, and the disappointing revenue productivity of the tax largely reflects this inadequate coverage. Taking elasticity of tax revenue as the annual compound rate of growth of tax revenue, the average elasticity of personal income tax revenue from the beginning of the Second Five Year Plan to 1970–71 comes to 3.7, as against an average for Union tax collections as a whole of 9.66. Defining the income elasticity of tax revenue as the ratio of the percentage change in tax revenue to the percentage change in national income, the performance of the perconal income tax is again disappointing, t,e income elasticity of personal income tax revenue emerpinv as 0.055 as against 1.4 for Union tax collections as whole.
1.4 for Union tax collections as a whole.

Revenue productivity may be increased by widening the definition of the tax base, increasing tax rates and/or lowering exemptions, and by ensuring that all those assessees intended to be covered are so covered up to full intended liability. Under the first of these heads, reform may be approached in a piecemeal fashion by moving to the inclusion of agricultural incomes within the tax base—such a move would require the cooperation of the State governments in view of the present constitutional exclusion of the Union from the taxation of agricultural income—and by the correction of a variety of loopholes such as the existing privileged treatment of Hindu undivided families, or might be approached in a grander, if more administratively formidable, fashion, by moving to the definition of a comprehensive tax base essentially as consumption plus increase in net worth. This latter definition would bring all forms of receipts, both in cash and in kind within the tax base.

Under the second head, the trend in India over the planning period has been toward the provision of relatively more generous exemptions (or equivalent tax credits), and this approach, although commendable in administrative terms, is one of the major reasons for the relatively slow growth of coverage and revenue productivity. This is particularly true in the light of the rather sharp increases in rate progressivity over the middle income ranges in the 1970–71 Union Budget, which effectively makes the rate structure the most progressive of the major developing countries and relatively harsh even in comparison to the sharpest progressive rate structures in developed countries.

Under the last head, what is required is a set of measures to diminish the chronic problem of tax evasion. Although there is some controversy over the magnitude of evasion, there is unanimity on the seriousness of the problem.[7] Many approaches to the dilemma of evasion have suggested,[8] the most intriguing remaining the completely self-checking tax return advocated by Professor Kaldor.[9]

The suggested broader tax base combined with the recent increases in rate progressivity should increase the built-in stabilizing effectiveness of the personal income tax and enhance its effectiveness as a discretionary stabilization instrument. The changes should also improve the performance of the tax as a means to the reduction of inequalities of income distribution.

The question that remains is whether these changes can be achieved without a serious trade-off against the second aspect of the growth objective—the effect on private sector saving and investment. The growth of "functionalism" or the favourable treatment for tax purposes of income saved and invested in certain ways, has progressed piecemeal in India over the last three or four Union budgets, the 1970–71 budget extending the list of preferential treatment at the same time as it sharply increased tax rates. The case remains, however, for a systematic programme of functional exemptions and preferences, and by development of provisions for generous loss offset for risk investment and for a scheme of averaging for tax purposes.

---

7 *Report of the Direct Taxes Administration Enquiry Commission* (1958) (Delhi: Manager of Publications, 1960), pp. 146–188.

8 Cutt, op. cit., Chapter 11.

9 N. Kaldor, *Tax Reform in India* (New Delhi: Ministry of Finance, 1958).

(b) *The Taxation of Agricultural Income*

As an extension of the principle of horizontal equity, it does not seem unreasonable, as a principle of taxation, to require inter-sectoral balance in the tax system. There are several historical cases—particularly in pre-revolutionary Russia and Meiji Japan—where inter-sectoral imbalance was deliberately used as an instrument of development, the agricultural sector being required essentially to finance industrial growth. The problem in many contemporary developing countries is quite the reverse. For a variety of reasons—often largely administrative—the relative tax burden on the agricultural sector tends to be light, the heavier tax burden falling on the more rapidly growing urban, industrial sector. India is a classic example of this problem.

Despite the still predominant role of the agricultural sector in national income and the high and increasing rate of government expenditure on agriculture over the planning period, resource mobilization from the agricultural sector—whether in the form of voluntary savings or taxation—has been relatively low and inelastic. Such limited evidence as is available on indirect tax burdens[10] suggests a lower relative burden and a diminishing relative share in the rural as against the urban sector. More precise evidence is available on the direct tax burden borne by agricultural incomes. Agricultural income is exempt from Union income tax but is subject to tax by a number of Indian States—significantly a diminishing number over the planning period. Although nominally progressive, agricultural income tax revenue has been relatively inelastic constituting approximately 8 per cent of total State tax revenue throughout the planning period. The more important direct tax on agriculture is land taxation, and the record is one of stagnancy, inflexibility, and diminishing relative burden. Revenue from land taxation has fallen from 73 per cent of State tax revenue in 1918–19 to 4 per cent in 1970–71, and revenue forecasts suggest a further relative decline. Mitra summarizes:

> ....the tax complex of the country is made up of two disparate fiscal systems. In the agricultural sector, barely 4 per cent of the aggregate income flows out to the state in the form of taxation. Outside agriculture, on the other hand, the government's tax claims are in the neighbourhood of 10 per cent. The current average tax revenue for the nation as a whole—about 8 per cent of national income—tells only part of the story and conceals the significant reality of two parallel tax structures.[11]

The growth objective of taxation in the agricultural sector may be defined in two parts. First, a reformed tax system should seek to siphon off an increasing proportion of the increases in agricultural income consequent on the programme of public investment in agriculture; the system should provide, in short, a productive and elastic source of revenue. Second, not only must the resource mobilization role of taxation of agriculture be carried out with the passive qualification of minimum adverse consequences, but taxation must be so fashioned as to complement positively the expenditure programmes designed to increase agricultural productivity.

The case for reform on grounds of resource mobilization is reinforced by considerations of the need to develop a fiscal tool to mitigate inequalities of income in the agricultural sector, and to contribute to the stabilization objective.

The theoretically most effective means of combining the tax objectives of increased and elastic revenue productivity, diminished inequalities, and enhanced flexibility and consequent stabilizing effectiveness (with the provision of a comprehensive assortment of incentives, allowances and exemptions designed to promote agricultural productivity) would be a progressive agricultural income tax

---

[10] Government of India, Ministry of Finance, *Incidence of Indirect Taxation in India* (1958–59) (New Delhi: 1961). *Report of the Taxation Enquiry Commission,* op. cit., Vol. 1.

[11] Ashok Mitra, "Tax Burden on Indian Agriculture" in R. Braibanti and J. Spengler (ed), *Administration and Economic Development in India* (Durham: Duke University Press, 1963), pp. 281–303.

based on ascertained net income—supported by the necessary accounting records—with a series of specific exemptions and allowances for reinvestment, land improvement, etc. But the history of attempts to levy tax on agricultural inromes is sufficiently discouraging to suggest that the agricultural income tax approac, be seen as a long-run aspiration to be arrived at after several stages of reform. The only practicable present procedure would seem to be the reform of the land tax base to accord with some notion of, at least, *presumptive* income or output, the long run intention being the transition from land taxation to agricultural income taxation and the integration of the latter with the Union income tax. To fulfil the three major tax objectives a revised land tax system would have to be determined on a standardized base, be flexible in response to changes in prices and output, be capable of personalization in terms of the individual circumstances of the taxpayer, and be adaptable to a comprehensive series of incentive and disincentive devices designed to promote agricultural productivity.

Given the necessary standardization of land classification procedures, the first essential step in the reform of Indian land taxation would seem to be the definition of a standardized tax base which is sufficiently flexible to fulfil the specified requirements. Such a base would have to correspond in some pre-determined manner with *presumptive* net income or output. Concern over the effect of taxation on agricultural productivity suggests, further, that presumptive income be defined not in terms of *actual output* but in terms of *productive capacity* or the output which the land should yield if managed with average efficiency. The tax would thus be based on *potential* output in relation to some regional average. Thus, the inefficient farmer whose production is less than the average for the region and/or for the type of land concerned would be penalized, whereas the efficient farmer would be correspondingly encouraged; the tax would also promote the transfer of land from inefficient to efficient hands and would penalize heavily underutilization, absentee ownership, etc.

The tax might be made *progressive* in terms of land holdings, though remaining proportional in terms of potential output for any given land size. In this way not only is the vertical equity criterion satisfied but there would be a sharp inducement to either the utilization of large land holdings—which are most likely to be held idle—or to the break-up of such large holdings into smaller units which would presumably be worked more efficiently. Allowance under the productive capacity criterion would have to be made for reduction or remission of land revenue in the event of extensive crop failure.

Tax yield under a reformed tax structure would clearly have to be responsive to price and production changes. What would appear most appropriate would be, say, a five-yearly re-assessment of regional average rated capacity to take account of growing conditions and price changes. Such adjustment of norms would seem unlikely to have serious incentive implications, inasmuch as the adjustments would be regional rather than individual. Effectively, the marginal tax rate on output would remain zero for an individual farmer but would be positive for farmers in the aggregate.

The proposed structure might be further refined to take account of the personal circumstances of assessees, to incorporate a variety of additional incentive devices, to distinguish the liability of landlords and tenants, and to reflect the process of land reform.

(c) *Other Direct Taxes*

(i) *Wealth Tax.* A tax on net wealth has been in operation in India since 1957 and is levied annually on the taxable net wealth of individuals and Hindu Undivided Families. In a series of reforms beginning in the 1968–69 Union Budget and culminating in the corresponding 1971–72 Budget the rate structure of the tax was made more progressive and the rate maximum raised to a quite remarkable 8 per cent on property value above Rs. 1.0 million. Additional wealth tax on urban real property reaches a rate maximum of 7 per cent on property value above Rs. 1.0 million. The generous exemption structure has also been truncated—the removal of jewellery being the most important of the changes—and, perhaps most remarkable of all, agricultural wealth has been brought within the purview of the Wealth Tax Act.

An annual tax on net wealth of the form taken by the Indian net wealth tax prior to the recent reforms is envisaged more in the nature of an additional income tax on income from capital than as a tax on capital itself. As such the tax is generally not a major revenue source, but is important for the redistributive objective as essentially a surtax on income tax, and has an interesting investment incentive effect inasmuch as the tax is directed to an assumed average rate of return on capital and thus provides an incentive to high-yield risk investment and a disincentive to hoarding and conservative investment. The structure of the tax now in force in India—if that structure is administratively enforceable—bears much more resembalance to a capital levy or a genuine tax on capital, inasmuch as the average rate of wealth-tax liability seems likely to exceed the average rate of return on all forms of taxable wealth. The new tax will certainly be more effective than the old in the diminution of inequalities of wealth and income, will yield more revenue, and will, in principle, provide a sharply increased incentive to high-yield risk investment. The question is whether the effects will all be positive, i.e. whether the new rates will be, in effect, confiscatory, acting to diminish private investment in the aggregate, and to promote evasion and capital flight.

(ii) *Expenditure Tax*. A tax on expenditure was first levied in the 1958–59 Union Budget, and, other than in the two fiscal years, 1962–63 and 1963–64, persisted till its abolition in the 1966–67 Budget. In its form prior to abolition, the tax was levied annually on expenditure incurred by individuals and Hindu undivided families. A basic exempt expenditure allowance of Rs. 30,000 was superimposed on an initial income level exemption of Rs. 36,000. A broad range of expenditures was exempt from tax, and tax rates on taxable expenditure were graduated to a maximum of 20 per cent.

The abolition of the tax was justified by its relatively low revenue productivity and its administrative awkwardness. It is arguable, however, that a really effective expenditure tax was never tried, and that a dramatically widened tax base—to be attained largely by the removal of the income exemption and the reduction of expenditure exemptions—and more severe rate structure would have been necessary to make the tax an effective fiscal tool with respect to the major tax objectives.

The role of an expenditure tax in a development context has several dimension; first, the tax serves to curtail the extent to which increases in income are directed to conspicuous consumption instead of saving, to diminish consumption inequalities, to assist in limiting consumption in an inflationary situation, and, finally, in the context of major income tax reform, to act as an integral part of a self checking personal direct tax return.

(iii) *Gift and Estate Taxation.* Estate Tax in India became payable on the capital value of property passing on the death of any person on or after 15 October, 1953, in accordance with the provisions of the Estate Duty Act of that year. The definition of taxable property transfers has been widened to encompass such transfers as gifts made in contemplation of death or within a short period before death. Above a minimum exemption level of Rs. 50,000 tax rates are graduated reaching a maximum of 85 per cent. A limited group of assets are tax exempt.

The estate tax has been complemented by a tax on *inter vivos* gifts since 1958. Graduated tax rates are imposed on transfers above a minimum exemption level of Rs. 5,000 by individuals, Hindu undivided families and associations of individuals. The range of exempt assets is considerably wider than under the estate tax, and the rate and exemption structures differ. The first Rs. 50,000 of the value of an estate passing at death is exempt, whereas the annual gift exemption is limited to Rs. 5,000—reduced from Rs. 10,000 in the

1971–72 Budget. The differences between the two rate structures were considerably reduced in the 1971–72 Budget, where gift tax rates were sharply increased, and the maximum rate of gift tax is now 75 per cent on gifts over Rs. 2 million—as against the maximum rate of estate tax on the corresponding slab of 85 per cent.

The existing estate and gift taxes in India and in developing countries generally—indeed, also in most developed countries—have not proved to be productive revenue sources, and would appear to have made little contribution to the diminution of inequalities of opportunity between generations. Within the standard structure of separate estate and gift taxes, the most effective reform would be the complete integration of gift and estate taxation into one transfer tax levied on a cumulative basis, and the use of an overall sharply progressive rate structure in the transfer tax. More liberal tax payment procedures and preferential tax treatment for "functional" assets would serve to moderate any adverse effects of the proposed changes on the private sector.

The optimal reform on both equity and revenue grounds would be of a more radical nature, and would go beyond such variants as the accessions tax to suggest the full incorporation of all gratuitous transfers—whether testamentary or *inter vivos*—in the cumulative taxable income of the recipient.

(iv) *Corporation Income Tax.* Corporations are regarded as separate entities for income tax purposes in India and have been subject to income taxation since 1860. Corporations are classified for tax purposes into four major categories, three covering domestic and one foreign corporations. The corporate tax rate structure is complex. Total corporation income—exclusive of a wide range of exempt receipts and deductible expenditures—is subject, according to its place in the four-group classification, to proportional tax rates of between 45 per cent and 70 per cent. Additional taxes imposed on corporations include a capital gains tax to which all corporations are subject, and a surtax imposed at a rate of 25 per cent—reduced from 35 per cent in the 1968–69 Union Budget—on all corporations the total income of which exceeds 10 per cent of the capital base, or Rs. 200,000, whichever is higher. A penalty tax on distributed profits in the case of public corporations was abolished in the 1968–69 Union Budget.

For many developing countries corporation income taxation is a more important revenue source than personal income taxation. In India, the corporation income tax has proved to be a relatively elastic and productive revenue source. Further, a separate, non-integrated corporation tax contributes to vertical equity—on the assumption that at least a portion of the tax is borne by capital owners—by taxing dividends and curtailing stock appreciation, and by dint of broad coverage and elasticity, is of great significance in automatic and discretionary stabilization policy.

The major disadvantage of the corporation tax is that it probably reduces funds for investment more than any other tax. However, this effect may be moderated by the introduction of extended loss-offset provisions and the use of selective accelerated depreciation (the latter is to be preferred to the frequently suggested alternative of replacement cost depreciation).

The proposal to integrate either fully or partially the personal and corporation income taxes has merit only on grounds of horizontal equity, and would considerably reduce the contribution of the corporate income tax to revenue productivity, vertical equity and stabilization.

(d) *Major Indirect Taxes*

Indirect taxes (taxes on commodities and transactions) are imposed in India by the Union Government and by all of the States. The Union Government levies a sales tax on interstate sales, manufacturers' and producers' excise taxes, and import and export duties; the States levy general sales or purchase taxes, excise taxes on alcoholic beverages and drugs, entertainment taxes, electricity duties, and taxes on sales or purchases of specific commodities. The most important indirect measures—in terms of their contribution to revenue—are Union customs duties, Union and State excise duties, and State sales taxes.

(i) *Union Customs Duties.* The Union Government levies import and export duties under its constitutional allocation of tax powers; revenue from the former is much greater than from the latter.

The Import tariff was rationalized in the 1965–66 Union Budget, and most of the duties across a wide range of commodities are now *ad valorem,* although some of the *ad valorem* duties are made specific by fixing the tariff values of the commodities to which they apply. Prior to devaluation in 1966, the basic rate of duty was 60 per cent on most intermediate goods and raw materials (other than primary raw materials), and 40 per cent on machinery and primary raw materials. Rates were much higher on consumer goods, generally 100 per cent, but ranging as high as 200 per cent. Following devaluation, the revised rates are generally 27.5 per cent on machinery and primary raw materials, 50 per cent on other raw materials, 60 per cent on processed materials and intermediate goods, and 100 per cent (unchanged) on consumers' goods.

Revenue from export duties had diminished to insignificance by 1965–66, and it would have been accurate to suggest that the export duty in India had been virtually replaced by the export subsidy. Devaluation in 1966 altered the situation, and export duties were imposed on a group of twelve commodities. Eleven of the duties were specific and one *ad valorem.* As might have been expected, the export duty on these commodities has been reduced and in some cases eliminated in subsequent budgets, and revenue from export duties seems likely again to diminish to insignificance by the end of the Fourth Plan.

(ii) *Union Excise Duties.* An excise tax is best seen as a true commodity tax, rather than as a transactions tax, since it is essentially imposed on the production of a commodity, and collected at the factory, rather than on the actual sale of the commodity. In this sense, an excise tax is distinct from a retail sales tax, the latter being strictly a transactions tax. Both taxes are, of course, intended to be shifted forward to consumers and are therefore ultimately incident on consumption.

Union excise duties are imposed under the Constitutional provision which reserves for the Union Government the exclusive power to impose excise taxes on tobacco and all other goods manufactured or produced in India, except alcoholic beverages and narcotics, the taxation of which is reserved for the State governments. The imposition and collection of the duties are governed by the Central Excises and Salt Act of 1944, as amended from time to time. The first excise duty in India was levied in 1894, and the device was extended to a wider range of articles in the 1930s, during World War II, and, particularly. following the recommendations of the Taxation Enquiry Commission in 1953–54. Revenue is derived from a broad range of commodities. Although the larger part of the set of rates remains specific, Union Budgets since the end of the Third Five Year Plan have moved increasingly toward the use of *ad valorem* rates, both in the treatment of new commodities and in the modification of tax rates on previously taxed commodities. Excise duties are levied at the manufacturing stage, and the basic duties are supplemented by *additional* and *special* excise duties and by a small group of *benefit excises.*

(iii) *State Excise Duties.* State Governments are empowered to levy excise taxes solely on alcoholic liquors for human consumption, and on opium, Indian hemp, and other narcotics. Excise taxes on medicinal and toilet preparations containing alcohol or narcotics are imposed by the Union Government but are collected by and accrue entirely to the States. Opium, Indian hemp, and other narcotics are subject to excise tax at varying rates in all States which have not prohibited their sale.

(iv) *State Sales Taxes.* A sales tax, as distinct from an excise tax, is a true transactions tax, and, further, is generally imposed at a uniform rate on the sale of a wide range of goods and services. A *universal* or *general* sales tax would cover the sale of all goods and services; a *selec-*

tive sales tax covers only specified or selected goods and services. In practice, most sales taxes are not general but exhibit varying degrees of selectivity; this is true of all the sales taxes levied by the Indian States. Another broad distinction made in India is between a sales tax proper and a *purchase tax*. A tax assessed on the aggregate sales of a registered dealer and collected from that dealer, is called a sales tax. If, on the other hand, the tax is assessed on the aggregate of a dealer's purchases, irrespective of his sales, it is referred to as a burchase tax. The sales tax is levied only on dealers, whereas the purchase tax is occasionally levied directly on consumers in the case of articles of conspicuous consumption.

A sales tax on motor fuel and lubricants was first levied in Madhya Pradesh in 1938 and the first general sales tax was introduced in Madras in 1939. Presently, all the States levy a sales tax of one form or another. The Constitution, as adopted in 1950, gave the States exclusive power to impose taxes on the sales of all goods except newspapers. Services are excluded from the ambit of the sales taxes.

The various sales taxes differ widely in their intended incidence and operation. In each system the most important characteristic is the point or points between production and retail sale at which the tax is levied, since this affects the qualifications of taxpayers, the classes of goods subject to the tax, rates of tax, and administrative procedures. The evolution and character of the sales tax system in each state has been conditioned by economic structure, financial needs, and adaptation to constitutional amendment.

In general terms, states which are characterized by substantial urban trade and significant industrial and manufacturing activities have tended to adopt a single-point tax imposed at only one point between production of goods and their sale to a consumer, and usually, on a limited group of dealers. In these States, a relatively high rate of tax is imposed on taxable sales and a large number of essential goods and basic raw materials are usually exempt. The incidence of a single point tax is closely controlled, in accordance with the largely urban commercial economy within which it operates. States with predominantly rural economies, on the other hand, have generally adopted multi-point sales taxes, imposed on every sale between production of the goods and their sale to the ultimate consumer. Since the incidence of such taxes is not controlled—so that the number of occasions on which different products are assessed before the retail level may vary considerably—the rates of tax are relatively low, exemptions are few, and most dealers are subject to the tax.

The rates at which the State sales taxes are levied depend on whether the tax is a single-point or a multi-point tax and on the nature of the goods sold. The rates applicable to each sale under single-point systems are generally higher than under multi-point systems, although the total of taxes imposed from producer to consumer under a multi-point system may be as high as the tax under a single-point system. Exemptions and concessionary rates vary widely between states. So-called "luxury" goods, such as motor cars, radios, electric appliances, watches, and cosmetics, are taxed at higher rates than other goods in most states.

The major group of indirect taxes are of great and increasing importance in the aggregate of Union and State tax revenue. From around 50 per cent of total (Union+State) tax revenue at the beginning of the Planning period, revenue from the four major tax heads constituted over 70 per cent of the total in the 1971–72 budgets. Union excises are the most important revenue source, followed by Union customs duties, State sales taxes and State excises.

The annual compound rate of growth of customs revenue from 1955–56 to 1970–71 has averaged 10.5 per cent; the income-elasticity of customs revenue over the same period was 1.096. The development context, with its requirements of foreign exchange and capital goods imports, suggests that revenue from customs will continue to decline relatively, and, possibly, absolutely.

The annual compound rate of growth of Union excise revenue from 1955–56 to

1970–71 averaged 12.1 per cent; the income elasticity of Union excise revenue over the same period was 1.7. The general conversion of excise taxes to *ad valorem* rates should increase the elasticity of excise tax revenue, and the possibility of increased revenue from rate increases and base widening is demonstrated annually in the Union Budgets. An interesting possibility which has not yet been tried is the formal planning of excise tax rates and base definitions on the basis of estimates of income elasticity of demand for groups of commodities.

The relevance of State excises emerged strongly in the Third Plan period with the apparent disintegration of prohibition. From the beginning of the Third Plan until 1970–71, the annual compound rate of growth of State excise tax revenue was a robust 13.25 per cent, and the income elasticity an equally impressive 1.6. The trade-off between revenue and prohibition is self-evident.

The annual compound rate of growth of State sales tax revenue from 1955–56 to 1970–71 was 11.13 per cent; income elasticity was 1.8. The possibility of increased revenue from rate increases—and indeed also base widening, since services are generally excluded from State sales tax bases—is so apparent that it seems certain that this form of tax will be one of the main revenue growth points throughout the 1970s.

In examining the contribution of indirect taxes to equity, the basic simple premise will be that indirect taxes are completely shifted forward and are borne by consumers in proportion to consumption expenditures on the taxed goods. On the basis of this assumption and further estimates of consumer demand patterns classified by income groups, the definition of indirect tax bases and rate structures can be designed to conform in principle to an intended distribution of burden by income groups. Such evidence as is available on the distribution of indirect taxes by income groups in India confirms not only that the burden of indirect taxes is progressive but has become sharply progressive.[12] Clearly the introduction of universal food exemptions under the State sales taxes and the gearing of Union excise rates to estimates of income elasticity could serve to further improve the progressivity of indirect tax devices in India, or at least to offset the regressive impact of the State excises on liquor and tobacco.

With respect, finally, to stablization, the signivcance of indirect taxation lies in reducing consumption through an initial once-for-all increase in the price of the taxed commodity. Indirect taxation is particularly significant in the growth context in India in that, at least directly, the diminution in demand is purely at the expense of consumption rather than investment. The potential stabilizing effectiveness of a mode of taxation is a function of the size of tax revenue in relation to national income, the movement of tax revenue in the same direction as national income changes, and the degree of responsiveness of tax revenue to changes in national income.

A measure of built-in flexibility—change in tax revenue other than from Budget changes, over change in national income—came to 0.055 for the aggregate of customs revenue, Union excises, and State sales taxes, over the period 1955–56 to 1970–71, indicating that the change in revenue from the major indirect taxes constituted 5.5 per cent of the change in national income over the same period. The most important of the indirect taxes is, of course, Union excises, the increased revenue from which constituted 3.3 per cent of the change in national income. The changes in customs revenue and State sales taxes were both 1.1 per cent.

Given the relatively high flexibility coefficient, and the fact that a large proportion of the flexibility of Union excises is the consequence of heightened rates and, to a lesser extent, coverage, it follows that indirect taxation in India offers an effective tool of both discretionary and automatic stabilization. A system of import duties, sales taxes and excise taxes set up to maximize responsiveness to income changes, with increased rates and coverage geared to movements in whole-

[12] *Incidence of Indirect Taxation*, op. cit.

sale or consumer prices index by a predetermined statutory automatic formula (formula flexibility), would offer increased effectiveness as a means of correcting inflationary price trends.

4. Summary and Conclusions

Important questions, pertaining to the principles of federal finance and the adaptation of the Indian tax system to the peculiar cultural and institutional context, were omitted in the preceding brief overview. Three broad, general issues of principle may, however, be considered to have emerged.

First, the role of taxation policy as an instrument of planned economic development can only be determined and evaluated in terms of the specification of a set of policy objectives. Further, the objective set can be meaningful only if the component objectives are operationally defined, and if the relationship between the component objectives, whether of conflict or complementarity, is clearly articulated.

Second, in terms primarily of resource mobilization and horizontal equity, a major deficiency in the Indian tax system lies in the problem of inter-sectoral imbalance, i.e. in the relatively light tax burden on the large agricultural sector.

Third, the development of the Indian tax system as a flexible, elastic policy instrument, which can be effectively related to objectives, requires the correction of the present relative decline of major direct tax instruments.

With respect to objectives, it was argued that the objective set might be defined at the highest level of aggregation to include growth, equity, and stabilization. The most acute area of conflict—for which the compromise solution of "functionalism" was suggested—was defined to lie between the desire to increase revenue productivity and diminish inequalities, on the one hand, and the desire to encourage private saving and investment, on the other.

With respect to inter-sectoral imbalance, a major overhaul of the agricultural taxation system was suggested, the first step in the reform involving the redefinition of the land tax base in terms of average potential output.

With respect to the direct tax : indirect tax ratio it was argued that the major scope for increased revenue productivity and increased effectiveness under the equity and stabilization objectives lay in the reform of personal direct taxation. It was argued, in particular, that the personal income tax and estate and gift taxes should be reformed by base widening and the extension of coverage. It was acknowledged, however, that indirect taxation, particularly Union excise taxes and State sales taxes, had provided a remarkably elastic and productive revenue instrument which could be reformed both in terms of tax bases and rates, in order to increase its stabilizing effectiveness and its contribution to vertical equity.

APPENDIX

Table 1. Total Tax Revenue (net and gross):

	1950-51 *Actuals*	1955-56 *Actuals*	TOTAL FIRST PLAN PERIOD	1956-57 *Actuals*	1960-61 *Actuals*	TOTAL SECOND PLAN PERIOD
I. TAXES ON INCOME AND EXPENDITURE (1+2+3)	1,257.0	1,132.3	5,869.5	1,441.7	1,919.7	8,106.0
Taxes on income other than corporation tax	1,327.3	1,313.5	6,640.7	1,517.4	1,673.8	8,036.8
LESS States' Share	475.2	551.6	2,782.4	587.5	873.7	3,746.7
1. Net Receipts	852.1	761.9	3,858.3	929.9	800.1	4,290.1
2. Corporatln Tax	404.9	370.4	2,011.2	511.8	1,110.5	3,792.5
3. Expenditure Tax					9.1	23.4
II. TAXES ON PROPERTY AND CAPITAL TRANSACTIONS (1+2+3+4+5)	38.1	25.5	136.9	24.1	134.9	584.4
Estate Duty		18.1	26.2	21.1	30.9	131.2
LESS States' Share		18.6	24.3	24.1	29.1	128.6
1. Net Receipts		—0.5	1.9	—3.0	1.8	2.6
2. Tax on Wealth					81.5	369.7
3. Gift Tax					8.9	26.8
4. Stamps and Registration	18.1	17.2	81.0	21.7	36.8	159.2
5. Land Revenue	20.0	8.8	54.0	5.4	5.9	26.1
III. TAXES ON COMMODITIES (1+2+3+4)	2,274.9	2,956.9	13,729.3	3,471.8	5,246.8	21,256.9
Customs	1,077.0	1,279.8	6,483.0	1,405.2	1,546.1	6,984.2
Imports						
Exports	473.6	377.6	2,643.7	286.7	131.2	1,043.5
Other Revenue	63.7	42.2	218.8	73.1	82.1	377.7
LESS Refunds	42.8	32.6	188.4	32.7	59.1	228.9
1. Net Receipts	1,571.5	1,667.0	9,157.1	1,732.3	1,700.3	8,176.5
Union Excise Duties	675.4	1,452.2	5,172.6	1,904.3	4,163.5	15,539.9
(of which additional excise duties)					336.0	806.5
LESS States' Share		165.7	640.6	182.2	751.0	2,812.3
2. Net Receipts	675.4	1,286.8	4,532.0	1,722.1	3,412.5	12,727.6
Tax on Ralway Passengers' Fares					158.9	446.2
LESS States' Share					137.9	421.6
3. Net Receipts					21.0	24.6
4. Other Taxes and Duties	28.0	3.1	40.2	17.4	113.0	328.2
IV. *TOTAL NET REVENUE* (*I+II+III*)	3,570.0	4,114.7	19,735.7	4,937.6	7,301.4	29,947.3
V. TOTAL GROSS TAX REVENUE (including States' Share)	4,045.2	4,850.6	23,183.0	5,731.4	9,093.1	37,056.5

SOURCES: Reserve Bank of India, *Report on Currency and Fiinance*,

Government of India, 1950-51—1970=71.

Rs. million

1961-62 (*Actuals*)	1962-63 (*Actuals*)	1963-64 (*Actuals*)	1964-65 (*Actuals*)	TOTAL 1965-66 (*Actuals*)	TOTAL THIRD PLAN PERIOD	1969-69 (*Actuals*)	1969-70 (*Actuals*)	1970-71 (Revised budget)
2,288.4	3,123.9	4,140.2	4,537.7	4,537.2	18,662.4	4,837.3	5,086.6	4,659.1
1,653.9	1,859.6	2,586.0	2,665.5	2,718.0	11,483.0	3,784.7	4,484.5	4,600.0
938.5	952.7	1,192.9	1,237.7	1,233.4	5,555.2	1,945.1	2,931.8	3,590.9
715.4	906.9	1,393.1	1,427.8	1,484.6	5,927.8	1,839.6	1,552.7	1,009.1
1,564.6	2,215.0	2,745.9	3,140.5	3,048.4	12,714.4	2,997.7	3,651.9	3,650.0
8.4	2.0	1.2	4.4	4.2	22.2	—	—	—
142.1	161.5	170.2	164.9			215.6	247.3	257.7
42.1	39.4	46.7	54.3	66.6	249.1	67.4	69.4	70.0
38.8	38.8	42.2	67.8	67.9	255.5	55.4	68.8	63.0
3.3	0.6	4.5	—13.5	—1.3	—6.4	12.0	—0.4	7.0
82.6	95.4	102.0	105.0	120.6	505.6	111.1	156.2	160.0
10.1	9.7	11.2	22.2	22.6	75.8	15.1	20.2	20.0
40.5	50.0	49.4	49.7			74.6	69.7	68.9
5.6	5.8	3.1	1.5			2.8	1.6	1.8
6,323.2	7,324.4	9,432.9	10,890.4	13,110.7	47,081.6	15,135.7	16,680.1	19,503.9
1,982.2	2,384.2	3,342.5	4,046.4	5,476.9	17,232.2	3,739.7	3,269.7	4,543.7
126.9	96.0	33.7	24.3	21.4	302.3	1,010.3	755.7	616.5
78.2	75.0	80.1	42.2	49.5	324.5	65.9	512.9	80.0
64.8	95.6	108.9	137.9	157.7	564.9	359.9	305.2	364.0
2,122.5	2,459.6	3,347.4	3,975.0	5,389.7	17,294.2	4,465.0	4,233.1	4,876.2
4,893.1	5,988.3	7,295.8	8,015.1	8,979.2	35,171.5	13,206.7	15,243.1	18,052.4
389.6	447.5	431.1	444.9	457.5	2,170.6	2,909.3	3,215.1	3,900.4
806.5	1,249.1	1,359.9	1,273.4	1,459.2	6,148.1			
4,086.6	4,739.2	5,935.9	6,741.7	7,572.0	29,075.4	10,297.4	12,028.0	14,152.0
114.1	125.6	149.6	173.7	257.4a	820.4	81.8	105.2	115.1
8,753.7	10,609.8	13,743.3	15,628.0	17,846.2	66,581.0	20,188.6	22,014.0	24,420.7
10,415.0	12,848.4	16,130.0	17,980.0	20,606.7	77,981.1	26,950.0	28,230.7	31,975.0

1960-70; *Reserve Bank of India Bulletin*, June, 1971.

Table 2. Total Tax Revenue of State

	1951-52 (*Accounts*)	1955-56 (*Accounts*)	TOTAL FIRST PLAN PERIOD	1956-57 (*Accounts*)	1960-61 (*Accounts*)	TOTAL SECOND PLAN PERIOD
I. TAXES ON INCOME	570.5	630.8	3,029.0	659.0	1,004.7	4,212.0
Shares of income tax	526.5	552.8	2,779.0	579.0	905.8	3,772.0
Agricultural income tax	43.3	76.7	246.0	79.0	94.9	425.0
Profession tax	0.7	1.3	4.0	1.0	4.0	15.0
II. TAXES ON PROPERTY AND CAPITAL TRANSACTIONS	754.0	1,110.4	4,740.0	1,190.0	1,444.1	6,619.0
Estate Duty		18.6	24.0	24.0	28.9	128.0
Land Revenue	479.9	780.1	3,267.0	832.0	971.9	4,550.0
Stamps and Registration.	255.6	290.8	1,354.0	313.0	433.3	1,839.0
Urban Immovable Property Tax	18.5	21.0	95.0	21.0	10.0	101.0
III. TAXES ON COMMODITIES AND SERVICES	1,486.0	1,820.1	8,327.0	2,108.0	3,799.0	15,239.0
Union Excise	7.0	165.7	646.0	179.0	751.1	2,809.0
State Excise	494.1	450.9	2,300.0	464.0	531.1	2,420.0
General Sales Tax	544.0	800.6	3,104.0	966.0	1,424.4	5,824.0
Sales Tax on Motor Spirit	45.3	15.4	266.0	10.0	163.0	518.0
Motor Vehicle Taxes	100.9	158.8	651.0	186.0	341.0	1,247.0
Tax on Railway Fares[a]					137.9	426.0
Entertainment Tax	63.9	73.4	319.0	86.0	131.1	523.0
Electricity Duties	33.9	58.2	226.0	69.0	125.1	489.0
Other Taxes & Duties[b]	196.7	97.1	815.0	150.0	194.3	982.0
IV. TOTAL (I+II+III) TAX REVENUE	2,810.5	3,561.4	16,096.0	3,957.0	6,247.8	26,070.0
V. TOTAL STATE TAX COLLECTIONS (Tax Revenue minus share of taxes from union)	2,277.0	2,834.3	12,647.0	3,175.0	4,562.0	19,361.0

Notes: [a]receipts in lieu of this head from 1961-62 are included under grants-in-aid; the Union tax on railway fares was abolished in 1960-61.

[b]includes sugar cane cess, purchase tax on sugar, tax on passengers and goods, tobacco duties, tax on prize competition and betting, interstate transit duties, etc.

Government 1951-52—1970=71

1961-62 (*Accounts*)	1962-63 (*Accounts*)	1963-64 (*Accounts*)	1964-65 (*Accounts*)	1965-66 (*Accounts*)	TOTAL THIRD PLAN PERIOD	1968-69 (*Accounts*)	1969-70 (*Accounts*)	1970-71 (*Revised budget*)
								Rs. Million
1,042.6	1,057.7	1,284.2	1,352.6	1,338.9	6,077.0	2,006.6	3,100.0	3,710.0
943.7	952.4	1,181.0	1,235.9	1,231.7	5,546.0	1,945.0	2,932.0	3,571.0
94.4	95.7	92.6	107.3	98.8	489.0	99.3	140.0	121.0
4.5	9.4	10.6	9.4	8.4	42.0	24.3	28.0	28.0
1,487.5	1,791.2	1,911.3	1,978.5	1,967.1	9,135.0	2,243.3	2,264.0	2,496.0
38.9	38.9	42.2	67.6	67.8	256.0	55.3	70.0	71.0
952.3	1,200.7	1,234.2	1,197.9	1,119.3	5,703.0	1,139.1	1,028.0	1,154.0
465.7	522.1	614.1	685.5	741.1	3,027.0	1,012.9	1,126.0	1,232.0
30.6	29.7	20.8	27.5	38.9	149.0	36.4	40.0	39.0
4,095.8	5,090.6	6,195.1	6,893.1	7,871.5	30,147.0	12,768.3	14,442.0	16,355.0
806.5	1,249.2	1,360.4	1,272.4	1,458.0	6,146.0	2,871.7	3,252.0	3,866.0
585.8	628.1	728.9	845.4	963.7	3,753.0	1,590.4	1,736.0	1,908.0
1,631.4	1,875.2	2,454.1	2,950.9	3,385.7	12,297.0	4,370.9	4,908.0	5,395.0
183.0	213.5	229.0	233.3	292.2	1,151.0	352.9	386.0	512.0
379.3	462.9	574.0	593.3	642.2	2,651.0	893.2	935.0	1,015.0
151.0	182.1	225.6	251.1	294.4	1,104.0	424.5	504.0	543.0
148.9	194.8	272.9	334.3	353.6	1,305.0	548.7	581.0	644.0
209.9	284.8	350.2	412.4	481.7	1,740.0	253.3	300.0	302.0
6,625.8	7,939.5	9,390.6	10,224.2	11,177.5	45,359.0	17,083.6	19,809.0	22,574.0
4,836.7	5,699.0	6,807.0	7,648.3	8,420.0	33,411.0	12,211.6	13,555.0	15,066.0

SOURCES: Reserve Bank of India, *Report on Currency and Finance*, 1969-70; *Reserve Bank of India Bulletin*, August, 1971.

Table 3. Tax Revenue as per cent of National Income: Twenty Selected Countries, 1950-64

COUNTRY	1950			1963			1964			
	Direct Tax	Indirect Tax	Total	Direct Tax	Indirect Tax	Total	Direct Tax	Indirect Tax	Total	Ramking (1964 figures)
Australia	10.0	6.6	16.6	12.8	7.3	20.1	12.5	8.5	21.0	12
Aus ria	8.2	8.5	16.7	15.5	16.2	31.7	12.4	19.8	32.2	1
Belgium	8.6	12.2	20.8	9.5	14.8	24.3	9.4	14.9	24.2	6
Burma	1.8	6.2	8.0	5.1	9.8	14.9	10.8	9.9	20.7	13
Canada	9.0	7.0	16.0	10.9	7.3	18.2	10.5	7.5	18.0	15
Ceylon	3.5	10.8	14.3	5.1	9.8	14.9	5.1	16.3	21.4	11
Denmark	6.7	8.9	15.6	9.2	13.0	22.2	9.0	13.5	22.5	9[a]
Fance	7.9	16.5	24.4	7.2	18.5	25.7	7.7	19.2	26.9	5
Geramny, West	10.4	11.3	21.7	14.0	14.2	28.2	15.0	14.2	29.2	2
Grecee	2.9	9.6	12.5	2.9	13.2	16.1	3.0	13.5	16.5	16
INDIA	2.4	4.2	6.6	4.0	9.5	13.5	3.8	8.8	12.6	18
Ireland	6.9	12.4	19.3	8.4	14.2	22.6	8.1	14.1	22.2	10
Italy	3.0	9.3	12.3	5.5	14.3	19.8	5.9	17.1	23.0	8
Japan	9.4	7.4	16.8	7.7	5.7	13.4	7.7	5.7	13.4	17
Netherlands	14.5	13.6	28.1	16.4	10.9	27.3	16.7	11.2	27.9	3
Norway	7.6	11.8	19.4	6.2	16.7	22.9	5.9	16.6	22.5	9[a]
Philippines	1.0	4.3	5.3	2.6	8.4	11.0	2.6	8.4	11.0	19
Sweden	9.9	7.8	17.7	12.5	13.0	25.5	11.0	13.0	24.0	7
U.K.	17.9	14.1	32.0	16.5	11.2	27.7	15.7	11.5	27.2	4
U.S.A.	13.2	3.4	16.6	19.1	6.1	25.2	13.9	6.7	20.6	14

Note: [a]equal ranking.

SOURCE: United Nations, *Statistical Yearbook* 1965 (New York: 1966).

Table 4. Tax Burden in Terms of per Capita Income, 1964

Country	Index	Ranking	Country	Index	Ranking
Australia	3.0	11[a]	INDIA	4.2	9[a]
Austria	5.9	5	Ireland	4.9	6[a]
Belgium	2.5	13	Italy	6.5	3
Burma	8.4	1	Jaean	6.0	4
Canada	2.0	14	Netherlands	4.9	6[a]
Ceylon	4.2	9[a]	Norway	4.3	8
Denmark	2.7	12	Philippines	2.1	14
France	4.8	7[a]	Sweden	3.4	10
Germany, West	4.8	7[a]	U. K.	3.0	11[a]
Greece	7.9	2	U.S.A.	1.4	15

Note: [a]equal ranking.

SOURCE: United Nations, *Statistical Yearbook* New (York: 1966).

Table 5. Average and Marginal Rates of Taxation over the Planning Period

1	2	3	4	5	6	7	8	9	10	11
YEAR	National Income at Current Prices Rs. Million	Total Union and State Tax Revenue Rs. Million	Gross Union Tax Collections Rs. Million	State Tax Collections Rs. Million	Average Tax Rate on (3) per cent	Marginal Tax Rate on (3) Per cent	Averagee Tax Rate on (4) Per cent	Marginal Tax Rate on (4) Per cent	Average Tax Rate on (5) Per cent	Marginal Tax Rate on (5) Per cen
1951-52	99,700	7,387	5,050	2,337	7.4		5.06		2.34	
1952-53	98,200	6,778	4,420	2,358	6.9		4.50		2.40	
						0.80		—3.33		2.5
1953-54	104,800	6,725	4,200	2,525	6.4		4.00		2.40	
						..		..		..
1954-55	96,100	7,204	4,560	2,644	7.5		4.74		2.76	
						12.75		7.83		4.92
1955-56	99,800	7,676	4,850	2,826	7.7		4.85		2.85	
						9.23		6.61		2.62
1956-57	113,100	8,904	5,730	3,174	7.9		5.06		2.84	
						193.25		153.75		39.50
1957-58	113,900	10,450	6,960	3,490	9.2		6.11		3.09	
						3.66		1.57		2.09
1958-59	126,000	10,893	7,150	3,743	8.6		5.67		2.93	
						36.31		19.71		16.60
1959-60	129,500	12,164	7,840	4,324	9.4		6.05		3.35	
						11.26		7.81		4.45
1960-61	141,400	13,504	8,770	4,734	9.6		6.20		3.40	
						29.18		24.24		4.94
1961-62	148,000	15,430	10,370	5,060	10.4		7.00		3.40	
						53.68		38.33		15.35
1962-63	154,000	18,651	12,670	5,981	12.1		8.22		3.88	
						25.38		19.11		6.27
1963-64	172,100	23,246	16,130	7,116	13.5		9.37		4.13	
						9.79		6.60		3.19
1964-65	200,100	25,988	17,980	8,008	13.0		8.98		4.02	

SOURCES: Resere Bank of India, *Report on Currency and Finance* 1965-66 (Bombay: Reserve Bank of India, 1967); Government of India, *Explanatory Memorandum on the Budget of the Central Government*, 1967-68 (New Delhi: Ministry of Finance, 1967); "Finances of State Governments 1967-68," *Reserve Bank of India Bulletin* (August 1967).

21

Centre-State Fiscal Relations in India

A. T. EAPEN

1. Introduction

Inter-governmental fiscal arrangements are of abiding interest in all federations. It is all the more so in the Indian federation where the federal and state governments are engaged in a concerted effort for a planned economic development of the nation. The planning process involves an assessment of the total resources to be mobilized by the Union and the states. Based on this assessment, the various state plans and the Union plan are put together to form a consistent national plan which would promote a balanced development of different parts of the country and extend the benefits of economic development to its less developed regions. Therefore, careful attention to centre-state fiscal arrangements becomes essential in order to ensure not only an effective mobilization of the national pool of resources, wherever they are, but also its deployment, wherever necessary within the confines of the federation, in order to achieve an appropriate balance between national and regional development.

In a discussion of the problems of intergovernmental fiscal relations in a federal framework, K. C. Wheare makes the following observation :

> There is and can be no final solution to the allocation of financial resources in a federal system. There can only be adjustments and re-allocations in the light of changing conditions. What a Federal government needs, therefore, is machinery adequate to make these adjustments and to make them also in such a way that the financial independence of the general and regional governments is preserved so far as possible.[1]

and he continues :

> ....It must be admitted, I think, that a political body is needed to take these decisions, although there is a strong case for the view that an independent body like the [Australian] Grants Com-

[1] K. C. Wheare, *Federal Government* (Oxford University Press, 1951), p. 123.

mission should have the final decision of the whole question.[2]

The architects of the Indian federation provided for an independent statutory body, namely, a Finance Commission,[3] to be appointed every quinquennium or earlier, entrusted with periodic review and resolution of federal-state fiscal problems. Such are inherent in a federal structure which characteristically exhibits an imbalance in the allocation of financial resources on the one hand, and functional responsibilities on the other, between federal and state governments.

Developments on the tax as well as expenditure sides of governments contribute to the imbalance in federal structure. As economic activity progressively gets integrated into a nationwide market, the more productive and equitable tax sources become increasingly better suited for exploitation by the national government both from the standpoint of efficient allocation of resources as well as administrative efficiency. This leaves the state governments with inadequate sources of independent revenue. On the expenditure side, the evolving transformation from a *laissez-faire* to a welfare state results in ever-increasing pressures for costly public services on all levels of governments, especially the state and local governments which are in a better position to tailor them to the preferences of citizens. Thus, the level of government which is most appropriate for providing many costly public services is not always the best for raising the necessary financial resources. The problem is further complicated by the wide interstate variations in income and wealth prevailing in all existing federations. Therefore, there is an imperative need for a mechanism which can resolve in an equitable manner the issue of the transfer of resources from the federal to the various state governments.

2. Taxation and Borrowing: Constitutional Provisions

The Indian Constitution vests in the federal government the exclusive power to levy the following taxes:[4] customs, taxes on corporations and non-agricultural income, estate taxes on property other than agricultural land, and all excises except those on alcohol and narcotic drugs. The states have the exclusive power to levy taxes on agricultural income and estate taxes on agricultural land. The Constitution permits the states to levy sales taxes; however, they are prohibited from imposing such taxes on transactions which occur outside their boundaries or which arise in the course of interstate or international trade.[5] Furthermore, a constitutional amendment made in 1956 empowers the Indian Parliament to restrict state sales tax laws concerning goods declared to be of "special importance" in interstate trade.

Borrowing powers of the states are limited by the provisions of the Indian Constitution. The state governments have no right to borrow outside India. Furthermore, if a state is indebted to the Union (as every state is now), it may not resort to further borrowing without the prior consent of the federal government.[6]

3. Methods of Financial Adjustment: Constitutional Provisions

The Constitution provides for three avenues for supplementing the financial resources of state governments. These are: (1) sharing of certain federal taxes, (2) grants-in-aid, and (3) grants for public purposes. The first two are designed to be integral parts of normal federal-state financial adjustments. The Constitution expects the Finance Commission to conduct periodic studies of federal-state fiscal problems and make recommendations with respect to the sharing of federal taxes and awards of grants-in-aid to state governments. It was the clear intention of the fathers of the Indian Constitution that all matters pertaining to normal federal-state financial adjustments should be scrutinized by the Finance Commission, which was given a pre-eminent role in

2 Ibid., pp. 124–25.

3 See *Constitution of India*, Article 280 (hereinafter cited as C.I.).

4 Ibid., Seventh Schedule.

5 Ibid.

6 Ibid., Art. 293.

the resolution of problems in fiscal federalism.

The third means of financial adjustment, namely grants for public purposes (permitted under Art. 282 of the Constitution), was intended to be resorted to only in emergencies. Since such grants are not envisaged as part of normal Federal-state financial adjustments, they are kept outside the purview of the Finance Commission.

Although grants for public purposes under Art. 282 were intended for meeting emergencies, with the advent of centralized economic planning, the federal government has chosen this avenue in order to award grants for the execution of various projects under the economic plans. These grants are made on the recommendation of the Planning Commission, which is essentially a political body. Thus, soon after the inauguration of the Indian Constitution, the Finance Commission has been bypassed in the determination of a vital part of the Federal-state financial adjustment mechanism.

Not only has the Finance Commission been excluded from the determination of significant aspects of fiscal federalism, but also the dominant role assigned to it in the Constitution has been progressively circumscribed. The directives to the second and third Commissions explicitly required them to take into account, among other things, the states' needs under the economic plans and their tax efforts before determining grants-in-aid of their revenues.[7] On the contrary, the fourth and fifth Finance Commissions were directed not to take into account the states' requirements under the economic plans for determining grants-in-aid. Furthermore, by implication they were even precluded from a study of states' tax efforts. For example, in assessing grants-in-aid for the five years ending with the fiscal year 1973–74, the fifth Commission was directed to consider not the tax efforts of states but the revenues available to them on the basis of levels of taxation likely to be reached at the end of fiscal year 1968–69.[8]

The rise of the Planning Commission with wide powers over the allocation of resources between the federal and state governments has resulted in a progressive downgrading of the role of the Finance Commission. Prior to the formulation of each economic plan, the Planning Commission is expected to make an assessment of all the resources available to the federal and state governments, including additional taxation, borrowing, deficit financing, and foreign assistance. Based on this assessment, the Planning Commission determines the size of the national plan which is composed of subplans for the federal government and each state government. To minimize overlapping between the Planning and Finance Commissions, the latter has been restricted to the non-plan sector of state budgets. This led the Third Finance Commission to observe:

> Against this background, the role of the Finance Commission comes to be, at best, that of an agency to review the forecasts of revenue and expenditure submitted by the states and the acceptance of the revenue element of the Plan as indicated by the Planning Commission for determining the quantum of devolution and grants-in-aid to be made; and, at worst, its function is merely to undertake an arithmetic exercise of devolution, based on amounts of assistance for each state already settled by the Planning Commission, to be made under different heads on the basis of certain principles to be prescribed.[9]

4. Tax-Sharing

The Indian Constitution spells out a wide variety of federal-state arrangements in regard to taxation. These dispositions

---

[7] *Report of the Finance Commission, 1957* (New Delhi, 1957), p. 2. (Hereinafter cited as *Second Report*) and *Report of the Finance Commission, 1961* (New Delhi, 1962), p. 2 (hereinafter cited as *Third Report*).

[8] *Report of the Finance Commission,* 1969 (New Delhi, 1969), p. 2 (hereinafter cited as *Fifth Report*). Also *Report of the Finance Commission, 1965* (New Delhi, 1965), pp. 1–2 (hereinafter cited as *Fourth Report*).

[9] *Third Report,* p. 35.

have stemmed from a desire to minimize a wide array of tax problems endemic to federal systems, such as duplicate tax administrations, double taxation, tax rivalry, tax evasion, excessive tax compliance costs, etc. Four types of arrangements may be readily identified:

1. Taxes which are levied by the federal government but collected and appropriated by the states;[10]
2. Taxes which are levied and collected by the federal government but assigned to the states;[11]
3. Taxes which are levied and collected by the federal government but mandated to be shared with the states;[12] and
4. Taxes which are levied, collected and retained by the federal government which, on its own volition, may share proceeds with the states.[13]

The Constitution enumerates the taxes that fall into each of the four groups mentioned above. However, the actual details with respect to sharing are left to the recommendations of the Finance Commissions.

The first two arrangements mentioned earlier are evidently not intended for making any financial adjustments between federal and state governments but for ensuring uniformity of taxation, minimization of tax evasion and tax compliance costs, and administrative convenience. In the first case, the taxes are collected and appropriated by the states; thus the allocation of the receipts among the various states is automatic. The taxes in this group are certain stamp duties and excises on certain medicinal and toilet preparations and a federal interstate sales tax.

In the second catagory, although the federal government levies and collects the taxes, it has no right to the revenues. In regard to the allocation of the receipts from these taxes among the various states, all the Finance Commissions have felt that the principles of distribution should be such as to secure, as far as possible, for each state the amount it would have collected, if it had the power to levy the taxes.[14] The only tax in this category which is levied and collected by the federal government is an estate tax on non-agricultural property.[15]

Under the third and fourth categories are, respectively, federal tax on non-agricultural income and federal excises. The former is mandated to be shared with the states. The latter may be shared with the states at the discretion of the Indian Parliament.

Progressively rising budgetary pressures have prompted the state governments to plead before the Finance Commissions for increasing shares of federal income tax and excises. In the case of income tax, the states have advanced two reasons for a larger share of the receipts. First, the Income Tax Act of 1959 reclassified income tax paid by companies as corporation tax, thereby excluding it altogether from sharing with states. Second, the receipts from income tax have proved to be less elastic than those from corporation income tax. Because of these two reasons, the states have felt justified in asking for a larger share of federal income tax. The Finance Commissions have responded to states' demands by progressively increasing the states' share from 50 to 75 per cent. The last three Finance Commissions have cautioned against further increases in the states' share of income tax, lest the federal government, which levies and collects the

---

10 *C.I.*, Article 268.
11 Ibid., Art. 269.
12 Ibid., Art. 270.
13 Ibid., Art. 272.

14 *Second Report*, pp. 51–52; *Third Report*, pp. 13–14; *Fourth Report*, p. 12; and *Fifth Report*, p. 237. For example, the estate tax on non-agricultural immovable property, which comes under this category, is distributed among the states in proportion to the gross value of such property assessed and located in each state.

15 A federal tax on railway passenger fares imposed in 1957 used to be in this category until 1961 when it was repealed. To compensate for the consequent loss of revenue to state governments, an *ad hoc* grant is made by the federal government. Moreover as a result of an extra-constitutional arrangement, the state governments have agreed to replace their sales taxes on three widely used commodities, namely factory-made textiles, sugar and tobacco, by additional federal excises on them. The net proceeds of these excises are distributed among the states.

tax, may lose interest in the yield of the tax.[16]

In the case of federal excises, the Finance Commissions' response to states' demand for a larger share has been to broaden the base by including more and more federal excises within the divisible pool. Although the earlier Finance Commissions restricted sharing to some selected federal excises, the later Commissions have found no justification for doing so. Moreover, if only some selected federal excises are shared, a reduction or even abolition of one of these may adversely affect the revenue position of the states. Furthermore, the larger the number of shared taxes, the greater the stability of shared revenues for state governments. Thus, all basic excises, additional excises on mineral oils, and special excises have been recommended to be included in the divisible pool. With the broadening of the base, the Finance Commissions have reduced the states' share from 40 to 20 per cent, although in absolute terms the divisible share has progressively increased.

In regard to the distribution of shared federal tax receipts among the various states, generally each state has advanced a formula which is most beneficial to it. For the distribution of income tax, states have urged the Finance Commission to take into account one or more of the following: contribution, population, area, proportion of scheduled castes and tribes in population, etc. In the case of federal excises, the criteria put forward include population, consumption, contribution, collection, and various other indices of financial need.

The Finance Commissions have generally felt that income taxes and excises should be allocated among the states on the basis of some broad index of need, such as population. In general, the special circumstances and needs of the various states are germane only to the determination of grants-in-aid and not to the distribution of taxes shared between the Union and the states.[17]

16 *Third Report,* p. 17; *Fourth Report,* p. 18; *Fifth Report,* pp. 25–26.

17 *First Report,* p. 75; *Second Report,* pp. 39–40 and 44; *Third Report,* pp. 17–18 and 22; *Fourth Report,* pp. 19 and 28–29; *Fifth Report,* p. 28.

Population is given predominant weight in the distribution of income tax; in addition, some weight is given to the respective contribution of the states to the receipts of the tax. In 1969, four relatively industrialized states alone accounted for about three-fourths of the income tax collections.[18] All the Finance Commissions except the second have been inclined to give some weight to the respective contributions of the states because of the fact that "there is all over the country a core of incomes—particularly in the range of personal and small business incomes—which could be treated as of local origin."[19] The fifth Finance Commission, for example, has recommended that 90 per cent of the divisible income tax pool be distributed on the basis of population and the remainder on the basis of contribution.[20]

Population of the states is the major factor in the formula for the distribution of federal excises, too. The Finance Commissions have been reluctant to give any weight to consumption of taxed commodities in the distribution formula because it would result in considerable disadvantage to the less urbanized states which are not in a position to raise revenues from sales taxes to the same extent as more urbanized states. The first Finance Commission distributed the states' share of excises solely on the basis of population.[21] The subsequent Commissions, while still holding population as the most important factor in distribution, have made some adjustments in favour of the relatively poorer states. The fifth Finance Commission, for example, distributed 80 per cent of the divisible excises on the basis of population and the remainder on the basis of a variety of indices of relative needs of states, such as per capita income, prop-

18 *Fifth Report,* p. 27.

19 *First Report,* p. 73; *Third Report,* p. 18; *Fourth Report,* p. 19; *Fifth Report,* pp. 26–28.

20 The first, third, and fourth Commissions had recommended that 80 per cent be distributed on the basis of population and the remainder on the basis of contribution. Since data for state-wide contribution to federal income tax are not available, proxy variables have been used to approximate state-wide contribution.

21 *First Report,* p. 82.

ortion of scheduled tribes in population, number of hospital beds per 1,000 of state population, etc[22]

Comments on Tax-Sharing

The Constitution gives the right to levy tax on non-agricultural income and most of excises exclusively to the federal government. The state governments have absolutely no right to impose them within their boundaries. The readiness of all Finance Commissions, except the second, to acknowledge the relevance of contribution in the distribution of income tax implies the recognition of the inherent right of each state to a part of the income tax contributed by it. Such right has no constitutional basis. If a broad index of need is the appropriate basis for distribution of the proceeds of a shared tax, then there is no justification for giving any importance to contribution in the scheme for distribution.

Also it may be argued that there is no reason for giving any consideration to the special needs of states in the formula for the distribution of shared taxes. Presumably, every state is entitled to a share of federal income tax and excises irrespective of need, but grants-in-aid are awarded only to those states which have demonstrated a need for such assistance. Therefore, it seems appropriate to take into account special needs of states for the determination of grants-in-aid rather than for the distribution of shared taxes. Moreover, if the absolute share of a state from the distributable pool of federal taxes is raised because of its special needs, the grants-in-aid received by it should be correspondingly reduced. At the margin, it should not make any significant difference whether the funds are received from shared taxes or grants-in-aid. Therefore, instead of making inadequate and haphazard provisions for special needs of states in the formula for distribution of shared taxes, the entire problem may be systematically considered in the determination of grants-in-aid. Hence, a strong case may be made for simplifying the method of distribution of shared taxes among the states on the basis of a broad index of need, such as population, leaving their special needs to be covered, if necessary, by grants-in-aid.

Furthermore, given the present formula for the distribution of shared taxes, it may be asked why contribution is not relevant for the distribution of federal excises, if it is relevant for the distribution of income tax? Likewise, if special needs of the states are relevant for the distribution of federal excises, then why are these same needs not significant for the allocation of income tax?

At present, the receipts from shared taxes add substantially to the surpluses in the non-plan budgets of several states, some of which have the highest per capita incomes in the country. The fourth Finance Commission found six states with surpluses[23] whereas the fifth Commission found eight states with substantially larger surpluses.[24] Swelling the surpluses in non-plan state budgets by receipts from shared taxes leads to a reduction in the overall federal resources that are made available to support the economic plans of *all* states, especially the less advanced ones.[25] More importantly, however, given the prevailing under-taxation even by the wealthier states, swollen surpluses in the non-plan budgets are certainly not likely to impel the state governments to intensify tax effort and enhance efficiency. This situation points to a need for reducing the states' shares of divisible taxes (which are now 75 per cent for federal income tax and 20 per cent for federal excises) so that large surpluses in non-plan state budgets may be avoided. Of course, such reduction should not affect the total amount payable by way of shared taxes and grants-in-aid to any state which currently receives grants-in-aid.

In the future, Finance Commissions may be well advised to fix states' shares of divisible taxes and adopt schemes for their distribution with a view to avoiding large surpluses in state budgets. They may also adhere to a broad index of need,

22 For details, see *Fifth Report*, p. 36.

23 *Fourth Report*, p. 59.

24 *Fifth Report*, p. 65.

25 See Minute by G. Swaminathan, *Fifth Report*, pp. 99–103.

such as population, as the basis for distribution of shared taxes. By doing so, they may avoid the ritual of states pleading for larger shares of federal taxes and presenting ingenious formulae for the allocation of shared federal levies. This would give future Commissions an opportunity to devote a greater part of their time and energy for an intensive study of state and local finance which is indispensable for making meaningful decisions with respect to federal-state fiscal problems in general, and sharing of federal levies and estimation of grants-in-aid in particular.

5. Grants-in-Aid

The first Finance Commission laid down some important principles governing the determination of grants-in-aid for states.[26] These principles have been generally endorsed by all the subsequent Commissions.[27]

The budgetary needs of a state are an important consideration for the determination of grants-in-aid; however, before assessing such needs several adjustments have to be made to the state budgets in order to make them comparable. Uniform treatment has to be accorded to commercial and business undertakings of the state governments, the separation of their capital and revenue (current) budgets, and interest and amortization charges of their debts. Unusual and non-recurring items of receipts and expenditures have to be eliminated from state budgets. Due allowance should be made for failure to maximize tax effort or to perform public services efficiently. Furthermore, special consideration may be given to less advanced states for improving the standards of certain basic social services.

Although all the Finance Commissions have been in agreement about the principles governing the determination of grants-in-aid, none has so far undertaken any detailed inquiry into the tax efforts, efficiency of administration, or relative needs of various states. They have been handicapped by a serious lack of time, resources, and statistical information necessary to make a meaningful study of state and local finance. Consequently, grants-in-aid have been based mostly on the budgetary gaps reported by the states. This led the third Finance Commission to observe:

> ....We have therefore been compelled, like our own predecessors, to cover the annual budgetary gaps of all states, whether caused by normal growth of expenditure, the maintenance cost of completed schemes and mounting interest charges or even by a measure of improvidence.[28]

In order to assess grants-in-aid on a realistic basis, the Finance Commission has to determine standards for tax effort and services provided by the state governments. On the basis of these standards, the Commission may determine the amount of resources that a state should raise on its own, the amount of resources required by the state to perform various public services at certain pre-determined levels, and the amount of grants-in-aid required by it.[29] To be sure, there are no precise criteria by which standards for tax effort or public services could be measured. However, an independent statutory body, such as the Finance Commission, entrusted with the responsibility for resolution of problems in fiscal federalism, has to persevere in the construction of reasonably satisfactory standards for tax efforts and public services.

Tax Efforts of States

It is practically impossible to devise objective indices for the determination of the relative tax efforts of various states.[30] What constitutes an adequate tax effort is open to debate. A comparison of tax performance of states may be obtained by comparing their per capita tax yields.

---

[26] *First Report,* pp. 69–97.

[27] *Second Report,* p. 23; *Third Report,* pp. 28–29; *Fourth Report,* pp. 46–47; *Fifth Report,* p. 47.

[28] *Third Report,* p. 38.

[29] The Commonwealth Grants Commission in Australia determines grants-in-aid in this manner.

[30] Ibid.

This, however, does not compare tax performance to fiscal capacity of states.

A comparison of the actual rates of various taxes prevailing in different states would give an indication of the relative use of their tax capacity.[31] However, such a comparison should be made with caution since seemingly similar taxes may have very different bases in the different states. A variation of this method would be to test actual tax performance against the yield of a model of tax programme for the states.

A reasonably satisfactory index of the relative tax efforts of the states may be obtained by comparing their tax performance to fiscal capacity. Tax performance and fiscal capacity may be respectively measured by per capita state and local tax collection and per capita state income adjusted for federal personal income tax drain.[32]

There are several methods by which tax efforts of states may be compared. But the first four Finance Commissions expended very little, if any, of their energy to make such comparisons. The directives to the fourth and fifth Finance Commissions implicitly precluded them from an examination of the states' relative tax efforts. In spite of this, the fifth Finance Commission made some cursory attempts to study the relative tax efforts by comparing per capita state and local tax collection to per capita income.[33]

Owing to lack of statistics on the states' current income, the fifth Finance Commission compared their per capita tax revenues in 1967–68 to average per capita incomes during the three years from 1962–63 to 1964–65. As seen from Table 1, there is considerable variation in fiscal capacity, tax performance and tax efforts of the different states. Comparing the states at the extreme ends of the distribution, average per capita income during 1962–65 in Punjab was somewhat less than double that of Bihar; per capita tax revenues in 1967–68 in Punjab and Maharashtra were about three times that of Bihar; tax efforts of Kerala—as indicated by the tax collected in 1967–68 from every Rs. 100 of average income during the period 1962–65—was double that of Orissa. Kerala had the highest tax effort in spite of the fact that its average per capita income during 1962–65 was lower than the national average. On the average, in 1967–68 the state governments taxed away about 6.4 paise from every rupee of average income received during 1962–65. Assuming a fifty per cent increase in average income in 1967–68 from that of 1962–65, average state taxation in 1967–68 amounted to only about 4 paise from every rupee of income received in the same year.

Wide differences in the tax efforts of states may be seen also from a comparison of the per capita yields of important state taxes. The per capita yields of general sales taxes in 1967–68 among the five states with the highest per capita incomes varied from Rs. 14 in Maharashtra to less than Rs. 7 in West Bengal and Haryana, whereas in Kerala, with a per capita income below the national average, it was Rs. 10.[34] There is considerable variation in the rates of sales tax on various goods and services among the different states.[35]

The most blatant case of state-wide undertaxation as well as interstate disparity in taxation is with respect to agri-

---

[31] The Commonwealth Grants Commission in Australia adopts this method to examine the states' relative tax efforts.

[32] Per capita income is an inadequate index of fiscal capacity. The fiscal capacity of a state depends not only on income but also on wealth; it depends not only on income *received* but on income produced within the state. Furthermore, the index does not make any allowance for difference in the distribution of income between states. Allowing for federal income tax drain is particularly important in view of the exemption of agricultural income from federal income tax in India. Also, per capita tax collection does not make any allowance for interstate shifting of state and local taxes.

[33] This index does not measure the relative degree of sacrifice of income for taxes borne by the residents of different states. Various attempts have been made to develop a measure of tax burden which incorporates an element of vertical equity. See Ved. P. Gandhi, *Tax Burden on Indian Agriculture* (The Law School of Harvard University, Cambridge, 1966), Chapter 2. See also K. V. S. Sastri, *Federal-State Fiscal Relations in India* (Oxford University Press, 1962), Chapter 2.

[34] *Fifth Report,* p. 82.

[35] For the rates of sales taxes on different commodities in different states, see *Fifth Report,* Appendix V, Tables 20–26, pp. 149–62.

Table 1. Fiscal Capacity, Tax Performance and Tax Efforts of States

(Amounts in Rupees)

	Fiscal Capacity Average State Per Capita Income, 1962-65		Tax Performance Per Capita Tax, 1967-68		Tax Effort State Tax Collection For Rs. 100 of State Income	
	Amount	*Index*[1]	*Amount*	*Index*	*Amount*	*Index*[1]
Punjab	492	133	37	168	8.4	131
Maharashtra	478	130	37	168	8.3	130
West Bengal	465	126	26	118	6.2	97
Gujarat	462	125	30	136	7.0	109
Haryana	445	121	29	132	7.2	113
Tamil Nadu	400	108	29	132	7.8	122
Assam	393	107	19	86	5.2	81
Andhra Pradesh	386	105	20	91	5.4	84
Mysore	373	101	23	105	6.7	105
Kerala	341	92	27	123	8.7	136
Madhya Pradesh	325	88	17	77	5.6	88
Rajasthan	314	85	20	91	6.8	106
Uttar Pradesh	306	83	15	68	5.1	80
Orissa	306	83	12	55	4.3	67
Jammu & Kashmir	302	82	19	86	6.8	106
Bihar	265	72	12	55	4.9	77
Average	369	100	22	100	6.4	100

[1]Indices are based on national average being equal to 100

Source: *Fifth Report*, Table 12, p. 141

cultural income, the taxation of which is exclusively reserved for the states. Comparing proceeds from land revenue and agricultural income tax in 1967–68 as a percentage of average state agricultural income during 1962–65, the fifth Finance Commission found that it was 2.5 per cent for the relatively very low-income state of Rajasthan; it was only 0.5 per cent for the most prosperous agricultural and also highest income state of Punjab, the same as for Bihar and Orissa, which are among the lowest-income states.[36] Undoubtedly, there has been a very significant increase in agricultural income in 1967–68 from 1962–65. Therefore, if the 1967–68 proceeds from land revenue and agricultural income tax are compared with the agricultural income of the same year, the picture would be considerably worse. Andhra Pradesh, Gujarat, Madhya Pradesh, Haryana, and Punjab do not levy any tax at all on agricultural income; even in those states where the tax is levied, there is a general feeling that it is inadequately enforced.[37]

[36] *Fifth Report,* p. 82.

[37] Ibid., p. 84. The undertaxation of the agricultural sector is all the more unjustified since a number of services are provided free or at subsidized rates to agriculturists by the federal and state governments. These services include improved seeds, fertilizers, pesticides, pumps and implements, rural electrification, agricultural credit, irrigation, etc. On the undertaxation of the agricultural sector in India, see Ved. P. Gandhi, op. cit.

Wide variations in tax effort, gross undertaxation of the agricultural sector, and rampant tax evasion appear to be chronic features of state taxation in India.[38] The Uttar Pradesh Taxation Inquiry Committee reported that in 1967–68 sales tax receipts increased by more than 50 per cent from 1965–66 without any increase in rates but by some improvements in the administrative machinery.[39] Substantial evasion of sales tax was found also by the Kerala State Taxation Inquiry Committee.[40]

The manner of determining grants-in-aid or the states' share of receipts from federal income tax and excises has done very little, if anything, to penalize states for their failure to maximize tax effort. On the contrary, it appears to have rewarded the states for their laxity in tax effort. This serious problem was alluded to by the third Finance Commission as follows:

> Secure in the knowledge that the annual budgetary gap would be fully covered by the devolution of Union resources and grants-in-aid, the states are tending to develop, as we have noticed, an allergy to tap resources in the rural sector on many considerations and also a disinclination to make up the leeway in others.[41]

The fifth Finance Commission made some allowance for the tax effort of a state if it "appeared to be considerably lower than that of other states with similar per capita income and particularly states with similar conditions of development." However, it seems that stronger measures are needed to raise the states' tax efforts to an adequate level.

38 See *Fifth Report,* Chapter 8. See also *Appraisal and Prospects of the Second Five-Year Plan* by Planning Commission (New Delhi, 1958), pp. 12 and 20; *Third Five-Year Plan Progress Report* by Planning Commission (New Delhi, March 1963), p. 39; *The Third Plan: Mid-Term Appraisal* by Planning Commission (New Delhi, November 1963) pp. 34, 105–6.

39 *Fifth Report,* p. 88.

40 Ibid.

41 *Third Report,* p. 38.

Standards for Public Services

None of the Finance Commissions has made any serious effort to study the standards of public services provided by the various states or to inquire into the efficiency with which they perform various functions.

Devising standards for public services is often more difficult than devising those for tax effort. Just as in the case of tax effort, it is impossible to formulate completely satisfactory indices for the standards of public services.

The fifth Finance Commission adopted a method used by the Commonwealth Grants Commission in Australia to compare the standards of public services provided by the states. The method involves a simple comparison of per capita expenditure of various services provided by the states. Per capita expenditure as an index of the standard of public services is subject to serious qualifications. Interstate differences in per capita expenditures for any service are not necessarily indicative of the differences in the quality of that service. For example, a given quality of police protection may cost more per capita in an urbanized state than in a rural one; per capita costs of highway construction depend on the terrain of a state, and so on. Where large differences in per capita expenditures for a particular service exist, the Finance Commission will have to investigate further in order to ascertain whether such differences are due to genuine variations in quality, inefficient administration, or other special reasons. If there are clear cases of inefficiency or extravagance, the Finance Commission should adjust the budgetary positions of the states correspondingly before determining their grants-in-aid.

There are wide variations in the 1967–68 per capita expenditures for various public services provided by the state governments, as seen from Table 2. Excluding the very special case of Nagaland,[42] and perhaps less so of Jammu and Kashmir.

42 The relatively very high figures for Nagaland do not significantly distort the national average since its population in 1967 was only less than one half of a million out of a total of 511 million.

Table 2. Per Capita Expenditures for Selected Public Services Provided by States, 1967-68.

(*Amounts in Rupees*)

	Per Capita Expenditures for									
	Civil Administration		Tax Collection		Education		Medicine and Public Health		Total Social and Development Sources	
	Amount	Index[1]	Amount	Index[1]	Amount	Index[1]	Amount	Index[1]	Amount	Index[1]
Andhra Pradesh	6.6	97	1.1	52	9.3	89	4.2	102	20.0	89
Assam	10.3	151	1.6	76	12.6	121	4.1	100	25.7	114
Bihar	4.1	60	1.2	57	5.0	48	1.7	41	12.8	57
Gujarat	7.1	104	2.8	133	10.9	105	4.8	117	23.5	104
Haryana	6.5	96	1.4	67	11.7	113	3.6	88	22.3	99
Jammu & Kashmir	16.9	249	2.8	133	17.1	164	9.2	224	38.4	171
Kerala	7.3	107	2.1	100	21.1	203	6.4	156	36.9	164
Madhya Pradesh	6.0	88	1.6	76	10.6	102	3.7	90	21.1	94
Maharashtra	9.7	143	5.4	257	12.3	118	5.2	127	27.6	123
Mysore	5.7	84	1.4	67	11.6	112	3.8	93	26.9	120
Nagaland	146.1	2149	0.7	33	46.1	443	20.3	495	100.5	447
Orissa	6.0	88	2.3	110	8.0	77	3.8	93	20.8	92
Punjab	8.6	126	1.6	76	15.8	152	4.5	110	29.8	132
Rajasthan	6.5	96	2.2	105	11.3	109	7.4	180	24.8	110
Tamilnadu	7.4	109	1.1	52	14.4	138	4.8	117	29.7	132
Utter Pradesh	5.0	74	1.9	90	6.4	62	2.4	59	15.6	69
West Bengal	8.0	118	2.1	100	11.2	108	5.2	127	24.5	109
Total	6.8	100	2.1	100	10.4	100	4.1	100	22.5	100

[1]Indices based on national average being equal to 100.

Source: *Fifth Report*, Table 30, p. 173.

The per capita expenditure for all social and developmental services[43] in Kerala is about three times that of Bihar.[44] The situation is quite similar with respect to education for which Kerala's per capita expenditure is more than four times that of Bihar.[45] Similar variations can be seen in expenditures for civil administration, tax collection, etc.

The fifth Finance Commission was of the opinion that a substantial part of the interstate variation in per capita expenditures for various services was due to

43 Social and developmental services are expenditures for the development of human and physical capital and include expenditures for education, public health, rural and community development, public works, etc.

44 It may be noted that Bihar has the lowest per capita income and one of the lowest tax effort. Kerala has the highest tax effort but a per capita income below national average.

45 Before a meaningful comparison of per capita expenditure for a particular service can be made, it is important that the service is defined uniformly for every state. In the case of education, even if the service is defined uniformly for every state, some of the variation in per capita expenditure may be due to variation in the proportion of school age children actually attending school.

differences in the quality of services and special circumstances prevailing in different states, such as sparseness of population, special problems of border states, proportion of scheduled tribes in state population, etc. After making allowance for these factors, the Commissioners felt that "where the level of expenditure in a State was substantially higher than that generally indicated by expenditure in other comparable States, it should be the State's responsibility to find further sources for meeting part of the extra expenditure and the budgetary deficit as assessed by us should not be covered entirely by grants under Article 275 unless we found that the tax effort of the State in relation to its per capita income was also substantially higher than that of State with similar per capita income and comparable conditions."[46]

Business Undertakings and Public Debt of States

Before grants-in-aid needed by a state is ascertained, allowance has to be made not only for the tax effort and standards of public services but also for the results of their commercial undertakings and interest charges and amortization provisions for their debts. The mounting debts of the states and losses from commercial undertakings and other investments have put their budgets under severe pressure.

In assessing the budgetary needs of states, a strong case may be made for excluding all their commercial undertakings and investments on the presumption that they should be so managed as to produce no loss. In the event of losses occurring, the states may be expected to cover them not by grants-in-aid from the federal government but by their own sacrifice. This salutory principle has not been applied to all the business undertakings by the Finance Commissions. The fifth Finance Commission has, however, extended its application to practically all commercial enterprises and investments of state governments.[47]

On the same principle, interest charges and amortization for public debt incurred for business ventures may be kept out of the current (revenue) budget altogether. They have to be met from the revenues from investment. However, if loan finance is used for non-revenue yielding capital expenditures, such as roads, hospitals, school buildings, flood control projects, it may be appropriate to meet interest cost and amortization from revenues. In actual practice, large items of such capital expenditures for social overhead capital (undertaken in many cases to fulfill projects in the economic plans) are placed in the capital budget which is financed by borrowing. But with the mounting capital expenditures financed by loans, the states have come to feel that interest charges and amortization for such loans should be provided by the federal government.

In assessing the needs of the states for grant-in-aid, it appears that the earlier Finance Commissions had allowed all interest charges including those on debts incurred for commercial enterprises.[48] The fifth Finance Commission was, however, more discriminatory in allowing interest charges. The Commissioners, as a rule, did not allow any interest charges on that part of states' debts which is utilized for business undertakings, loans to other parties, and unauthorized overdrafts from the Reserve Bank of India; but interest charges on debt incurred for expenditure on social overhead capital (which do not yield any revenue) were allowed subject to certain uniform limits laid down by the Commission.[49]

The treatment accorded to amortization of states' debts has varied from one Commission to another. The second and third Commissions did not allow for amortization when such provision had to come from shared taxes or grants-in-aid. The fourth Commission, however, felt that amortization for all *market* borrowings of states should be allowed as legitimate charges against revenue. It took the Fifth Commission to stress the proposition that the principle that governs the eligibility

46 *Fifth Report,* p. 57.
47 *Fifth Report,* p. 59.

48 *Second Report,* p. 37; *Third Report,* p. 41; *Fourth Report,* p. 51.
49 *Fifth Report,* pp. 58–59.

or otherwise of interest cost as a legitimate charge against revenue also governs the disposition of amortization. The Commissioners, therefore, allowed amortization only for that part of the states' debt which was incurred for capital expenditure of a non-revenue yielding nature, subject to certain uniform limits.[50]

Special Assistance to Low-Income States

Wide variations among states with respect to resources and standards of public services have been discussed earlier. In view of this, the first Finance Commission felt that grants-in-aid should be so designed as to bring about a certain measure of equalization among the states. As a modest beginning, the Commissioners recommended special grants-in-aid for the promotion of primary education in eight less advanced states.[51]

The second Finance Commission did not, however, recommend any special grants-in-aid for low-income states. The Commissioners were of the opinion that where the national and state governments cooperated for planned economic development, priorities and provisions in the plan itself should determine the fiscal needs of the states for the period of the plan. Although equalization is a valid criterion for the assessment of grants-in-aid, the Commissioners felt that it was the function of the Planning Commission and the National Development Council to ensure equalization of the standards of essential public services provided by the states. Having accepted the plan as ensuring an equitable standard in the field of social services, there was no room for any grants for the expansion of any particular public service in any state, such as the primary education grants recommended by the first Commission.[52]

The position taken by the second Finance Commission with respect to special assistance to low-income states did not, however, deter the third Commission from recommending special grants for the maintenance and construction of roads and other communications to some less advanced states.[53] But the later Commissions have endorsed the second Commissions's position and put the burden of ensuring equalization of the Planning Commission.[54]

Comments on Grants-in-Aid

No Finance Commission has so far made a serious study of state and local finance with a view to a realistic determination of grants-in-aid needed by the states. As a result, the determination of grants-in-aid has so far been, as the Third Commission stated, mostly an exercise in covering the budgetary gaps reported by the states. Very little effort has been devoted to examing the adequacy of the states' tax efforts and the efficiency with which they perform public services or manage business ventures. The Finance Commissions have thus, unwittingly, rewarded those states which have been lax in tax effort or improvident in fiscal management and provided no incentive to any state to improve tax performance or enhance efficiency in administration.

Although grants-in-aid are intended for those states "in need", it is ironic that both Bihar and Uttar Pradesh, two of the most populous and low income states in the Union, were not eligible for grants-in-aid as determined by the fourth and fifth Commissions. In both these states, the levels of public services, as judged by the indices in Table 2, are far below national average; in Bihar especially the levels appear to be appallingly low. It must be mentioned that the tax efforts too of both these states are below the national average (Table 1). Presumably, public needs are relatively inadequately reflected in the budgets of these states. With the burden for equalization placed on the Planning Commission[55] and a narrow interpretation of "need" by the Finance Commissions, receipts from shared taxes have proved to be more than adequate to cover

50 Ibid., p. 63.
51 *First Report,* pp. 103–104.
52 *Second Report,* p. 25.
53 *Third Report,* pp. 32–33.
54 *Fourth Report,* pp. 48–49; *Fifth Report,* p. 12.
55 It is interesting to note that per capita plan outlays for Uttar Pradesh and, more so, for Bihar are well below the national average. See *Fifth Report,* p. 101.

gaps in the non-plan budgets of these states.

6. Modifications in Centre-State Fiscal Arrangements

After more than twenty years of experience in Federal-State financial relations under the new Constitution, what possible suggestions for modifications of the existing arrangements can be made? The second, third, and fourth Finance Commissions strongly felt that modifications should be made in the existing arrangements for federal-state financial adjustments.[56] The wide variations that continue to prevail in the states' tax efforts and levels of public services stress the need for a re-examination of the machinery as well as the methods adopted to deal with problems of fiscal federalism.

The mechanism of an independent statutory body, such as the Finance Commission, to deal with all evolving problems of fiscal federalism in a non-political environment is indeed worth preserving and promoting. But the rise of the Planning Commission with wide powers over the allocation of resources in the Indian Union has almost led to a total eclipse of the Finance Commission. The relegation of the Finance Commission to the non-plan sector of the state budgets and the implicit restrictions placed on it with respect to scrutinizing the tax efforts of the states have practically made it impotent. It is highly desirable to restore the Finance Commission to the pre-eminent status intended for it in the sphere of fiscal federalism.

In order to restore the Finance Commission to the role destined for it in the Indian Constitution, the first step would be a clear demarcation of the roles of the Planning and Finance Commissions. The Planning Commission may continue to have the responsibility for formulating the national economic plan with its constituent state plans. But the Finance Commission should have the responsibility to determine the resources the states should raise by existing and new taxation and how much residual federal aid should be given by way of shared taxes, grants-in-aid, and loans so that the state governments may meet the needs of their plan as well as non-plan budgets. Undoubtedly, this requires very close coordination between the Planning and Finance Commissions.

If such a demarcation between the roles of the Finance and Planning Commissions is agreed upon, it is clear that the Finance Commission, as envisaged in the Indian Constitution, cannot fulfill the responsibility placed on it. It would have to be transformed into a permanent body with an adequate research staff to undertake continuing studies of state and local finance in India. The Commission will have to determine the adequacy of the tax effort of each state; it will have to determine the efficiency with which states perform public services and manage their business undertakings. It is only by an intensive study of state and local finance that the Finance Commission can fulfill the responsibility placed on it by the Indian Constitution. It is indeed a serious indictment of fiscal federalism in India that no earnest efforts have been made so far in this direction, even twenty years after the inauguration of the Indian Constitution.

It may be added that the proposed demarcation of the roles of the two Commissions would promote more effective planning as well as better mobilization of resources. The Planning Commission would be able to concentrate on physical planning as well as ensuring an appropriate regional balance in economic development. The Finance Commission would be concerned with the fiscal aspects of the plan and non-plan budgets of states which would include a careful assessment of the resources that should be raised by every state and the additional resources that should be transferred to it in the form of shared federal taxes, grants-in-aid, loans, etc. The Finance Commission would thus be able to spur the states' efforts to improve tax performance and enhance efficiency in the provision of public services. This would promote a better mobilization as well as allocation of resources.

---

[56] *Second Report,* p. 72; *Third Report,* pp. 35–36; *Fourth Report,* pp. 86–93.

Lastly, it is very important to modify the existing arrangement with respect to taxation of agricultural property and income. Under the Constitution, state governments have the exclusive power to tax agricultural income and property. This is, indeed, a very serious inequity in the Indian tax structure.[57] Moreover, this has led to considerable undertaxation of the agricultural sector of the Indian economy at a stage in the economic development of the country when that sector, in fact, should be making a substantial contribution towards capital formation. The distinction between agricultural and other income should be done away with and taxation of all income should be placed in the hands of the federal government.

57 See Government of India, Ministry of Finance, Department of Economic Affairs, *Report of the Taxation Inquiry Commission,* 1953–54, Vol. III (New Delhi, 1955), pp. 220–36.

BIBLIOGRAPHY

Adarkar, B. P., *Principles and Problems of Federal Finance* (London: P. S. King & Son, Ltd., 1933).

Bhargava, R. N., *Union Finance in India,* 1956.

Bhatt, V. V., "On The Magnitude and Allocation of Federal Assistance to The States in India: Some Rational Criteria," *Public Finance,* XXIV, No. 4/1969, pp. 563–72.

Birch, A. H., *Federalism, Finance, and Social Legislation in Canada, Australia, and the United States* (London: Oxford University Press, 1955).

Clark, D. H., *Fiscal Need and Revenue Equalization Gants* (Toronto; Canadian Tax Foundation, 1969).

Commonwealth of Australia, *Report of the Commonwealth* Grant Commission (Annual).

Dwivedi, D. N., "A Critique of Indian Fiscal Federalism—A Comment," *Public Finance,* XXVI, No. 3/1971, pp. 498–501.

Eapen, A. T., "A Critique of Indian Fiscal Federalism," *Public Finance,* XXIV, No. 4/1969, pp. 537–57.

———, "On the Magnitude and Allocation of Federal Assistance to The States in India: Some Rational Criteria-Comment," *Public Finance,* XXV, No. 3/1970, pp. 430–32.

———"A Critique of Indian Fiscal Federalism-Reply," *Public Finance,* XXVI, No. 3/1971, pp. 502–04.

Musgrave, R. A., *The Theory of Public Finance* New York: (McGraw-Hill, 1959).

——— "Approaches to Fiscal Theory of Political Federalism," *Public Finances: Needs, Sources, and Utilization,* A Conference of the Universities-National Bureau Committee for Economic Research, 1961, pp. 97–122.

Oates, W. E., *Fiscal Federalism* (Harcourt Brace Jovanovich, Inc. 1972).

Prest, W., "Fedral-State Financial Relations in India," *Economic Record,* April 1960, pp. 191–219.

Report of the Finance Commission: 1952, 1957, 1961, 1965, and 1969 (Delhi: Manager of Government Publications).

Sastri, K. V. S., *Federal-State Fiscal Relations in India* (Oxford University Press, 1962).

U. S. Advisory Commission on Intergovernmental Relations, *Measuring the Fiscal Capacity and Effort of State and Local Areas* (Washington, D. C., March 1971).

Part Seven

INTERNATIONAL ECONOMIC RELATIONS

22

Foreign Trade and Balance of Payments

JALEEL AHMAD*

1. Introduction

The purpose of this chapter is to highlight the important characteristics of the pattern of India's international trade and balance of payments, particularly in regard to their implications for her economic development. This is done in a framework provided by: (a) the neo-classical theory of international trade and payments; (b) the nature of structural constraints that modify the processes of continuous and smooth "transformation through trade"; (c) the over-all strategy of Indian economic planning; and (d), finally, the similarity and the divergence of India's experience from the experience of today's developed, industrialized countries on the one hand, and the less developed, semi- or non-industrialized countries on the other. The discussion attempts a clarification of central issues involved and avoids the elaboration of their myriad ramifications. Clearly, no attempt at exhaustiveness is made. Merely quantitative and descriptive material has been kept at a minimum.

The quantitative magnitude of India's foreign trade in terms of its value, volume, and prices during 1948–1970 is shown in Tables 1 and 2 in the appendix to this chapter. The development programmes embodied in the Five Year Plans since 1950 gave utmost priority to the import of capital goods for capacity creation. As a result, imports rose both in absolute terms and relative to national income, particularly since 1956 and at least until 1968. On the other hand, India's export earnings from traditional commodities like jute and tea have either remained stagnant or have risen insignificantly. These differential growth rates of imports and exports have created a fundamental disequilibrium in India's balance of payments, necessitating large inflows of capital, mainly in the form of inter-governmental grants and loans. The magnitudes of various items in India's balance of payments are summarized in Table 2.

This chapter attempts to systematically analyze the major economic forces that ex-

* The author wishes to thank Professor Peter Miles for reading the draft and making valuable comments and Miss Lise Brault for secretarial assistance.

plain the behaviour of foreign trade and balance of payments during the recent past. In particular, we discuss such critical factors as the domestic transformation difficulties, high propensity to import, limitations on demand and supply of exports and the effect of devaluation on balance of payments.

2. Static and Dynamic Gains from Trade

In open economies, international trade plays an important role by providing alternative sources of demand and supply in the form of a country's exports and imports. It is through the expedient of international trade that a country specializes in the production of goods and services for which its resource endowments are best suited, and exchanges them for other goods and services whose domestic opportunity costs are higher than prices at which they can be obtained from other countries. Thus, participation in international trade has far-reaching implications for efficient utilization of domestic resources and the level of economic welfare in the country concerned. The study of the pattern of a country's international trade and the means for financing of such trade is, therefore, an integral part of the study of a country's economic development.

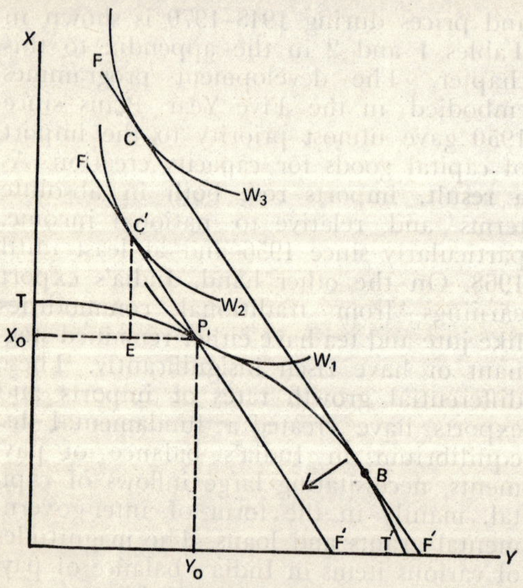

Fig. 1

The important normative implication of international trade is that a relatively free trade will make a country "better off," in the sense that more goods and services will be available for consumption than under a regime of "autarky" or of a less free trade. The neo-classical trade theory usually illustrates the welfare possibilities of trade by means of a diagram such as Figure 1, using the production possibilities and the community indifference curves.[1]

The production possibilities curve TT′ of a country indicates all the possible combinations of any two goods, say tractors (X) and wheat (Y), that could be produced with existing resources and technology. The production possibility curve, in turn, is derived from a "contract curve" which is the locus of all points of tangency of the isoquants and is inscribed in a box diagram whose axes represent the fixed quantities of the two factors of production, labour and capital. The two factors of production are assumed to be freely substitutable for each other and, being non-specific, are transferable from one sector to the other. The transformation curve so derived is drawn concave to the origin, implying an increasing opportunity cost of transformation of one good into the other.

The production possibility curve is combined with a set of community indifference curves which reflect the collective pattern of demand as determined by consumers' tastes and the distribution of income.

In the absence of trade, resources are optimally allocated and welfare maximized at a point where the community indifference curve is tangent to the production possibilities curve. This occurs at point P in Figure 1, where Y_0 of wheat and X_0 of tractors are produced and consumed. The domestic price ratio of Y and X is represented by the slope of the tangent at P.

[1] For details, the reader should consult any standard text on international trade, such as B. Sodersten, *International Economics* (New York: Harper & Row, 1970).

Now, trade will take place between two countries whenever the domestic price ratio differs from the price ratio prevailing in the trading-partner country. Thus, if a country faces an international price ratio (FF′), it can profitably specialize in the production of Y and exchange it for X. Production would take place at B and consumption at C. In doing so, the country would have moved to a higher community indifference curve W_3.[2]

This conclusion of the trade theory has significant implications for resource allocation in the developing economies. The productivity of domestic resources will be maximized if they are invested in line with a country's comparative advantage, and the subsequent exchange of these commodities in accordance with consumer preferences maximizes national income. It must be clearly understood, however, that the allocation analysis of trade described in the preceding paragraphs is completely *static* and reveals what the structure of foreign trade should be at a given point of time. But a country's comparative advantage undergoes a constant change in response to underlying changes in the supply and prices of production factors, technological developments, and the process of "learning by doing," and could in itself be modified by domestic economic policies otherwise desirable. There is thus no presumption in trade theory that the present comparative costs reflect long-run advantages and not susceptible to changes in the course of time.

Given the static nature of trade theory, it does not give any guidance as to what a country should produce and export in order to increase its *dynamic* efficiency or its rate of growth.[3] This neglect of dynamic aspects in trade theory is partly a reflection of the enormous conceptual difficulties in handling the consequences of "time," and partly a reflection of the fact that non-economic objectives undertaken for legitimate reasons frequently modify the economic ones and require different methodological tools for their analysis.

In a country where the composition of production factors and technology is rapidly changing, the production possibility curves and the domestic cost ratios can undergo substantial changes. These purely domestic changes eventually bring about changes in the volume and composition of international trade, as well as in the terms at which a country trades with others. For example, the economic development of the United States during 1850 and 1900 caused a perceptible shift in its production possibility curve away from resource-based production, viz. agriculture, forestry and fisheries, and towards capital-based manufacturing output. During this period, the share of manufactures in the United States exports almost doubled from 12.6 to 23.3 per cent of total exports.[4]

There is, therefore, no presumption that since India has in the past been exporting primary commodities, she will continue to have a static comparative disadvantage in the production of manufactures. Nevertheless, problems of adjustment are bound to arise as resources are reallocated and the economy strives to attain a new equilibrium. These structural problems take many different forms.

[2] It should be noted that the welfare gains from trade arise from two distinct sources, viz., from specialization, and from exchange of goods at price ratios different from those prevailing at home. Thus, strictly speaking, specialization is not essential for gains from trade. If we abandon the assumption of non-specificity of factors of production and their transferability between sectors, we obtain a single-point production possibilities curve at P instead of the curve TT′ as before, where production and consumption before trade take place. International trade in the face of non-transferability of factors forces the production to remain at P, i e., there is no specialization; nevertheless, consumption moves up to C′ on the higher indifference curve W_2. The country exports PE of Y in exchange for EC′ of X. The inability to transform resources reduces the gains from trade, but it does not eliminate them.

[3] A few attempts have been made to relate the static to dynamic efficiency in trade by separating the production and consumption problems of a developing economy, but the results are unsatisfactory. For a recent discussion, see Bent Hansen, *Long and Short Term Planning in the Underdeveloped Countries* (Amsterdam: North Holland Publishing Company, 1967).

[4] Richard E. Lipsey, "Foreign Trade" in Lance E. Davis et. al., *American Economic Growth—An Economist's History of the United States* (Harper & Row, 1972). Table 14.4.

Firstly, the development theorists have argued that current market prices frequently diverge sharply from the long-run social costs and, therefore, fail to reflect "potential" costs of production.[5] The disadvantage in the export of manufactures attributed to the presently less developed economies may consequently be more apparent than real, and may persist only as long as the price system remains a poor allocation guide.[6]

Secondly, adjustment problems may arise because in the critical short-run, the domestic factors of production are non-homogenous, durable, and non-shiftable from one sector to the other. Once a particular structure of production is in place, capital (and labour) become specific and immobile and cannot readily be transferred from one sector to the other. A country has, therefore, little flexibility in determining the range of feasible outputs and cannot instantly and without cost adjust to a new production pattern. This problem of domestic transformation can be overcome only through a radical restructuring of economic policies designed to obtain a pattern of production and trade which is in line with the real, long-run social costs.

In developing countries like India, the static gains arising from the reallocation of existing resources may be outweighed by the impact of trade on such factors as the supply of additional resources, the savings/investment process, a fuller utilization of capacity, the extent of markets, and ultimately, the rate of economic growth. But perhaps the most critical role of foreign trade in India consists in its ability to provide capital equipment and other materials necessary for investment. Without trade, such goods may be obtainable only at prohibitive cost or, in extreme cases, not at all. This point underscores the fact that international trade comprises of not only the finished products intended for the final consumer, but also the factors of production in the form of equipment, semi-processed goods, and raw materials.

International trade and economic growth interact in many different and significant ways. A rapid economic growth is usually accompanied by a high rate of growth in both exports and imports, and often by an increasing share of foreign trade in national income. Rising exports may act as a cause of economic growth by enlarging the markets and thus inducing a larger employment of domestic resources. Similarly, imports in a growing economy, in addition to being a source of vital capital goods, help to widen the consumer's choice with respect to the range of goods and services available.

In addition to these direct effects, there are other, more subtle and indirect relationships between international trade and economic growth. The cumulative effect of any change in the quantities exported and imported is transmitted to other sectors of the economy via inter-industry transactions involving purchases and sales between a group of sectors. These effects depend on the intensity of input-output relations between sectors and are likely to be quite complex in a rapidly growing economy. Similarly, the "external economy" effects of domestic production in any particular sector—either through export expansion or through import substitution—singularly influence the mutual profitability of investment in related sectors. The production changes in turn favourably influence and are influenced by corresponding changes in technological knowledge.

3. Structural Obstacles to Transformation through Trade

International trade has traditionally occupied a relatively small part of the Indian economy as far as the quantities of her exports and imports are concerned. This is partly a reflection of the fact that large countries generally tend to be self-sufficient in producing the bulk of their supplies and trade plays only a marginal

[5] S. Chakravarty, "The Use of Shadow Prices in Programme Evaluation" in P. N. Rosenstein-Rodan (ed.), *Capital Formation in Economic Development* (M. I. T. Press, 1964), as well as his *Logic of Investment Planning* (Amsterdam: North Holland Publishing Company, 1960).

[6] Keith B. Griffin, *Underdevelopment in Spanish America* (Cambridge: M.I.T. Press, 1970), Chapter 2.

part. But it is also partly a symptom of her under-development in the sense that long periods of economic stagnation and, until recently, the absence of any planned economic development effectively reduced the demand for imports and the supply of her exports. In a state of underdevelopment, i.e. at a level of income lower than that necessary to generate self-sustaining growth or to raise the living standards, an economy is likely to attain a balance of payments equilibrium, and may even have a trade surplus as did India between the two World Wars.

Small quantitative magnitudes notwithstanding, India's imports are vital to the operation and development of her economy. It is not difficult to demonstrate that, in the absence of imports of certain key raw materials and industrial components, the resulting loss in national production would be a large multiple of the cost of imports.[7] This extreme dependence on imported supplies is a characteristic which India shares in large measure with other less developed countries and is of enormous consequence for her future development. The matter is of sufficient importance to deserve further analysis.

It is difficult to think of a developing country that does not face intolerable balance of payments problems. Oddly enough, these problems are the result of development itself. The process of development increases the demand for capital goods to a level and a rate that is beyond the production capacities of most less developed countries. A policy of accelerated capital accumulation, therefore, requires adequate quantities of foreign exchange, to an extent that the rate of economic growth becomes dependent on the ability to finance the "development" imports.

The high propensity to import arises basically due to an internal disequilibrium connected with the structural inability to transform domestic resources into capital goods required for development. India's immense resources of manpower cannot, in the short run, be transformed into industrial machines and equipment necessary for growth. This transformation rigidity would not in itself be a bottleneck if production functions were sufficiently flexible to allow possibilities of substitution between the domestic and imported inputs. But the dominant technological constraints give rise to a factor proportions problem, in the sense that there is little or no substitutability between domestic and imported inputs along an isoquant.[8]

Why does the problem of non-substitutability arise? Clearly, a primary product qualifies as a "non-competitive" import if it cannot be produced at home and must be imported in a certain, more or less, fixed proportion to existing domestic factors. The imports of crude oil in India belong in this category. However, the non-substitutability with respect to capital goods—both for capacity expansion and maintenance purposes—is more subtle and less tractable. First of all, the problem may arise simply because in many industrial operations there may be only a limited number of technologically feasible processes, requiring inflexible factor proportions. Production techniques that could intensively use the domestic resources are simply not available, or alternatively the international "demonstration effect" may influence the choice of imported technology.

Secondly, non-substitutability may be the indirect result of the divergence between market and shadow rates of wages and foreign exchange. In India, like in other less developed countries, the market wage rate is likely to be higher than the shadow price of labour, while the "official" rate of exchange of domestic for foreign currency may be lower than its shadow price, the latter being a function of the marginal productivity of imports in their most optimal uses. Given the dichotomy between the market and shadow prices, a profit-maximizing entrepreneur is likely to choose a factor proportion which is relatively more import-intensive and relatively less labour-intensive than is desirable from the point of view of the eco-

---

7 W. B. Reddaway, *The Development of the Indian Economy* (George Allen & Unwin, 1962), Chapter 3.

8 Steffan B. Linder, *Trade Policy in the Less Developed Countries* (New York: Praeger Publishing Company, 1967).

nomy as a whole. It must be clearly understood that, while the shadow prices are relevant from a social standpoint, an individual entrepreneur's factor proportion decisions are made on the basis of market prices of labour and foreign exchange. The problem is accentuated by the frequent tendency to maintain over-valued rates of foreign exchange, as well as by the almost universal practice of keeping low tariffs on imported capital goods, with a view to encouraging domestic capital formation. In any event, domestic production becomes relatively import-intensive and requires increasingly larger quantities of imports.

In addition, the inequalities that characterize the distribution of income in India tend to aggravate the factor proportions problem. The more skewed the income distribution, the greater the proportion of increases in demand that leaks directly or indirectly into imports. India's trade policies directed at switching the demand for imports towards domestic substitutes as a means of conserving scarce foreign exchange have led to just the opposite result. Import substitution policies, designed to produce domestically the consumer goods hitherto imported, often require further imports in the form of raw materials, components, and capital goods. As a consequence, the domestic production of these commodities, often involving no more than an assembly of imported components, conceals the real costs to the economy and allows the more affluent consumers to bid away scarce foreign exchange from socially more desirable production.

Limited domestic transformation possibilities and the resulting rigidity in factor proportions would not be much of a problem if the economy could generate sufficient exports to finance the imports.[9] Our earlier discussion of the welfare aspects of trade theory had implied that, as long as there are relative differences in productivities, a country can export goods in the production of which it has a comparative advantage in exchange for those in which it does not. Thus, there would seem to be no obstacle, other than inappropriate domestic expenditure and exchange policies, to the maintenance of an export level sufficient to ensure external balance. In reality, however, the current structure of international trade provides no such built-in mechanism for expanding India's traditional exports.

For an economy to utilize the escape route of international trade, one will have to assume that the reciprocal foreign demand for its exports is perfectly elastic.[10] This condition is far from being fulfilled, since India's major exports are faced with either falling or slow expanding world demand, with the result that without a drastic change in export composition, it is difficult to maintain the value of her export earnings. Almost all primary-oriented less developed countries suffer from the combination of export concentration, export dependence, and price fluctuations.[11] Quite different problems are faced in the export of manufactures and semi-processed goods. These problems are due partly to low absolute productivities and other production bottlenecks in the newly created industrial sector and, partly to the existence of virtually impregnable tariff and non-tariff barriers on the entry of such products in the industrially advanced countries.

In any event, significant expansion of exports of manufactures, with the possible exception of handicrafts, requires a corresponding increase in imports of essential inputs from abroad, and we are back at the original factor proportions problem. In extreme cases, production functions may be such that input-imports for export production demand the use of more foreign exchange than the exports even-

9 We are, at the moment, ignoring the problem of capital transfers which may serve to finance a deficit in the balance of trade. These problems are considered later in the section on balance of payments.

10 This is the well-known "small country" assumption of trade theory which means that in an atomistic world market a country can sell as much as it likes to, at an unchanged world price.

11 See, for instance, M. Michaely "Concentration of Exports and Imports: An International Comparison," *Economic Journal* (December 1958).

tually yield, and may give rise to negative value-added.[12]

4. Economic Planning and Foreign Trade

The characteristic features of India's international trade are greatly conditioned by these and similar structural disabilities. The underlying constraints had become particularly acute following an articulate policy of economic development embodied in the successive Five Year Plans since 1950. The trade picture has since then been dominated by rapidly rising imports and virtually stagnant export earnings. It is doubtful whether any conceivable strategy of development could have substantially reduced the import requirements without seriously affecting the rate of growth. It is a matter of some controversy, however, as to whether India could have pursued a more vigorous programme for export expansion and thus avoided the large trade deficits.

Before answering this and other questions, it is worthwhile examining the undercurrents of trade policy and to trace their logical relationship to the Indian planning procedures. The Indian planning procedures, from the very start, have been concerned with the over-all size of the savings/investment in public and private sectors as well as with the allocation of investment among alternative uses. The sectoral allocations, initially determined by the *ad hoc* availability of worthwhile projects, came to develop a tenuous relationship with the two-sector[13] and four-sector models which provided the theoretical framework for the Indian Plan.[14]

The time path of growth in these models is determined by the proportion of capital goods output devoted to the further production of capital goods. Since the models assumed the absence of international trade, the growth rate of the economy effectively became a function of the capacity of the domestic capital goods industry. This assumption had the effect of significantly restricting the scope of domestic transformation possibilities only to those permitted by the domestic capital goods sector, since the "closed economy" precluded an enlargement of transformation possibilities through recourse to international trade. This feature of the model has been much criticized for ignoring an important means of solving the domestic transformation problem.[15]

In any event, a major objective of the Indian economic policy came to be the development of the domestic capital goods industry by allocating a higher proportion of total investment to such sectors. This policy clearly implied a declining role of foreign trade in obtaining such goods from abroad, and envisaged an eventual independence from imports. It was thus natural that a policy of import substitution in the manufacturing sectors came to occupy a central place. While it is quite clear that in primary-oriented economies like India, any industrial development necessarily has to take the form of import substitution, the wisdom of indiscriminate reliance on import substitution as a growth strategy may be questioned. But first let us turn to the rationale of import substitution.

5. Foreign Exchange Constraint and Import Substitution

The traditional justification for import substitution in India, as elsewhere, seems

---

12 Jagdish Bhagwati and Padma Desai, *India—Planning for Industrialization* (Oxford University Press, 1970), have suggested the possible existence of negative value-added at international prices in such manufacturing sectors as leather goods, non-ferrous metals, iron and steel and automobiles. They caution, however, that the phenomena could have arisen because of statistical difficulties which are substantial.

13 P. C. Mahalanobis, "Some Observations on the Process of Growth of National Income," *Sankhya* (September 1953), and "The Approach of Operational Research to Planning in India," *Sankhya* (December 1955).

14 For further details on Indian planning models, the reader should consult A. Ghosh, *Planning, Programming and Input-Output Model* (Cambridge University Press, 1968).

15 For a recent discussion of these and other issues connected with trade and development policy, the reader is referred to J. Bhagwati and

to have been provided by the "two gap" models of development,[16] although it has been suggested that this may have been an *ex post* rationalization for the development of heavy industry on other than strictly economic grounds.[17] The two-gap approach postulates limited substitution possibilities between domestic savings and foreign exchange. Given this rigidity in production functions, it is stated that a high potential saving is by no means a sufficient condition for growth of national product since its (domestic savings') optimal use may be prevented by a shortage of imported inputs. By the same token, a large capacity to import may fail to stimulate growth if the requisite domestic savings do not materialize.

The critical conclusion of the model is that a developing country is likely to be faced with two structural constraints of enormous significance, viz. (1) a minimum requirement for imports to sustain a given rate of growth of GNP; and (2) an actual or a potential ceiling on export earnings which are insufficient to finance the required imports. The "foreign exchange" gap,[18] the difference between minimum required imports and total exports, is given by

$$\overline{M}_n - \overline{E}_n = M_0 + \beta(V_n - V_0) - E_0(1+e)^n$$

where the symbols have the following meaning:

M_0 = the observed initial level of imports.

V_0 = the Gross National Product in the initial year.

$V_n = V_0(1+r)^n$, r being the compound growth rate and n the number of years after 0.

E_0 = the initial level of exports.

β = the marginal rate of imports per additional unit of GNP.

e = rate of growth of exports.

The gap can be seen in Figure 2.[19] In situations where the foreign exchange gap is dominant, the existing total import capacity, i.e., $E_n = E_0\ (1+e)^n$ will effectively set the upper limit to the increase

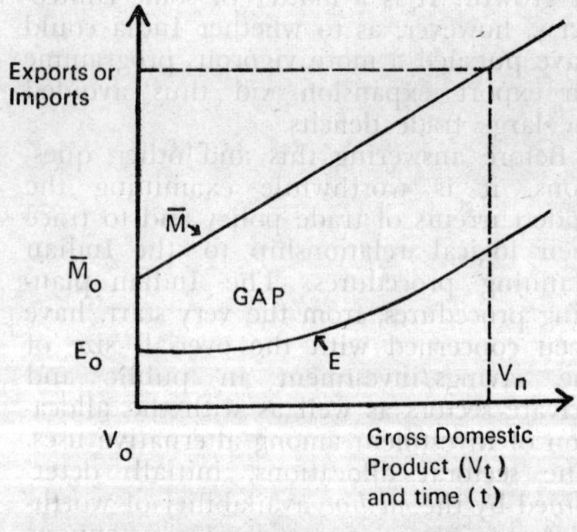

Fig. 2

in GNP.[20] Barring foreign aid, the development of the domestic capital goods industry may be the only viable solution for closing the foreign exchange gap. It must be remembered that in this model, exports are assumed to take their highest value and thus cannot eliminate the gap.

P. Desai, *India–Planning for Industrialization* (Oxford University Press, 1970).

16 There is a growing literature on the "two-gap" models of development, of which the following are representative: R. I. McKinnon, "Foreign Exchange Constraints in Economic Development and Efficient Aid Allocation," *The Economic Journal* (June 1964); H. B. Chenery and A. Strout, "Foreign Assistance and Economic Development," *American Economic Review*, September 1966); J. Vanek, *Estimating Foreign Resources for Economic Development: Theory, Method and a Case Study of Colombia* (McGraw-Hill, 1967); and A. Martens, "The Two-Gap Theory of Development Reconsidered with Special Reference to Turkey," *European Economic Review* (Summer 1970).

17 J. Bhagwati and P. Desai, op. cit., p. 236.

18 The following illustration will clarify the concept. An initial value of M_0=2000 and β=.15, V_0=10,000, V_n=16,289 and n= 10 will give the value of minimum imports $\overline{M}_n$ =2943. Similarly, given E_0 =1500, e=.04, E_n=2220. The foreign exchange gap will equal 2943–2220=723.

19 Since we are primarily concerned with trade problems, any discussion of savings gap is ignored in this analysis.

20 For details of this formulation, see OECD, *Quantitative Models as an Aid to Development Assistance Policy* (Paris 1967), Annex. III.

In practical terms, the United Nations had calculated the "trade gap" (including factor income payments) for India in 1962–63 to the tune of $ 950 millions in 1960 prices. On the basis of a projected growth rate of the economy of 5.0 per cent per year, the trade gap was estimated to be as high as $ 2500 millions in 1975–76.[21]

Foreign aid inflows in India have always been regarded as something one can do without in the long run when the economy is able to cope with the structural adjustments necessary for self-sustaining growth. One such adjustment can be effected through a process of import substitution whereby the continued dependence on massive imports of capital goods and equipment can be reduced or eliminated.

Import substitution in open economies may be recognized when, *ceteris paribus*, an increase in the domestic production of a commodity results in a decline of competing imports. However, if the increase in domestic production is less than the growth of demand—both for final and intermediate consumption—imports will continue to rise and import substitution may not be obvious. Yet it is clear that import substitution has been positive in the sense that domestic production is now supplying a part of the output that would have otherwise been imported. In order to overcome this difficulty, import substitution may be defined as "the difference between growth in domestic output with no change in the import ratio and the actual growth."[22] Symbolically, import substitution in the *i*th sector is measured as :

$$S_i = Z_i^2 (u_i^2 u - u_i^1)$$

and $u_i^2 = X_i^2 / Z_i^2, \quad u_i^1 = X_i^1 / Z_i^1,$

$$Z_i = X_i + M_i \text{ and } X_i = D_i + W_i + E_i$$

and the symbols have the following meaning : X_i =domestic production, D_i =domestic final demand, W_i =intermediate demand, E_i =exports and M_i =imports.[23] Subscripts refer to sectors or industries and superscripts refer to time periods.[24]

Summary estimates of import substitution for the Indian economy following the above method are given in Table 1.[25] These estimates suggest that for the 15-year period, 1950–51 to 1965–66, import substitution accounts for roughly one-fourth of the total growth in output, and for nearly one-half of the growth of output of the capital goods sector. This is not surprising since import substitution is an independent source of economic growth in much the same way as export expansion. Indeed, in the early stages of industrial growth, the contribution of import substitution may be the more important one. Econometric analyses of Japanese industrial growth show that import substitution, and not exports as popularly believed, accounted for nearly 40 per cent of the growth of manufacturing industry during 1914 to 1954.[26] Table 1 also shows that of the three broad groups of industries, import substitution in the capital goods sectors seems to be the most pronounced.

India's experience in this regard is by no means unique; many of the less developed countries for much the same reasons have resorted to import substitution as a development strategy. In Latin

21 United Nations, *Trade Prospects and Capital Needs of Developing Countries* (New York, 1968), p. 76.

22 H. B. Chenery, "Patterns of Industrial Growth," *American Economic Review* (1969), p. 640.

23 These measures represent a simplification from a comprehensive national income model for the study of structural changes. For details, see J. Ahmad, "Import Substitution and Structural Change in Indian Manufacturing Industry," *Journal of Development Studies*, Vol. IV, No. 3, (April 1968).

24 None of the possible measures of import substitution is completely free from ambiguities. The present measure is by far the most straightforward and widely accepted in literature. For a discussion of this problem, see Robert B. Sutcliffe, *Industry and Underdevelopment* (Addison Wesley, 1971).

25 For alternative definitions and measurement of import substitution in India, the reader is referred to J. Bhagwati and P. Desai, op. cit., Chapter 5. Though sensitive to the choice of measures, the orders of magnitude are roughly the same.

26 H. B. Chenery, S. Shishido and T. Watanabe, "The Pattern of Japanese Growth, 1914–1954," *Econometrica*, Vol. 30, No. 1 (January 1962).

Table 1. Import Substitution in the Indian Economy

Period and Industry Group	Import Substitution		
	Value (Rs. Crores)	Share in Total Growth (percentage)	Ranking in Group
1950/51–1955/56			
Consumer goods	25.27	10.4	3
Intermediate goods	46.11	47.9	2
Capital goods	65.74	54.4	1
Total	137.12	29.8	
1955/56–1960/61			
Consumer goods	90.29	16.2	1
Intermediate goods	62.63	12.1	2
Capital goods	48.18	10.9	3
Total	201.10	13.3	
1960/61–1965/66			
Consumer goods	87.99	12.2	3
Intermediate goods	152.47	20.1	2
Capital goods	376.16	38.9	1
Total	616.62	25.2	
1950/51-1965/66			
Consumer goods	163.31	10.8	3
Intermediate goods	207.79	12.6	2
Capital goods	705.30	42.0	1
Total	1076.40	22.3	

SOURCES: J. Ahmad, "Import Substitution and Structural Change in Indian Manufacturing Industry," *Journal of Development Studies*, Vol. IV, No. 3, April 1968, Tables 4–5, pp. 333–364.

America, notably in Argentina and Brazil, import substitution has been the chief element of economic change and industrialization. India is relatively fortunate in possessing one of the important preconditions of successful import substitution—that of a large potential market. Given her vast potential consuming and producing resources, India can initiate large-scale industrialization on a number of fronts and meet the requirement of minimum efficient scale for most industries.

Although the immediate justification for import substitution was provided by the necessity to conserve foreign exchange, the Indian planners had more in mind than a mere saving of foreign exchange. Even a cursory reading of the policy documents leaves little doubt that the planners were interested in initiating structural changes of far-reaching significance which could not have been possible without drastically changing the pattern of trade inherited from a long history of colonial relations with her major trading partners.

The manner in which a deficit on balance of trade is financed has important implications for the domestic economy and is, therefore, not a matter of indifference to the country concerned. The command over foreign exchange is desired not for its own sake, but to further other objectives, e.g. changes in production structure, to which it contributes by allowing increased imports. The point is that a country's objectives in acquiring foreign exchange should be kept in mind while evaluating the alternative means of earning them. The planning authorities have to constantly evaluate the impact of foreign exchange earning activities on as many economic and social parameters as possible. Suppose that India could "earn" an equivalent amount of foreign exchange by exporting either commodity A or commodity B, or by displacing the imports of commodity C. Now, the production of commodities A, B or C is likely to have different consequences both for her domestic structure and the trading position. The production and export of commodity A, for instance, may imply a movement toward the country's long run comparative advantage, while the export of B may tend to perpetuate a situation where potential gains from trade and other dynamic considerations are ignored. Similarly, the domestic production of C may attempt to correct an inefficient production structure resulting from past misallocation of resources. In addition, the production of the three commodities may have different implications for labour productivities, resource use, and technological progress. If so, the country can hardly remain indifferent as to the source of its foreign exchange;[27] a choice has to be made between the commodities or, most likely, an optimal output mix has to be determined. This choice inevitably forces attention to the values and weights implicit in a country's "demand function" for foreign exchange.

In India, this kind of function was never made explicit since the trade policy during the last 25 years had only a tenuous relationship with Plan objectives and was itself simply a collection of *ad hoc* measures taken from time to time to deal with problems as they arose. Yet, it is quite clear that the policy of import substitution was embedded in the desire to create a large scale domestic industrial structure which was expected to lead the economy to a "self-reliant and self-generating stage." It was, therefore, no accident that the Second Plan of 1956 embodied far-reaching social and political goals in its allocations and its priorities. These goals and priorities have undergone only minor revaluations, due more to expediency than to any basic rethinking.

By any reckoning India's industrial performance during the past twenty years has been impressive. Apart from the fact that the index of industrial production has trebled since 1950, the industrial structure has achieved diversification and depth needed for future growth. The process of import substitution has been extended both vertically and laterally to include a larger proportion of value-added in the gross value of Indian output, and the average import coefficient in most manufacturing sectors has witnessed a dramatic decline. This relative independence from imports may be seen in the illustration that in 1956, India only "assembled" motor trucks, while in 1971 it manufactured them with an import content of barely one per cent.

6. Import Substitution and Efficiency

India's vast potential, both as a producing and a consuming unit, leaves little doubt as to the viability of large-scale import substitution; yet, some questions may be raised about its efficiency. These questions concern not so much the supposed incompatibility of import substitution with export expansion,[28] but rather its indiscriminate extension to a wide range of sectors without regard to costs, productivities or the growth of demand. Again, India is in the company of a large number of countries which have succumbed to the temptation to import-substitute in as many lines as possible without carefully considering the role of international trade. It is certainly possible to grow bananas on the North Pole (in the hot houses) but it would not be optimal to do so in view of the possibility of acquiring them through trade. Similarly, even though a country may be capable of import-substituting in all sectors from A to Z, its comparative advantage of doing so may lie in only a few of them.

Little analytical work on these lines has been done in India, so that emphatic answers are hard to come by.[29] But there

---

27 To the extent that self-reliance and self-sufficiency in economic matters may be desirable objectives in themselves, a country may be reluctant to finance its balance of payment deficits through foreign capital inflows. Presumably, this reflects a desire to reduce the influence of foreign private and governmental, and sometimes international, agencies implied by the foreign borrowing.

28 On this supposed conflict, see Ian M. D. Little, Tibor Scitovsky and Maurice Scott, *Industry and Trade in Some Developing Countries* (Oxford University Press, 1970).

29 Exercises of this kind in India have been limited generally to ascertaining the "saving" in foreign exchange which would result by initiating substitute domestic production, both with reference to direct and indirect inputs. If one could produce, let us say, chemical machinery worth Rs. 10 crores, the saving of foreign exchange may be greater or lesser than this amount depending upon the import intensity of such production as well as of the indirect requirements.

can be little doubt that valuable resources could have been saved if the process of import substitution had been more selective with a limited number of strategically chosen sectors and industries where a concentration of effort and resources could have maximized the gains in efficiency. Particularly in the heavy industry sector, simultaneous development of a plethora of manufacturing activities may have deprived the economy of the advantages of large-scale production and of meeting the minimum critical thresholds. In addition, a proliferation of industries has deprived her of specialization and an eventual development of comparative advantage in selected lines. This lack of specialization can be seen in the fact that after 20 years of vigorous development of heavy industry, there is hardly any line of production in which India could claim decided cost advantages relative to international prices.

The process of import substitution ran into a structural difficulty of another sort. As the imports of most luxury consumer goods were restricted by prohibitory tariffs, the profitability of their domestic production automatically increased. If this production had required the use of only the domestic factors, the initial cut in imports would have conserved foreign exchange for "essential" uses. But their domestic production required additional imports of components and spare parts—a process which was extended to other sectors of the economy via inter-industry repercussions. Hazari has estimated that for the years 1961–62 and 1963–64, the proportion of India's total imports which supported the domestic production of "luxuries" was 7.6 and 8.3 per cent respectively. The corresponding figure for "necessities" was 28.7 and 32.9 per cent respectively.[30]

The above illustrates a frequently observed phenomenon in countries which rely on import substitution strategies for "saving" foreign exchange. Trade policies designed to exclude the imports of "inessential" goods automatically create incentives to channel domestic investment into their production. At the same time, since exchange rates are frequently overvalued, the cost of importing the inputs for their production is kept artificially low. This accentuates the tendency toward import intensive techniques of production, and further aggravates the factor proportions problem, discussed earlier in this chapter. India's predicament in this regard may be compared with Argentina where the intermediate import requirements per composite unit of final output were higher in 1960 than in 1953, despite considerable import substitution in the intervening years.[31] In other words, the desire to import less builds up pressures to import more—a process that may continue unabated. In the longer run, however, the cumulative direct savings of foreign exchange are likely to exceed the cumulative indirect expenditures of foreign exchange.[32]

Given a built-in incentive to domestically produce luxury goods whose imports have been curtailed and the political pressure of the affluent to satisfy this demand, the establishment of a wide range of import-substituting consumer goods industries presumably at high opportunity costs, has been a prominent feature of the industrial landscape in India since 1955. Most of these industries catered to the demand of the affluent few for sophisticated and highly diversified products, totally out of line with the average per capita income in the country. The present structure of income distribution in India means that the demand for these products is not enough to cross the minimum threshold for exploitation of the economies of scale. Moreover, the demand tends to fall off beyond a certain point resulting in unutilized capacity and higher average costs. This same sort of demand insufficiency

---

30 B. R. Hazari, "The Import Intensity of Consumption in India," *Indian Economic Review* (October 1967).

31 David Felix, "The Dilemma of Import Substitution—Argentina," Gustav F. Papanek (ed.), *Development Policy—Theory and Practice* (Harvard University Press, 1968).

32 This conclusion requires certain assumptions about the rate of investment, its import-intensity and the output-capital ratios. For a comprehensive treatment of this problem, see Carlos F. Diaz-Alejandro, "On the Import Intensity of Import Substitution," *Kyklos*, 1965.

has plagued the Argentinian consumer goods industry during the last decade. It was estimated, for instance, that the cross-sectional income elasticity of demand for a large number of durable goods, including refrigerators, vaccum cleaners, and television sets, was below unity.[33] The remedy in both cases lies either in scrapping the domestic production of some of these goods and let imports fulfil the demand or in changing the structure of income distribution in a way which makes these industries viable through large increases in demand.

Indiscriminate import substitution without basic changes in income distribution inevitably leads to a slowing down, as seems to be the case currently with the industrial sector in India. Since the Indian economy was subject to excess demand initially, investment continued to grow at its maximum rate determined by the marginal savings ratio and the rate of import of capital goods. But the full capacity income seems to have caught up with potential real aggregate demand. In a large number of industrial sectors, particularly in the consumer goods sector, supply seems to have outstripped demand, with the result that investment has ceased to grow because of excess capacity. It would be instructive to draw a parallel with the experience of Brazil where a vigorous process of import substitution seems to have led to a slackening, for the same reasons. This has been explained in terms of a growing inequality in the functional distribution of income in Brazil which is directly attributable to the growth of highly protected domestic industries. During 1955–1965, the growth rate of real wages per worker in the Brazilian industry was 2.8 per cent per year, while the index of industrial productivity during the same period grew at 5.0 per cent.[34] These differential growth rates suggest that the distribution of income tends to be biased against the working class and inhibits the growth of income. Indeed, the proportion of value-added in manufacturing attributable to wages declined from 34 per cent in 1957 to 23 per cent in 1965.[35]

The point is simply that a given bundle of consumer goods may require, for their domestic production, a larger volume of imports than an alternative bundle. Thus, even if there are fixed proportions between domestic and imported inputs in each industry, it is unlikely that this proportion would be the same for all industries. Variations in product-mix will, therefore, give some flexibility in import requirements. India could significantly reduce her overall import requirements by redistributing income in favour of poorer classes who are likely to spend a greater proportion of their income on goods that require less imported inputs. It should be noted, however, that possible variations in the product-mix will be constrained by the extent to which growth must be balanced between the different sectors of the economy, for any given distribution of income.

7. Import and Exchange Controls

The over-all import policy that has dominated the entire planning period in India is one of a fairly tight regime of import and exchange controls, which alternated with occasional periods of liberalization. The principal feature of the regime has been the allocation of permissible imports by categories, e.g. capital goods, raw materials, etc., among sectors and industries by means of an elaborate

33 David Felix, op. cit., offers the following explanation. The cross-sectional income elasticity tends to be high when durables are being newly acquired by upper income families. The lower half of the upper income family units in 1962 bought under 50 per cent of all refrigerators and washing machines sold, almost 40 per cent of all T. V. sets and about one-third of all stoves, radios, and vaccum cleaners, while the upper 25 per cent of all income recipients purchased from two-thirds to three-fourths of the automobiles sold. In total, 44 per cent of expenditures on durable goods were on automobiles alone, and another 18.6 per cent on television sets, leaving little more than one-third of total expenditures to be shared by a large number of remaining items.

34 Werner Baer and Andrea Maneschi, "Import Substitution, Stagnation and Structural Change: An Interpretation of the Brazilian Case," *The Journal of Developing Areas* (January 1971).

35 Ibid.

administrative machinery which was gradually evolved over a period of time.[36]

The procedures followed for allocation of foreign exchange had two ostensible criteria: (1) the principle of "essentiality" and (2) the principle of "indigenous non-availability." Thus, if an import was deemed essential and if it could be shown that there was no competing domestic production, it was permitted. In practice, however, it is not clear as to how the actual priorities were determined for industry-wise and plant-wise allocations. This is not surprising, since the large number of sectors and industries involved precluded any clear notions of priority. Bhagwati and Desai conclude "that the agencies involved in determining industry-wise allocations fell back on vague notions of "fairness," implying pro rata allocations with reference to capacity installed or employment, or shares defined by past import allocations and similar rules of thumb without any clear rationale."[37] These simple *ad hoc* rules of allocation seem to have little relationship to productivity, and have probably resulted in large scale inefficiencies in the allocation of a scarce resource. One measure of this inefficiency may be the fact that large foreign exchange resources were allocated to consumer goods industries at the expense of vital producers' goods industries.

Quota restrictions on imports, implied by the criterion of "non-availability," have meant "automatic and anticipatory" protection to all industries that qualify, regardless of relative prices in domestic and foreign markets. It has been estimated that the resulting effective rates of protection for some industries during 1960–62 were as high as 10,000 per cent.[38] Moreover, the reliance of AU allocations of foreign exchange on the level of installed capacity may have been partially responsible for underutilization of existing capacity. Insofar as import allocations under the AU licensing were directly related to the additional capacity *installation,* while the materials necessary for additional *utilization* of existing capacity must be purchased at import-premium-carrying prices, there would result a bias in favour of creating capacity even when excess capacity exists.

8. Export Structure and Policy

Like all less developed countries, India's export trade is heavily concentrated in a few traditional commodities. This lack of diversification is reflected in the fact that only five commodities—jute, tea, cotton textiles, vegetable oils, and tobacco—account for over 80 per cent of her total export earnings. These commodities have not only shown a poor rate of growth, but are also losing their share in the world markets.[39] Sticky export earnings in turn have seriously impaired India's capacity to import.[40] This is particularly significant when one considers the fact that the

---

[36] The allocation has taken the form of CG licensing for imported capital goods and the AU ("actual user") licensing for imported inputs and raw materials.

[37] J. Bhagwati and P. Desai, *India—Planning for Industrialization* (Oxford University Press, 1970), p. 290.

[38] For details of this and other research into these problems, see Jagdish N. Bhagwati and Sukhamoy Chakravarty, "Contributions to Indian Economic Analysis: A Survey," *American Economic Review,* Vol. LIX, No. 4 (September 1969), Part 2, p. 64.

[39] For example, the earnings from the export of jute manufactures declined from a value of Rs. 1,633 millions in 1952 to Rs. 1,255 millions in 1960. There was some improvement in later 1960s, but by 1970 they had merely regained a value approximately equal to the one in 1952, viz., Rs. 1,707 millions. The export earnings from tea grew from Rs. 1,236 millions in 1960 to a mere Rs. 1,447 millions in 1970—a change of 17 per cent in ten years. Similarly there has been a reduction in India's share of world trade in these commodities. India's share of world trade in jute manufactures declined from 95 per cent in 1950–51 to 45 per cent in 1969–70. Her share of world exports of tea declined from 50 per cent to 21 per cent during the same period. These declines in individual commodity exports are in line with an overall decline of India's share of world exports from 2.0 per cent in 1950 to 0.9 per cent in 1966.

[40] Export earnings financed 83 per cent of India's total imports during the First Five Year Plan (1951–55), while this proportion fell to 56 per cent during the Second Plan period (1956–60). The percentages, of course, conceal the fact that imports had dramatically increased during the Second relative to the First Plan.

reduction in the value of her exports and of her share in world exports have occurred in a setting of rapidly rising value and volume of world trade.

This unsatisfactory performance raises the question whether India's stagnant export earnings are due to unfavourable demand conditions for her exports, or as a result of her own economic and commercial policies. Few systematic analyses are available to provide a categorical answer.[41] There is little doubt, however, that India's export commodity composition is heavily biased toward commodities whose world demand is either stagnant, as of jute, or rising only slowly, as of tea. These exports belong to the group of commodities which not only have an income elasticity of demand of below unity, but are also largely unresponsive to price changes. It is, therefore, not surprising that India is experiencing difficulty in maintaining the value of her exports. Part of the difficulty seems to be the presence of a number of competing suppliers from other parts of the world attempting to expand their exports from very low initial levels. The relative decline in India's share of world exports of tea between 1950 and 1970 is partly the result of highly competitive policies on the part of Ceylon, Indonesia, and countries in Africa which have markedly increased their share of the world total. In a stagnant world market the gain of one country is the loss of another.

India's export policies since the 1950s have been based on two broad assumptions: (1) stagnant world demand for her major export commodities provides no optimism for any appreciable increases, and (2), in any event, it would be desirable to reduce her dependence on a few resource-based commodities, and to encourage the export of new industrial goods, particularly the products of the rapidly growing light engineering industries.

The first assumption is immensely valid in the sense that it would have been extremely difficult, if not altogether impossible, to increase export earnings from traditional commodities where external demand factors call the tune as to the quantities sold and prices paid. This is true of export commodities of which India is a major world supplier, and hence, has to operate in an oligopolistic world market, constrained by the actions of a small number of rival producers. Under these circumstances, it is very difficult for a single producer country to increase its share of world trade, without disturbing the hierarchy of market shares and provoking retaliatory measures. Thus India could have no control over its export earnings from commodities like tea and cotton textiles, and has to abide by world demand and supply constellations determined by the combined actions of a small number of producers.[42]

In the case of other commodities, of which India is either a marginal supplier or holds a near monopoly, her domestic policies may have influenced her export earnings by influencing the volume of their production, the terms on which they are exported, and their domestic demand. All these factors seem to have played their part in making the supply of Indian exports inelastic. By far the most significant factor limiting the export growth seems to have been the growth in domestic consumption of exportables in the wake of growth of incomes and population. This phenomenon can be illustrated by the example of cotton textiles. The high income-elasticity of demand for cotton textiles coupled with a high rate of population growth assures the domestic industry of a steadily rising domestic demand.[43] Certain other important exports, like vegetable oilseeds, were in demand at home in increasingly large quantities to serve as raw materials for the growing Indian vegetable-oils industry.

---

41 However, the reader is referred to the very detailed study by Manmohan Singh, *India's Export Trends and the Prospects for Self-Sustaining Growth* (Oxford: Clarendon Press, 1964).

42 For a detailed commodity-by-commodity account of these problems, the reader is referred to Manmohan Singh, op. cit.

43 The income elasticity of demand in India for cotton textiles is estimated to be 1.4, cf. B. R. M. Chatterjee, "A Statistical Study of Consumption of Cotton Textiles in India," *Monthly Abstract of Statistics*, Vol. 13, No. 10 (New Delhi, 1960).

This is also true of raw cotton and leather. Thus the conclusion is inescapable that exports in most cases have succumbed to the overwhelming pressure of competing domestic demand.[44] This is despite the fact that India has been fairly successful in holding the price line and had the mildest inflation of all developing countries in recent times.[45] The inflationary pressures were kept in check partly by increasing the domestic absorption of exportables. Undoubtedly, the maintenance of over-valued exchange rate has created disincentives for exports, thereby raising the profitability of domestic sales.

India's experience in this regard is fairly in line with that of all other developing countries who are faced with the dilemma of maintaining a viable rate of growth of exports in the face of a rising domestic demand. In certain countries domestic demand has been restrained by imposition of excise duties in order to keep export sales rising. In India, however, political pressures for effecting reasonable increases in consumption have always been strong. The Five Year Plans themselves have consistently planned for a monotonic rise in private consumption, whereas a more restrictive consumption policy would obviously have avoided the strain on balance of payments.

The second assumption, viz. the desirability of the exports of manufactures rather than those of primary commodities, is rooted in the desire to provide structural support to domestic industrialization through broadening of the markets. There can be no doubt that from the point of view of long-run efficiency, it is desirable for India to reduce her dependence on traditional commodity exports, which suffer from adverse factors on both demand and supply sides. Such a diversification could arise through the development of "new" exports of what has come to be known in India as the "engineering industries" sector.

India's record in this respect has been quite satisfactory, though by no means exceptional. The exports of a large number of newly established industries have shown rapid rates of growth, even though the absolute quantities involved are as yet quite small. Completely new lines of exports have emerged, and there is some evidence that the range of commodities entering export trade is gradually increasing. This diversification can be seen by comparing the commodity-concentration index of the engineering industries. For eighty commodity sub-groups within the engineering industries, this index declined from 27.2 in 1956–58 to 17.8 in 1962–64, implying that a larger assortment of commodities are being exported.[46]

It is worth noting also that the growth in exports of manufactures has been accompanied by a growth in the domestic consumption of these commodities. Exports of manufactures seem to have been subject to the same kind of restraining influence from domestic demand noticed in the case of resource-based commodities. It is quite possible, therefore, that the growth rate of exports of manufactures would have been much higher were it not for the inelasticity of supply caused by the competition between domestic and foreign sales. Nonetheless, export performance of the industrial sector has been encouraged by the export promotion measures undertaken since the Third Five Year Plan. These promotion measures have taken the form of "import entitlement" schemes,[47] exemption from

44 See Benjamin Cohen, "The Stagnation of Indian Exports," *Quarterly Journal of Economics* (November 1964).

45 The All-India Wholesale Price Index rose by only 6.8 per cent during the ten-year period, 1950–51 and 1960–61, while the Consumer Price Index during the same period rose roughly by 18 per cent. The degree of inflation revealed by these indices is infinitesimal compared to price rises in some of the Latin American countries, where a 30 per cent inflation in one year is not uncommon.

46 The Commodity Concentration Index is defined as $100\sqrt{\Sigma \frac{x_{ij}^2}{x_j}}$

where x_{ij}=India's exports of sub-group i within group j, and x_j=the country's total commodity group j, cf. J. Bhagwati and P. Desai, op. cit., p. 429.

47 Import entitlement schemes are a form of hidden subsidy to exports, in so far as they entitle the eligible exporters to premium-carrying import licenses in proportion to the value of exports.

sales and excise taxes on inputs, "draw-back" of import duties on raw materials, direct tax concessions, special allocation on controlled rates of scarce inputs like iron, steel, transportation, etc. At the same time efforts were made to increase the trade in manufactures with the U.S.S.R. and other socialist countries.[48]

Although exports of manufactures have now become an important feature of India's foreign trade, serious production and trade problems continue to hamper their development. Not the least of these concern the external impediments which pose a problem of "entry" of such manufactures both in the markets of the developed, industrialized, and of the less developed, semi-industrialized countries. The single most inhibiting factor to the development of exports of manufactures from the less developed countries is the system of tariffs adopted by the industrial countries. The characteristic features of this system is that the tariff rates on imports rise successively with the degree of product elaboration.[49] For example, the tariff rates become increasingly higher as one moves from iron ore to raw steel to machine goods.[50] This tariff discrimination against products with high value-added content makes it difficult for the less developed countries to compete in the world market for manufactures. In addition, there is a bewildering array of quota restrictions and other non-tariff barriers on products of existing and potential interest to the less developed countries.[51]

Potential Indian exports to the other less developed countries also present problems insofar as the process of import substitution in other countries encompasses virtually the same range of goods which India is trying to export. The case of the cotton textile industry in this respect is typical. The cotton textiles industry in practically all less developed countries is the first casualty of the domestic import substitution process, due both to the rising profitability of home production and its relative technological simplicity. The Indian cotton textiles industry which emerged after World War II as the largest among all the less developed countries has now serious rivals for supplying both the home demand and the exports.

Quite apart from the limitation on the trading possibilities, the young Indian manufacturing industry has to cope with production problems of serious dimensions which prevent any significant entry into foreign markets. The world trade in manufactured goods is not simply a matter of inter-country differences in costs of production, so that the cheaper Indian costs are not sufficient to generate exports. Potential export items, particularly in the western countries, have also to meet standards of quality, homogeneity, and speed of delivery, etc. to go over the hump. These products have also to be sufficiently "differentiated" from close substitutes in the international market-place[52] in order

---

The important feature of these schemes is that a specified percentage of the f.o.b. value of exports is allowed to be used for the import of raw materials and components necessary for the production of the exports or of allied products.

48 Bilateral trade and payments agreements with a limited number of countries have become a regular feature of India's foreign trade since 1959, when the five year bilateral agreement between India and the U.S.S.R. came into force. These agreements provide for trade in specified commodities during a given period of time on the basis of a self-balancing monetary mechanism. The local currency balances arising out of such trade are in general not convertible into "hard" currencies.

49 Bela Balassa, *Trade Liberalization Among Industrial Countries* (McGraw-Hill, 1967), pp. 180–181.

50 Consider the following example from the United States imports tariff schedule:

Commodity	*Tariff Rate*
(a) Iron ore	Free
(b) Pig iron	\$ 1.12 per ton
(c) Bar iron	\$ 20–\$ 30 per ton
(d) Machine goods	
(i) Mining machinery	27.5% ad valorem
(ii) Machine tools	30% ad valorem
(iii) Textiles machinery	40% ad valorem

51 The most organized form of non-tariff barriers is embodied in the Long Term Arrangement for Trade in Cotton Textiles, popularly known as LTA, which was negotiated under the auspices of GATT and lays down specific quota ceilings, by commodity and by destination, for the import of cotton textiles in North America and Western Europe.

52 A recent analysis suggests that the itensity of international trade in manufactures depends on the similarity of income and demand patterns. As a result, countries with broadly similar demand

to develop strong consumer preferences.

It is thus difficult to escape the conclusion that India's export promotion efforts are beset with serious difficulties both at home and abroad. One may even assert that the export problem could not be solved independently of the more fundamental structural problems that India has to grapple with in the early stages of her economic growth. One can maintain this general position without implying that India has done everything possible to increase her exports or that all efforts in this direction are bound to be fruitless. One could go further and claim that there may indeed be no export problem at all, but that is another story.

9. Balance of Payments

Having described at some length the pertinent structural features of India's foreign trade, it is now a straightforward matter to draw their balance of payments implications. The "factor proportions" rigidity between domestic and foreign resources, combined with the unfavourable commodity composition of exports implies that development efforts in India have a built-in tendency to generate balance of payments pressures. These pressures, reflecting an excess demand for imports, can be eliminated only by scaling down the development effort which, in the Indian context, means abandoning the targets embodied in the Five Year Plans.

These pressures have resulted in a continuing deficit in India's trade balance since 1955, and the recurrent crises with respect to the means for covering such deficits. In all the years since 1956, India had an excess of imports over exports of goods and services to the tune of nearly of $ 14 billions or an average yearly deficit of $ 900 millions. The deficit had increased dramatically in the last years of the Third Five Year Plan, but is in a downward trend since 1968 as seen in Table 2. The quarterly data for 1971 estimated from IMF sources indicate that India's commodity trade is now nearly in balance.[53]

It is important to realize, however, that the deficits or surpluses on the trade balance should not, in themselves, be a cause for alarm or jubilation. This is because of the equilibrating role of the autonomous and induced capital movements between nations. While India was saddled with huge deficits on its current account balance, the capital account has shown correspondingly large inflows of capital. Capital inflows embody a "real" transfer of goods and services which increase national income and assist in capital formation. On the other hand, a balance on trade account is not necessarily a blessing, since it may signify (as it does in the contemporary Indian scene) a petering out of profitable investment opportunities due to insufficiency of demand rather than a genuine structural viability.

This relationship between the trade and capital accounts is not accidental; it is characteristic of capital-importing and capital-exporting nations. A capital-importing country must generate trade deficits in order to offset the surplus on capital account, while a capital-exporting country must have a surplus on trade account in order to balance the deficit in capital account. In other words, deficits and surpluses on trade and capital accounts are companion phenomena that offset each other so as to yield an overall balance.

The phenomenon of "real transfer" rests on the fundamental proposition that a country cannot invest, for domestic purposes, beyond the level of its own savings, except to the extent of its ability to secure

structures tend to trade with each other in products which are close substitute for each other, though sufficiently differentiated to have a slice of the world market in an oligopolisbic fashion. It must be stressed that this analysis refers to only the manufactured products in international trade, and does not attempt to explain the pattern of trade in natural commodities. For details, the reader is referred to S. B. Linder, *An Essay on Trade and Transformation* (Stockholm, 1967).

53 IMF, *International Financial Statistics,* Vol. XXV, No. 3, (March 1972). Other data based on annual *International Financial Statistics* and the *Balance of Payments Yearbook.*

Table 2. Balance of Payments
(Millions of U. S. Dollars)

	1960	1961	1962	1963	1964	1965	1966	1967	1968	1969	1970
Goods and Services	−881	−792	−945	−890	−1246	−1473	−1147	−1304	−840	−463	−608
Trade Balance FOB/CIF	−945	−751	−876	−870	−1232	−1307	−1069	−1134	−635	−220	−341
Investment Income	−90	−134	−171	−189	−214	−260	−254	−276	−278	−292	−299
Central Government	86	43	70	110	155	86	150	83	37	19	6
Other	68	50	32	59	27	8	26	23	36	30	26
Transfers	148	93	170	223	335	159	305	183	176	233	233
Private	79	74	72	88	87	85	178	139	160	176	163
Central Government	69	19	98	135	248	74	127	44	16	57	70
Capital Flows											
Private	146	−11	10	38	35	−2	14	3	−13	−34	−24
Central Government	552	668	620	709	1066	1109	837	1199	927	695	625
Commercial Banks:											
ASSETS	−3	1	−9	4	−16	17	−57	36	36	−13	−9
LABILITIES	29	−26	10	20	15	−15	−13	−7	−19	8	—
Monetary Authorities	67	59	136	−23	−25	103	10	14	−76	−385	−320
Monetary gold	—	—	—	—	—	−34	38	—	—	—	—
I. M. F. Accounts	−69	126	29	−20	−44	33	74	95	−83	−133	−251
Other assets	125	7	116	−16	18	18	−96	−85	−24	−236	−16
Other liabilities	11	−74	−9	13	1	−14	−6	4	31	−16	−9
Net Errors and Omissions	−58	8	8	−81	−146	102	51	−124	−191	−41	−22

Minus sign indicates debit

SOURCE: *International Financial Statistics* and *Balance of Payments Yearbook.*

investments from abroad.[54] Assuming fixed prices and no government, output (Y) in an open economy consists of consumption (C), investment (I) and exports (X),

$$Y = C + I + X \qquad (1)$$

Similarly, income received (Y) is spent, on consumption of domestic goods (C) on imports (M), or it is saved (S),

$$Y = C + M + S \qquad (2)$$

Combining the two equations results in the identity:

$$I + X = S + M \qquad (3)$$

and therefore,

$$S = I + (X - M) \qquad (4)$$

It can be seen from (4) that

$$S \gtrless I = X \gtrless M = \pm FI \qquad (5)$$

where FI=net foreign investment. What this means is that a country can increase domestic investment beyond the level of domestic savings to the extent that it has a deficit on merchandize account, i.e., $X < M$, or in other words, has a net foreign

54 For details, the reader should consult a standard textbook on the theory of balance of payments, e.g. B. J. Cohen, *Balance-of-Payments Policy* (Penguin, 1969).

capital inflow, i.e.$-FI$. If a country is willing to let its international payments position deteriorate, it can dissave, i.e., $-FI=S<I$.

It should, therefore, come as no surprise that continuous deficits on merchandize trade in India for the past fifteen years have been accompanied by large inflows of capital.[55] These capital inflows have permitted the total of domestic expenditures—"real absorption"—to remain at a level higher than real income. This should not be construed to mean that a country can permanently live beyond its means by running trade deficits. Such deficits in the short and the intermediate-run can be financed by accumulating debts to other countries. In the long run, however, an adjustment process must set in to eliminate the deficit. In practice, the limit to foreign borrowing is set by the increasing burden of debt servicing and repayment of capital to foreign lenders, which requires generation of ever-increasing trade surpluses. The annual outflow of repatriated earnings on foreign capital in India grew to a total of $ 362 millions in in 1970 from a low of 90 millions in 1960.[56] Debt-service charges account for approximately 20 per cent of her total export earnings in 1970. The problem can be postponed for a while by further borrowings to pay for the earlier debts.

The other significant constraint on India's external borrowing capacity arises due to a greatly reduced supply of foreign private capital. During the period 1950–69, India received capital inflows to the tune of Rs. 90 billions. Out of this, only Rs. 12 billions are private, direct and portfolio investments, and the rest is external assistance and loans from foreign governments and international agencies, chiefly the Aid India Consortium which includes twelve industrial countries and the World Bank group. Actually, loans constituted about 80 per cent of all non-private capital inflows—a circumstance which explains an increasing repayment burden. For the years 1966–69, nearly 32 per cent of fresh external assistance was used up for amortization and interest payments.

On the whole, foreign assistance "authorizations" in India have tended to correspond with the actual deficits on the current account, including the debt service and other repayments. Long-term, autonomous private capital inflows have been far less insignificant than in many other less developed countries of India's size and potential. The future prospects of high assistance levels are not promising, both from India's standpoint as well as of her donors, and the burden of adjustment for potential deficits will increasingly have to be borne by autonomous capital inflows. Eventually, however, the adjustment will have to be done through trade surpluses. An important part of the process of development is, therefore, to ensure that the sequence from a trade deficit position to one in which there is a net outflow of goods and services can be followed through smoothly.

10. Balance of Payments Adjustment Policies

This brings us to the question of policy instruments available to a developing country like India to bring about an equilibrium in the balance of payments. An initial difficulty arises with respect to the nature of such disequilibrium. Should one treat an *actual* deficit (or surplus) in the balance of autonomous transactions as evidence of disequilibrium, and attempt to correct it by eliminating the external assistance and other accommodating capital inflows? Or, should one define disequilibrium with respect to a *potential* deficit on the assumption of a high rate of growth, full employment, and free trade?[57] A full scale discussion of these issues will take us afar and will raise more questions than it will solve. In the Indian context, Manmohan Singh suggests that an equilibrium in the balance of payments must be

55 The subject of foreign aid and foreign capital in India is being discussed in a separate chapter in this volume.

56 I.M.F., *Balance of Payments Yearbook* (August 1971).

57 A discussion of some of these issues is contained in a well-known paper by R. F. Khan, "The Dollar Shortage and Devaluation," *Economia Internazionale*, Vol. 3, No. 1 (1950).

consistent with a rate of economic growth of at least 5 per cent per annum, with a minimum amount of import controls to eliminate the excess demand for foreign exchange.[58]

The classical prescription for dealing with payments imbalances rests on the proposition that a disequilibrium contains the seeds of its own reversal. A newly developed deficit results in a multiple reduction in income, which in turn, lowers imports (and expands exports) and may thus offset whole or part of the deficit.[59] Since this "automatic" contraction in the level of economic activity following a deficit is likely to correct the situation only partially, the governments are urged to reinforce the automatic tendencies by "expenditure-reducing" policies through fiscal and monetary means.[60]

Recent discussions have tended to put a greater reliance on "expenditure-switching" policies like devaluation to bring about balance of payments adjustments through changes in relative prices, i.e., the ratio of import prices to domestic prices. Thus the effect of devaluation of the Indian Rupee is to lower the prices of goods and services produced in India relative to prices in other countries, making Indian products more competitive both at home and abroad. In other words, Indian imports become more expensive in terms of rupees, inducing a "switch" to the cheaper home-produced substitutes, while Indian exports become cheaper in terms of foreign currencies in which they are brought. A devaluation, therefore, is a two-pronged remedy: it reduces imports and expands exports in a way that the total effect is in the direction of eliminating the deficit.

The condition that must prevail, if devaluation is to bring the foreign balance back into equilibrium, is that the sum of the two demand elasticities must exceed unity, and further, that the two supply elasticities must be infinite. These are known as Marshall-Lerner conditions.[61] But if the balance of payments deficits arise due to deeply rooted structural causes, the Marshall-Lerner conditions are not going to be satisfied in practice. It will be recalled that balance of payment deficits in structurally weak economies arise not so much because their prices are out of alignment with those of the rest of the world, but because of the "transformation problem" where domestic resources cannot be transformed into importables. This rigidity in production functions is reinforced by further rigidities in indirect transformation through trade which requires that foreign demand for a country's exports be perfectly elastic. In these circumstances, devaluation may not only be irrelevant; it may even make the balance of payments worse.

This is likely to occur if the domestic demand for imports (particularly, of capital goods) is inelastic and devaluation simply raises their cost in terms of exportables. Similarly, if the foreign demand for exports is relatively inelastic—price reduction produces a less than proportionate increase in quantity demanded—the total earnings from exports decline.[62] In either case, the effect on balance of payments is to increase the deficit. The deficit can only be avoided by reduction in capital imports, which in turn, will reduce the rate of growth and further aggravate the structural problem. The remedy in this case may be worse than the disease.

Devaluation is usually urged for a country suffering simultaneously from unemployment and a deficit—a situation characteristic of India as well as of most less developed countries. It is important

---

[58] Manmohan Singh, op. cit., p. 323.

[59] Analogous reasoning would apply to a surplus situation: the multiple rise in income due to trade surplus brings about an increase in imports (and a reduction in exports) that wholly or partly offset the surplus.

[60] An example is the British "stop-go" policy during 1950s and 1960s: contractionary monetary and fiscal measures in times of deficits and expansion in times of surplus.

[61] For details, see F. Machlup, "The Theory of Foreign Exchanges," and Joan Robinson, "The Foreign Exchanges"—both reprinted in American Economic Association, *Readings in the Theory of International Trade,* 1950.

[62] Consider the example of India's exports of jute manufactures. Their volume increased from 746,000 metric tons in 1952 to 850,000 metric tons in 1960—a gain of 14 per cent—while their value during the same period declined from Rs. 1,600 millions to Rs. 1,100 millions—a fall of 30 per cent.

to realize, however, that unemployment in these countries is due to complex structural causes and not due to a lack of effective demand. Thus, devaluation, which basically relies on a simple price-quantity relation, cannot be expected to increase the degree of employment. Even if the unemployment is of the "effective demand" type, it is easy to see that devaluation cannot reduce it if complementary imports are reduced and exports do not increase, or increase marginally. For devaluation to be effective, the demand elasticities must not only be greater than unity but they must be considerably greater.[63]

In any event, the "reversal factors" attendant on any policy of devaluation must be reckoned with. One such reversal factor is that devaluation leads to an increase in the domestic price level by raising the prices of imported commodities. If imports enter into the production process as inputs, a cost-price inflationary spiral may arise as the producers attempt to pass on the increases in costs to the consumers in the form of higher prices. This will wipe out the competitive gain, exports will suffer and imports will begin to rise.

The burden of the above discussion has been to show the futility of devaluation as a policy, without considering its structural context. Orthodox exchange rate adjustment solutions are not very applicable under these conditions and may aggravate the problem. It is not uncommon to find a less developed country simultaneously experiencing a balance of payments deficit, inflation, unemployment and slow growth. In fact, the Indian economy six years after the devaluation of the Rupee in June 1966, closely approximates this situation.

It is obvious that the foreign exchange devaluation of 1966 (from a par value of 4.76 rupees to 7.50 rupees per U.S. dollar) has failed to stimulate exports, since now sufficient time has passed to allow for the lags in price-quantity adjustments to work themselves out. It is also true that the *note* devaluation in 1966 may have been much less than the apparent one, since almost all export subsidies, chiefly the import entitlement schemes, were withdrawn with the devaluation. Thus the devaluation was largely a measure for the rationalization of the maze of administrative procedures and allocations designed to subsidize exports and implying a *de facto* devaluation. Indeed, it was argued then, that a devaluation can be simulated by equivalent import duties and export subsidies and was, therefore, not necessary.[64] On the other hand, it may have been necessary just for this reason—to avoid the bureaucratic delays, lack of coordination among agencies and other administrative deficiencies which such a simulation involves. In any event, the empirical questions relating to the precise manner in which devaluation would help—either through price-quantity adjustment or as part of a general rationalization—and how much devaluation was required, were not discussed either before or after the devaluation.

11. Conclusion

In foreign trade as in other sectors of the economy, India's emphasis since Independence in 1947 has come to rest on fundamentally different considerations than those which dominated her development experience over most of the earlier two decades. It is doubtful whether any conceivable development strategy could have reduced her heavy capital imports since 1950, without seriously impairing the total development effort. Similarly, import substitution in key sectors to an extent and degree permitted by potential domestic capabilities was inevitable, even though one may quibble whether the transformation difficulties were as severe as implied in the Plans. But one must not lose sight of the fact that in initiating import substitution processes, planners had more in mind than a mere saving on foreign exchange. The major reason has undoubted-

[63] The question is discussed in greater detail in Keith B. Griffin, *Underdevelopment in Spanish America* (M.I.T. Press, 1969), Chap. 5.

[64] P. M. Bardhan, "The Case Against Devaluation," *The Economic Weekly* (September 1962).

ly been the desire to reorient the country's production and trade structure in line with projected changes in demand conditions and resource availabilities.

The burden of the analysis in this chapter has been to highlight the structural features that prevent an attainment of balance of payments equilibrium. We have shown the built-in features that lead to excess demand for imports and the role of foreign demand and domestic supply elasticities that put severe limits on the growth of export earnings. The policy implications that emerge from this analysis are scattered throughout the discussion. As an overall assessment, it is quite clear that a long-run attainment of India's balance of payments presupposes a solution to the structural problem that affects her foreign trade. In any event, a balance of payments equilibrium is not desired for its own sake; a single-minded concern with balance of payments, to the exclusion of basic structural disequilibria in the foreign trade sector, is misplaced.

Table A. 1. India's Imports 1948–1970

(Value, Volume and Prices)

YEAR	1948	1949	1950	1951	1952	1953	1954	1955	1956	1957	1958	1959
Value of Imports C.I.F. (Millions of Rupees)	5678	7167	5547	8538	8074	5752	6175	6729	8215	10683	8778	9459
Volume of Imports (Index, 1963 = 100)	61	75	58	71	69	55	62	67	83	95	85	94
Import Prices (Index, 1963 = 100)	91	88	95	117	119	106	100	99	100	110	103	96

YEAR	1960	1961	1962	1963	1964	1965	1966	1967	1968	1969	1970
Value of Imports C.I.F. (Millions of Rupees)	11083	10845	11241	11795	13694	13926	17100	21060	18823	15333	15940
Volume of Imports (Index, 1963 = 100)	91	95	103	100	106	129	127	129	126	103	103
Import Prices (Index, 1963 = 100)	101	102	97	100	103	105	134	159	151	153	154

SOURCE: I. M. F., *International Financial Statistics*, 1971 Supplement, pp. 120–121.

NOTE: Figures for 1970 are taken from I.M.F., *International Financial Statistics*, Volume XXV, No. 7 (July 1972), pp. 178–179.

Table A. 2. India's Exports 1948–1970

(Value, Volume & Prices)

YEAR	1948	1949	1950	1951	1952	1953	1954	1955	1956	1957	1958	1959
Value of Exports (Millions of Rupees)	4509	4661	5458	7670	6167	5312	5627	6077	6192	6565	5817	6229
Jute	1768	1487	1201	2401	1622	1106	1213	1262	1125	1034	924	987
Tea	558	786	714	956	803	1024	1307	1165	1405	1243	1368	1261
Volume of Exports (Index, 1963 = 100)	67	68	77	76	71	73	75	83	80	87	79	85
Export Prices (Index, 1963 = 100)	85	85	93	135	110	94	96	94	95	95	94	94

YEAR	1960	1961	1962	1963	1964	1965	1966	1967	1968	1969	1970
Value of Exports (Millions of Rupees)	6338	6607	6682	7766	8328	8031	9920	12100	13153	13754	15198
Jute	1156	1316	1502	1485	1566	1599	1880	2218	1998	2029	1707
Tea	1201	1240	1240	1323	1242	1027	1362	1881	1651	1181	1447
Volume of Exports (Index, 1963 = 100)	80	83	89	100	106	99	102	99	111	110	121
Export Prices (Index, 1963 = 100)	103	105	100	100	100	106	139	160	154	163	163

SOURCE: I. M. F., *International Financial Statistics*, 1971 Supplement, pp. 120–121.

NOTE: Figures for 1970 are taken from I. M. F., *International Financial Statistics*, Volume XXV, No. 7 (July 1972), pp. 178–179.

BIBLIOGRAPHY

Ahmad, J., "Import Substitution and Structural Change in Indian Manufacturing Industry," *Journal of Development Studies* (April 1968).

Baer, W. and A. Maneschi, "Import Substitution, Stagnation and Structural Change: An Interpretation of the Brazilian Case," *The Journal of Developing Areas* (January 1971).

Balassa, B., *Trade Liberalization among Industrial Countries* (McGraw-Hill, 1967).

Bardhan, P. K., "The Case Against Devaluation," *The Economic Weekly* (September 1962).

Bhagwati, J. and S. Chakravarty, "Contributions to Indian Economic Analysis: A Survey," *American Economic Review* (September 1969), Part 2.

Bhagwati, J. and P. Desai, *India–Planning for Industrialization* (Oxford University Press, 1970).

Chakravarty, S., "The Use of Shadow Prices in Programme Evaluation," P. N. Rosenstein-Rodan (ed.), *Capital Formation in Economic Development* (M.I.T. Press, 1964).

Chakravarty, S., *Logic of Investment Planning* (North Holland Publishing Company, 1960).

Chatterjee, B.R.M., "A Statistical Study of Consumption of Cotton Textiles in India," *Monthly Abstract of Statistics* (New Delhi, 1960).

Chenery, H. B. and A. Strout, "Foreign Assistance and Economic Development," *American Economic Review* (September 1966).

Chenery, H. B., S. Shishido and T. Watanabe, "The Pattern of Japanese Growth, 1914–1954," *Econometrica* (January 1962).

Chenery, H. B., "Patterns of Industrial Growth," *American Economic Review* (1960).

Cohen, B. J., *Balance of Payments Policy,* Penguin Modern Economics (1969).
Cohen, B., "The Stagnation of Indian Exports," *Quarterly Journal of Economics* (November 1964).
Diaz-Alejandro, C. F., "On the Import Intensity of Import Substitution," *Kyklos* (1965).
Felix, D., "The Dilemma of Import Substitution—Argentina," G. F. Papanek (ed.), *Development Policy—Theory and Practice* (Harvard University Press, 1968).
Ghosh, A., *Planning, Programming and Input-Models* (Cambridge University Press, 1968).
Griffin, K. B., *Underdevelopment in Spanish America* (M. I. T. Press, 1969).
Hansen, B., *Long and Short Term Planning in Under-developed Countries* (North Holland Publishing Company, 1967).
Hazari, B. R., "Import-Intensity of Consumption in India", *The Indian Economic Review* (October 1967).
Kahn, R. F., "The Dollar Shortage and Devaluation," *Economia Internazionale,* Vol. 3, No. 1, (1950).
Linder, S. B., *Trade Policy in the Less Developed Countries* (Praeger Publishing Company, 1967).
Linder, S. B., *An Essay on Trade and Transformation,* (Stockholm, 1967).
Lipsey, R. E., "Foreign Trade," L. E. Davis et. al. (eds.), *American Economic Growth—An Economist's History of the United States* (Harper & Row, 1972).
Little, I. M. D., T. Scitovsky and M. Scott, *Industry and Trade in Some Developing Countries* (Oxford University Press, 1970).
Machlup, F., "The Theory of Foreign Exchanges" R. D. Irwin (ed.), *Readings in the Theory of International Trade* (American Economic Association, 1950).
Mckinnon, R. I., "Foreign Exchange Constraints in Economic Development and Efficient Aid Allocation", *The Economic Journal* (June 1964).
Mahalanobis, P. C., "Some Observations on the Process of Growth of National Income," *Sankhya* (September 1953).
Mahalanobis, P. C., "The Approach of Operational Research to Planning in India," *Sankhya* (December 1955).
Martens, A., "The Two-Gap Theory of Development Reconsidered with Special Reference to Turkey," *European Economic Review* (Summer 1970).
Michaely, M., "Concentration of Exports and Imports: An International Comparison," *Economic Journal* (December 1958).
Organization for Economic Development and Cooperation, *Quantitative Models as an Aid to Development Assistance Policy* (Paris, 1967).
Reddaway, W. B., *The Development of the Indian Economy* (George Allen & Unwin, 1962).
Robinson, J., "The Foreign Exchanges," R. D. Irwin (ed.), *Readings in the Theory of International Trade* (American Economic Association, 1950).
Singh, M., *India's Export Trends and the Prospects for Self-Sustained Growth* (Clarendon Press, 1964).
Sodersten, B., *International Economics* (Harper & Row, 1970).
Sutcliffe, R. B., *Industry and Underdevelopment* (Addison Wesley, 1971).
United Nations, *Trade Prospects and Capital Needs of Developing Countries* (1968).
Vanek, J., *Estimating Foreign Resources for Economic Development: Theory, Method and a Case Study of Colombia* (McGraw-Hill, 1967).

23

Foreign Private Investments in India

V.N. BALASUBRAMANYAM

1. Introduction

The role of foreign private investment in the development process has evoked considerable interest and debate in recent years. The arguments for and against such investment often range to extremes. The proponents envisage a multi-faceted role for it, emphasizing the part it can play in providing the much needed foreign exchange and technical skills to the less developed countries. It is argued that, at a time when official aid flows are becoming sluggish and the burden of repayment and service charges on the less developed countries from past flows are mounting, private foreign investment may provide an alternative source of development finance. Further, the development of productive skills and capabilities by the less developed countries depend to a considerable extent on massive international transfer of managerial, entrepreneurial, and technical skills. It is contended that, to the extent that such skills are rooted in the private sector of the industrialized countries, private foreign investment may be a more effective mechanism of transferring such skills than official aid flows. The opposition to private foreign investment springs from not only nationalistic and ideological considerations, but also from a genuine concern regarding its possible adverse economic effects on the countries playing host to private foreign capital. It is argued that the relatively high profits earned by the foreign firms and the scope for extension of ownership of industry provided by the opportunity to re-invest such profits may result in the eventual domination and control of the economy by the foreigners. As Peter Ady succinctly puts it, private foreign investment is seen by some as no more than a mere twentieth century refinement or economic outcome of the gunboat-diplomacy of the imperialist powers of the last century.[1] It is pointed out that increasing ownership of capital stock by the foreigners may significantly

[1] Peter Ady (ed.), *Private Foreign Investment in the Developing World,* Praeger Special Studies in International Economics and Development (New York, 1971), p. 3.

affect the distribution of income in favour of the foreigners, impose a balance of payments burden on the host countries resulting from the outflows of profits and dividends on foreign investment, result in a misallocation of resources and adversely affect employment opportunities for the local population.

However, between the ardent advocates of private foreign investment and its trenchant critics, there are the "strategic pragmatists," who advise the governments of the less developed countries to pursue policies and explore novel methods of foreign enterprise participation designed to harness the beneficial effects of foreign investment and at the same time, control or curtail its damaging effects. It may, however, be difficult to achieve a right balance between the incentives to be provided to attract foreign capital and the restrictions and regulations designed to curb its harmful effects. Nevertheless, the philosophy of moderation has not come too soon. The international flow of private capital has not been on the increase in recent years. The reduced significance of extractive industries and plantations—the traditional strongholds of foreign capital in the last century—and the fears of nationalization and expropriation of foreign interests by local governments have acted as a damper on the private capital flows to the less developed countries.

The official policies of many of the less developed countries reflect the recognition of these facts. On the one hand, they have been offering a variety of incentives to foreign investors in the form of tax concessions, guarantees against expropriation, and assurances regarding repatriation of profits and their capital. On the other hand, they have attempted to curb the harmful effects of foreign capital by demarcating its areas of participation, stipulating conditions regarding the extent of foreign capital ownership and enjoining the foreign firms to employ and train the domestic nationals and allow for domestic capital participation in their ventures. Further, they have also been encouraging novel methods of foreign enterprise participation like joint business ventures, management contracts, and technical collaboration agreements between the domestic and foreign firms.

The Indian experience with private foreign capital participation since independence provides a case study of not only the evolving patterns of private foreign capital participation in the less developed countries, but also illustrates the possible role that foreign enterprise participation can play in the development process and the problems associated with it. The purpose of this chapter is to analyse the role of private foreign capital and enterprise participation in the development process with particular reference to the Indian experience. Section I describes the nature and organizational pattern of private foreign capital and enterprise. Section II examines the arguments regarding the benefits and costs of private foreign capital in the development process. Section III analyses the recent developments in the field of private foreign capital and enterprise in India. Section IV provides a summary of the discussion.

2. Nature and Pattern of Foreign Capital and Enterprise

Portfolio capital flows and direct foreign investment constitute the two main forms of capital participation. Portfolio capital flows refer to the acquisition of securities by individuals or institutions issued by foreign institutions, without any associated control over, or participation in their management.[2] Much of the international capital flows of the last century—nearly three-quarters—took this form. Although foreign direct investment is of comparatively recent origin, it has been expanding rapidly. Foreign direct investment differs from portfolio capital flows in that it confers on the investing entity an ability to exercise control over the decision-making process of the entity in which it invests. The investor acquires this power to exert control over operations by virtue of its owning the capital stock of the entity in which it invests in a major

[2] J. H. Dunning, *Studies in International Investment* (George Allen & Unwin, 1970), p. 2.

way. The distinguishing features of direct investment, then, are the majority ownership of capital stock by the foreign entity and the ability to exercise control over operations which flows from it.[3]

The ability to exert control over decision-making immediately suggests that something more than mere flows of financial capital are involved in the case of foreign direct investment. These relate to the transference of resources other than mere financial capital like technical and managerial skills or, more generally, knowledge and ideas. It is this characteristic of foreign direct investment that renders it a powerful mechanism for the dissemination of technology. With the growing recognition of the role that technology plays in the growth process, emphasis has shifted from the role that direct investment plays in transferring capital to the less developed countries, to the contribution it makes in terms of technology and managerial know-how. It is, indeed, argued that a major factor motivating a firm to undertake direct investment abroad is the monopoly over technology and skills it possesses. If it is only a question of earning a higher rate of return on capital abroad than at home, it could be achieved by portfolio investments rather than by setting up a wholly owned venture abroad or by purchasing a controlling interest in a foreign entity. It is the need to exploit the monopoly over technology and skills of some kind or the other in foreign markets that necessitates foreign direct investment. The extent to which the countries playing host to direct investment can benefit from such transfers of skills and technology depends to a large extent on governmental policy and the efficiency of the local firms in imitating and improvising the techniques and skills of the foreign firms. In other words, it depends on the efficiency of the competitive mechanism in the host countries and the terms and conditions on which foreign capital is allowed into the host country. However, the role played by foreign direct investment in transferring technology to the less developed countries may not be an unmixed blessing. Although the critics concede the potential of foreign direct investment to transmit technology, they take issue with the ownership of capital and exercise of control over operations that it involves.

It is this recognition of the technology-transmitting capabilities of foreign direct investment on the one hand and the concern with ownership of capital and control over operations by the foreigners that it involves on the other, that has led to a search for alternative methods of foreign enterprise participation. Joint business ventures, management contracts, and technical collaboration agreements are the new major forms of foreign enterprise participation that are becoming increasingly popular in recent years. A feature of these arrangements that renders them so appealing is the absence of majority capital ownership by the foreigners and the absence of complete control over operations by the foreign entity. A joint business venture is defined as one in which there is the commitment, for more than a short duration, of funds, facilities, and services by two or more legally separate interests to an enterprise, for their mutual benefit.[4] The emphasis in this form of organization is on the commitment of resources by both entities. The resources committed by the foreign firm need not entirely be financial resources. Its contribution in terms of managerial and technical skills may be more important than its financial contribution. There is indeed no hard and fast rule specifying the share of the two partners in the equity structure

---

[3] India, for example, classifies as direct investment all the net assets of branches of foreign companies in India, as well as the ordinary shares held abroad of those Indian joint-stock companies which can be identified as "foreign controlled." Under the branch form of investment, no local capital participation is involved and the management functions are exercised by the personnel appointed by the parent firm. All those joint stock companies which are incorporated in India, but in which more than 50 per cent of the shareholding is held by a single foreign company, are classified as foreign subsidiaries and identified as foreign controlled.

[4] J. W. C. Tomlinson, *The Joint Venture Process in International Business: India and Pakistan* (MIT Press, 1970).

of the venture. It may be 50-50 or it may be skewed to some extent in favour of one of the partners. Even if the financial contribution of the foreign firm is less than that of the local firm, its contribution in terms of organizational and technical resources would give it an equal status in the venture. The important point to note, however, is that neither of the two partners exercise exclusive control over operations. A technical collaboration agreement is defined broadly as an agreement between a foreigner and an entity created under local law and owned by local public or private interests, in which the foreigner provides management services, technical information, or both, and receives payment in money.[5] The significant points to be noted in this definition are that a technical collaboration agreement precludes foreign ownership of capital and the payment received by the foreigner is in return for technical services rendered and not for equity contributions. Insofar as the foreign firm has no equity interests in the venture, it follows that a technical collaboration agreement also precludes the exercise of formal control over operations by the foreign firm. Although these evolving patterns of foreign enterprise participation represent an attractive alternative to direct foreign investment, their efficiency in transferring technical skills is subject to qualification. First, the extent of knowledge transferred under these arrangements may be less than under direct investment. Second, the absence of control exercised by the foreign firms under these arrangements may be more apparent than real. Third, both joint ventures and technical collaboration agreements may pose problems of conflict between the foreign and the local firms. However, these arrangements are gaining in popularity in the less developed countries and their significance as an alternative to foreign direct investment cannot be ignored altogether. The problems associated with these arrangements will be discussed in greater detail in the context of the Indian experience in Section III.

[5] J. S. Fforde; *International Trade in Managerial skills* (Oxford: Blackwell, 1957).

3. Benefits and Costs of Private Foreign Capital

An assessment of the contribution of private foreign capital to the development process, has to weigh its benefits against its costs. In the final analysis, it is the net contribution that the presence of foreign capital makes to the real income and employment of the recipient country that is important. In Section I the external economies that accrue from foreign investment, in the form of technical skills it provides, was shown to be a major argument in its favour. However, the direct benefits of foreign capital inflows in terms of higher real incomes to local factors of production, lower prices and improved products to consumers, and the increased tax revenues it yields to the Government, need also to be considered.

Although based on restrictive assumptions, the following formal exposition illustrates the direct benefits accruing from the inflows of foreign capital.[6] Assuming perfect competition, constant returns to scale, and only two factors of production—labour and capital—the effects of an inflow of foreign capital on the incomes accruing to the domestic factors of production can be illustrated by the following diagram:

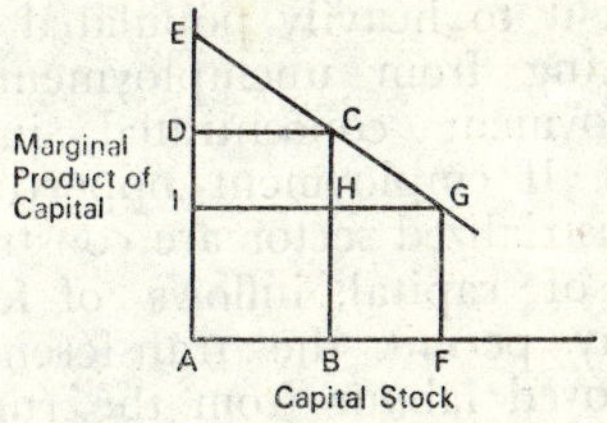

Fig. 1

The line EG relates the marginal physical product of capital to the capital stock, given the amount of labour. To begin with, if the total capital stock is AB, total output is ECBA. On the assumption that

[6] This exposition is taken from G. D. A. McDougall, "The Benefits and Cost of Private Investment from Abroad—A Theoretical Approach," *Bulletin of the Oxford University Institute of Statistics*, Vol. 22, No. 3 (1960).

profits per unit of capital equal the marginal product of capital and that the total capital stock AB is domestically owned, total profits are equal to ABCD and the wage-income accruing to labour is CDE. If there is now an inflow of foreign capital of the amount BF, total output increases by the amount BFGC. Foreign capital earns BFGH of this amount. The addition of BF of new capital to the total capital stock results in a fall in the marginal product of capital and hence, its profit rate. The total profits accruing to domestic capital are now reduced to ABHI. However, the total wages accruing to labour is now GIE. This increase in wages of the amount DCGI is, however, mostly made possible by a redistribution of income away from the domestic capitalists which amounts to DCHI. In addition to this redistribution effect there is also a net gain to domestic factors represented by the triangle CGH. Further, the governmental revenues can also be increased by taxing the profits accruing to foreign capitalists. Given the marginal product curve, both the redistribution effect and the gain to domestic factors will be larger, the larger the inflow of capital.

In addition to the contribution that foreign capital makes to labour productivity, it may also contribute to increased employment. This may be a very significant benefit to heavily populated countries suffering from unemployment and underemployment concentrated in the rural areas. If employment opportunities in the industrialized sector are constrained by a lack of capital, inflows of foreign capital may permit the transference of underemployed labour from the rural to the industrial sector. This would be a clear social gain to the economy, as the newly employed labour in the industrial sector would be earning a wage rate higher than their marginal product in the rural sector.

Against these benefits of foreign capital must be posited its possible adverse effects. Apart from the fears of possible foreign domination and control of the economy, its possible adverse effects on employment, domestic savings and balance of payments must also be considered.

The formal analysis of the benefits of foreign capital presented earlier assumes full employment. In this situation, foreign investment may cause unemployment by drawing away resources from other sectors in the economy, causing the factors of production there to be unemployed or underemployed. In other words, foreign investment may simply displace other resources instead of being an addition to them. However, even in an economy suffering from unemployment, private foreign investment may adversely affect employment opportunities, (a) if foreign firms introduce labour-saving capital-intensive techniques to the economy; (b) if their products compete with those of traditional labour-intensive industries; (c) if it contributes to a general increase in the wage rate for skilled workers, forcing the local firms to adopt capital-intensive labour-saving methods of production. Whether or not foreign firms employ relatively capital-intensive methods of production is largely an empirical matter. It is, however, the presumption based mainly on casual empiricism that the techniques of production adopted by foreign firms may be those perfected in the capital-rich and labour-scarce western industrialized countries and would have little relevance to the factor endowments of the less developed countries. Foreign firms may pay relatively high wage rates both because they employ relatively skilled labour and from a desire to appease local national and trade union sentiments against their operation. Though there is not much empirical evidence available to substantiate these arguments, they nevertheless, rob much of the steam in the formal analysis on the beneficial effects of foreign investment in increasing employment opportunities.

Apart from its deleterious effects on employment, inflows of private foreign capital may also adversely affect the balance of payments of the host country. It is argued, and data is presented, to show that the outflows of foreign exchange in the form of dividends and profits on private foreign investment may exceed the inflows of fresh private capital. In other words, the cost of servicing the past flows may far exceed fresh inflows of foreign capital. Further, if the foreign firms tend to draw away resources employed in foreign exchange earning or saving activities the foreign exchange contribution of private foreign investment may indeed be negative. However, a mere comparison of the fresh inflows of capital with the outflows in the form of dividends, royalties, and repatriation of capital, with the latter being in excess of the former, may not justify this conclusion. The effects of foreign direct investment on productivity, savings in foreign exchange occurring due to import substitution, the impetus it provides to exports, and the other external effects of imported capital and technology on the economy need to be considered in arriving at a judgement on the balance of payments effects.

A more serious criticism of private foreign investment, however, rests on the argument that foreign firms, more often than not, earn monopoly profits in the less developed countries. The formal analysis of the benefits of foreign investment outlined earlier assumes perfect competition. This assumption is hardly realistic. Much of foreign investment may occur in sectors where competition is weak. As Carlos Diaz-Alejandro puts it, "much of direct foreign investment in Latin America has occurred in areas and sectors where markets and competition are weak. Pure competitive models would miss most of what the argument is about."[7] Weak competitive structures in the less developed countries may, in part, be a reflection of the backwardness of their economies. But lack of effective competition may also be due to political factors and the type of trade and industrial policies pursued by the governments of the less developed countries. A recent writer on the subject contends that the foreign firms are able to earn high monopoly profits because of an unholy alliance that exists between the foreign investors and the political power-groups in the less developed countries. These power groups, according to the writer, are shaped, nourished, and sustained by foreign economic power, an external constituency," whose interests coincide with the interests of the indigenous ruling groups.[8] Whether or not indigenous power groups, who may benefit from the operations of the foreign firms, connive to provide monopolistic havens for foreign firms, is debatable. It is, however, possible that the protectionist measures involving tariffs and quotas on imports pursued by many of the less developed countries as a part of their import substitution policies may have provided profitable sheltered markets for foreign firms. While the controls on imports limit competition from abroad, domestic industrial licensing policies may hinder domestic firms from entering the field, thus permitting entrenched foreign firms to enjoy monopoly profits. Further, a xenophilic preference for foreign products and machinery by domestic consumers and producers may be a factor enabling the foreign firms to enjoy high profits.

The "exploitation thesis" centring on the argument that foreign firms earn monopoly profits in the less developed countries, is an old one. It is, however, to be recognized that the high profits earned by the foreign firms may in part be due to the kind of industrial and trade policies pursued by the less developed countries themselves.

It is hard to arrive at any firm conclusion on the question whether the benefits of foreign investment outweigh its costs or not. Even if it is possible to quantitatively assess the direct benefits and costs of foreign investment, it would be impossible to measure all its indirect benefits and costs. The foregoing summary of the benefits and costs of private foreign capital underlines the need to be wary of either undue optimism or pessimism regarding its contribution to the development process. It is, however, clear that it has a role to play in the development pro-

[7] Carlos Diaz-Alejandro, "Direct Foreign Investment in Latin America," in C. P. Kindleberger (ed.), *The International Corporation* (MIT Press, 1970), p. 31.

[8] Richard B. du Boff, "Transferring Wealth from Underdeveloped to Developed Countries via Direct Foreign Investment," *Southern Economic Journal*, Vol. XXXVIII (July 1971) pp. 118–123.

cess and much depends on the policies pursued by the host countries. Effective utilization of private foreign investment in the development process calls for not only policies which discriminate among the various uses to which it can be put, and minimize its costs, but also for institutional changes which foster competition in the economy. Finally, effective utilization of foreign investment in the development process calls for regulation of such investment in the context of the entire development programme.

The Indian experience in the field of private foreign capital and enterprise participation illustrates several of the issues in this section.

4. Private Foreign Capital and Enterprise in the Indian Economy

India has had a long experience with inflows of private foreign capital, especially from Britain. Three-quarters of the foreign capital in India on the eve of Independence was British-owned. As is typical of the colonial pattern of investment, it was mostly concentrated in extractive industries and processing of raw materials for export, and international trade and ancillary industries. It is estimated that in mid-1948, a little over one-quarter of foreign capital was in tea and jute, 17 per cent in trading, 8 per cent in finance and management and about 6 per cent in utilities and transport. Thus, no more than one-fifth was invested in manufacturing other than jute.[9] The predominance of foreign capital in the Indian economy is illustrated by the following figures cited by Michael Kidron: In 1949–50, 85 per cent of the area planted to tea was foreign controlled and more than half of the paid up capital of plantation industries in general, was foreign owned. Foreign control in jute is estimated to have been around 70 to 95 per cent. Similarly, in the case of wool and hides and mining, nearly 60 to 70 per cent of the capital was foreign owned. Overseas shipping was a completely foreign preserve until 1946. Nearly 40 per cent of the import and export trade was handled by foreign firms and much of the financing of international trade was done by foreign exchange banks.

Since Independence, however, significant changes have occurred in the nature and pattern of private foreign capital participation in the Indian economy. Its areas of interest, its volume, and organizational pattern, have all altered considerably. The total outstanding value of foreign direct investments, which stood at Rs 2559 million by mid-1948, had increased to Rs 6547 million by the end of 1967. The share of plantations, mining, and the services, which was around 64 per cent of all such investments in 1948, had declined to 31 per cent by the end of 1967. On the other hand, the share of the manufacturing sector, which was around 28 per cent in 1948, had increased to nearly 49 per cent by the end of 1967.[10] Thus, foreign capital and enterprise have been fanning out towards technologically intensive fields of manufacturing and away from its traditional strongholds of extractive and plantation industries. Another prominent development in the field of foreign enterprise participation in India has been the advent of joint business ventures and technical collaboration agreements between Indian and foreign firms.

Indian Official Policy towards Foreign Capital

The Indian official policy towards foreign capital and enterprise may have considerably influenced these developments. Fears of foreign economic and political domination, founded on the colonial experience, is indicated by the initial hostility towards private foreign capital, expressed by Indian private business interests and political parties alike. Such expressions of hostility, which even demanded that the then existing foreign capital in India should be bought out and eliminated, are well documented in Michael Kidron's excellent annotated account of the evolution of Indian attitudes towards foreign

---

9 Michael Kidron, *Foreign Investments in India* (Oxford University Press, 1965), p. 9.

10 Details of the sectoral distribution are given in Table 2 on page 22.

capital.[11] Such initial hostility and fears of foreign domination found official expression in the Government of India's Industrial Policy Resolution of 1948. While recognizing the value of private foreign investment, the resolution emphasized that in cases in which such participation was allowed, majority ownership and effective control should always rest in Indian hands. The resolution also promised to constrain foreign investment and avoid its adverse effects by legislation. This resolution was, however, not enacted into law and a fully fledged policy statement on foreign capital was issued by the Prime Minister in 1949. This statement held out the promise of a much more liberal policy towards foreign capital than the 1948 resolution. According to this statement, existing foreign capital was to be treated on a par with national enterprises, mutually advantageous conditions for fresh inflows of capital were to be framed, repatriation of capital and remittances of profits were to be allowed, and fair compensation in the event of nationalization was assured. Further, the 1948 stipulations regarding the majority ownership of capital and Indianization of personnel were considerably toned down. The 1949 statement conceded majority ownership to foreign enterprises for a limited period, if it was to be in the national interest. Though speedy Indianization of personnel was still required, the government was prepared to allow non-Indians in top positions if Indians of requisite skill were not available.

This official welcome to foreign capital did not, however, find favour with domestic business interests in the early years following Independence, as Michael Kidrons's documentation shows. However, despite opposition from private business interests, the official attitude of liberalization continued, with the Government relaxing its policy concerning majority ownership in several cases and negotiating double-tax agreements and tax concessions for foreign personnel. Indeed, by the mid-fifties, as industrialization gathered momentum, even the hostility of Indian businessmen towards private foreign enterprise began to wane. The quotas and tariffs on imports imposed by the Government to promote import substitution provided profitable sheltered markets for Indian enterprise. Private foreign capital and enterprise came to be increasingly looked upon as a means of obtaining the much needed foreign exchange and technical know-how.

This change of heart on the part of private interests was accompanied by a stiffening in certain aspects of policy by the Government. Although the broad framework of policy continued to be liberal, specific regulations governing the sectoral allocation and nature of foreign enterprise were stipulated. These stipulations have been prompted both by economic and political considerations. The balance-of-payments effects of private foreign capital has been a prime concern of the official policy-makers. The need to limit the drain on foreign exchange resources that foreign capital and technical participation entails, (in the form of dividends, royalties, and technical fee payments) has been one of the major considerations governing the specific regulations. Added to this is the desire to delimit the areas of possible foreign economic domination. The regulations not only demarcate the industries and sectors where private foreign capital participation is allowed, but also require each act of foreign investment to be subjected to detailed official scrutiny and approval. In 1961 and 1968, the government published lists of industries in which foreign capital and technical participation was to be allowed. While certain key industries like steel were barred from foreign capital on political grounds, it was also to be discouraged from participating in certain 'inessential' consumer goods and service industries on economic grounds. The latest press note of the government categorises industries into three groups: those in which both foreign financial and technical participation may be permitted, industries in which only technical collaboration may be permitted, and industries in which neither technical nor financial participa-

[11] Michael Kidron, op. cit.

tion is considered necessary.[12] The note states that the objective of regulating foreign technical and financial collaboration is to ensure that "foreign capital and technical know-how is utilized in the manner most advantageous to the country, having regard to the current and future needs and specially to strengthen effectively its balance-of-payments position without injuriously affecting the growth of Indian and foreign enterprises already well established in India."[13]

The imports of foreign capital and technology are thus essentially subject to three factors: (1) non-availability of comparable indigenous resources; (2) essentiality in the sense of contributing to development; (3) effects on balance-of-payments. The regulation of the effects of foreign capital participation on the balance-of-payments is to be achieved by stipulations regarding equity participation, royalty payments on technical collaboration agreements, duration of such agreements, and the priorities announced for export-oriented industries. Foreign equity participation is to be in a minority and limited to 40 per cent, save in cases where the project requires sophisticated technology not available in India, or involves a substantial amount of foreign exchange, or is essentially export-oriented.

The tax policies of the Government can be an important instrument both for providing incentives to foreign capital and for its regulation. The tax policies of the Government of India with respect to foreign capital reflect the preference for joint business ventures and the need to attract foreign capital and technology into new industries.[14] The tax rates applicable to foreign companies have been revised from time to time, but a differential has been maintained between the rates applicable to dividends arising out of foreign investment in Indian companies and those arising out of other operations in India. Tax on income from Indian companies is charged at 41.5 per cent whereas other income is charged at 61.5 per cent. Similarly, rates charged for new companies (those incorporated after 1961) are lower than those charged for old companies. The tax on royalties and technical fees is 50 per cent for agreements entered into prior to 1961. Further, income from certain designated priority industries is taxed at a lower rate. New industrial undertakings are also granted a tax holiday on profits up to 6 per cent per annum for a period of six years. A development rebate of 20 per cent of the value of plant is also given. All these concessions are designed for the development of new and priority industries. Tax concessions are also granted to foreign personnel relevant to foreign collaborations. They are exempt from income taxation up to a certain period after their arrival in India—six months for managers and three years for engineers.

The foregoing embodies the general policies of the Government with regard to private foreign capital. However, there are no objective set of criteria on the basis of which applications for foreign collaboration are screened. Each case is to be judged on its merits by the authorities. This involves a cumbersome procedure requiring the applicants to submit a host of information to several ministries and licensing authorities screening the applications.[15] The cumbersome nature of these procedures, the lack of any objective criteria for approving applications, and the inordinate delays involved in screening applications have been noted by more than one writer on the subject. In the case of twenty-three firms surveyed by the National Council of Applied Economic Research

[12] Government of India, Press Note, July 20, 1968, printed in *Foreign Investment and Collaboration—Guide Lines* (New Delhi: Indian Investment Centre).

[13] Ibid.

[14] For a detailed discussion of Indian tax policies towards foreign capital see *Foreign Technology and Investment—A Study of their Role in India's Industrialization* (New Delhi: National Council of Applied Economic Research, June 1971). Ch. 6.

[15] A succinct summary of the procedures governing the approval of applications for foreign collaboration is given in *Foreign Collaboration in Indian Industry* (Bombay: Reserve Bank of India), p. 9. A penetrating critique of Indian industrial policies is found in J. N. Bhagwati and P. Desai, *India—Planning for Industrialisation* (London: Oxford University Press, 1970).

it was found that the average time taken by the Government to approve their proposals for collaboration was a year and nine months.[16] The Estimates Committee of the Government of India (1967–68) stated that "the Committee regrets to note that there is considerable delay in finalizing applications for foreign collaboration. As many as 42% of the applications in 1965 and 39% in 1966 remained undecided after six months of their receipt. Out of these, over 12% in 1965 and over 16% in 1966 were undecided after more than a year."[17] It is to be noted, however, that the Government has set up a central agency in 1968—the Foreign Investment Board—to deal with all matters relating to private foreign investment and collaboration. The Board is to supervize the activities of the various ministries involved in screening the applications for collaboration and to endeavour to dispose of all applications within a period of three months from the date of submission.

Magnitude and Composition of Private Foreign Capital in India

What has been the impact of official economic policies on the magnitude and composition of private capital flows? Considering the fact that India provides heavily protected and very profitable domestic markets, one would expect it to attract a sizeable amount of private foreign capital. However, compared to other developing countries like Mexico, Taiwan, and Malaysia, whose markets are much less protected than those of India, the inflows of private foreign capital into India have been meagre. Over the period 1956–61, net inflows of private foreign capital into the economy accounted for only 4.4% of the total investment in the private sector and this figure stood at 7.5% over the period 1961–66. In the case of Malaysia, on an average over the period 1960–63, for which data are available, private foreign capital flows accounted for nearly 30% of the domestic fixed capital formation in the private sector.[18] Further, much of the foreign investment that has occurred in India in recent years has been on account of reinvested earnings and investment in kind (Table 1).

Table 1. Pattern of Foreign Direct Investment Inflows into India

(Rs million)

	Cash Inflow	Reinvested Earnings	Non-cash Inflow	Gross Inflow
1956-61 (Annual Average)	45.0	137.0	170.0	352.0
1963-64	40.0	98.0	141.0	279.0
1964-65	22.0	204.0	190.0	416.0
1965-66	26.0	188.0	121.0	335.0
1966-67	26.0	149.0	73.0	248.0

SOURCE: *India's Foreign Liabilities and Assets*, 1961, (Bombay: Reserve Bank of India, 1964) and "India's International Investment Position," *Reserve Bank of India Bulletin* (August 1969).

The investments in kind are accounted for by the imports of equipment and know-how by the foreign subsidiaries operating in India from their parent companies.

The meagre inflows of fresh foreign capital into the country go to show that the existence of profitable sheltered markets alone may not be enough to attract foreign capital. The "climate for foreign investment" that prevails in the country may be more important than profitable markets resulting from protectionist policies. The phrase "climate for foreign investment" embodies a number of elements. The tax policies enunciated by the government, its strictures regarding the em-

[16] National Council of Applied Economic Research, op. cit., p. 55.

[17] Quoted in J. N. Bhagwati and P. Desai, op. cit., p. 262.

[18] These estimates are taken from A. I. MacBean and V. N. Balasubramanyam, *Benefit Cost Analysis of Foreign Direct Investment with Special Reference to Asia*, unpublished study prepared for the UN.

ployment of local nationals by the foreign firms, its ability to provide social overheads, its policy on repatriation of profits, the assurances it gives regarding compensation in case of nationalization and its attitude towards private enterprise in general, all fall under the head "climate." The Indian policy statements, though not lacking in incentives for private foreign capital, display an ambivalent attitude towards it. Assurances regarding repatriation of profits and compensation in case of nationalization and tax incentives are proffered. But the protracted negotiations which a policy of judging each case on its merits involves, the insistence that majority ownership of capital should rest in Indian hands, and the stipulations regarding employment of local nationals may have discouraged foreign investors. Further stipulations barring entry for foreign firms into consumer goods industries may also have acted as a factor inhibiting capital inflows. The logic of barring entry of foreign capital into such industries is questionable. As Bhagwati and Desai argue, "if a foreign investor buys up a restaurant, this will bring into the economy foreign exchange which can be used to import 'essential' machinery. To argue, therefore, that foreign investment should be excluded from the restaurant industry is just a simple and widespread fallacy."[19]

It does not, however, follow that all regulation of foreign investment was ill conceived. As shown in the earlier section, there is a need for policies designed to curb the adverse effects of foreign investment. Regulation of foreign investment in the interests of guarding the balance of payments position of the country and protecting small-scale domestic entrepreneurs against the competition from large-sized international firms may have been necessary. Demarcating the sectors of foreign capital participation and the insistence on the need for foreign firms to contribute to the exchange earnings of the country may be justified. But it is the policy of judging each case on its merits, which involves protracted negotiations and the expenditure of managerial time and resources by the prospective investors, that is questionable.

Although fresh capital inflows into the country have been relatively low, there have occurred some significant changes in the composition and organizational pattern of foreign capital participation in India. First, foreign capital has increasingly moved into technologically intensive fields of activity. Secondly, joint business ventures and technical collaboration agreements have gained in importance. Table 2 shows the changes in the sectoral distribution of direct foreign investment in India since Independence.

The data in Table 2 show the increasing bias of foreign direct investment towards the manufacturing sector. Within the manufacturing sector, chemicals, metals and metal products, machinery and tools, and transport equipment, have grown in importance. The explanation for this changing composition of foreign investment is to be sought both in the profitable sheltered markets these manufacturing industries provide and the official policy of discouraging such investment in the services sector and consumer goods industries. This is evidenced by the decline in the percentage share of investment going into food, beverages, and tobacco and textile products. The case with plantations and mining is similar.

Significant changes have also occurred in the sources of supply of private foreign capital. Traditionally, the UK has been the major source of direct investment. Although it still leads the field, its share declined from 80 per cent of the total of foreign investment in India in 1948, to 48 per cent at the end of March 1967. The U.S. investments, on the other hand, increased from 4.2 per cent of the total in 1948 to 25.2 per cent by the end of March 1967. Japan and West Germany, which did not figure at all in 1948, had shares of 3.7 per cent and 5 per cent respectively, by the end of March 1967. While the past political and economic ties of India with U.K. explains her predominant position, new entrants may have been attracted by the profitable markets and the relatively stable political climate that prevails in India. New entrants may also be more

[19] J. N. Bhagwati and P. Desai, op. cit., p. 224.

Table 2. Sectoral Distribution of Foreign Direct Investment in India 1948, 1961 and 1967 (Rs million)

	Mid 1948: Investment	%	End of 1961 Investment	%	End of 1967 Investment	%
1 Plantations	523	20.4	1038	17.9	1072	16.4
2 Mining	115	4.5	124	2.1	44	0.7
3 Petroleum	223	8.7	1486	1276		
4 Manufacturing of:	710	27.8	2194	37.8	3226	49.0
Food, Beverages & Tobacco	101	14.2	361	16.0	350	10.8
Textile Products	280	39.4	207	9.4	161	5.0
Transport Equipment	10	1.4	130	5.9	229	7.1
Machinery & Tools	12	1.7	114	5.2	213	6.3
Metals & Metal Products	80	11.3	321	14.6	495	15.3
Electrical Machinery	48	6.8	147	6.7	284	8.8
Chemicals	80	11.3	505	23.0	946	29.3
Others	99	13.9	409	18.6	548	17.0
5 Services	988	38.6	962	16.6	929	14.2
TOTAL	2559	100.0	5804	100.0	6547	100.0

SOURCE: *Reserve Bank of India Bulletin* (various issues)

willing to explore and make the best of the opportunities than old investors, whose attitudes and judgements may have been crystallized and even fossilized. John P. Lewis's observation with regard to the contrasting reaction of the American and British investors to the official policies requiring speedy Indianization of personnel is worth recording in this context: "In this regard they [the Americans] differ almost comically from the managers of some of the old line, pre-Independence British businessmen who soberly assure their interviewers that Indians, while capable of good routine management, simply lack the capacity for handling breakdowns and other stress situations in the industrial process."[20] The influx of several countries into the field may have broadened the choice of sources of supply of capital and technology to the Indian entrepreneur and strengthened his bargaining position.

Technical Collaboration Agreements and Joint Business Ventures

A major development in the field of private foreign enterprise participation in India has been the advent of technical collaboration agreements and joint business ventures. The characteristic features

[20] John P. Lewis, *Quiet Crisis in India* (Brookings Institution, 1962), p. 230.

of these arrangements were described in Section 2. Table 3 shows the number and distribution of these arrangements by country of participation.

A total number of 3557 collaboration agreements were approved by the Government of India over the period 1948–70. Of these only 366 agreements were approved between the years 1948–56. Indian industrialization gathered momentum with the inception of the second Five Year Plan in 1956. The need for technology and know-how on the part of the Indian entrepreneurs and the attraction of sheltered markets provided by the stringent controls on imports explains the upsurge in foreign collaboration agreements since 1956. The growth in collaboration agreements also illustrates the tendency of private foreign enterprise to veer away from financial collaboration. Out of the 75 agreements finalized between Independence and 1949, only 41 were for pure technical collaboration. However, over the period 1957–63 more than 1700 collaboration agreements were approved, but only 246 of these involved foreign financial participation.[21] Thus, though joint ventures involving foreign capital participation have occurred, pure technical collaboration agreements have been the most important form of participation. Further, even in cases where foreign financial participation is involved not all of the agreements may involve inflows of capital from abroad. The equity held by the foreigners may merely represent an allotment by the Indian firms, of a part of their equity to

Table 3. Number of Collaboration Agreements Approved by the Government of India, Classified According to Countries of Participation

	1957	1958	1959	1960	1961	1962	1963	1964	1965	1966	1967	1968	1969	1970	Total
UK	17	34	52	120	126	79	70	105	60	44	50	19	34	39	849
USA	6	4	10	61	77	57	67	78	48	42	34	36	18	41	579
W. Germany	2	6	13	58	67	42	48	68	44	41	24	22	28	28	491
Japan	1	3	8	39	30	24	32	35	26	18	21	12	17	15	281
Switzerland	—	2	1	13	19	19	19	19	18	19	6	6	7	13	152
France	2	1	2	9	16	14	16	11	12	11	9	8	7	7	125
Italy	4	4	4	9	13	11	6	8	7	3	6	3	3	8	89
E. Germany	—	—	1	5	4	5	10	24	6	3	2	2	5	5	72
Sweden	1	—	1	13	—	6	1	6	3	5	8	4	2	3	53
Netherlands	1	—	—	6	10	7	4	5	2	3	4	2	3	3	50
Denmark	—	—	—	6	5	1	5	4	3	3	1	4	1	5	38
Others	47	49	56	35	37	32	22	25	15	21	17	13	9	20	414
TOTAL	81	103	150	380	403	298	298	403	242	202	182	131	135	183	3191

SOURCE: Compiled by the Indian Investment Centre, New Delhi.

[21] M. Kidron, op. cit., p. 260.

Table 4. Technical Collaboration Agreements Classified by Industry, 1957-70

	1957	1958	1959	1960	1961	1962	1963	1964	1965	1966	1967	1968	1969	Jan. to Dec. 1970	Total 1957 to Dec. 1970
1. Electrical Equipment, Apparatus, components etc.	4	6	9	46	69	63	52	35	22	21	24	16	16	21	404
2. Industrial Machinery (other than textile machinery)	6	3	8	34	47	29	40	68	40	44	19	25	32	43	433
3. Machine Tools & accessories	—	4	6	26	35	17	26	33	14	19	21	15	3	12	231
4 Transport equipment	5	7	13	38	23	26	24	26	7	12	11	4	6	14	261
5. Basic Chemicals	7	8	18	25	37	4	4	26	14	10	11	7	4	4	179
6. Chemical products	3	2	9	8	13	38	24	25	20	5	12	5	7	10	181
7. Heavy Electrical Equipment (Generation and Distribution	7	6	4	35	27	—	2	20	10	8	13	10	4	5	151
8. Iron & Steel Products	2	5	11	25	17	12	13	21	9	12	2	7	2	6	124
9. Instruments	—	—	1	19	9	12	21	20	17	7	8	—	7	1	124
10. Textile Machinery	1	1	4	15	15	4	5	15	18	10	1	7	3	6	105
11. Material Handling & Construction Equipment	1	1	4	18	19	4	4	13	8	8	9	3	7	5	104
12. Castings & Forgings	1	—	1	9	10	5	12	27	5	6	1	1	1	—	79
13. Drugs & Pharmaceuticals	4	8	4	11	7	9	6	6	5	3	5	5	1	3	77
14. Ceramic & Glassware	2	3	2	10	11	10	5	8	3	4	—	2	3	2	65
15. Paper & Paper Products	2	2	—	9	10	5	5	4	5	2	1	2	1	1	49
16. Metal & Metal Products	2	1	1	3	6	6	8	5	1	1	5	2	2	4	47
17. Technical Consultancy	—	2	1	—	—	5	9	6	1	1	4	2	2	5	38
18. Agricultural Machinery & implements	1	—	3	4	2	3	3	2	2	3	2	4	9	4	42
19. Fertilizers	—	—	—	—	2	1	1	—	3	3	—	1	—	1	12
20. Pesticides	1	2	2	1	1	—	—	—	—	—	1	2	—	—	12
21. Others	32	42	49	44	43	43	37	47	38	23	32	11	25	36	500
TOTAL	81	103	150	380	403	298	298	403	242	202	182	135	135	183	3191

the foreign firms, in lieu of royalty and technical fee payments to be made for imports of technology, or in addition to such payments.

These collaboration agreements have also been heavily concentrated in technologically intensive fields of manufacturing activity. Table 4 shows the distribution of collaboration agreements by industry. Electrical machinery, non-electrical machinery and machine tools, transport equipment and chemicals accounted for more than 50 per cent of the agreements approved during the years 1957–70.[22]

The growth in the number of technical collaboration agreements has given rise to several important issues. First, it has been argued that it has resulted in an over-import of technology and often, repetitive borrowing of the same technology has occurred. It is argued that imports of technology from abroad may have had adverse effects on indigenous research and development effort. Secondly, there is the more general issue relating to the viability of technical collaboration agreements as mechanisms for transferring technical know-how to the less developed countries. By viability is meant the scope they offer for effectively transferring technology on an enterprise-to-enterprise basis, their effects on the balance of payments of the borrowing countries and the extent of control the foreign firm can exercise over the operations of local firms.

On the basis of available information it is difficult to assess whether or not over-imports of technology have occurred. In the early years, a number of agreements were approved in "inessential" consumer goods industries like toys, footwear, ink, toothpaste, etc. But the number of agreements is a poor guide to the nature of technology imported. The assistance rendered may have been confined to marketing the product or the mere use of foreign brand names. Further, as Bhagwati and Desai point out, the argument is better made against the very establishment of these industries than arguing that imports of technology should not be allowed into these industries.[23]

The more important issue relates to the viability of these agreements as transfer mechanisms. The success of these agreements as transfer mechanisms depends on the will to transfer on the part of foreign firms and the ability to assimilate and utilize the borrowed technology on the part of the local firms. The extent of knowledge transferred may depend on the degree of lender involvement through asset ownership and managerial control. Technical collaboration agreements are by definition bereft of foreign participation and control. The knowledge transferred under these agreements may not be very extensive. In the Indian case much of the knowledge transferred under the technical collaboration agreements has been limited to the loan of blueprints, drawings, designs, process charts, flow sheets, etc. The technical involvement of the foreign firms was much higher in the case of joint ventures involving foreign financial participation. It included the training of Indian engineers and managers abroad, assistance in plant construction and help in procuring raw materials and marketing the product.[24]

The success of a technical transplant also depends on the ability to absorb the knowledge on the part of the knowledge-importing firms. The effective utilization of imported knowledge depends on the ability of local firms to restructure and adapt the imported knowledge to suit

22 It is to be noted that the number of agreements approved in each industry group may not provide a correct guide to the importance of these groups in the field of technical collaboration. The number of agreements need to be weighted by some index indicating the relative size of each of the industry groups in order to arrive at a correct judgement regarding the relative importance of the different industries in the field of technology imports. Moreover, the number of agreements in itself does not indicate anything about the quality and magnitude of the technology imported. Limitations of space preclude a detailed discussion of these problems in this paper. One should, however, be aware of these limitations in drawing conclusions about the relative importance of different industry groups in the field of foreign collaboration.

23 J. N. Bhagwati and P. Desai, op. cit., p. 226.

24 V. N. Balasubramanyam, *International Transfer of Technical Knowledge to India* (Praeger Special Studies in International Economics and Development, March, 1973).

local conditions, and the availability of local sources of supply for components which meet the specifications and standards required by the foreign technology. The often cited success story of Japanese industry in the field of technology-imports illustrates the significance of these factors.[25] The distinguishing characteristic of Japanese industry has been its ability to restructure and adapt imported knowledge by means of indigenous research efforts. The presence of a well-integrated sector of small subcontractors that could produce components to prescribed engineering standards and under tight production schedules also explains the success story of Japan. These basic ingredients are yet to take shape in India. Paradoxically enough, the success of technical collaboration agreements seems to call for the very skills and abilities which many of the less developed countries lack. The foreign firms entering into technical collaboration agreements may have been of very little assistance in restructuring the knowledge to suit the local conditions. In the Indian case it was found that such assistance, if it had occurred at all, was mostly in the case of joint ventures.[26]

Further, there is the issue of control exercised by the foreign firms. Theoretically, the foreign firms cannot be expected to exercise control over operations when their involvement is confined to technical assistance. However, in practice they may be able to stipulate various restrictive clauses in the agreements which enable them to exercise a certain degree of effective control over operations. These restrictive clauses relate to exports, sources of supply of raw materials, production standards, and minimum royalty payments. Table 5 summarizes the data on restrictive clauses stipulated by foreign firms in the case of Indo-foreign collaboration agreements. The data relates to a sample of 1951 agreements surveyed by the Reserve Bank of India. The agreements are classified according to (a) for-

25 See T. Ozawa, "Imitation, Innovation and Japanese Exports," in P. B. Kenen Lawrence (ed.), *Open Economy* (Columbia University Press, 1968).

26 V. N. Balasubramanyam, op. cit.

Table 5. Restrictive Clauses in Indo-foreign Technical Collaboration Agreements

Type of Restriction	Number of agreements with restrictive clauses: Subsidiaries	Minority foreign equity participation	Pure Technical Collaboration	Total
1 Export restrictions:	56	230	169	455
(*a*) Total prohibition exports	3	15	18	36
(*b*) Area restrictions	19	118	102	239
(*c*) Permission of collaborators needed	32	80	37	149
2 Sources of supply of materials & equipment	14	46	94	154
3 Restrictions on production pattern	2	36	27	65
4 Payment of minimum royalty	1	14	40	55
5 Restrictions sales procedure	6	7	5	18
6 Others	1	1	1	3
TOTAL NUMBER OF AGREEMENTS WITH RESTRICTIONS	63	251	213	527
TOTAL NUMBER OF AGREEMENTS	144	445	462	1051

SOURCE: *Foreign Collaboration in Indian Industry—A Survey Report* (Bombay: Reserve Bank of India) p. 106.

mal technical collaboration agreements entered into by foreign subsidiaries in India with their parent firms; (b) agreements involving both foreign technical and financial participation; (c) purely technical collaboration agreements contracted by Indian firms.

Restrictions relating to exports are the most important. Total prohibition of exports are in a minority, while area restrictions, stipulating the countries to which Indian firms may or may not export, obtained in more than 53 per cent of the agreements surveyed. Of the other type of restrictions the most important one is that relating to sources of supply. Nearly 30 per cent of the agreements surveyed by the Bank were of this type. Further, pure technical collaboration agreements involving no foreign financial participation accounted for a majority of the agreements with such restrictions. Export restriction clauses are a device by which the foreign firms attempt to guard the markets for their own products or the sales of firms in foreign countries to whom they may have sold licences. Such restrictions may, therefore, not only be necessary to shelter their own markets from competition by Indian firms, but also to preserve their market for technology. The foreign firms may permit exports to certain countries the markets of which they find difficult to service. Thus, such export restrictions are in the nature of a market-sharing device. They are, however, a control device to the extent they can influence future market prospects for India. The restrictions on sources of supply of raw materials and components may not only tie the Indian firms to a particular source of supply but also enable the foreign firms to charge a mark-up on the plant and equipment they supply. Such mark-ups may provide the foreign firms with an additional avenue of returns, especially when the government has imposed a ceiling on the rates of royalty to be paid.

It is difficult to assess whether or not the growth in technical collaboration agreements has resulted in widespread technological gains to the economy. A study on foreign investment and technology by the National Council of Applied Economic Research has concluded that "imported technology has been widely diffused in the economy....imports of technology and associated equipment have played an important role in industrial expansion as well as in the prevention of monopolistic conditions."[27] On the other hand Michael Kidron, in his study on foreign investments in India, states that imported skills do not permeate the economy to any great extent."[28] The conclusion of the National Council Study is based on a comprehensive examination of the distribution of collaboration agreements and royalties paid on imported know-how by different industrial groups and different size classes of firms in Indian industry. Michael Kidron's conclusion is based on casual observation and case studies. As argued earlier, the number of agreements approved in different industry groups does not provide a satisfactory guide to the nature and extent of technology imported, the terms and conditions on which it is imported and its effective utilisation. Similarly, casual observation and stray case studies may not provide enough evidence to pass an adverse judgement on the role of technical collaboration agreements. However, an examination of the nature and characteristics of these agreements raises a more general issue. Are such agreements, which are of an arm's length nature, preferable to direct foreign investment? It can be argued that in view of the many limitations that beset these agreements, they may not be a very effective mechanism for transferring technical know-how to countries at an intermediate stage of development, such as India. They may be more suited to relatively developed economies like Japan which have the requisite skills and resources to restructure and utilize the imported know-how. Furthermore, these agreements also pose problems of regulation and control. It is, therefore, possible that direct investment with more lender involvement through asset ownership and joint ventures involving foreign financial participation may be a prefer-

[27] National Council of Applied Economic Research, op. cit., p. 17.

[28] Michael Kidron, op. cit., p. 303.

able mechanism for importing foreign skills and know-how. This conclusion is, however, predicated on the assumption that the host countries undertake measures to enlarge effective competition in their own economies and judiciously regulate the sectoral distribution of foreign capital participation. This is not to say that technical collaboration agreements should altogether be discarded. The need to accelerate development being paramount, none of the means available to do so can be dismissed. They can be effectively utilized if domestic research and development efforts are directed towards improving the absorptive capacity of the economy. Such agreements may be eminently suitable in the case of sectors and industries which are capable of restructuring and assimilating imported know-how.

The Balance-of-Payments Issue

A major cause of concern with imports of private foreign capital and technology are their effects on the balance-of-payments of the country. The argument that it adversely affects the balance-of-payments of the country is usually supported by data to show that the outflows in the form of dividends, profits, royalty, and technical fee payments exceeds the inflows of private foreign capital. Table 6 shows data

Table 6. Net Inflows of Private Foreign Capital and Outflows of Investment Income
(Rs million)

Year	Inflows on a/c of Direct Investment	Portfolio capital Inflows	Outflows of Investment Income
1963-64	224.0	449.0	1029.0
1964-65	429.0	389.0	1197.0
1965-66	219.0	223.0	1343.0
1966-67	216.0	830.0	2039.0

SOURCE: "India's International Investment Position," *Reserve Bank of India Bulletin*, August 1969.

for India on net inflows of capital (including reinvested earnings) on account of direct investment and outflows of investment income for the years 1960–65 for which data are readily available.

The outflows in each year have been in excess of the inflows. Furthermore, payments for imported know-how in the form of royalties and technical fees also show a rapid increase, and indeed they have grown much faster than dividend payments on direct investment (Table 7).

Table 7. Royalty Technical Fee Payments and Dividend Payments
(Rs million)

Year	Dividend Payments	Royalty & Technical Fee Payments
1956-57	71.0	67.0
1957-58	88.0	56.0
1958-59	83.0	57.0
1959-60	117.0	76.0
1960-61	126.0	117.0
1961-62	185.0	155.0
1962-63	215.0	167.0
1963-64	188.0	184.0
1964-65	220.0	223.0
1965-66	194.0	253.0
1966-67	288.0	338.0

SOURCE: Reserve Bank of India, *Foreign Collaboration in Indian Industry.*

Dividend payments, which averaged around Rs 97 million per year over the five year period 1956–60, had increased to an annual average of Rs 200 million over the period 1961–66. Royalty and technical fee payments which average around Rs 71 million over the first period had increased to Rs 219 million over the second period. The relatively higher rate of growth of royalty and technical fee payments attests to the profitability of technical collaboration agreements for the foreign firms.

It may, however, be far-fetched to conclude, on the basis of the above data, that imports of private foreign capital and technology have resulted in a net foreign exchange cost to the country. This would be too partial an analysis. At the very least the effects of such imports in terms of increased exports and import replacement must be taken into account. In addition, the external economies and diseconomies resulting from imports of capital and technology on foreign exchange flows need to be considered. Moreover, the high foreign exchange costs may have been due to poor project selection and the over-protective policies of industrialization followed by the country, rather than the fault of the form of financing. Some of the projects in which foreign capital and technical collaboration have been allowed may have been in inefficient ventures producing on too small a scale with high-cost imported components.

5. Conclusions

The foregoing review brings to the fore the major developments and issues in the field of private foreign enterprise participation in India. First, the inflow of new private foreign capital into India has been relatively meagre. Much of the increase in direct investment that has occurred is accounted for by reinvestment of profits and investments in kind. Secondly, there has occurred a significant change in the sectoral distribution of private foreign investment in favour of technologically intensive manufacturing industries. Thirdly, though Britain continues to lead the field both as a supplier of capital and technology, other countries, principally the USA, Japan, and West Germany, have been important new entrants to the field. The attractive markets provided by India and the relatively stable political climate that prevails in the country explains the entry of these countries. Fourthly, Indian official policies have had a significant impact on the organizational pattern of foreign enterprise participation in India. Technical collaboration agreements and joint ventures have grown in importance since the late fifties.

The role of private foreign capital and enterprise in the development process is a subject with complex ramifications. The nature of the subject precludes settled conclusions. It cannot, however, be denied that it has an important role to play in the development process. The record of India in attracting private foreign capital relative to that of other developing countries like Malaysia, Mexico, and Taiwan has not been encouraging. It is debatable whether technical collaboration agreements which have grown more significantly than direct foreign investment have resulted in net gains to the country. However, as argued earlier, they cannot altogether be discarded. The remedy for the future lies not in abjuring private foreign capital and enterprise altogether but in making sure that the social rates of return from such investment exceed the marginal cost of obtaining it. Attraction and effective utilization of foreign capital and technology calls for a more effective policy framework and institutional change. The recent streamlining of official policies and liberalization of industrial licensing and import policies may go a long way in this direction. Effective utilization of imported technology also calls for indigenous research and development efforts directed at restructuring and assimilating imported technology.

24

Economic Integration in South Asia

PREM P. GANDHI

1. Introduction

The events in the past couple of years have moved so swiftly on the Indian subcontinent that they have marked the end of the old geopolitical structure of that area. Though it is too early to discern the full impact of the far-reaching consequences of the chain of events that started at the close of 1970, yet one can, with some certainty, note some early signs. For one thing, the creation of Bangladesh, along with the disintegration of Pakistan's political and economic structure, has written a new political equation in the area. India's victory in its recent conflict with Pakistan over East Bengal (formerly East Pakistan) has brought a new mood of national confidence and a strength to its role as a regional power in South Asia. Moreover, the resultant Simla Accord reached by India and Pakistan visualizes the peaceful settlement of thorny political problems between them and suggests the possibility of increasing trade and economic cooperation. With a background of such optimism prevailing in the subcontinent we may cautiously explore in this study the possibility of economic integration, not only between India and Pakistan, but in the whole of South Asia which also includes Nepal, Burma, and Malaysia. At the same time the study also suggests the possibility of Bangladesh's membership in any viable integration scheme in this region at some future date.

The increased strength of India in the subcontinent may have made the possibility of integration more difficult by causing uneasiness among its neighbours. It may also have revived old political frictions. The dominant position of the Indian economy in South Asia causes nervousness and suspicions about its objectives and motives regarding any regional integration plans. At the same time, though the type and extent of cooperation is by no means defined or clearly appreciated in India, its attitude towards regionalism has been ambivalent, at least in the past. It is surprising to find that India has enthusiastically supported economic cooperation in the South Asian region and Asia as a whole, while rejecting any stronger regional grouping. The explanation lies in her foreign policy objectives, in particular the idea of non-alignment. This conflict between economic and political objectives has made the question of India's role in economic integration ambiguous. This is not to suggest that the pursuit of both the economic and political objectives is mutually exclusive, but it does involve some changes and adjustments in order to achieve the foreign policy results.

This paper, by surveying the major foreign policy objectives and India's responses in the past, intends to show the role which India can play in promoting economic integration in South Asia and the resultant benefits to India. The paper is divided into two major sections. The first section is concerned with the scope of economic integration and is mostly definitional in order to lay out the broad outlines of regional cooperation. In other words, this segment of the paper deals with the question: "What are we talking about?" The second section explores the broad foreign policy objectives, divided into political, economic, and socio-cultural groups. Since such a vast topic needs detailed research and interdisciplinary expertise in the area of foreign policy, we would limit our analysis to the more basic and obvious factors.

2. Definition and Types of Economic Integration

Definition

In surveying some of the interpretations given to economic integration, Balassa concludes that it is both a process as well as a state of affairs. "Regarded as a process, it encompasses various measures abolishing discrimination between economic units belonging to different national States; viewed as a state of affairs, it can be represented by the absence of various forms of discrimination between national economies."[1] However, the mere abolition of discrimination may not be enough to achieve the optimum efficiency that underlies the justification for economic integration. In fact, Tinbergen distinguishes between negative and positive integration. Negative integration involves the abolition of a number of restrictive or trade impediments and thus results in a better division of labour and specialization in products most suited to the domestic conditions of the member countries. But it is the positive integration that thrusts in the kind of cooperation and coordination of national economic policies to make economic integration a more meaningful entity. Positive integration requires the creation of new institutions and their instruments; or the modification of existing instruments. In Tinbergen's definition, then, integration is the creation of the most desirable structure of the international economy, removing artificial hindrances to the optimal operation and introducing deliberately all desirable elements of coordination or unification.[2] Economic integration, *par excellence,* of all the countries, would imply "one world" in political terms, which goes much beyond what the classical economists had either envisaged or advocated.

Having so defined economic integration, it should also be distinguished from economic cooperation. Though ECAFE (Economic Commission on Asia and Far East) has used the two interchangeably in its studies, the terms differ, both qualitatively and quantitatively. Economic cooperation is by far the looser version of the two. Economic integration, on the other hand, involves a substantial degree of formal commitment to remove economic barriers and other quantitative restrictions in the way of economic interaction. The higher forms of economic integration may also involve some loss of national sovereignty through substantial governmental commitments in changing domestic economic policies. This may not be the case in economic cooperation, though the distinction here becomes rather thin. In any event, as Balassa notes, "distinguishing between cooperation and integration, we

[1] B. Balassa, "Towards a Theory of Economic Integration", *Kyklos,* No. 1 (1961), p. 4.

[2] J. Tinbergen, *International Economic Integration* (Amsterdam: North Holland Publishing Company 1958), Chap. 1.

put the main characteristics of the latter—the abolition of discrimination within an area—in clearer focus and it becomes possible to give the concept definite meaning without unnecessarily diluting it through the inclusion of diverse actions in the field of international cooperation."[3]

Types of Economic Integration

With this background, we can distinguish between a number of different types of economic integration involving various degrees of economic association and the resultant abrogation of national sovereignty. ECAFE lists the following types of economic integration schemes in descending order of political significance and the degree of governmental commitments:

1. Economic union
2. Customs union
3. Free trade union
4. Sectoral or partial integration
5. Preferential application of quantitative restrictions
6. Preferential applications of tariffs
7. Long-term trade contracts.[4]

This range of proposals for economic integration differs from each other not only in terms of the commitments, but also in the resultant benefits. Each succeeding scheme on the list is less formal than the previous one. Thus, the pros and cons of any given proposal would depend upon the participants' assessment of the relative economic, political, and social costs and benefits of regionalism.

On the one extreme of this spectrum of integration is economic union, which represents complete economic integration of a group of countries. Under this scheme there is not only a complete freedom of movement of goods and services, but also of the factors of production. Except for land, the factors of production move unrestricted between the member countries in order to gain the maximum returns. Along with this unrestricted mobility, economic union necessitates coordination and harmonization of national economic policies with the possibility of political integration. The best known example is the European Economic Community, popularly called the Common Market, comprising of France, West Germany, Italy, The Netherlands, Belgium, and Luxembourg.

Customs union differs from the economic union in the sense that here the integration is limited to the customs, i.e. elimination of tariff barriers between the participating countries, along with the establishment of a common external tariff wall against the non-members. The Central American Integration Programme, when finally matured, may be one example of customs union, another being the Benelux in the past.[5]

Free trade area differs from the first two in that it maintains national external tariffs against the non-members while eliminating the internal tariffs against the member nations. In a way, it implies the establishment of a common market in the trade of all the constituent territories while retaining the freedom of individual tariff preferences or arrangements with outsiders. The establishment of the EFTA (European Free Trade Association) in 1959, and LAFTA (Latin American Free Trade Association) in 1960, are examples of such a proposal of economic integration.[6]

Sectoral or partial integration implies the establishment of a common market only in one sector or industry, like in the case of European Coal and Steel Community in 1951, or the Free Trade Agreement between the U.S.A. and Canada in automobiles in 1965.

---

3 Balassa, op. cit., p. 5.

4 ECAFE, "Economic Bulletin for Asia and the Far East," Vol. XII, No. 1 (June 1961), p. 3.

5 Countries in the Central American Integration Programme are Guatemala, Honduras, El Salvador, Nicaragua and Costa Rica. Benelux represented the Association of Belgium, The Netherlands and Luxembourg.

6 EFTA was organized in the face of establishing The Common Market to which England was opposed in the beginning. It includes Austria, Denmark, Norway, Portugal, Sweden, Switzerland, and the U. K., and is popularly called the "outer seven" as contrasted from the "inner six" which is generally applied to the members of the Common Market. LAFTA is comprised of Mexico, Columbia, Ecuador, Peru, Brazil, Chile, Argentina, Paraguay, and Uruguay.

The fifth form of integration scheme only talks about the removal of quantitative restrictions such as quotas, on the inter-member trade, while retaining the customs duties on such trade. Customs union, or free trade arrangement, implies the removal of all kinds of restrictions either tariff or non-tariff.

Preferential tariff arrangements, as exemplified by the British Commonwealth countries, extend only to the mutual tariff preferences. They neither involve any reductions in tariff, nor any elimination of such tariffs on Commonwealth trade. As the name implies, they simply allow for a margin of preference in favour of goods originating within Commonwealth countries as against those of the outsiders.

The last scheme is only a form of bilateral trade contracts arranged between any two countries. Since it is the weakest of all proposals, the results on economic integration are also the least. Such a proposal may be considered as a scheme for economic cooperation rather than for integration.

3. Asian Experience with Economic Integration

The main justification for economic integration is built on the grounds of potential gains revolving around resource allocation and efficiency. In the traditional analysis, an increase in productive efficiency is tantamount to the rise in real income and thus economic welfare. The argument runs along the idea of comparative advantage, i.e. countries produce those products in which they have a relative advantage. Exchanging such products with other countries for those in which they have a relative disadvantage, each country is naturally benefited. The idea of comparative advantage as proposed by Ricardo and followed by other classical economists, was, in fact, a static theory in as much as it was based upon a constant technology or a fixed production function. However, based on it the classicists advocated universal free trade as an international economic policy believing that it would result in an optimum allocation of a given stock of resources and in the process leading to higher levels of real income.

With the reductions in tariffs and rapid improvements in transportation, international trade grew rapidly in the 19th century, leading to a tremendous rise in economic growth, a side effect which the classicists had not suspected. In the light of this record, trade was later labelled, by Sir Dennis Robertson, an "engine of growth." The principle of comparative advantage in its dynamic aspect of affecting economic growth thus assumed the pivotal role in the economists' belief in, and advocacy of, universal free trade until the experience of the developing countries started to shake it in the late 1950's. To be sure, the 19th century experience meant economic growth with trade not only for the advanced countries of Europe, but also for the less developed countries through a process of increased demand by the developed countries for the primary products of the underdeveloped countries. Nurkse called this process "the transmission of growth." In a way it is this aspect of trade that changed after the Second World War.

This part in the chain of thought has been popularized by economists like Nurkse, Myrdal, Prebisch, Singer, and others who have been concerned with the process of development in the developing countries and the role that international trade plays in it. Thus, arguments run on the lines that trade based on comparative advantage, both in its static and dynamic aspects, is not conducive to economic development. In its static version trade may reallocate resources in the developing countries, mostly in the primary producing sectors. The reallocation runs counter to the very process of economic development, aiming as it does, at the diversification of the economic base. In the dynamic context, trade contributes to the growth process only where exports lead the imports so as to provide greater resources to help expand the economic base. However, in reality, exports of the developing countries suffer due to a lag in the growth of demand in the developed countries for the products of the developing countries. Imports of the underdeveloped countries, on the other hand, rise rapidly under the necessities of development which requires greater amounts of capital goods and other manufactured items, leading to a net import balance. The result then is that if trade is left free, as the classical economists believed it should be, this unfavourable balance of trade would imply an outflow of productive resources which actually retards economic development instead of helping it. ECAFE sums up the discusssion: "Thus, the limitation imposed on the possible rate of economic growth by the slow growth of exports finds its expression in a growing gap between export prospects and import needs. The gap may be bridged to some extent by foreign capital imports and external assistance. But, from the point of view of selfsustained growth, external economic aid should not constitute a permanent basis for economic development, and in so far as foreign loans necessitate interest and repayment servicing in the future, the extent to which capital imports can be made use of depends ultimately upon export earnings prospects."[7]

Besides the argument presented above, the structure of world trade has itself changed. While in the 19th century the pattern of international division of labour had resulted in the exchange of manufactured goods, raw material, and foodstuff in approximately the same proportion, in the 20th century almost two-thirds of such trade is between the industrialized countries involving manufactured products. Moreover, a bulk of the trade among the developed countries is set within a framework of a regional block of western European countries belonging to the Common Market. The very success of the European Common Market is itself an important reason for the increasing interest in economic integration, so much so that there are serious discussions and schemes of regional integration in every part of the world, e.g. Free Trade Area between the U.S. and Canada, or its wider version of the Atlantic Free Trade Area composed of the U.S., Canada, the six countries of the European Common Market, the U.K. and Japan; Latin American Free Trade Association; Central American Common Market; Casablana Common Market scheme in Africa; ComeCon (Eastern European Countries and the U.S.S.R.) In Asia itself there are at least half a dozen schemes of regional cooperation between the various countries, some of which overlap each other.

ECAFE has been in the forefront of advocating regional integration and increased economic cooperation between the various nations of Asia. In fact, the success of the European economic community has had such a tremendous impact on the thinking of international institutions such as ECAFE that most of them have come to accept regional groupings as a way to multilateralism. It is creditable that ECAFE, ever since its establishment in 1947, has persisted in generating a regional approach to the solutions of its members' problems. One of its areas of stress has been to promote understanding among its members to coordinate their national plans in order to "take full advantage of the possibilities of trade, of exchange of services and technical skill, and of each country's comparative advantages, with a view to achieving a balanced industrial development of the region as a whole."[8] But it made the first serious attempt for integrated regional development when its executive secretary, Dr. Lokanathan, prepared and presented an aide-memoire on regional economic cooperation for consideration by a closed meeting of the heads of delegations at the Commission's eleventh session in March 1955. However, the document was not approved for the agenda and has remained a confidential document. But with the initiation of schemes for economic integration in Europe and Latin America, a new mood ushered in the politics of the member nations who then favoured the idea of regionalism and instructed the Secretariat for this task. Since that time the Secretariat

7 ECAFE, "Economic Development and Planning in Asia and the Far East," Vol. XII, No. 3 (December 1961), p. 56.

8 L. P. Singh, *The Politics of Economic Co-operation in Asia: A Study of Asia International Organizations* (Columbia, Mo.: University of Missouri Press, 1966), p. 143.

has produced thoughtful studies on the subject for its members' consideration.[9]

One of the chief problems for ECAFE and others in pushing the idea to reality has been the political climate prevailing in Asia. Asia after the Second World War has been an arena of both hot and cold war where the big powers have pushed their ideological controversies to ride above the interests of the region. At the same time the political turmoil within and the vested interests of the various Asian nations have added to the complexities and the confusion. As stated previously, regional integration involves an adjustment in national interests and, because of the prevailing conditions, it has been difficult for the individual countries to make such concessions to others. This, however, has not hindered the like-minded countries and their governments to promote various schemes of regional cooperation in economic and technical, political and defense, and socio-cultural areas. In fact, there are at least a dozen different regional groups, mostly among the South East Asian countries. These include security agreements like SEATO (South East Asia Treaty Organization), and ANZUS (Australia, New Zealand, and the U.S.), ASA (Association of Southeast Asia including Malaya, the Philippines and Thailand), MAPHILINDO (A stillborn agreement between Malaysia, the Philippines, and Indonesia), ASEAN (The Association of Southeast Asian Nations of Indonesia, Singapore, Malaysia, Thailand, and the Philippines), and ASPAC (Asian and Pacific Council comprised of Japan, Taiwan, Australia, New Zealand, The Republic of Korea, Malaysia, Thailand, the Philippines, and South Vietnam). A rather different and loose form of economic cooperation scheme in Asia has been the Colombo Plan which covers almost all of the countries of Asia. However, the most successful scheme of the economic integration plan involving three Asian countries has been the RCD (the Regional Cooperation for Development comprising of Pakistan, Iran and Turkey).

[9] For a detailed historical background of ECAFE's efforts in promoting regional cooperation in Asia, see Singh, op. cit., chapters 7 and 8.

Though it is tempting to discuss these schemes in detail in terms of their strength and weaknesses, yet such a discussion would be outside the scope of the present study. However, in analyzing the prospects of economic integration in Asia, various writers have mentioned certain critical factors that may be relevant for our purposes.

One writer on the subject of economic integration in Asia has grouped the obstacles to such an initiative under three headings: psychological, economic, and political, in reverse order of importance. In Asia in the past colonialism forged strong links between the colonies and imperial countries at the cost of establishing intraregional cooperation. The result is that Asia, unlike any other continent, lacks both the tradition as well as the institutions for fostering regional cooperation. That is why "even after the end of the colonial period, no serious attempt was made by influential groups of Asian leaders to propagate in Asia the need for closer contacts between the national elites in order to create a psychological basis for cooperation as was done in Europe by Jean Monnet of France and his Committee for Action on European Economic Unity."[10] Similarly, in Latin America, Raul Prebisch and ECLA (Economic Commission on Latin America) did much to train such an elite as that existing in Europe. Moreover, the elite that does exist in Asia is a product of different ideologies that can be identified with their colonial past. This has developed into a condition where the elite groups in Asia find little in common with each other, but are more comfortable with imported European values and preferences. In countries where such an elite has been responsible for articulating the foreign policy, as Nehru did in India, it has pushed these processes of emotionally linking themselves with the West, rather than with the region to which they belong. This "unnatural" association with Europe has been further strengthened by the corresponding lack of asianization due to language barriers, topographical and geographical difficulties, limita-

[10] Singh, op. cit., p. 227.

tion of transportation and communication, and so on.

Among the economic factors that retard the progress of regionalization are those connected with the economic structure of the Asian economy—underdeveloped and largely homogenous. Though neither of the economic factors taken alone preempts the possibility of economic integration, together they raise serious problems. Economic backwardness can be cured by industrialization which necessitates the heavy importation of capital, machinery, and technology. These are the very areas where the intraregional trade is of no help because of the economic homogeneity of the Asian countries. All of them are underdeveloped and primary producing countries with very little diversification. These economies have little to contribute to the solution of each other's problems. In fact, their solutions lie with their interrelationship with the developed countries. Thus, in surveying the scope of regional cooperation among the developing countries of the world, one always points to the lack of international trade between them as one of the basic factors hindering such a step. Since each one of the developing countries has little to offer the other, they have little to gain from integrating with each other. To secure concessions by liberalizing trade with each other is not so important as arranging credit, aid, investment from the developed countries. Therefore, one witnesses the various preferential trade arrangements which the developing countries of Asia have with the developed and industrialized countries of Europe and America, which, incidentally, have been developed or helped again by their past close association with the developed countries as ex-colonies. However, none of these arguments should be considered as permanent because of the very fact of their changing economic structure.

But the key to the prospects of economic integration lies in the political factors. In Asia, unlike that in Europe and Latin America, there have been mutual suspicions and distrust among the regional countries. Strangely, in political life, Asia is much less homogeneous than any other region. The range of heterogeneity is from representative governments to communist regimes, including in-between monarchy and military dictatorship. All of this accounts for differing political values and ideologies. Moreover, while in other continents there have been forces present for political integration and cooperation, particularly since the end of the Second World War, Asia has witnessed the trend toward political fragmentation. The division of India and Pakistan in 1947, separation of Burma in 1937, the split of French Indo-China into Laos, North and South Vietnam, the division of Korea into North and South, and their respective disintegration from Japan, separation of Malaysia and Singapore, and so on have all contributed to the political disintegration of Asia. At the same time their involvement with the two superpowers has widened the political cleavage between the Asian countries. Since all of them have gained political independence after the Second World War, the internal political conditions and economic reality are forcing them not only towards economic independence through development programmes, but also towards political and economic nationalism. The manifestation of this last item is that the Asian countries have developed the strategy of national self-sufficiency at any cost in every field, a situation which runs counter to the fundamentals of economic integration and cooperation.

Over and above the obstacles mentioned here, the scope, nature, and type of economic integration schemes are not very clear to most Asian countries. Should the regional integration scheme be extended to the entire Continent, all but Mainland China, North Korea, and North Vietnam, or to some subregional groupings? Should it take the form of customs union, free trade area, or sectoral integration? In view of the diversity of socio-economic-political structures in Asia, what role should be assigned to the non-regional members or the advanced countries of Asia itself?

In view of the various considerations and the problems involved in wielding an organization comprising such a diverse group, it may be more practical to initiate a scheme of regional integration involving only a few countries. The present study proposes to concentrate on the South Asian region composed of six countries: Burma, Ceylon, India, Malaysia, Nepal, and Pakistan.

Table 1 presents the region's economic profile. The region and the component economies contain the essential elements of economic underdevelopment—smaller output, the predominance of the primary sector, lower per capita income. At the same time, the region, as a whole, represents one of the heaviest concentrations of population outside Mainland China. The rate of population growth in the region is one of the highest in the world. The "dual" characterization of the region is given by the fact that the agricultural sector accounts for 35–45 per cent of the gross national product of the individual countries.

The significance of this can be placed in perspective when one understands that a small increase in the agricultural production, the kind this region has witnessed since 1967, can have appreciable effect on the economic growth rates which for the region's economies has been between 5.5 and 8.5 per cent in 1968 and 1969. By the same token, over 2/3 of the region's population live in the rural areas. Overall, the region suffers from economic poverty which is reflected in the lower per capita income in the member countries. The explanation of the low per capita income again lies in terms of the predominance at subsistence level due to the low productivity. Foreign trade is very important for the region both in terms of attaining the necessary capital and industrial products as well as for increasing the domestic output. Its significance varies in individual countries–40 per cent in Malaysia to less than 5 per cent in India. For most of the countries in the region, the bulk of export earnings are derived from a single commodity—rubber in Malaysia, tea in Ceylon, rice in Burma. The bulk of foreign

Table 1. South Asia at a Glance, 1966-67*

Country	1 Area (km)	2 Population (,000)	3 Growth (63-67)	4 Density (per sq km)	5 GNP (Million $ 1966)	6 Per Capita GNP	7 Share of Agriculture in GNP % (1967)[a]
India	3,268,090	511,125	2.5	156	43,842	88	45.6
Burma	678,033	25,811	2.1	38	1,740	69	—
Ceylon	65,610	11,701	2.4	178	1,722	151	37.2
Malaysia	332,633	10,071	3.1	30	3,057	314	30.7
Nepal	140,797	10,500	1.9	74	1,015	99	—
Pakistan[b]	946,716	107,258	2.1	113	13,106	125	45.7

*SOURCE: United Nations, *Statistical Yearbook*, 1968 (New York: 1969)
For col. 1, 2, 3, 4 See Table 18
For col. 5, 6 See Table 191

[a] Data collected from: United Nations: ECAFE: *Economic Survey of Asia and the Far East*, 1969 (Bangkok: 1970), p. 11

[b] Figures include those of E. Bengal, now Bangladesh.
No separate figures for Bangladesh exist at present.

of agriculture which for the most part is trade is carried on with the industrialized countries along with a very small amount of intraregional trade.

In other respects, in spite of the national differences in their outlook, the group is relatively more homogenous. For one thing, all of these countries, except Nepal, are the former colonies of Britain with a common bondage of English language, civil service, administration, and the legal framework. The countries involved are also geographically contiguous. There has been a great deal of population movement between them in the past. Till the recent past, Nepal had a common market with India, with special and economic interests due to its land-locked position. Moreover, it is this region where India, despite the announced objectives of its foreign policy, has been more cautious and ready to lend help in strengthening it. In a way, India's policy has been to secure this region within its orbit of influence. This is not to suggest, one way or another, India's success in this venture. But even as a total, the South Asian region is an important link between the East and West, and India is a kingpin in this link. India understands its position and role so far as South Asia is concerned. It is in this light that we may analyze India's objectives, its position, and the results in promoting regional integration in South Asia.

4. India's Foreign Policy Objectives

Its Attitude towards Regionalism

Foreign policy is a product of the interactions of varied factors, often those that tend to go in opposing directions. Ideally speaking, one would tend to think of foreign policy as a "reasoned product of creative leadership—concerted action arising out of a rational perception of the fundamental interests of the nation state."[11] Since the nation-state is composed of institutions and organized groups who view the national interests in terms of their own self interests, foreign policy then evolves out of the tensions and conflicts of these vested interests. Such interests by no means are only foreign or external, but also include domestic or internal ones. Therefore, foreign policy reflects, in the same manner, the essentials of domestic policy. In a way, both the foreign and domestic policies are interrelated as a nation-state attempts to control and manipulate the external forces beyond its own national frontiers and sovereignty to achieve the desirable national objectives. Nowhere is such a marriage of domestic and foreign policy so clear and complete as in the economic field. Nevertheless, the same is true, to a greater extent, in political and social areas.

However, foreign policy experts tend to view the above framework as too limited in scope. Such a conception of foreign policy does not take into account the various interests that the State itself may have, paramount among which is national security, or the survival of the sovereign itself from both the internal and external subversive forces.

The other objectives of the state may be related to this prime interest and may include such objectives as economic development and growth, equitable distribution of income and wealth, equal opportunities to all to work and share in the society, social and economic uplift for the backward regions, or people of the nation, and so on. All these objectives may be considered as the preservation and perpetuation of the nation-state itself. Thus, foreign policy includes two components: (a) the decision about the national objectives and the strategy to achieve them; and (b) the identification of various instruments to operate that strategy. In one sense, then, the latter includes the choice of techniques or the means to accomplish the ends, the former involves the recognition of the ends themselves. Put in another way, the first component requires an operational strategy to achieve the desired objectives; the second one is merely a technical matter of choosing between the various alternatives to accomplish the same objectives.[12]

[11] B. J. Cohen, *American Foreign Economic Policy, Essays and Comments* (New York: Harper & Row, 1968), p. 2.

[12] For a detailed analysis of the foreign policy objectives see Cohen, op. cit., pp. 1–35.

If foreign policy, so defined, points to the combination of diverse thoughts, impulses or the imprints of various dedicated individuals, vested groups and the deliberation of institutions, that may be so. But in India, till the recent past, foreign policy was the product of a singe brain—Jawaharlal Nehru. It bore his concept of a nation, his understanding of events, and its history, his vision about its future, his recognition of its friends and foes, or simply his imagination of national good and welfare. There is hardly any doubt that, as one writer has put it, "it was tempered by his brilliance and his compromises," and one may add, for better or for worse.[13] Though it may be too early in the paper to conclude the success or failure of India's foreign policy, yet, as the successive treatment would show, throughout the post-Independence period there has been a confusion between the means and the ends. Neither were the ends clearly defined or understood, nor were the means to accomplish them carefully chosen. For all practical purposes, the lofty ideals of a single man, Nehru, were first translated into the national objectives, and then the strategy and means to accomplish them were influenced by his pragmatic weaknesses.

It has been noted by the commentators on India's foreign policy that it has been influenced by a variety of factors—"the traditional values of Indian society, the commitments of the Indian national movement during the struggle for freedom, the nature and structure of elite opinion in India, the geopolitical realities of the State as it emerged after partition, the economic needs of a society urgently in need of a take-off, and the internal political pressures and pulls generated by a democratic system."[14] However, all of these factors were themselves vented through the appreciation and judgements of Nehru and the Congress party, and in managing the affairs of the state they hit upon the twin policy of secularism at home and non-alignment in foreign policy. In more than one respect the two are very similar. The socio-economic and political aspects of these policies are closely related. The basic tenets of secularism are individualism, openness, and equality. They require the tolerance and appreciation of individual beliefs and dignity without being pressurized into some other alien social fabric or being judged by outside moral values. Socially, it means diversity of opinion and culture, freedom from regional or communal biases. Politically, it implies the freedom to choose and govern. Economically, it advocates the equality to work and share the fruits of labour. Non-alignment, to be effective, would require all these. In enunciating the foreign policy objectives of India, Nehru stated in a speech at Columbia University: "The main objectives of that policy are: the pursuit of peace, not through alignment with any major group of power, but through an independent approach to each controversial or disputed issue, the liberation of subjected peoples, the maintenance of freedom, both national and individual, the elimination of racial discrimination and the elimination of want, disease, and ignorance, which afflict the greater part of the world's population."[15] Students of India's foreign policy have remarked that "in this sense, India's foreign policy is inextricably bound up with the internal approach to her problems. The three basic planks of India's state policies—non-alignment in world affairs, a democratic and liberal political system, and an increasing governmental participation in the economic life of the community in order to force the pace of economic growth—are all meant to serve the twin objectives of unleashing the revolution and phasing it, objectives which would become the basis for her friendly posture to both the great powers of the world."[16] Thus, both secularism and non-alignment were meant to reinforce each other in moulding and channelizing the revolutionary ferment that came into being after the Second World War in Asia

[13] P. Singh, *India and the Future of Asia*, (New York: Alfred A. Knopf, 1966), p. 115.

[14] S. Gupta, *India and Regional Integration in Asia* (New York: Asia Publishing House, 1964), p. 1.

[15] Gupta, op. cit., p. 9.

[16] Gupta, S., ibid., p. 10.

and Africa as the old world order started to crumble.

Though it is tempting to look deeper into this phenomenon to analyze the strength or weakness of these policies, yet we must break at this point to concentrate on the immediate issue of India's attitude toward regional integration in South Asia. In a nutshell, India's attitude has been shaped by its foreign policy posture, its motivations and assumptions. Needless to say that neither the motivations nor the assumptions have changed much over the period, though the operational strategy has differed in successive years.

Some of the underlying assumptions of India's foreign policy have been:[17]

1. Asia is the most important continent in terms of the conflicting political ideologies and where the two superpowers—the U.S.A. and the U.S.S.R.—both have a high stake.
2. If Asia is important, India's position in Asia is special and unique both in terms of the traditional meeting point of East, North and West, and being the largest democratic country in the world.
3. India, because of its resources and population, is an actual or potential power.
4. The Communist bloc is neither monolithic, nor is there any inevitable expansionist tendency of the Communist bloc as a whole. Moreover, sooner or later, liberal forces would develop within the Communist world that would lead to its ultimate disintegration.
5. The political debates and international conflict transcend political ideologies and live along national interests. Therefore, by taking positions on issues would mean involvement in the inner bloc politics both of the Communist and of the Western world—"the attempt to remain a factor in inner-bloc politics while remaining generally non-aligned in the Cold War."
6. In politics, ideology is of little importance or relevance, except as a propaganda weapon. Therefore, efforts should be made to make India a focal point of East-West coexistence and detente.

Within these broad avenues, India's position toward the rest of Asia was to blunt China's appeal by clearly presenting a viable alternative in terms of its own socio-political economic system. Thus, if India could be made attractive for both the Communist and the non-Communist world to coexist, it would have gone a long way toward the containment of China, irrespective of its potential military strength. At the same time India, by the designs of its foreign policy presented a lower profile so as not to frighten the smaller nations of Asia by its own potential power or by its motivation to dominate them. Thus, in pursuing that policy, India emphasized discussion of the liberation of the depressed people of Asia, not only from economic poverty, but also from the political and socio-cultural deprivation. All of these factors influenced India's strategy to talk about economic and technical cooperation between the Asians while avoiding all discussions about regionalism in Asia.

In setting a strategy and measuring the results of that strategy, one finds a big cleavage between the two in the case of India. India's foreign policy and its operational strategy for all its noble character failed to achieve its objectives. In Asia converge the vital interests of the three major Asian powers—India, China, and Japan. One writer on the subject has put the matter in the following manner:

> India's tragedy is that while China, through manipulation and militancy, and Japan, through her excellence in the sciences, finance, and industry, have created their spheres of influence in most of the Southeast Asian countries, India, through desultory and indifferent diplomacy, has lost the status she gained in the first ten years of independence. In the absence of any fundamental political objectives in Southeast Asia, India's attempt to get a firm foothold there has lacked drive. In Indian estimation Arab and African

[17] S. Gupta discusses some of these assumptions in detail and their relevance to India's foreign policy in *India and Regional Integration in Asia,* Chap. 1.

> countries overshadowed Southeast Asia in importance—though no tangible gains accrued from her great flirtation with the Afro-Arab world—while little was done to prevent China's shadow from hanging low over the small, but vital, countries of Southeast Asia.[18]

India's policy has been rather confused in Asia. Its indecisiveness in dealing with its neighbours, its inability to project or stress the national objectives, and its lack of diplomatic initiatives have left the countries around it in a state of uncertainty. This has been equally exploited by China to its advantage, so much so that the countries like Ceylon, Pakistan, Nepal, Burma, Malaysia, and others who would normally have fallen within India's orbit, sometimes show their leanings towards China. After the Sino-Indian War of 1962, China acted promptly to settle the territorial boundaries with Pakistan and Burma. At the same time China has extended her diplomatic front with Ceylon, Malaysia, and Nepal and is becoming closely linked with Pakistan.

What would economic integration of South Asia mean to India and to the region? In order to assess the merits of this proposal, a definable set of objectives must be stated. These objectives can be listed under political, economic, and socio-cultural heads.

5. Political Objectives

In spite of all the rhetoric on the geopolitics of the region, the foremost consideration here is the very survival of India and its political system. Though national survival is an ambiguous term and hard to be quantified, yet there can be little argument in suggesting that national security must involve the twin objectives of national independence and territorial integrity. National independence may itself include the preservation and perpetuation of certain "core-values," be they cultural and religious, economic or political.[19] All of these are a set of subjective judgements collectively achieved in a given society. For India, the preservation of its sovereignty includes not only the prevention of China's direct incursion into its territory, but also to look beyond its national frontiers to discourage it from having any such designs. Thus, India in this respect has a vital stake in the political situation of its neighbours, whether she likes it or not. Besides blocking China, India should also deter the big powers to influence the geopolitics of this region. Though both of these objectives have been understood, the success to achieve them has not been so clear. As our analysis so far has revealed, the hesitancy on the part of India has confused her neighbours. Economic integration as we have stressed has to have political backing, both for its initial acceptance and for its future success. If India has been withdrawn or hesitant in the past so as not to alarm its neighbours, it has neither been able to convince them as Indo-Pakistan Wars have revealed, nor has it been able to prevent China from influencing them. In short, due to its own diplomatic flabbiness, India has failed in both exposing the Chinese designs in this region and in making its own aims clear to them.

In the early years of its Independence, the foreign policy of India was dictated by the fact that nothing should be done to stop the forces of national independence in Asia and Africa. India, therefore, regarded the Communist takeover of China as a sign of that political Independence and was critical of the United States policy of containment through military aid and security pacts. In India's judgement, most often such military aid was given to strengthen the corrupted national governments in many Asian countries and to stifle the domestic opposition in the guise of anti-Communist pressures. Though India, in the estimation of some writers, was aware of the danger that Communist China, under its present leadership, posed to India's own security, yet she undertook to contain China not through the security pact or regionalization, but by involving China in facing the common tasks of economic develop-

[18] Singh, op. cit., p. 166.

[19] Cohen discusses this and other points in Chap. 1.

ment in Asia and elsewhere.[20] However, many other countries in Asia viewed China in different terms and opposed both China's entry into the regional bodies, e.g. ECAFE, and India's efforts to do so. For precisely the same reasons, India opposed their efforts for regional blocks to augment their own national security and to strengthen their economies. During this period, the favourite rhetoric of the Indian governments was to ask "security from what?" It is now history that the price which India paid for such a policy was the annexation of Tibet by China, thus bringing China's threat to its own borders, forcing the smaller countries around its periphery to befriend China, China's attack on India's border, and the occupation of India's territory, and a constant threat of China's military might in its own backyard. The effect of India's foreign policy in Asia was that by the mid-1960's, China had close relations with Pakistan, Ceylon, Nepal, Burma, Indonesia, and Cambodia, the same countries that with the help of a vigorous foreign policy by India could have fallen into its sphere of influence. At the same time China also tried to stir up trouble in Sikkim and Bhutan in exposing India's weakness to defend its own borders.

Though much has changed since then, yet for India to suceed in the gamesmanship against China it would require a complete reversal in its fundamental assumptions about regionalism. While China has lost some of its special appeal to Asia by its setbacks both in Indonesia and Cambodia, India has gained new optimism in the wake of its recent confrontation with Pakistan. The establishment of military regimes both in Indonesia and Cambodia that are careful about China's motives along with the domestic upheavals in China by its "cultural revolution" have revealed to Asia the domestic instability in China. At the same time China's recent entry into the United Nations, the rapprochement between the U.S. and China following the summit meeting, its cautious and moderate response during the Indo-Pak war and China's recent pronouncements in internatioal organizations, have created the impression of China's cooperation in international diplomacy. On the other hand, the emergence of Bangladesh after the 1971 Indo-Pak war, India's help to Ceylon during the latter's domestic trouble, better relations with Nepal, the Simla Accord following the Indo-Pakistani summit meeting, have accorded India a powerful position in Asia. All the developments in China and India have contributed to an easing of tensions in Asia which can be used by India to chalk a different course than it has in the past and it may be time for India to think anew on regional integration. A strong and peaceful South Asia is not only a deterrent to China's military power, but also will go a long way towards keeping the big powers out of the area, a goal long desired by India. Some of the big powers have often talked about their legitimate interests in South Asia and have also intervened in the region. Pakistan, historically, has provided a base for big power activities in South Asia. With a new government and mood prevailing in Pakistan since the end of the Indo-Pak war, it remains to be seen how sincere Pakistan is in forging ahead the common tasks of economic development. But the successful negotiations between India and Pakistan on various outstanding problems between the two countries would also go a long way in subduing the fears which the neighbouring countries may have about India. By holding diplomatic negotiations for reaching understanding and compromise with Pakistan, India can assure its smaller and weaker neighbours of its objectives and interests in regional cooperation.

6. Economic Objectives

A strong political system needs economic power to support it. Moreover, economic objectives are to be geared to achieving the political benefits. An aggressive foreign economic policy is to be followed for achieving the immediate economic objectives, but also the political ends. Whereas the political aims are subjective and non-

[20] Both Gupta and P. Singh discuss this point more thoroughly in their respective books. See particularly Gupta, op. cit., Chapter 1 and P. Singh, op. cit., Chap. 5 and 6.

quantifiable, economic goals are definite and definable.

The paramount consideration for India and its neighbours is economic development. Since international trade is an important part in the economic development process, a trade surplus is considered desirable because of its effect in raising the national income. To achieve this surplus, exports are encouraged and imports are restricted to only those necessities, such as the capital goods, that would aid the developmental process. However, as stated earlier, the process is not that simple since the exports lag behind the imports, causing severe balance of payments problems consequently an increasing emphasis is laid on import substitution which is practised with little consideration of the cost and prices. That is, if a country like India finds it difficult to increase its exports, due either to low foreign demand or short domestic supply, and has to import manufactured goods, capital equipment, machinery, and industrial raw materials to develop industrially, it has to resort to rationing its limited foreign exchange by controlling or licensing imports, curtailing foreign travel, etc. The result of such controls is the encouragement of domestic production of the previously imported products, a process that gives no consideration to the comparative advantage or the cost of production. If such import substitution continues, the real cost to the country could be quite high. On the other hand, if the domestic market of a product such as steel is not large enough to absorb the output of an efficient-size plant, it would lead to excess capacity (the underutilization of the plant) and wastage of the scarce capital which the country can ill afford in the initial stages of its developmental process. Thus, in order to have import substitution, the industries would continue to need protection on the basis of the "infant industry" consideration.

Both of these arguments are put forward in support of economic integration or regionalism. Economic integration would require a mutual relaxation of trade barriers and exchange controls which would lead to the expansion of trade. Since the increase in trade causes demand for the country's exports to rise, it would also help in overcoming the smallness of the market so that plants could be able to produce the desired maximum output, and the surplus would be exported. Thus, economic integration of the region is viewed as the strategic weapon to combat economic underdevelopment. There is more discussion on this subject in the previous chapter on Foreign Trade and Balance-of-Payment.

However, the case for regional integration among the underdeveloped countries is not so simple and straightforward. For one thing, regional integration in South Asia may lead to the mutual increase in trade, but the bulk of the present regional trade is not among themselves, but between the countries of South Asia and the industrialized countries of the Western Hemisphere and Japan. As Table 2 suggests, this lack of intraregional trade is attributed to the competitiveness of their economic structure, from the homogeneity of their economies which are mostly agricultural, with a small industrial base. At the same time, the needs of industrialization are such that the countries have to trade with the developed countries. Thus regional integration among the South Asian countries would not only involve little expansion of intraregional trade, but, if steps are undertaken to increase this mutual trade between, say, India, which is relatively more industrialized than others in the region, it would imply diverting trade from the low cost countries (e.g. Japan and the western economies) to the high cost Indian products. This has been called a "trade diversion" effect in the literature.[21] Moreover, the develop-

[21] The terms "trade diversion" and "trade creation" were first used by Viner in discussing the effects of economic integration. Trade-creation refers to the newly created trade between the member countries of the Union while trade-diversion refers to the trade diverted from a foreign country to the member country. The net effect of the two may be positive, negative or unchanged, depending upon a host of assumptions. See J. Viner, *The Customs Union Issue* (New York : Carnegie Endowment for International Peace, 1950), and the subsequent literature especially J. E. Meade, *The Theory of Customs Union* (Amsterdam : North Holland Publishing Company 1955).

Table 2. Intraregional Trade in South Asia, 1967*

Country	Imports to Exports From: Total value of Imports (Millions)	Total value of exports (Millions)	Value of Intraregional Exports (Millions): India	Burma	Ceylon	Malaysia	Nepal	Pakistan[a]	Regional Exports % total
INDIA (Rupee) IR 1=13.333c	IR 20076.1 ($ 2.808)	IR 11928.2 ($ 1.613)	..	IR 38.21 (Ky 36.38)	IR 147.8 (CR 123.2)	IR 69.0 (M$ 45.50)	IR 150.8	IR 0.11 (PR 1.5)	3.4
BURMA (Kyat) Ky=21c	Ky 741.42 ($ 156.0)	Ky 587.41 ($ 124.0)	Ky 75.73 (IR 92.41)	..	Ky 50.60 (CR 62.8)	Ky 8.99 (M$ 12.70)	..	Ky 28.82 (PR 19.0)	27.9
CEYLON (Rupee) CR 1=16.8c	CR 1738.4 ($ 360.0)	CR 1630.9 ($ 348.0)	CR 16.2 (IR 33.31)	CR 0.3 (Ky .72)	..	CR 2.0 (M$ 1.86)	..	CR 30.9 (PR 26.9)	3.0
MALAYSIA (Dollar) M$=1=32.66c	M$ 3451.38 ($ 1127.0)	M$ 3831.37 (1252.0)	M$ 38.78 (IR 93.01)	M$ 0.68 (Ky 18.50)	M$ 11.77 (CR 18.8)	..	..	M$ 6.43 (PR 19.4)	1.5
NEPAL (Rupee)	..	..	..	..	..	..			..
PAKISTAN[a] (Rupee) PR 1=21c	PR 5243.4 ($ 1101)	PR 4472.2 '($ 645)	PR 1.3 (IR 2.11)	PR 42.2 (Ky 62.24)	PR 37.4 (CR 34.3)	PR 7.5 (M$ 8.98)	..	..	1.9
Regional Imports % of Total	..	..	11.0	9.1	13.7	1.9	..	..	

*SOURCE: United Nations, *Yearbook of International Trade Statistics*, 1969 (New York: Dept. of Economic and Social Affairs, 1971).

[a] Figures include those of E. Bengal, now Bangladesh. No separate figures for Bangladesh exist at present.

ment process requires a total increase in exports of a country rather than a diversion of the existing trade. On this account, whether or not regionalism would mean a total expansion of the export base of the countries in South Asia is an open question.

In recent years the idea of regionalism has been recommended on other grounds, some of which are interesting for our purposes. ECAFE, for example, does not consider the lack of complementarity as a hindrance to regionalism. In fact, as it puts it, "What is relevant to the possibility of further expanding this volume of intra-group trade is not the degree of complementarity as such, as the extent to which the full volume of intra-group trade, determined by that degree of complementarity, is prevented from realizing itself by the interposition of artificial barriers or other means of economic policy."[22] In other words, what regional cooperation has to achieve is increasing the flow of intraregional trade between the less, rather than the more, complementary economies of the region. Under such a consideration, countries like Malaysia and Japan, having a highly complementary economic system, would have already exploited the trade possibilities between them. But the competitive economies of Burma and India, or India and Pakistan, have more to gain by trading with each other, if they can mutually relax their economic or trade and other artificial barriers.

Specialists on regional integration among the ECAFE countries also argue that mere relaxation of trade barriers is not enough in the context of the present economic conditions of the region. Free trade requires an efficient price and market system to provide the necessary incentives for the firms to produce. In the context of South Asian economies, the market system is not only inefficient but it is also fraught with inelastic supply curves, imperfect mobility of resources, and governmental interference. In such a case, there is no guarantee that free trade would encourage production and economic growth. Free trade itself leads to the concentration of gains to those countries that have the initial advantage of industrial infrastructure, such as India. This possibility alone would mitigate any attempt on India's part to push for a scheme, especially when the mood of its neighbours is dictated by the political suspicions and hostility. Free trade also runs counter to economic planning as the main instrument of economic development. Therefore, regional economists stress the idea of "plan harmonization" as a method of regional integration.

Plan harmonization refers to the coordination of national developmental plans. ECAFE and the other specialists have consistently stressed this aspect of cooperation which is defined as "partial or comprehensive extension of national economic planning to a regional or sub-regional plan for the allocation of productive resources."[23] Such a scheme would require intergovernmental consultation, exchange of information, and negotiation. Sooner or later this may lead to agreements on production and investment policies which may be undertaken on the regional, rather than national, level. Regional investment plans would involve intergovernmental agreements on national specialization which itself would push the idea of economic integration. Thus, "the goals of integration can be attained, at least in principle, by the alternative means of "agreed specialization" through intergovernmental negotiations without subjecting the participating countries to brutal and blind market forces and to the disruptive side-effects of free trade."[24]

In a way, this approach is a complement to the trade liberalization method of economic integration. The only difference between "plan harmonization" and the classical prescription of free trade is that "freedom of commodity movements will be a dictated rather than a dictating circumstance in the plan harmonization strategy."[25] This would help the participating governments to develop the habit of consulting and trusting each other, a rare habit in the present context of South Asian politics. Moreover, by agreeing to a regional investment strategy, the members will gain the benefits of avoiding wasteful competition among each other, conserve and better allocate scarce capital, apply import-substitution on a regional rather than a national level, derive better distribution of the gains from integration, achieve the economies of scale, and hence receive the benefits from greater efficiency and economic growth.

For India and its neighbours to receive such benefits, economic integration schemes must be carefully considered. With proper organizational machinery and establishment of regional institutions,

22 ECAFE, *Economic Development*, p. 53.

23 H. Kitamura and A. N. Bhagat, "Aspects of Regional Harmonization of National Development Plan" in Theodore Morgan and Nyle Spoelstra (ed.), *Economic Interdependence in Southeast Asia* (University of Wisconsin Press, 1967), p. 44.

24 Kitamura and Bhagat, op. cit., p. 42.

25 Ibid., p. 44.

most of the fears of unequal distribution of integration gains and the supremacy of any one member, India, can be dispelled. It is often argued in India that because of its vast market, there are not many benefits which India can reap from regional integration. Though the argument is true to some extent, there are other considerations that are far more important. The crucial ones are that India, like any other country, cannot and does not have the advantage in producing everything. Import substitution, having gone to a large extreme, has created serious misallocation of resources. The existing excess capacity in most of the sectors is one sign of the inefficiency of the Indian economy.[26] Though it is hoped that this excess capacity is only for the short run, the timelag involved in the creation and the full utilization of capacity can be much longer in the developing economies. It is worth noting that a large population is not the same thing as a large domestic market. Low per capita income does not generate sufficient demand to realize the economies of scale. One must also be concerned here with the effects of a closed economy, i.e. where the import competing industries have been protected from foreign competition by the tariffs. A closed economy creates monopolistic or oligopolistic situations that are detrimental to the realization of low cost benefits. It causes undue restrictions on the output and hence high prices. Openness in competition through regional integration would help such situations. But all this has to be considered against the background of the Indian economy where the foreign sector only accounts for 5 per cent of the total production. Moreover, as studies indicate, even this low ratio has been falling, as the exports have grown more slowly than the total output.[27] The result is that the sluggish export sector has been unable to meet the requirements of import substitution and industrialization, causing serious balance-of-payments gaps. It should also be borne in mind that the foreign sector, though small in India, is an important sector, since the needs of industrialization in the initial stages are heavily dependent on the imports of capital from abroad. This had been traditionally handled by the Indian government, until the Third Plan, by external assistance rather than exports promotion.

A final comment on the Indian position is based on the benefits that would accrue to the private sector. Since economic integration would involve the harmonization of national economies, this will act as a direct incentive for India's private sector. Some of the countries, notably Ceylon, Malaysia, and Pakistan, until recently, have had a more dominant private sector and are much more market-oriented than India, which aims at a Socialist Society with a dominant role played by the public sector. There is no doubt that the fears of the private sector are more imaginary than real, yet the result is that the private investment has not been readily coming. This hesitancy of the private sector has been notable in the past couple of years.[28] India's private sector, that in many cases possesses the necessary management skills, investment ability, and the inspiration to take a larger role in economic development can be stimulated to a greater extent by India's willingness to open up both domestically and internationally. This may prove to be highly beneficial to India in the long run since Indian investors have a tradition of dealing with the countries of South Asia. No doubt in this venture the excesses of the Indian private sector can be checked by the overall regional economic policy and institutions.

For the rest of the members in this regional scheme the gains can be equally great. With no exception the five mem-

---

[26] For example, it has been estimated that railwagon building capacity was working at 39 per cent of installed capacity in 1970–71. Other manufacturing industries like cement machinery, printing, paper, tea, leather and rubber products used only about 70 per cent or less. See *Far Eastern Review: 1972 Year Book* (Hong Kong: 1971), pp. 180–192.

[27] One ECAFE study estimates the post-war growth rate of exports at 2.7 per cent per year and employs this figure for long-term projections of the Indian economy. ECAFE, *Review of Long-Term Economic Projections for Selected Countries in the ECAFE Region.* Development Programming Techniques, series no. 5, 1964, pp. 137–39.

[28] *1972 Year Book*, op. cit., pp. 184–185.

bers are small, with limited production capabilities and market. Each one trying to stimulate economic development will meet these limitations and thus would be handicapped. These limitations are particularly true for the capital goods, industrial raw materials, and petro-chemicals. Moreover, the necessary availability of skilled manpower and management cadres are extremely limited in these countries. Thus, in order to achieve a more rational allocation of their limited resources, it remains in their interest to cooperate in such a scheme. Needless to say that the fears of economic dominance, real or fancied, can be allayed with the proper regional institutions. A more realistic regional political and diplomatic cooperation will go a long way in soothing and overcoming the initial hostilities.

7. Social Objectives

Regional integration requires geographic contiguity, a certain degree of socio-cultural cohesion, absence of political tensions and a potential for economic complementarity and cooperation. Though economic integration could be a cohesive factor in welding the diversity in such areas, the process of integration depends heavily upon regional similarities. Despite the many obvious differences among the proposed membership of South Asian integration scheme, there are many unifying elements, i.e. the socio-cultural similarity.

One of the main reasons for the existence of this cohesion has been the historical ties between India and the other members. The Buddhist missionaries that travelled from ancient India to the neighbouring countries contributed a lot to the process of religious and cultural assimilation. In modern times the movement of surplus Indian labour to these countries helped in modernizing their backward economies. From the Indian point of view, the mass-scale migration of Indian labour was a sort of rediscovery of these lands and contributed to the rise of Indian foreign assets and the inflow of factor income in its balance-of-payments. There is no doubt that the existence of this Indian community and their aggressiveness in the economic penetration of those countries have created hostilities among the native populations, resulting in the anti-Indian sentiment of their governments. Indian labour migration is one area of political suspicion and equally an avenue of future cooperation. A fair and equitable resolution of this problem between India and the concerned countries would do much to clear the air of hostility and mistrust. For India, such a settlement would also imply an extension of its sphere of influence. For countries like Burma, Ceylon, and Malaysia, this would mean the availability of a pool of labour with entrepreneurial talent, administrative skills, and investment funds. Moreover, this problem should be considered from the wider angle of liberalizing factor mobility, that is, where labour, capital, and management are unrestricted in moving between the various areas, a problem which at some point in economic integration would have to be tackled.

One of the common characteristics of the South Asian countries is the widespread presence of underemployment and unemployment. Though unemployment is the manifestation of a lagging growth rate, yet there are vast social and political consequences that flow from it. It means a pool of restive people that can be exploited for purposes of an anti-social character, e.g. crime, prostitution, delinquency, and petty thefts, as well as potential for political unrest. In South Asian countries, where the growth of population is taxing the economic resources as it generates more demand for education, health and housing, a concerted effort has to be made in cooperating with each other to solve such problems. Economic integration can bring this sort of cooperation, while increasing the growth rate and conserving the wasteful expenditure of scarce resources in duplicating industrial facilities, which exist in the context of economic nationalism. The resources released by importing such a product as steel cheaply from a member nation rather than constructing a relatively inefficient domestic industry can then be channelled into fields of social welfare.

For India, these areas are highly important. In spite of the fact that India is one of the highly industrialized countries in the region, the population growth is eating up the gains in its output. At the same time the increased unemployment among its educated and literate population, mostly young people concentrated in urban areas, is itself a source of social tension. Economic integration and cooperation could provide an opportunity to use them in training and educating the people of other countries, i.e. a sort of Indian Peace Corps. India can also open its universities to foreign students and industrial facilities for training labour from the member countries. The exchange of such visitations among the people of South Asian countries would not only aid in the better understanding of each others' cultures, but would also turn their attention to Asia in contrast to the Westernization of their earlier generations.

8. Conclusion

The study is by no means inclusive of all aspects and problems involved in economic integration in South Asia. What it attempts to show is that the important factor for the absence of regionalization is the lack of leadership, at least in the past. In this context, this study places the blame on India which is the only regional power that can undertake this responsibility. Though the reasons for the unenthusiastic response of India are contained in its foreign policy objectives, yet one must critically analyze the effectiveness of this policy. The paper also contains the optimism due to the tremendous changes that have occurred on the subcontinent. Such changes present a new opportunity for the countries of that region to think afresh on the prospects of economic integration. In our judgement the benefits in taking such a step far exceed the risks involved. No doubt the responsibility in initiating such a scheme lies with India which is the only country that can assure its neighbours of the benefits of regionalization and allay their fears of its dominance. The successful achievements of the Simla Accord may be such a step in the right direction.

BIBLIOGRAPHY

Berrill, Kenneth, *Economic Development: with Special Reference To East Asia* (New York: St. Martin's Press Inc., 1964).

ECAFE, Various publications starting as early as 1957.

Ganguli, B. N., *India's Economic Relations with the Far Eastern and Pacific Countries In the Present Century* (Bombay: Orient Longmans, 1956).

Ghosh, Alak, *Indian Economy: Its Nature And Problems* (Calcutta: The World Press Private Ltd., 1971).

Gupta, Sisir, *India and Regional Integration in Asia* (New York: Asia Publishing House, 1964).

Kang, Shin Joe, *Economic Integration In Asia* (Hamburg: The Hamburg Institute For International Economics, Verlag Weltarchiv Gmbh, 1969).

Morgan, Theodore, (ed.), *Economic Interdependence in Southeast Asia* (Madison, Wis.: University of Wisconsin Press, 1969).

Onslow, Cronley, *Asian Economic Development* (New York: Frederick A. Praeger, 1965).

Singh, Lalita P., *The Politics of Economic Cooperation in Asia* (Columbia, Mo.: University of Missouri Press, 1966).

Singh, Manmohan, *India's Export Trends: and its Prospects for Self-sustained Growth* (London: Clarendon Press, 1964).

Singh, Patwant, *India And the Future of Asia* (New York: Alfred A. Knopf, 1966).

Index